THE SAN FRANCISCO SCHOOL OF ABSTRACT EXPRESSIONISM

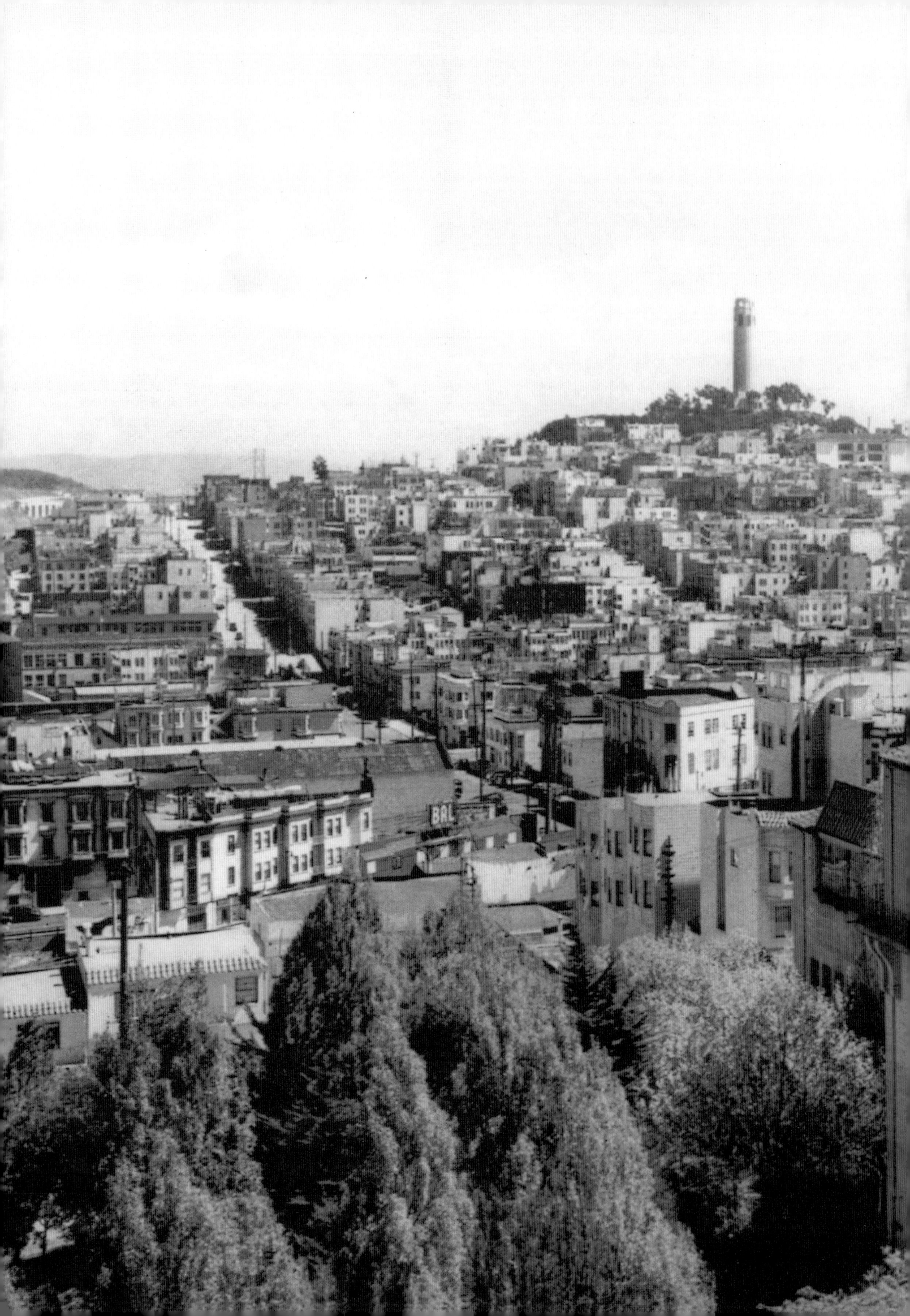
BAL

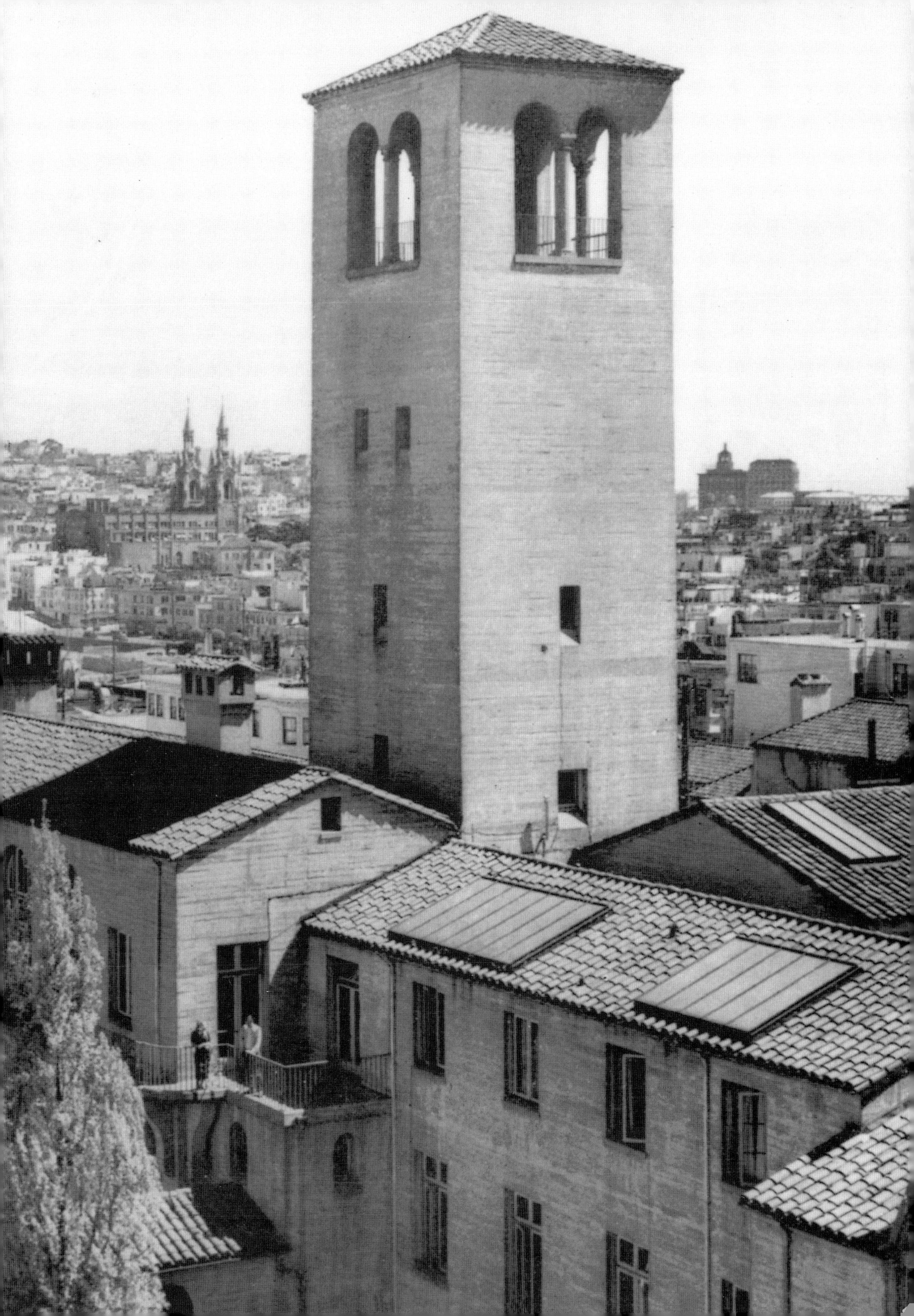

THE SAN FRANCISCO SCHOO

LAGUNA ART MUSEUM   LAGUNA BEACH

F ABSTRACT EXPRESSIONISM

SUSAN LANDAUER

With an Introduction by Dore Ashton

UNIVERSITY OF CALIFORNIA PRESS   BERKELEY   LOS ANGELES   LONDON

University of California Press
Berkeley and Los Angeles, California

University of California Press, Ltd.
London, England

Laguna Art Museum
Laguna Beach, California

Library of Congress Cataloging-in-Publication Data
Landauer, Susan.
    The San Francisco school of abstract expressionism / Susan
Landauer ; with an introduction by Dore Ashton.
        p.   cm.
    Includes bibliographical references and index.
    ISBN 0-520-08610-4. — ISBN 0-520-08611-2 (pbk.)
    1. Abstract expressionism—California—San Francisco.
2. Painting, American—California—San Francisco.   3. Painting,
Modern—20th century—California—San Francisco.   4. California School
of Fine Arts, San Francisco.   I. Title.
ND235.S27L36   1996
759.194'61'09045—dc20   94-47988

Printed and bound by Dai Nippon in Hong Kong
9 8 7 6 5 4 3 2 1
The paper used in this publication meets the min-
imum requirements of American National Standard for Information Sciences—Permanence
of Paper for Printed Library Materials, ANSI
Z39.48-1984.

Frontispiece

California School of Fine Arts, San Francisco, ca. early 1940s.

Gabriel Moulin Studios Archives.

This book serves as a catalogue for an exhibition organized by the
Laguna Art Museum, Laguna Beach, California

Laguna Art Museum

27 January – 21 April 1996

San Francisco Museum of Modern Art

18 July – 8 September 1996

The exhibition and catalogue were made possible through the generous support of the following foundations, agencies, and individuals:

The Henry Luce Foundation, Inc.

The National Endowment for the Arts, a Federal agency

The Peter and Madeleine Martin Foundation for the Creative Arts

David J. and Jeanne Carlson, Carmel, California

Michael J. and Katherine Coggiano

Franklin A. and Linda P. Ferratta

The publisher gratefully acknowledges the contribution provided by the Art Book Fund of the Associates of the University of California Press, which is supported by a major gift from

The Ahmanson Foundation

FOREWORD

Laguna Art Museum was founded in 1918 by California artists who saw the need for an exhibition space that would generate dialogue on indigenous painting and its relationship with mainstream international art movements. In subsequent years, exhibitions organized here began to foster genuine understanding of the significant contributions made by California's own painters and sculptors, both locally and among national audiences. We are delighted to present *The San Francisco School of Abstract Expressionism,* which continues and extends this venerable tradition.

By telling the story of San Francisco Abstract Expressionism and its complex, interactive involvement with the New York School, this exhibition and book will forever alter the emphasis given to West Coast studios in critical thinking and writing about the period. It will also bring to the forefront of historical consciousness the work of a number of painters whose names are not yet as well known as those of Pollock, de Kooning, Rothko, and Still.

Guest curator Susan Landauer had the foresight and the perseverance to bring this story to light and to see it into print, and all of us at Laguna Art Museum are grateful for her painstaking research and insightful writing. I also want to thank Charles Desmarais, former director of Laguna Art Museum, for recognizing the significance of this project and for supporting its development during the crucial planning period. Susan M. Anderson, our curator of exhibitions, was instrumental in bringing *The San Francisco School of Abstract Expressionism* to this institution and has overseen the organization of the exhibition and accompanying publication.

The Henry Luce Foundation, Inc., this country's leading champion of scholarship in American art, has played an integral role in this entire project, having supported Susan Landauer's research as well as providing major funding for the exhibition and catalogue. It is impossible to express our gratitude adequately to the Luce Foundation's board and staff, not for this project alone, but also for their ongoing vision and hard work, which continues to enrich the intellectual and aesthetic lives of Americans everywhere.

The San Francisco School of Abstract Expressionism was also supported in part by a grant from the National Endowment for the Arts, a Federal agency. Generous contributions to help underwrite this publication were made by the Peter and Madeleine Martin Foundation for the Creative Arts, David J. and Jeanne Carlson of Carmel, Michael J. and Katherine Coggiano, and Franklin A. and Linda P. Ferratta.

We are deeply indebted to the many lenders whose willingness to share treasures from their collections has made this exhibition possible. The participation of the University of California Press has greatly enhanced the quality of this book, and will ensure broad dissemination of the knowledge it contains. For this, we are particularly grateful to Deborah Kirshman,

Fine Arts Editor, who has seen the project through its entire development.

The successful realization of an exhibition this complex requires the professional contributions of many talented individuals, and Laguna Art Museum's staff expertly executed their responsibilities. Bolton Colburn coordinated all the loans and the exhibition tour, arranging for shipping, insurance, and myriad other details. Lisa Buck helped arrange the tour, Serge Armando designed and oversaw the installation of the exhibition, Margaret Maynard researched and prepared exhibition labels and other educational materials, and Lynn Allinger-Barr kept the museum's offices running smoothly with her calm, good-natured skill and charm. Together, they have produced an exhibition and catalogue that make a valuable contribution to the history of American art.

—Naomi Vine
Director

PREFACE

From the mid-1940s to the late 1950s, San Francisco and, in particular, the California School of Fine Arts, provided the setting for an important wing of Abstract Expressionism, commonly known as the San Francisco School. Many modern movements earning the appellation "school" are somewhat artificially constructed from disparate artistic expressions. One might ask, for example, what Ad Reinhardt's minimalist black paintings have to do with Willem de Kooning's women. In the case of San Francisco Abstract Expressionism, however, there was a clear sense—which was neither retrospectively applied nor artificially imposed by contemporary critics—that the artists belong together. In part, this resulted from the institutional setting provided by the California School of Fine Arts on Chestnut Street in San Francisco, where most of the artists either taught or studied. Ultimately, despite the fact that the darkest paintings of Frank Lobdell, the overwrought canvases of James Budd Dixon, the quiet meditations of Edward Corbett, and the whimsical lines of Hassel Smith cover a wide aesthetic spectrum, there is reason for art historians to confirm the understanding of the time that whether or not the term "school" makes a comfortable fit, the artists were certainly members of a common enterprise.

San Francisco Abstract Expressionism differs from the New York version in certain respects. Not being a product of a frenzied metropolis, it is perhaps slower, less flashy, and more deeply rooted in nature. At the same time, it is equally expressive of the post–World War II experience, with its peculiar ambivalences and swings of mood between ecstatic expansiveness and painful introspection. Like most of the New York artists, the San Franciscans believed that strokes of paint on canvas could express their innermost feelings—even, some thought, their spiritual essence—while functioning as a kind of pictorial Esperanto. But what seems to have provided them with their greatest source of energy was a complete faith in the revolutionary character of their art. Certainly, there were instances of reinventing the wheel, but nearly all the San Francisco Abstract Expressionists believed with Elmer Bischoff that they had access to a "limitless variety of undreamt of ways of coming alive on canvas."

Despite the artists' sense of a shared mission, the story of San Francisco Abstract Expressionism cannot be told without considering the various personalities and sensibilities of the individual artists. Thus, although the study points to recurring motifs, both stylistic and ideological, individual artistic expression plays a significant part. I found it necessary to interweave biographical material with my discussion of the artists' work, for the story of San Francisco Abstract Expressionism required an analysis of the formative elements in the lives of its individual participants. At the same time, to understand the development of the movement meant examining a variety of forces, from broad cultural currents to the intricacies of the curriculum of the California School of Fine Arts and the exhibition policies of Grace McCann Morley of the San Francisco Museum of Art.

In large part I have sought to recover truths that seemed common knowledge at the time but have fallen victim to critical and historical mythology. Besides the well-entrenched fiction that Abstract Expressionism was the inspiration of a heroic few, I have examined numerous minor myths in the narrative of the San Francisco School. It is a story in itself to see how many of these myths gained momentum from publication to publication, as in the case of the oft-repeated tale of the director of the California School of Fine Arts having symbolically rung down the curtain on 1930s-style Social Realism by covering the school's Diego Rivera mural.

Until relatively recently, the literature of San Francisco Abstract Expressionism could be described as folkloric in that much of it is based on oral narrative. Until 1985 the most extensive publication on the subject was essentially a compilation of interviews with the artists conducted in the mid-1960s: Mary Fuller McChesney's *Period of Exploration* (1973), which will remain an indispensable resource for research on San Francisco Abstract Expressionism. In 1985 Thomas Albright devoted two chapters of his *Art in the San Francisco Bay Area* to the movement, and subsequently the topic has been explored in Caroline A. Jones's introduction to *Bay Area Figurative Art* (1990) and a chapter in Richard Cándida Smith's *Utopia and Dissent* (1995). This publication, then, represents the first attempt to provide a comprehensive history of Abstract Expressionism in San Francisco. I should mention that it is not my intention to join the current vogue for canon bashing. The purpose of this study is not to reject the achievement of the New York School but to rethink and expand our conception of Abstract Expressionism to include the perspective of the San Francisco artists. I hope that it will lay the groundwork for future studies of this rich and vital episode in the history of American art.

From inception, this study has met with tremendous support. I would like, first of all, to thank the Henry Luce Foundation, which has done so much to further scholarship in American art, for its extraordinary generosity in funding the project at every stage. The Smithsonian Institution enabled me to do crucial archival research at the Archives of American Art, and the National Endowment for the Arts, a Federal agency, provided generous support for both the book and the accompanying exhibition. Special thanks go to the Peter and Madeleine Martin Foundation for the Creative Arts and to David J. and Jeanne Carlson of Carmel, Frank and Linda Ferratta, and Michael and Kathy Coggiano for their much-needed and timely contributions to the publication.

Reconstructing such a thinly documented art movement would have been much more difficult without the cooperation of its participants. With few exceptions, they were unstinting with their time, their recollections, and their art. In this regard, I would especially like to thank Edward Dugmore, John Grillo, George Stillman, and Walter Kuhlman, who brought out of storage paintings that had not been unrolled in decades. Also helpful were Jerrold Ballaine, Joel Barletta, Richard Bowman, Bruce Conner, Zoe Etigson, Lilly Fenichel, Sonia Gechtoff, Dimitri Grachis, Wally Hedrick, Al Held, John Hultberg, Jack Jefferson, Jess, James Kelly, Dong Kingman, Adelie Landis, Frank Lobdell, Robert McChesney, Byron McClintock, George Miyasaki, Ann Morency, Deborah Remington, Frann Spencer Reynolds, Philip Roeber, Peter Shoemaker, Nell Sinton, Charles Strong, Hassel Smith, Sam Tchakalian, and Horst Trave. Above all, I am grateful to Mary Fuller McChesney, who so generously shared her rich archive of interviews conducted for *A Period of Exploration*.

In working on this publication and exhibition, I have had a tremendously talented and dedicated staff. I would like to thank Shannon Rowan, Coordinator of Rights and Reproductions, for her diligence, hard work, friendship, and moral support. Andrea Feeser, Project Researcher, did a remarkable job of researching and fine-tuning the extensive appendices and bibliography, a daunting responsibility. Mara Skov, Assistant Curator for the exhibition, carried out her duties admirably and with much enthusiasm. And Emily Gerser, Curatorial Intern, lent a welcome hand.

Numerous librarians and curatorial staff have contributed important information. I would like to thank especially Jeff Gunderson, librarian of the San Francisco Art Institute, and Judy Throm of the Archives of American Art at the Smithsonian Institution. Both were extremely helpful in locating key documents at critical junctures of the project. Mary Gonella of the San Francisco Public Library also went out of her way to provide assistance. Other individuals who aided the research include Karen Brungardt, Jane Glover, Corine Jennings, Linda Krenzin, Joey Kuhlman, Susan Roberts Manganelli, Jeff Nathanson, Allison Pennel, Stephanie Smith, Cherie Summers, Tim Taylor, and Janine Van Becelaere.

Many other individuals have played an important role in bringing this publication to fruition. They include Michael Schwager, Director of the Sonoma State University Art Gallery, for his guidance, encouragement, and belief in the project from the beginning. For helping me to locate paintings, special thanks go to Grace Borgenicht, David and Jeanne Carlson, Adrienne Fish, John Natsoulas, Sandy Parkerson, Anita Shapolsky, Manny Silverman, Charles Campbell, Paul Thiebaud, and Joan T. Washburn. Janice Capecci, Therese Heyman, Harvey Jones, Arthur Monroe, and Terry St. John spent generous amounts of time showing me the Oakland Museum's considerable holdings of San Francisco Abstract Expressionism.

Other individuals who helped along the way include Anna Abend, Michael Agron, David Anderson, Pauline Armstrong, Anne Arnold, Phyllis Ayer, Scott Baker, Bill Berkson, Denise Bibro, Stephen Bischoff, Rena Bransten, Ruth Braunstein, Kathan Brown, Michael Brown, Gerald Buck, Diane Caudillo, Tulip Chestman, Benjamin Chinn, Silas Cook, Ciro Cozzi, Alison de Lima Greene, James Delman, Mag Dimond, Dick Ebert, Jim Eakle, Betty and Monte Factor, M. Lee Fatherree, Allan Federman, Morgan Flagg, Patricia Foster, Eddie Fumasi, Tom Gibson, Gretchen Grant, Laurie Bischoff Hall, Reine Hauser, William Heick, Linda Hooper-Kawakami, F. Herbert Hoover, Norman and Mary Jackman, Diana Roosevelt Jaicks, Nola Jay, Drew Johnson, Tamara Jost, Paul Kantor, Ann and Paul Karlstrom, Kara Kirk, Ann Lee, Anthony Lee, Leah Levy, Ben Lowe, Fred Lyon, Fred Martin, Cathy Medeiros, Paul Mills, Diana Morley, Jean Moulin, Juliet Nations-Powell, Elizabeth Neuman, James Newman, Gertrud Parker, Nata Piaskowski, Elizabeth Quandt, Clinton Reilly, Connie Reyes, Steve Richards, William Roth, J. Budd Sage, Magda Salveson, Will Shank, Jennifer Small, Adele Suslow, Jean and Bill Tickle, Patricia Trenton, Wendy Turner, Elaine Wechsler, Susan Williams, Beryl Wright, and Diana Young.

I would also like to thank the professors at Yale University who suggested useful avenues of inquiry when I began my research: Jules Prown, Creighton Gilbert, Susan Fillin-Yeh, Anne Coffin Hanson, John Agnew, and Howard Lamar. Peter Selz, Professor Emeritus at the University of California, also provided important early guidance. And I would like to express appreciation to my advisor, Professor Ann Gibson, for her counsel and support.

For reading my manuscript and making useful suggestions, I am grateful to David Anfam, David Beasley, Nancy Boas, Phyllis Diebenkorn, Ann Gibson, Creighton Gilbert, Lynn Klein, Barbara Klein, Walter Kuhlman, Carl Landauer, Jules Prown, Shannon Rowan, George and Lillian Stillman, and Jonathan Weinberg.

A number of talented individuals at the University of California Press contributed their time and expertise to this book. I would like to thank Deborah Kirshman, Fine Arts Editor, for her initiative and vision, and for the considerable energy and dedication she gave to steering the publication through to completion. Kim Darwin Manning, Fine Arts Editorial Assistant, also deserves thanks in this regard. And I would like to express my appreciation to Stephanie Fay for her expert editorial work; independent editor Fronia W. Simpson for her sharp eye; and Steve Renick for bringing his extraordinary design talent to the project.

In closing, I would like to thank Naomi Vine, Director of the Laguna Art Museum, and curators Susan M. Anderson and Bolton Colburn, for their enthusiasm about the project. I would also like to thank the museum's administrative staff, including Lynn Allinger-Barr, Serge Armando, Jennifer J. Harper, Lisa Buck, Nancy Hightower, and Margaret Maynard, for providing the resources for the exhibition.

And finally, I would like to thank Carl Landauer, for his thoughts and insights throughout.

—Susan Landauer

In their more ingenuous moments, most artists I know readily concede that in the light of history the factional quarrels through which they have passionately battled their way will fade, and that the works that seem so diverse will come to resemble each other more and more. Although the historical concept of a Zeitgeist has lost favor with art historians and critics, it has been my experience that most artists assume that it exists. Not only does it exist, but it sponsors a lingua franca that develops of necessity. Those ancient sailors and merchants touching distant ports needed a common language simply to keep things going. For as long as men have ventured forth to strange places there has been an international pidgin. Culturally speaking, there has been a psychological and formal lingua franca called modern art for more than a century, and a dialect called Abstract Expressionism for a half-century. Within that subdivision there is yet another called San Francisco Abstract Expressionism. Although no one is quite sure how precisely to define Abstract Expressionism, everyone, even European rivals, recognizes that after the Second World War something happened in America. And, as Susan Landauer stresses, what happened was not an autochthonous event in a certain place—New York, for instance—but a seemingly spontaneous phenomenon throughout the country.

The Second World War effected a dramatic caesura in the story of modern art. In America, which had not directly experienced its furious destruction, the war produced a strong impetus to change everything. This craving to begin from degree zero that typically overtakes cultures that have experienced great upheavals, such as revolutions and wars, was felt perhaps even more keenly in Europe, but, as most historians agree, conditions there were hardly favorable to burgeoning art movements. In the physical wasteland of postwar Europe, it would take a decade to gather force and create a milieu suitable to the support of vanguard art movements. In America, on the other hand, everything was in place: the psychological need, the institutions, and, above all, the material means. The cultural effect of war, seen in one way or another as catharsis, was to release a high-voltage charge of creative energy.

In a large description of any artistic period, all points of the compass matter. Artists have always been restless scanners, casting glances back into history and far into geographic distances. Several of the protagonists of Landauer's story were aware of coast-to-coast developments in postwar painting, and even of their relatives in Europe, such as Jean Dubuffet, Hans Hartung, and Jean Fautrier. But, through a concatenation of circumstances, which Landauer gathers for the first time into a coherent account, they were in a position to form a distinctive "school." Landauer comes as close as is possible to defining that awkward term through her study of San Francisco artists. For what is a school? There are schools of fish, of thought, of poetry, and, as a forty-year-old Webster's tells us, of art. "A group, as of painters or musicians, under a common local or personal influence producing a general similarity in their work." By this handy definition, the painters whom Landauer describes certainly constitute a school, while the painters supposedly belonging to the "New York School" fall far short. Only to the degree that one artist ignited another, or ten artists egged each other on, can New York painting of the postwar decade be said to be a school or, for that matter, can Abstract Expressionism be said to be a style. At best we can say it was a cultural mood in which artists throughout the United States found their discrete voices, and some, for a time, sang in unison. The brief moment that Landauer describes had its own peculiar intonation, while still sharing in the mood of postwar rebelliousness, and devil-may-care experiment. The two coasts were more like André Breton's communicating vases than either coast ever cared to admit.

Standing back, we might see the postwar events Landauer describes as part of a seismic shift in the Western world that we are still painfully experiencing. The artists called Abstract Expressionist, east or west, were beset with conflicting longings. On the one hand, they longed to have an identity: to belong to something, anything, school or movement or place. On the other, they longed to spring free of everything, to be quintessentially human, which, in their view, meant to be free to transcend even art. A hidden idealism spurred them on, an idealism that posited *universal* human values, although they would have been ashamed to articulate that tired abstraction. (By idealism I mean quite concrete ideas that had a long history. An example of how such ideas endure despite all cynical critiques is best taken from some other field: the First World Peace Conference in Paris in 1889 proposed an international arbitration system, and we are still trying to realize it.) Abstract Expressionists, wherever they were, drew upon a long tradition of modernism while longing to be somewhere else spiritually, as each individual story Landauer recounts clearly indicates. All of them were affected by public events, such as the attack on modern art launched by Truman and prosecuted by the infamous congressman George Dondero in 1947. The Don Quixotism that followed among the more volatile artists is also part of the story. All of them were prey to hidden hopes that at last America would be freed of its semicolonial state of

mind and become a significant player in the worldwide renewal of artistic life. And all of them, I would venture to say, shared certain assumptions: that the experimental character of modern art—try this, try that, what if . . .—had to be honored; that, as John Dewey suggested, they had to see "Art as Experience"; that matter in itself had expressive potential; that, as Clyfford Still emphatically declared, "Hell, it's not just about painting"; and finally, that art, as Landauer says, had to be seen as "an experience of adventure, discovery, and evolving consciousness."

Once the commonalities are duly noted, the cultural historian is bound to discern differences and to take into account the quirks of contingency. Landauer's work is particularly helpful in this respect, for she has provided a succinct account of the individuals whose idiosyncrasies and energies put a distinctive mark on the San Francisco School. Several strong personalities, who until now enjoyed a more or less local renown, are seen in Landauer's work in their proper dimensions. By recounting in accurate detail the evolution of the San Francisco School and the personalities that most shaped it, Landauer inevitably offers material for comparison and confirms that no "school" is impermeable—there are always influences from elsewhere, always mutual interchanges, and always a kind of artistic reciprocity that historians often fail to perceive.

Several of the characters in this story certainly affected the larger history of Abstract Expressionism. There was, on an institutional level, the presence of a truly exceptional museum director, Grace L. McCann Morley, director of the San Francisco Museum of Art since 1935, who, like Alfred H. Barr on the East Coast, methodically educated the San Francisco public, and of course artists, in the history of modern art. Morley, with characteristic aplomb, also opened her museum to major figures in the burgeoning Abstract Expressionist movement, offering Arshile Gorky, Robert Motherwell, Jackson Pollock, and Still their first museum exhibitions. Gorky's excursion to San Francisco for the 1941 exhibition was for him a signal event, pulling him out of an aesthetic lull and offering him a desperately needed mark of esteem that New York had not managed to supply. It was Morley, also, who found the dynamic young curator Douglas MacAgy, who would soon galvanize the community by establishing a new institution on the ruins of an old California School of Fine Arts. Moreover, MacAgy was the husband of another extraordinary museum figure, Jermayne MacAgy, who, with access to the grand halls of the California Palace of the Legion of Honor, would demonstrate her great originality and her ability to highlight aspects of painting culture that others overlooked. Jermayne MacAgy was thoroughly familiar with artists working all over the world and knew how to suggest telling parallels between artist friends in her local life and those operating on the international stage. She also knew how to synthesize the shifting currents in grand statements that were easily transportable, as in her 1950 catalogue foreword in which she declared that "while each artist shares the spirit with the others represented here, he acts alone."

Both MacAgys were patient and admiring friends of perhaps the most influential of the San Francisco School artists, Clyfford Still. Sophisticated denizens of the larger world, the MacAgys recognized not only Still's innate talents as a painter, but also his undeniable value as a homegrown Savonarola. Still's moralistic rants enlivened the Bay Area scene, and provided the yeast for the fast-rising loaves of many students in MacAgy's school. No matter that artists such as Richard Diebenkorn and James Budd Dixon were less than enthralled by Still's apocalyptic pronunciamentos, especially his puritanical denunciations of the great European masters of modern art. His presence as an *exalté* gave them the urgent impetus to examine their own aesthetic beliefs.

There is another aspect of Landauer's account of Still's proprietary role in the San Francisco School that merits attention: Despite his disdain for almost everybody in the art world, Still was not above seeking his own fortunes on the East Coast, where, through the diligence of another painter, Mark Rothko, he exhibited in one of the most important public crucibles of Abstract Expressionism, Peggy Guggenheim's Art of This Century gallery. Although Still, characteristically, soon sought to dissociate himself from the group and showed little gratitude to Rothko, he did find enough common cause with Rothko to arrange for him to come to MacAgy's school for the summer sessions of 1947 and 1949. As Landauer points out, these visits would be of inestimable value to Rothko, who each time found the distance from his usual haunts inspiring. In his letters

to another influential teacher at the school, Clay Spohn (who, incidentally, finds his rightful place for the first time in this text), Rothko made it clear that his sojourns in San Francisco were important to his artistic life. Certainly his exchanges with Still fortified him in his own stubborn choices and emboldened him in his public statements of disaffection from received ideas of the nature of abstract art.

By offering carefully documented evidence of the interchanges between the two regions, east and west, and describing the areas of mutuality, Landauer performs a necessary service to historians of good faith seeking to illuminate the phenomenon of Abstract Expressionism. To take one example: In the summer of 1947, it appears that Rothko discussed the idea of the Subjects of the Artist school with Still, MacAgy, and Spohn. A year later, Still came to New York to join others, such as Motherwell, William Baziotes, and Rothko, in setting up the highly informal program. The history of the short-lived school has been mired in conflicting accounts (Still, of course, claimed to be its principal founder), and it has been difficult to disentangle its origins and the reasons for its quick dissolution. In their efforts to sort out details, commentators have too often forgotten to note that the stated purpose, rather than the personality conflicts, remained the catalytic fact, and that no matter how brief its life, this school made its mark. The idea that even abstract artists were committed to the principle that there had to be a subject, and that abstract art could never be merely decorative but carried with it certain moral imperatives, was what mattered. And in the event, Still's hyperbolic utterances made a difference. By setting Still's life in San Francisco in its full cultural expanse, and by discussing just what went on in his so-called graduate class, where such artists as Edward Dugmore and Ernest Briggs flourished, Landauer gives us a means, not only of weighing Still's impact on the New York School, but also of evaluating the ideas that activated the formation of an identifiable group of artists.

In most accounts of the Abstract Expressionist cultural ambience of the decade after the war, there has been little information about shared enthusiasms. Historians have been too busy trying to find out who did what first and, to some degree, trying to locate its origin firmly in one place—New York. I think it is reasonable to place a greater weight on the metropolis that, like Paris between the wars, functioned as a large amphitheater in which to present ideas coming from many far-flung sources. But it is not helpful to ignore the fluid interchanges, and the larger cultural opportunities offered in the rush of postwar artistic activities. For instance, while artists in New York had long been interested in jazz and one of the early avantgarde leaders, Stuart Davis, had insisted on its influence on the plastic arts (but then, so did Mondrian!), those on the West Coast had actively participated in the revival of Dixieland, and the small clubs in San Francisco were filled with roistering artists who took their jazz seriously and personally. New Yorkers were just as busy consuming Henry Miller's racy prose in the late 1940s as the San Francisco contingent, but the West Coast had the honor of Miller's personal presence, as well as that of Kenneth Rexroth, whom New Yorkers were also aware of, but not nearly so intimately. Both coasts saw a rise in interest in things and thoughts hailing from Asia. In New York, a few artists attended Daisetz Suzuki's lectures in the late 1940s on Zen Buddhism, and a few were regulars in John Cage's informal salon on Grand Street, where koans were rife. San Francisco had even closer connections, thanks to its geographical situation and its own local Zen popularizer, Alan Watts. Side by side with the interest in Zen was a growing tendency to reinvent Dadaism on both coasts. In New York it ripened in the early 1950s and made darting appearances in the poetry of Frank O'Hara and Kenneth Koch, whose comic iconoclasm paralleled the tendencies in San Francisco art that eventually gave rise to the peculiar junk art the Bay Area liked to call Funk Art. Clay Spohn, as Landauer brings to our attention, had all along sponsored a kind of Dada perspective at the California School of Fine Arts, and not a few of his students were inspired by the more amusing aspects of his lessons. Even more, they were affected by Spohn himself, who had been a buddy of Calder's on the Left Bank between the wars and whose vast knowledge was always in the service of a libertarian view of existence.

Finally, both coasts mistrusted intellectualization and the role of theory in the evolution of painting. Many studio discussions in lower Manhattan centered on the blight of verbalization that tended to displace attention to the role of intuition in the creative process. At times these exchanges bordered on anti-intellectualism, which was certainly at work among the more innocent participants but was sometimes assumed disingenuously by more knowing artists just to keep the critics at bay. In San Francisco the fierce, scourging rhetoric of Clyfford Still certainly inflamed his listeners. Landauer quotes from his diary of 1945: "verbiage becomes a substitute for comprehension." This thought did not stop Still from producing ample verbiage or from helping to establish a preternatural impulse on the part of his acolytes to renounce just about everything anyone else had proposed in discussions of modern art. It was perhaps just this exalted negativism that produced an identifiable style, at least for a time.

I say identifiable, but Landauer is at pains to pay attention to the variety of approaches within the San Francisco School. All the same, it becomes demonstrable, when we follow in detail the individuals associated with that school, that there were a few common tendencies peculiar only to them. Above all, it becomes obvious that the painters in the West were in a better position than their confreres in the East to pursue the ineluctable American myth of the great frontier. Throughout the crucial postwar decade there were West Coast artists celebrating their place. The wide-open spaces, even if somewhat debased by Hollywood, were still metaphorically present in their painting. Many of the artists Landauer interviewed conceded the importance of their geographical place, their physical space, in their painting adventures. New Yorkers could only dimly conjure the sweep of a view of San Francisco Bay, or the vistas that later would profoundly absorb Richard Diebenkorn. Their commitment was more often to a kind of transcendental landscape, while the San Francisco School veterans, even when they wished to find other situations, usually sought out still more stunning wide spaces, as when both Diebenkorn and Corbett headed for New Mexico, and Dugmore for Mexico. The evidence of their strong attachment to the magnificent vistas of the West lies in their paintings, and as Landauer reports, it was noticed time and again by commentators. Moreover, there is legitimate reason to associate this nature-based surge of feeling with the culture of California. In all the arts, and perhaps most tellingly in the art of poetry, the California landscape has figured deeply, from the school of poetry developed in the last years of the nineteenth century by Joaquin Miller to Robinson Jeffers to Kenneth Rexroth.

Everyone knows by now that history is subject to constant revision, and that new interpretations have a tendency to become the stuff of history itself. It is always a delicate matter to balance the incontrovertible facts—in this case, the works of art—against the variegated thoughts they have generated. It is my conviction though, that the close and disinterested examination of documents, which is to say paintings, and the character of their authors yields a semblance of truth that is indispensable to a healthy culture. Landauer is aware that with slight adjustments, with the shift of a light or shadow, there is a possibility of coherence, or intelligibility. She has a tonic sense of measure and has not been swayed by the hidden rivalries, the regional pride of place, that so often mar historical accounts. In this work, she adjusts the imagery of accumulated testimony, both spoken and written, to the real data—the works themselves—and emerges with an eminently intelligent account of a specific aspect of the Abstract Expressionist epoch (for by now, a half-century later, we can discern the lineaments of an epoch). Too many commentators know how to make a scaffold, but not how to lay the bricks with their own hands. Landauer took on the problem of dealing with a style that was not a style, and a school that was not a school—at least they have never been satisfactorily classified. She isolated and highlighted those elements that could be verified and shaped into a coherent story. In this, she makes a contribution to history in the best tradition. In so many recent historicizing commentaries, the authors commence with the hyperbolic assumption that Abstract Expressionism "changed the course of painting throughout the world." Landauer does not traffic in such simplistic boasts, and is careful to bear in mind the larger issues and, above all, the larger world of Western culture, not to mention Eastern culture, that inevitably tinctured the attitudes of even the wildest macho painters building a milieu in San Francisco. The story of Abstract Expressionism is heightened and given an authentic continental dimension in Landauer's essential study.

—DORE ASHTON

1

Mapping a Movement

Among the various group portraits reproduced in the catalogue for the Albright-Knox Art Gallery's lavish survey of Abstract Expressionism is one taken by Fred McDarrah in a dimly lit room of the Club (fig. 1.1).[1] Most of those listening that night to the discussion entitled "What Is the New Academy?" are obscured in darkness. But behind the panel of speakers with their glasses of water is a large homemade sign bearing New Year's greetings from the San Francisco group.[2] Although the Albright-Knox survey was intended "to give as comprehensive a view of the movement as possible," it locates that movement exclusively in New York.[3] San Francisco has no place in the catalogue except where history unexpectedly intrudes in the photograph opposite the first page of the introduction. Admittedly, the new year celebrated in the poster was 1958, quite late in the life cycle of Abstract Expressionism, but the fraternal relationship between the two cities dates from more than a decade earlier. San Francisco was involved in the early stages of the movement's development, and the photograph represents only a trace of the participants absent from the dominant narrative of Abstract Expressionism.

The Albright-Knox catalogue is, of course, only the result of a well-worn pattern that has been followed by all the major surveys of Abstract Expressionism.[4] The image of Abstract Expressionism has gone through various mutations, but membership in its pantheon has remained basically intact. Although the lists of "first-generation" Abstract Expressionists vary slightly from survey to survey, the force of canon has confined the roster to a relatively stable group. So ingrained is the habit of exclusion that "Abstract Expressionism" has become synonymous with the "New York School." The conflation is so complete that it seems no longer important which term appears in the titles of books and articles. When painters from outside the New York milieu do find their way into standard discussions of Abstract Expressionism, they are treated as second-generation artists and routinely dismissed as derivative. Because the San Francisco artists Richard Diebenkorn, Edward Dugmore, Ernest Briggs, and Edward Corbett made their debuts on the East Coast in the early 1950s, Irving Sandler relegated them to the appendix of his book on the second-generation New York School.[5] A similar assumption led the critic Michael Kimmelman to call Diebenkorn a "San Francisco apostle of the New York School" and William Rubin to label Hassel Smith a second-generation Abstract Expressionist whose "morphology is Gorky's" and "manner is de Kooning's."[6] This view has been so pervasive that even studies devoted to California artists—works that should show full familiarity with the artists' chronologies—tend to depict their subjects as spin-offs of a movement begun in New York.[7]

The presumption of derivation rests on the unquestioned belief that painters working outside New York missed the germinal period of Abstract Expressionism. The standard account revolves around a story of a small band of heroized artists who created an artistic revolution inside the borders of Manhat-

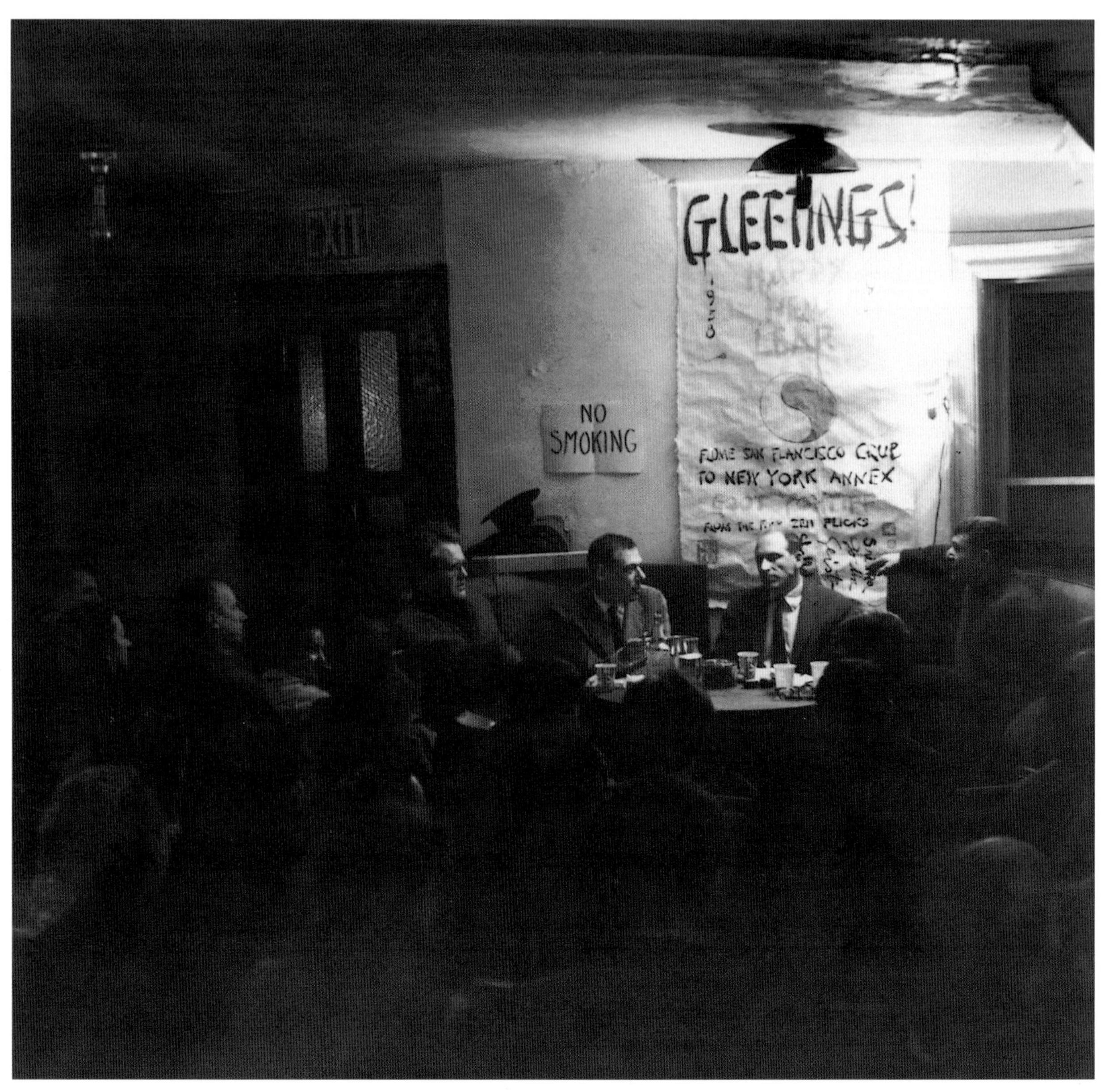

EXIT
NO SMOKING
GLEETINGS!
FUME SAN FRANCISCO CLUB
TO NEW YORK ANNEX

Figure 1.1

Panel discussion "What Is the New Academy?" at the Club, Fourth
Avenue and Tenth Street, New York, with (*left to right*) the critic
Hubert Crehan, *Art News* editor Thomas Hess, the critic Harry
Holtzman, and the painter Herman Cherry. Rice-paper poster
from San Francisco was a Christmas gift to the Club. Photograph
© Fred W. McDarrah.

tan. Eugene Thaw, for example, began a recent essay for the Metropolitan Museum of Art as follows: "From about 1945 to 1950, the years immediately following the Second World War, in one of those mysterious transformations of cultural history, a small group of American painters working mostly in New York became the leading edge of avant-garde art and changed the direction of painting throughout the world."[8] In a remarkably similar vein, the jacket of the Albright-Knox catalogue sets these first words before the casual museum-shop browser: "In the years following World War II, a small group of painters working principally in New York City became the founders of an original, avant-garde art movement that changed the course of painting throughout the world."[9] Clearly, the same story is being told.

While conceptions of fraternity remain relatively fluid, most scholars propose some version of the model outlined above. Only recently has the validity of group identity been questioned, by Serge Guilbaut, Ann Gibson, and Michael Leja. Guilbaut's thesis that the New York School was the product of bourgeois liberal propaganda compelled him to challenge the "hagiography" of Abstract Expressionism, asking, "What has become of all the Byron Brownes, the Carl Holtys, the Karl Knaths, the Balcomb Greenes, and Charles Seligers?"[10] Gibson has also challenged the rigidity of the canon, noting that until very recently it "excluded nearly everyone who wasn't white, male, and apparently heterosexual."[11] Leja made the issue of group cohesion the central question of his essay on the formation of New York's avant-garde. After an exhaustive search for signs of communal effort, Leja found little evidence that the artists conceived of themselves as a discrete entity. He concluded that while they "expended considerable energy on behalf of other aesthetically amorphous artists' groups" in the late 1940s, they "made no effort to organize or promote the particular constellation that was beginning to take shape and would later become the New York School."[12] The only clear consensus Leja found was a commitment to "the idea of abstraction-Surrealism synthesis."[13]

Although Leja, Gibson, and Guilbaut have challenged the immediate boundaries of the New York School, they have not looked far beyond them.[14] I would like to argue that the evolutionary stages of Abstract Expressionism in New York occurred in roughly the same pattern and sequence across the nation. While Leja has suggested that by most accounts "the essential fact was the simultaneous emer-gence of a group of individuals capable of and committed to engaging and extending the modernist tradition in roughly compatible ways," I have found a much broader simultaneous emergence.[15] Basically, one can detect a nationwide trend toward adopting European modernism during the Second World War, followed by a burst of radical experimentalism.

Such an understanding of the national artistic climate is not, however, merely an exercise in revisionism, for it was shared by artists on both coasts at the time. It seems that the commentaries and expressions of the period have been lost in the urgency to make the remarkable work of a small group of New York artists more remarkable still. Contemporary discussions of the national scope of experimentation like that taking place in New York were so numerous and compelling that I think it worth dwelling on them here.

Toward the end of the war a number of critics, art dealers, and curators began to notice that a new trend was under way in American art. Nationally, modernism, in both its figurative and its abstract forms, had been gaining ground since the beginning of the war, but in both guises it had generally been dismissed as imitative of European modernism.[16] The new tendency, by contrast, was viewed as an innovative hybrid of modernist idioms, as in the exhibition *Abstract and Surrealist Art in the United States,* organized in 1944 by the art dealer Sidney Janis and Grace McCann Morley, director of the San Francisco Museum of Art.[17] More than identifying two branches of vanguard painting, this survey revealed for the first time the substantial overlapping of abstraction and Surrealism occurring across the nation. Robert Coates, writing for the *New Yorker,* was among the first critics to comment on this development, characterizing it as a fusion of abstraction, expressionism, and Surrealism: "I feel some new name will have to be coined for it, but at the moment I can't think of any," he wrote in 1944.[18] A little more than a year later, Coates came up with the now-familiar term "Abstract Expressionism."[19]

Coates's phrase did not catch on until the early 1950s, but in the meantime there was an increasing awareness that the development he identified was gathering force across the country. Although expressive abstraction was still marginal in comparison with figurative painting, the Art Institute of Chicago's Fifty-eighth Annual Exhibition of 1947–48, surveying abstract and Surrealist painting in the United States, found that such abstraction, drawing some of its vocabulary from Surrealism, was scattered across the nation, in isolated villages as well as metropolitan art centers. After the exhibition's curators, Katherine Kuh and Frederick Sweet, had traveled more than twenty-five thousand miles visiting galleries, studios, and art departments from Louisville, Kentucky, to Walnut Creek, California, the institute's director, Daniel Catton Rich, reported: "Hundreds of men and women throughout America are working vigorously with abstract means, attempting to convey their personal emotion through lines, colors, effects of light and texture, rather than through transcriptions of nature. As for American artists under thirty, abstraction, together with a moody form of expressionism, has become one of the two most popular approaches to painting."[20]

This trend appeared not only in surveys with designated modernist themes, but also in museum annuals treating broader regional and national developments. In the late 1940s the annual exhibitions at the Carnegie Institute, the University of Illinois, the San Francisco Museum of Art, and the Seattle Art Museum were just as likely as the annuals at the Whitney to display experimental painting of the type Coates and Rich described.[21] Even the University of Iowa found in its survey of 1946 that "young painters are boldly experimenting in conjuring up a host of unfamiliar shivers . . . Both abstract and semi-representational artists are fusing formal and surrealistic values, resolving the ageless polarity of the classic and the romantic."[22]

Until the early 1950s, the future members of the New York School were undifferentiated from this broad-based modern movement, even by the critics, museum officials, and gallery dealers who would become most instrumental in their success. One of the New York School's most powerful patrons and supporters, Alfred H. Barr, the director of the Museum of Modern Art, made no attempt to define the artists as a group, but designated them as part of a pan-national, even international, avant-garde. In 1948 he spoke of a category of contemporary abstract painting he called "free form, free symbol," characterized by "spontaneity of line, form, and color," and "freedom of imagery and metaphor" combined with "free intuitive association emerging from the unconscious and practiced with a high degree of automatism."[23] Although Barr mentioned some of the painters who would later compose the New York School, he did not designate them leaders of the movement. Jackson Pollock, Robert Motherwell, and William Baziotes shared equal honors with Knud Merrild, Janet Sobel, and other names less familiar today. To emphasize the broad scope of the movement, Barr included a number of Latin American and European artists, among them Carlos Mérida, Joaquín Torres-García, and Graham Sutherland. As late as 1950 he described Pollock and de Kooning as belonging to a worldwide phenomenon thriving most vigorously "in those countries where cultural freedom still survives."[24]

For critics in New York, the painters now identified as the leaders of Abstract Expressionism were subsumed by a much larger population of artists.[25] Even Clement Greenberg and Harold Rosenberg, the critics most responsible for canonizing the movement, initially viewed artists like Pollock and de Kooning as members of a vanguard that extended well beyond the small coterie now recognized. In the late 1940s Rosenberg stressed that painters such as Baziotes, Motherwell, and Adolph Gottlieb were "attached neither to a community nor to one another" but were participants in a far-flung spontaneous tendency.[26] And Greenberg described the work of Pollock and de Kooning as manifesting a broad and deep avant-garde trend in contemporary art loosely amalgamating Cubism, expressionism, and Surrealism.[27] In Greenberg's estimate, that avant-garde was fairly large: in 1947 he counted roughly fifty painters in New York alone.[28]

What Greenberg saw reflected the way the art was assembled for public display in the galleries and museum annuals. Looking back at the pioneering shows of Abstract Expressionism, one finds, not a small heroic group, but rather an unmanageable number of artists, often as many as fifty or sixty. The shows organized by David Porter, Howard Putzel, Sidney Janis, and Samuel Kootz in the mid to late 1940s—now considered the first group shows of Abstract Expressionism—included many figures now obscure.[29] Interestingly, the Metropolitan's national exhibition *American Painting—1950*, boycotted by the self-named "Irascibles"—Pollock, de Kooning, Motherwell, Mark Rothko, and others—turned out to present art much in the same style as their own.[30] Reviewing that show, a critic for the *Art Digest* observed:

> There are some rooms in which the nonobjectivity takes the form of linear weaving over a matrix of solid color; there are other rooms in which the checkered technique is prominent; still others show a preponder-

ance of broad bold areas. If those 18 advanced artists, who earlier refused to enter this exhibition because of an imagined bias by the juries, had submitted their paintings, undoubtedly many would have been accepted. Their paintings would have been lost, though, in the welter of similar work by many, many other artists. Is it possible that some of their fears lay in that direction?[31]

The two shows the Abstract Expressionists themselves helped to organize were also marked by wide parameters. Motherwell's *Seventeen Americans: The School of New York,* held at the Frank Perls Gallery in 1951, included only some of the artists presently associated with the New York School. And the famous "Ninth Street Exhibition," organized the same year as the Metropolitan show, placed many familiar names next to those of a large number of artists now unknown. Officially entitled *Today's Self-Styled School of New York,* the exhibition included more than fifty artists.

In the catalogue for *Seventeen Americans,* Motherwell was careful to emphasize that the term "School of New York" was not a geographical designation but only a general "direction" in American painting.[32] Similarly, when the term "New York School" was used some years later as the title of the movement's first museum retrospective, Barnett Newman complained: "Don't those who use this label realize that, by doing so, they succeed in seceding from America? Actually New York had nothing to do with it."[33]

In Motherwell's case the nomenclature was doubtless intended to provoke comparisons with the "School of Paris," implying an equivalence of breadth and diversity as well as vitality. In his book *Modern Artists in America,* certainly the most extensive and significant publication by the New York Abstract Expressionists, he made this objective abundantly clear.[34] Compiled in 1951 with Ad Reinhardt, *Modern Artists in America* presents the achievements of a sweeping transcontinental modernist assembly, as the opening sentence declares: "Today the extent and degree of Modern Art in America is unprecedented. From East to West numerous galleries and museums, colleges and art schools, private and regional demonstrations display their mounting interest in original plastic efforts."[35]

Although the book gives priority to New York, taking most of its reproductions from galleries on Fifty-seventh Street, it makes an effort to demonstrate the continental span of the "new American school of non-representational painting."[36] Clearly, the editors were celebrating a triumph not only for New York but for the nation as a whole. To substantiate their claims, they included work from several regions of the country and quoted the French sculptor Michel Seuphor's observations on the national annuals of 1950 at the Whitney and Metropolitan museums: "Both were brilliant proof that it is indeed abstract art that holds first place in the States . . . This is not only true in New York City, but throughout the country. In the Metropolitan I saw abstract paintings of unquestionable worth from 13 different states."[37]

But if *Modern Artists in America* testified to the abstract art being done in various parts of the country, the two focal points of the book were unquestionably New York and San Francisco. San Francisco was clearly the other capital of abstraction, represented by the work of Richard Diebenkorn, Edward Corbett, Frank Lobdell, Hassel Smith, Elmer Bischoff, Charles Howard, and James Budd Dixon. Perhaps more symbolic than the number of West Coast artists was the inclusion of transcripts of two symposia, one held in New York and the other in San Francisco: the artists' discussions at Studio 35 were thus complemented by Douglas MacAgy's Western Round Table on Modern Art in San Francisco. Symbolizing their parity, the transcripts were edited to precisely the same length.[38]

By the time *Modern Artists in America* appeared in 1951, San Francisco's reputation as a center of experimental abstraction was well established, both locally and nationally. This reputation may have been due in part to the exhibitions held at the San Francisco Museum of Art, which was then the only museum west of Chicago devoted to promoting modern art. Its director, Grace McCann Morley, was perhaps more pioneering than Barr and his immediate successors in exhibiting contemporary art, giving experimental artists all over the country their first museum exhibitions, including many New York artists such as Gorky, Motherwell, and Pollock.[39]

More important in nurturing avant-garde art in San Francisco was the California School of Fine Arts (renamed the San Francisco Art Institute in 1961; fig. 1.2). Douglas MacAgy, the school's charismatic and well-connected director, invited artists, photographers, and filmmakers from around the country. With a faculty that included Clyfford Still, Clay Spohn, Diebenkorn, Corbett, and Smith—and a roster of

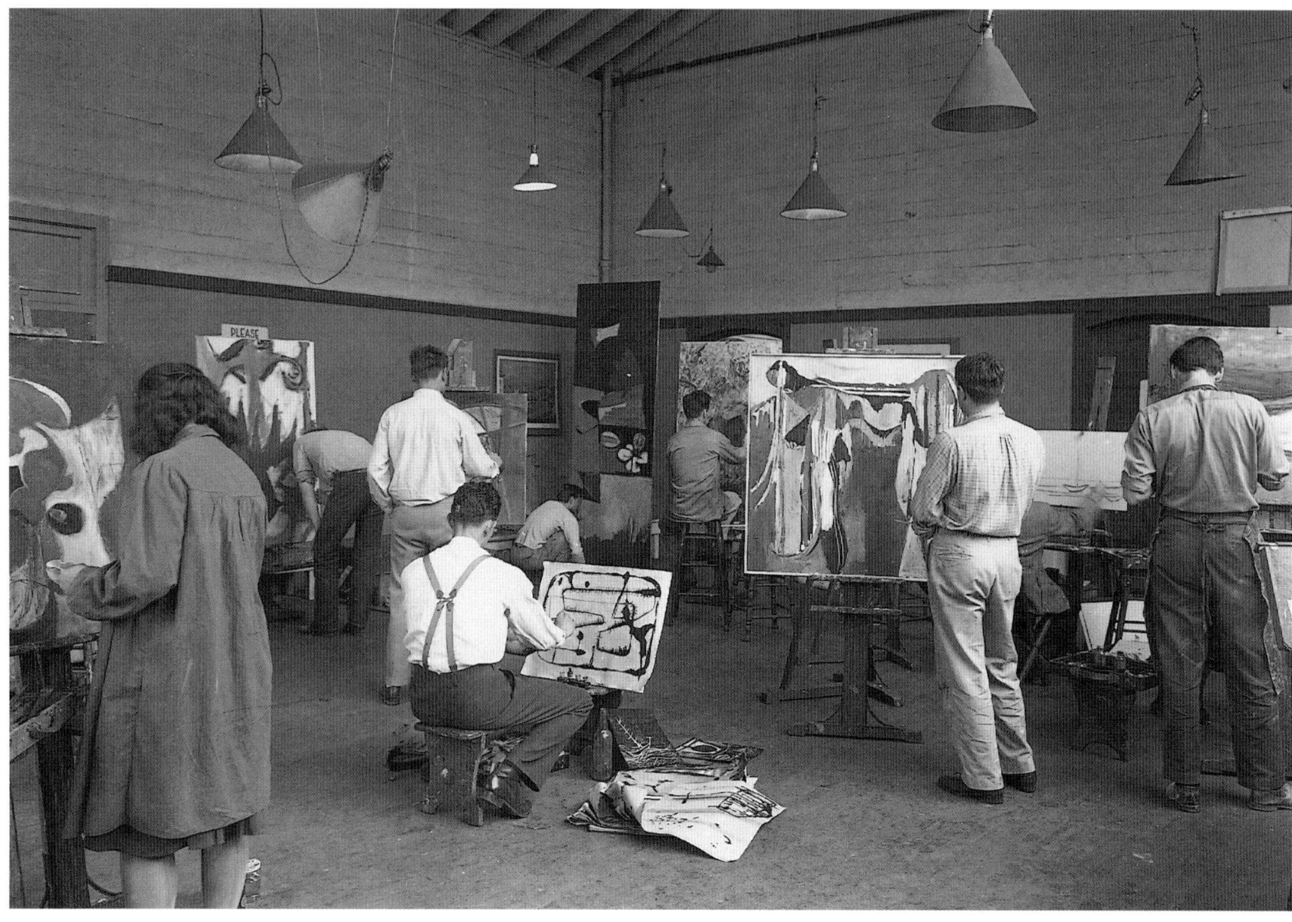

Figure 1.2

Classroom, California School of Fine Arts, San Francisco, 1948

(Frank Lobdell, *second from right*). Photographer:

William Heick.

visitors such as Rothko, Reinhardt, Man Ray, and Stanley William Hayter—the school became a center of experimental painting after the war. Equally responsible for the infusion of artistic energy into the school was the influx of veterans, whose age, experience, and motivation transformed the student body. The combination of mature students and extraordinary teachers gave the California School of Fine Arts a reputation as the most progressive art school in the country. A survey conducted by the Addison Gallery in 1948 found that of the twenty-five leading art programs in the United States—including the art department at Black Mountain College—the California School of Fine Arts was the most committed to experimental abstraction.[40] Thus Weldon Kees in 1950 observed in the *New York Times* that next to New York, "San Francisco strikes at least this observer . . . as the liveliest center of art activity in the country today." Singling out Corbett, Smith, George Stillman, and Philip Roeber as the best of San Francisco's painters, Kees asserted: "Work by any one of these men would set New York's avant-garde seismographs aquiver."[41]

A number of critical questions need to be addressed before charting a geography of Abstract Expressionism, perhaps the most crucial being a definition of the term itself. Thus far I have tried to avoid the phrase "Abstract Expressionism" because of its variation in meaning over time. Coates's "Abstract Expressionism" was not precisely Barr's, and neither of their conceptions is synonymous with the current one. From early on, definition has been a source of heated debate, one that shows few signs of cooling. The difficulty of defining the movement has resided primarily in the unwillingness of the canonical artists to describe themselves as a discrete unit, and in their striking heterogeneity of style and ideology. Attempts to define them along formal lines have failed to account for a grouping that includes artists as dissimilar as Baziotes and Reinhardt, and efforts to group them in ideological categories have run into similar problems. These pitfalls have sometimes been cleverly circumvented by identifying the artists as a "collection of individual voices," but such a view fails to address the question of unity.[42] Another common tack has been to describe the movement as a social fraternity. For purposes of mapping a broad development, however, this definition is inadequate, and even in the New York context, other problems arise, such as whether to admit Stuart Davis or John Graham into the movement's ranks. More recently, some scholars have suggested grouping the artists by their common politics, but that cannot do justice to the breadth of their political allegiances, which range from the Marxism of Reinhardt to the right-wing conservatism of Still.[43]

Many of these definitional problems, I would like to suggest, can be traced to the New York School's centrality in the scholarship. Essentially, a definition of Abstract Expressionism shaped by the personalities of the New York School has necessarily incorporated the idiosyncrasies of the major figures. The very stylistic disparities between Pollock and Rothko, for example, have led many scholars toward iconographic interpretation and away from formal analysis.[44] But if one looks beyond the group of artists who have dominated our understanding of Abstract Expressionism and surveys the broader landscape of mid-century American painting, certain lines of analysis become clear.

I have described a broad national trend toward experimental abstraction, mixing aspects of Surrealism, abstraction, and expressionism. This blend—the blend that appears in the Carnegie Institute's annuals, for example—could be described as an early stage of Abstract Expressionism. But in the late 1940s, these experiments developed to a point where the work of some American artists became further removed from European sources. Rothko's field paintings, Pollock's drip paintings, and de Kooning's black and white enamel paintings are the archetypes of this mature Abstract Expressionism, while Baziotes's work shows more obvious Surrealist, and Reinhardt's, more obvious Neoplastic roots.[45]

Such a conception of Abstract Expressionism encompasses a wide range of formal possibilities, but there are enough characteristics in common to constitute an identifiable aesthetic. That "elusive stylistic core," as William Seitz aptly called it, consists of abstraction that is either multidirectional and nonspecific in subject matter or, in its purest state, fully nonobjective.[46] It shies away from geometric forms with static hard edges in favor of organic shapes or brushstrokes that are fluid and indeterminate. Forms are generally unbounded by delineation and sometimes even by the canvas itself through implied projection. Space is for the most part flat or shallow, and compositions are bold and dynamic rather than fussy and meticulous. The emphasis is on directness of expression, usually involving a spontaneous and intuitive process of painting.

This focus on stylistic characteristics may seem an unfashionable return to Greenberg's privileging of formal matters, but the formal properties of Abstract Expressionism are themselves carriers of cultural and historical meaning. The real explosion of what I have described as mature Abstract Expressionism occurred just at the fever pitch of a national debate on modern art, following the attack in 1947 led by President Truman and Congressman George Dondero on the appropriateness of modern art as an American expression.[47] Far from an art-for-art's-sake development, the plastic language of Abstract Expressionism expressed an ideology formed in response to specific historical pressures brought about largely by the war. Briefly summarized, the ideology of Abstract Expressionism embraced a globalist perspective that equated modernism with universal humanism. It was an essentially romantic movement committed to individual vision and intuitive, subjective expression. Like other romantic ideologies, it rejected mechanistic materialism in favor of spiritual values and viewed the world, not in terms of fixed absolutes, but as an inchoate process or flux. Art was seen as an experience of adventure, discovery, and evolving consciousness. Above all, the Abstract Expressionist ideology passionately rejected all constraints upon the free spirit. The exaltation of freedom was expressed in the unbounded, expansive painting language, and in the reluctance to systematize meaning. Ambiguity of form and content can thus be read as metaphors for noncoercion and self-determination.

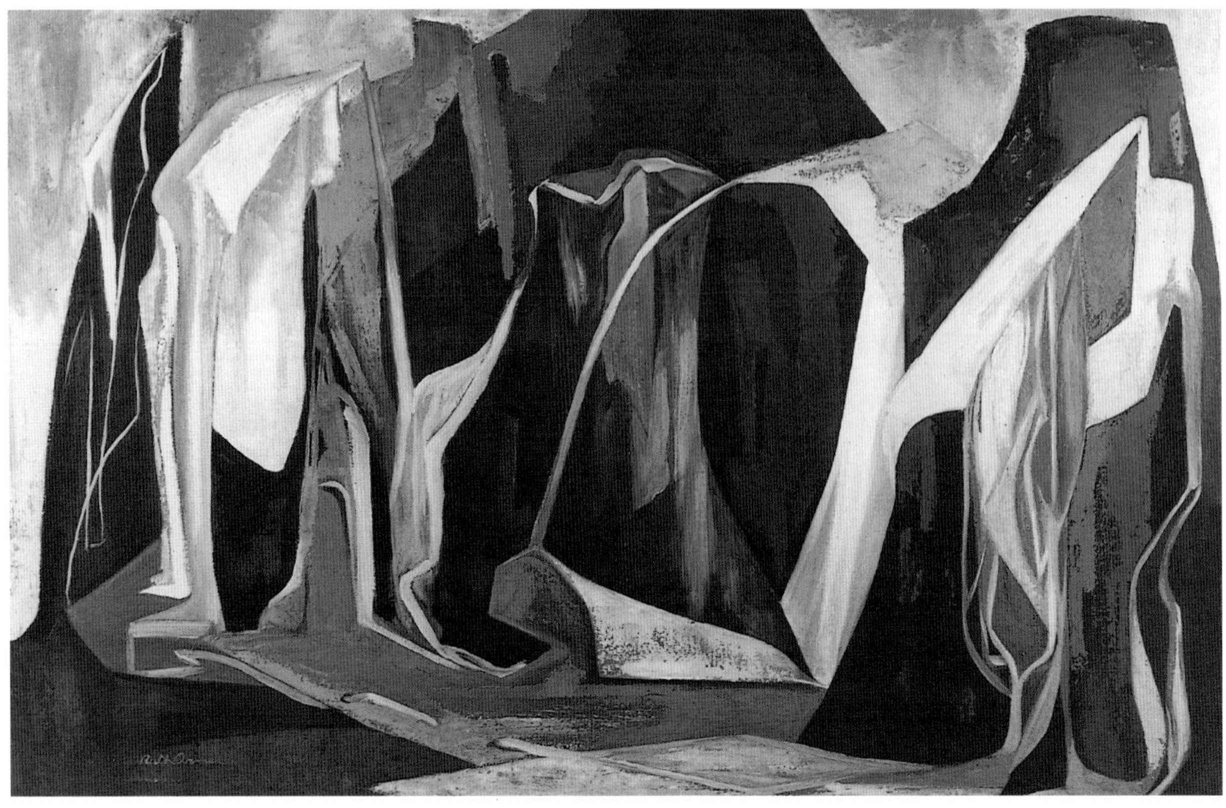

Defined as such, Abstract Expressionism in San Francisco and New York followed a remarkably parallel course. In San Francisco, as in other parts of the country, expressionism, Cubism, and Surrealism had begun to make inroads during the late 1930s, and by the end of the war a vigorous cross-fertilization was taking place. Although figurative painting and an imitative form of Synthetic Cubism still predominated during the war, more than a dozen painters loosely affiliated with one another were working along the same lines as their contemporaries in New York, combining biomorphic forms in a fluctuating, relatively shallow space, with a subject matter only vaguely suggested. Their approaches ranged from the swirling linear matrixes of Philip Pinner and John Holland to the shadowy abstractions of Ruth Armer (fig. 1.3) and the paint-spattered canvases of Harold Christopher Davies (fig. 1.4).[48]

Such abstraction took root and spread more quickly in San Francisco than in most other American cities. As early as 1945, this sort of hybrid abstraction had begun to eclipse figurative painting in regional exhibitions of contemporary art,[49] and by 1947 the

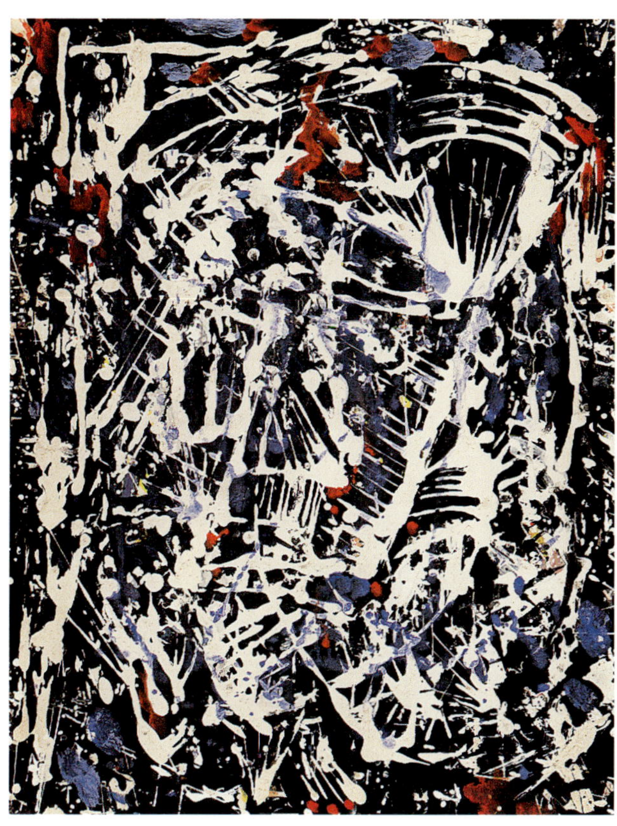

critic Alexander Fried found that a mass adoption of abstract styles had "totally obliterated" representational painting from the local repertoire.[50] The annual exhibitions at the San Francisco Museum of Art were the first in the nation to be dominated by abstraction.[51] As Peter Selz has noted, "to paint abstractly was not really a matter of choice for young San Francisco artists: it was what everyone was doing. In 1949 the entire San Francisco Annual was totally abstract, which could hardly be said of that year's Whitney Annual."[52]

But as early as 1947, a bifurcation was occurring in San Francisco between what was becoming a mainstream tendency and the more radical abstract painters. This group, centered at the California School of Fine Arts, had achieved a sufficiently extremist presence to seriously trouble the public and critics. Erle Loran, the San Francisco correspondent for *Art News,* described the response to a group show at the San Francisco Museum of Art in 1948: "It was like seeing the French cartoons illustrating the public reaction to the first Impressionist shows in Paris to watch the faces of the bewildered visitors. The more timid would look furtively at others as if to seek companionship in their bewilderment; the sophisticated were often quite frank about their stupefaction. Nothing like this had been seen in such large amounts in one place . . . It was the most complete release from restraints of all kinds that had ever occurred."[53]

Interestingly, the East Coast press noticed the San Francisco group before it identified a coherent New York School. In 1948, while Greenberg and Rosenberg were describing a fairly amiable dialogue with European modernism diverse enough to encompass symbolic fantasy and geometric abstraction, Aline Louchheim was reporting in the *New York Times* a controversial "first sensation" movement in San Francisco whose "ardent champions" painted abstractions with "slap-dash gusto."[54] "First sensation" was one of many names for the new nonobjective expressionism in the late 1940s; it was also known as "free-form" or "open-form" abstraction, "Spiritism," "Amorphous Chromatism," and, in less hospitable quarters, the "drip and drool school."

Such critical notice suggests that the San Francisco painters were not second-generation followers of a

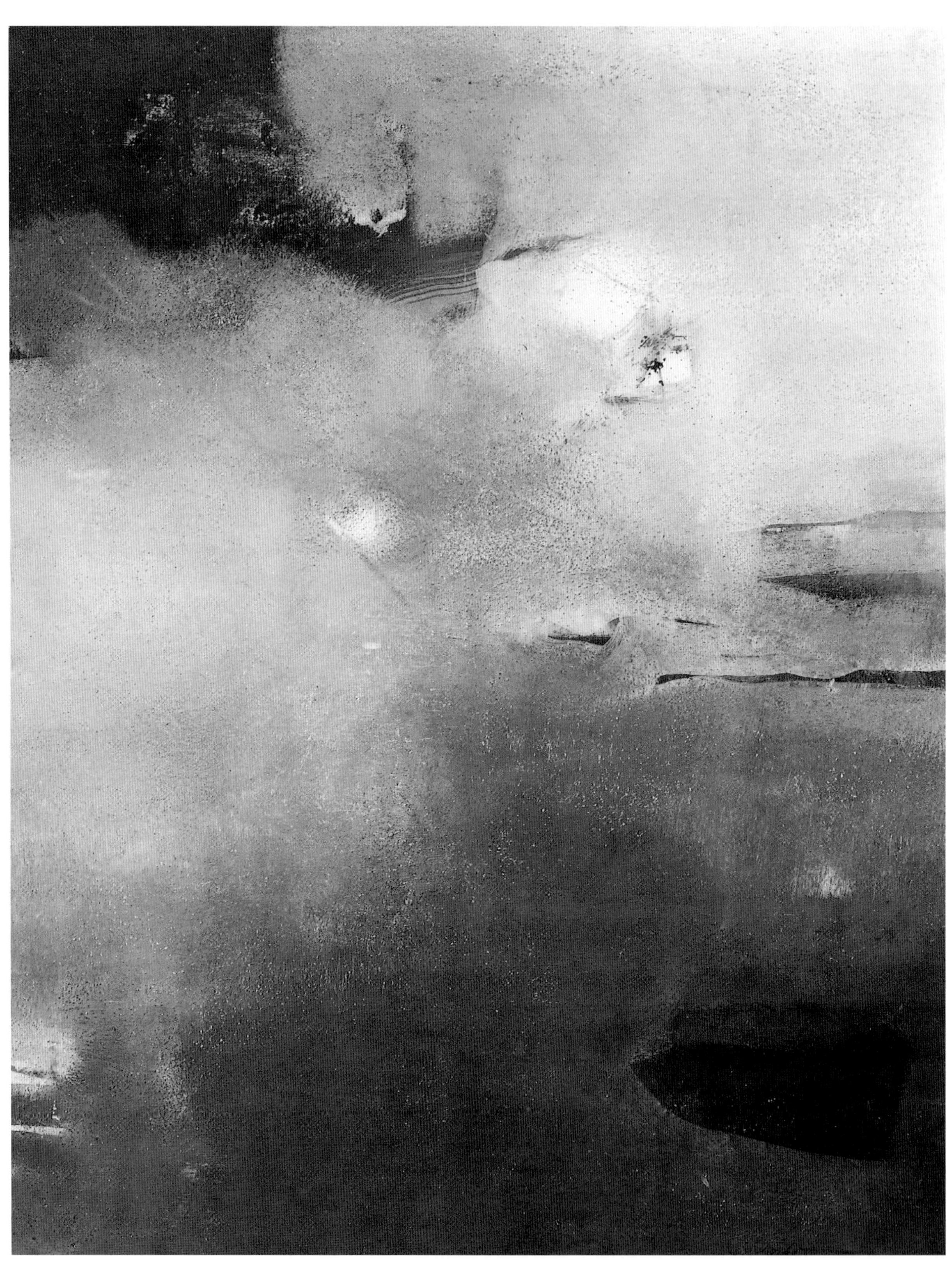

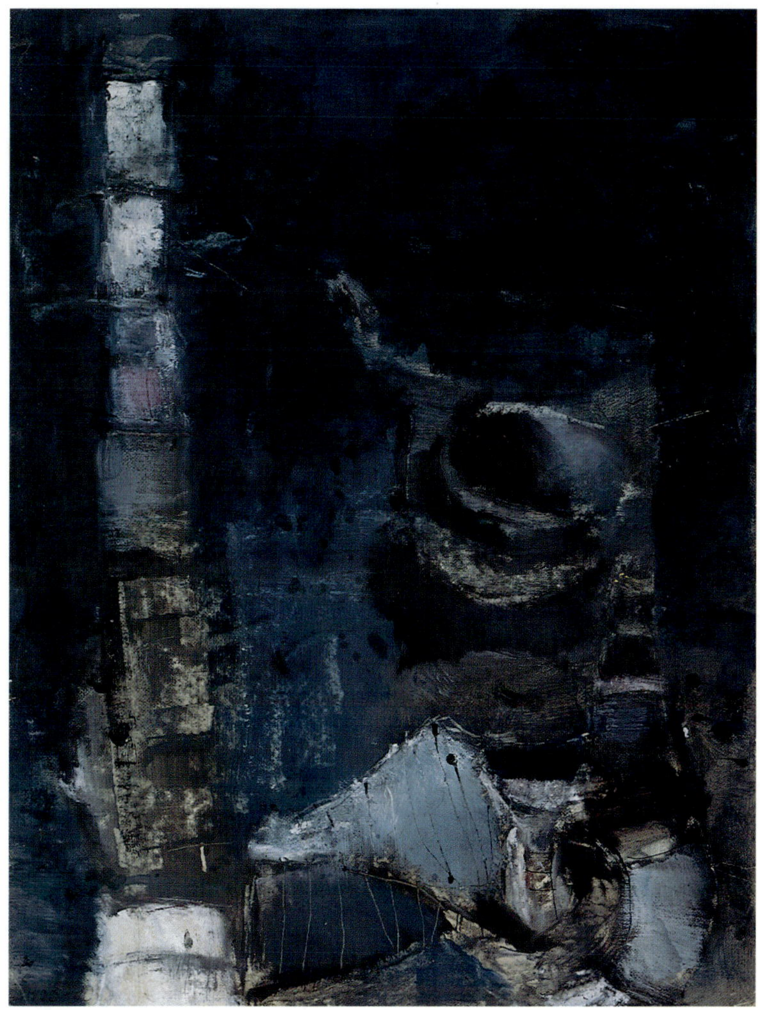

movement begun in New York, as they are so often perceived. Although they were perhaps less compelled by market pressure to secure trademark images, and less bound by success to repeat themselves, the majority of artists in San Francisco evolved individual styles by the late 1940s. Corbett's smoky mists (fig. 1.5), Stillman's spidery scaffolds (fig. 1.6), Smith's playful whiplash lines (fig. 1.7), and Lobdell's hulking forms had emerged by that time. This is not to say that the San Francisco painters were untouched by developments in New York. Still's contact with some of the artists represented by Art of This Century and the Betty Parsons Gallery provided an important conduit of ideas between San Francisco and New York in the late 1940s. While teaching at the California School of Fine Arts from 1946 to 1950, Still kept in close touch with Rothko and Newman, and it was through his urging that Rothko visited the school as a guest instructor in the summers of 1947 and 1949. Moreover, many San Francisco artists were avid readers of the New York little magazines *View* and *Tiger's Eye.*[55] But the chronology of influences is often complex and reciprocal: Rothko was as much a recipient as a transmitter of ideas during his San Francisco trips.[56] And Reinhardt, who taught at the California School of Fine Arts in the summer of 1950, made no appreciable impact in San Francisco, though his own work was inspired by the black monochromes of Corbett.[57] As much as the San Francisco artists may have admired certain New York Abstract Expressionists, one would

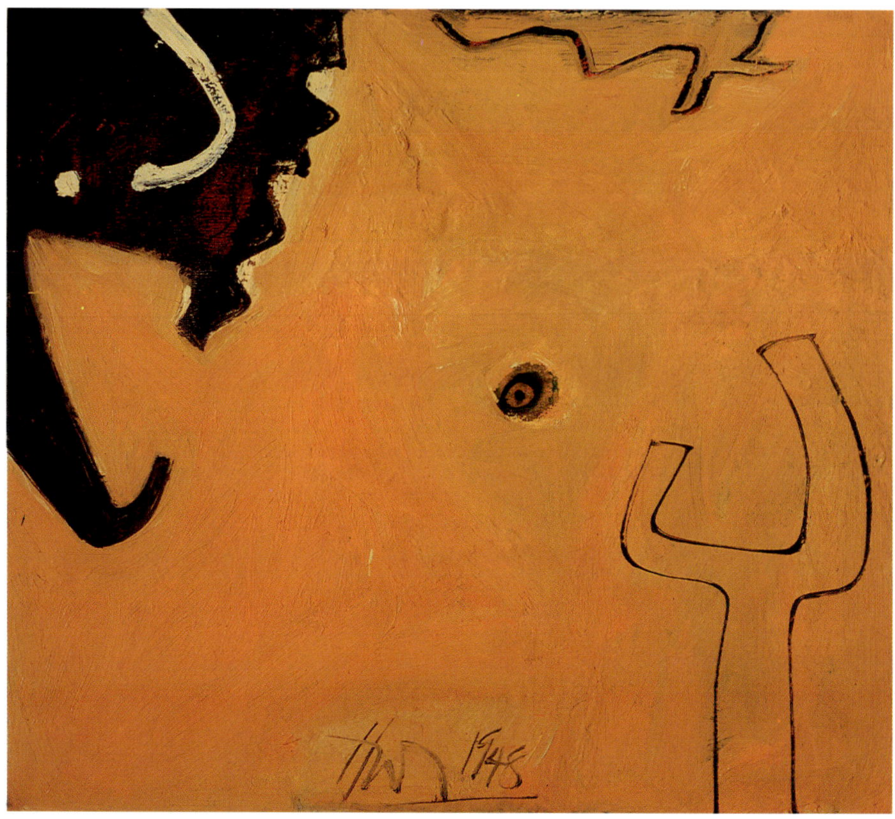

search in vain for the lacy skeins of Pollock, the shattered fields of de Kooning, or the slashing diagonals of Franz Kline; until the 1950s there are few signs of these artists' influence.

Such questions of precedence are less important, however, than what this simultaneity of developments suggests: that we need to rethink our causal explanation for Abstract Expressionism in general. The sources of inception particular to Manhattan, such as urban angst and the presence of the European émigrés, may have to take a back seat to much broader national, and perhaps international, cultural influences.

The breadth and depth of the movement's wellsprings are evident in the mainstream art trends that developed following the outbreak of the Second World War. Contrary to conventional art-historical wisdom, abstraction was not the only alternative for artists who found themselves disillusioned by prewar nationalist, socialist, or utopian ideologies and their artistic counterparts: Regionalism, Social Realism, and geometric abstraction.[58] In fact, these ideologies had lost their credibility for most American artists, whether abstract or figurative. One of the more striking aspects of American art from the 1940s is the absence of the social protest and regional reportage that had characterized the previous decade. Artists of all political persuasions and aesthetic inclinations responded to the war by turning inward, away from social and political reality, to the realm of private vision and individual imagination, a tendency loosely designated "neo-romanticism."[59] Moreover, techniques such as dripping, kneading, incising, and impasto, often presumed to be the special province of Abstract Expressionism, suited many representational artists as appropriate ways to express the angst of the period.[60] Figurative and abstract painting thus mirrored the same reality: a world in crisis, ferment, and transition. Both expressed an ideology that gave primacy to the interior realm of personal emotion and individual revelation. In short, the core ethos of Abstract Expressionism was far from being limited to a small segment of abstract painters; it was fundamental to the larger population of postwar artists.

Yet Abstract Expressionism was a good deal more than a nonrepresentational variation of the neoromanticism prevalent in the 1940s. Despite its ostensible neutrality, abstraction did carry significant political connotations. The tendency among commentators of the time to equate modernism—especially in its more experimental forms—with democracy is well known by now.[61] In addition to its association with freedom, modernism became identified with an internationalism that matched the global outlook and cosmopolitan vision of the period. Postwar literature is filled with praise for modern art's transcendence of the narrow isolationism of the 1930s.[62] The universalism of Abstract Expressionism —its ambition to speak a content generic to all cultures, to speak a "visual Esperanto," as Elmer Bischoff succinctly put it—was inextricably linked to the globalism of the period, and was shared by many more traditional painters.[63]

But to see Abstract Expressionism as a reflection of mainstream values is to misunderstand an essential premise of the movement, its subversive spirit. If modern art stood for principles of democracy, nonetheless the public, many critics, and even government officials greeted it with considerable hostility. The outburst of antimodernism in 1947 leading to the State Department's recall of an exhibition of modern American painting from its scheduled tour abroad has been well documented.[64] The exhibition's cancellation provoked a heated national debate over freedom of expression that lasted several years. Guilbaut has examined how the controversy ultimately made Abstract Expressionism a potent tool for politicians. But no one has examined the role of the debate in fueling the modern movement, in providing what Renato Poggioli called the "antagonistic moment" that ignites an avant-garde.[65] With both the Congress and President Truman attacking modern art as unintelligible, and much of the public rallying behind them, modernists across the country found themselves assaulted from all sides. The controversy not only gave them common cause and collective momentum, but in certain quarters served as a cata-lyst for rebellion. It seems more than sheer coincidence that the shrillest denunciations were met with some of the most unbridled experimentation in the arts.[66] This was particularly noticeable in San Francisco, where the explosion of nonobjective painting came in late 1947, just when the California School of Fine Arts was launching a campaign to defend modern art,[67] and the local papers were full of attacks on the San Francisco Museum of Art for exhibiting abstract painting.[68]

Abstract Expressionism, then, evolved under conditions that affected artists well beyond the confines of Manhattan. The movement's pattern of development, from the synthetic modernism of the war years to the experimental radicalism of the late 1940s, did not spring from the genius of a gifted few. When Reinhardt and Motherwell summed up the movement by quoting Wallace Stevens—"It is not that there is a new imagination, but that there is a new reality"—they understood that this reality was faced as much in San Francisco as in New York.[69]

On the Question of a San Francisco School

I have described how Abstract Expressionism in San Francisco fed into broad national currents, and I have mentioned the close interaction among the artists of the California School of Fine Arts. But thus far I have not examined the question of regional distinction. The scholarly and critical literature is divided on whether the collective efforts of the San Francisco artists constituted a regional school of art. Most recently, Caroline A. Jones has argued that a San Francisco School did indeed exist, noting that it was more "sensual, emotionally supercharged, painterly in an intuitive way, and connected with nature" than its counterpart in New York.[70] By contrast, Thomas Albright, the critic who has written the most on San Francisco Abstract Expressionism,[71] denied the existence of a unified regional school, arguing that the movement "was no more homogeneous in the Bay Area than it was on the East Coast" and, more generally, that Northern California's art cannot be separated from the communal experience of the United States.[72]

The issue of regionalism is admittedly tricky for the period in question, because the very notion of a local school conflicts with Abstract Expressionism's crusade against cultural chauvinism. Sympathizers viewed abstraction in the 1940s as the "international idiom of twentieth-century painting"; to embrace it was to condemn regionalism in both art and politics.[73] As Mark Tobey remarked in 1946, regionalism could be stressed only "at the expense of the inner world" and "the understanding of this single earth."[74] Most artists in San Francisco would doubtless have agreed with Motherwell that "to fail to overcome one's initial environment is never to reach the human."[75]

Given this prevailing viewpoint, the San Francisco painters did not strive to emulate local traditions. On the contrary, their intent was to make a clean break with the past and to transcend the particulars of time and place. Ironically, by reacting against indigenous conventions, the San Francisco painters produced a kind of reactionary regionalism. At the height of the movement in the late 1940s, most of them seem to have repudiated the bright, sunny colors associated with West Coast painting, notably the popular California Watercolor School of the 1930s and 1940s. In essence, their regionalism is defined by their attempts to avoid a local identity. In this context, Elmer Bischoff's description of the California School of Fine Arts as a monastery standing as "a fortress against the dissuading and subverting forces of the outside" carries special meaning.[76]

As I will later suggest, certain aspects of the Northern California experience made their way into San Francisco Abstract Expressionism. But it is not the force of the region that lent cohesion to the artists in San Francisco. For a brief time—roughly from the end of World War II to early in the Korean War—there is little doubt that the cluster of artists at the California School of Fine Arts possessed many of the traits historians of modern art assign to schools: group interaction, joint exhibitions, critical recognition, and a commonality of ideals, attitudes, and artistic practice. By the early 1950s their collective efforts were distinctive enough for French art journals to acknowledge an *école du Pacifique,* in part because of the zealous promotional tactics of the Parisian critic Michel Tapié.[77]

Tapié learned of the San Francisco artists in the early 1950s, when a group of expatriates from the Bay Area that included Sam Francis, Claire Falkenstein, Frank Lobdell, Walter Kuhlman, and Lawrence Calcagno exhibited together in Paris.[78] Excited by their work, he conceived of an *école du Pacifique,* its center at the California School of Fine Arts and its circumference stretching as far as Seattle, incorporating the Northwest painter Mark Tobey.[79] Tapié's

notion was picked up by at least one art critic in Paris, the *Herald-Tribune*'s correspondent Kenneth Sawyer, whose article on the subject in *Cimaise* in 1954 ventured that "at least for a brief period—between 1946 and 1949—the San Francisco Bay Area was the most aesthetically advanced region in the United States."[80]

Not long after news began circulating in Paris of an *école du Pacifique,* critics and curators in New York began speaking of a West Coast school of Abstract Expressionism. The Paris correspondent for *Time* magazine was among the first to discuss some of the San Francisco painters Tapié was promoting in 1953, and the following year James Johnson Sweeney devoted a section of his *Younger American Painters* show at the Solomon R. Guggenheim Museum to California artists.[81] By 1956, the *Art News* critic Hubert Crehan reported that "hardly a month goes by when there is not some talk in the art press about the 'California school of painting' or 'School of the Pacific.'"[82] Although Crehan, himself a former CSFA student, felt that San Francisco artists like Corbett, Still, Calcagno, and Briggs did not have enough in common to constitute a school, many critics in New York accepted the idea of a West Coast variant of Abstract Expressionism.[83] Writing for the San Francisco issue of the *Evergreen Review* in 1957, Dore Ashton described the close interchange at the California School of Fine Arts, the seminal influence of Still, and the artists' predilection for a pictorial space evoking the expansive western landscape.[84]

Critics such as Ashton were following a familiar pattern in identifying and defining a West Coast school of art. The emergence of the Pacific Northwest School, spearheaded by Tobey and Morris Graves, had prepared the way for this critical interest during the war. But while the Pacific Northwest School was defined externally, sparking resistance from some of its participants, several of the San Francisco artists argued the case for a distinct West Coast movement themselves.[85] One month after Crehan's contentious article appeared in *Art News,* the Oakland Art Museum sponsored an exhibition and panel discussion entitled *California School—Yes or No?*[86] Crehan, who was invited to defend his article, found himself embroiled in a debate. After prolonged discussion, the conclusion of the panel, which included Diebenkorn, Smith, and David Park, was that while Tapié's notion of an *école du Pacifique* embracing the Northwest was inaccurate, there was some justification in acknowledging a San Francisco School.[87] Even Still, notorious for his aversion to aesthetic categories, wrote to the Oakland Art Museum's curator Paul Mills, applauding his effort to accurately record the history of the movement: "I look forward to the time when a clarification of the principles I laid down which made this work possible can be established . . . in fact, the Bay Area, in certain respects and among the few who were informed, anticipated by over nine years both New York and Paris."[88]

Among the San Francisco artists, the most vocal advocate of a distinctive West Coast school was Smith. In response to Crehan's article, he outlined an energetic defense of a San Francisco School of Abstract Expressionism. Circulated among his friends before an Italian art journal agreed to publish it in 1958, the essay argued that a regional school of painting existed in San Francisco if the term "school" were taken to mean "a group of painters living in a common locality, sharing some common ideals, aspirations, and experiences, studying with and/or being influenced by one another, and having a common 'style.'" That style, according to Smith, had a number of recognizable features, chief among them a lack of Cubist influence and an inclination toward humor and deliberate crudity. The San Francisco School, Smith contended, was "marked by its ungraciousness, its positive unwillingness to please. In no other locality will you find so many paintings produced [about] which it can be said, 'I wouldn't put *that* on my shit-house wall.'"[89]

Not all the San Francisco artists agreed with Smith about the attributes common to their art. Smith's description certainly fit the work of some artists, but not that of others. It is difficult, for example, to find humor in the painting of Still or Corbett. One senses a certain jockeying for centrality in Smith's interpretation; that it matched his own painting better than anyone else's is probably not coincidental, nor is his exclusion of a number of artists from his version of the school.[90] Yet while there was some disagreement about specifics, most of the San Francisco artists felt that their work differed from New York Abstract Expressionism in significant respects.[91] The consensus was that the West Coast variation had been rougher, more concerned with nature, and less influenced by French art. Most agreed with Bischoff that while the San Francisco group's ideology mirrored the same national currents and impulses that produced the New York School, it took on a distinctive character in the hands of the artists at the California School of Fine Arts.[92] San Francisco Abstract Expressionism

had its own history and its own cast of characters. The art not only filtered through different temperaments but also reflected a unique set of geographical, cultural, and historical circumstances.

Among the most decisive circumstances to shape the art in San Francisco was the presence of Still on the faculty of the California School of Fine Arts from 1946 to 1950. Still's hostility toward European modernism—particularly French modernism, which he saw as spiritually hollow—made a strong impression on artists in San Francisco. Although many had reached the conclusion on their own that European art was stagnant, Still prodded them to go further than they might have in circumventing Surrealist and Cubist vocabularies. Still's animus toward the politics of the art market, which he expressed through an all-out assault on aesthetic standards, was also persuasive in San Francisco. It was in part because of Still's leadership that artists such as Smith outdid themselves to become "apostles of ugliness."[93] As much as Still belittled the mechanics of picture-making, the brutal style of his work (fig. 1.8) was highly influential at the California School of Fine Arts. Indeed, by the end of the 1940s there were so many artists turning out paintings composed of ragged patches of color that Alfred Frankenstein, the art critic for the *San Francisco Chronicle,* began referring to a "Still school" in San Francisco, an idea later adopted by Clement Greenberg and Thomas Hess.[94]

Still was not the only forceful presence in San Francisco. In a very different sense, Clay Spohn, who taught at the California School of Fine Arts from 1945 to 1950, was just as influential.[95] A painter and sculptor who had worked with Alexander Calder in Paris during the 1920s, he is credited with bringing Dada to San Francisco between the wars. Spohn's witty Dadaesque assemblages of the 1940s, along with his exuberant philosophy of art, provided a much-needed alternative to the weighty seriousness of Still. Spohn encouraged artists such as Smith, Diebenkorn, and Bischoff to develop a playful variety of Abstract Expressionism that had no real counterpart in the first-generation New York School. Indeed, Spohn was the first in a considerable line of artists dedicated to irreverent whimsy in the Bay Area, including James Kelly (fig. 1.9) and Roy De Forest, and such Funk ceramicists and assemblagists as Robert Arneson, Clayton Bailey, and William T. Wiley.[96]

The toughened veterans who dominated the faculty and student body of the California School of Fine Arts after the war also contributed to the distinctive charac-

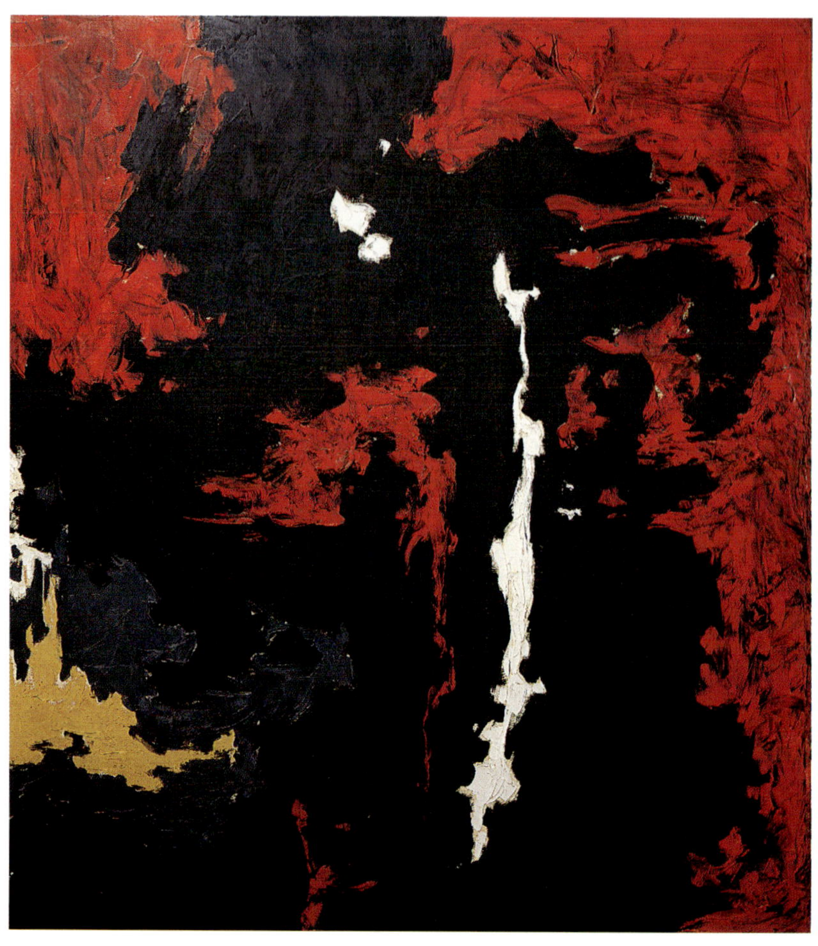

Figure 1.8

Above: Clyfford Still, *Untitled,* 1949. Oil on canvas,
80 × 68¾ in. Collection, Adriana and Robert Mnuchin,
Washington, Connecticut. Photograph courtesy, C & M Arts,
New York; photographer: Thomas Powel, Jr.

Figure 1.9

Opposite, above: James Kelly, *Shillelagh,* 1952. Oil on paper,
23 × 29 in. Collection of the artist. Courtesy, The Art Museum
of Santa Cruz County.

Figure 1.10

Opposite: John Grillo, California School of Fine Arts, San
Francisco, 1947. Photographer: William Heick.

ter of San Francisco Abstract Expressionism.[97] The
presence of so many former GIs, who as William Ivey
recalled, were inclined to settle arguments with their
fists, gave the school an atmosphere of machismo that
profoundly affected the group aesthetic.[98] Painting
was measured by its virility and raw power. As Bischoff
observed, "A strong painting or sculpture would likely
be described as a hell-raiser or blockbuster or even in
some coarser, more aggressive term."[99] The use of
expletives was a direct carryover from the barracks culture of the military, where profanity was rampant.[100]
Such tough, unsentimental attitudes caused some
artists to disapprove of comparatively elegant painters
such as Tobey, Baziotes, and Gorky, despite their
renown in the East.[101] Still considered masculinity so
important to his work that for a time he refused to
paint horizontal canvases or rounded forms because of
their feminine associations.[102]

Attitudes such as these made it difficult for women
artists to find acceptance among the CSFA artists.
Dorr Bothwell, a Surrealist painter on the school's
staff, described being "shoved over in the corner to
talk to the wives" at faculty parties when discussion

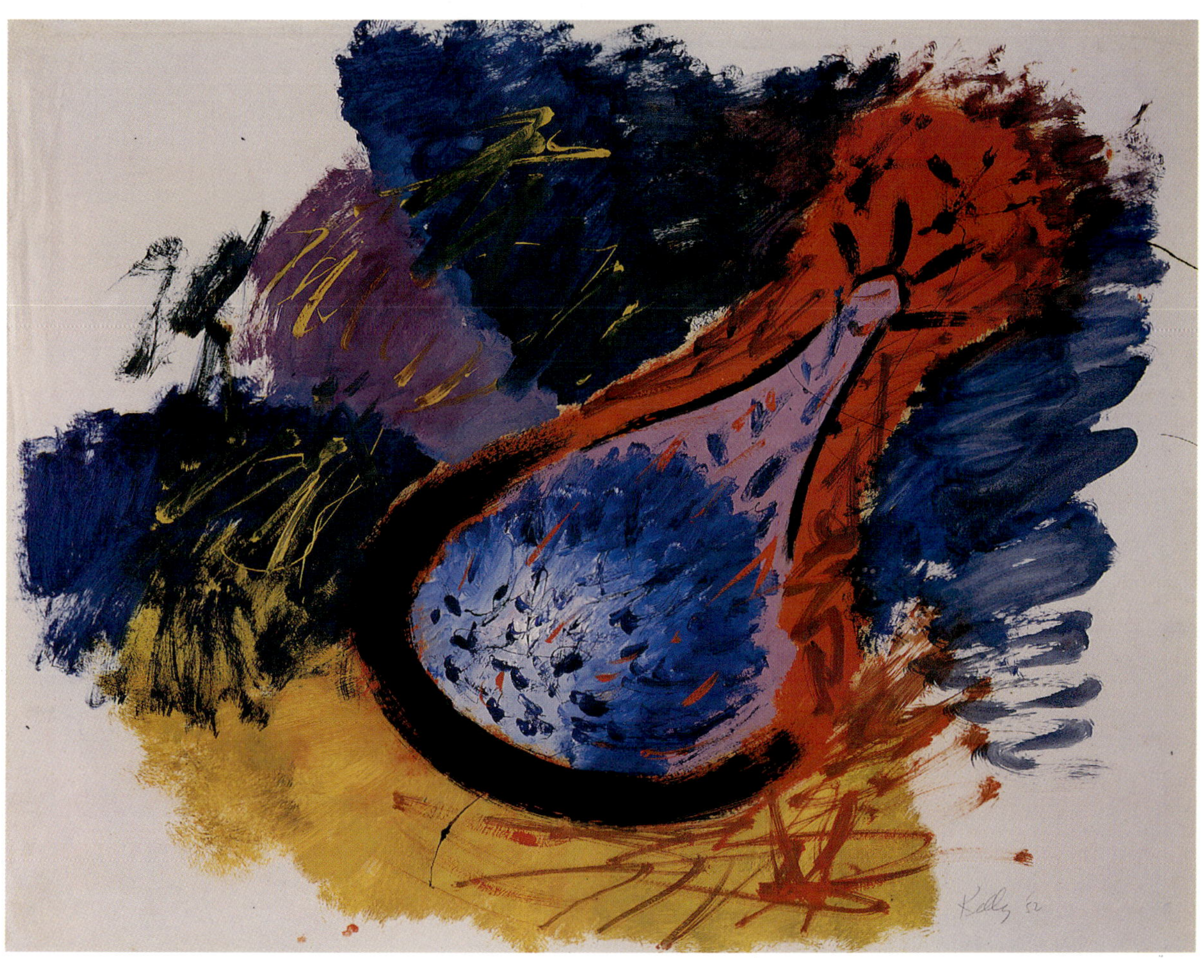

got around to art and the men deemed their four-letter terminology too crude for her sensitive ears.[103] Lilly Fenichel remembered that the only teacher at the California School of Fine Arts who gave her "permission to be soft and feminine" was Corbett.[104] Fenichel, however, could not help being excluded from director MacAgy's highest praise, which according to John Grillo (fig. 1.10) was a slap on the back and the assurance that "you paint with your cock."[105]

Although the individual styles of artists varied greatly, by the end of the 1940s a discernible San Francisco look had emerged, the product of mutual influence and a shared sensibility that valued toughness over taste. In general, the painting emphasized rough surfaces and broad areas of color. "A moving mass, not quite porous, not quite solid" was Gifford Phillips's apt description of the style.[106] The terms "gesture painting" and "color field," classifications Irving Sandler devised for the New York School, cannot generally be applied to this work.[107] While instances of both can be found—and indeed one

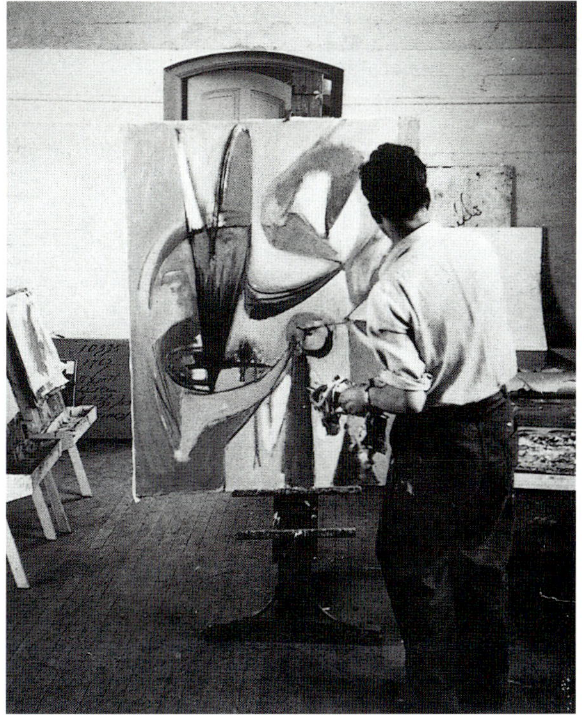

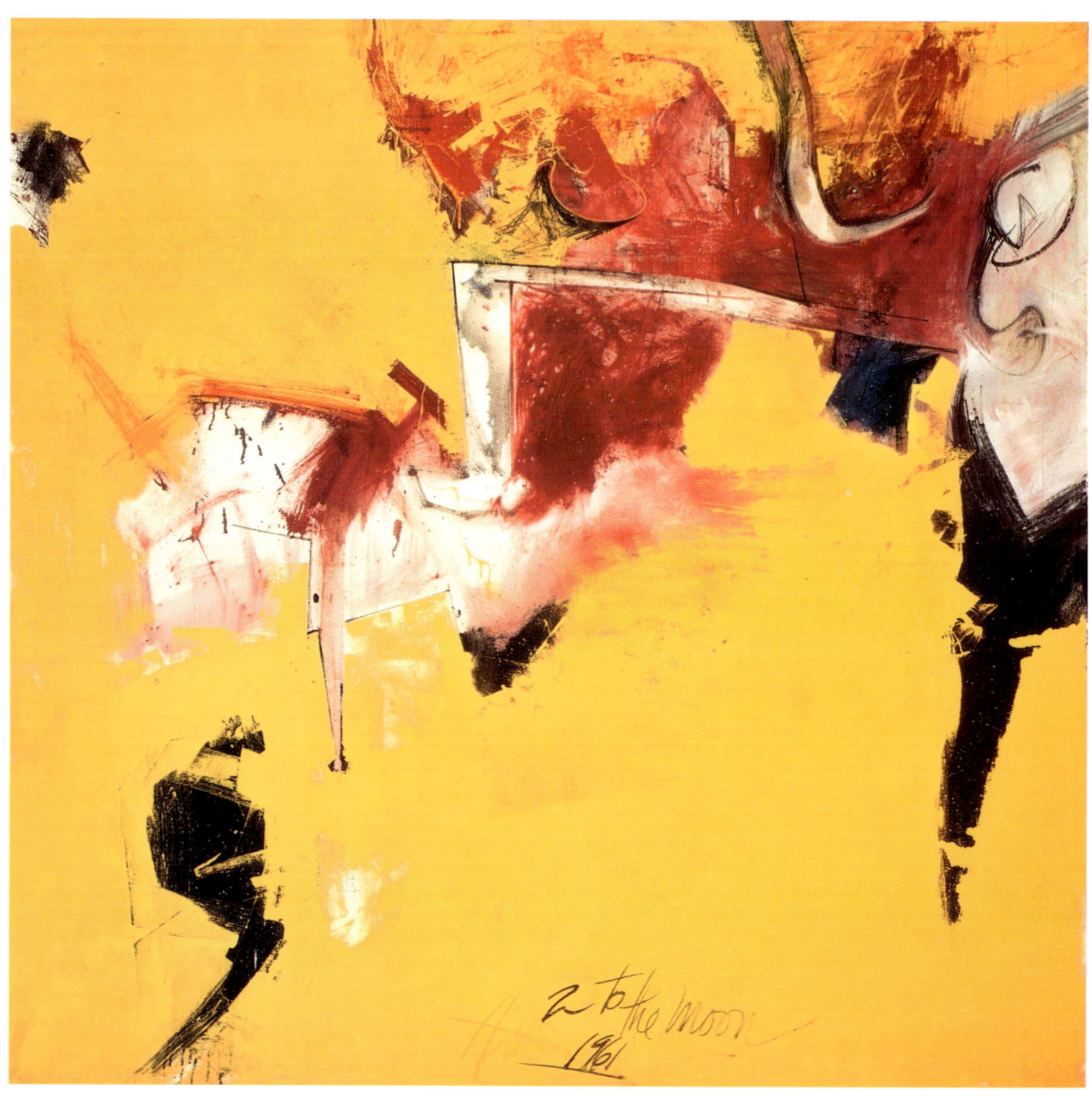

might argue that the latter was first developed in San
Francisco by Still—most painting from the region lies
somewhere between Sandler's categories. Two obvious
cases of a poor fit are Smith and Diebenkorn, whose
painting, like that of many artists in their group, com-
bines painterly brushwork with broad expanses of
unbroken color (figs. 1.11, 1.12).

The San Francisco painters also developed a distinctive palette to match their rugged paint handling.
Harry Jacobus, a student in the early 1950s, remembered that in San Francisco, "the colors had to be only
dirty, acid ones. They could never be what you might

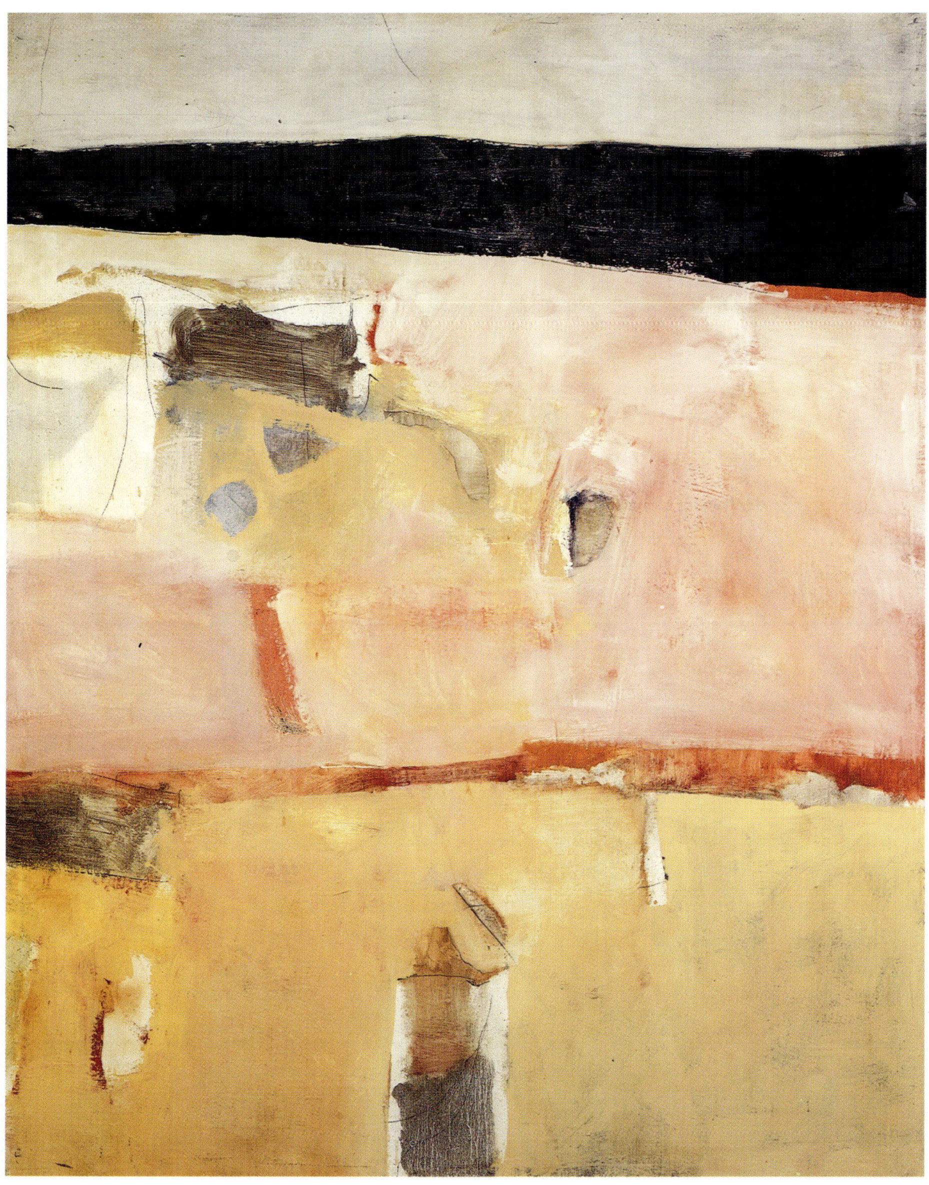

call beautiful, or pretty, or decorative."[108] There was a similar preference among the San Francisco artists for unpolished textures and raw, undisguised materials. Ronald Bladen's densely piled canvases, some of which have the appearance of caked mud (fig. 1.13), and his "earth drawings"—composed literally of dirt —exemplify this tendency.[109] Significantly, the only French artist the San Franciscans generally approved of was Jean Dubuffet, whose sludgy impastos made of mud and pebbles sometimes resembled their own.

In a broad sense, the predilection of the San Francisco painters toward an earthy organicism was char-acteristic of abstraction nearly everywhere in the decade Lawrence Alloway called the "biomorphic for-ties."[110] But the CSFA artists generally avoided the swirling biomorphs associated with Miró, Arp, and other Surrealist-influenced artists of the time. Instead, their paintings were deeply rooted in the landscape around them, and in this sense the San Francisco group differed from the New York School. Although references to nature can be found in the paintings of Gorky, Baziotes, Pollock, and Theodoros Stamos, they generally carried complex metaphoric meanings that removed them from the subject of nature

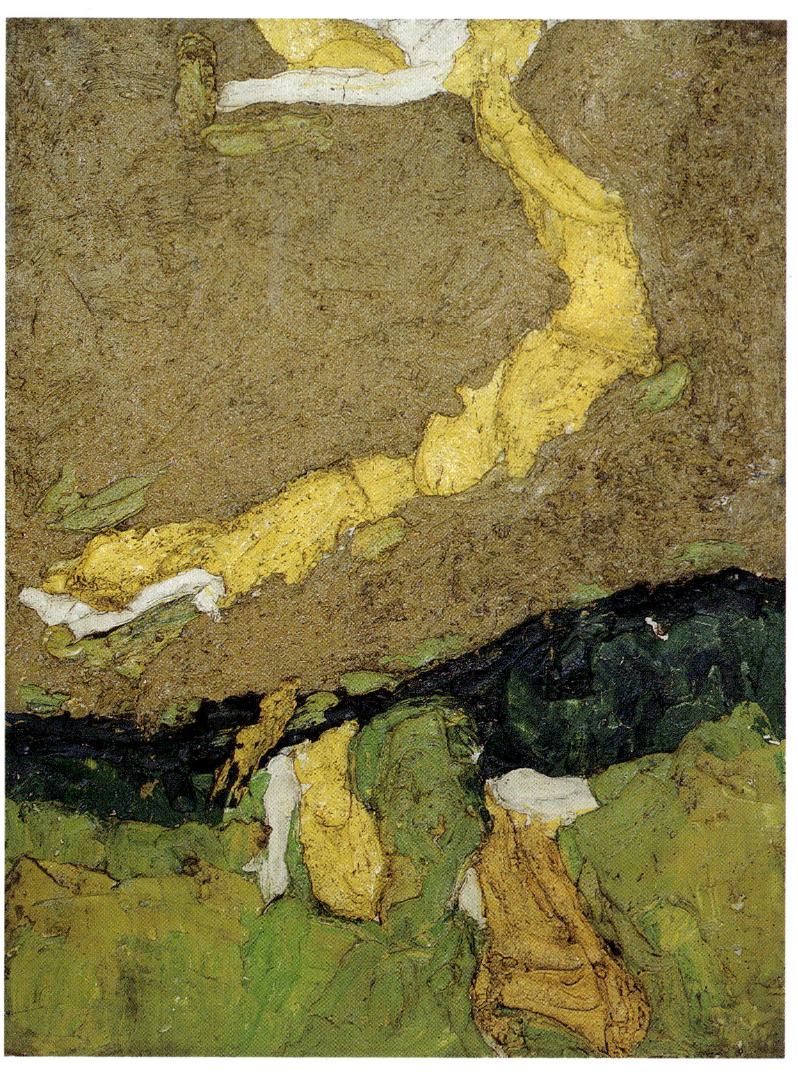

itself.[111] And while artists in New York often resorted
to illustrations in books or to specimens in the glass
cases of the Museum of Natural History, the San
Francisco painters generally addressed themselves to
their own experience of living nature. Some found
inspiration in the hills, fog, and wide-open spaces of
San Francisco; others took trips to the deserts of Mexico and the Southwest, to the Sierra Nevada, and the
Mendocino coast. Approaches to these subjects varied
considerably, from Corbett's velvety charcoals (fig.
1.14) to Grillo's luminous solar disks. John Hultberg
distilled the patterns he found in nature (a technique
he attributed to the photographer Edward Weston),
while Robert McChesney painted abstract corollaries
to such sensory experiences as the cold dampness of
fog or the shimmering heat of the desert (fig. 1.15).
Diebenkorn approached landscape formations more

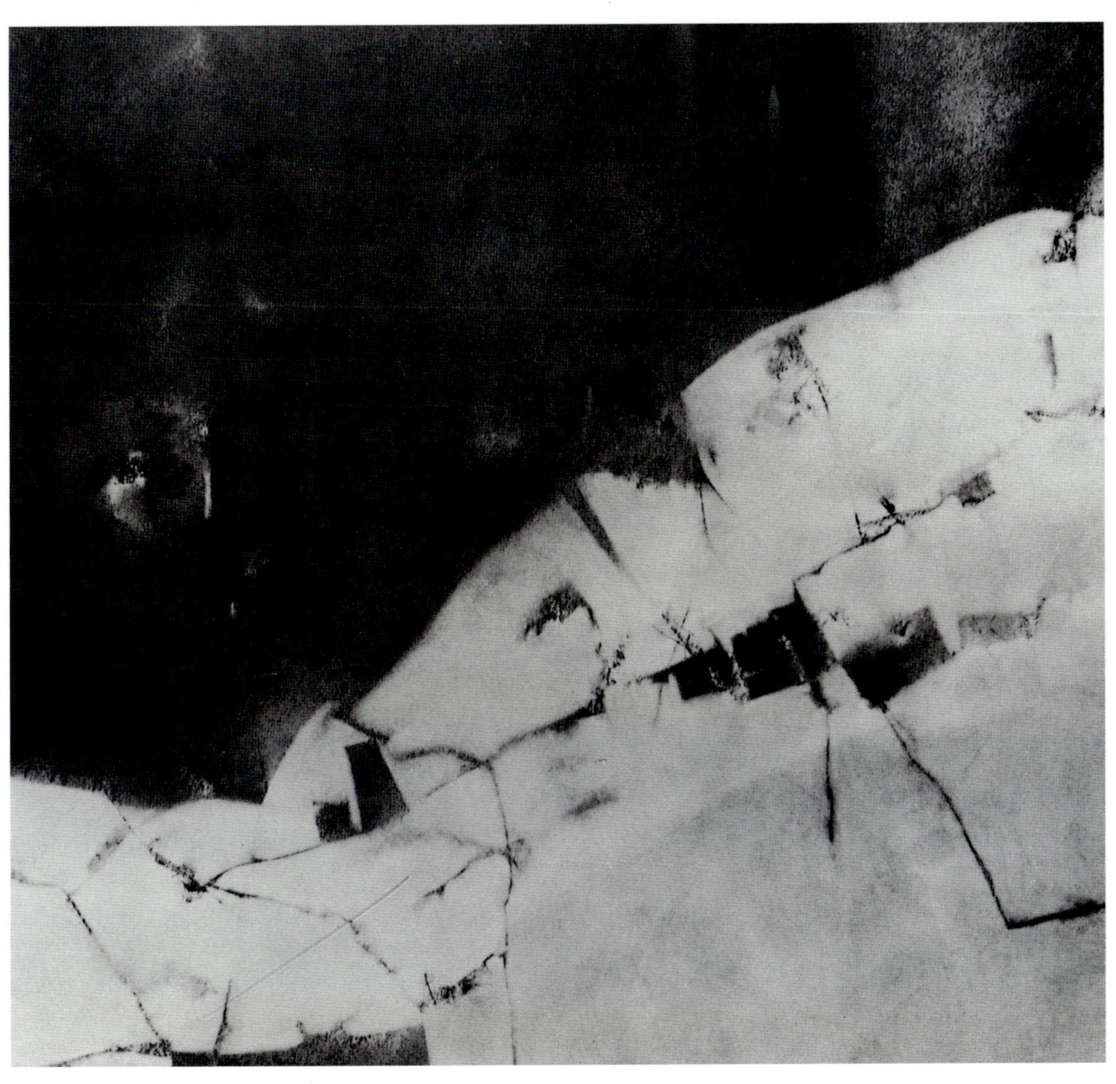

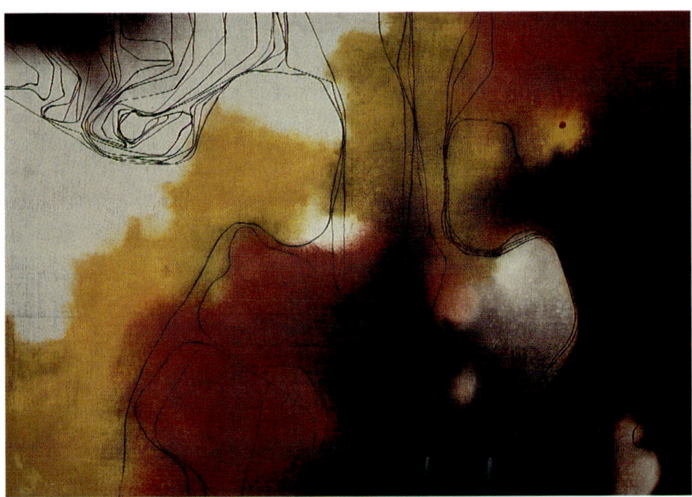

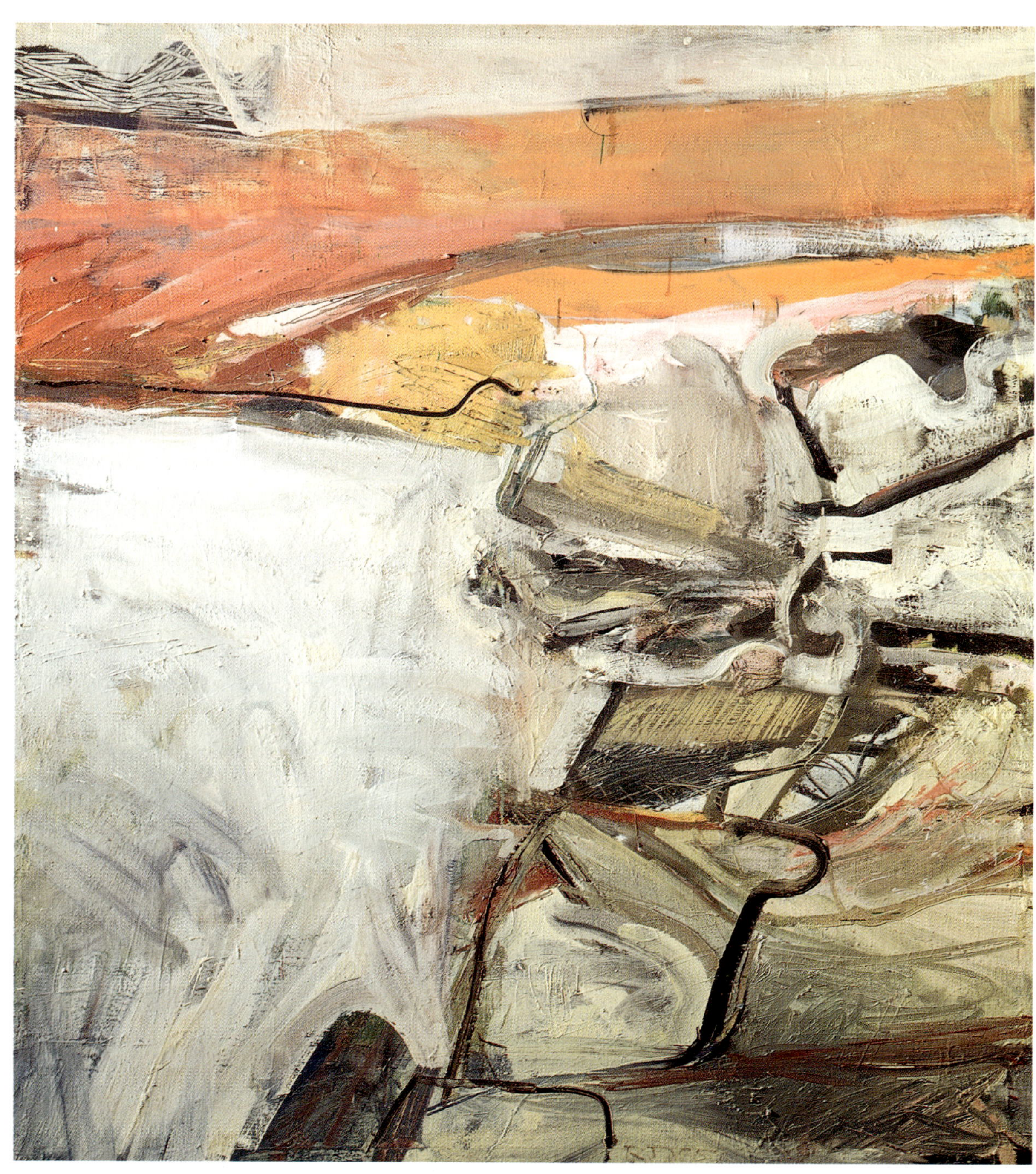

Figure 1.16

Richard Diebenkorn, *Berkeley #42,* 1955. Oil on canvas, 57½ × 51½ in. The Cleveland Museum of Art, Contemporary Collection.

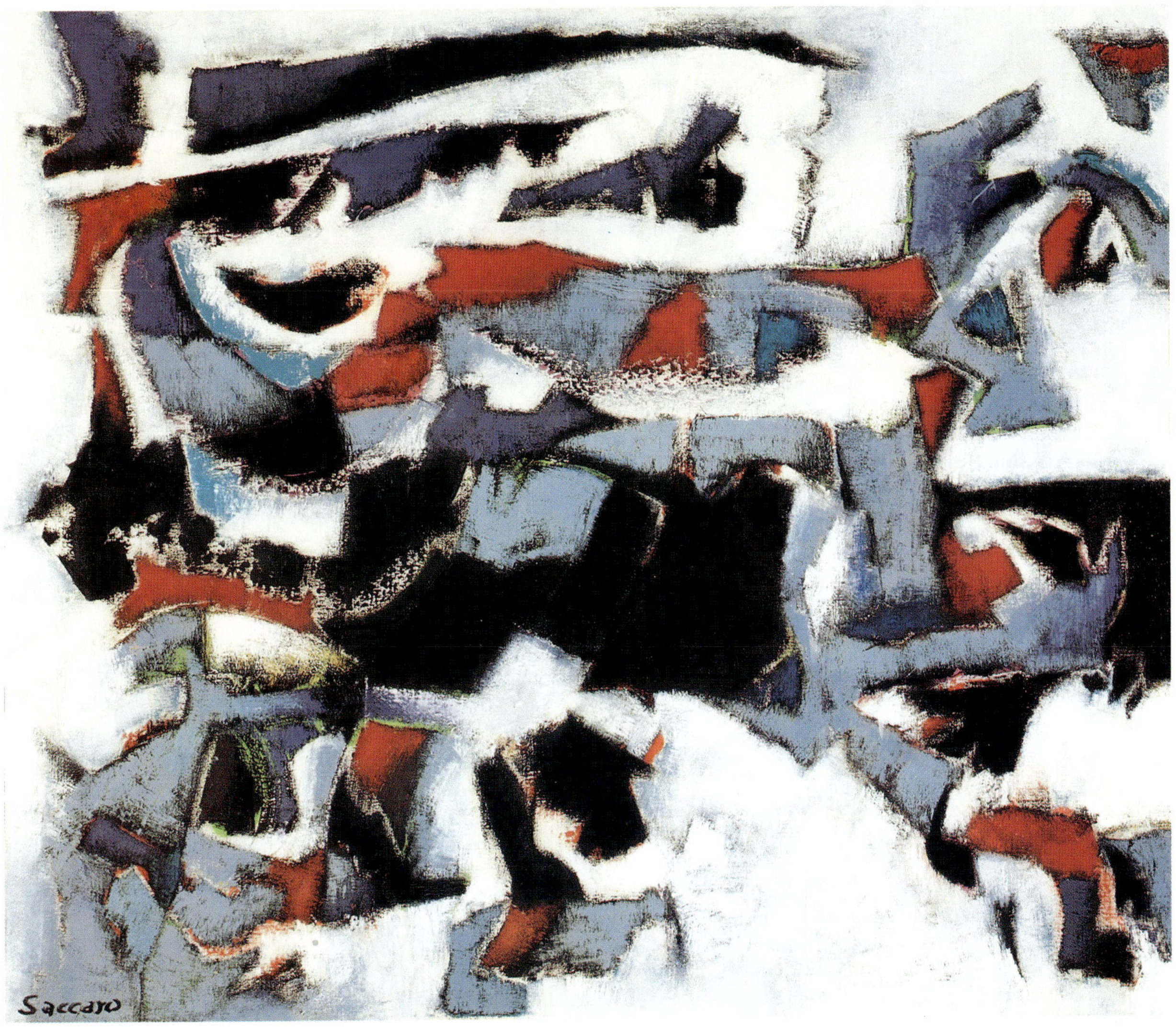

Figure 1.17

John Saccaro, *Rock, Branch, and Winter,* 1953. Oil on canvas, 41½ × 47¼ in. Collection, The Oakland Museum, gift of John Saccaro in memory of James Budd Dixon. Photographer: M. Lee Fatherree.

topographically, taking his cue from the patchwork of city and bay beneath the Berkeley hills (fig. 1.16). These paintings, begun in the early 1950s, closely paralleled New York's own brand of abstract impressionism in the work of artists such as Helen Frankenthaler and Joan Mitchell.

In their emphasis upon natural themes (as in fig. 1.17) the San Francisco Abstract Expressionists were drawing upon a long tradition in Northern California, perhaps the only truly regional tradition they adopted. Henry Hopkins, among others, has noted that an awareness and incorporation of the natural environment is "the unbroken string that not only separates the look of the art of this region from most of that of the East Coast but that of Southern California as well."[112] The local landscape was a principal

subject of Bay Area poets, too, from the eulogies of
the Sierras by Joaquin Miller and John Muir in the
nineteenth century to the nature poetry of Kenneth
Rexroth and William Everson. The revival of the environmental movement in the Bay Area after the Second World War (San Francisco was the birthplace of
the Sierra Club, the country's leading conservation
organization), sparked a renewed enthusiasm for
wilderness themes.[113] Poets such as Everson, Rexroth,
Michael McClure, and Robinson Jeffers wrote of
the untamable forces of nature. Many San Francisco
painters, including Still, were particularly drawn to
Jeffers's majestic paeans to primordial nature.[114] His
grand, almost Miltonic, evocations of the vastness of
the Pacific Ocean and the jagged shoreline of Big Sur
have much in common with Still's own soaring vision
of the sublime.

Certainly the sheer breadth and scale of open space
was among the strongest environmental influences on
artists in San Francisco. Although New York artists
such as Pollock were developing an expansive pictorial
language of their own in the late 1940s, the San Francisco painters were inspired directly by the surround-
ing landscape. The California School of Fine Arts
itself was ideally situated on Russian Hill to take
advantage of San Francisco's sweeping vistas of the
bay. Until the school was expanded in the late 1960s,
its northern face was lined by studio windows with
views that swept down to Fisherman's Wharf and several miles across the bay to Marin County. While the
impact of such visual stimuli is difficult to quantify,
many of the artists insisted that it had a tremendous
impact on their work. Edward Dugmore, for example, maintained that the horizontal tension found in

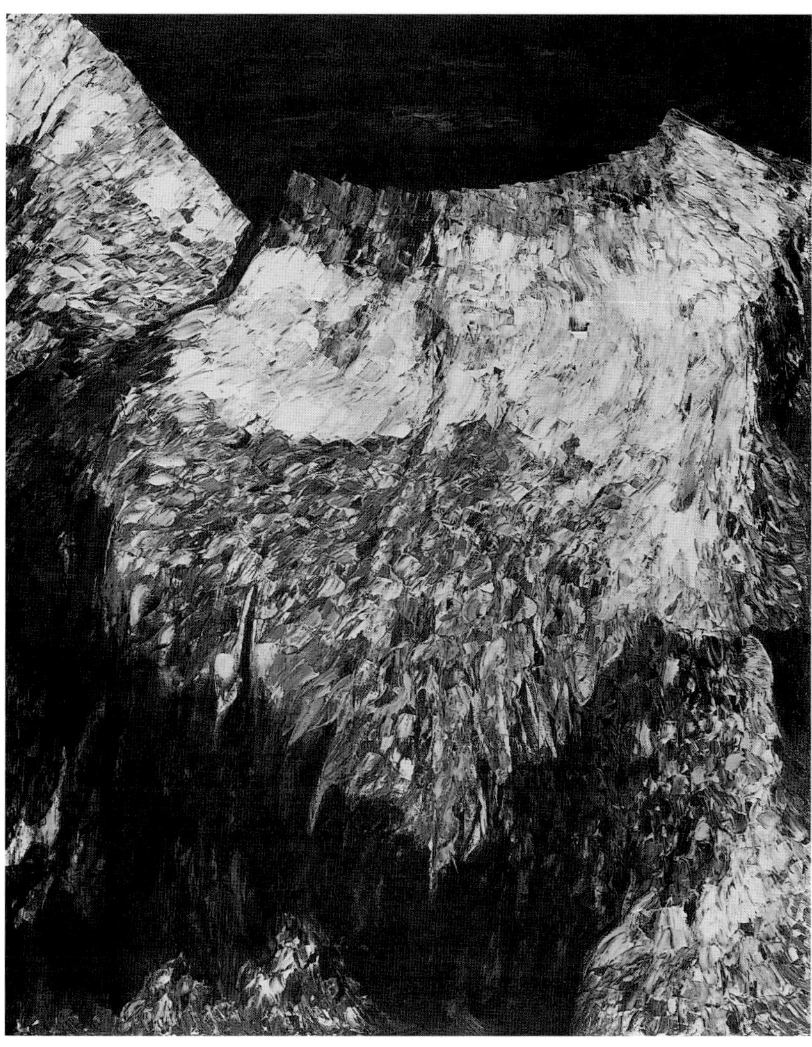

much San Francisco Abstract Expressionism, including his own (fig. 1.18), was the result of gazing at the water's horizon line day after day.[115]

Other aspects of San Francisco Abstract Expressionism can be traced specifically to the milieu of the city. The Dixieland jazz revival in San Francisco during the 1940s played an important part in the formation of Smith's aesthetic, based on the pulses and rhythms of such favorite jazz musicians as Lu Watters and Earl Hines. San Francisco's proximity to Asia and its large population of Asian immigrants made an impact as well. A number of artists were drawn to Eastern philosophies, particularly to Zen Buddhism, which was a popular topic of discussion at the California School of Fine Arts.[116] Asian painting and calligraphy were sources of inspiration for many San Francisco artists, notably Briggs, Dixon, Jay DeFeo, Sam Francis, and John Saccaro.

Of greater significance, however, was the presence of the Beat writers in San Francisco. With the departure of MacAgy and Still from the California School of Fine Arts in 1950, the center of artistic activity in San Francisco increasingly shifted to North Beach, where the Beat poets and writers had been gathering since the late 1940s. A period of intense interaction followed that lasted through the next decade. Lawrence Ferlinghetti became a spokesman for the San Francisco artists as the West Coast correspondent for *Art Digest*. A series of galleries and coffeehouses run jointly by artists and writers sprang up around North Beach, where poetry readings took place against a backdrop of Abstract Expressionist paintings. It was

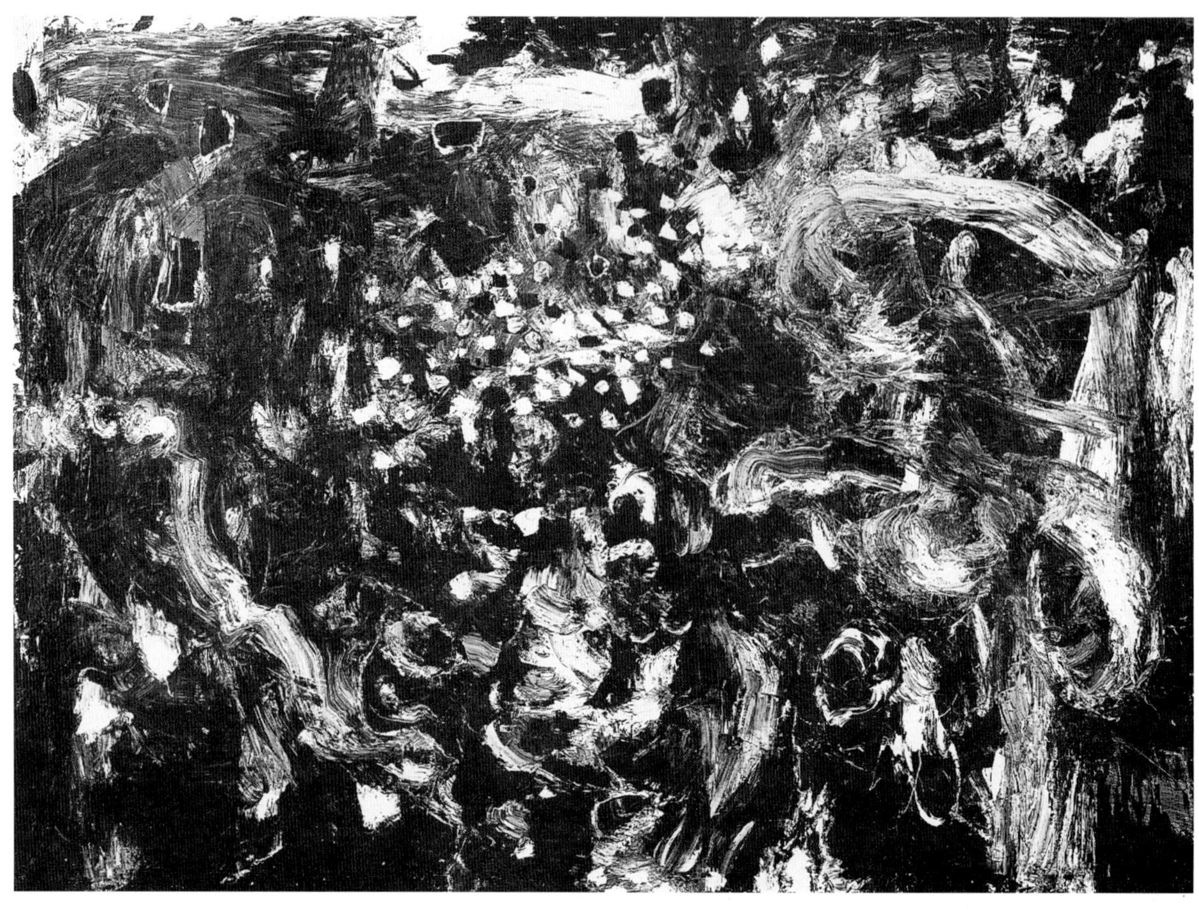

James Kelly, *Last Days of Dylan Thomas,* 1953. Oil on canvas, 64 × 87½ in. Private collection. Photographer: Leon Kuzmanoff.

in one of these alternative galleries that Allen Ginsberg gave his celebrated reading of "Howl" in 1955.[117]

This final chapter of San Francisco Abstract Expressionism has been virtually ignored, largely because the Bay Area Figurative and Funk movements diverted the attention of critics in the late 1950s. Thomas Albright, in *Art in the San Francisco Bay Area,* mentions the interchange briefly,[118] but he fails to ask the critical question: was this a marriage of convenience—a coexistence of two like-minded avant-gardes, or did the Beat writers and poets significantly influence the San Francisco painters? The question is answered by the artists who were closest to the move-

ment. Jay DeFeo, Sonia Gechtoff, James Kelly, and Deborah Remington considered their paintings visual equivalents of poetry and sometimes referred explicitly to passages of Beat writing or the poetry of such Beat heroes as Dylan Thomas (figs. 1.19–1.21). Their paintings share the wry, ironic, and sometimes morbid humor that was a hallmark of the Beat sensibility. No doubt this rapprochement was facilitated by San Francisco's permissive attitude toward representation in the 1950s. While the literary reference was for the most part taboo in New York's artistic circles, it slipped easily into the repertoire of the San Francisco painters.

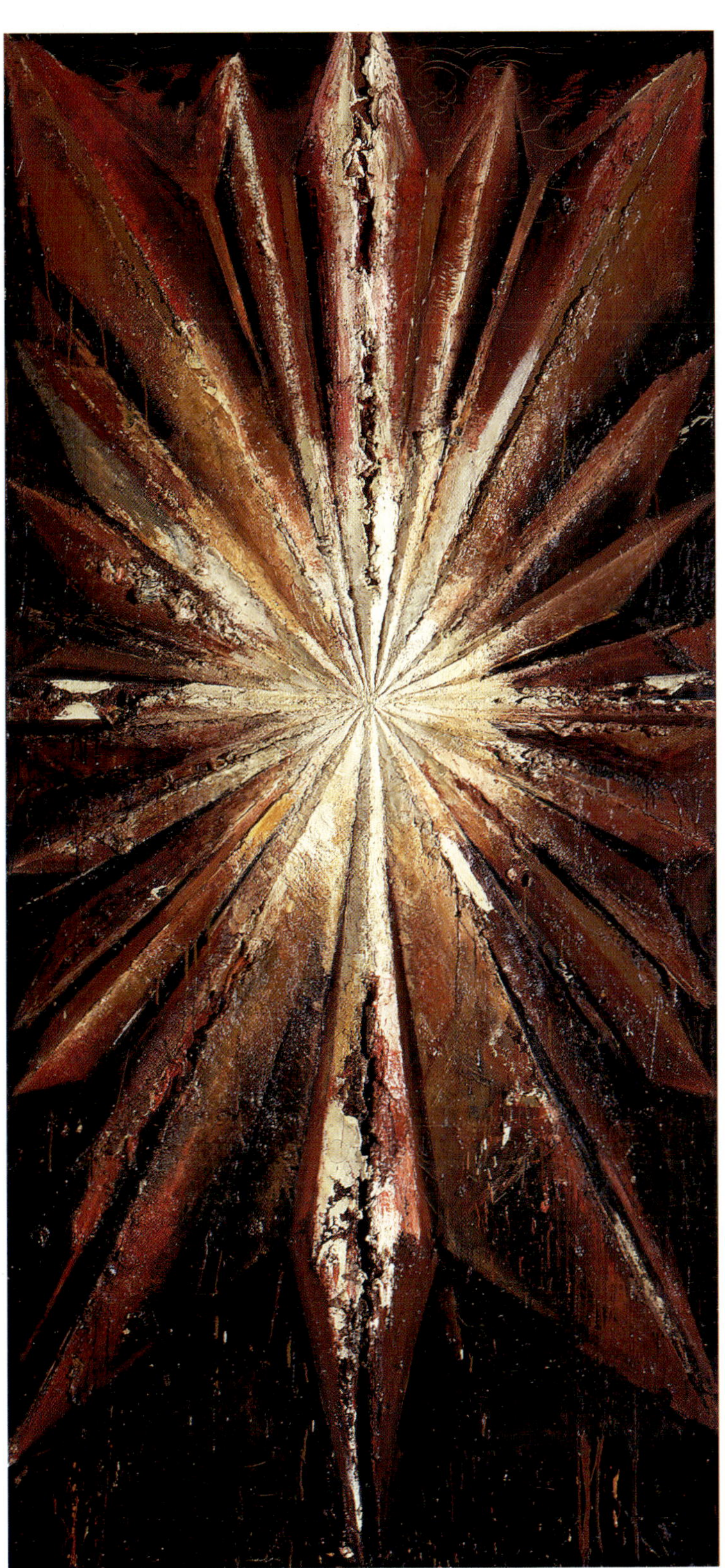

Figure 1.21

Jay DeFeo, *Jewel,* 1959. Oil and mixed media on canvas,
120 × 55 in. Collection, the Estate of Jay DeFeo.
Photographer: M. Lee Fatherree.

2

The Modernist Prologue

For several weeks in the spring of 1945, the art columns in San Francisco newspapers could speak of little besides what promised to be the city's most important art event of the year, perhaps of the decade. San Francisco had been chosen as the site of the founding conference of the United Nations, and the conference was to be accompanied by a national survey of contemporary American art. The museum selected for the exhibition was, appropriately, the stately California Palace of the Legion of Honor, a replica of Napoleon's neoclassical Palais de la Légion d'honneur, built in 1924 by San Francisco's sugar baron, Adolph Spreckels.

In a number of important respects, Jermayne MacAgy's *Contemporary American Painting* delivered its promise, signaling a new era for American art. The bicoastal exhibition proclaimed abstraction the language best suited to the international attitude and cosmopolitan vision of the postwar age. Unlike Regionalism, MacAgy wrote in the exhibition catalogue, modern art recognizes "the interdependent condition of all nations in a culture of the world."[1] For San Franciscans, these words had special resonance. More than ringing down the curtain on the nationalism of American Scene painting, which had by then been out of vogue for several years, MacAgy gave voice to San Francisco's most deeply held aspiration: to transcend its narrow identity as a regional center. San Francisco could now join the mainstream of contemporary art.

MacAgy's exhibition expressed this sense of coming of age, for only a few years earlier San Francisco's claim to cultural cosmopolitanism would have sounded hollow. For decades, San Francisco lagged behind artistic developments in Europe and other major American cities, especially New York and Chicago. Until the beginning of World War II, modernism had fared relatively poorly in San Francisco. After an auspicious start with the Panama-Pacific International Exposition of 1915, which presented a sampling of Fauvism, Cubism, Orphism, and Futurism, modern European painting stimulated no more than a conservative strain of Post-Impressionism in Northern California.[2] Even during the 1920s, when modernism was flourishing on the East Coast, the most radical modernists the Bay Area could claim were the Society of Six, an Oakland-based group of plein-air landscape painters inspired primarily by Post-Impressionism. Meanwhile, in San Francisco's bohemia—a cluster of studios on the southern flank of Telegraph Hill and lower North Beach—a barely updated style of late Impressionism and Symbolism prevailed. Gottardo Piazzoni, Maynard Dixon, Rinaldo Cuneo, Ralph Stackpole, and others who showed at Beatrice Judd Ryan's Galerie Beaux Arts in the late 1920s and early 1930s are often cited as pioneering modernists, but by East Coast standards these artists were rather timid. That Piazzoni and Stackpole could return from a trip to Paris in 1922 bubbling over with excitement about "the ascendancy of the Impressionists and their followers" suggests how far behind the times these artists were.[3] San Francisco possessed no counterpart to the Stieglitz circle in New York or the Synchromists in Los Angeles; not even the more domesticated Precisionists, such as Charles Sheeler or Louis Lozowick, won followers in the 1920s.

Northern California's first significant acknowledgment of twentieth-century European modernism took place, not in San Francisco as one might expect, but across the bay in Berkeley and Oakland, where the faculties of the University of California, the California College of Arts and Crafts, and Mills College began exploring Cubism and German Expressionism at the close of the 1920s.[4] Hans Hofmann's two summers teaching at Berkeley, in 1930 and 1931, followed by a show of his drawings at the California Palace of the Legion of Honor in the summer of 1931, encouraged a blend of modernisms incorporating the teachings of Cézanne, Matisse, and Kandinsky. Nevertheless, the efforts of these artists in the East Bay were barely noticed in San Francisco and the larger art community of Northern California. Glenn Wessels, an instructor at the California College of Arts and Crafts, remembered that he and a handful of college professors were "voices shouting in the wilderness" for most of the 1930s: "Worth Ryder and I were maybe the only two people around here who knew very much about Picasso, for instance, who knew anything about Cubism. Everything we did was lampooned in the newspapers and made fun of. When Hofmann was introduced to the San Francisco Art Association at that time, he was a figure of fun. Walters, the sculptor, got up and mimicked him in public."[5]

Admittedly, the early 1930s were not the best of times for modernists anywhere in the country, but more than reflecting the conservative sensibility of the decade, Wessels's anecdote underscores the fundamentally insular nature of the San Francisco art community. Artists in San Francisco had virtually no firsthand access to modern European art without traveling to the East Coast or abroad. Until the mid-1930s, the only museum in the Bay Area that showed modern European art was the Oakland Art Gallery, a cramped exhibition space in the Municipal Auditorium.[6] Knowledge of modernists from the East Coast was even more restricted. Alfred Maurer had been the solitary American modernist included in the Panama-Pacific Exposition in 1915, and during the 1920s, only Beatrice Judd Ryan's Galerie Beaux Arts served as a reliable conduit for contemporary art from New York, occasionally showing modernist prints and watercol-

ors from the Downtown Gallery.[7] Not until the mid-1930s would San Franciscans have the opportunity for a good look at representative works of Precisionism or the abstractions of Stuart Davis.

All of this changed with the opening of the San Francisco Museum of Art in 1935 and the appointment of Grace McCann Morley (fig. 2.1) as its director. Morley, a native of Berkeley, had studied French and Greek at the University of California before receiving a doctorate in French literature from the Sorbonne. After a brief stint as chief curator of the Cincinnati Art Museum, she returned to California to direct the new San Francisco Museum of Art.[8] Morley's international leanings, which she would later trace to hearing Woodrow Wilson speak on the League of Nations as a freshman at Berkeley, were apparent from the moment she took the post.[9] The inaugural exhibition at the museum was a survey of contemporary European and American art,[10] followed by a series of exhibitions featuring Picasso, Miró, Kandinsky, and Klee. Its program for the next ten years emphasized modern European and Latin American art, as well as the art of Oceania and Africa (the museum was officially called San Francisco's "museum of contemporary art and its sources").[11] Between 1935 and 1945 Morley was the only museum director in the country to approach the pace of Barr at the Museum of Modern Art.[12] In that period she arranged to show the majority of MOMA's landmark exhibitions, including *Fantastic Art, Dada, Surrealism* (1936), *Cubism and Abstract Art* (1936), *Picasso: Forty Years of His Art* (1940), and the Braque, Cézanne, Gauguin, Klee, Kandinsky, Matisse, and Tanguy retrospectives as well as the first showing of Picasso's *Guernica* in an American museum.[13]

The effects of Morley's crash course on modern art were felt almost at once. San Franciscans proved unusually receptive to modernism. A small exhibition of paintings by Miró at the San Francisco Museum of Art allegedly drew gasps in 1935,[14] but only five years later the public was so enamored of MOMA's visiting Picasso retrospective that officials had trouble closing the show. One newspaper reported: "This city believes it can claim the honor of having staged the first art sit-down strike in history. When the 10 o'clock closing hour at the San Francisco Museum of Art, where an extensive collection of Picasso's paintings were being shown, arrived for the last day of the display, 1,300 visitors sat down and refused to leave till they had had their fill."[15]

Public sentiment was matched by the dramatic

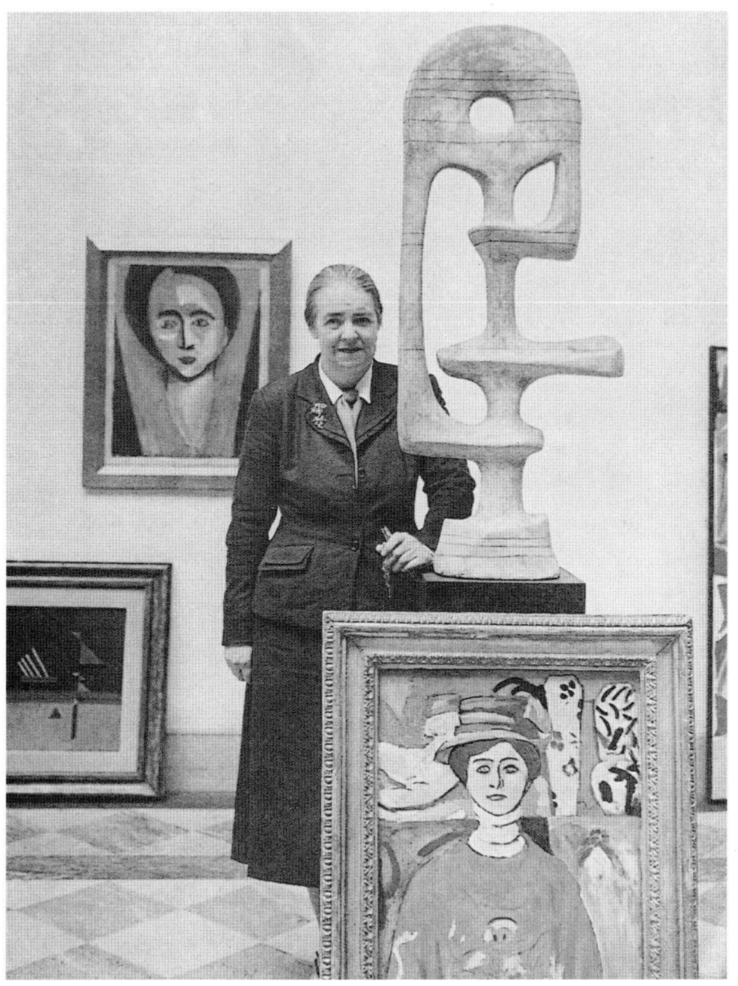

surge of modernist experimentation in the city's art community. The San Francisco Museum of Art's first survey of Bay Area painting, in 1935, presented a few works in which there was a visible turning toward abstraction, but they constituted an almost imperceptible trend.[16] A few years later, abstraction was becoming commonplace in the annual exhibitions—so much so that in 1941 *Art Digest* proclaimed San Francisco "the capital of ultra-modern art in America."[17] By the end of the war, various European strategies were conspicuous in the work of San Francisco artists: the fractured shapes of Synthetic Cubism, the childlike pictographs of Klee, the squiggling biomorphs of Miró, and the architectonic grids of Mondrian. Like their contemporaries in New York, San Francisco painters were eclectic in their borrowings, mixing and combining European motifs in a plurality of styles.

By the early 1940s, however, it was evident that Surrealism had emerged as the dominant force in San Francisco's modernist circles. Clearly, Surrealism had arrived in 1940 when the *Montgomery Street Skylight* called for artists to "awaken the potentialities of subconscious vision, visualize as it were, the essence and substance of the soul of this becoming process," and declared that "so-called technics of form, color, composition, perspective are the chains which bind art to a dead and unawakening past."[18]

With the formation of the Los Angeles–based Post-Surrealist group in 1934, ultimately composed of Grace Clements, Philip Guston, Knud Merrild, Helen Lundeberg, Reuben Kadish, Lorser Feitelson, and the San Francisco artist Lucien Labaudt, Surrealism made an earlier debut in California than in the rest of the country.[19] The work of these artists, for the most part a veristic brand of Surrealism (with the exception of Merrild's poured "flux" abstractions),[20]

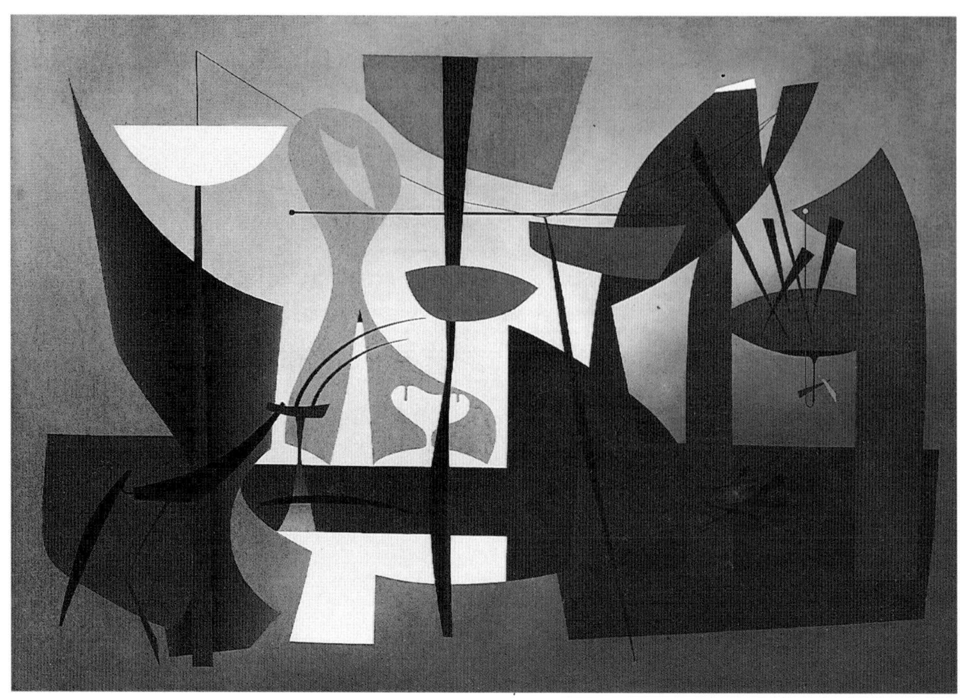

was shown in an exhibition at the San Francisco Museum of Art in 1935.[21] Local interest in Surrealism was further nurtured by Barr's controversial survey *Fantastic Art, Dada, Surrealism,* which came to San Francisco in 1937, and by a series of shows of work by Surrealist émigrés organized by Howard Putzel and Julien Levy in the late 1930s for the Paul Elder and Courvoisier galleries in San Francisco.[22] With the outbreak of World War II, the San Francisco Museum of Art also began to showcase the Surrealist émigrés. Beginning with a solo show of Tanguy in 1940, Morley presented at least one exhibition per year of the work of an exiled member of the Surrealist group or an artist working in the Surrealist mode,[23] as well as several group shows of Surrealist émigrés.[24]

Surrealism took a variety of forms in San Francisco, some reflecting national tendencies, others, regional characteristics specific to the area. One local variant was the highly disciplined, formalist Surrealism of Charles Howard. Howard had exhibited with the Surrealists in London during the 1930s, where he married the Surrealist painter Madge Knight. In 1940 he returned to California with a style of hard-edge abstract Surrealism that became especially influential in San Francisco. *First War Winter* (1939–40; fig. 2.2) is typical of Howard's enigmatic yet severely classical imagery. Among the artists who worked in this mode were Spohn, André Moreau, Leah Rinne Hamilton, and Robert McChesney (fig. 2.3).

Closer to the abstract Surrealism found in New York were the swirling André Masson–like abstractions of Dan Harris (also known as Zev), John Holland, W. Edwin Ver Becke, Philip Pinner, Ralph Du Casse, and Bezalel Schatz. Were it not for their diminutive scale and semifigurative elements, some of these works might pass for full-blown Abstract Expressionism.[25] Schatz's work in particular parallels Pollock's automatic paintings of the 1940s. From 1947 on Schatz executed a series of torrential works in which paint was violently squeezed and flung upon his canvases.[26]

Despite his stylistic kinship with certain members

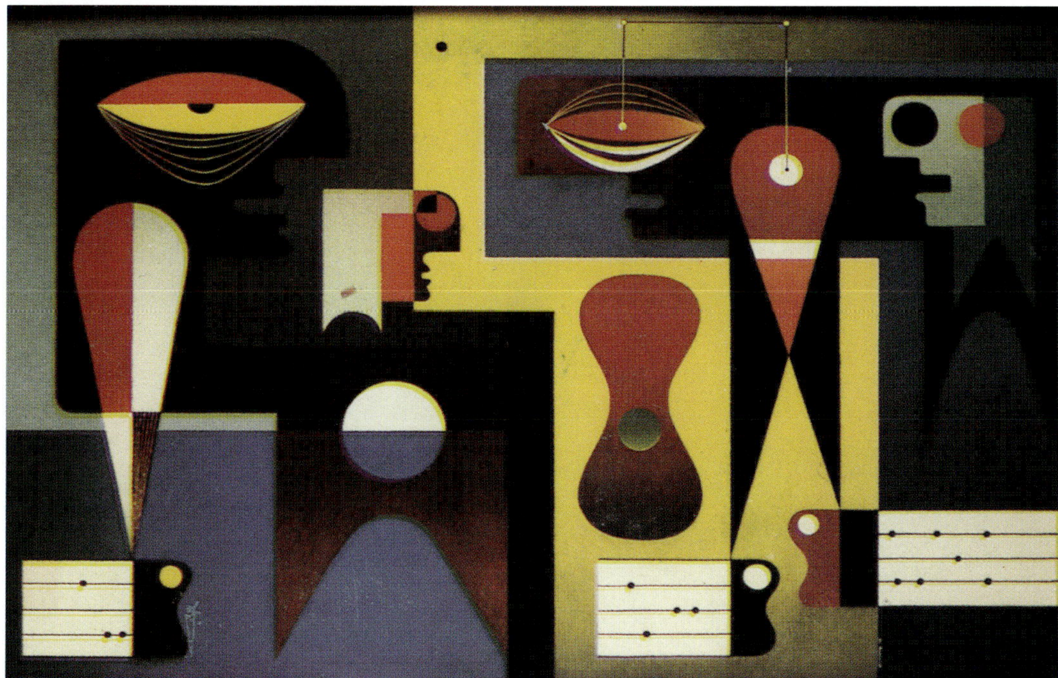

Figure 2.3

Robert McChesney, *Morning, Noon, Nite,* 1946. Oil on board,

25 × 37 in. Collection, James and Linda Ries. Photograph

courtesy, 871 Fine Arts, San Francisco; photographer:

Don Felton.

of the future New York School, Schatz was never part of the Abstract Expressionist movement in San Francisco. Indeed, very few of the artists who came to prominence in the late 1940s at the California School of Fine Arts participated in the Surrealist discourse that governed San Francisco's avant-garde during the war. Most of them (probably even Still) experimented with Surrealism at some stage in their careers, but their engagement was mostly cursory. Unlike their counterparts in New York, few San Francisco Abstract Expressionists inquired into the unconscious mind or explored the primitive, archetypal subject matter of late Surrealism.[27]

Scholars have generally argued that this relative lack of involvement reflected a paucity of Surrealist influence in San Francisco.[28] As I have suggested, however, not only was Surrealism well established in San Francisco, but a number of important exiled Surrealists visited the region during the 1940s. Indeed, two of the Surrealist émigrés most influential for the New York School—Stanley William Hayter and Gor-

don Onslow-Ford—developed high profiles in the Bay Area during the 1940s. Morley gave Hayter his first one-man show in the United States in 1940 before he moved to New York and introduced Surrealist concepts to Pollock, Rothko, and Motherwell. Hayter also taught painting and printmaking at the California School of Fine Arts in 1940 and 1948 and throughout the 1940s made visits to the Bay Area, where his wife, the sculptor Helen Phillips, had been born and raised.[29] Onslow-Ford also became a familiar figure in San Francisco after moving there in 1947 with the Surrealist émigré Wolfgang Paalen and renting an apartment just up the street from the California School of Fine Arts. Two years later, Onslow-Ford took a studio on the Sausalito ferryboat *Vallejo,* which he shared with the CSFA instructor Jean Varda (soon to be joined by Alan Watts). Morley was immediately receptive to Onslow-Ford's work and published one of his most important theoretical tracts, *Towards a New Subject in Painting,* in 1948 to accompany his largest museum exhibition to date. Soon afterward,

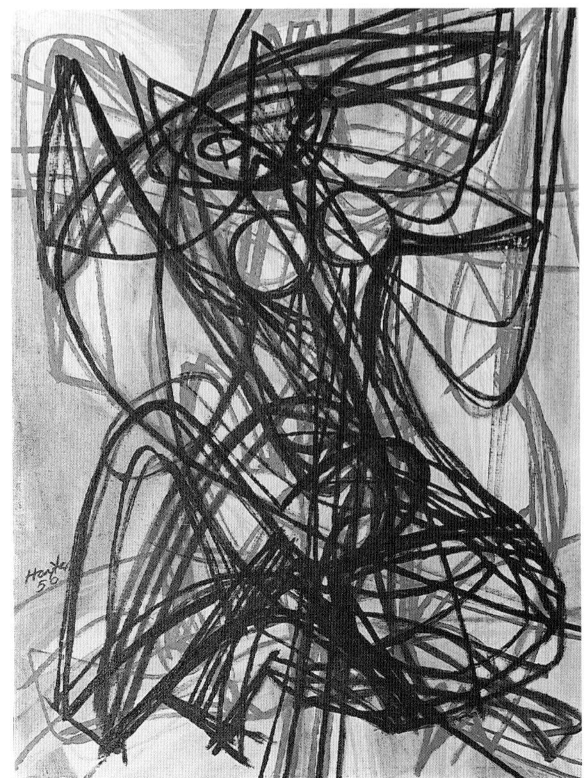

Figure 2.4

Stanley William Hayter, *Marionette,* 1950. Oil on canvas, 39¼ × 28⅞ in. Collection, San Francisco Museum of Modern Art, gift of Mr. and Mrs. Archibald Taylor.

Onslow-Ford joined forces with Paalen and the local Surrealist Lee Mullican to form the abstract Surrealist Dynaton group, which premiered at the San Francisco Museum of Art in 1951.

Thus, rather than being insufficiently acquainted with Surrealism, it would seem that many of San Francisco's Abstract Expressionists deliberately set themselves apart from the movement. Still was especially vocal in his antagonism toward what he called "Surrealist theology," but Corbett, Lobdell, Smith, Dugmore, and Jefferson were also among those skeptical of Surrealism's elaborate theoretical doctrine and its preoccupation with psychoanalytic archetypes.[30] For these artists such subject matter was ultimately inhibiting and irrelevant to personal expression. Symbolic allusions were something to be purged from their art rather than coaxed into being through automatism.

Although spontaneity was an important feature of Abstract Expressionism in San Francisco, it related less to the Surrealist technique of automatism than to the broader championing of immediacy that runs through the modernist tradition beginning with Impression-ism.[31] Stream-of-consciousness poetry and prose, improvisational jazz, and the expressionist methods of such figurative artists as C. S. Price were collectively more influential than Surrealism in encouraging a spontaneous approach to painting.[32] Indeed, the technique of automatism was sometimes frowned upon in San Francisco.[33] Lobdell recalled that in the late 1940s, automatism was viewed with suspicion at the California School of Fine Arts: "Anything that became a formula was suspect, and being spontaneous could be a formula."[34] Even Hayter's innovative automatic techniques were rejected as overformulaic (fig. 2.4). In the summer of 1948, Hultberg and Lobdell walked out in disgust after two weeks of Hayter's painting class. Stillman later explained that Hayter was "trying to make everybody paint curves."[35]

Although these artists were perhaps more indebted to Surrealism than they liked to admit—certainly their organic-form vocabulary and ambiguous sense of space owed something to Surrealist art—the rebellious attitudes they cultivated resulted in a greater distancing from Surrealism than that found among New York's Abstract Expressionists. Not only did they consciously reject myth-conferring titles and symbols, but their work rarely showed such Surrealist commonplaces as swirling arabesques and curvilinear shapes.[36] And perhaps because automatism was not fundamental to their painting process, the work they produced was somewhat less linear and gestural than Abstract Expressionism in New York.

The genesis of Abstract Expressionism in San Francisco raises provocative questions about the role of Surrealism in the development of Abstract Expressionism in general. Art historians have been inclined to assume along with Jeffrey Wechsler that the Abstract Expressionists "developed their mature style because of their contact with Surrealism."[37] Yet while this assumption seems at least partially plausible for some of the New York painters—although not for de Kooning or Hofmann, whose roots were too securely expressionist—it is certainly not applicable to the majority of San Francisco's Abstract Expressionists. San Francisco's relationship to Surrealism is characterized more by rupture than seamless continuity. Rather than build upon the achievements of the European movement, the San Francisco painters meant to supplant it, to "unseat the reigning king," in the words of Ernest Briggs.[38] The story of that dethroning must first acknowledge the particular complex of personalities and circumstances brought together by the California School of Fine Arts at the close of the war.

Douglas MacAgy and the California School of Fine Arts

Douglas MacAgy's appointment as director of the California School of Fine Arts in the summer of 1945 marked the beginning of the school's transformation from a relatively undistinguished art academy into the headquarters of Abstract Expressionism on the West Coast.[39] Financially strapped since the Depression, the California School of Fine Arts had nearly closed twice during the war because of low enrollment. In this "rather desperate" situation, MacAgy recalled, the Board of Trustees gave him virtually free rein to appoint a new faculty and redesign the curriculum.[40]

MacAgy had been interested in modern art for many years before taking the position at the California School of Fine Arts (fig. 2.5). By his own account, he had spent the better part of a decade being "over-educated" in art history and psychology—at the University of Pennsylvania and the University of Toronto,

the Barnes Foundation, the Courtauld Institute, and the Cleveland School of Art—before finding employment as a curator at the Cleveland Museum of Art in the late 1930s.[41] His imaginative installation of Barr's traveling Picasso show there in 1940 led Morley to hire him the following year as her assistant in San Francisco.[42] As a member of Morley's staff, MacAgy soon developed a strong interest in Dada and Surrealism, which led him to make the acquaintance of a number of New York artists, including Gorky, whose first museum exhibition took place at the San Francisco Museum of Art in 1941. His wife, Jermayne MacAgy, also became a forceful advocate of vanguard art while on the staff of the California Palace of the Legion of Honor, where she was influential in promoting contemporary abstraction. Her annual exhibitions there in the late 1940s put San Franciscans in touch with some of the latest achievements of East Coast artists. By all accounts, she was a remarkably creative curator whose exhibitions included a landmark survey of kinetic sculpture in 1948 and a show of large-scale drawings in 1950 that required submissions of no less than six feet in height or width.[43] Many of the Abstract Expressionists associated with the California School of Fine Arts in the late 1940s and early 1950s—including Bischoff, Diebenkorn, and Smith—would have their first solo museum exhibitions at the Legion of Honor.

Although some artists recall that Jermayne was the more influential of the pair, she has been overshadowed by her husband.[44] Decades of local veneration have created a mystique around Douglas MacAgy. One of the most celebrated legends recounts that his first act upon taking over the school was to cover the Diego Rivera mural in the auditorium with a curtain—interpreted invariably as a visionary gesture ushering in a new era of painting.[45] The gesture, however, could hardly have been visionary considering that Social Realism had gone out of fashion with the beginning of the war, and actually the fresco remained uncovered for most of MacAgy's tenure.[46] Similarly, MacAgy is credited with liberating the school from its traditional institutional structure by abolishing grades, holding faculty meetings over cocktails, and allowing the school to function essentially as a cluster of studios. In reality, he did none of these things. MacAgy did create a freer atmosphere than that of previous administrations by allowing studios to remain open twenty-four hours a day, by making himself personally available to students—"he was not a

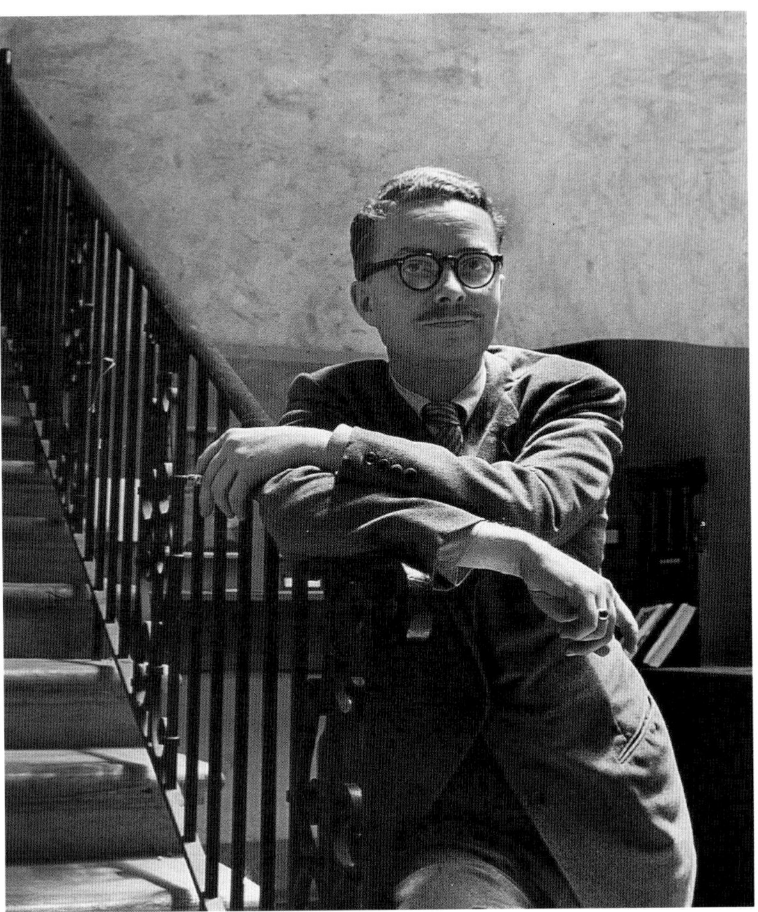

Figure 2.5

Douglas MacAgy, California School of Fine Arts, 1947. Photograph courtesy, San Francisco Art Institute Archives.

character shut up in an office somewhere," one student recalled—and by organizing raucous parties, where the faculty's Studio 13 Jazz Band played Dixieland jazz (MacAgy himself played drums).[47] But Still's depiction of MacAgy as an autocratic individual who reminded him of "a small army officer" is telling.[48] By nature, MacAgy was a strict disciplinarian who despised slovenliness in artists, a man who told a reporter in 1948 that "the day of the Bohemiantype artist is dead."[49] Accordingly, the program MacAgy instituted reflected an exacting personality. As the school's records make clear, students who did not take their work seriously were promptly expelled.[50]

But recognizing MacAgy's concern with discipline should not subtract from his pivotal role in promoting and nurturing experimental art in San Francisco.

Indeed, he was deeply devoted to avant-garde ideals. His stated aim as director was to make the school a "laboratory" or "proving ground" for experimentation while encouraging his students to study the past carefully—"not to conform to it, not to acquire taste, but to discover loopholes for escape from its dead hand."[51] Most important, the school was not to "impose a ready-made set of visual arrangements or prescribed meanings" and would pay respect "at all times to the ultimate integrity of the individual artist."[52]

MacAgy's emphasis on personal freedom and his emphatic denunciation of a priori standards seem to have been in large measure a response to the oppressive policies of art academies under Hitler, Stalin, and Mussolini. In the late 1940s MacAgy frequently compared his own catholic program to the rigid prescriptive standards of these dictators. In MacAgy's opinion, the classical revival flourishing in their institutions was intended to assist political ambitions and "rationalist, materialist, and mechanistic modes of action."[53]

MacAgy seems to have been determined as well to give the California School of Fine Arts a national rather than regional outlook, to make it a place where artists could encounter the essential forces of American art. His most significant step in that direction was to appoint a group of teachers more attuned than their predecessors to the latest developments in contemporary art. Because the faculty had dwindled during the financially disastrous war years, MacAgy was able to begin with a virtually clean slate.[54] He put Minor White and Ansel Adams in charge of a new photography department dedicated to expressive photography,[55] and he hired the abstract Surrealist Robert Howard to head the sculpture program. He brought in Sidney Peterson to teach an experimental filmmaking workshop stressing vanguard techniques.[56] And in the painting department, MacAgy gave full-time appointments to Bischoff, Smith, Park, and Spohn.

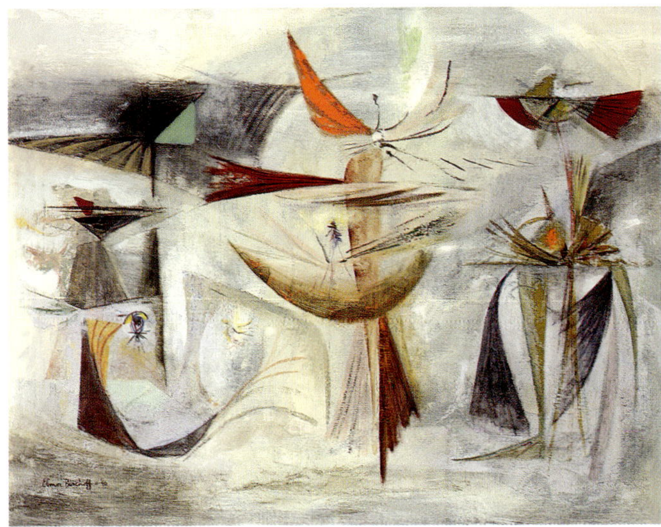

Figure 2.6

Elmer Bischoff, *Untitled*, 1946. Oil on canvas, 21⅞ × 27⅞ in.

Collection, Stephen Bischoff. Photographer M. Lee Fatherree.

Faculty I: Bischoff, Smith, Park, and Spohn

Elmer Bischoff was the youngest of MacAgy's new faculty members. Born in 1916, the son of an architect, Bischoff was raised in a comfortable middle-class family in Berkeley. In the mid-1930s he studied art at the University of California under the "Berkeley School" modernists Worth Ryder, Erle Loran, and Margaret Peterson and became an ardent admirer of Cézanne and Synthetic Cubism. The Picasso retrospective at the San Francisco Museum of Art confirmed that direction. He would later recall that the show made a tremendous impression, for Picasso represented "the maximum of aliveness on canvas."[57] The encounter led to a series of self-described "homages to Picasso," which lasted until he was drafted into the military.[58] After spending several years in the Army Air Corps with an intelligence unit stationed in England and France, Bischoff returned to California; a few months later, in January 1946, he began teaching at the California School of Fine Arts.

During his first year on the faculty, Bischoff's paintings no longer paid homage to Picasso but incorporated much of the Surrealist spirit found in San Francisco during the war. The critic Alfred Frankenstein described the oils and watercolors Bischoff displayed in 1946 as "beautifully and subtly handled studies of twirling, strutting, and flying forms."[59] The pastel colors and delicate use of line in paintings such as the untitled canvas in figure 2.6 call to mind the Surrealist abstractions of Matta and Rothko.[60] But Bischoff's Surrealist phase would be short-lived. By 1947 his soft ethereal abstractions had given way to vigorous, brutal paintings on a much larger scale (fig. 2.7).[61]

Hassel Smith was similarly recruited from the Bay Area, but his background differed from Bischoff's (fig. 2.8). Smith had come to California with his parents as a teenager, settling in San Mateo, a suburb south of San Francisco. His initiation to modern art came while he was an undergraduate at Northwestern University in the early 1930s, when he saw a large survey of European painting and sculpture at the Art Institute of Chicago. His rapport was instantaneous, and after completing a bachelor's degree in art history and practice, he returned to San Francisco to enroll at the California School of Fine Arts.[62] At that time the school was still a traditional academy of art, offering the usual courses in life drawing and figure painting. Smith studied with Spencer Macky, Otis Oldfield, and Lee Randolph, old-line modernists working largely in the tradition of the Post-Impressionists. Far more significant for his development were the courses he took with the guest instructor Maurice Sterne. Sterne's expressionist paint handling (he was a great admirer of Soutine) and his fluid draftsmanship had a lasting impact on Smith.

Smith's work of the late 1930s consisted primarily of spontaneous plein-air scenes of San Francisco and the local countryside. When the war broke out, his 4-F status kept him out of the service, and between odd jobs working as a timber scaler and social worker, he joined the artists who frequented the bohemian bars and cafés of North Beach (fig. 2.9). Smith's membership in the group was confirmed when he moved into Maynard Dixon's old studio in the Montgomery Block, a popular address for artists and writers since the late nineteenth century. His first solo show, held at the neighboring Iron Pot restaurant in 1946, was organized by Henri Lenoir, the impresario of North Beach who later opened the Vesuvio Café, the legendary haunt of the Beat poets. Smith's work at the time concentrated on riotous tavern scenes and proto-Pop Americana (fig. 2.10). Some of his favorite subjects were ice-cream cones, American flags, and cigarstore Indians. Frankenstein described Smith's richly

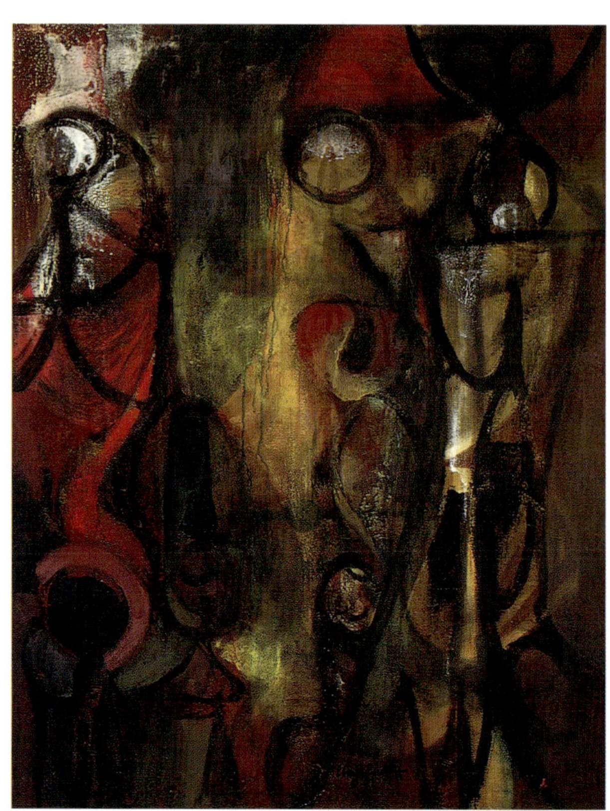

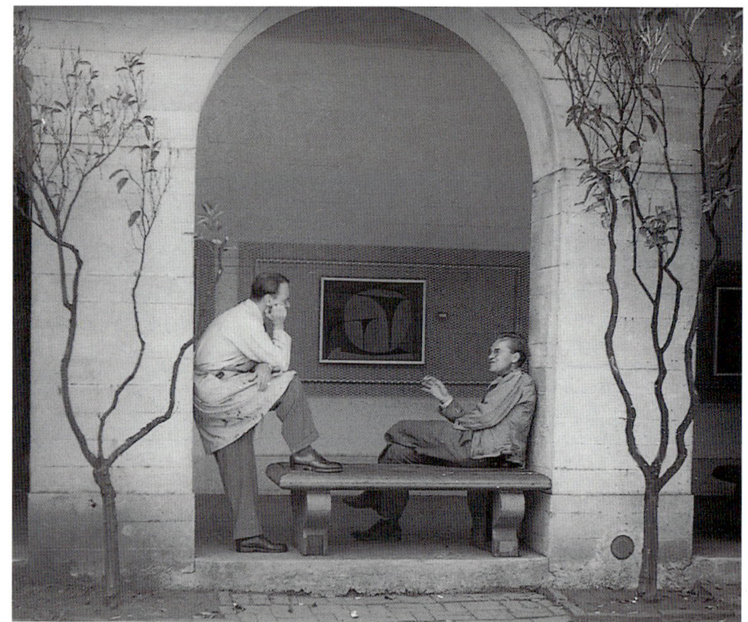

Figure 2.7

Above: Elmer Bischoff, *Vertical Assemblage,* 1947. Oil on canvas, 49 × 36¾ in. Collection, Laurie Bischoff Hall. Photographer: M. Lee Fatherree.

Figure 2.8

Right: Elmer Bischoff (*left*) and Hassel Smith, California School of Fine Arts, San Francisco, 1948. Photographer: William Heick.

Figure 2.9

Opposite: Hassel Smith, ca. early 1940s.

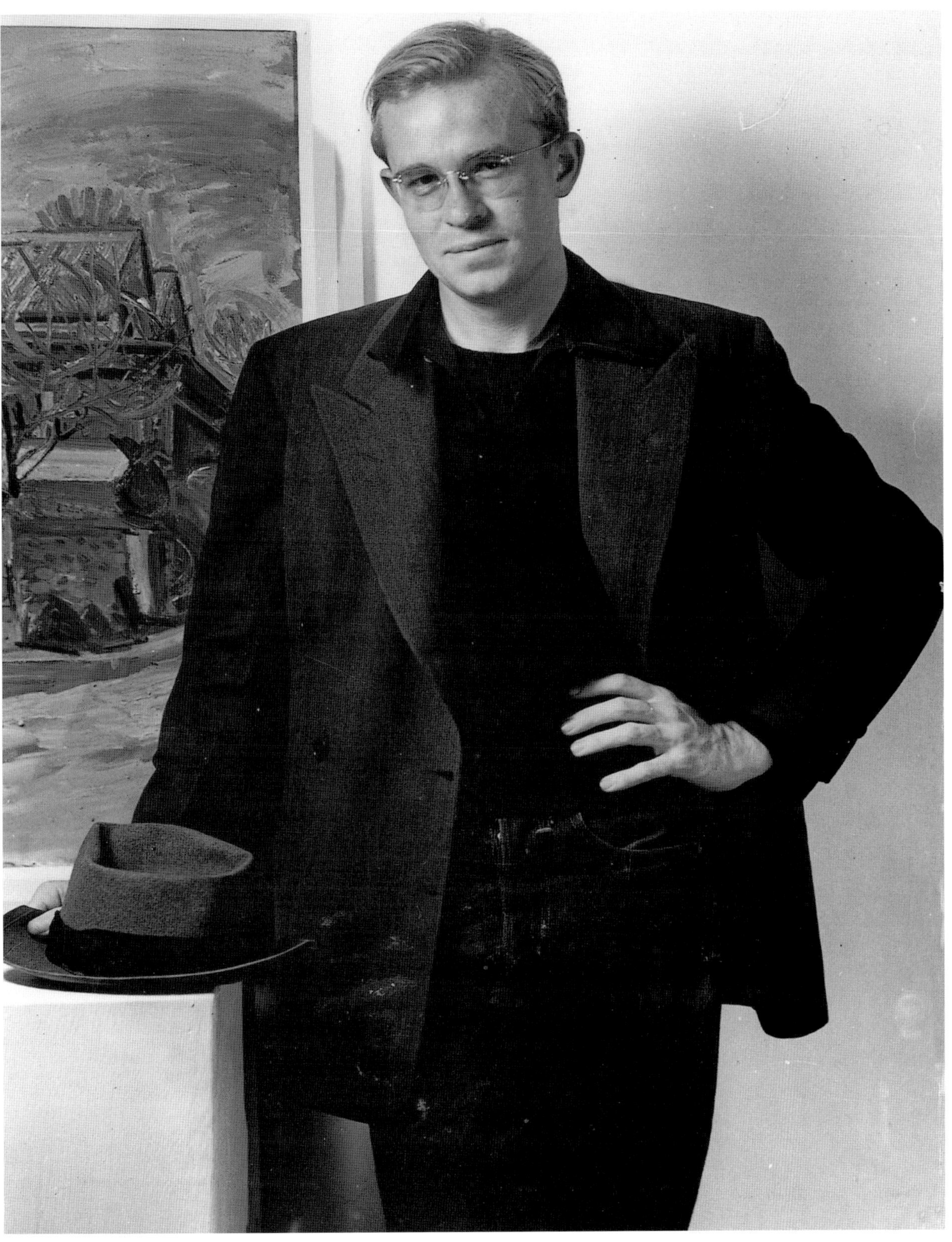

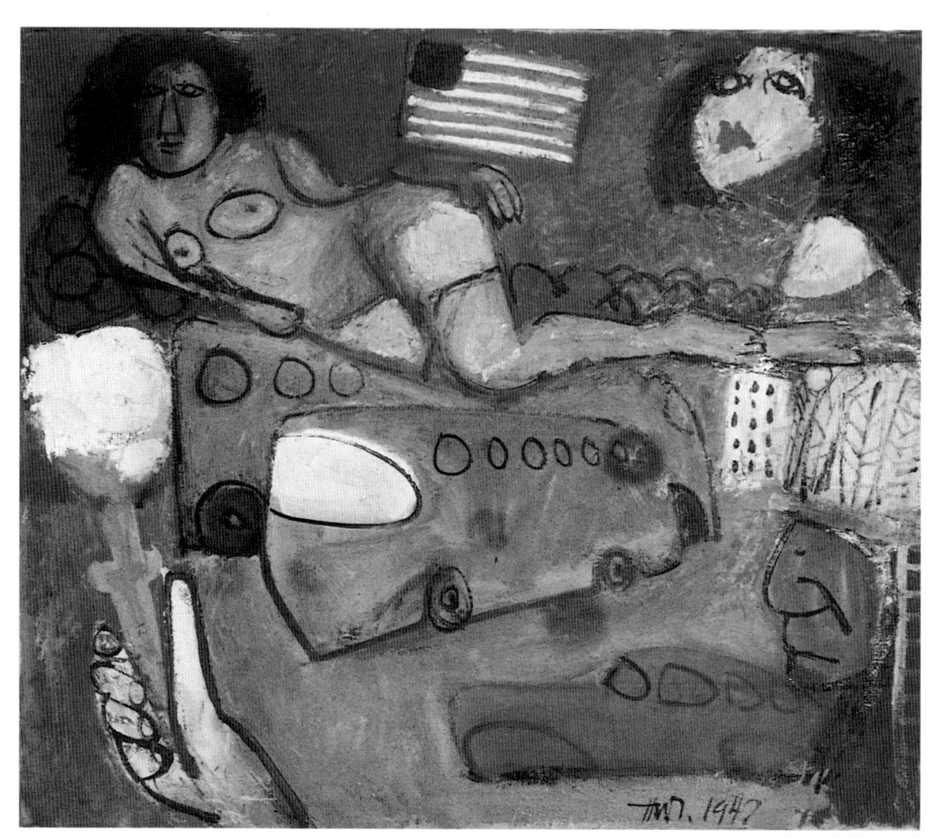

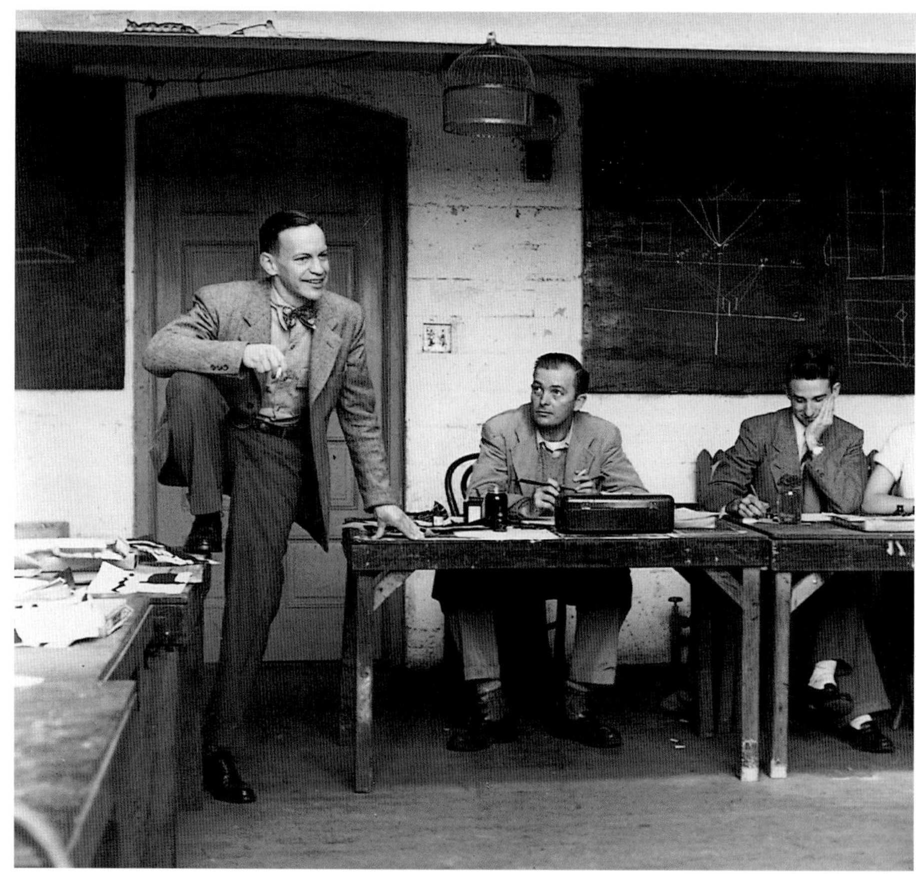

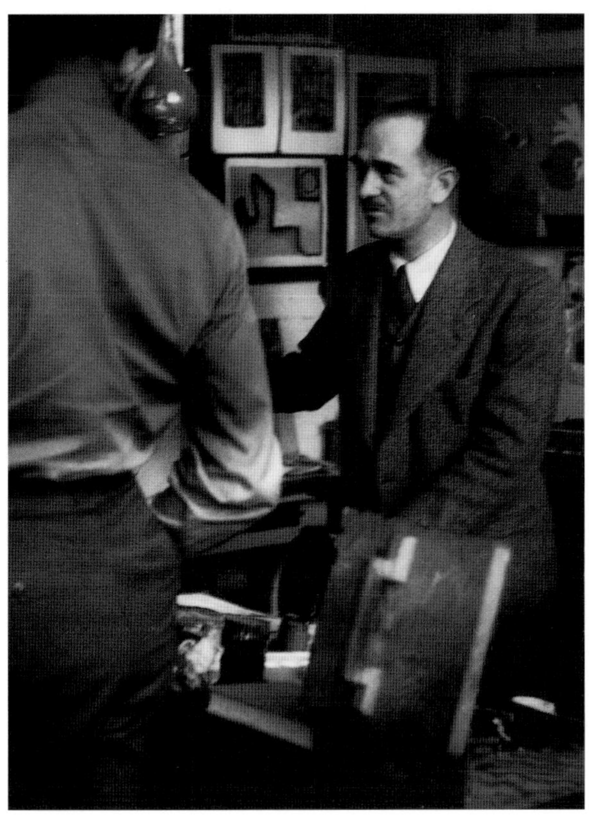

colored paintings as "brusque, violent, heated, and turbulent canvases."[63] Smith was working along these lines when he joined the teaching staff at the California School of Fine Arts in 1945.

David Park (fig. 2.11), another of MacAgy's initial recruits, also had strong roots in the Bay Area. Park began his career as an apprentice stonecutter in Ralph Stackpole's open-air sculpture studio in North Beach in 1929, and by the early 1930s he was painting murals in the Rivera style for the Works Progress Administration (WPA). Around 1936, Park's work began to show the influence of Picasso. The flattening of form into contoured panels suggests that he was studying Picasso's "studio" abstractions of the early 1930s.[64] Toward the end of the war, Park had also begun to incorporate the biomorphic vocabularies of Jean Arp and Miró.

By the time Park joined the faculty of the California School of Fine Arts in 1945, his career was well established, with one-man shows to his credit at the Oakland Art Gallery, the East West Gallery of Fine Arts, and the San Francisco Museum of Art. The paintings Park displayed in a faculty exhibition shortly after his first year at the California School of Fine Arts were typical of formative Abstract Expressionism, combining vaguely Surrealist imagery with the spatial ambiguities of late Cubism.[65]

Clay Spohn (fig. 2.12) had the most versatile background of any of the artists MacAgy hired that first year. Nearly a generation older than the rest of the faculty, he had been born in 1898, just in time to serve as an apprentice seaman for the U.S. Navy in the First World War. Spohn was raised in the East Bay hills of Piedmont and during the 1910s attended the California College of Arts and Crafts and then the California School of Fine Arts when it was still housed on Nob Hill. In the early 1920s he studied painting, first at the Art Students League in New York with George Luks, Kenneth Hayes Miller, and Guy Pène du Bois and then in Paris, where he took classes at the Académie Moderne under Othon Friesz. Spohn spent most of his time in Paris on the Left Bank, in cafés such as the Dôme and the Select Bar, where he met Marcel Duchamp and Stanley William Hayter along with the fashionable set Hemingway described in *The Sun Also Rises.* It was in one of these cafés that he ran into

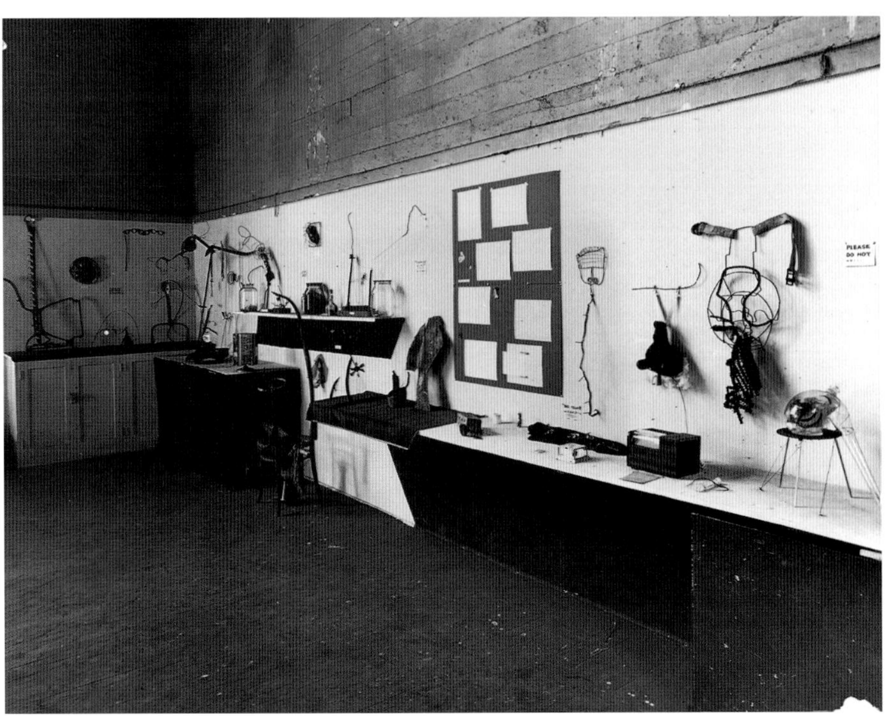

Figure 2.13

Clay Spohn, *Museum of Unknown and Little-Known Objects,*
exhibited at the California School of Fine Arts, San Francisco,
1949. Photograph courtesy, The Paul Chadbourne Mills
Archives of California Art, The Oakland Museum.
Photographer: F. W. Quandt.

Alexander Calder, an acquaintance from his days at the Art Students League. Calder was then making sculptures out of broom handles on wheels, and the two met in his studio to discuss the possibilities of kinetic sculpture. Calder described his impression of Spohn:

> I remember him for several reasons; having a meal with him often took a long time because he would order a dish and eat it when it came, and then decide whether or not he was still hungry. This often dragged things out. If he was brought fried eggs that were insufficiently cooked, he would ask for the waiters to "blow their noses," probably in English . . . Of course, the main thing was that it was he who suggested I make things entirely of wire.[66]

In the late 1920s Spohn himself was devising sculptures from found materials. Among his inventions was the "feeling piece," a construction of wood,

metal, nails, and sandpaper that was meant to be experienced in the dark.[67] At the same time, Spohn was working through the European movements, absorbing Fauvism, Cubism, and Surrealism. All these investigations were cut short when he returned to San Francisco and found no appreciable interest in modern art. Spohn spent a good part of the 1930s painting portrait commissions and murals for the WPA, depicting subjects from classical mythology and American Indian folklore. In the early 1940s, however, with the reviving interest in modern European art, he returned to his earlier explorations in abstract painting and sculpture.

In 1941 Spohn made his debut at the San Francisco Museum of Art with a whimsical piece called *Wake Up and Live,* a kind of Funk assemblage *avant la lettre.* The jury had trouble deciding whether to classify the entry as sculpture or painting because it consisted of a red flyswatter that the spectator could operate to whack a meticulously painted housefly on a varnished

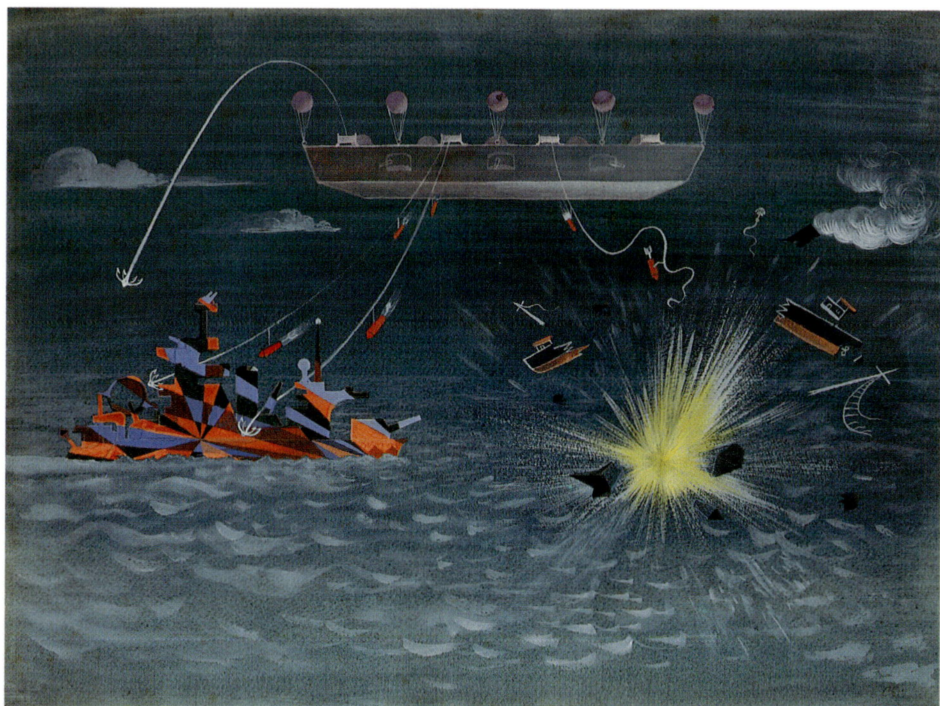

Figure 2.14

Clay Spohn, *Hover Machine (Fantastic War Machine)*, 1942.

Gouache on paper, 15 × 20 in. Collection, The Oakland

Museum, gift of the Estate of Peggy Nelson Dixon.

Photographer: M. Lee Fatherree.

board.[68] Throughout the 1940s, Spohn created witty and imaginative sculptures from outlandish materials. His most famous was a 1949 tableau of forty-two assemblages for the *Museum of Unknown and Little-Known Objects* (fig. 2.13), made from materials culled everywhere from back-alley garbage cans to Spohn's personal cupboard. Some of the highlights of his "museum," designed for a fund-raising ball at the California School of Fine Arts, were *Forking Situation,* a group of forks with intertwined tines, mock-erotically placed on a bed of velvet; *Old Embryo,* a rubber Halloween mask floating eerily in a chemical flask, and *Mouse Seeds,* a jar of mildewed rice.

Spohn is generally viewed as having provided a Dadaist alternative to Abstract Expressionism in San Francisco, and he is remembered primarily as a forerunner of Bay Area Funk Art.[69] But Spohn's zany assemblages of the 1940s, which he considered merely a playful diversion, have obscured his more serious ambitions as a painter.[70] Since the late 1920s Spohn

had been evolving an elaborate philosophy of visionary abstraction that incorporated ideas from his wide-ranging reading in science, metaphysics, literature, psychology, anthropology, religion, and art. A prolific writer, Spohn amassed dozens of manuscripts detailing his own theories. Although he spent many years preparing these treatises for publication, he seems to have been plagued by an inability to concentrate on a single project. Similarly, his painting never followed a solitary course but shifted restlessly from one idea to the next. His work of the 1940s ranged from a group of watercolors called *Fantastic War Machines* (fig. 2.14), depicting colorful Rube Goldberg contraptions, to austere hard-edged compositions and florid expressionist abstractions.[71]

Years later, smarting over criticism of his eclecticism, Spohn conceded that his mercurial temperament had probably damaged his career and perhaps prevented him from finding a personal means of expression.[72] In an important sense, however, this very quality was Spohn's greatest virtue as a teacher, and it was as a teacher that he made his most significant contribution to Bay Area art. William Ivey, a student at the California School of Fine Arts in the late 1940s, remarked that "almost everybody I know that was at the school at that time will mention his name as being perhaps the most exciting teacher they had . . . The sense of art as an *adventure,* a mental adventure, was something he gave as much as anybody . . . Still was kind of magisterial. Rothko was kind of Buddha-like. But Clay was like a child, bubbling with ideas all the time."[73]

Spohn encouraged his students to find inspiration wherever their whims led them. Class discussions covered a broad spectrum of subjects from Dylan Thomas to Sir James Jeans, who wrote popular books on science. Spohn likened the role of the artist to that of the explorer, alchemist, or scientist: "The elements of art are similar to the elements in matter," he insisted. "All the artist has to do is discover them and rearrange them into concoctions according to his own formulae, creating new and powerful magic."[74] The one thing Spohn cautioned his students not to study too closely was the work of others.[75] Picasso, he felt, posed a particular threat to the young imagination. Spohn implored his students never to follow the precepts of a master but to leave themselves an infinite range of possibilities: "Art is not only free of anything that has to do with the dogmatic, but it is the essence and spirit of freedom. It can be developed only when the mind and spirit are completely free and released. Limitation is the enemy of free expression."[76]

For the students at the California School of Fine Arts just returning from the war, Spohn's message was precisely what they wanted to hear. "We had all been fed up with regimentation, with being put in a uniform and told what to do," George Stillman explained. "We were looking for a way out of that discipline—a way to be individual, a way to be human."[77] Besides intensifying the need for freedom and personal identity, the war profoundly altered conventional attitudes and perceptions. As Edward Corbett observed, most artists who had been through combat no longer felt bound to "the comfort and conformity of tradition."[78] The returning GIs were restless, rebellious, and in a mood to challenge conventions. After the war, this feeling was infectious. Dorr Bothwell recalled: "It was in the air, definitely in the air. It was in the air to throw everything over, to make a new start."[79]

Perhaps this new strain of student, even more than MacAgy's innovative teaching staff, was responsible for the energy and imagination at the California School of Fine Arts. Smith remembers that the school before the war had been "a debutante kind of place . . . just crawling with socialites,"[80] but by the end of 1946 the student body was composed primarily of veterans subsidized by the GI Bill of Rights.[81] Self-sufficient, highly motivated, and intensely serious about their work, they were mostly in their late twenties, ten years older than the school's previous art student. Many of them had already been to art school, and some, like Kuhlman, Lobdell, Dixon, and Dugmore, had worked as professionals before the war and were enrolled at the California School of Fine Arts primarily to collect the government subsidy.[82]

This situation created a special challenge for the instructors, since many students were older and more knowledgeable than they were. In some cases the instructors found the GIs intimidating. Rothko referred to his class at the school as a group of "gangsters,"[83] and William Ivey remembered that Still was "scared to death" of the veterans: "Most of us had been in combat [and] we had been through things he couldn't even imagine. We felt superior in most ways to the faculty."[84] But for the most part, the closeness in age and experience promoted exchange rather than intimidation. The blurring of roles was no doubt encouraged by the leveling effects of the war. As Bischoff remarked, those who had served in uniform generally felt "there were not really instructors and students as much as there were older artists and younger artists."[85]

A striking example of a student who contributed more to his instructors than they taught him was John Grillo (fig. 2.15). Grillo was among the first veterans to arrive at the California School of Fine Arts at the close of the war.[86] MacAgy described him as a "fiery young sailor" who showed up at the school with a folio of tattered paintings from overseas.[87] Grillo had had extensive art training before coming to San Francisco and had completed a degree nearly ten years earlier at the Hartford Art School, where he acquired some of the techniques of the Old Masters and learned to render human experience in the expressionist manner of Robert Henri. Under the tutelage of the Ash Can School and its lineage—most of the Hartford faculty had studied at the Art Students League—Grillo painted portraits, landscapes, and circus scenes.

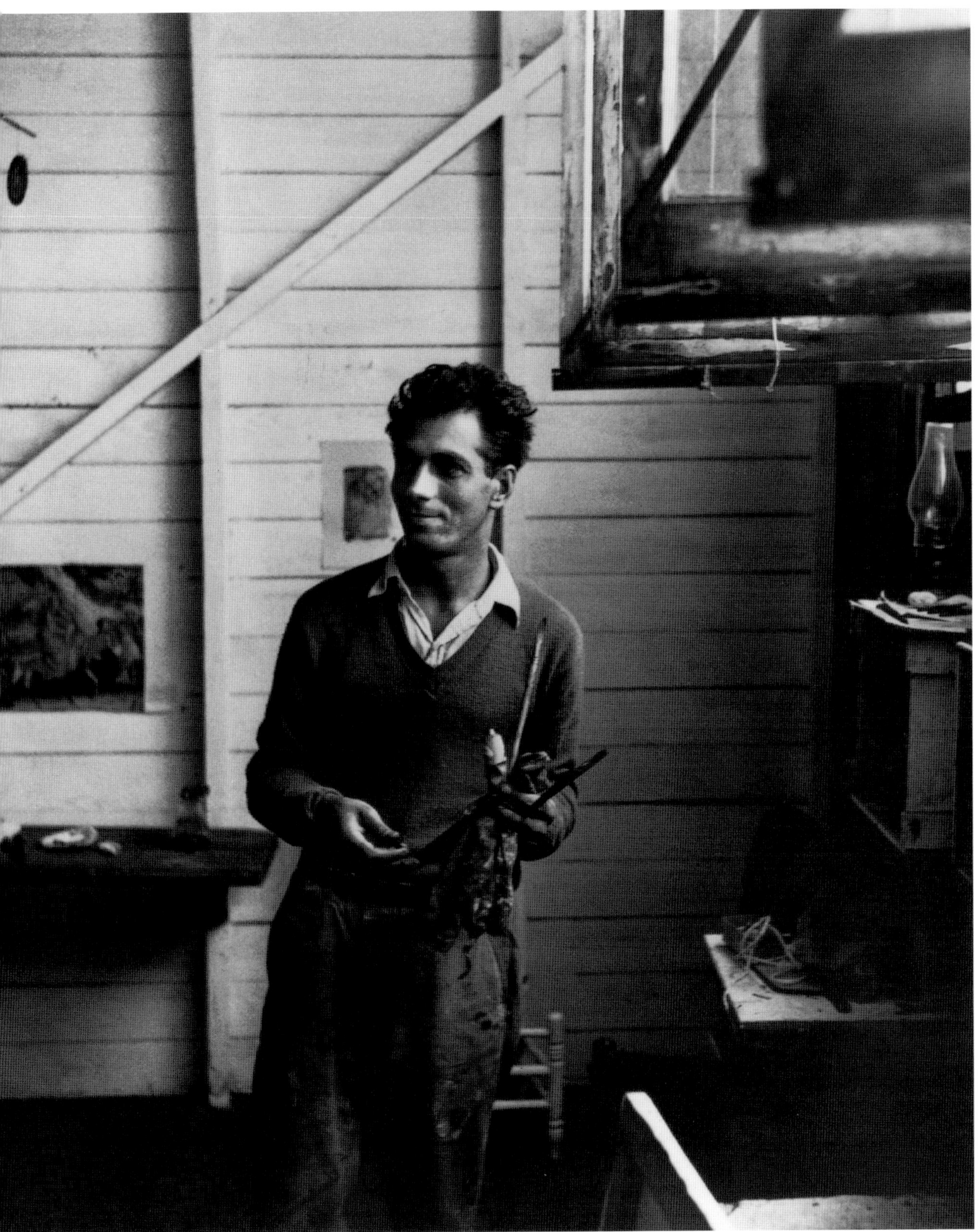

Figure 2.15

John Grillo, 1949. Photographer: Bill Witt.

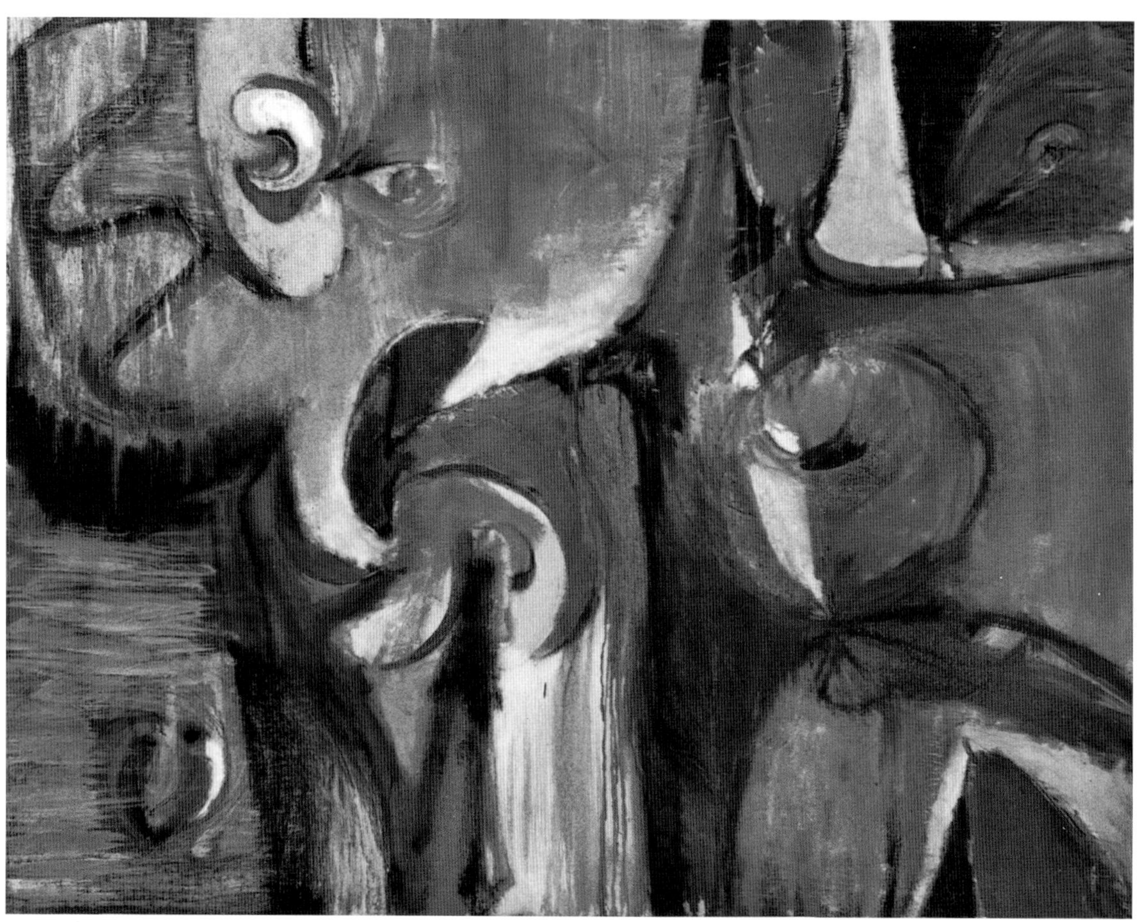

Figure 2.16

John Grillo, *Untitled*, 1946. Oil on canvas, 45 × 58 in.

Whereabouts unknown. Photographer: William Heick.

Although he was well versed in European modernism through frequent visits to the Wadsworth Atheneum and galleries in New York, Grillo's decisive move into abstraction occurred while he was in the South Seas during the war. While stationed on Okinawa, he began a series of free-flowing nonobjective abstractions that were relatively independent of the European influence visible in much early Abstract Expressionism. Short on art supplies, Grillo used whatever was on hand, throwing cocoa and coffee grounds on sheets of paper to make speckled abstract patterns, then tying the compositions together with washes and linear designs. Someone told him his work looked like Mark Tobey's, although he had not yet learned of Tobey.

The Okinawa paintings Grillo brought with him to the California School of Fine Arts impressed MacAgy enough so that he gave Grillo his own studio—the only student then receiving such a privilege. Grillo remembered that his teachers gave him free rein to paint what he wanted and encouraged him to experiment. John Hultberg, a student at the time, recalled watching Grillo work in 1947: "He'd stand back about three feet and throw paint at the canvas, let it drip, turn it over. They'd never heard of it in New York."[88]

Few oil paintings of Grillo's have survived from that period, but photographs of them and a large number of remaining works on paper tend to support Hultberg's recollections (figs. 2.16, 2.17). From 1946 to

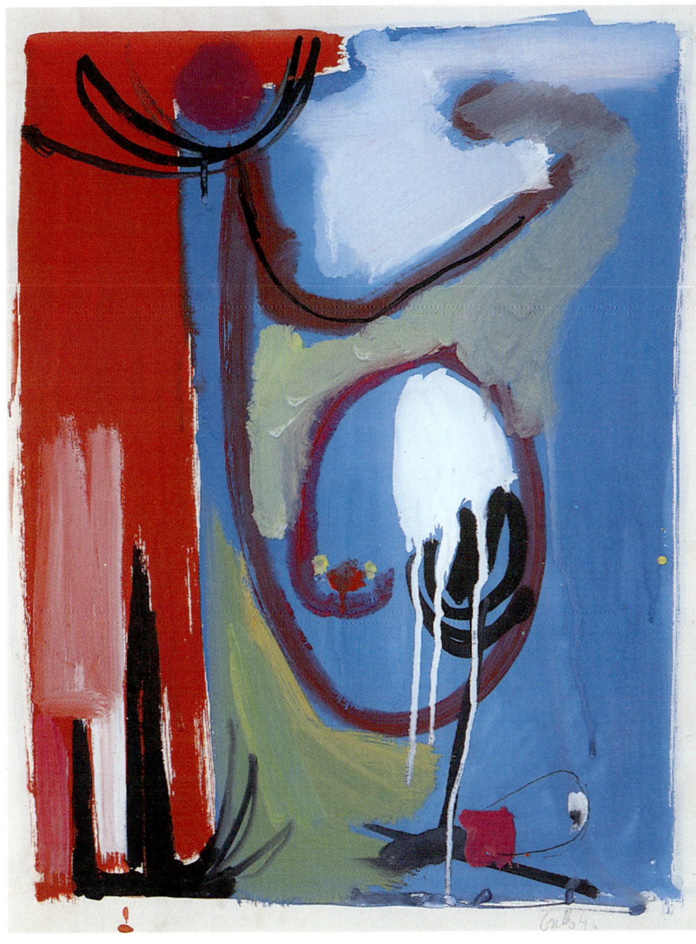

Figure 2.17

John Grillo, *A Dripping Form*, 1946. Poster paint on paper,
23 × 18 in. Collection, Andrew G. Newman. Photograph
courtesy, Carlson Gallery, Carmel, California.

1947, Grillo produced a series in poster paint that for
sheer inventiveness of technique rivaled vanguard
developments on the East Coast. In their spontaneity
and dramatic intensity, many of these paintings bear
the hallmarks of classic Abstract Expressionism.
Grillo animated his surfaces in a variety of ways, ranging from broad gestures to streaked and spattered
paint. These works show none of the anguish of Pollock or de Kooning; instead, they exude a sensuality
and delight in the manipulation of paint, with colors
that are radiant and in some cases phosphorescent.

In the summer of 1947, Grillo left for the East
Coast to study with Hans Hofmann, whose love of
dazzling color matched his own. Although Grillo's
stay in San Francisco had been short, his legacy was
considerable. Grillo's freewheeling and unorthodox
approach opened fresh possibilities of expression and
served as an important catalyst for liberating the
painting of artists like Richard Diebenkorn.[89]

Faculty II: Varda, Corbett, and Diebenkorn

The flood of veterans into San Francisco during the
first year after the war filled the classrooms of the California School of Fine Arts to capacity. By the end of
1946, the student body was triple the size of the previous year, with an average of fifty applicants per
week.[90] To accommodate the deluge, MacAgy hired a
number of additional faculty members, including
Jean Varda (fig. 2.18), Corbett, and Diebenkorn.

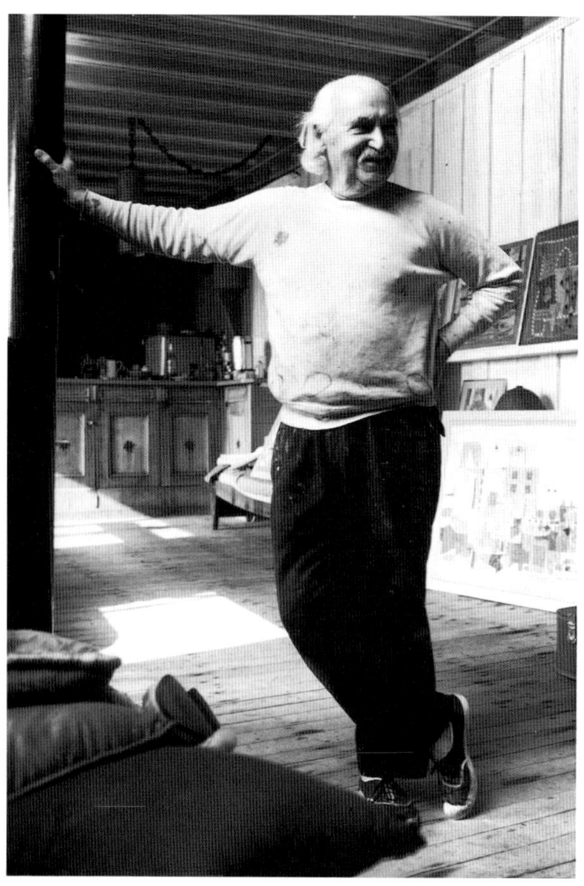

Jean Varda, in his Sausalito ferryboat studio. Photograph

© 1996 Fred Lyon.

Varda, an émigré from Smyrna, had associated with Braque, Picasso, and Miró as well as the literary group around Anaïs Nin and Henry Miller in Paris before World War II. When France was invaded in 1939, Varda and Miller fled to the United States, Varda settling in Monterey, Miller in Big Sur, where both developed prodigious followings around their salons for visiting European artists. Varda's house in Monterey, which Miller described vividly in his tribute to the artist in the Berkeley-based little magazine *Circle,* was made almost entirely of refuse: boxes, rockers, discarded iron pipes, and dismantled hulls and masts of wrecked ships, decorated with inlaid bits of tin, glass, pewter, wood, and stone.[91] His collages and mosaics, mostly colorful carnivalesque friezes suggesting medieval pageantry, partook of a similar aesthetic, incorporating broken bottles, mirrors, and other assorted debris, much as Kurt Schwitters had in his *Merz* constructions of the 1920s. Although Varda would never be part of the Abstract Expressionist movement in San Francisco—his work was finally too festive and decorative in style—he was, along with Spohn, highly influential in promoting an imaginative, experimental approach to materials. His discourses on the metaphysics of art, filled with aphorisms such as "modern painting is the last sanctuary of magic," struck a responsive chord among the artists at the California School of Fine Arts.[92] Varda also contributed to the ethos of spontaneity at the school. He considered it something of a rite of passage for his students to practice what he called "the labyrinth," a process of total release not unlike the orgiastic outpourings of Miller, which he compared to the Dionysian purification rituals of the ancient Greeks.[93]

More significant for the future of painting in San Francisco was the appointment of Edward Corbett (fig. 2.19) in the summer of 1947. Corbett had informed opinions about contemporary art in the East, having spent the last years of the war in Manhattan, where he befriended Jack Levine and Ad Reinhardt. Widely respected in San Francisco as an intellectual with a far-ranging knowledge of philosophy and literature, he was notorious for confusing his students with arcane lectures on Sartre and Kierkegaard. Corbett was also an aspiring poet with a social orbit that included almost as many writers as painters. Some of his literary friends in the late 1940s included Weldon Kees, Robert Duncan, Henry Miller, and Kenneth Rexroth.

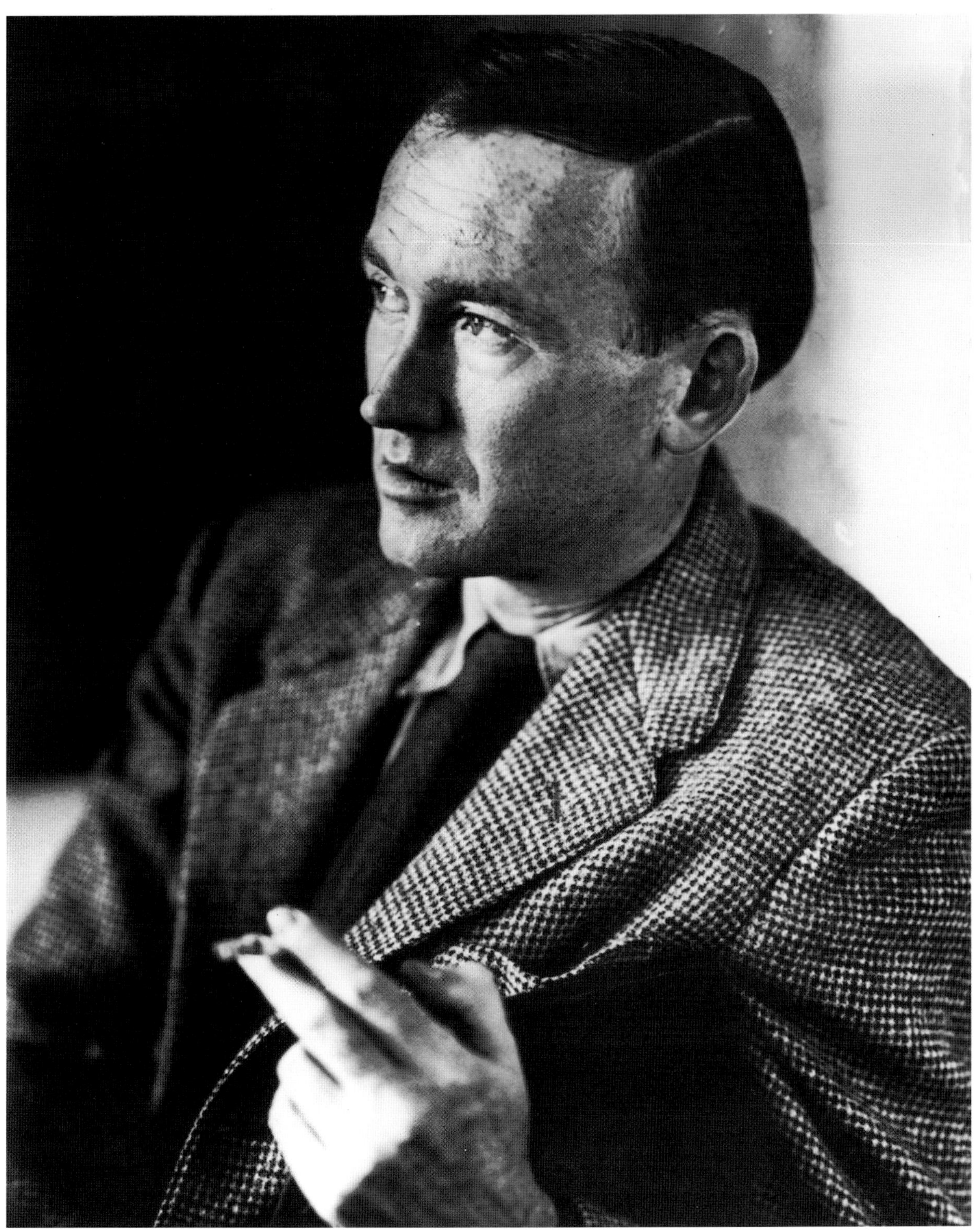

Figure 2.19

Edward Corbett, Studio C Gallery in Berkeley, 1950.

Photographer: Marshall Douglas.

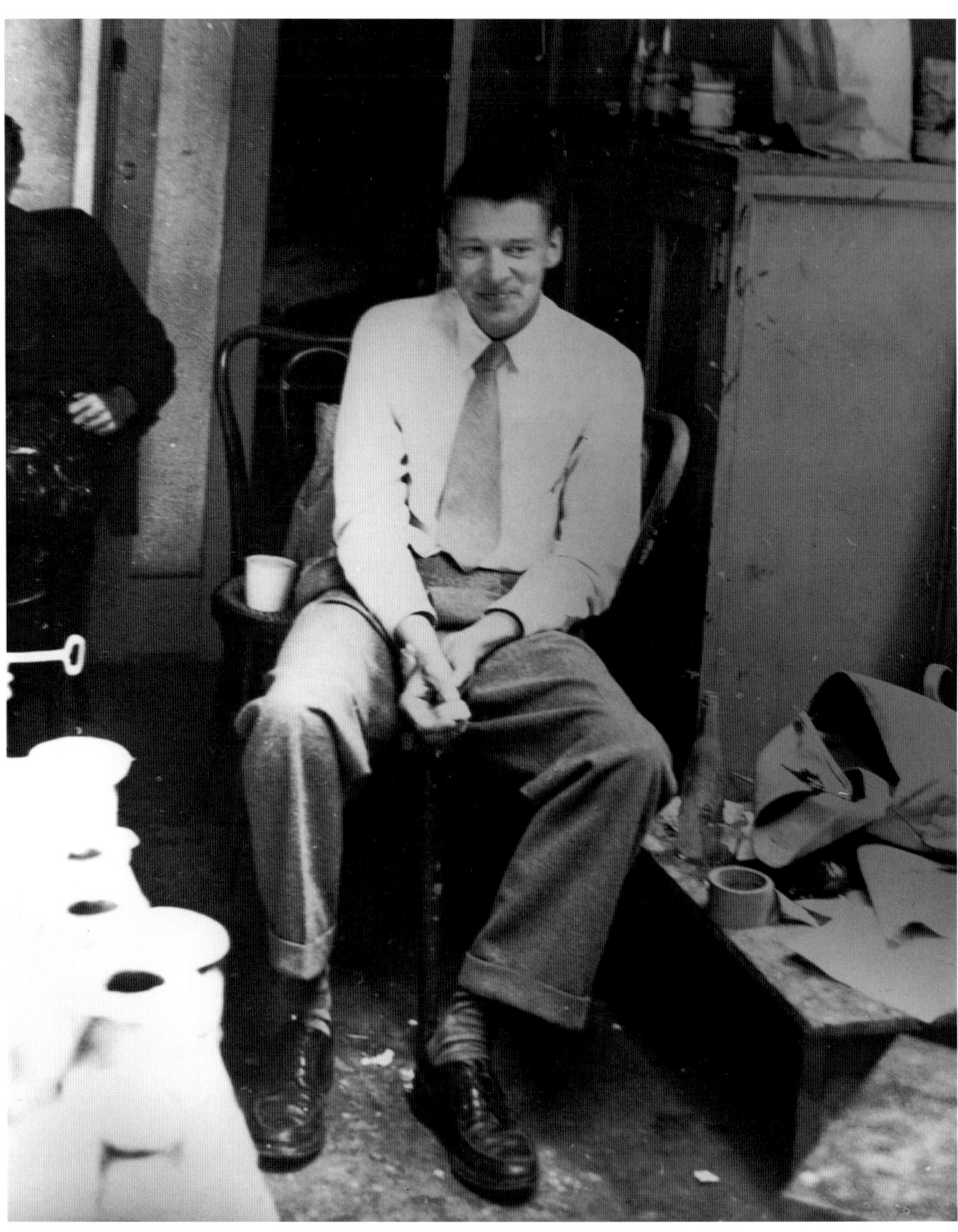

Figure 2.20

Richard Diebenkorn, California School of Fine Arts, San
Francisco, ca. 1948. Photographer: George Stillman.

Corbett's connections to the San Francisco art world dated back to 1936, when he and Smith were classmates at the California School of Fine Arts. There, Corbett was unusual in gravitating toward Cézanne and Picasso, whose work he had seen at the newly opened San Francisco Museum of Art. In 1944 Corbett moved to New York, where, after viewing the large Mondrian retrospective at the Museum of Modern Art, he became a self-professed "disciple" of Neoplasticism and, with Reinhardt's sponsorship, joined the American Abstract Artists.

Corbett's oils and temperas of the mid-1940s were starkly geometric in style, with neon colors and offbeat compositions sometimes closer to the Op Art of the 1960s than to mid-century Neoplasticism.[94] Occasionally, Corbett digressed from geometry and produced flowing, allover linear designs. Many of these works resemble the meandering line of André Masson, but Corbett was never seriously interested in Surrealism. Although he flirted briefly with an Odilon Redon–inspired figurative Surrealism during the war, he later described that stage as marked by confusion and a conflict of intentions.[95]

When Corbett returned to San Francisco in 1946, he took a teaching job at San Francisco State College and moved to North Beach, where he became acquainted with William Saroyan, Hilaire Hiler, and other habitués of the Black Cat Café. In the Bay Area, Corbett's Neoplastic work met with immediate success. He took part in a show of abstract work along with Diebenkorn, McChesney, Ellwood Graham, and Philip Pinner at one of the few galleries in the area that exhibited modern art, the Pat Wall Gallery in Monterey. With at least one critic calling him the best of the group, Corbett was invited back for a one-man show.[96]

Despite these signs of success, Corbett was becoming increasingly dissatisfied with the narrow art-for-art's-sake goals of his geometric abstractions, finding these works could not fulfill what he described as a growing desire for the "romantic" and "inspirational" in painting.[97] By the time he joined the faculty of the California School of Fine Arts in 1947, Corbett had concluded that the future of American art lay in a synthesis of formalism and expressionism.[98] Although he was unsure how that synthesis might be achieved, he knew that he wanted to "discover expressive values in painting without recourse to subject matter . . . to accomplish a personal or subjective emotional release through form . . . not evangelically for the world but for myself."[99]

Another of MacAgy's new appointments, Richard Diebenkorn (fig. 2.20), was destined to become one of the most highly acclaimed artists associated with the California School of Fine Arts, but when MacAgy hired him in 1947, he had barely shed his status as a student. Diebenkorn had been enrolled at the school just a little over a year before and had taken classes with Park and Spohn. Both would continue to be important mentors after he joined the faculty. Shy and introspective, with a lanky build that sometimes gave him the awkward appearance of a teenager, Diebenkorn would continue through the 1940s to occupy an uncertain role somewhere between student and teacher.

Raised from the age of two near Twin Peaks in San Francisco, Diebenkorn entered Stanford University in 1940 expecting to study medicine or law. Instead, the courses he took in painting and drawing affirmed that his future lay in art. Diebenkorn's studies at Stanford were interrupted in 1943 by the war; and he was stationed at the University of California for officer candidate training. The experience proved important, introducing him to the work of the "Berkeley School" modernists Worth Ryder, Margaret Peterson, and Erle Loran, who gave him his first substantial exposure to the ideas of Picasso and Cézanne. When Diebenkorn left Berkeley for Quantico, Virginia, via Parris Island, South Carolina, Loran's book on the compositional principles of Cézanne was among the few items he carried in his duffle bag.[100] Loran's painstaking analysis of the formal structure of French abstraction would make a deep and lasting impression on him.

Diebenkorn also brought to Quantico a copy of *Dyn* magazine, published in Mexico by the Surrealist painter Wolfgang Paalen.[101] The issue, purchased from the bookstore at the San Francisco Museum of Art, contained abstract Surrealist works by Motherwell and Baziotes. This marked the beginning of Diebenkorn's brief encounter with Surrealism, which lasted until just after the war. The few examples of his painting while he was stationed in Virginia show the influence of Bonnard, Matisse, Klee, and other European painters he admired on trips to the Phillips Collection in Washington. But while Diebenkorn was in Woodstock, New York, on a fellowship for independent study in the winter of 1946–47, his work began increasingly to reflect the Surrealist imagery of Picasso and Miró.[102] Some of his Woodstock paintings also show a familiarity with the latest Surrealist-inspired work of Motherwell, Baziotes, and Rothko, which he saw during visits to Manhattan galleries (fig. 2.21).[103]

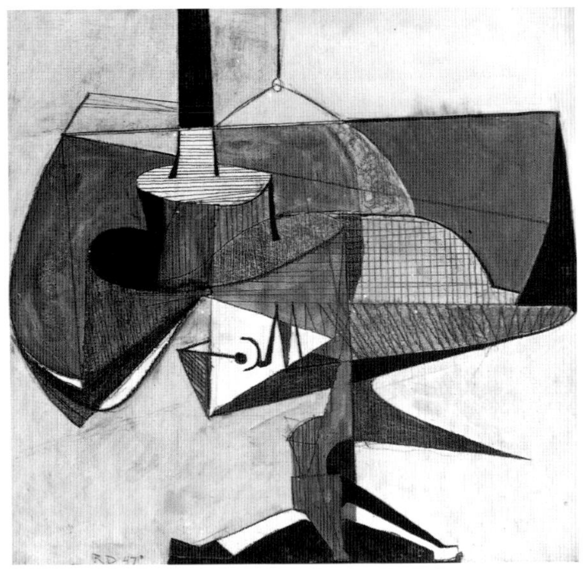

Figure 2.21

Richard Diebenkorn, *Untitled* (*Magician's Table*), 1947. Oil on

Masonite, 14½ × 15⅛. Private collection. Photographer:

M. Lee Fatherree.

Figure 2.22

Opposite: Clyfford Still, 1951. Photograph © Hans Namuth.

When Diebenkorn returned to San Francisco in the summer of 1947 to teach at the California School of Fine Arts, he found that the school had changed dramatically. The Woodstock work, which he had considered so "advanced," suddenly appeared staid and academic next to the freewheeling experimental painting he saw around him at the school. Diebenkorn remembered feeling somewhat ashamed to show his modest canvases to Grillo, who was then painting explosive mural-sized abstractions. Diebenkorn told Gerald Nordland that he "felt like a hermit returning to the world where things were happening."[104] The experience, he said, "was very exciting, but at the same time, it made me very uncomfortable."[105]

Clyfford Still: Background and Early Work

Certainly among the more significant events that took place while Diebenkorn was away in New York was the arrival of Clyfford Still (fig. 2.22) at the California School of Fine Arts in the fall of 1946. The story of his sudden, mysterious appearance in a long black coat with crumpled snapshots in hand to apply for a job that had opened up by chance just two days before is by now legendary. MacAgy is said to have been so electrified by the force of Still's personality that he hired him on the spot.[106] Spohn recalled the incident somewhat differently:

> Douglas [MacAgy] came to my office and said, "I want to show you something. A man phoned yesterday from Sacramento or Davis looking for a teaching job." Douglas set up the two paintings against various pieces of furniture. They were exactly the same size, about 36 inches by 28 inches. Each was done as large, bold strokes of rather dull color, more or less monochromatic with slight changes in the hue and occurring well inside the borders of the white canvas background. No attempt had been made to represent anything other than the strokes of pigment and the way they were applied—thick, heavy strokes, one into the other, applied in a more or less vertical direction to be sympathetic to the longest dimension of the canvases, which were to be regarded as seen vertically. Frankly, I don't know what I thought. Yes, they did have spirit and zest, they were strong with a certain gusto and flair that gave them vitality. I wasn't able to say anything more than, "Yes, they're interesting" . . . Well, of course, it turned out to be Clyfford Still.[107]

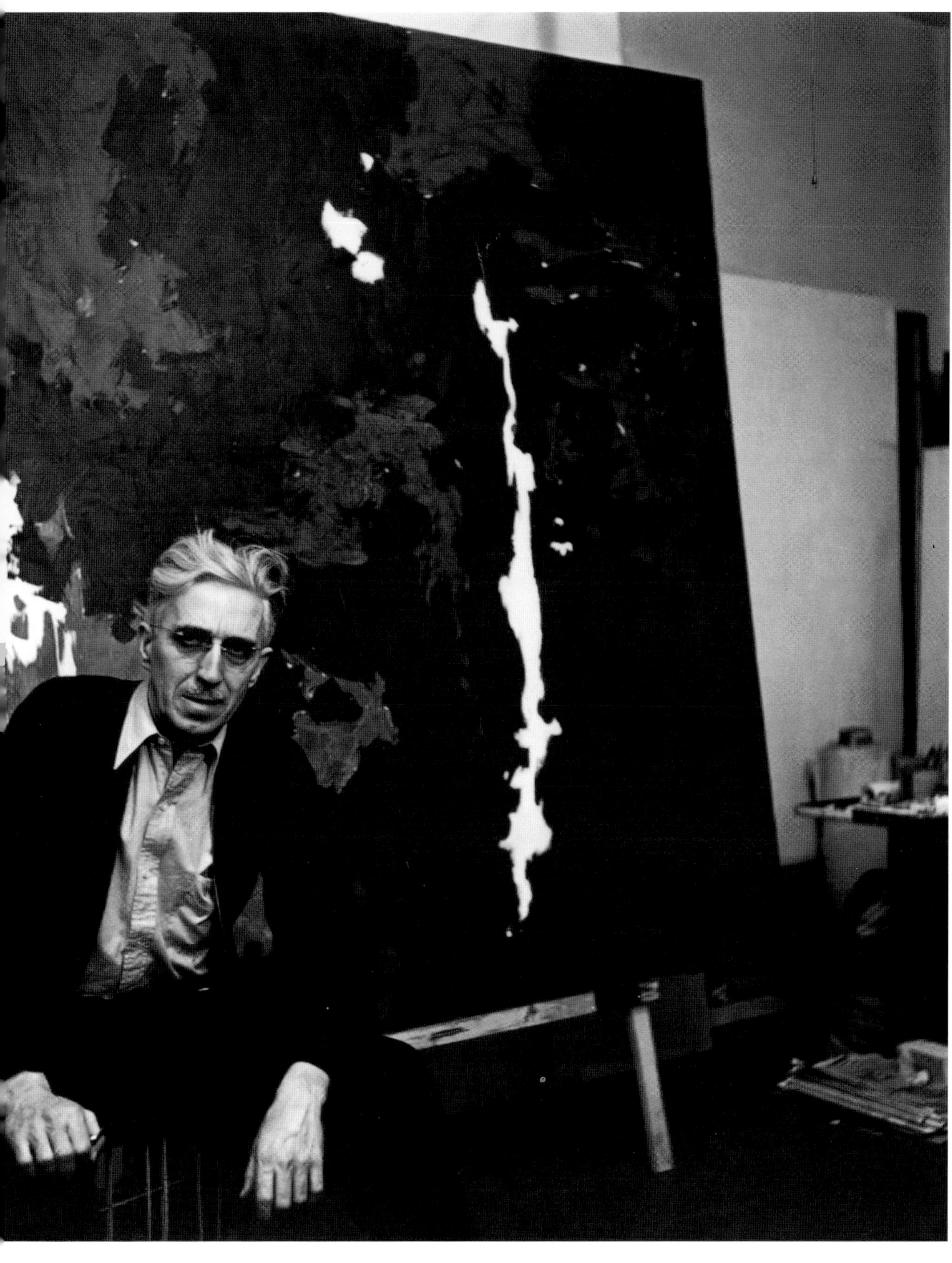

In truth, Still was hardly a stranger to San Francisco and certainly not an obscure painter from the Sacramento Valley. He had spent most of the war working in the Bay Area as a steel checker for the navy and an engineer for Hammond Aircraft, and Morley had given him his first museum exhibition at the San Francisco Museum of Art in 1943. Although the show drew mostly negative reviews, Morley was impressed enough to accept a painting of Still's for the permanent collection, his first museum acquisition.[108]

The major complaint leveled at Still's San Francisco exhibition—that his work looked technically naive—was to plague him for the rest of his career, perhaps in part because there was a measure of truth to the charge: he had virtually no formal art training. If his own account can be believed, aside from forty-five minutes of instruction at the Art Students League in 1925, after which he allegedly walked out in disgust, Still was entirely self-taught.[109]

Still's independence may have been fostered by an exceptionally hard life on a homestead in the remote plains of southern Alberta, where his family moved in 1910, when Still was six. Alberta at that time had been a province for only five years and was among the last of the true frontiers on the North American prairies. Although Still often spent the frigid Canadian winters at his parents' second home in Spokane, his education was continually interrupted by the strenuous demands of the farm, where his arms were sometimes "bloody to the elbows shocking wheat."[110] A high-strung mother and an abusive, autocratic father made the environment inhospitable for a young man with dreams of becoming an artist.[111] Nonetheless, from his early teens Still devoted his spare time to teaching himself to paint. His earliest works—on barrel tops, windowpanes, and whatever he could find—were inspired by reproductions gleaned from magazines and books. Botticelli, Titian, and Rembrandt were among his early idols, whose paintings he diligently copied.

Still's work of the late 1920s and early 1930s falls well within the Regionalist genre prevalent at the time, although most of it comes closer to the debunking spirit of Sherwood Anderson's fiction than the buoyant optimism of Thomas Hart Benton. Many of his subjects seem to reflect the harshness of life on the prairies. His *Row of Grain Elevators* (1928), for example, shows a squalid agrarian landscape with a sour yellow sky and a swamp littered with wreckage. Other paintings depict grim, even brutal, scenes such as the gutting of livestock or darkened, deserted buildings in the snow.[112]

In 1933, at the age of twenty-nine, Still graduated from Spokane University with a bachelor of arts in literature and philosophy and began teaching art at Washington State College in Pullman. His master's thesis on Cézanne, completed two years later, reveals his newfound interest in European modernism. For the next several years, Still seems to have schooled himself in most of the major European movements. His work of the 1930s shows a close study of Cubism and a preoccupation with German Expressionism, which had become fashionable in Washington after an exhibition entitled *Contemporary German Painting* at the Henry Art Gallery, University of Washington, Seattle, in 1934 and subsequent shows of works by Carl Hofer, Alexej Jawlensky, Lyonel Feininger, and Karl Schmidt-Rottluff.[113] Still's dry, sludgy paint handling and his earthen palette of grays, umbers, and browns are reminiscent of the work of such well-known Pacific Northwest expressionists as C. S. Price.

Around 1934 Still took one of the central tenets of German Expressionism to heart and decided "to begin again"—to embark on a voyage of inner revelation from which he could develop a personal aesthetic.[114] His work after the mid-1930s concentrates almost exclusively on what Still loosely called "self-portraits"—sometimes male and female personages intertwined, but more often a solitary figure set in a barren, lonely wasteland. With their elongated bodies, enormous hands, and deep eye sockets, many of these images call to mind African and Oceanic sculpture. Twisted and deformed, alternately bloated and starved, they seem to have been wrenched from a profoundly tortured psyche.

By the time the war began, Still's paintings had taken on a truly nightmarish cast. The light of day had for the most part vanished, and in its place was a midnight world inhabited by hideous apparitions suggesting hooded red-eyed demons, howling wolves, nimbed saints, and long-necked, cleft-headed creatures. The vaguely mythical and ritualistic connotations of these paintings have compelled a number of scholars to link them to specific texts, such as Jung's *Modern Man in Search of a Soul,* James Frazer's *Golden Bough,* and Jane Harrison's *Themis.*[115] Yet Still's imagery seems at once too general and too personal for such a literal reading of his work. The urge to view Still's iconography of the war years as deriving from ancient mythology stems in part from the prevalence of such subjects in late Surrealism, specifically in the work of Rothko, Pollock, and other artists commonly associated with Still. Although Still doubtless drew

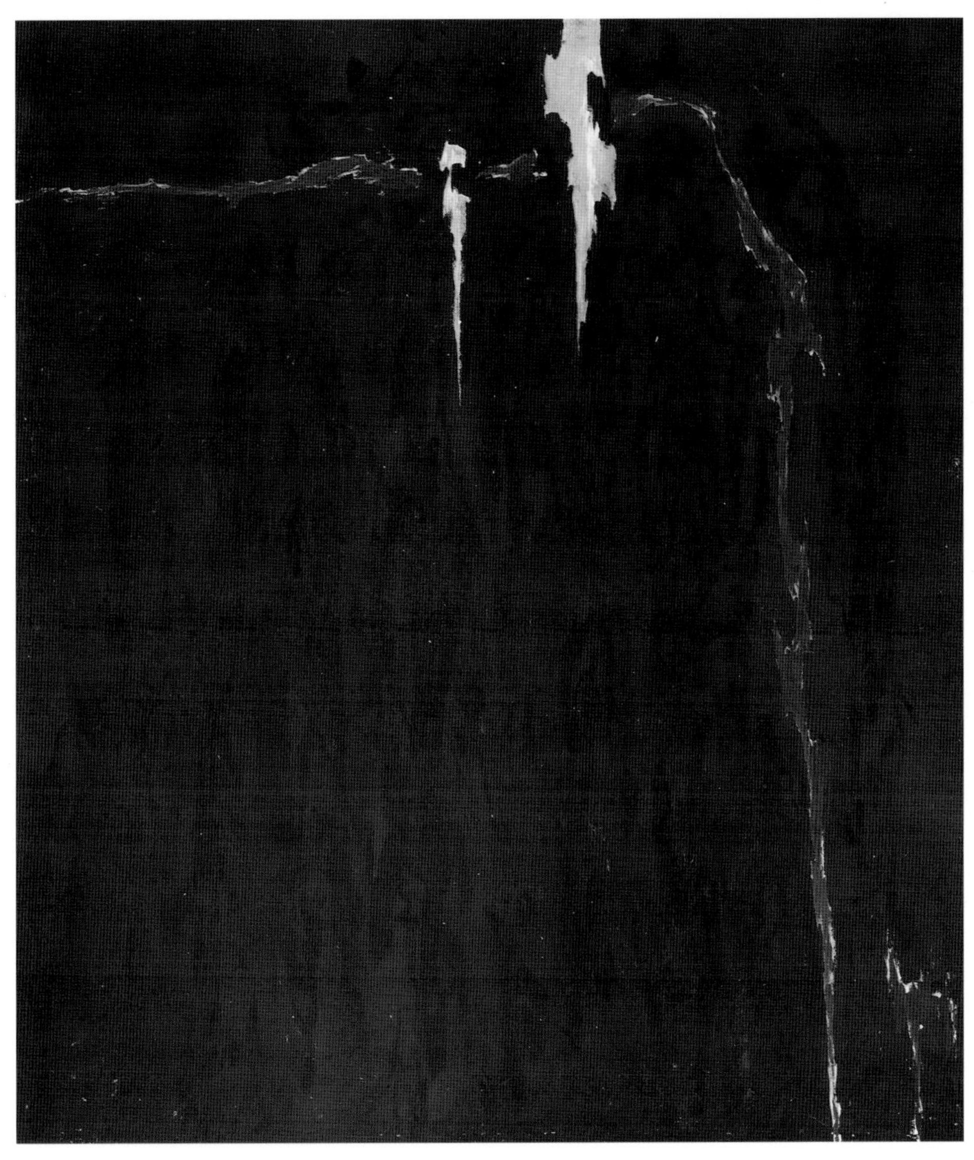

Figure 2.23

Clyfford Still, *Painting 1944-N,* 1944. Oil on canvas, 8 ft. 8¼ in.

× 7 ft. 3¼ in. The Museum of Modern Art, New York, The

Sidney and Harriet Janis Collection.

some of his ideas from sources in classical mythology—and probably Native American mythology as well—his vision is closer to that of the apocalyptic phantasmagorias of Blake and perhaps closer still to that of Goya, whose hallucinatory *Black Paintings* on the walls of his Quinta del Sordo (deaf man's house) outside Madrid Still particularly admired. Certainly, one of the themes that runs through Still's work of the early 1940s—the epic struggle between good and evil—is more in line with nineteenth-century Romantic ideas than with Surrealist ideology, where right and wrong tend to be conflated. Indeed, the subject of one of Still's favorite poems, Blake's "Tyger," might be his own: humankind's tragic conflict between the divine and the bestial in the soul.[116]

But it is perhaps not necessary to reach back so far in time to find sources for Still's imagery, since there were many painters occupied with such themes during the war. Solitary figures in nocturnal landscapes, visions of religious revelation and of nature's violent forces were among the typical subjects of neoromantic figurative painters such as Raphael Gleitsmann and Rico Lebrun. Even Still's formal vocabulary has a good deal in common with that of these artists. The craggy shapes, eerie back-lit silhouettes, and somber reds, browns, and blacks can be found in numerous other paintings.[117]

When Still began teaching at the California School of Fine Arts in late 1946, at least some of his work continued in this semifigural vein.[118] Shortly before his arrival, his show at Peggy Guggenheim's Art of This Century gallery in New York featured paintings that included what one reviewer called "a primaeval serpent-like figure in front of a stormy grey sky with a red sun."[119] But Still had also painted a number of fully nonobjective works. The earliest of these appear to be several canvases he executed between 1941 and 1943 while living in the Bay Area. Most of them contain familiar shapes, some resembling the Eskimo designs then popular in the Northwest.[120] Still's *Oil on Canvas, 1942,* however, presents little more than a yawning dark ground with a shaft of pale pigment racing up the canvas.[121] This painting looks very much like the "zip" paintings that Barnett Newman would later use to build his career.

Closer to Still's mature oeuvre are the paintings executed in Richmond, Virginia, from 1944 to 1945, when Still was teaching at the College of William and Mary. One of the most startling works from that period is the large *Painting 1944-N* (fig. 2.23) in the collection of the Museum of Modern Art, New York. Almost nine feet tall, it consists of a field of sooty black—probably meant to look charred by fire—pierced by a jagged crimson line in the shape of a thunderbolt. While ostensibly "dropping the known image," Still's stated intent for these nonobjective works, this painting projects much of the *terribilità* of his contemporaneous semifigurative efforts.[122]

This was the trajectory Still would follow during his first year on the faculty of the California School of Fine Arts. During that year his painting became increasingly abstract, and while tenuous figurative associations continued to surface, by the end of 1947 his work was almost entirely nonobjective.[123] The paintings Still displayed at the California Palace of the Legion of Honor in 1947, the fruits of his initial year at the California School of Fine Arts, show many features of his trademark style (fig. 2.24): the encrusted vaults of pigment—sometimes appearing ripped and flayed like flesh (fig. 2.25), other times rising majestically as if to exceed their framing borders—and the ghastly palette of acid yellows, lurid reds, and dour browns and blacks.[124]

Still's show at the Legion of Honor in San Francisco took many artists by surprise. Few had seen his work before, for Still kept his studio off-limits to all but a select number of individuals. Kenneth Sawyer, an aspiring artist and writer who was visiting San Francisco in 1947, recalled the shattering experience of seeing Still's new paintings for the first time:

> It was the show in San Francisco that introduced Still's work to a number of young people—myself included—who were either studying at the California School of Fine Arts or gloomily concerned with the state of painting in America. Our first response to these potent, utterly original oils was one of disbelief: then came shock, then admiration. Most of us, veterans of the Second World War, had stern convictions as to the nature of modern painting; it must be Mondrian, Miró, or Picasso. What we were confronted with on the walls of the Legion museum was unrelated to those preconceptions—unrelated in the most unsettling fashion . . . His works were marked by a violence, a rawness, which few of us—though we naturally accepted the violence of the current Europeans—were prepared to recognize as art. It was unnerving to have one's preconceptions so efficiently shorn in a single exhibition. Here was painting that instructed as it destroyed: the School of Paris had died quite suddenly for us; something new, something that most of us could not yet define, had occurred.[125]

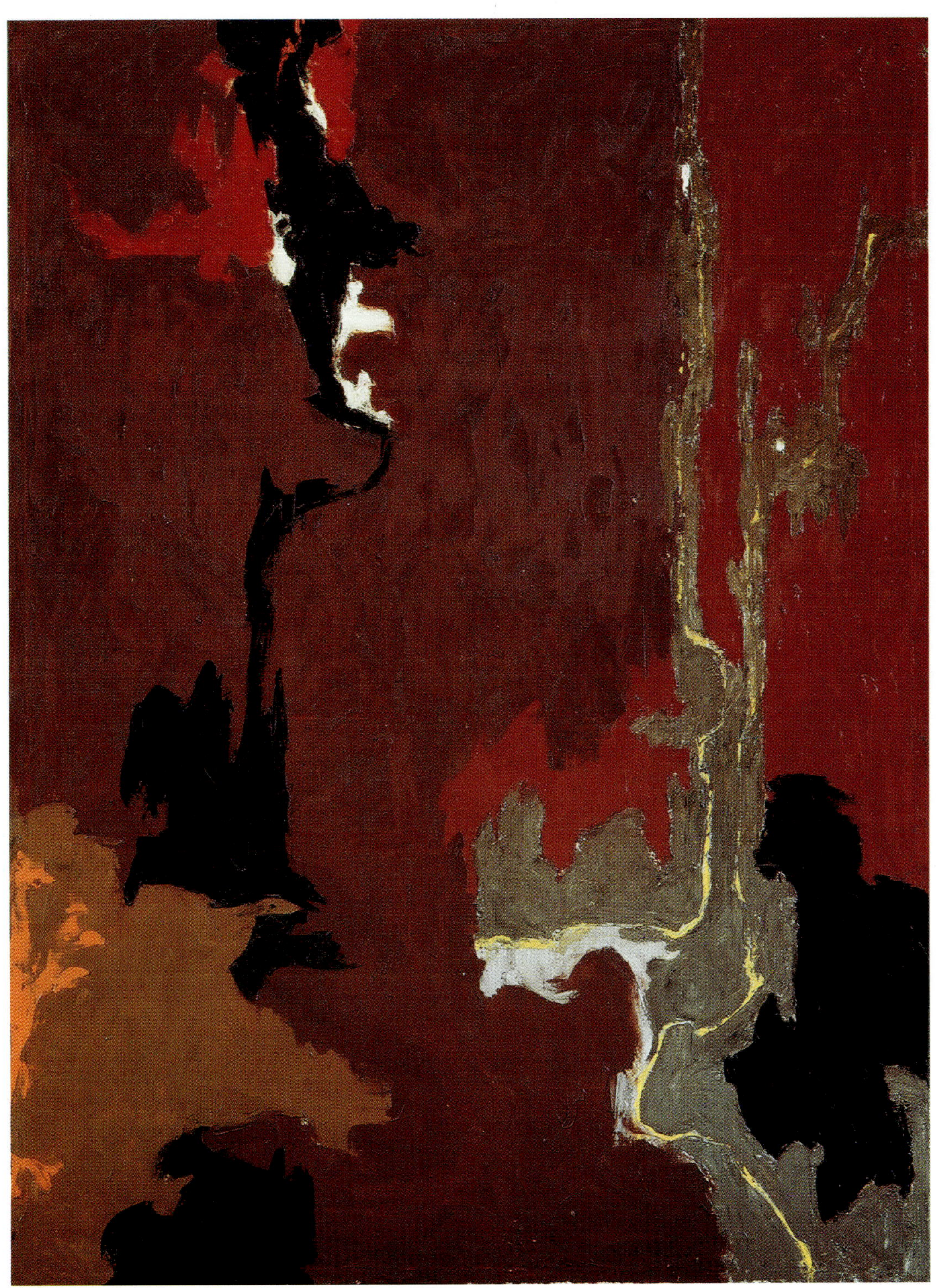

Figure 2.24

Clyfford Still, *Untitled,* 1946. Oil on canvas 61¾ × 44½ in.

Collection, The Metropolitan Museum of Art, George A.

Hearn Fund and Arthur Hoppock Hearn Fund.

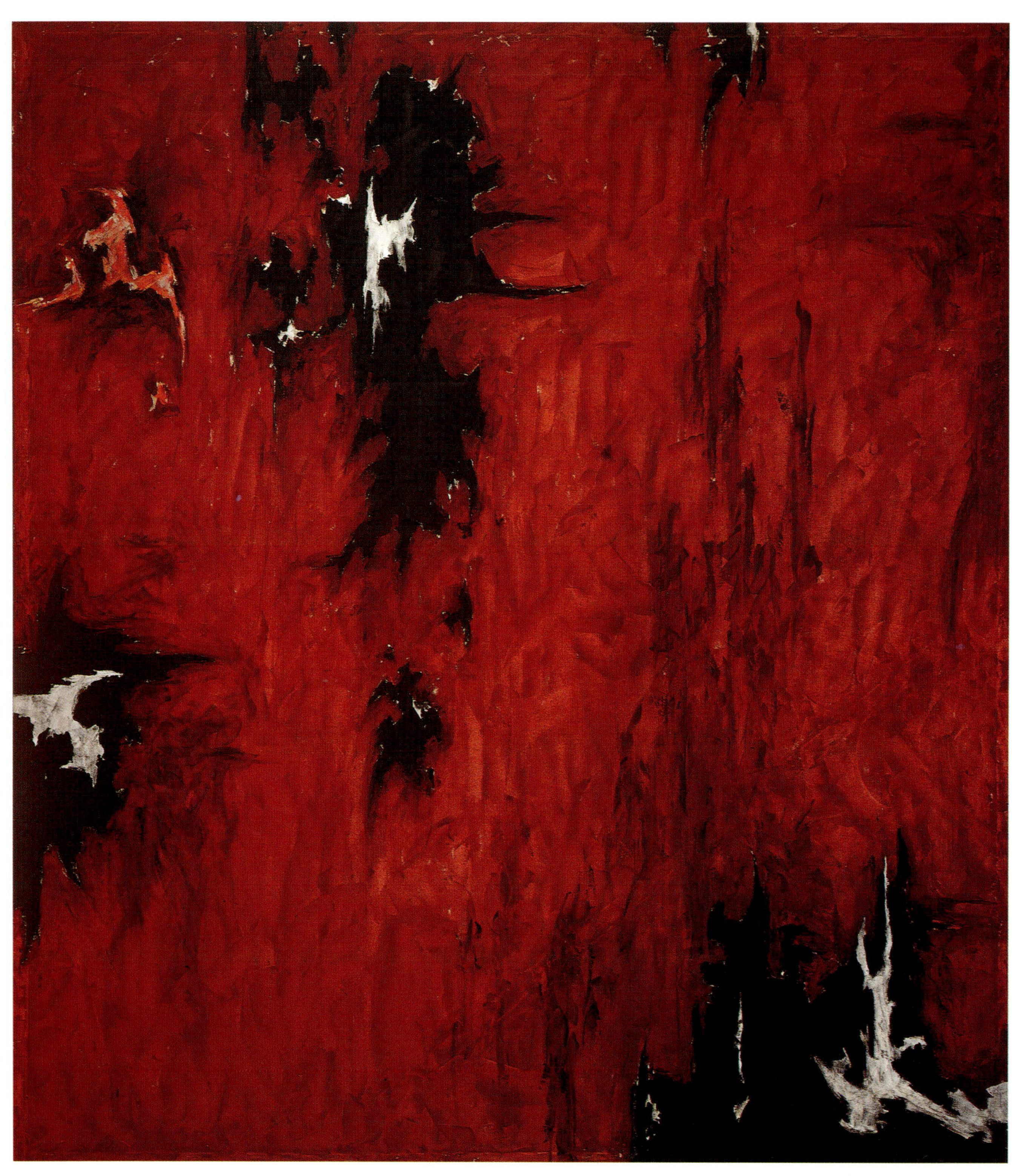

Figure 2.25

Clyfford Still, *Untitled* (*1947-R-No. 2*), 1947. Oil on canvas,

105 × 92 in. Gagosian Gallery, New York.

Not everyone in San Francisco shared Sawyer's admiration for Still; some artists, like Bischoff, Varda, Park, and Dixon, disliked his work intensely and remained vigorously opposed to it. Few, however, could deny that he had made the most radical break with French modernism they had encountered. And Still's rhetoric went even further than his work in its assault on European hegemony. To achieve "a truly free vision," he insisted on rejecting all European "isms" as "gimmicks of the past" that served only to tyrannize individuality and suffocate the spirit.[126]

Still's call for a total liberation from the past had a tonic effect on many of the artists associated with the California School of Fine Arts. At a time when San Francisco artists—especially the veterans who had just returned from the war—were looking for expressions of individuality, Still's ideas about the personal integrity of the artist and his willingness to reject received traditions found fertile ground. As I mentioned earlier, a number of artists in San Francisco had become increasingly experimental before their contact with Still. Bischoff, Diebenkorn, and Spohn had already begun to investigate versions of expressive abstraction. Grillo provides perhaps the most convincing example of an artist who seems to have discovered full-blown Abstract Expressionism on his own. A number of San Francisco painters, then, could claim to have pursued their own lines of exploration. But it was Still who channeled much of the experimentalism of the San Francisco artists. Because of the extremism of his canvases and his sharply articulated ideas, Still galvanized the artistic radicalism already under way in San Francisco.

3

Limitations establish security. Limitations should be temporary and imposed by the individual and not by governments, museums, dealers or critics. A creative idea is a revolutionary act. A creative idea is an expression of the dignity of a man. The painter knows this. It is the tradition of painting.

—FRANK LOBDELL, 1950

Disdain for the Thesis

When the artists of the San Francisco School described their movement in later years, they often intoned the same themes and even the same phrases. Their recollections are full of references to original invention and are punctuated by the words "discovery," "exploration," and "adventure." Frank Lobdell remembered that "once the hegemony of Cubism had been broken, anything was possible; new and endless possibilities for discovery were opened" (fig. 3.1).[1] Corbett insisted that the late 1940s had been "a period of exploration as much as anything else, an effort to find out what painting could be without merely repeating what had been already accomplished."[2] Dixon, not content to confine himself to a single image, declared that he "felt like an adventurer, a discoverer, an inventor" (fig. 3.2).[3] It seems that nearly all the artists associated with the movement at the California School of Fine Arts believed they had access to what Bischoff called a "limitless variety of undreamt of ways of coming alive on canvas."[4]

Such recollections should not be taken as mere nostalgia, for they drew upon an inventory of ideas current at the movement's high point. Some of the New York Abstract Expressionists similarly described their project as one of "self-discovery."[5] The notion of painting as a process of self-revelation—revealing, to use a buzzword of the 1940s, the "unknown" contents of the mind—was a mainstay of the Surrealist discourse imported to America during the war. The Surrealists themselves had resurrected the preoccupation with the terra incognita of the mind from nineteenth-century Romanticism. Thus artists such as Still, Corbett, and Spohn, who were students of Romantic thought, did not need to look to Surrealism for this idea. They could find it in Goya, Blake, or Redon.

In the case of most San Francisco painters, however, the process of discovery was less a matter of questing for self-knowledge than a search for a new painting language. This more general notion of art-as-discovery is, of course, a staple of avant-gardism, whether in its extreme manifestations, as in Futurism, or its more traditional and moderate tendencies, such as the prose of André Gide. Indeed, this concept has been identified as the unifying trait of modernism.[6] In the realm of modern painting, the term "adventure" became generic after Apollinaire used it to describe the enterprise of the Cubists. This ancestry suggests that the artist John Ferren's interpretation of the New York School's obsession with "searching" as a sign of futility and alienation seems wide of the mark. Ferren's simplistic comparison of the attitudes of American and European artists has been misleading for scholars of Abstract Expressionism. In his "Epitaph for an Avant-garde" (1958), Ferren stated: "We discovered a simple thing, yet far reaching in its effects: 'the search is the discovery.' Picasso had said, 'I don't search. I find.' We lacked the confidence for such an arrogant remark. We discovered instead that searching was itself a way of art."[7] This comment has led Stewart Buettner, among others, to conclude that such a "strange regard for art as an act of self-discovery" was "the result of a lack of confidence, an insecu-

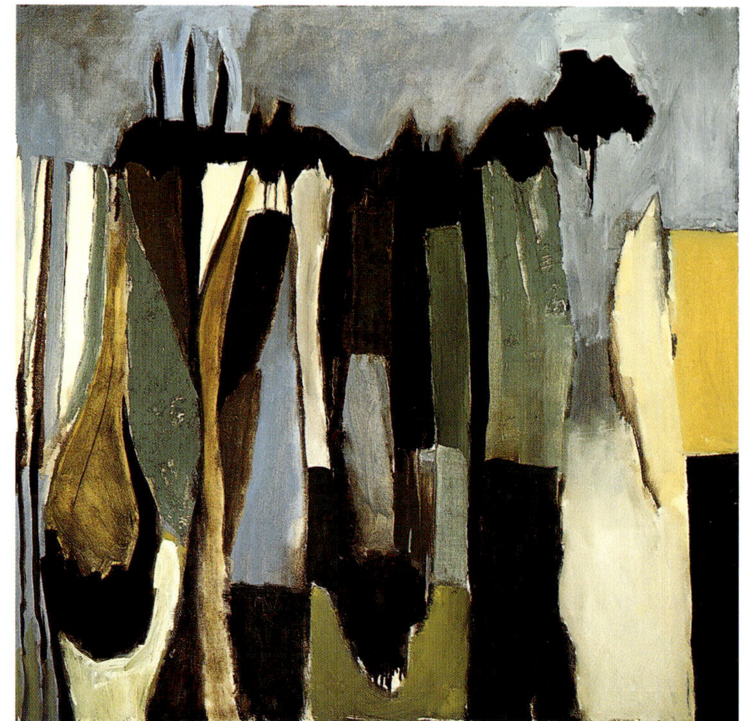

Figure 3.1

Frank Lobdell, *Untitled,* 1948. Oil on canvas, 36 × 36 in.

The Buck Collection, Laguna Hills, California.

Bliss Photography.

rity not only about the course of art, but about the artists' place along that course."[8] Ironically, both Buettner and Ferren have used one trope of modernism, "agonism,"[9] to lay claim to the originality of another, art-as-discovery. Certainly, Buettner's characterization is inappropriate for the San Francisco artists, who spoke of giddiness and excitement in their endeavor.[10] Their preoccupation with exploration indicates their consciousness of belonging to the avant-garde, collectively engaged in extending, perhaps even superseding, European modernism.[11]

But if the San Francisco painters around Still in the late 1940s emulated the essential dynamic of European modernism, they did not accept all of its rhetorical devices. Like their counterparts in New York, they did not organize their movement as a campaign, nor did they issue manifestos. Although their refusal to articulate preconceptions can be seen as an embrace of the modernist ethic—as taking the open-endedness of avant-gardism to its logical conclusion—there was some ambivalence about modern European art. The general feeling was that European modernism, especially Surrealism, had been corrupted by rhetoric, program, and exposition. The aim

of the San Francisco artists, as Hultberg described it, was to "divest ourselves of all intellect, to get back to painting as a non-verbal thing."[12]

Hultberg's statement underscores a strain of anti-intellectualism, a mistrust of reason—and specifically of the systems generated by reason, both ideological and technological—that emerged with the profound disillusionment resulting from the war. It was the "rational" side of the human mind that could, as Corbett wrote, "decide, quite logically, that extermination camps are the solution to political problems."[13] This antirationalism took many forms in the 1940s, from the rise of existentialism to what Joseph Warren Beach called the "cult of the simple," the wide appreciation for plain-spoken writers like Hemingway and Saroyan.[14] Henry Miller's "New Instinctivism" was another manifestation of the postwar preference for intuition over intellect. Hemingway, Saroyan, and Miller were all highly regarded, even emulated, at the California School of Fine Arts, where copies of Miller's contraband *Tropic of Cancer* (1934) were prized possessions.[15] Miller's "religion of instinct," to borrow a phrase from his biographer, Robert Ferguson, was also widely disseminated through the Bay Area avant-

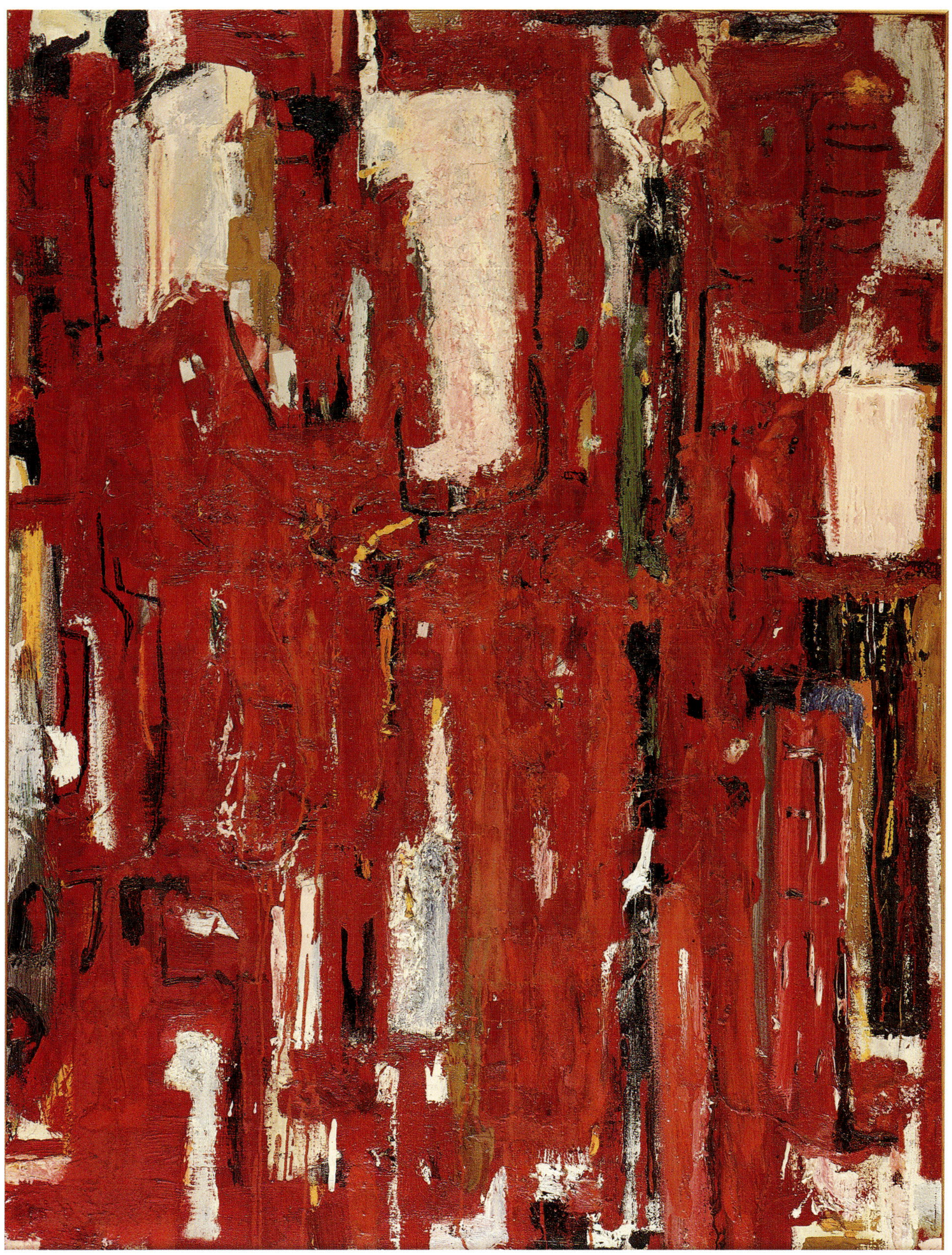

Figure 3.2

James Budd Dixon, *Untitled,* 1951. Oil on canvas, 48 × 36 in.

Collection, Clinton Reilly. Photograph courtesy, 871 Fine Arts,

San Francisco.

garde journals, *Berkeley* and *Circle,* during the 1940s. But as Walter Kuhlman pointed out, these ideas were so much "in the air" during the late 1940s that it was not necessary to read such writings firsthand.[16]

This "disdain for the thesis" dovetailed with another cluster of attitudes about the impotence of words and their irrelevance to painting.[17] A diary entry of Still's toward the close of the war sums up the prevailing view:

> I deplore most the overemphasis on words. Not the poet's words, but words that explain, reason, debate, deduce, make "fact." Words have become omnipotent because so facile a tool have they become for the utilitarian and the practical. It is not that they are perfect instruments. The opposite is the case as any mathematician will verify or musician insist. It is simply that in the social intercourse of man, words are unconsciously burdened with significances that rebound dangerously on the user. They simulate the very alpha and omega of understanding . . . Verbiage becomes a substitute for comprehension . . . From the state of the weather to an interpretation of the picture, words bear the burden of our stuttering life.[18]

As Still observed, it was not merely a matter of the old modernist bromide that words were extraneous to the visual facts of painting, but rather that they placed unwanted boundaries on meaning.[19] This is why so few of the San Francisco painters in the late 1940s entitled their works.[20] It was not so much to prevent the paintings from referring to something beyond themselves as to extend and expand their import, to allow each viewer to discover a personal message. The act of naming would close off the multitude of possible meanings that could spring from a single canvas.

This sensibility exemplifies the commitment to individualism and self-determination in cultural and intellectual realms produced by the encounter with totalitarianism—whether expressed as existentialism, the fascination with Renaissance individualism,[21] or the growing critique of mass culture. Although primarily associated with the 1950s through publications like David Riesman's *Lonely Crowd* (1950) and William Whyte's *Organization Man* (1956), the concern that mass culture posed a threat to the creative individual was an important theme for American artists and intellectuals during the 1940s.[22] The menace of authoritarian culture became a central preoccupation of MacAgy, who blamed what he called the "depersonalized structure of modern life" on an ever-increasing bureaucracy and praised Miller's *Tropic of Capricorn* (1939) for attacking "the metropolis which not only frustrates [man's] desires, but stultifies his capacities."[23]

If the San Francisco artists extended the privilege of free interpretation to the viewers of their art, they did so because of their aversion to any system that might impinge upon their own will, an aversion so intense that many of them refused to state and thereby codify their objectives.[24] Thus, even the intellectual Corbett could insist, "I have no systematic philosophy of art, and I do not intend to have one. The areas of mystery and indecision are precisely where art, for me, begins."[25] And Kuhlman could maintain in 1949, despite all evidence to the contrary, that the movement was not "a question of abstract painting versus representational work. Each artist works in the medium he believes in at the moment."[26]

Spohn was more inclined to theorize about his art than Corbett or Kuhlman, but he was no less concerned with the perils of exegesis. "Fine, provocative, and revelatory feelings, experiences, and realizations," he warned, "are always damned when they are explained or capable of analysis, measurement, and explanation . . . To take any one position toward a thing relegates it to the damnable position of being relative, finite, and material, a thing or an object. Only the intangibles have real meaning, for they alone deal with basic truths."[27]

Such a preference for the boundless over the measurable, for the spiritual over the empirical, echoes the Romantic struggle against Neoclassicism and Lockean rationalism, a theme frequently recited by the critic Alfred Frankenstein in his attempts to explain the painting of Still and others in San Francisco.[28] The analogy was appropriate considering the interest in Romantic thought shared by a number of artists in the group, including Still, Corbett, Kuhlman, Spohn, and Philip Roeber.[29]

Consensus by Negation

The ideological themes I have sketched thus far—the antirationalism, the insistence on self-determination, and the corollary mistrust of words, categories, and systems—are all encapsulated in the statement, written by Jermayne MacAgy, probably with the help of Still, for a group exhibition at the Henry Art Gallery in Seattle in early 1950:

If the observer is able to shed expectations that are appropriate to most painting in the European tradition, he may find himself stirred in this exhibition by an invocatory spirit that is rare. The authoritarian will be challenged and the doctrinaire confounded. For the forms this spirit takes neither establish a given "style" nor identify themselves by a name. They elude the clutch of critical systems in a world that is sick with erstwhile humors. Yet while each artist shares the spirit with the others represented here, he acts alone. Expressions are divergent. In the presence of these paintings, we may find new forces within ourselves.[30]

As the statement suggests, the dreaded "clutch of critical systems" included the aesthetic category. To espouse a collective style constituted an a priori judgment, and thus a form of dogma. Moreover, style was viewed as incidental to expression, and not an end in itself. Spohn described the common attitude when he wrote in 1949: "A painting must transcend the material or physical elements; the shapes, spaces, color, and tactile or aesthetic qualities; the skill, craftsmanship, manner, style, and historical chronology are irrelevant . . . A great painting always transcends itself."[31]

On this point, the San Francisco painters found themselves in agreement with the Surrealists, whose axiom "Thought is supreme over matter" meant that painting should always be placed at the service of the mind.[32] A similar view was held by many New York Abstract Expressionists, who considered formalist abstraction guilty of sacrificing human values to materialist concerns.[33] But taken as a group, the San Francisco painters may have been more extreme in their anti-aestheticism than their East Coast contemporaries. Stylistic critiques like those taking place at Hans Hofmann's school, for example, would have been frowned upon in San Francisco. Not only were discussions about aesthetics discouraged, but there seems to have been a tacit agreement that no value judgment should be made about completed works.[34] Even Spohn's pedagogical-sounding "Handbook of Abstract Expressionism," part of which he mimeographed for his students in 1948, made no stylistic recommendations but focused on methods of freeing the imagination.[35]

Among the San Francisco artists, Still was perhaps the most adamant in this regard. In his classes, he refused to discuss the mechanics of picture-making or comment on individual paintings, and he was known to lose his temper if another artist so much as implied an aesthetic judgment. Diebenkorn remembered inviting Still to lunch at his Sausalito home and, before sitting down to eat, showing the older artist a recent painting. When Still said he liked the work, Diebenkorn was embarrassed by the compliment and stammered that he "wasn't sure the color really worked." He recalled: "Unfortunately, this wasn't the sort of thing you could say to Clyfford Still. What was this about color *working?* That sort of talk was for pedants and old-fashioned art teachers. Clyfford didn't believe in craftsmanship—only in the emotional impact of the entire image. He got up, put on his coat, and, without saying a word, walked out."[36]

Yet while the artists at the California School of Fine Arts never formed an express consensus about the physical characteristics of their painting, they were nearly unanimous about how and what *not* to paint.[37] And these prohibitions were, for the most part, closely observed. It was obvious from the inside who did not belong to the movement: those who did not share the same prejudices and objects of disdain. Paradoxically, this consensus by negation amounted to an aesthetic program that was no less predictable than the canons the artists scorned.[38]

At the core of the San Francisco aesthetic was the nonobjectivity of the new painting. Out of roughly twenty-five artists associated with the San Francisco movement in 1948, only three—John Hultberg, Peter Shoemaker, and Lawrence Calcagno—commonly employed recognizable, if ambiguous, symbolic imagery, which may help to explain why many of their contemporaries viewed them as peripheral to the group.[39] Explicit representation of natural objects, on the other hand, was axiomatically forbidden. In the late 1940s the taboo was so complete that many painters felt constrained to repaint or destroy their canvases if they discovered a fragment of figurative imagery ex post facto.[40]

The preference for a nonreferential mode of painting was reflected in the terminology the artists chose to describe their work. "Nonobjective," "nonfigurative," and "nonreferential" were generally favored over "abstract," which implied a distillation of forms from nature. In Still's case, the issue also had to do with dissociating the movement from its European parentage. In his view, "abstraction" carried an inescapable French connotation and was thus inappropriate as a designation for painting that was American.[41] Spohn was dissatisfied with all existing terms. "Abstraction" was too ambiguous, and "nonobjective" implied a form of painting without intention or function. As an alternative, Spohn coined the phrase "subjective realism," explaining:

> As far as I am concerned, all painting is a form of realism which falls into either of two very general classifications. Some paintings could be called objective realism. That is where the material used deals with the visual appearances of reality in some degree or another. The other kind . . . is what I would prefer to call subjective realism. That is where the material used deals entirely with subjective things, with feeling meanings, with living experiences . . . The principal difference between these two, to put it simply, [is] that the objective realist believes in (or accepts) only what he sees, whereas the subjective realist may believe in what he sees, but for his world of creation, he chooses only to accept that which he knows to be true, because it is that which he feels, and he regards the experience of feeling . . . as being very real.[42]

For some San Francisco artists, painting nonobjectively meant exalting the medium. Hultberg, for example, considered it largely a matter of "keeping the religion of pure paint."[43] Yet few of the San Francisco Abstract Expressionists would have agreed with Motherwell that Abstract Expressionism was primarily about "paint itself."[44] The decision to paint nonobjectively was a matter of liberating content, in much the same way that leaving works untitled kept the lines of communication open. But as Spohn's commentary suggests, the avoidance of natural appearances was most important because it interiorized meaning. In essence, it asserted the belief, echoed in existentialism, that the subjective perception of reality had greater validity than the objective definition. The idea differed from earlier European subjectivist theories of abstraction primarily in the greater distance from the superficial features of nature. If one were to devise a spectrum shading from nature to feeling, with abstraction (being a synthesis of the two) in the middle, the position of most San Francisco Abstract Expressionists would hover somewhere between abstraction and feeling.

This conception leaves some room for the San Francisco painters' differing views of the role nature played as a source for their work. Despite their overwhelming bias against figuration, only Still categorically denied the influence of nature on his painting. None of the other San Francisco artists were willing to assent to Still's pronouncement: "I paint only

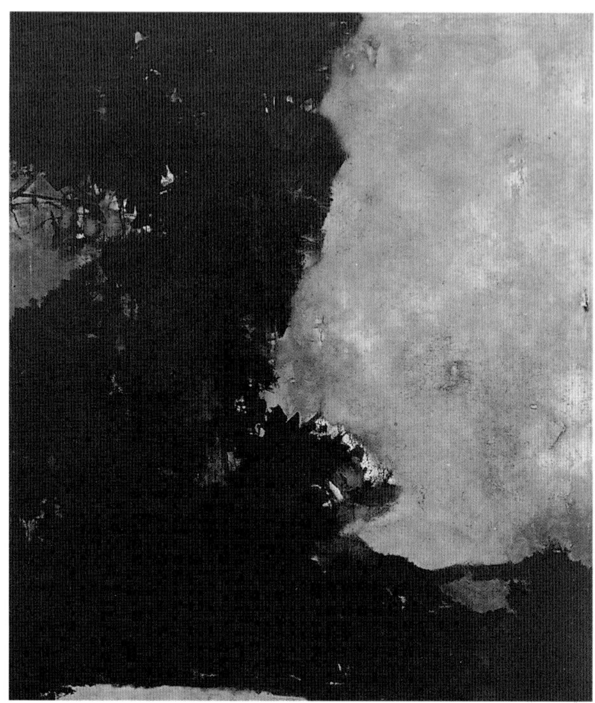

myself, not nature."[45] In fact, many of them considered the natural world a primary inspiration. As Spohn pointed out, nature could be a rich and meaningful subject as long as the artist filtered it through his imagination and dealt only with "living abstract elements . . . those elusive things such as atmosphere, space, and relationships that cannot be pinned down or measured."[46] Corbett's paintings of the late 1940s convey a strong feel for the intangibles of nature. The soft, misty texture of works such as *Untitled (Black Painting)* (1950; fig. 3.3) suggests the San Francisco fog Corbett liked to watch over the bay. Stillman also evoked natural textures, particularly the cracked and pockmarked surfaces of rocks and scorched earth (for example, fig. 3.4). Fissure motifs like those in Still-

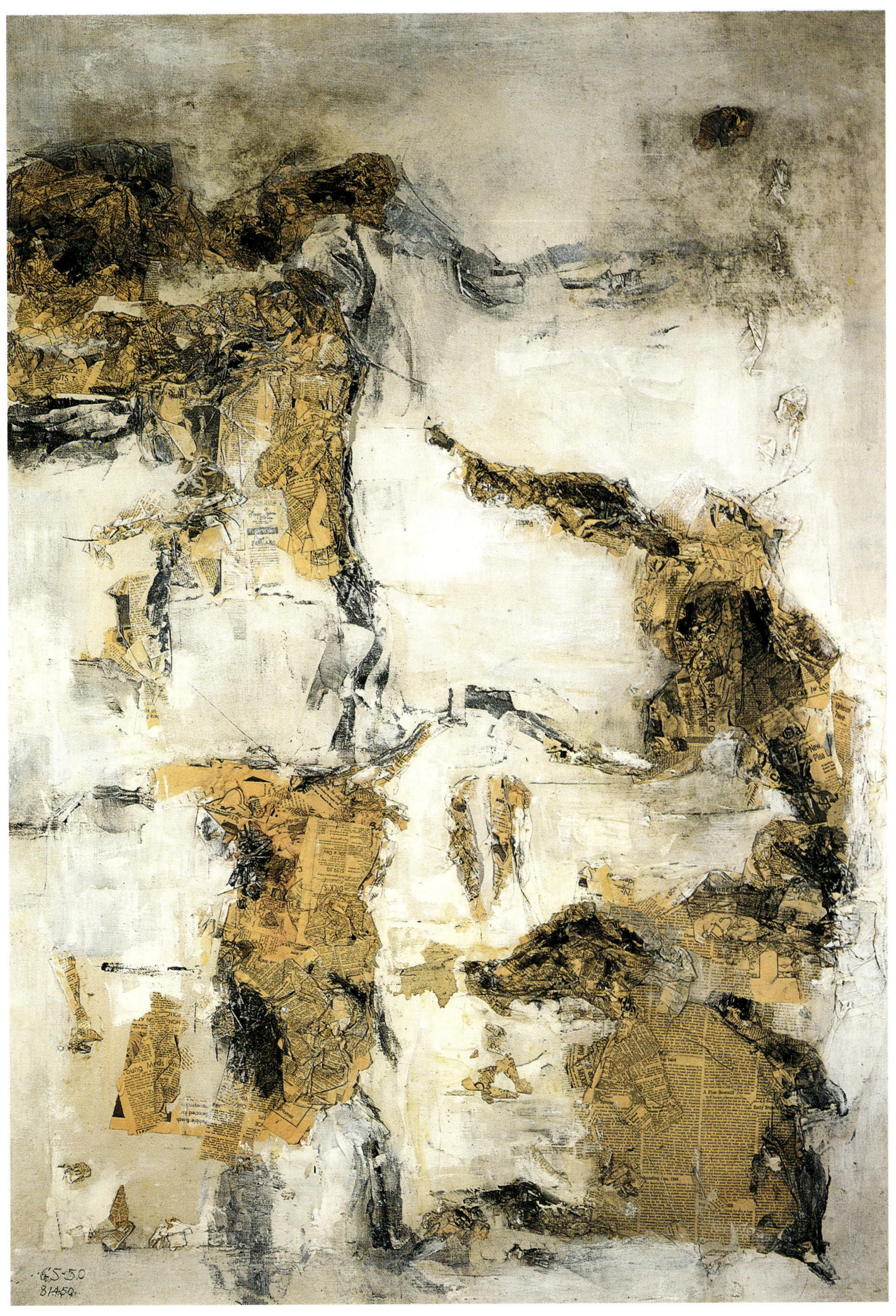

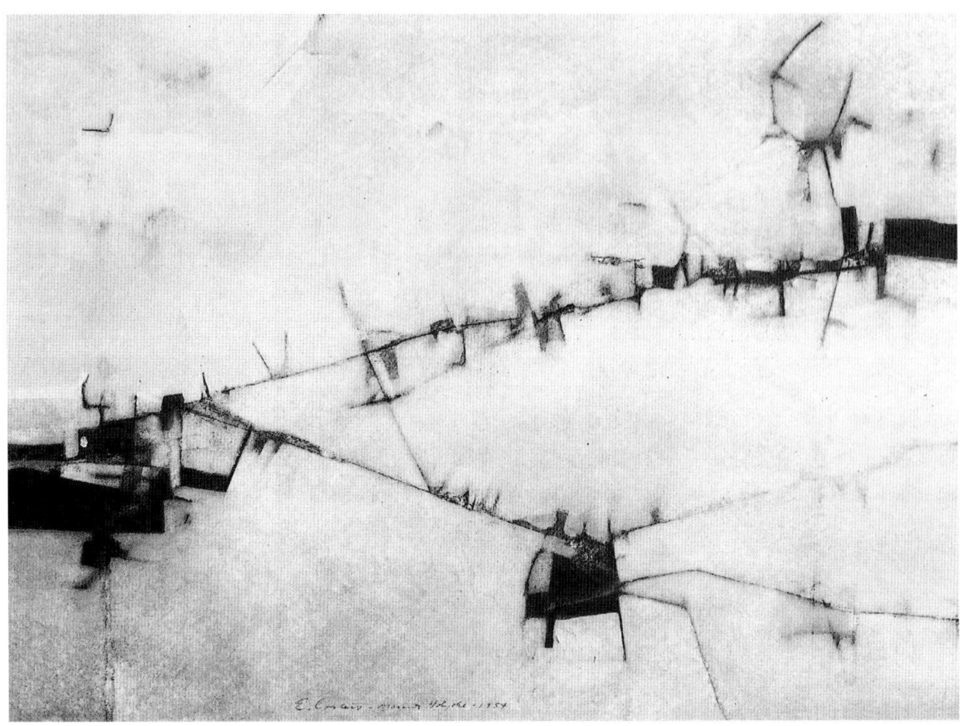

man's work were explored by a number of San Fran-cisco artists in the late 1940s and 1950s, with versions of this theme varying widely, from the delicate frac-tures of Corbett and Diebenkorn (figs. 3.5 and 3.6) to the glacial force of Jay DeFeo (fig. 3.7). Kuhlman's paintings offered yet another treatment of the natural world, one that involved highly subjective memories of his personal encounters with nature. While on the surface *Untitled #9* (1948; fig. 3.8) may present no more than a nonobjective design, the painting recol-lects Kuhlman's experience scuba diving in the Virgin Islands, suggesting bottom-dwelling fauna such as starfish and spiky sea anemone.[47]

Regardless of nature's role as inspiration, all the San Francisco Abstract Expressionists, including Still, drew from a language of color and form that was essentially organic. Once again an aesthetic tendency was largely a response to a widely discussed antipathy. Whether in the form of Cubism, Neoplasticism, or Bauhaus design, most San Francisco artists felt that geometric abstraction was hermetically isolated in its aestheticism and incapable of commenting on the world. It is not surprising to find in artists eager to assert the human an impulse to distance themselves from the formalism that was increasingly coming

under attack for its dehumanizing qualities.[48] The cool, impersonal machine aesthetic of Fernand Léger and many American artists since the 1920s had become associated with a sympathetic view of indus-try, technology, and science that was no longer ten-able after the war.[49]

Geometric abstraction, as a subset of classicism, had long been perceived as an enemy of the free spirit. Herbert Read defined classicism as an age-old mani-festation of political and social repression. In an essay composed shortly before the war, he wrote:

> Classicism, let it be stated without further preface, rep-resents for us now, and has always represented, the forces of oppression. Classicism is the intellectual coun-terpart of political tyranny. It was so in the ancient world and in the medieval empires; it was renewed to express the dictatorships of the Renaissance and has ever since been the official creed of capitalism. Wherever the blood of the martyrs stains the ground, there you will find a doric column or perhaps a statue of Minerva.[50]

Read's words were given fresh meaning by the forcible revival of classicism in the official architecture and art academies under Stalin, Hitler, and Mussolini.[51] It

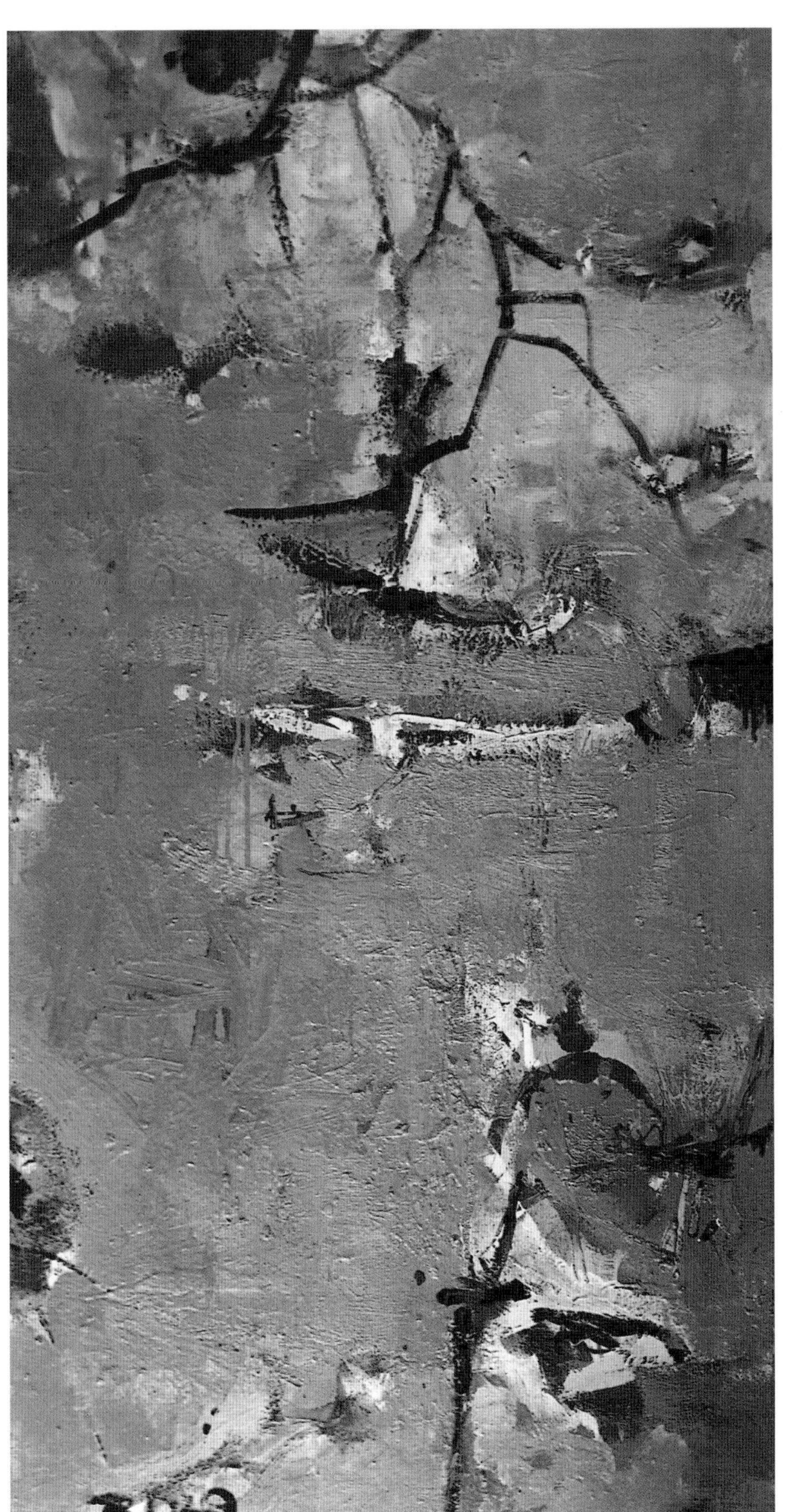

Figure 3.5

Opposite: Edward Corbett, *Mount Holyoke #36,* 1954.
Gouache, charcoal, and crayon on paper, 18$\frac{1}{16}$ × 24 in.
Collection, Hirshhorn Museum and Sculpture Garden,
Smithsonian Institution, gift of Joseph H. Hirshhorn, 1966.

Figure 3.6

Left: Richard Diebenkorn, *Sausalito,* 1949. Oil on canvas,
dimensions and whereabouts unknown. Photographer:
George Stillman.

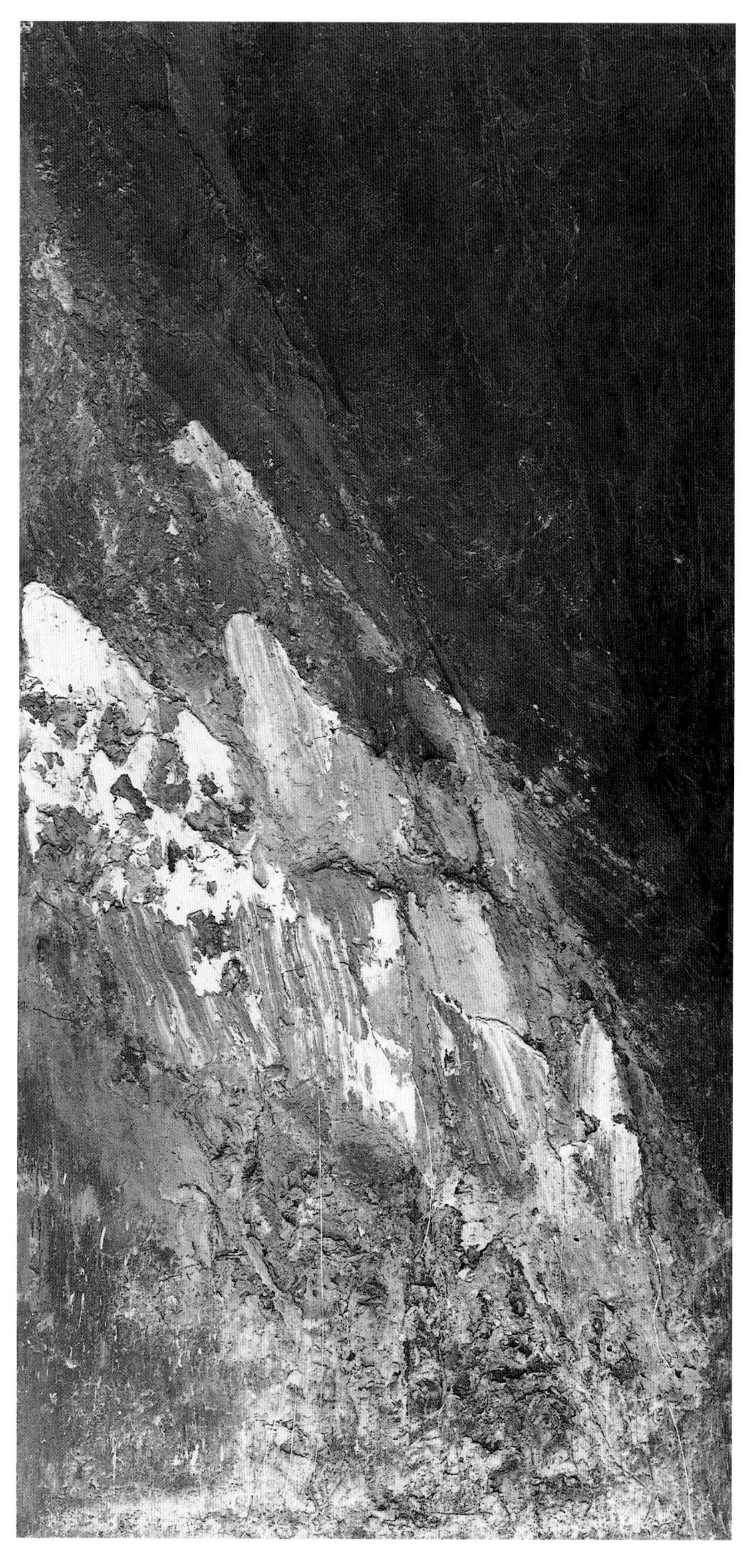

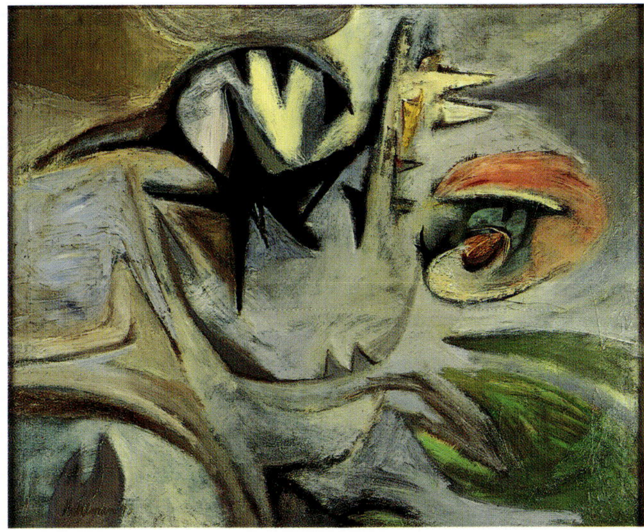

seems that the San Francisco artists rejected geometry in symbolic opposition to such blatant curtailment of artistic freedom. Indeed, they consistently expressed their belief that the language of classicism signified tyranny and oppression. Thus, for Diebenkorn, geometry "equalled sterility"; for Corbett, it represented a "strait jacket"; and for Still, it stood for nothing less than "totalitarian hegemony."[52]

Devices of Dissension

The aesthetic ramifications of this anticlassicism were far-reaching and involved more than a mere refusal to paint geometric shapes. Indeed, nearly every aspect of the San Francisco School's sensibility can be seen as antithetical to classicism. Clarity, order, and stasis gave way to the contrary romantic qualities of dynamism, ambiguity, and imprecision. Clean, smooth surfaces and clear hues were rejected in favor of rough textures and earthy, sometimes muddy colors. The compositions of the paintings, as well as their component parts, show a penchant for the irregular and indistinct (figs. 3.9, 3.10). This distaste for static forms even included a reluctance to fix edges with delineating lines. As MacAgy observed, the function of line as an instrument of quantitative expression made it a paramount symbol of classicist rationality.[53]

The San Francisco artists' passion for boundlessness involved more than a liberation of form within the canvas; for many, it entailed a projection beyond the framing borders of a painting. This effect was most frequently achieved by creating an edge-to-edge expanse of color or by placing shapes along the periphery of the canvas to imply their continuation on the other side (figs. 3.11, 3.12). Margins were either eliminated or violated by allowing the paint to trespass in the form of drips and spatters (fig. 3.13).[54] Another common tactic was to increase the scale of the paintings to create an expanded presence, although limited studio space and finances often restricted that possibility.[55]

The theme of expansion, as art historians have often noted, was important for some of the New York color-field painters, notably Rothko and Newman, but also for Pollock, who liked to think of his drip paintings as creating a spatial continuum without "any beginning or any end."[56] This projective environmental space, generally understood as creating a sense of intimacy between the viewer and the work, is commonly considered the most significant innovation of Abstract Expressionism.[57] But, in fact, the notion of enveloping spectators through implied projection into their space had been explored by a number of Surrealists during the war, including Wolfgang Paalen, Max Ernst, and Frederick Kiesler. As members of Peggy Guggenheim's stable of artists in the mid-1940s, Rothko, Pollock, and Still would have been familiar with Kiesler's "spatial exhibition" design for the Art of This Century gallery, which eliminated frames, pedestals, and even walls to bring the viewers

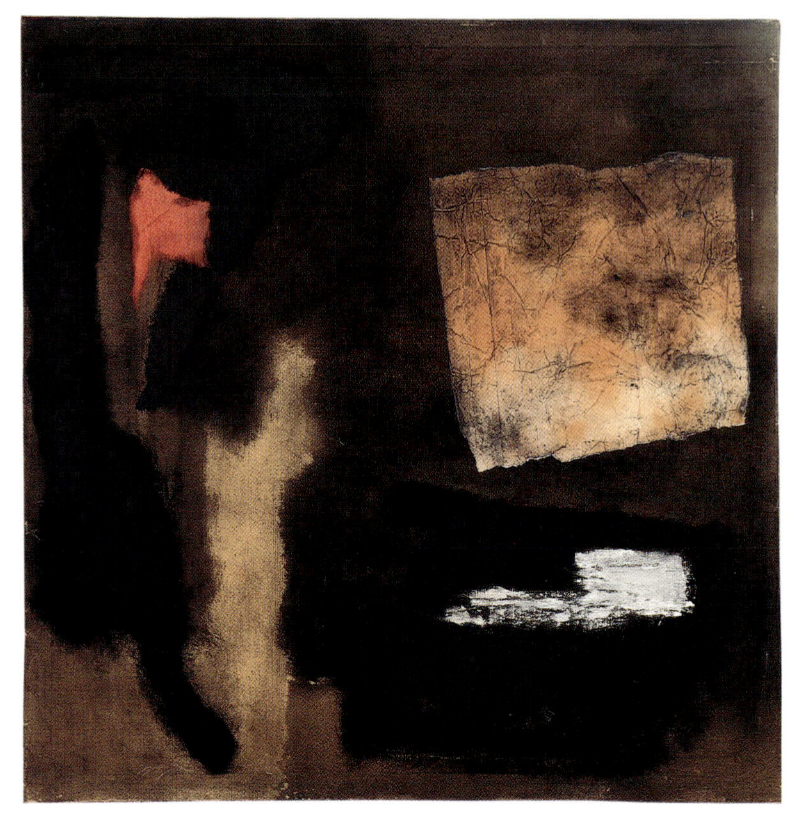

Figure 3.9

Right: Philip Roeber, *Untitled,* 1950. Oil and paper on canvas, 48 × 46 in. Collection, Mag Dimond. Photographer: Ira D. Schrank.

Figure 3.10

Below: Robert McChesney, *Mountain Series, Number 2,* 1953. Oil on canvas, 38 × 53 in. Collection, Whitney Museum of American Art, New York. Photographer: Geoffrey Clements.

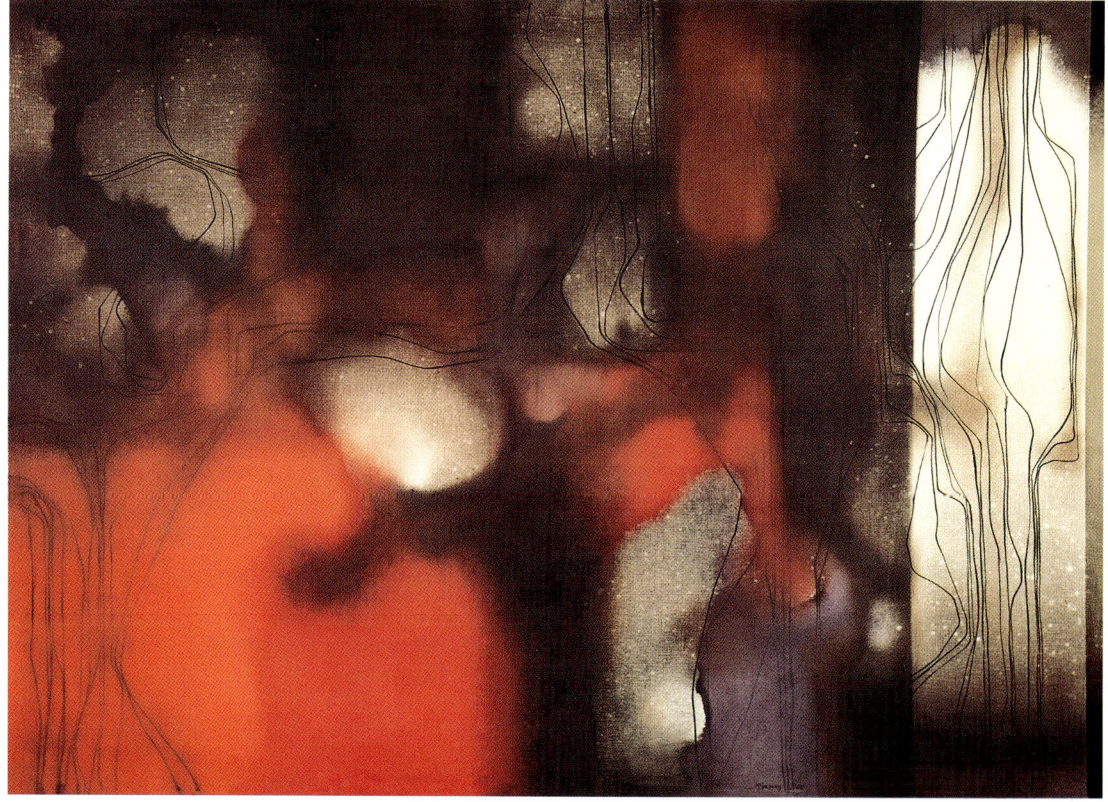

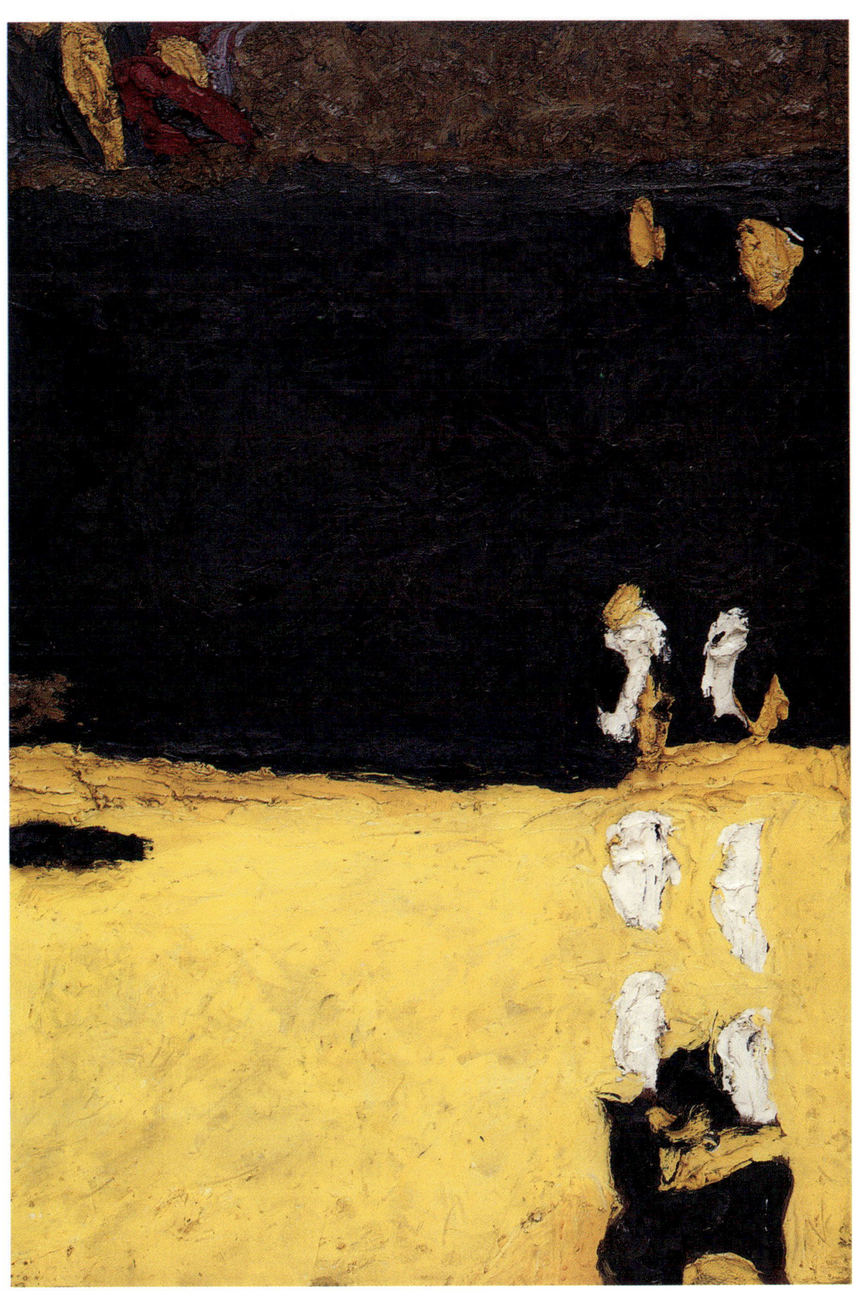

Figure 3.11

Ronald Bladen, *Untitled #4,* 1956–59. Oil on canvas, 72 × 48 in.

Collection, Lannan Foundation, Los Angeles. Photographer:

Susan Einstein.

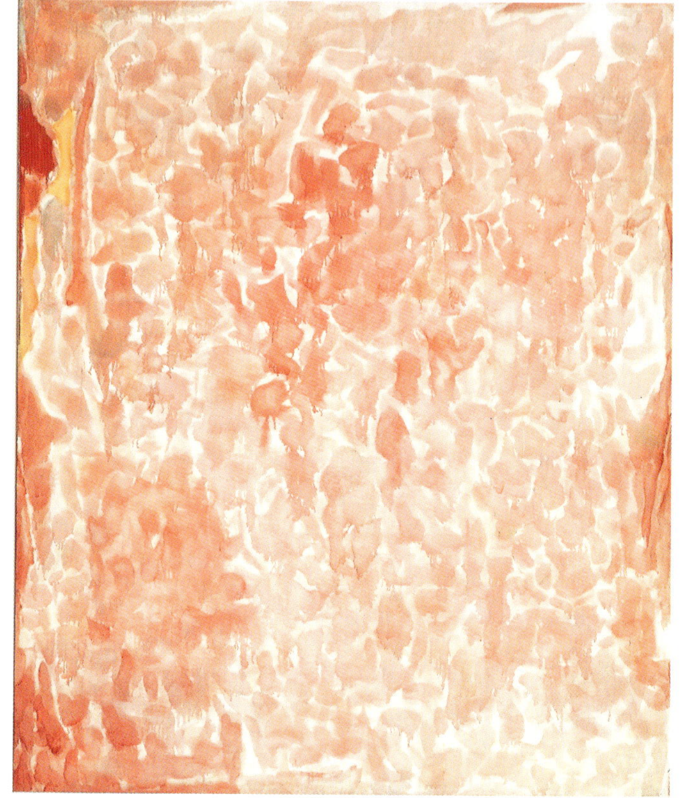

Figure 3.12

Right: Sam Francis, *Red and Pink,* 1951. Oil on canvas, 80 × 66 in. San Francisco Museum of Modern Art, partial gift of Mrs. Wellington S. Henderson. © 1995 Sam Francis / Artists Rights Society (ARS), New York.

Figure 3.13

Below: James Budd Dixon, *Archetypes,* ca. 1948. Oil on canvas, 37⅞ × 37⅞ in. Collection, The Oakland Museum, extended loan of Dean Mawdsley. Photographer: M. Lee Fatherree.

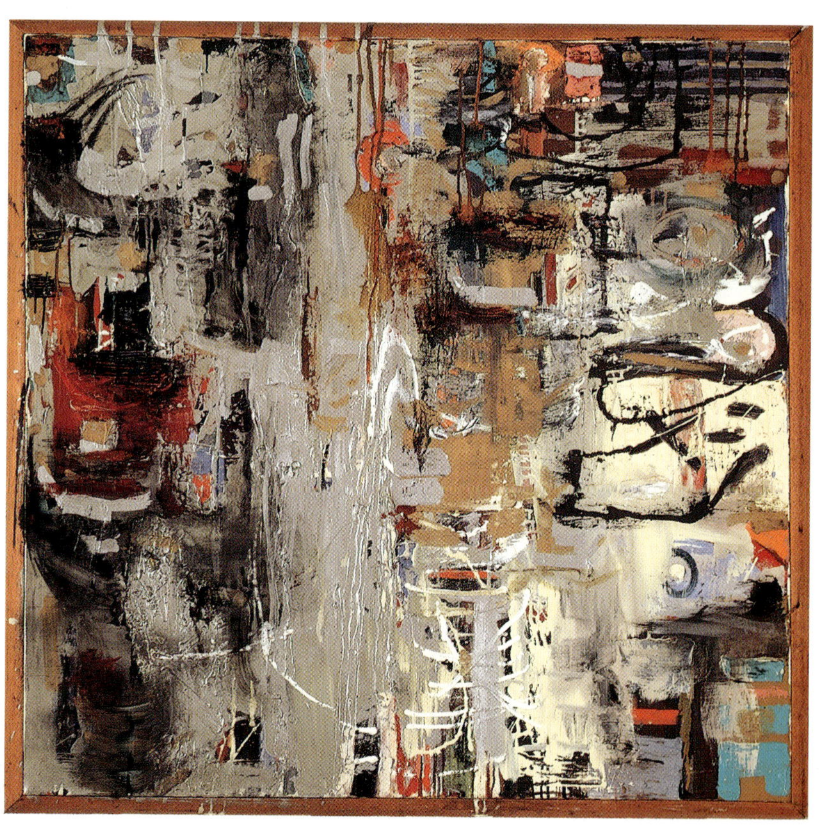

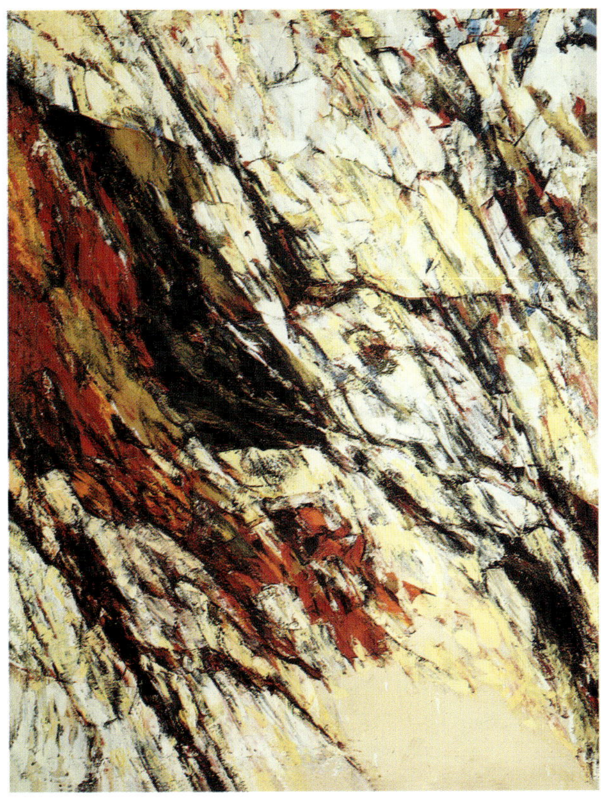

Figure 3.14

Ernest Briggs, *Number 1107,* 1955. Oil on canvas, 69 × 50½ in.

Collection, Whitney Museum of American Art, New York,

purchased with funds from the Friends of the Whitney

Museum of American Art. Photographer: Geoffrey Clements.

into the closest possible contact with the work on display.[58] These ideas were current in San Francisco as well during the war through such Surrealist poets and artists as Bern Porter, who proposed a concept he called the "New Projection" in the early 1940s.[59] Some of Porter's ideas closely resemble the aims of Pollock's drip paintings. In a 1944 article entitled "All Over the Place," Porter declared that "splashing over the frame or overlapping it and giving the appearance of spreading out to adjacent walls is quite feasible and wholly justifiable when the objective is the union of the artist's creative consciousness and the spectator's environment."[60] While Porter's theories about pictorial projection were clearly an important precedent for the San Francisco painters, there is little evidence that the CSFA artists were particularly interested in producing an encompassing environment for the spectator.[61] For most of the artists, the aim was rather to produce a feeling of freedom. Sometimes they achieved this by suggesting ascension with upward trajectories of paint (fig. 3.14, 3.15).[62] At other times the implication was a gentler horizontal expansion (fig. 3.16). In all these instances, however, the central

idea was to create a spatial metaphor for human aspiration. "To be stopped by a frame's edge was intolerable; a Euclidean prison," Still exhorted in his typical Nietzschean fashion. "It had to be annihilated, its authoritarian implications repudiated."[63]

While the sources for this idea in Romantic thought, particularly the aesthetics of the sublime, have often been discussed in connection with Still, as well as in relation to his closest associates in New York, Rothko and Newman, they may also pertain to many San Francisco artists.[64] The notion that a limitless expanse could induce spiritual exaltation is at the heart of Edmund Burke's concept of the sublime and subsequent recastings of Romantic thought, including American transcendentalism. In the writings of Emerson and Thoreau, however, the complex of ideas associated with the sublime took on an added dimension that held particular meaning for artists and writers in the West. For writers of the American Renaissance, particularly for Whitman, the expansive western frontier not only symbolized spiritual exaltation, but also embodied the principle of individual liberty at the very core of American democracy.[65]

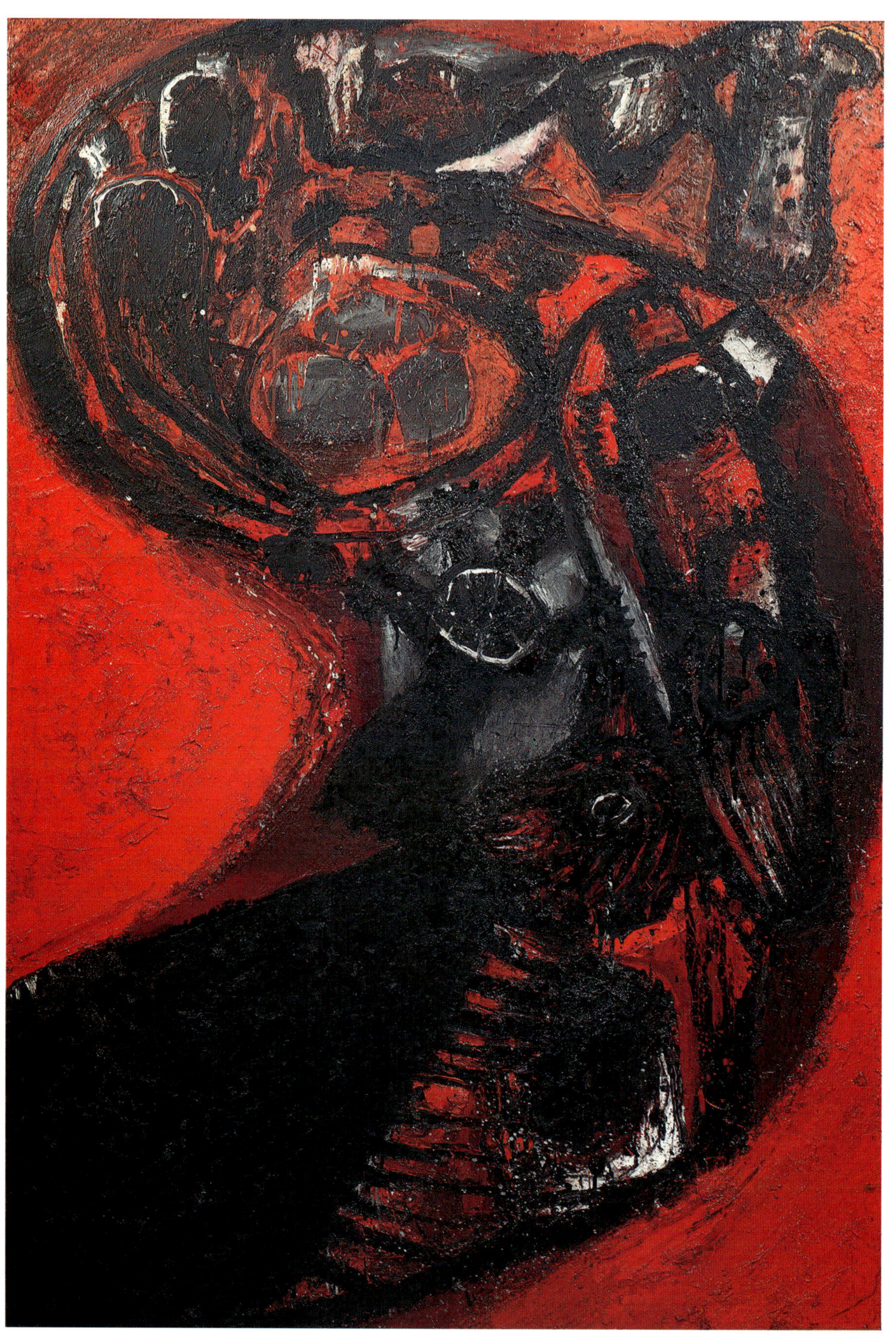

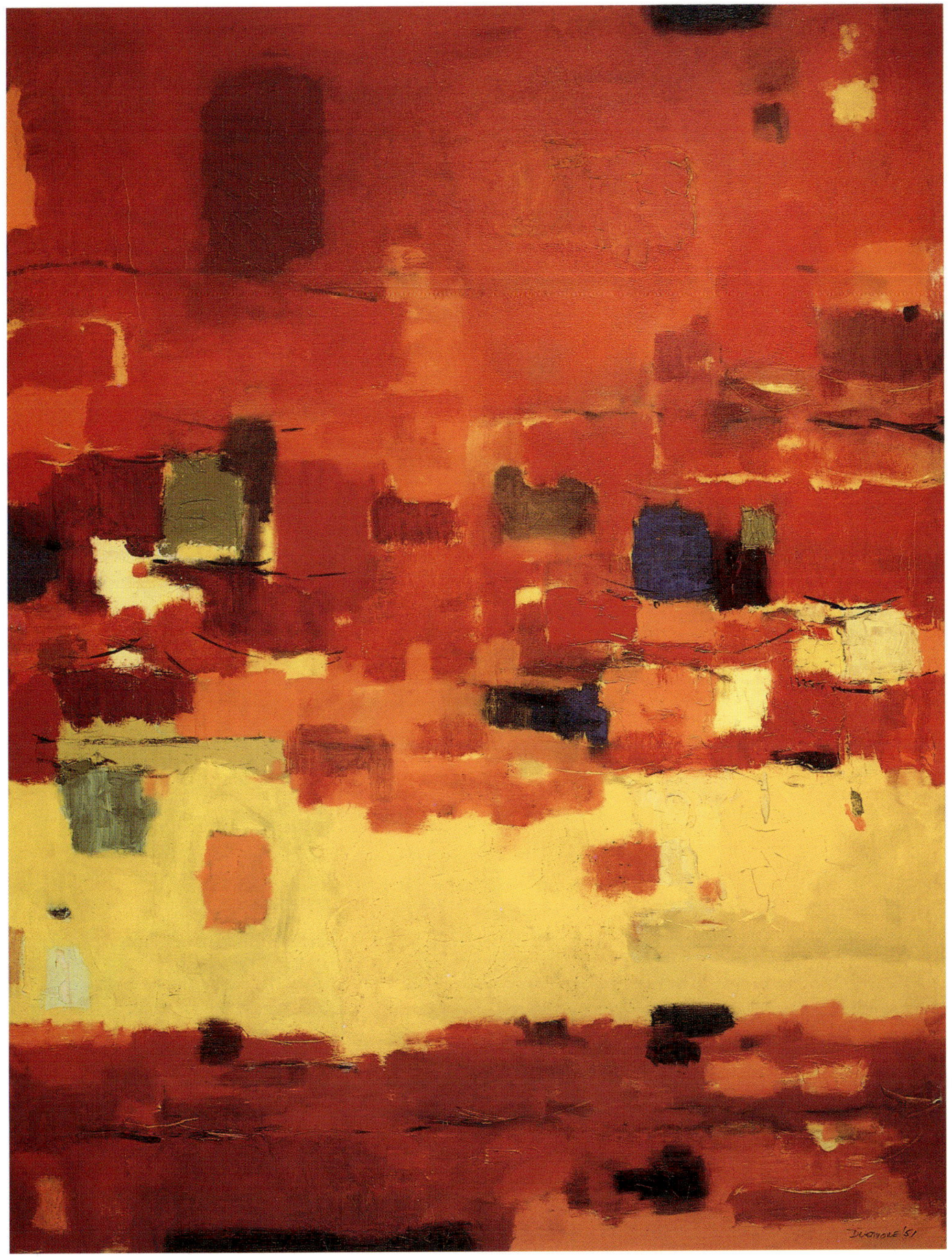

Figure 3.15

Opposite: Frank Lobdell, *Ascent (Red),* 1962. Oil on canvas,
73 × 49 in. Collection, Anderson Gallery, Buffalo, New York.

Figure 3.16

Above: Edward Dugmore, *Tlaquepaque #12,* 1951. Oil on
canvas, 72 × 54 in. Collection, Abner D. and Roslyn Goldstine.
Photographer: Antoni E. Dolinksi.

Considering the importance of such values after the war, it is not surprising that many poets and writers in California resurrected these themes. Robinson Jeffers, Kenneth Rexroth, and Gary Snyder are just a few of the literary figures during the postwar period whose writings allude to the expansive western landscape as a symbol of freedom and individualism.[66] These sentiments invoke the mythology of the West as a paradigm of pioneering self-sufficiency dating back to the nineteenth century, but they also reflect a specific postwar moment. California's image as a cultural frontier, expanding the limits of human activity, reached unprecedented intensity in the years just after the Second World War. With the population nearly double its prewar size and the standard of living suddenly the highest in the country, California found itself transformed from a province dependent on the East to a powerful, self-sufficient state. Youthful, experimental, and above all, free from the weighty tradition that bound the cities of the eastern seaboard, Californians briefly envisioned assuming the nation's economic and cultural leadership.[67] With the decimation of the Japanese fleet, Governor Earl Warren revived California's "passage to India" dream of international economic supremacy through trade with Asia. Expressing California's newfound optimism, Warren declared: "We have sniffed our destiny . . . never before have there been quite so many people possessed of faith in our future or quite so intent on giving voice to the conviction that we have our foot in the door of an era of dream realization."[68] The art collector and publisher Gifford Phillips conjured visions of cultural leadership when he compared the frontier of the forty-niners to the pace-setting cultural frontier of 1949:

> The frontier which lured the '49ers to California had plenty of bright, yellow gold at the end of the rainbow . . . Today, one hundred years later, that frontier has vanished. But in its place has arisen a new and even more exciting frontier. This new frontier no longer involves large unexplored tracts of land. Its undiscovered areas lie in the realm of the mental, moral and social—rather than the physical . . . People living in other parts of the country have already formed most of their attitudes, customs and institutions . . . That's one reason why some three million of them left home and came to California during the last seven years. These people seek to establish a way of living that is truly modern—modern in the sense of benefiting from the past but not being bound by it.[69]

Whether or not the artists in San Francisco felt any special claim to artistic leadership, many of them believed their work reflected the cultural and geographical expanse of the West. William Morehouse, a student of Still's in the late 1940s, remembered that Still in particular identified with the West, returning "again and again to the theme of the artist-as-pioneer and of painting as the last frontier—where the individual had the opportunity to explore new territory and create himself."[70]

This reverence for freedom was expressed in the pictorial expansiveness of the San Francisco artists, but it was also communicated in their spontaneous manner of painting. Some artists were more unrestrained than others; approaches ranged from Smith's unbridled abandon (fig. 3.17) to Still's more deliberate methods. But all the San Francisco Abstract Expressionists embraced a spontaneous ideal of painting. Bischoff summed up the common view when he explained: "Broadly speaking, the spontaneous, unpremeditated act was seen as connecting with a richer, more profound—some would have even said: more authentic—source in the individual than an act which was consciously controlled and deliberate . . . This was a world of paint brushes, palette knives and hands. The straight edge, the compass, masking tape, tracing paper, spray guns, photographs, duplicating techniques all were scorned."[71] An unhampered process of painting could thus convey at once the artist's expressive freedom and his personal identity. The San Francisco artists accepted unquestioningly the expressionist tenet of empathy, that color, space, line, and shape inherently embodied the feelings, temperament, and spirit of the artist.[72] This belief in the indivisibility of subject and object was most fanatically expressed by Still, who claimed that stretching his canvases was physically painful, and that letting go of his paintings was as excruciating as losing his skin.[73]

Yet as essential as the ideal of immediacy was for these artists, it would be a mistake to see their work as the product of unchecked impulse and chance. Most executed their paintings over an extended period of time and thoughtfully reworked them. "You didn't make a painting a day," Dixon explained. "It would take you two or three months, sometimes six months to get it to the point where you felt it was finished."[74] Experimentation and improvisation were significant sources of invention, but only in tandem with a disciplined formal rigor. As Bischoff noted, "Talent, tech-

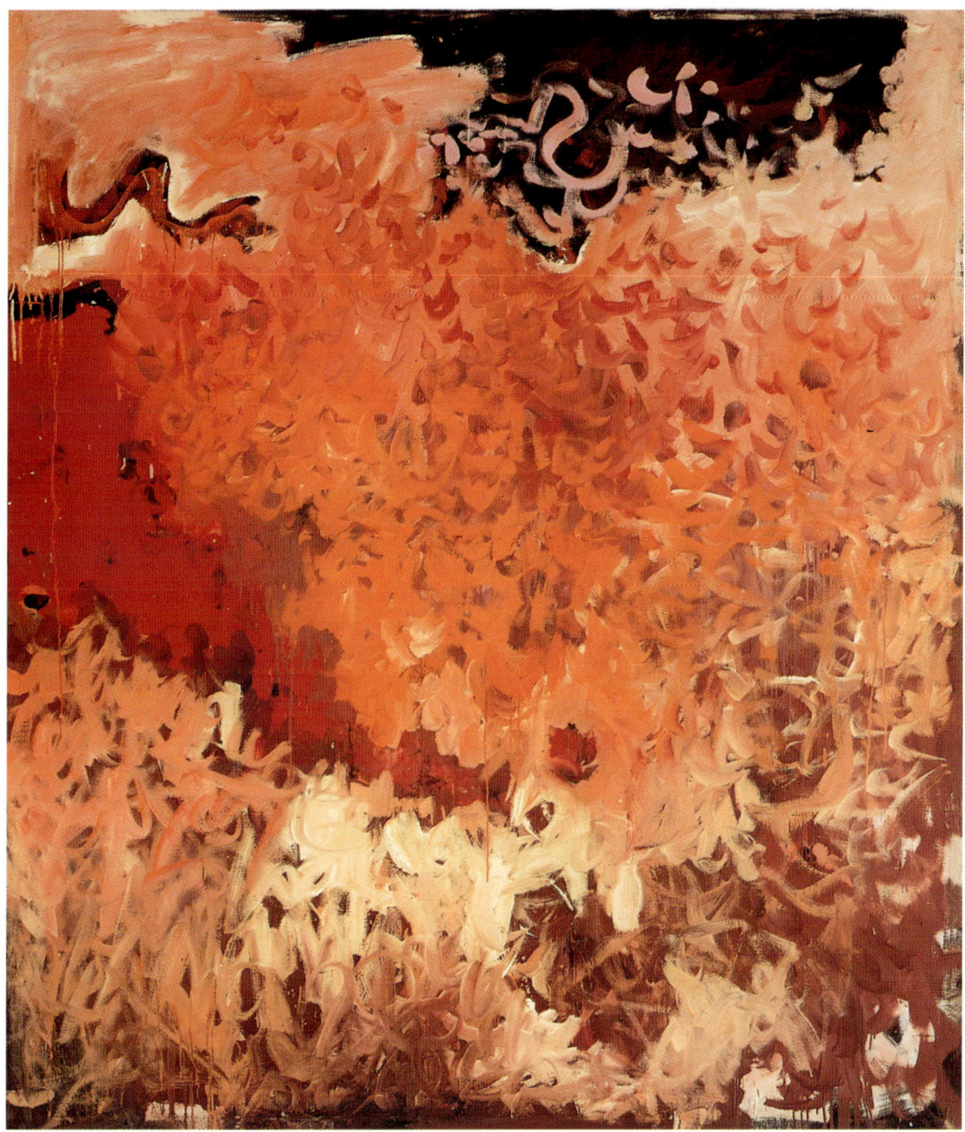

Figure 3.17

Hassel Smith, *Little Big Horn,* 1953. Oil on canvas, 85 × 70 in.

Collection, Museum of Fine Arts, Museum of New Mexico,

gift of Mr. and Mrs. Gifford Phillips.

nical skill and control, experience, intensity of concern, capacity for disciplined, dogged work—these were all considered important."[75] Facility was decidedly not a virtue; on the contrary, painting was expected to be hard-won and hard-wrought. William Morehouse remembered learning this lesson after receiving a D in a course with Spohn even though he had dutifully completed all of the assignments. Stunned, he went to Spohn to ask if there had been a mistake, and was told: "You are too glib; painting has become too easy for you."[76]

In this light, it is not surprising that Harold Rosenberg's notion of "action painting," with its exaltation of process over product, of the act over the object, was almost universally rejected in San Francisco. To be sure, there was a strong antimaterialist ethos among the San Francisco artists; as Still put it, the movement was not "just about painting—that's

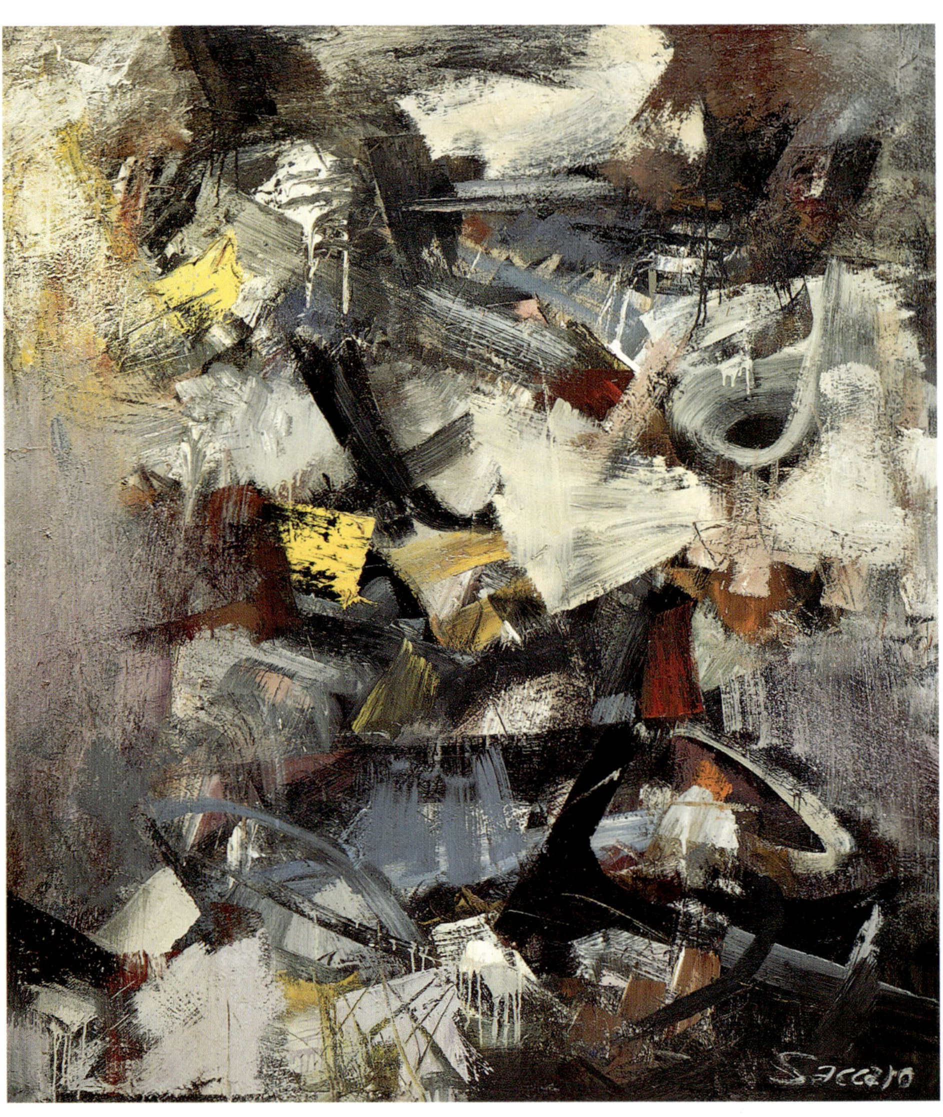

Figure 3.18

John Saccaro, *Settebello,* 1963. Oil on canvas, 68 × 58 in.

Private collection. Photographer: M. Lee Fatherree.

one trap it was necessary to get this instrument out of."[77] But color, form, and composition were not to be abandoned, as Rosenberg suggested, nor was painting to be a "liberation from Value."[78] On the contrary, the idea was to put painting to the service of value—to make painting an instrument for political, philosophical, and moral purposes. The glorification of the aleatory and unconscious painting process that was fundamental not only to "action painting" but also to its European cousin, automatism, was also problematic for many of the San Francisco painters.

Indeed, some, notably Still, Lobdell, Jefferson, and Corbett, were violently opposed to Rosenberg's ideas.[79] In Corbett's opinion, the basic premise of both automatism and "action painting" was not only self-defeating but fraudulent. It was impossible for the artist to draw entirely from the unconscious, he argued, since the truly creative process required all the artist's faculties.[80] Corbett liked to quote the psychologist Lawrence Hatterer, who observed: "To maintain that the artist creates exclusively in a state of reduced or disturbed consciousness, that is, from his unconscious or preconscious, is not an accurate reflection of the extremely organized, disciplined, and at times' highly conscious state of the creative mind. Inevitably, all levels of consciousness are involved."[81] John Saccaro, one of San Francisco's most gestural Abstract Expressionists (fig. 3.18), spoke for many artists when he said:

> Most critics that I've read talked about action, the spontaneity. Sure, spontaneity is valuable; it's valuable in any kind of painting and especially in abstract painting. But spontaneity has never been the thing. For Christ's sake, there must be some sort of energy besides the energy of the tracks of the paint, the rushing up there and splattering the damned canvas. There has to be another kind. Some artists call it feeling. Some call it sensation. It has several names. For myself, I always thought of it as occult energy.[82]

On close inspection, it appears that the San Francisco artists, as a group, like their counterparts in New York, were not a great deal more spontaneous than the Fauves or German Expressionists or, for that matter, such figurative contemporaries as Abraham Rattner or C. S. Price.[83] As we have seen, each of the painters worked within a set of strictures dictated by both the aesthetic of the group and the artist's own stylistic inclinations. The employment of drips, spatters, unmixed paint, and gestural brushwork was as deliberate as their decision to use organic forms and colors. In many cases, such painterly mark-making was not a by-product of spontaneous execution at all, but a calculated device. Some of Corbett's Point Richmond paintings, for example, such as an untitled work of 1950, contain delicate drips that could only have been painstakingly applied (fig. 3.19).

If the painterly language of the San Francisco artists was not always the result of rapid-fire methods, it was no less expressive of the ideal of spontaneity—or, to be more specific, of artistic freedom. The drip and gesture served much the same function as the use of centrifugal compositions and open-form shapes, and the elimination of framing margins; all were symbolic weapons of protest against ideological coercion. The drip occupied a special place in this arsenal. In the pre-McCarthy battle over the legitimacy of modern art—with abstract painting attacked as un-American by conservative and even not-so-conservative artists, critics, and museum officials—the dripping and spattering of paint became the ultimate insignia of artistic radicalism. Although not all the San Francisco artists

consistently used drips in their work—Still is the notable exception—there was something of a drip explosion at the California School of Fine Arts at the height of the modern art controversy in early 1948.[84] The phenomenon lasted less than a year, but evidently involved a number of artists.[85] The paintings that survive suggest how audacious and confrontational the works in this genre must have appeared in the late 1940s. Smith's *Untitled* (ca. 1948), with its dark, runny streaks and irreverent disregard for pictorial structure, still carries an aura of protest (fig. 3.20). Shown by Smith in a joint exhibition with Bischoff and Park at the San Francisco Museum of Art in 1948, this painting caused a furor in the local art community, provoking shocked opponents to coin the unflattering phrase "drip and drool school."[86]

Smith's defiance of conventional taste was in part an expression of the strong sentiment of anticommercialism among the San Francisco artists. As Stillman explained, decorative functionalism was anathema: "To fall into the trap of providing social entertainment on the level of drawing room decoration was to be avoided at all costs."[87] No artist in San Francisco was more preoccupied with this than Still. His jeremiads against the corruption of the art world were notorious even in the 1940s. In Still's view, the artist was threatened on all sides by polluting, emasculating forces, from the art dealers who turned paintings into commodities to the critics who distorted their meaning. Only the most uncompromising stance could preserve the integrity and effectiveness of the work. In the late 1940s, Still frequently adopted the analogy of guerrilla warfare to explain the only tenable position of the contemporary artist: "You're not going to win and you can't withstand the forces," he told his students, "but you *can* harass them."[88] Few, though, could match the vehemence of Still's attacks: critics were "verminous scribblers," galleries were "brothels," and the Museum of Modern Art was a "gas chamber."[89]

Still's protest against the decoration of fashionable interiors was an important element of his work, probably the one that made the greatest impact in San Francisco. Jack Jefferson observed that the "antibeauty" in Still's painting, the "willingness to use something really raw and brutal," appealed to many painters (he was himself among them; see fig. 3.21).[90] A number of Still's techniques for assaulting the protocols of decor became pervasive, including his exposure of bare canvas (sometimes intentionally dirtied), and his use of dry, parched paint, which naturally lent

Figure 3.19

Above: Edward Corbett, *Untitled,* 1950. Oil on canvas, 49 × 45 in. Collection, Robert Duncan Estate. Photograph courtesy, Richmond Art Center.

Figure 3.20

Opposite: Hassel Smith, *Untitled,* ca. 1948. Oil on canvas, dimensions and whereabouts unknown. Photographer: George Stillman.

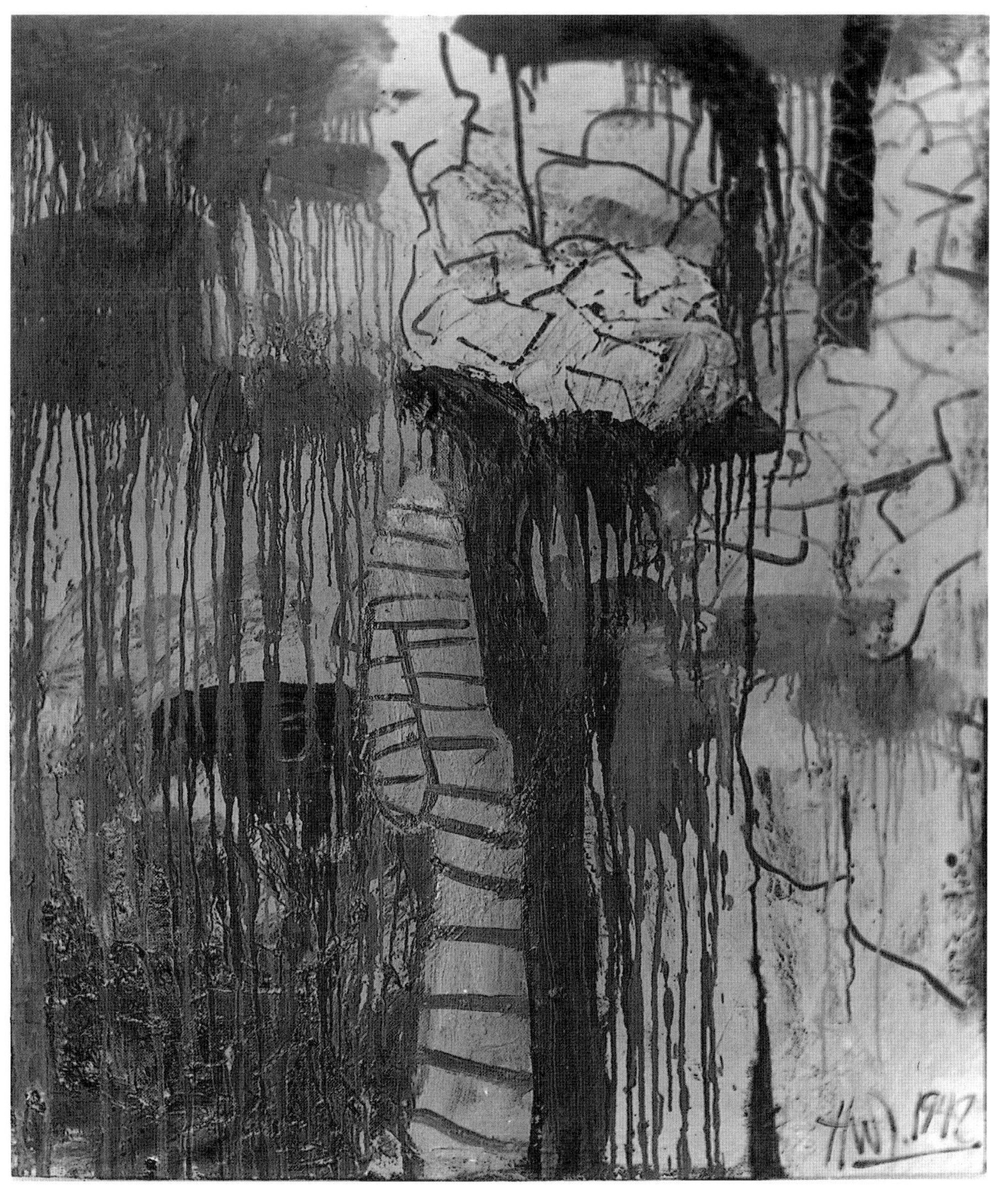

itself to a thick buildup of clotted, accretionary sur-faces. Even Still's palette, designed to counter all that was sensuous and appealing, became the standard of many San Francisco painters. Dull browns, gummy blacks, and leaden grays took precedence while deco-rative pastels—especially pink and baby blue—were often avoided, since, as Still told his students, they were too closely associated with Madison Avenue advertising.[91]

Some painters took Still's contempt for painterly finish to further extremes than Still himself. Indeed, it would not be an exaggeration to say that a cult of the ugly arose in San Francisco. According to Briggs, stu-dents used to compete "to see who could make the nastiest painting, get the greasiest black."[92] Symbolic of this tendency were Mel Weitsman's unsightly effi-gies composed of tar, mattress ticking, and other per-ishable proto-Funk materials. Such crudeness was encouraged in part by the lack of an art market in San Francisco, which allowed artists to make particularly brazen departures from middle-class taste.[93] It was a source of considerable pride for artists in San Fran-cisco that their work was less marketable than the most radical painting from New York. When Pollock's first major retrospective was held at the Museum of Modern Art in 1956, Smith noted with obvious satis-faction that "while critics in New York have only recently discovered that Jackson Pollock looks 'tame,'

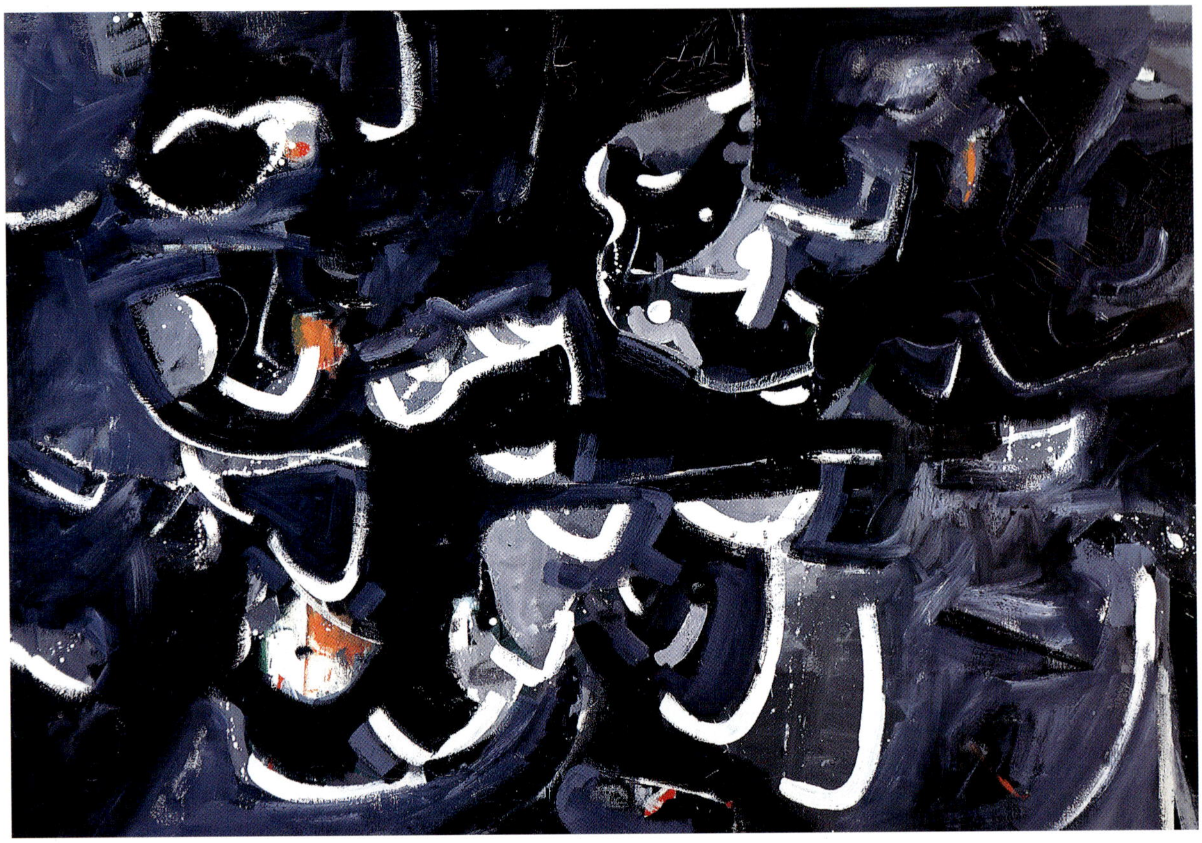

Figure 3.21

Jack Jefferson, *Chestnut Street #10,* 1952. Oil on canvas, 48 × 72 in. Collection, Laguna Art Museum, gift of Jack and Zena Jefferson.

'graceful' and even 'pleasant,' he has always appeared to be so in San Francisco."[94]

Beyond encouraging a general flouting of good taste, this antipathy toward the art establishment had far-reaching consequences in San Francisco, profoundly affecting the development of its artists. Corbett, for example, decided to make his paintings more delicate and refined just as the American art market called for brash gesture. Other artists refused to show their work if asked to compromise their ideals. Stillman remembers storming out of the Museum of Modern Art in New York when the curator Dorothy Miller pointed to one of his paintings and suggested that he put together an exhibition of "work like that."[95] Because of the commercial forces at work in the art world, some artists, like Still, ultimately became deeply reclusive, refusing to sell their work or show it publicly. Still even boycotted the annual exhibitions at the San Francisco Museum of Art and encouraged his students to do likewise: "We're grown men, not like children who put their paintings on the wall and hope for a gold star. I told them to wait until the museum came to them."[96]

Not all the artists could afford to shun the annuals, but a group of them expressed their antagonism to the art market by founding the Metart Galleries in the spring of 1949. The cooperative, nonprofit exhibition space on Bush Street at the entrance to Chinatown set a precedent for a Bay Area tradition of artist-run galleries. Some of the Metart's immediate heirs were the King Ubu, the Six, and the Spatsa galleries, all of which served more as meeting places than as venues for sales in the 1950s.

The origins of the Metart Galleries are the subject

of some debate. Still claimed that the gallery was his idea, but several of the participating artists have disagreed.[97] Edward Dugmore insists that the Metart (short for metaphysical art) was the brainchild of Ernest Briggs, Hubert Crehan, Jorge Goya, and himself.[98] Nonetheless, elements of the gallery's philosophy were clearly inspired by Still, especially the idea that the individual artist's work should not be diluted in group exhibitions. Each of the twelve original members—nine men and three women—had the two-room gallery for one month, with full control over their work and its display.[99] This arrangement, the Metart's initial press release explained, followed "from the belief that only in a full statement of his work can the artist advance toward that form of 'communication' possible in the plastic arts" and that "anything less than a one man show is merely a concession to the unimportant decorative aspects of art, the dealers' interest in 'selling a painting,' or the museums' practice of collecting and exhibiting the isolated 'facts' without understanding their 'meaning.'"[100] The Metart, by contrast, was committed to "in no manner limiting, coercing, or examining the individual's artistic, social or moral freedoms."[101]

Of course, the Metart also served an eminently practical function; when it opened in 1949, there was only one other gallery in San Francisco that consistently catered to experimental abstraction, the Lucien Labaudt Gallery on Gough Street.[102] Although the Metart denied having a party line—in fact, Dugmore claimed the gallery's intention was specifically to encourage individuality, to "break up this idea that we were all a gang of nonobjective painters"—only one of the twelve artists, W. Cohantz, painted in a representational manner.[103] The rest were devoted, as Frankenstein observed, to "an extremely free kind of nonobjective painting."[104]

In its brief life span of fifteen months, the Metart Galleries provided an important venue for the San Francisco School, giving a number of artists, notably Briggs, Jefferson, and Dugmore, their first solo shows. The Metart also hosted Still's last exhibition in San Francisco, organized as a farewell gesture by some of his former students before he moved to New York. Opening in October 1950, the exhibition revealed that Still's work had changed considerably since his last San Francisco show at the Legion of Honor in 1947. The rude gashes and molten surfaces had for the most part given way to a lighter, airier sensibility. Replacing the brutal blood and tar colors were placid fields of golden yellow and sapphire blue. This shift

was by no means definitive; it was never Still's habit to follow a steady line of development. But as the following chapter will show, the contrast between these two exhibitions reflected the gamut of ideas that Still had explored and refined with his colleagues in San Francisco during the crucial years from 1946 to 1950.

4

Clyfford Still, 1947–50

It is difficult to trace the chronology of Still's development with certainty because of his manipulation of public access to his work and his reputation for predating paintings.[1] Nevertheless, Still's claim that his work was "fully evolved" by 1940, and that his San Francisco paintings were merely extensions of preestablished concepts, is clearly inaccurate.[2] Not until late 1947 or 1948 did Still paint his first "field" paintings—expanses of color modulated by little more than the tracks of his palette knife. The shapes that formerly crackled like an electric storm through his canvases were now sometimes reduced to wisps of color clinging to the edge of what Clement Greenberg aptly called a "pregnant" void.[3] Around 1949, Still further compressed these forms into strips of pigment climbing up the sides of his canvases (fig. 4.1). The *terribilità* of his earlier work would resurface from time to time well into the 1950s, but in general, a milder mood characterized his output after 1950.

Still's recollections of the 1940s provide few clues to the sources of inspiration he might have found in San Francisco. He asserted that the California School of Fine Arts had been little more than a place for him to paint, and that he had remained emotionally detached from San Francisco: "My interest in the city, its artists, and its history was zero. I had work to do."[4] Still's posture of indifference, an important facet of his ideology, can be traced to such Romantic thinkers as Goethe, Schiller, and Nietzsche.[5] He seems to have emulated the Romantic ideal of the creative genius, the supremely original artist who gives birth to new forms of art rather than passively reflecting his culture. Still, like his heroes, aspired to a solitary vision, defiant of convention and free from the imperatives of his time. His ideal approximated Nietzsche's *überhistorische* or suprahistorical, man, unfettered by the claims of environment and impervious to influence.

Yet as much as Still hoped to achieve a transcendental vision, he could not help being a product of his time. Indeed, as we have seen, his very involvement with Romantic ideology places him firmly in the context of postwar cultural developments. But Still did succeed in attaining a significant degree of artistic independence in San Francisco. None of his colleagues at the California School of Fine Arts appear to have influenced him, although his own work made a tremendous impact on many of them. Still was inspired by some of the Mexican modernists he saw at the San Francisco Museum of Art. He particularly liked José Clemente Orozco, whose brooding palette and slashing brushwork often resembled his own.[6] But for the most part, Still's artistic sources remained safely in the distant past.

One of the artists Still admired most was Rembrandt, whom he regarded as among his "early gods," more for the force of his personality and his image of unflagging individualism than for any technical aspect of his work.[7] Still's practice of signing his paintings with his first name was probably modeled after Rembrandt's.[8] Another artist important for Still was Tintoretto, whose epic murals full of sweeping movement may have inspired his own monumental scale.

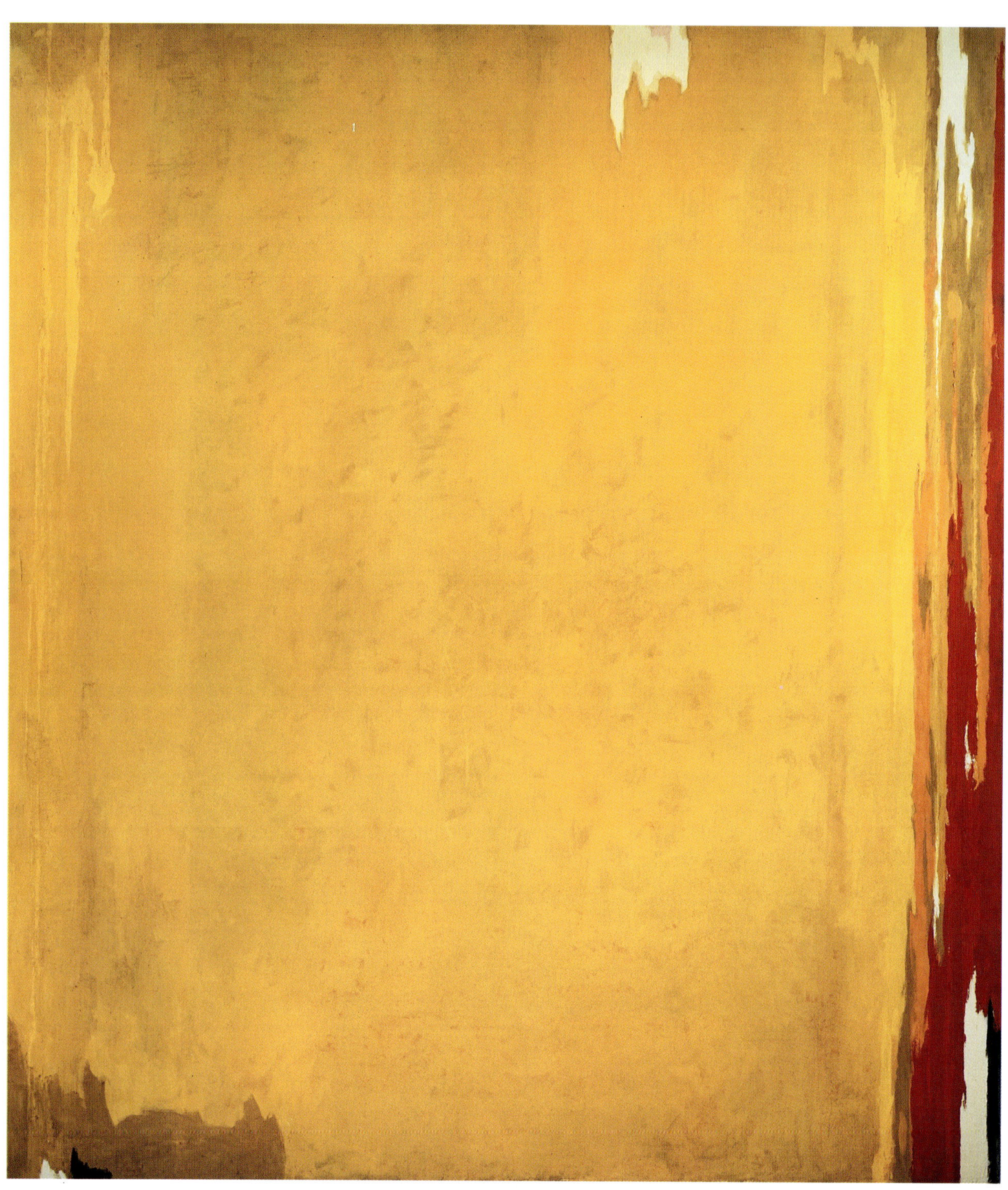

Figure 4.1

Clyfford Still, *Untitled,* 1951. Oil on canvas, 108 × 92½ in.

Collection, National Gallery of Art, Washington, gift of

Marcia S. Weisman in honor of the Fiftieth Anniversary of the

National Gallery of Art.

Figure 4.2

Clyfford Still, *1947-M,* 1947. Oil on canvas, 105 × 92 in.

Collection, Frederick Weisman Company, Los Angeles.

The boundless sense of space in Turner's cloud studies also provided an example for Still's field paintings of the late 1940s. Still kept a number of reproductions of Turner's late works tacked to the walls of his studio at the California School of Fine Arts in 1948, occasionally bringing them to class to show his students.[9] But Still's most significant artistic mentors were the Spanish masters Goya, Velázquez, and El Greco. Indeed, Still identified with their work so deeply that he was convinced that he had Spanish blood that could be traced on his Scottish side to the Spanish Moors.[10] Stylistically, the Spanish masters seem to have made a powerful imprint on Still's painting. A number of quintessential Spanish characteristics appear in his work: the limited palette, the tenebrous rendering of light, the ascending flamelike shapes (fig. 4.2), which are especially reminiscent of El Greco, and, above all, the Spanish *duende,* or intense devotion to matters of the soul.[11]

Still's artistic isolation in San Francisco was certainly encouraged by his steadfast independence. Temperamentally, he could not have been more out of sync at the high-spirited California School of Fine Arts, with its Studio 13 Jazz Band and rollicking, hard-drinking parties.[12] Still had a deeply conservative strain in his personality, an uncompromising moral rectitude that set him apart from other artists in San Francisco. Indeed, there was nothing bohemian in his demeanor. While other instructors wore jeans and army fatigues, Still came to class dressed in old-fashioned double-breasted suits and spats.[13] In the studio he was just as fastidious; palette knives and brushes were always in meticulous order and nothing was wasted—any paint that spilled on the floor was promptly retrieved. Similarly, the tools in the trunk of his vintage Jaguar were carefully spread out on a bed of velvet.[14]

Still's insistence upon absolute discipline and control had its impact on his painting. Predictably, accident played no part in his creative process and what improvisation there was had none of the jazz-inspired abandon of many other artists in San Francisco. Certainly the exalted aims of Still's art were far removed from the whimsical humor of Spohn or the joyful whiplash calligraphy of Smith. Still's approach was closer to that of certain nineteenth-century *alla prima* masters, relying only upon an image in his mind to complete a painting in a single virtuoso performance.[15]

Still's aristocratic radicalism,[16] his Nietzschean disdain for the masses, also ran counter to the populist views of many San Francisco painters, who believed with Bischoff that "gestures in paint on canvas" could "become a sort of visual Esperanto, liberating to all who had eyes."[17] Still's elitism may have played an important part in souring his relationship with Bischoff, Diebenkorn, and Park, all of whom turned away from Abstract Expressionism in the 1950s. In fact, few of the San Francisco artists could stomach his sweeping repudiation of European modernism. Although many agreed that French art lacked what Lobdell called "substance and guts," and was thus ill-suited to express the postwar experience, Still's moralizing diatribes against the decadence of European art alienated many San Francisco painters.[18]

Yet in spite of his maverick personality—or perhaps in part because of it—Still developed an ardent following in San Francisco. His very aloofness, combined with his messianic intensity, proved an irresistible draw for many of the younger artists. Indeed, he seems to have cultivated the mystique that rapidly grew around him in San Francisco. His practice of enshrouding his work in secrecy and taking only favored students to his studio had the effect of an initiation rite. The studio itself became the subject of much mythologizing. Nicknamed "the cell," reinforcing Still's ascetic, clerical image (he once came to a Halloween party in a monk's cowl), the studio was located at the base of the school's bell tower, next to the boiler room.[19] Jon Schueler recalled his bewilderment when he visited the studio for the first time in 1948: "It was the God damndest cell you ever want to see. You could look straight up and never find the ceiling . . . You got this sense that he was at the bottom with something going on endlessly above."[20]

Ultimately, Still's painting became widely known and imitated, not only at the California School of Fine Arts but throughout the Bay Area.[21] His followers continued to proliferate long after he left San Francisco. Lilly Fenichel reported that in the 1950s "just about everyone at the school started out by painting like Still."[22] Apparently, however, this was not Still's intent; when Alfred Frankenstein suggested the existence of a "Still school" in 1949, the painter became enraged and launched a public protest.[23]

Mark Rothko, who was teaching in San Francisco that summer, wrote to the *San Francisco Chronicle* denouncing its "rhetoric of confusion." Another writer on Still's behalf accused Frankenstein of "yellow journalism at its most vicious and false," insisting that "the implications in the words 'Still school' are the very antithesis of Mr. Still's entire philosophy of teaching, as any student he has ever had in his class will testify."[24]

Still did try his best to discourage followers and was careful not to proselytize on matters of style. In his classes he went to great lengths to avoid prescriptive teaching, seldom commenting on individual paintings and rarely discussing the mechanics of picture-making. His classroom lectures tended to focus on topics only tangentially related to art—subjects like bullfighting, baseball, and the poetry of Robinson Jeffers.[25] For the most part, Still left his students to work out their own ideas, whether abstract or figurative. His celebrated "graduate painting class" offered little more than a communal studio space and forum for dialogue and exchange.[26] It was really more of an informal club with tacit membership, for Still initially gave no assignments, credits, or grades.[27] Approximately fifteen artists—including Kuhlman, Jefferson, Briggs, Stillman, and Dugmore—participated, from the fall of 1948 to the spring of 1950. For Still, the class afforded the chance to carry out his ideas for the Subjects of the Artist, the short-lived Eighth Street loft school in New York.[28]

Still had taken part in the early stages of planning the Subjects of the Artist school, initially discussing the idea with Rothko, Spohn, and MacAgy in the spring and summer of 1947.[29] A little more than a year later, he left San Francisco to help set it up in New York. It was to be, according to Still, a program very much like the California School of Fine Arts, "a center of free activity for imaginative effort" that would give instructors complete freedom to teach whatever they wanted and students the liberty to come and go as they pleased.[30] In fact, Still had hoped not only to teach there himself, but to recruit other CSFA instructors. According to Still, however, the Subjects of the Artist quickly became a platform for self-promotion, and he returned to San Francisco in disappointment.[31]

Still's association with the New York art world was, of course, an undeniable part of his appeal, especially for the younger students at the California School of Fine Arts. In the time that he was in San Francisco, he had three one-man shows in New York—first at Peggy

Guggenheim's Art of This Century in 1946, and then at the Betty Parsons Gallery in 1947 and 1950. Both galleries were important spawning grounds for Abstract Expressionism in New York. Although Still's alliance with the New York School has been somewhat overemphasized—he did not meet its most influential figures, Pollock and de Kooning, until after moving to New York in 1950—he did form significant friendships with Rothko and Newman. It is easy to understand why Still might have been particularly drawn to them, since both had developed high profiles for their combative relationship to the art establishment.[32] And they were the most outspokenly anti-European of the New York Abstract Expressionists, although it could be argued that Still inspired much of their xenophobic rhetoric in the late 1940s (Newman's insistence upon "freeing ourselves" from the "devices of Western European painting" sounds very much like Still).[33] However, all three were prone to dramatic proclamations, which no doubt became increasingly clamorous with mutual encouragement.

Mark Rothko's Visits to San Francisco

Still's relationship with Rothko was the first and closest of his New York associations. The two had met in 1943 at the home of a mutual friend in Berkeley, and a few years later, Rothko introduced Still to Peggy Guggenheim and wrote the essay for Still's New York debut at the Art of This Century gallery. Throughout the late 1940s Rothko served as Still's New York liaison, installing his shows, storing his work, and keeping him abreast of the latest machinations on Fifty-seventh Street. Still reciprocated by arranging for Rothko to teach two summer sessions at the California School of Fine Arts, in 1947 and 1949, and by giving him free use of his San Francisco studio.

Rothko's students and fellow instructors at the California School of Fine Arts remember him as a brilliant conversationalist and speaker, whose discussions were peppered with allusions to classical mythology and literature. Witty and personable, Rothko seemed to embody the very image of the sophisticated New Yorker. He was the temperamental opposite of Still, who tended to be reclusive and inaccessible.[34] MacAgy described Rothko as an inspiring teacher, whose "elusive talk" was like the curling smoke of his ever-present cigarette (fig. 4.3).[35] Rothko's Friday afternoon discussions in the summer of 1947 drew capacity crowds to the classroom normally reserved

for Ansel Adams.[36] His illustrated lecture course of 1949, "Views of Painting Today," was also widely attended, since it offered a rare chance to see slides of work being done by contemporaries in New York. According to Hultberg, Rothko showed paintings by de Kooning, Pollock, Motherwell, and Milton Avery. "We were surprised to find out we had been doing the same things they had been doing," he recalled. "It must have been in the air."[37]

On the whole, Rothko seems to have bolstered Still's views on art. Like Still, he publicly rejected historical precedents and encouraged personal exploration. Painting for him was less a matter of pictorial relations than an instrument of thought expressing a transcendent vision.[38] But in Rothko's estimation, that vision was not, as Still maintained, the exclusive province of the individual creator. Rather, it communicated the common—and in his view, tragic—condition of man. Rothko's universalism, couched though it was in Jungian terminology, struck a powerful chord of sympathy in San Francisco.[39]

Rothko's work seems to have impressed the CSFA artists as much as his theoretical discourse. Many of them particularly admired the subtle paint handling and elusive imagery in early paintings, such as *Slow Swirl at the Edge of the Sea* (1944; fig. 4.4), then in the San Francisco Museum of Art's collection.[40] His *Multiforms* series of the late 1940s was also highly regarded in San Francisco (fig. 4.5). Briggs remembered that in the summer of 1949, these paintings triggered "an instantaneous release of pink and blue and reds and soft edges," a welcome respite from the "enormous emphasis on dark earth colors, blacks and umbers."[41] The influence of Rothko's style can be seen in the soft, transparent washes of Dugmore (fig. 4.6).

Rothko's visits to San Francisco proved consequential for his own painting as well. After his initial summer of teaching at the California School of Fine Arts, in 1947—an experience he described as "momentous"[42]—Rothko resolved to divest his work of its automatist calligraphy and symbolic allusions, as well as descriptive titles.[43] Shortly after leaving San Francisco, he wrote that for art to express "transcendental experiences," all recognizable associations would have to be eliminated: "With us the disguise must be complete. The familiar identity of things has to be pulverized in order to destroy the finite associations with which our society increasingly enshrouds every aspect of our environment."[44]

Rothko's second trip to San Francisco appears to have had a significant impact on his painting as well.

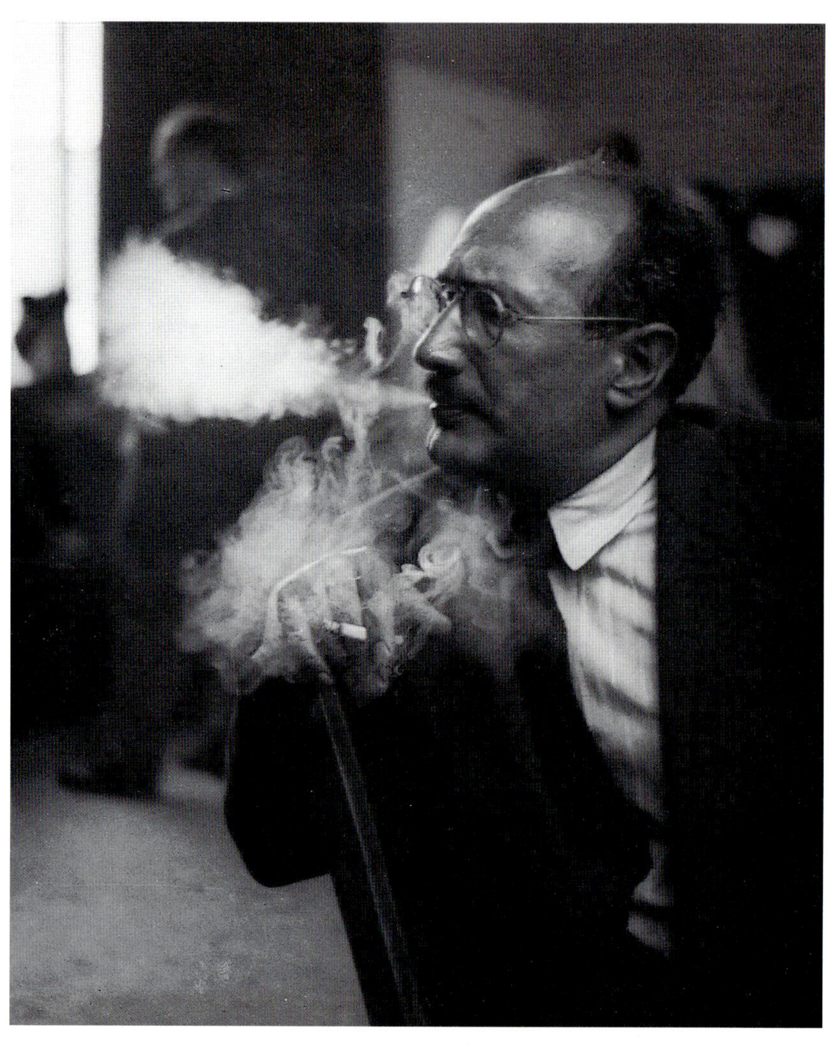

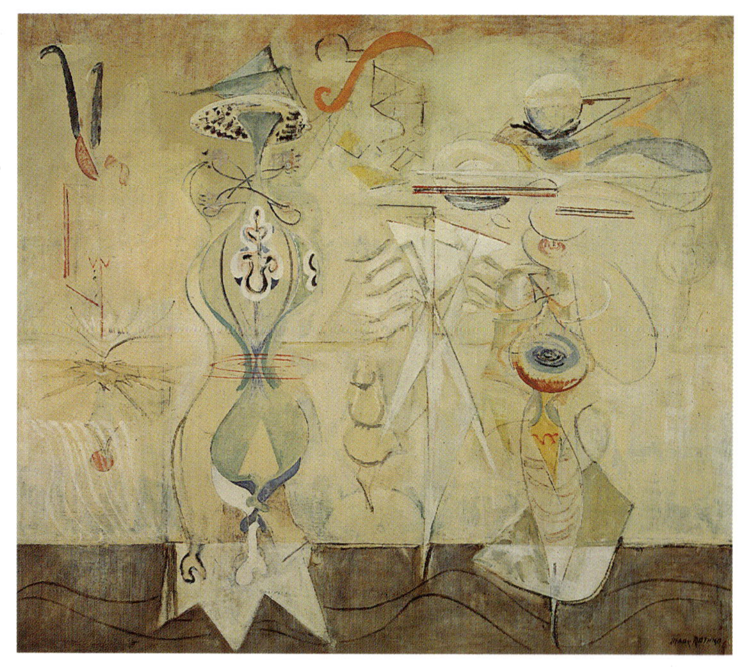

Figure 4.3

Above: Mark Rothko, California School of Fine Arts, San Francisco, 1949. Photographer: William Heick.

Figure 4.4

Right: Mark Rothko, *Slow Swirl at the Edge of the Sea,* 1944. Oil on canvas, 75 × 84¾ in. Collection, The Museum of Modern Art, New York. © 1995 Kate Rothko-Prizel and Christopher Rothko / Artists Rights Society (ARS), New York. Photograph courtesy, PaceWildenstein, New York.

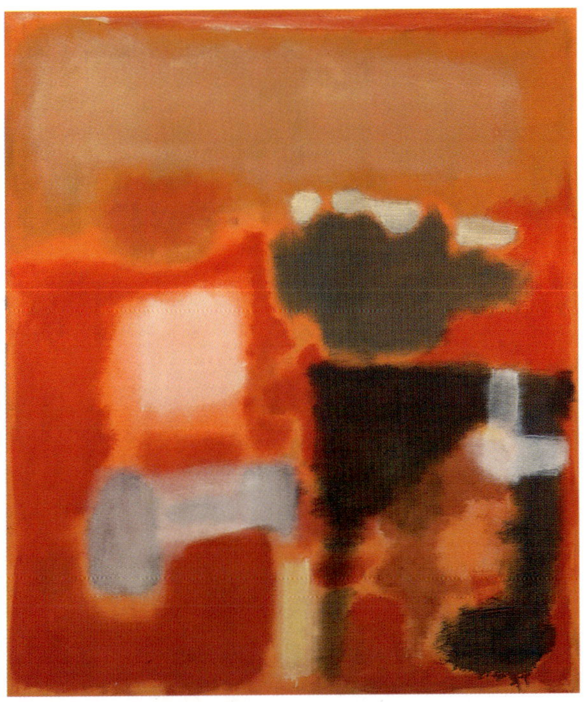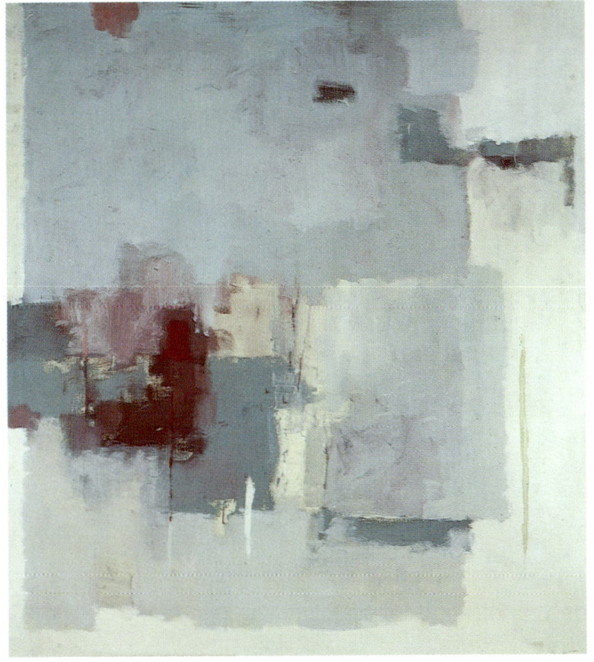

According to Spohn, he was working closely with Still and along very similar lines in the summer of 1949.[45] Some of the paintings he produced that year fit comfortably within the "blistered-slab" style prevalent at the school, with broad swaths of dark, heavy pigment.[46] But that summer, Rothko seems to have hit upon his signature style. Briggs remembered seeing a recent work by Rothko stretched in Still's studio with two or three large pink and blue color zones.[47] Rothko told Briggs that he was "arriving at his big style" and that Still had been instrumental in helping him to achieve it.[48] During the next few months, in the winter of 1949–50, Rothko further refined what would become his characteristic format, the billowy rectangles of luminous color stacked one on top of the other.

Edward Corbett, 1947–50

Corbett's work also underwent a dramatic shift after he began teaching at the California School of Fine Arts in 1947. Few works survive from the beginning of his move away from the Neoplastic style that characterized the paintings of the mid-forties.[49] Corbett later explained that from late 1946 to 1947 he "went underground," exhibiting infrequently because of

Figure 4.5

Above, left: Mark Rothko, *Number 18, 1948,* 1949. Oil on canvas, 67¹¹⁄₁₆ × 55⅞ in. The Frances Lehman Loeb Art Center, Vassar College, Poughkeepsie, New York, gift of Mrs. John D. Rockefeller, 3rd (Blanchette Hooker, class of 1931). © 1995 Kate Rothko-Prizel and Christopher Rothko / Artists Rights Society (ARS), New York.

Figure 4.6

Above: Edward Dugmore, *Untitled,* 1950. Oil on canvas, 61 × 54⅝ in. Collection, Edward Dugmore. Photograph courtesy, Manny Silverman Gallery, Los Angeles.

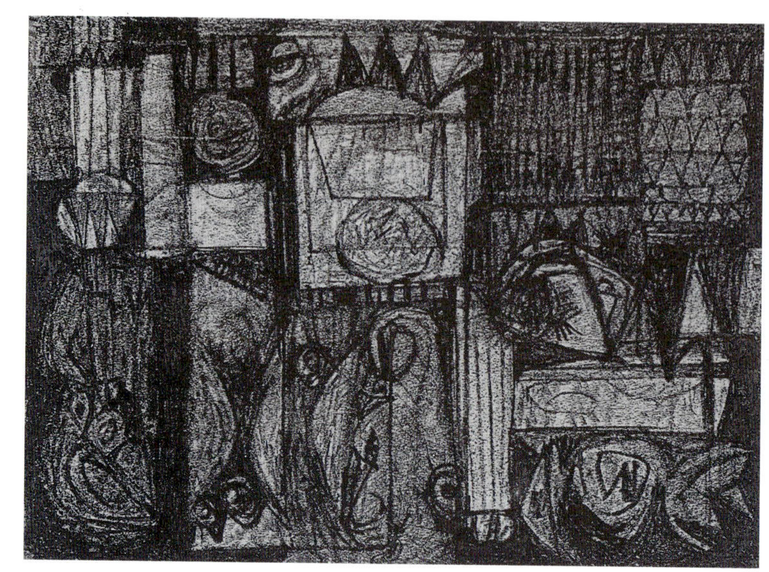

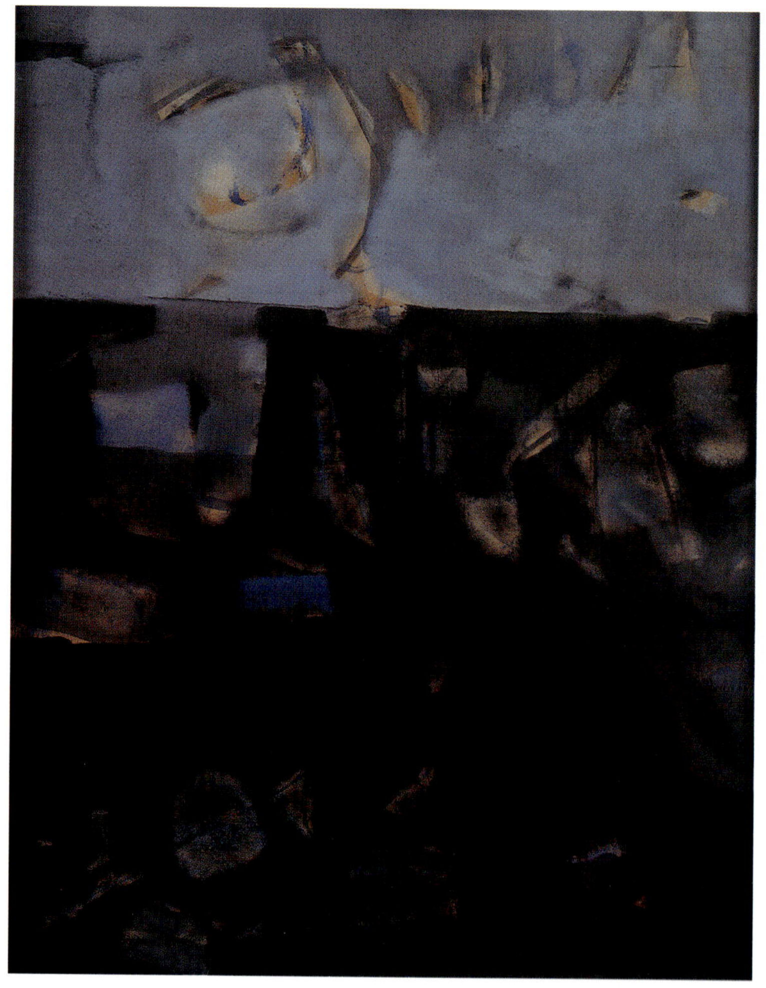

Figure 4.7

Edward Corbett, *Composition,* 1948. Litho crayon on paper,
14¾ × 19⅞ in. The Buck Collection, Laguna Hills, California.
Bliss Photography.

Figure 4.8

Edward Corbett, *Improvisation,* 1949. Ink and chalk on paper,
32¼ × 25 in. Private collection. Photograph courtesy,
Richmond Art Center.

Figure 4.9

Edward Corbett, *Untitled,* 1949. Oil on canvas, 61 × 39¼ in.

Collection, The Oakland Museum, gift of Dr. and Mrs. Victor

Calef. Photographer: M. Lee Fatherree.

anxiety about the coherence of his work.[50] In early 1948, however, he won first prize for *Composition* (1948), a litho-crayon drawing he submitted to the *Twelfth Annual Drawing and Print Exhibition* at the San Francisco Museum of Art (fig. 4.7). Composed of half-formed rays, spirals, scales, and other mysterious elements imbedded in a dark, murky grid, this work demonstrates that by then Corbett had made a radical departure from his previous hard-edged style.[51] The pictographic forms of the drawing show a debt, possibly to Adolph Gottlieb or Joaquín Torres-García, but more likely to Spohn, who was also exploring the artistic potential of the pictograph in the mid-1940s.

In 1948 Corbett's work began to show increasing confidence. He experimented with a variety of imaginative compositions, combining diffused organic shapes with softened blocks of color, sometimes laced together with crisscrossing lines. The jigsaw structure, loose calligraphy, and patches of spring green amid pastel colors compare with elements of Diebenkorn's *Berkeley* series of the early 1950s.[52] By 1949 Corbett had largely abandoned the grid of his previous work in favor of freer methods of expression. *Improvisation*

(1949; fig. 4.8) is representative of these new works. Here, Corbett has used chalk to create muted soft-focus forms. The composition is divided into two strata. In the lower level, a multitude of blue forms is imbedded in a dark field like precious stones. The shapes above, by comparison, seem to hover and dissolve.

Corbett's distinctive style began to emerge with increasing force in the latter part of 1949. By that time, discrete units of color appeared with less frequency, and instead, form and space fused into one continuous field (see fig. 1.5). Still's painting may have been the source for this edge-to-edge expansion, but Corbett transformed Still's example into something very much his own. Corbett's paintings have none of the aggressive upward thrust of Still's paintings but imply a gentle lateral expansion, suggestive of the abstract landscapes that would become his central theme in the 1950s. Critics have often compared Corbett's serene simplicity with that of Zen Buddhism and Chinese landscape painting. It appears, however, that Corbett had no particular interest in Asian art or philosophy. His reduced palette owes

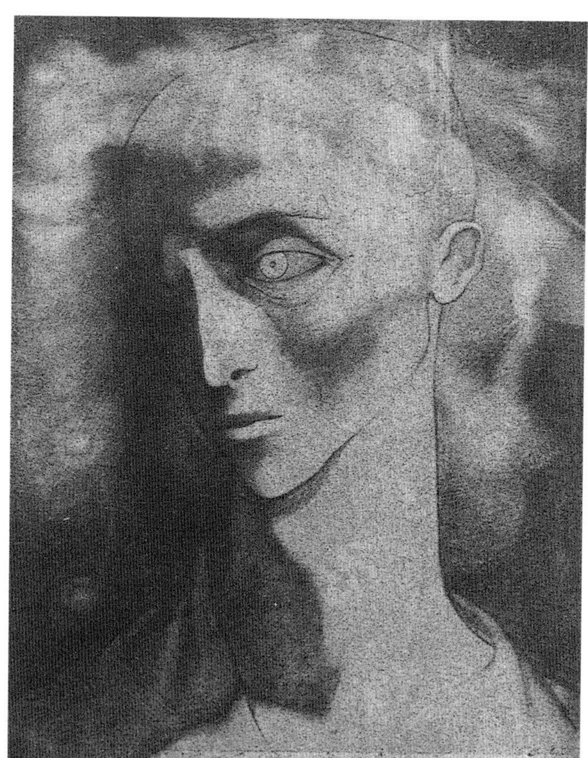

more to the Western tradition of grisaille than to Asian monochrome.

In one untitled painting of 1949 (fig. 4.9), in the collection of the Oakland Museum, the dark, nebulous mists that appear in much of Corbett's work at this time have given way to light-filled vapor. The thin coats of diaphanous paint invite comparison with Rothko's soft scrims of color. Although the two did not become friends until after Corbett left San Francisco, Corbett was well acquainted with Rothko's work through Rothko's visits to the California School of Fine Arts. Yet, while it is possible that Rothko's *Multiforms* of 1948–49 encouraged Corbett to soften his brushwork, he had sources of his own for this aspect of his work. In the painting illustrated in figure 4.9, for example, Corbett has clearly returned to the sfumato technique of his early charcoals, which he derived from his study of Leonardo (compare with fig. 4.10). As in those earlier works, the softness here was achieved through minute gradations of color and tone, as pink shades almost imperceptibly to gray. Rothko's method was different: rather than add graded amounts of pigment, Rothko applied washes of paint so thin that they feathered and bled along the edges, creating softened patches of color. Thus while Corbett's primary instrument was the delicate contrast of values, Rothko's was the drama of luminous color. It is perhaps in their approach to color that the two artists diverged most sharply. While Rothko favored hot, glowing hues, Corbett gravitated to the cooler side of the spectrum, a distinction that reflects the differing aims of their work. Whereas Rothko intended to stimulate powerful, almost Wagnerian, feelings ("I'm interested only in expressing basic human emotions—tragedy, ecstasy, doom," he once said) Corbett preferred to induce quiet contemplation.[53]

In the spring of 1949, Corbett moved from San Francisco across the bay to Berkeley, where he taught two semesters at the University of California. One of his outstanding students was Sam Francis, who had himself begun to explore expressive abstraction in 1947. Although Francis was never a student at the California School of Fine Arts, he knew Park and had been spotted, according to Still, "hanging around the school on weekends, talking with the students."[54] The expansive handling of space in Francis's paintings of the late 1940s reflects his encounter with the CSFA artists; the overall wash of paint in *Red and Pink* (1951; see fig. 3.12), for example, seems to want to flood the borders of the canvas. The work of Rothko is often deemed a primary artistic influence on Francis.[55] But

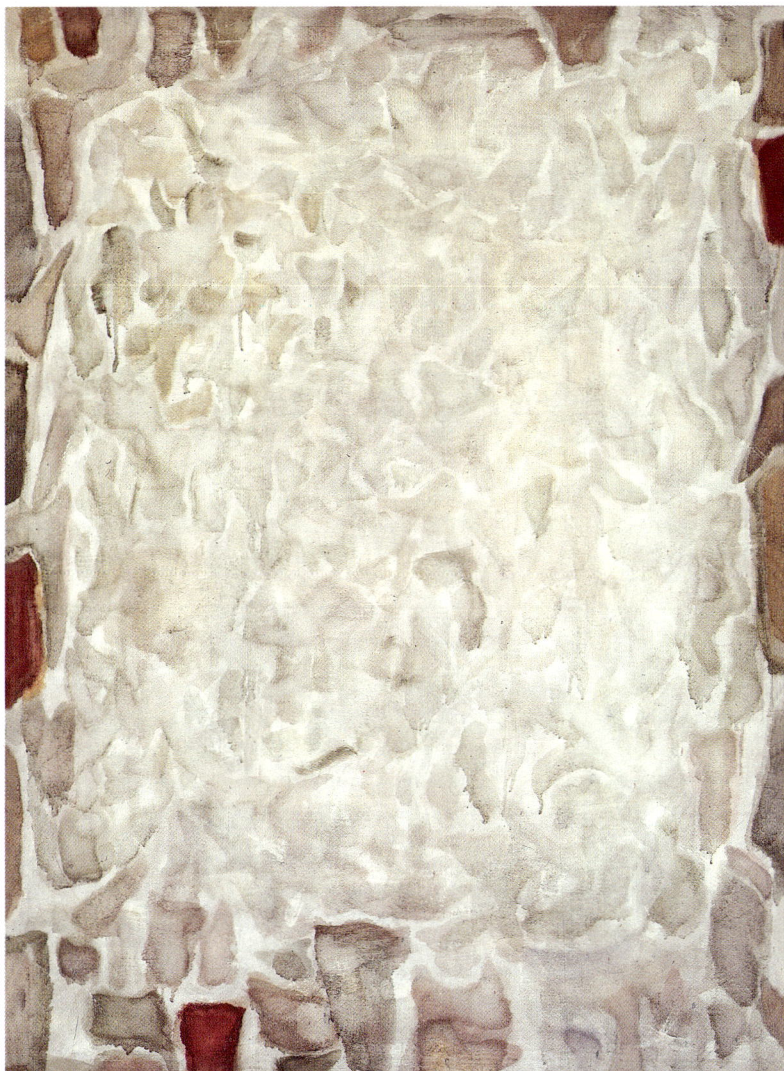

Figure 4.11

Sam Francis, *White*, 1951. Oil on canvas, 56 × 40½ in.

Collection, Frederick R. Weisman Art Foundation, Los Angeles.

© 1995 Sam Francis / Artists Rights Society (ARS), New York.

the subdued palette and soft, atmospheric quality of paintings such as *Composition in Pink* (1949)[56] and *White* (1951; fig. 4.11) are closer in spirit to the work of Corbett.[57] Indeed, the former painting bears a striking resemblance to Corbett's untitled pink painting of the same year (see fig. 4.9).

Francis left the Bay Area for Paris in 1950 and soon joined the French Tachisme group around Jean-Paul Riopelle. His subsequent devotion to the "Watteau to Matisse tradition of hedonism" places him more in a European framework than in the context of the San Francisco School.[58] One of Francis's most celebrated compositional strategies, however, the clustering of forms around a central void, as well as his use of black (fig. 4.12), has roots in the work of Corbett, Still, and other San Francisco artists.

Corbett stayed in Berkeley for only a few months before moving into a house on the Point Richmond waterfront with Smith, McChesney, the sculptor Mary Fuller, and the poet Weldon Kees. In Point

Sam Francis, *Black in Red,* 1953. Oil on canvas,
76¾ × 51 in. Collection, Frederick Weisman
Company, Los Angeles. © 1995 Sam Francis /
Artists Rights Society (ARS), New York.

Richmond, Corbett entered one of the most productive periods of his career. Although he had already produced a number of mature works, most critics and scholars agree that his first major paintings were the *Black Paintings* of 1950 (figs. 4.13–4.15). A number of San Francisco artists experimented with black-on-black and mostly black paintings in the late 1940s and early 1950s, notably Still, Lobdell, and Jefferson, but none of them explored the idea as fully as Corbett did in Point Richmond. In Corbett's Point Richmond paintings, color has been replaced by rich, deep blacks produced by combining oil and enamel. By ladling this mixture in generous quantities and tipping his canvases, Corbett created broad expanses of black pigment, perforated by glimpses into complex underlayers of interlacing paint. The texture resulting from this process varied from painting to painting: in some, the paint flowed over the surface like thick molten lava, smothering everything in its wake; in others, the paint was soaked into the very fiber of the canvas, leaving a filmy coat thin enough to expose the woven threads of the canvas (see fig. 4.15).

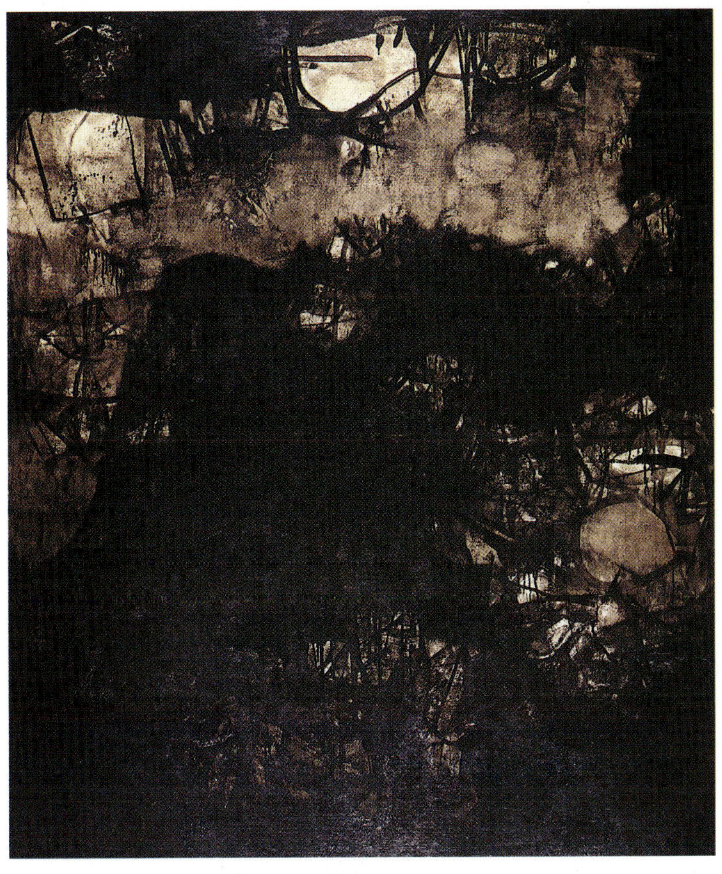

Figure 4.13

Left: Edward Corbett, *Untitled* (*Black Painting*), ca. 1950. Oil and enamel on canvas, 60 × 50 in. Collection, William Roth. Photograph courtesy, Richmond Art Center.

Figure 4.14

Below, left: Edward Corbett, *Untitled* (*Black Painting*), 1950. Oil and enamel on canvas, 54 × 50 in. Whereabouts unknown. Photographer: F. W. Quandt.

Figure 4.15

Below: Edward Corbett, *Untitled* (*Black Painting*), 1950. Oil and enamel on canvas, 60 × 40 in. Collection, Mag Dimond. Photographer: Duane Faubion.

Edward Corbett, *Untitled #3,* 1950. Oil and enamel on canvas,
46 × 43⅞ in. Collection, San Francisco Museum of Modern Art,
purchased with the aid of funds from Peter Haas, Jr.

Not all of Corbett's paintings from the Point Richmond period were restricted to black. Although he rarely strayed from dark, earthen colors, Corbett occasionally turned to soft shades of gray. In these paintings he presents an expanse of misty gray but punctures the surface and rudely breaks off its atmospheric character with edges that are shredded and chewed. This technique appears in a number of Corbett's paintings of the late 1940s, such as the softer *Untitled* (1949; see fig. 4.9), and in some of the *Black Paintings* of 1950 (see fig. 4.14). Another painting outside the black series, *Untitled #3* (1950; fig. 4.16), is composed of vertical bands of muted grays, blacks, and browns. This painting appears to signal a return to the geometry of Corbett's Neoplastic period, but if Mondrian's presence can be detected, it makes no more than a ghostly appearance. Far from the precision of Neoplasticism, the close tonal range of the colored bands and their wavering edges create an effect of indeterminacy rather than clarity. The gritty texture of this painting also rejects the polished, machine-edged surfaces of Mondrian.

The expansive monochromatic surfaces, rough paint handling, and rugged, stubbly texture place Corbett well within the San Francisco School. Yet when his work was exhibited in group shows during the late 1940s and 1950s, reviewers readily singled him out as the most elegant and refined. Even his *Black Paintings* came across as delicate and lyrical compared with the work of Smith: "It is easy to see," Frankenstein wrote in a review of their joint show at the California School of Fine Arts, "that the bold, enormous shattery pictures that leap from the walls and knock you down are all by Smith, and the smaller sensitive cloud-like paintings are all by his colleague."[59]

Self-effacing rather than egocentric, restrained rather than impulsive, Corbett's work in many respects seems the very antithesis of expressionism and its excessive offspring "action painting." Emotional indulgence is nowhere to be found in Corbett's art. He seems to have deliberately emptied his painting of gesture—the signs of the artist's creative process, active presence, and temperament. Indeed, his painting is resolutely antiphysical. Devoid of tangible form, incident, and even color, some of Corbett's paintings are statements of stillness and vacancy. The theme of absence is explored by means of nonforms: empty pockets, cavities, lacunae, areas where paint is nonexistent. Corbett's Point Richmond charcoals take this subtractive process to extremes. In an untitled work of 1950 in the collection of the San Francisco collagist Jess, Corbett makes as much use of an eraser as of charcoal.[60] Composed of nearly invisible wisps of vapor, with hints of lavender so pale they can be seen only in strong light, these drawings seem the very essence of incorporeality.

Corbett's *Black Paintings* and charcoals may nullify color and form, and they may suggest the absence of physicality, but they are not about negation. Far from being vitiating, Corbett's works are meant to be generative. His denial of physicality, like that of the Symbolists, was intended to prod the spirit and awaken the imagination. In this sense, his *Black Paintings* represent a return to Redon's *Noirs,* which Corbett had admired and studied since the late 1930s. Indeed, Corbett's canvases resonate with Redon's words of appreciation for black, words reprinted in a museum publication that Corbett saved: "Black is the most essential color . . . One must respect black. Nothing prostitutes it. It is the agent of the mind far more than the most beautiful color of the palette or prism."[61]

For the Symbolists and their Romantic precursors, black signified a realm of night, dreams, and the infinite—the unfamiliar terrain of the mind. All these associations are invoked in a series of "Black Poems," which Corbett began writing in the 1950s.[62] In his poems, black clearly suggests not only these Romantic themes, but also a strong feeling of death, solitude, and desolation. The recurring image of a black crow—whether it alludes to a common French Symbolist motif or to the raven of Edgar Allan Poe—appears to be a metaphor for the artist himself expressing his feelings of isolation and estrangement. Corbett's *Black Paintings* and "Black Poems" articulate the increasing sense of alienation shared by artists and writers during the gloomy McCarthy era, when blacklists and Senate hearings symbolized the conformity and conservatism of the age. Black, of course, would become an emblem of disaffiliation for the Beat poets and novelists of the 1950s and their entourage of black-turtlenecked devotees, the Beatniks.

Corbett intended his black paintings as protest works, as a means for putting his "personal-social self into painting" without resorting to the commonplaces of Social Realism.[63] In a statement made when his *Black Paintings* were shown in 1951, he explained his objective:

> Art in our time may have a special meaning in addition to its usually accepted aesthetic meaning. As an act of assertion of humane values, art may be the expressive complement of its present social origin, a critical work of individuals in a static and institution-ridden society.

Art can be proof, at any rate, that specific virtues may grow from vast conglomerates of evil. Something of this sort must be possible—if not possible, the artist is doomed to be the mere reflection of the reality which he hopes to criticize.[64]

Corbett's belief in a socio-political mission for art makes a striking contrast with the strict aestheticism of his good friend Ad Reinhardt, who found in Corbett's work a primary source of inspiration for his own signature black paintings. Shortly before he died in 1967, Reinhardt revealed the importance of Corbett's influence in a letter, reproduced here as Reinhardt wrote it:

> *Howdy ol' friend Corbett!*
> *("mention" your name in my catalogue?)*
> *How do I "mention" that in 1950*
> *(Everybody note the date)*
> *in San Francisco*
> *(Everyone mark the place)*
> *I saw ol' friend Corbett's*
> *Black Paintings and*
> *White Paintings?*
> *I joked about the black—*
> *"subterranean-oceanic-quality"*
> *(your work didn't need*
> *"poetry," word I didn't like)*
> *I didn't joke about the white*
> *which (looking back now)*
> *seemed more "extreme" (good word)*
> *than the black*
> *(my black from your white?)*
> *Who would have thought (not me)*
> *in 1950*
> *that 3 or 4 years later*
> *I would programme, academicize*
> *and dogmatize*
> *All-black-all-over-dark-paintings*
> *from Velazquez, Wu Tao-tzu, Corbett?*
> *From your ol' friend Reinhardt , Ad*
> *1967 (New York)*[65]

Reinhardt became well acquainted with Corbett's work during the summer of 1950, when he taught at the California School of Fine Arts and made frequent visits to Corbett's house in Point Richmond.[66] Comparing Reinhardt's paintings with Corbett's work of this period yields some similarities. Beyond their use of black, both often employed a restricted palette of close-valued hues. And Corbett's charcoal drawings, like Reinhardt's black paintings, contain faint hints of color that emerge only after careful examination. None of Corbett's white-on-white works, which Reinhardt indicates particularly influenced his aesthetic, appear to have survived, but descriptions suggest a resemblance to Reinhardt's faintly visible squares of color.[67] It is also worth noting that Reinhardt began confining himself to near-monochrome in 1950, the year he taught in San Francisco.

Formal similarities aside, Corbett and Reinhardt took very different approaches to painting, especially regarding content. Whereas Reinhardt meant to drain his work of all extra-aesthetic associations, Corbett hoped to stimulate the imagination. Reinhardt's uncompromising formalism ran against the grain of a number of artists at the California School of Fine Arts and was a source of irritation for Still.[68] Reinhardt's views on the moral integrity of the artist were well received,[69] but his tendency to speak in paradoxes spiked with sarcasm alienated many San Francisco painters.[70] Briggs, who took Reinhardt's summer course at the California School of Fine Arts, remembered that "his attitude was something nobody could quite figure out. Whether he was putting the whole thing down or whether he was really unable to talk or what. He'd just sort of mumble and show some slides and speak in these little epigrams, you know, that sort of canceled themselves out."[71] McChesney recalled that most of the San Francisco artists regarded Reinhardt with suspicion. He attributed this response in part to Reinhardt's social incompatibility, which became especially conspicuous at gatherings in Point Richmond:

> We'd have these parties out there and Hassel [Smith], who lived upstairs, would come down. We'd be slopping up the good juice and you know, Reinhardt wouldn't drink a drop, but he'd look around and if the booze was all gone, he'd run down to the corner, about five blocks away, and buy some booze so everybody could keep going. And this just bugged Hassel to death. Hassel said, "What the hell is this sonofabitch doing anyway? He's a spy."[72]

For his own part, Reinhardt could not identify with the machismo and deliberate crudity of many of the San Francisco artists.[73] He also felt very much like an outsider amid the excitement at the school: "Even while on the West Coast," he later confessed, "I didn't really understand or certainly share the enthusiasm for what was going on out there. Everybody was really hopped up and I didn't know quite what about."[74]

Stillman, Kuhlman, Dixon, and the Sausalito Six

Around 1948, George Stillman, Walter Kuhlman, James Budd Dixon, Frank Lobdell, Richard Diebenkorn, and John Hultberg began meeting in one another's studios, mostly in Sausalito. Sometimes they had pen-and-ink "jam sessions"; other times they set up academic problems to keep their figurative painting skills honed.[75] Within a short time, some of them began showing together at the Schillerhaus, Seashore, and Contemporary galleries in Sausalito (fig. 4.17). They also had group shows at the California College of Arts and Crafts and at Reed College in Oregon in 1948 and collaborated on a portfolio of lithographs.[76] Although their alliance was informal—and Dixon lived in San Francisco and Stillman in Berkeley[77]—the six artists became increasingly identified as a group.[78]

According to Hultberg, the Sausalito painters were spontaneously drawn together by a common desire to separate themselves from the artists associated with the Metart Galleries, some of whom were following Still's example too closely.[79] As a group, they were mostly older and more artistically experienced than the Metart painters. With the exception of Hultberg, they were comparatively self-sufficient and by the late 1940s had evolved strong abstract idioms of their own.[80] But while mutual influences can be detected, the Sausalito artists did not form a stylistic entity separate from the San Francisco School. Nor were they ideologically distinct from the larger movement, although they seem to have been less inclined to attach metaphysical meanings to their work.[81]

George Stillman (fig. 4.18) was one of the youngest and least experienced of the Sausalito artists, but he was also among the most independent. "You could never pin him down," Dugmore recalled. "He had this wild imagination. He was able to put blinders on in a sense and just paint what he wanted to paint, no influence at all from anybody."[82]

Stillman came to the California School of Fine Arts with an extensive background in photography but little knowledge of painting. In Ontario, California, where he spent much of his childhood, he experimented in his father's darkroom and became something of a prodigy with the camera.[83] At twelve he was already published, and at seventeen he took first prize for creative photography at the 1939 Golden Gate International Exposition. By the early 1940s Stillman had discovered Edward Weston's f64

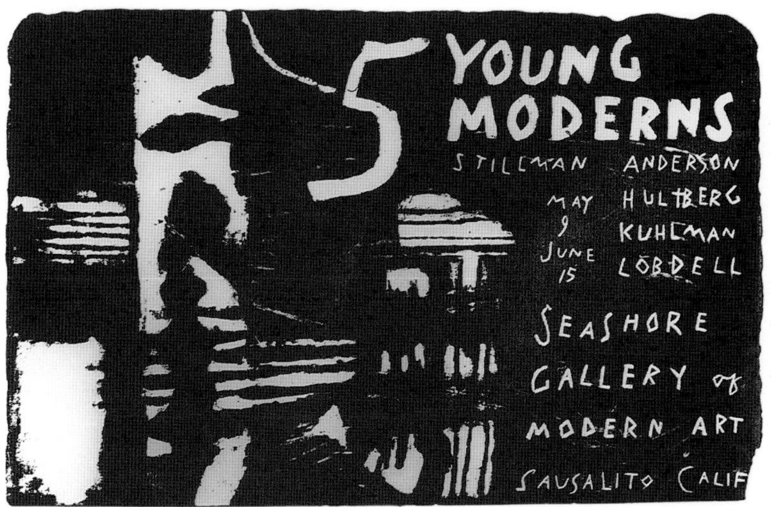

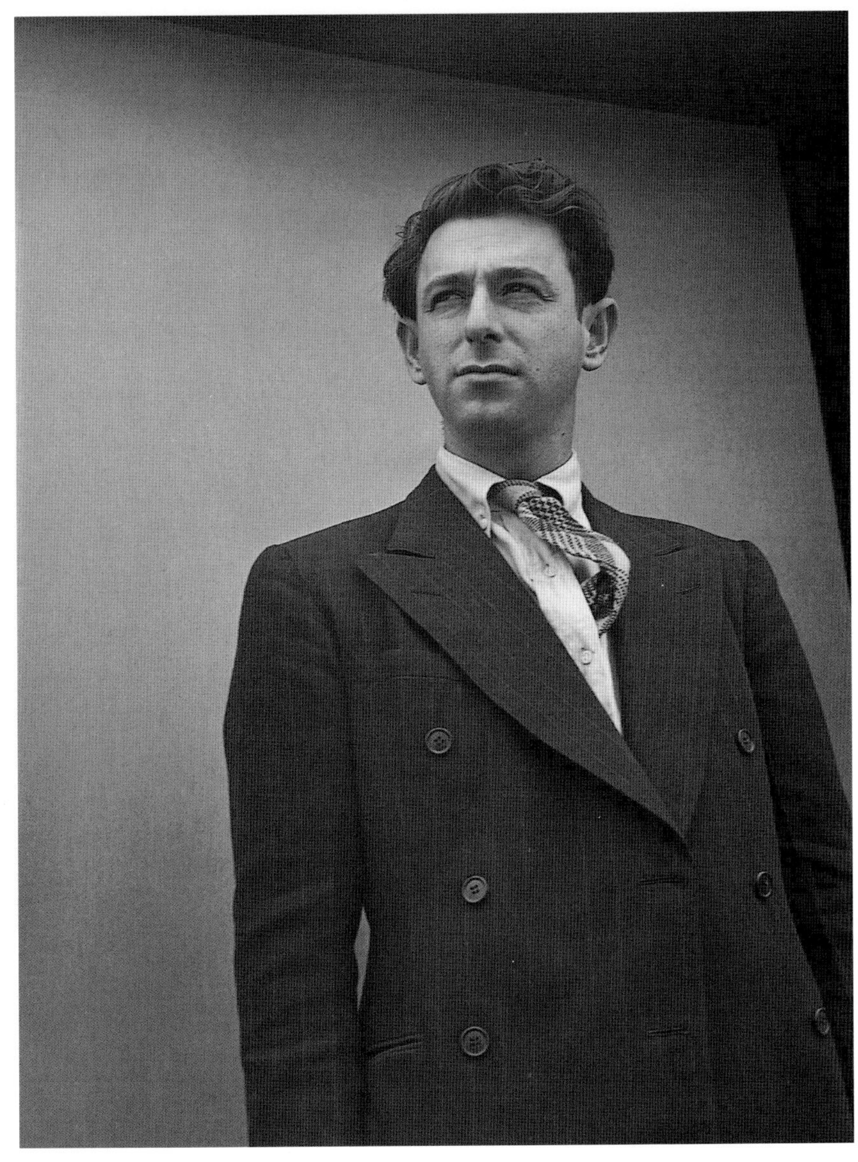

Figure 4.17

Left: Poster for Seashore Gallery of Modern Art, Sausalito, *5 Young Moderns,* 1948, designed by Frank Lobdell. Collection, George Stillman. Photographer: George Stillman.

Figure 4.18

Below: George Stillman, Berkeley, ca. 1948–49. Photographer: Nate Stillman.

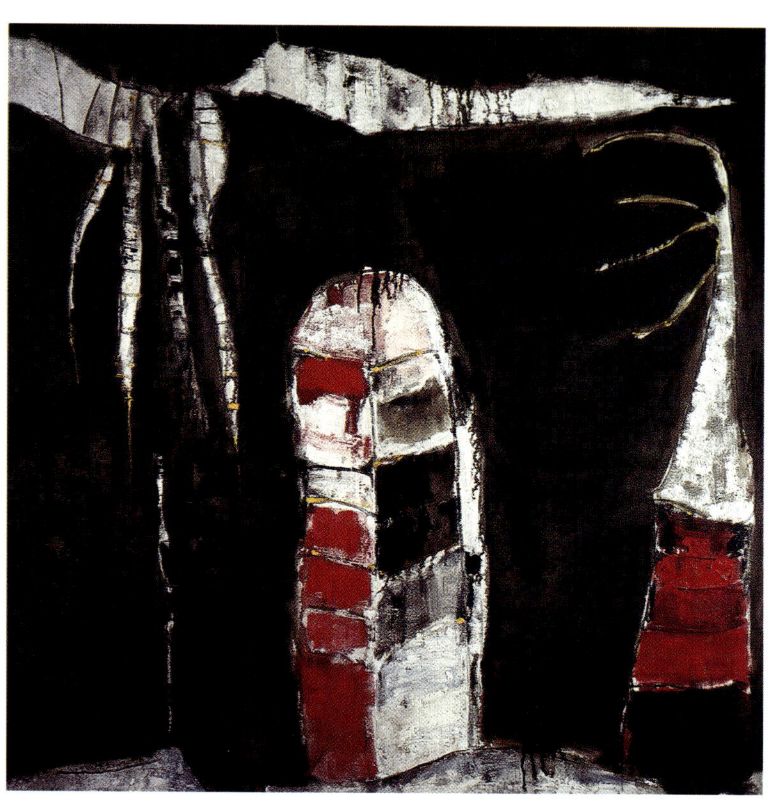

school and was well on his way to becoming a professional photographer. But after spending leave time from the army visiting the Museum of Modern Art in New York, he began to consider a career in painting. When the war was over, Stillman moved to the Bay Area and enrolled at the California School of Fine Arts. Throughout the 1940s, he continued to work as a photographer, operating a commercial studio in Oakland to support his wife and child, but his creative efforts were exclusively directed toward painting. Stillman's first one-man show in 1948 at the Artists' Guild Gallery in San Francisco displayed paintings with vivid colors and heavy, Tamayoesque contours, much in the spirit of the Mexican moderns of the 1940s. Many of these early works exhibited the childlike simplicity of Georges Rouault.[84] By 1948, however, Stillman had moved away from decorative, colorful patterns and had reduced his palette to a range of murky browns, greenish blues, reds, and blacks. His imagery also took on a vaguely Surrealist cast, mostly nonfigurative but sometimes suggesting phallic forms and underwater organisms (fig. 4.19).

This phase proved little more than a brief segue to Stillman's fully nonobjective work. The Oakland Museum's *Untitled* (1948; fig. 4.20) may be considered an important turning point. The painting features Stillman's signature scaffold motif, but the sense of depth and volume, comparatively secure in previous works, is now radically reduced. By flattening his space and confining his imagery to the picture plane, Stillman has denied his forms their status as objects. This three-step evolution, from figuration to a nonfiguration that retains some degree of spatial definition and, finally, to an imagery with no appreciable depth or volume, was typical of the San Francisco painters.

The Oakland painting also signals Stillman's newfound interest in surface effects. It was painted during a forty-five-minute impromptu session at the school, using whatever materials were at hand. After laying a ground of fast-drying enamel, Stillman scattered handfuls of dry pigment someone had left behind in a

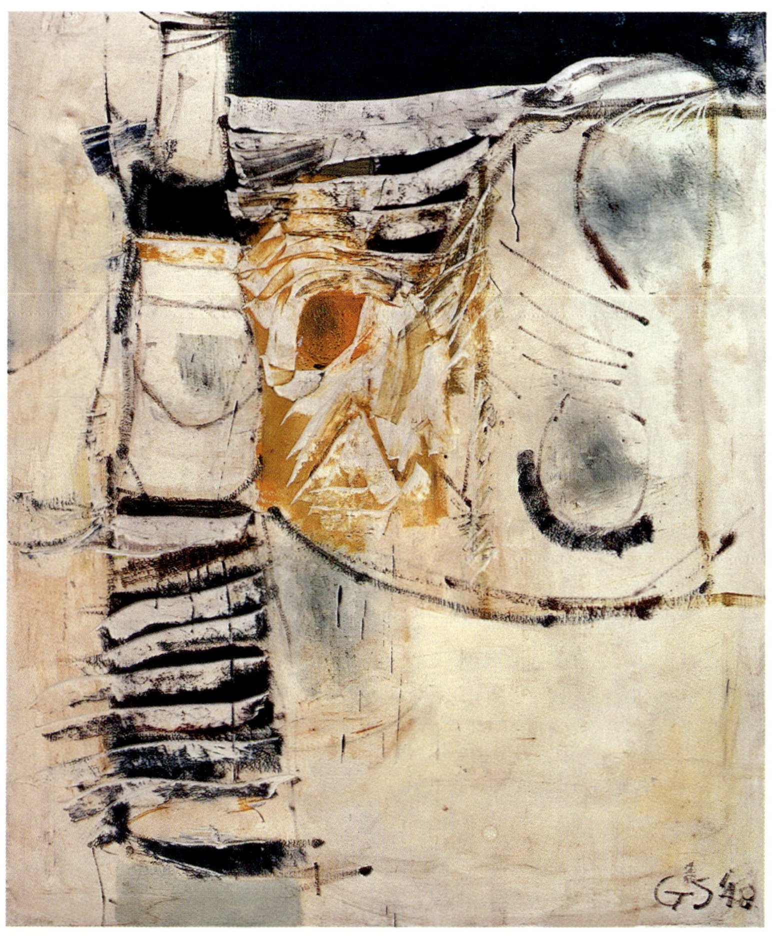

Figure 4.20

George Stillman, *Untitled*, 1948. Oil on canvas, 48 × 40 in.

Collection, The Oakland Museum, gift of George Stillman.

Photographer: George Stillman.

classroom. He then applied a coat of oil paint, worked it with a palette knife, and finished the painting with a few slashes of the brush and a smattering of paint. The result is a work of rich textural variation and subtlety.

Technical resourcefulness was one of the hallmarks of Stillman's work of the late 1940s. His background in photography as well as in chemistry, his major at the University of California at Berkeley before the war, seems to have furnished him with an unbounded curiosity about the properties of paint and the material limits of visual expression. To create some of his paintings, he applied a layer of wallpaper paste and brushed on a wash of paint and india ink while the paste was still wet. Networks of white lines were then produced by scraping the canvas with a palette knife. Another technique of Stillman's involved ammonium bichromate, a component of photo emulsion. By coating his surface with this chemical and then flooding it with ink, Stillman achieved unorthodox and sometimes striking textural effects.

Stillman's paintings after 1948 were generally monochrome or near-monochrome, for the most part in shades of brown. In many of them, the scaffold of previous paintings has exploded over the surface in a network of spidery lines. To produce these spare tracings, some barely visible at first glance, Stillman used mechanical pens with tips of varying thickness. Some of Stillman's most successful works are monotypes and etchings (fig. 4.21). Stillman, like many other artists in San Francisco, produced a significant number of graphic works. Paper was much cheaper than oil and canvas and could easily be obtained at the school. In addition, the San Francisco artists, unlike their contemporaries in New York, had ready access to printmaking equipment, a factor that may help to explain why printmaking played an important role in the San Francisco movement, while it remained largely unexplored by the New York School before the 1960s.[85]

After Stillman leased a large studio in Berkeley in 1950, his work increased dramatically in scale, from

George Stillman, *Untitled*, 1949. Monotype, 10 × 3½ in. Collection of the artist. Photograph courtesy, The Art Museum of Santa Cruz County.

paintings that were typically no more than four or five feet tall to canvases twice that size. He also began to concentrate on collage, using bits of crumpled and torn newspaper. An untitled work of 1950 (fig. 4.22) is characteristic of this period. The wrinkled, lumpy surface is the result of a heavy buildup of paper beneath a coat of paint. Many of these works are as much bas-relief as collage; Stillman wadded paper thickly enough so that it protrudes from the canvas. Another collage from 1950 (fig. 4.23) shows Stillman's predilection for twisting, meandering rivulets and canyons of crumpled paper. With their earthen colors and encrusted surfaces, these collages epitomize the raw, indecorous look of San Francisco Abstract Expressionism.

Toward the end of 1950, Stillman took a teaching position at the University of Guadalajara in Mexico. Soon after, he put his artistic career aside for more than a decade to provide for his son, who had been diagnosed as schizophrenic. Stillman's years in San Francisco were prolific; between 1947 and 1950, he produced over one thousand paintings and works on paper. But before he left, Stillman rented a trailer truck, filled it with as many canvases as he could, and hauled them to the city dump.[86] The incident says as much about San Francisco's market for contemporary abstraction as it does about the artist's paint-for-the-moment attitude. Unfortunately, fewer than fifty of Stillman's San Francisco works remain.

Next to Stillman, with his seemingly insatiable thirst for technical experimentation, Walter Kuhlman (fig. 4.24) looks very much the traditionalist. Unlike many of his contemporaries in San Francisco, Kuhlman was deeply respectful of his craft. Rather than using the unorthodox materials that so often resulted in premature cracking and warping, he worked with fastidiously mixed oils on well-primed canvas.[87] Kuhlman took great pleasure in studying the techniques of the Old Masters. Indeed, a good part of Kuhlman's appeal lies in his application of such time-honored methods as glazing and scumbling to abstract painting.

Born in 1918 to Danish immigrants in Minnesota, Kuhlman spent his formative years in the fishing village of Jutland, Denmark. His first art studies were at the St. Paul School of Art from 1936 to 1939, with the Midwest Regionalist Cameron Booth. Kuhlman's paintings of the 1930s were mostly emotion-laden landscapes, combining the expressionist handling of the Fauves with a dark melancholy that would later

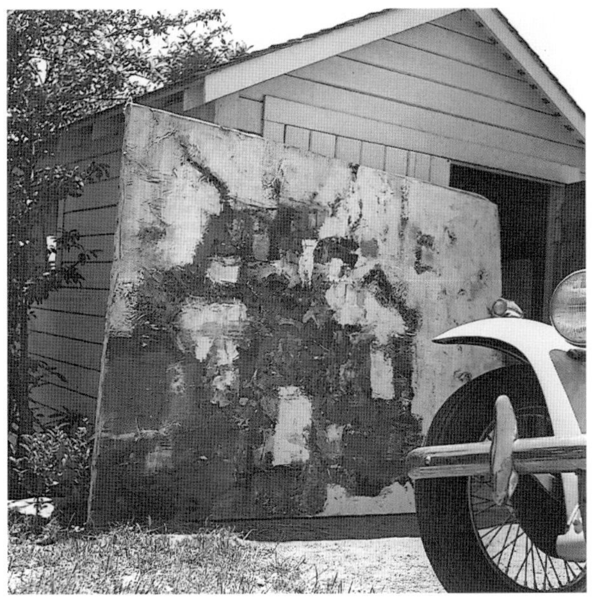

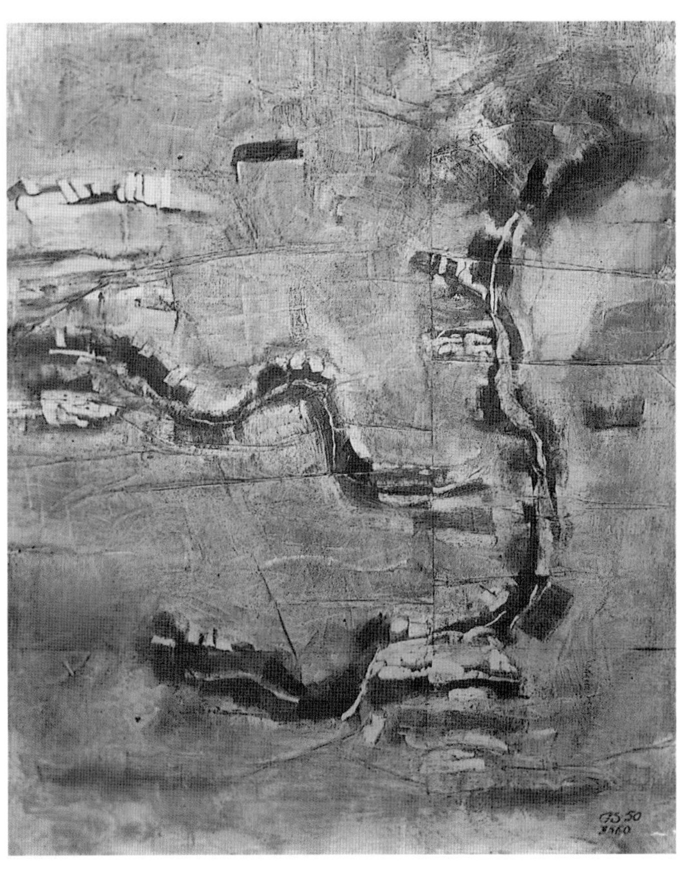

Figure 4.22

Above: George Stillman, *Untitled*, 1950. Oil, ink, and paper on canvas, 8 × 10 ft. Destroyed. Photographer: George Stillman.

Figure 4.23

Right: George Stillman, *3-5-50,* 1950. Oil, ink, and paper on canvas, 51 × 37 in. Collection of the artist. Photographer: George Stillman.

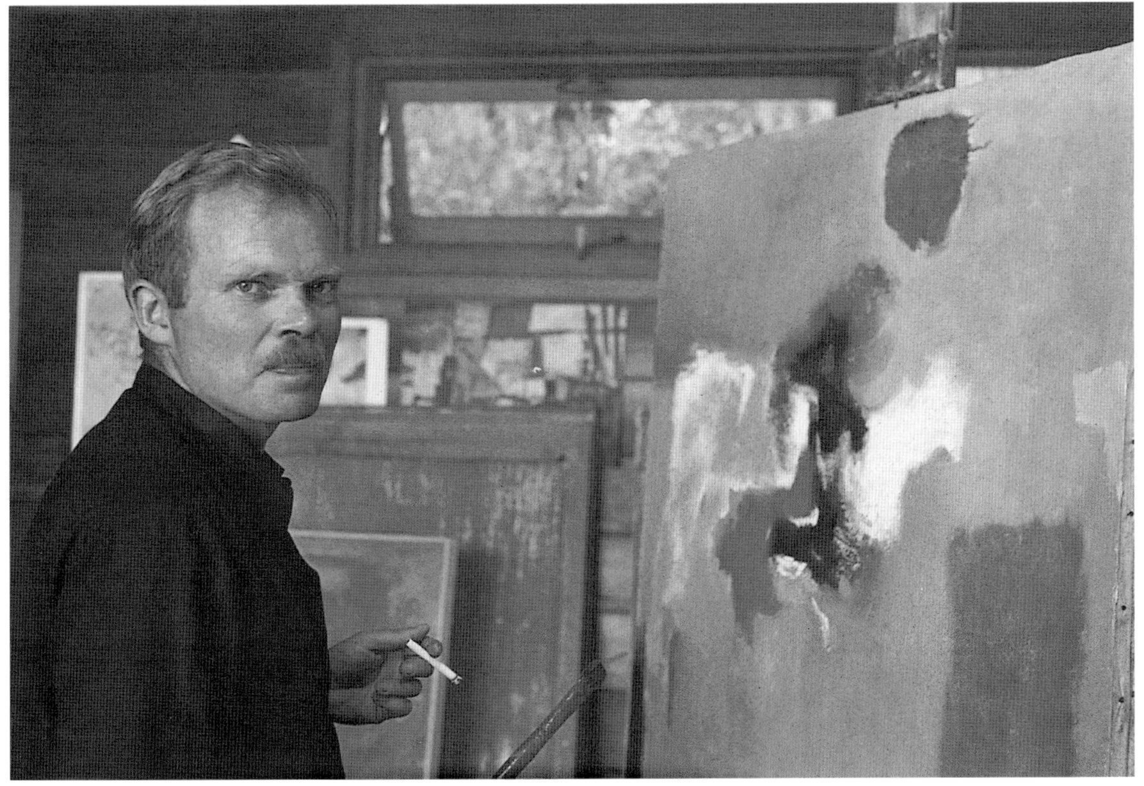

Figure 4.24

Walter Kuhlman, Sausalito studio, 1949. Photographer: Milton Farris.

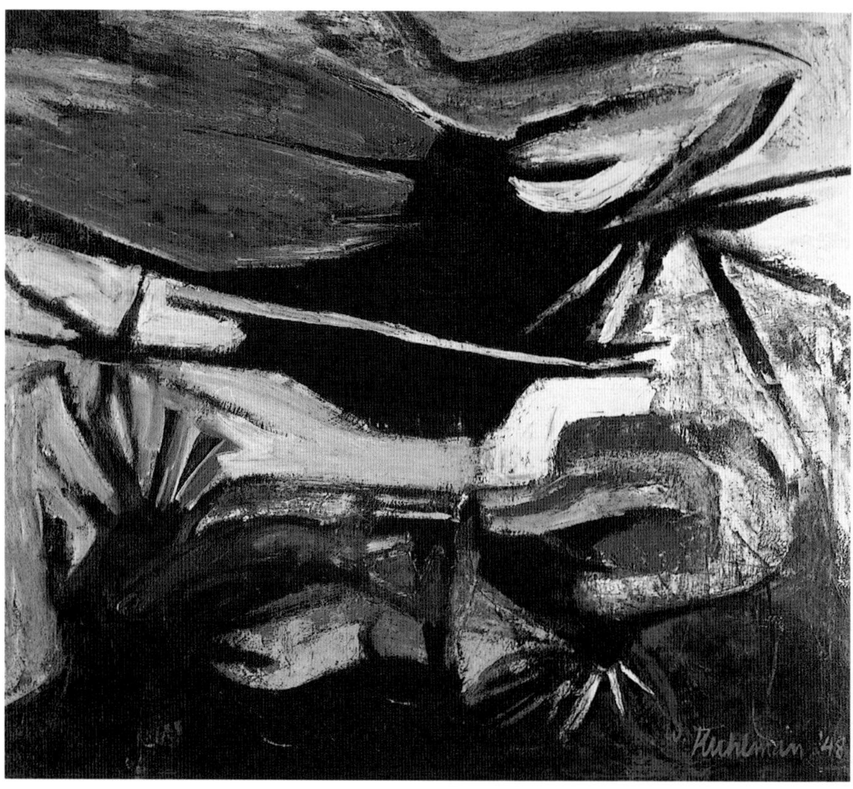

reappear in many abstract paintings of the 1950s. With their swirling clouds and twisted, agitated trees, some of these paintings call to mind the Romantic landscapes of Ryder, Blakelock, and Cole, Kuhlman's favorite American painters.

Kuhlman was relatively successful as a landscape painter before the war, showing in national exhibitions throughout the Midwest and the East.[88] After a retrospective at the Walker Art Center in 1940, he was invited to join the faculty of the St. Paul School of Art, where he taught for two years before he was drafted into the navy. Kuhlman, an unshakable pacifist, refused combat duty and was assigned to the medical corps as an illustrator, sketching the dead and wounded in operating rooms and hospital wards. He would later recall that this daily encounter with suffering and death made a profound impact on his art.[89] Following a pattern common among artists traumatized by the war, Kuhlman's response was delayed; it would be several years before he could express what he termed the fearful "shadow side of human nature."[90] The tormenting memories began to surface only at the end of the 1940s in the slashing forms of abstractions like *Untitled* (fig. 4.25) evoking the specter of surgical knives.[91] Some of his paintings

from that time also conjure images of rotting flesh in their yellowed whites tinged with blue and green.[92]

Kuhlman's initial foray into abstraction began in the Virgin Islands after the war, with a group of Picasso-inspired figurative works that combined aspects of Cubism and Surrealism.[93] After hearing glowing reports about the California School of Fine Arts from Lobdell, who had studied with him in St. Paul, Kuhlman moved to San Francisco in 1947. In his painting of this period he continued to draw from what he called a "storehouse of color memory" that included high-keyed yellows, reds, and turquoise greens from scuba diving in sun-drenched tropical waters.[94] But the diving may have affected more than Kuhlman's palette; the aquatic feel of such early works as *Untitled #9* (1948; see fig. 3.8) suggests underwater plant life.

It is difficult to summarize Kuhlman's creative development in the years 1948 to 1950 because he followed so many avenues of expression. Kuhlman's works in 1948 alone ranged from evocative marine imagery to the playful primitivism of *Untitled* (1948; fig. 4.26). Only toward the end of 1949 did Still's painting make an impact in the ragged shapes of works like *Yellow Painting #1* (fig. 4.27). Here,

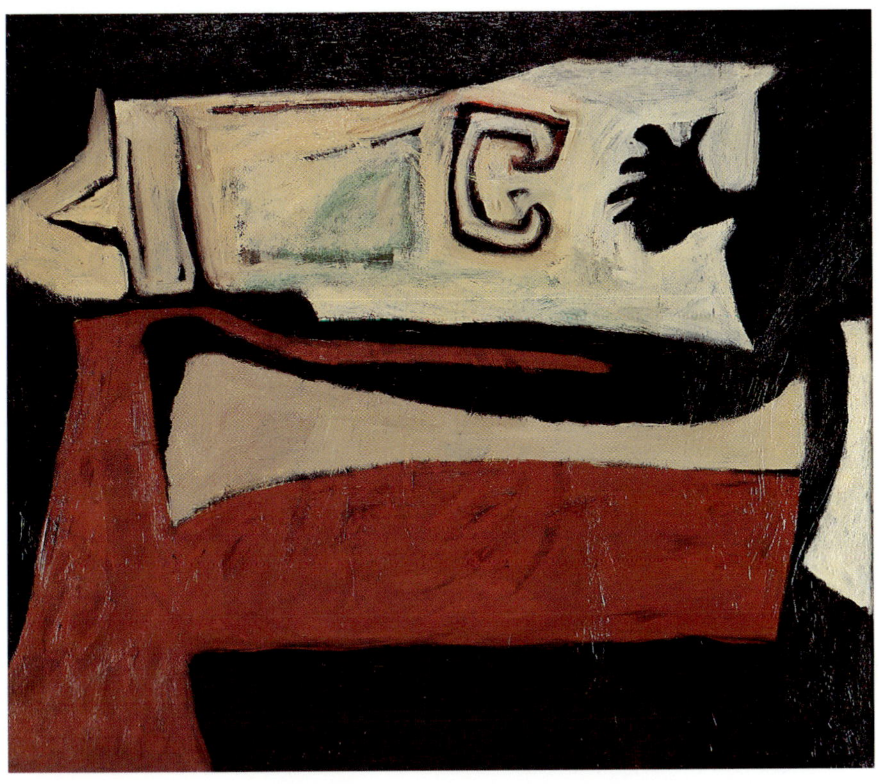

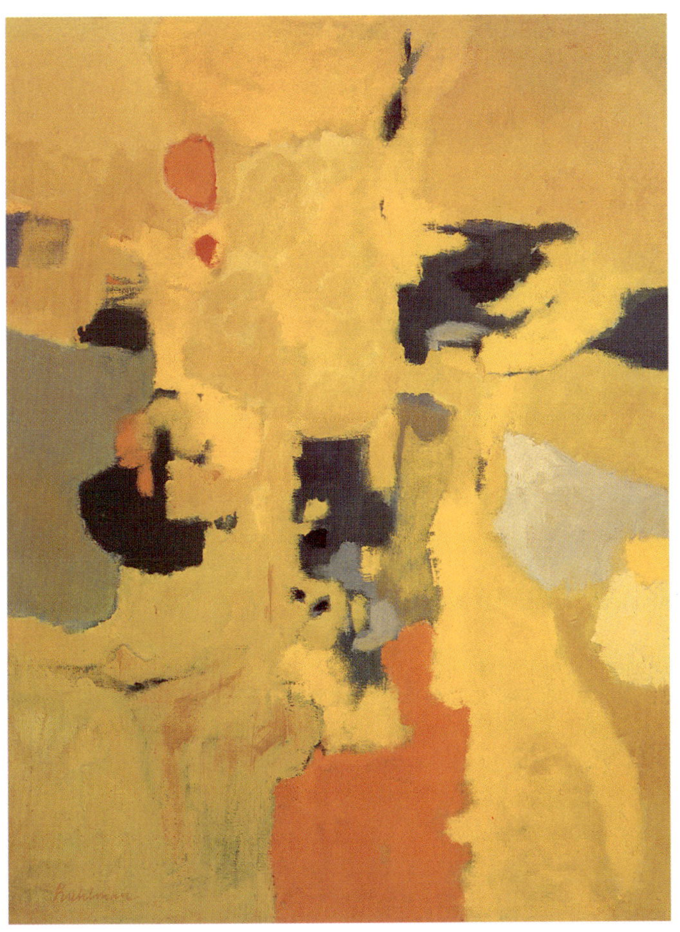

Figure 4.25

Opposite: Walter Kuhlman, *Untitled,* 1948. Oil on canvas,
35 × 39 in. Photograph courtesy, John Natsoulas Gallery,
Davis, California; Axiom Photography.

Figure 4.26

Above: Walter Kuhlman, *Untitled,* 1948. Oil on canvas, 36 × 40
in. Private collection. Photograph courtesy, John Natsoulas
Gallery, Davis, California; Axiom Photography.

Figure 4.27

Left: Walter Kuhlman, *Yellow Painting #1,* 1949. Oil on canvas,
57³/₈ × 41¹/₁₆ in. Private collection. Photographer:
M. Lee Fatherree.

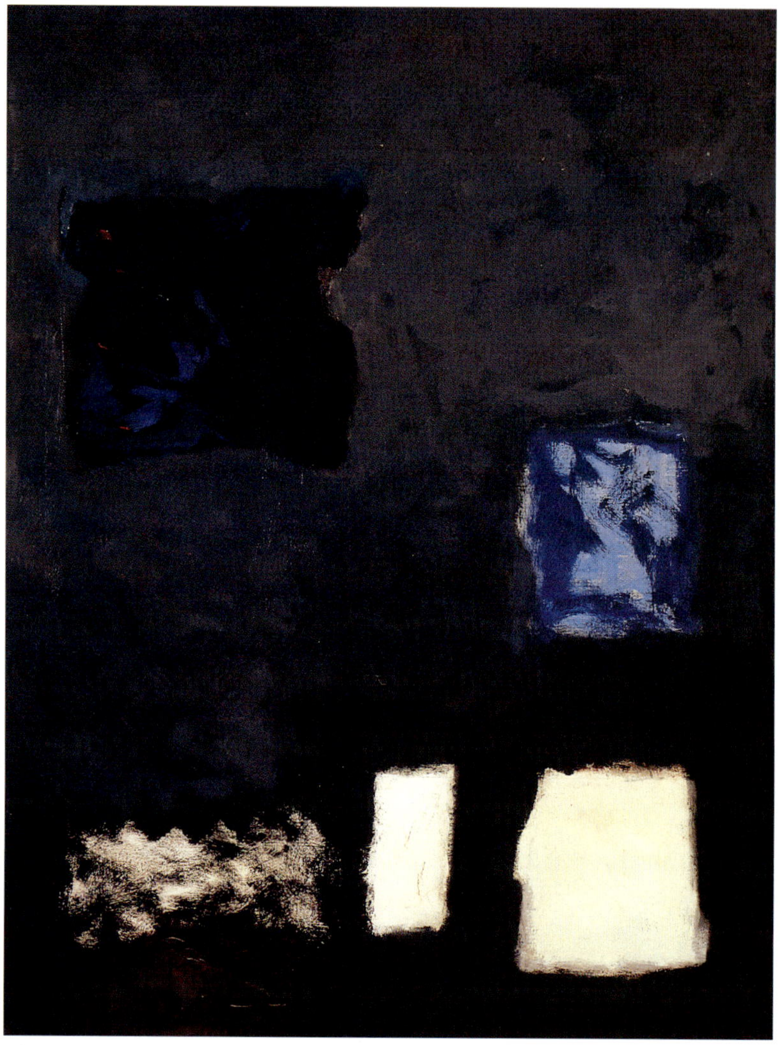

Figure 4.28

Right: Walter Kuhlman, *Untitled,* 1957. Oil on canvas, 47 × 35 in. Collection, The Oakland Museum, gift of Walter Kuhlman, in memory of James Budd Dixon. Photographer: M. Lee Fatherree.

Figure 4.29

Opposite: Walter Kuhlman, *Untitled (Brown Painting),* 1957. Oil on canvas, 47 × 35 in. Private collection. Photograph courtesy, John Natsoulas Gallery, Davis, California; Axiom Photography.

Kuhlman hit upon one of the central themes of the San Francisco School; the feeling of expansion, of inexorable centrifugal movement, is as intense as in much of Still's work of the same period.

In the 1950s, Kuhlman's imagery flattened and simplified. The untitled work of 1957 in the Oakland Museum's collection (fig. 4.28) is typical of his later paintings. As in much of Kuhlman's work, irregular squares of color float over a bed of painterly brushwork. His paintings of the 1950s have sometimes been compared to Rothko's, but Kuhlman's handling of paint is more lush and complex.[95] Many of his works also have a very un-Rothkolike palette of opaque browns, blacks, and deep blues, which tend to absorb rather than reflect light. *Untitled (Brown Painting)* (1957; fig. 4.29), for example, has the dense, impenetrable skin of paint characteristic of much San Fran-

cisco Abstract Expressionism. Its cryptic imagery, at once phallic and talismanic, recalls the mysterious, vaguely ritualistic work of Still during the war. As the 1950s progressed, Kuhlman's painting became increasingly dark and enigmatic, with allusions to the cross and other sacred symbols. His figurative work after 1961 would draw heavily from the myths and legends and his own childhood memories of Denmark.

James Budd Dixon (fig. 4.30) was the senior member of the Sausalito group. In 1946, when he attended classes at the California School of Fine Arts on the GI Bill, he was forty-six, four years older than Still and more than fifteen years older than most of his fellow students. He had also been earning a living as an artist for nearly two decades, longer than most of his instructors. Dixon had been born to a well-to-do family in San Francisco at the turn of the century. His

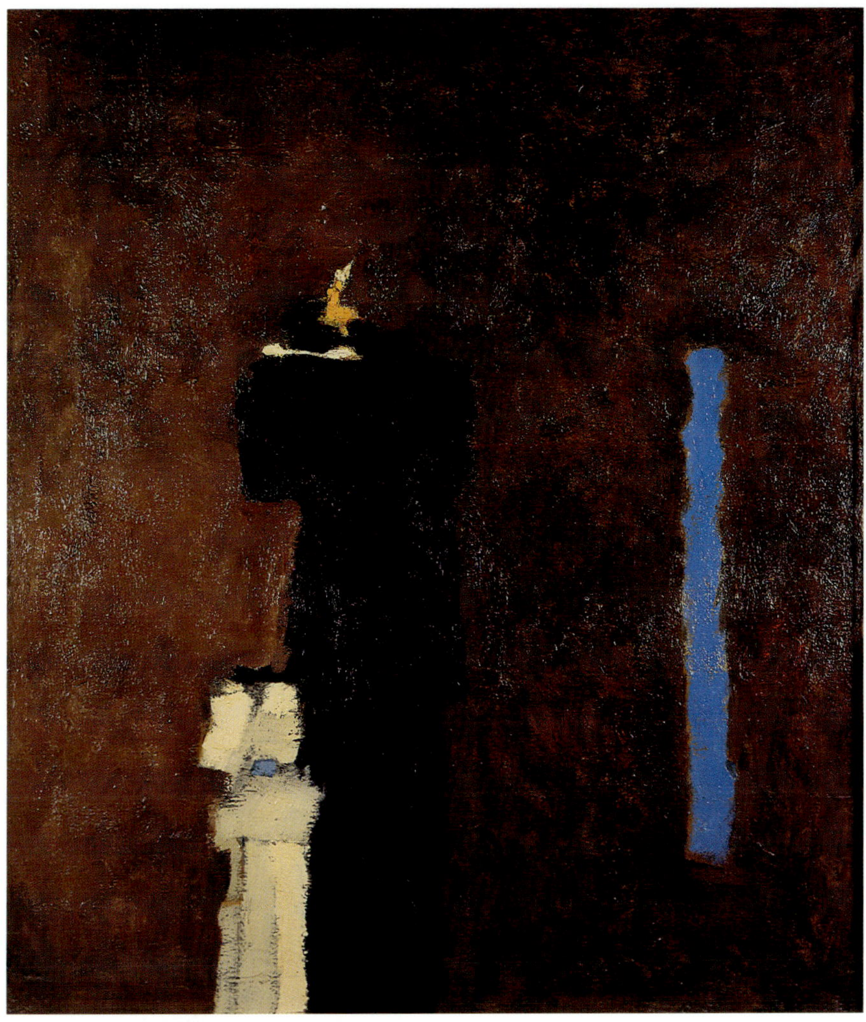

great-uncle, James H. Budd, for whom he was named, had been California's first Democratic governor in the late 1890s. Dixon's father prospered in agriculture in the San Joaquin Valley and raised his children on a sprawling farm estate just outside Stockton.[96] At thirteen, Dixon inherited from his aunt what the *San Francisco Examiner* termed a "fortune," money his stepfather subsequently squandered in gambling and poor investments.[97] Dixon did, however, attend the University of California in high style, reputedly vying for attention with Randolph Hearst, Jr., with his flashy Stutz Bearcat roadster and rakish good looks.[98] He worked as a cartoonist on the campus humor magazine, but left without earning a degree and began attending the California School of Fine Arts, where he studied sporadically throughout the decade.[99]

Dixon's earliest efforts were Beardsley-style book illustrations inspired by Art Nouveau. By the 1930s he had established himself as an accomplished adherent of the California Watercolor School, a West Coast variant of American Scene painting with an emphasis on plein-air coastal scenes and cityscapes.[100] Among Dixon's subjects of the period were deftly drawn views of Telegraph Hill, when the summit was still relatively uncluttered by the frame houses that would cling to its bluffs in the 1940s and 1950s.

By the time the San Francisco Museum of Art gave him his first one-man show in 1939, Dixon had departed from his previous realist style with colorful abstractions blending Cubist, Surrealist, and expressionist motifs drawn from Picasso, De Chirico, Tanguy, and Kandinsky.[101] Dixon's newfound interest in modern art may have been inspired by his friendships with Spohn and Reuben Kadish, although such

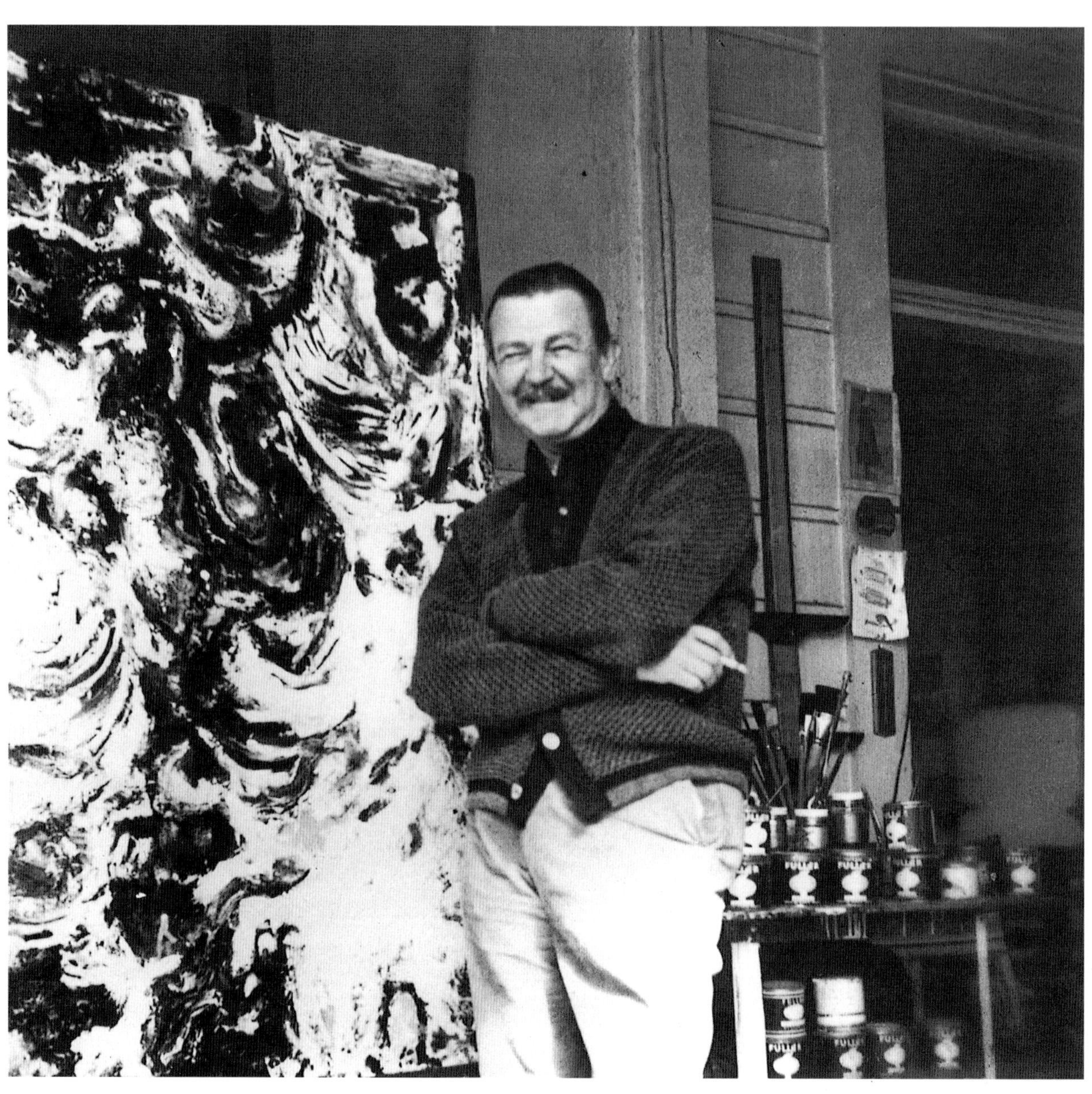

Figure 4.30

Above: James Budd Dixon, San Francisco studio.
Photographer: Peggy Dixon. Photograph courtesy, The Paul
Chadbourne Mills Archives of California Art,
The Oakland Museum.

Figure 4.31

Opposite: James Budd Dixon, *Untitled,* ca. 1948. Oil on canvas,
36 × 30 in. Private collection.

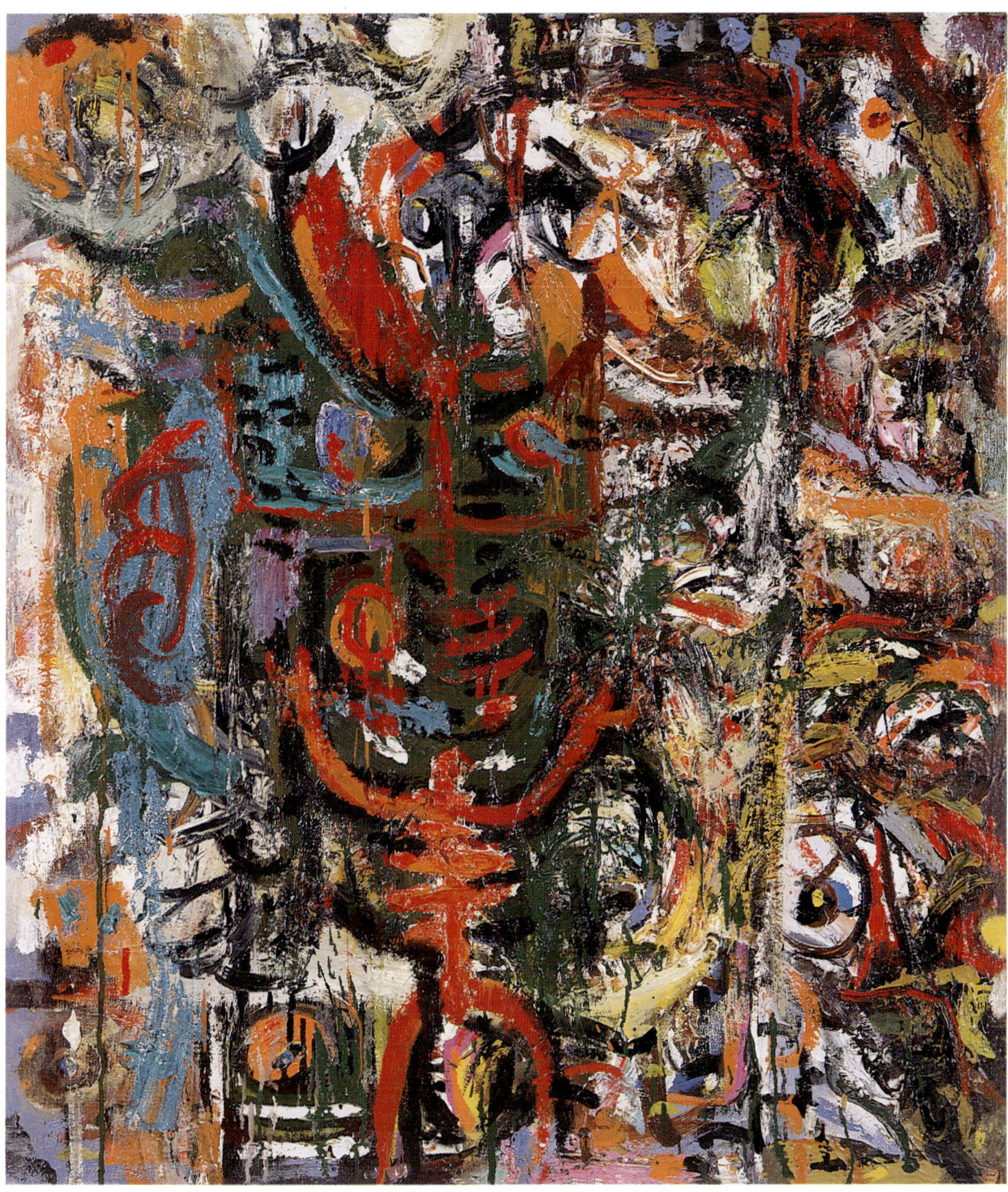

hybrid modernist forms were becoming increasingly commonplace in San Francisco at the start of the war. Dixon's work continued along these lines for the next several years. In the mid-1940s he began a series of satirical drawings resembling Picabia's Dadaist object-portraits.[102] These drawings were executed entirely with drafting tools, which he had learned to use while serving as chief draftsman for a shipbuilding company during the war.

Around 1947–48 Dixon's work took a decidedly expressionist turn. From this point through the end of the decade, his paintings would be characterized by sweeping lines and vertiginous movement. In some works, the tracks of Dixon's brush are interlocked so tightly that they form a matted fabric of paint (fig. 4.31). Dixon was the only San Francisco Abstract Expressionist in the late 1940s to look to Pollock for inspiration. He had seen Pollock's one-man show at the San Francisco Museum of Art in 1945 and was profoundly impressed by the emotive power of paintings like *Guardians of the Secret* (1943; fig. 4.32), in the museum's permanent collection. Dixon's paintings of the late 1940s have a similar feeling of raw brutality. As in Pollock's early work, the effect is achieved through dissonant colors and a seemingly indiscriminate alternation of wet and dry paint.

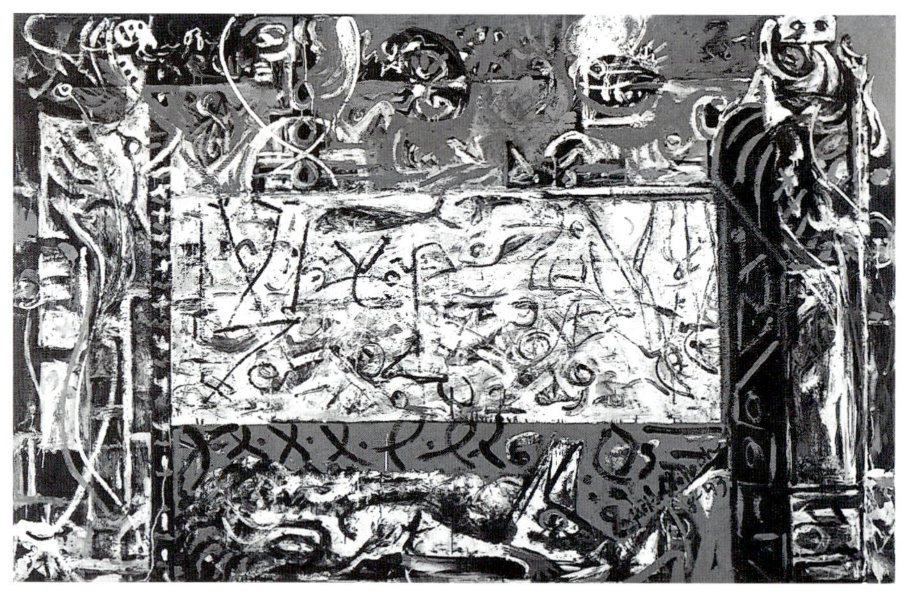

Figure 4.32

Above: Jackson Pollock, *Guardians of the Secret,* 1943. Oil on
canvas, 48⅛ × 75⅜ in. San Francisco Museum of Modern Art,
Albert M. Bender Collection, Albert M. Bender Bequest Fund
Purchase. Photographer: Don Myer. © 1995 Pollock-Krasner
Foundation / Artists Rights Society (ARS), New York.

Figure 4.33

Right: James Budd Dixon, *Untitled,* ca. 1948. Oil on canvas,
48¹/₁₆ × 37⅜ in. Collection, J. Budd Sage. Photographer:
M. Lee Fatherree.

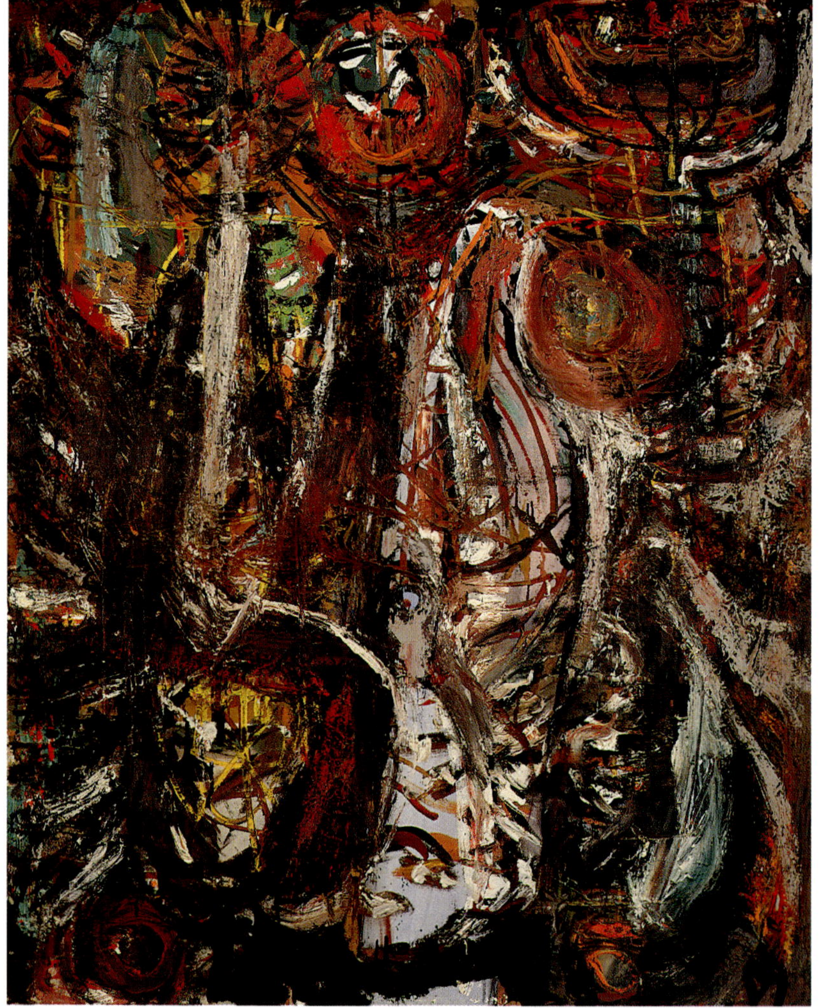

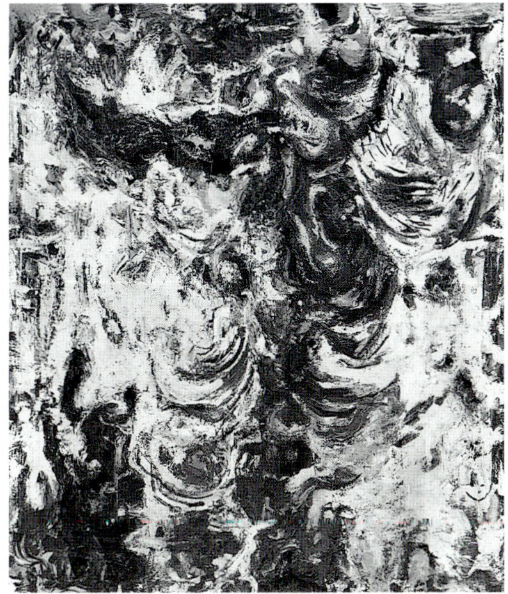

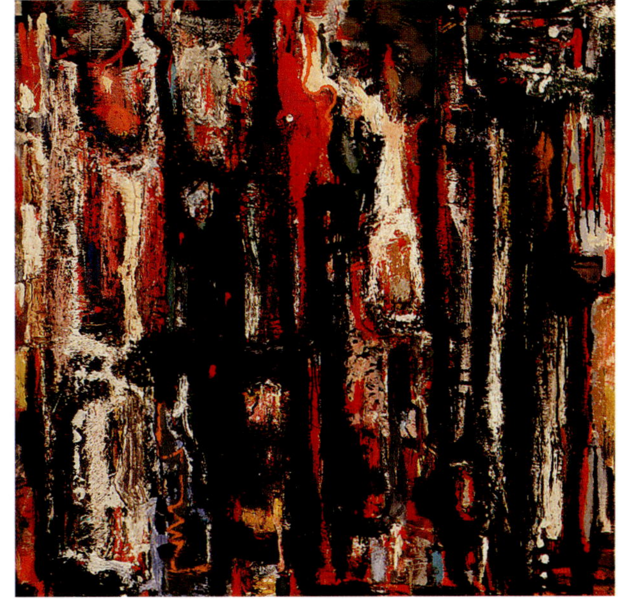

One of the hallmarks of Dixon's paintings in the late 1940s is their vague suggestion of a totemic presence, comparable to some of Tobey's paintings of roughly the same period. Dixon never made explicit figurative references in his paintings, and, strictly speaking, his work falls well within the nonobjective mainstream of the California School of Fine Arts.[103] Yet, like the work of Tobey and Pollock, Dixon's paintings sometimes contain ghostly allusions to the figure within their tangled webs (fig. 4.33). Many of his paintings from the late 1940s also make use of abstract designs taken from primitive art. Zigzags, tiger stripes, and corkscrew motifs are staples of these paintings. Dixon collected Polynesian art and developed a passion for tribal music in the 1940s.[104] His rhythmic, staccato brushwork has been compared to the pulsating beat of the African tom-toms Dixon played for parties at his studio.[105]

In the 1950s these tribal allusions disappear entirely. Line, too, seems to dissolve in a thicket of densely interwoven paint, sometimes embellished with squirts directly from the tube. Most of Dixon's paintings have the familiar sweep of the San Francisco School, but compared with the work of Still, Dixon's canvases are torrential. Paintings such as *White with Red Violet* of 1960 (fig. 4.34) present maelstroms of paint, heaving and swelling, curling and unfurling. Even more complacent works like *Study in Red and Green #13* (1958; fig. 4.35) have surfaces that appear to seethe and boil. Dixon's paintings often make star-

Figure 4.34

Above, left: James Budd Dixon, *White with Red Violet,* 1960. Oil on canvas, 58 × 50 in. Collection, The Oakland Museum, gift of the Estate of Peggy Nelson Dixon. Photographer: M. Lee Fatherree.

Figure 4.35

Above: James Budd Dixon, *Study in Red and Green # 13,* 1958. Oil on canvas, 48 × 48 in. Collection, The Oakland Museum, gift of the Estate of Peggy Nelson Dixon. Photographer: M. Lee Fatherree.

tling, even disturbing, use of color. As Albright observed, the "convulsive cacophonies of flaming reds and oranges, icy blues and shrill greens" made Dixon one of the more daring colorists of the San Francisco School.[106]

Dixon taught printmaking at the California School of Fine Arts from 1949 to 1955, and while many of his own prints have been lost, the works that remain show a highly imaginative approach to etching and lithography.[107] His prints make an interesting comparison with those of Stanley William Hayter, who was one of his teachers at the California School of Fine Arts in the summer of 1948.[108] Hayter's technical influence is apparent in Dixon's pressing of netting and coarse-woven fabrics onto soft grounds to create complex textural effects in his etchings. He also skipped drills across his plates to create stippled lines—standard fare at Hayter's Atelier 17 in New York. Some of Dixon's prints also feature Hayter's sinuous free-flowing line. But like most of his San Francisco colleagues, he preferred a rugged approach to Hayter's finesse. Dixon's lithographs show his cultivation of the uneven edges of printing stones and his signature "chewed" corner—a quirk picked up by several other San Francisco artists.

As a teacher, Dixon never achieved the stature of his younger peers Corbett, Diebenkorn, and Still, but he was an important figure for many second-generation Abstract Expressionists in San Francisco. During the 1950s his storefront studio on Lombard Street in North Beach was a popular rendezvous for CSFA artists such as James Kelly, Sonia Gechtoff, Deborah Remington, Julius Wasserstein, and Roy De Forest. Dixon made his Los Angeles debut with this group in Walter Hopps's fabled *Action I* show on the Santa Monica Pier in 1955, but poor health and alcoholism began to take their toll soon after.[109] Dixon had only one major solo exhibition during his lifetime, at the San Francisco Museum of Art in 1939, well before his work reached maturity. In the 1950s, he was better known in Paris than in San Francisco, mainly through the efforts of his primary patron, the French critic Michel Tapié.[110]

Richard Diebenkorn, 1947–50

Richard Diebenkorn was closely associated with Dixon and the Sausalito artists, but he was also involved with another informal group that included Park and Bischoff. In 1947, the year he moved to Sausalito, Diebenkorn began meeting regularly for drawing sessions with Bischoff and Park, mostly at Bischoff's house in San Francisco.[111] Almost every weekend, the artists visited one another's studios to view and discuss their work.[112] Ultimately, Park, Bischoff, and Diebenkorn would initiate the Bay Area Figurative movement that critically eclipsed the San Francisco School during the late 1950s. In the beginning, however, the trio may have been drawn together by a disaffection from Still. According to Smith, a rift developed shortly after Still's one-man show in the summer of 1947:

> When Clyff showed his paintings at the Legion of Honor in San Francisco in 1947 something very interesting happened! Almost immediately a kind of schism developed around that situation, with Elmer Bischoff and David Park and Dick Diebenkorn taking a very adverse attitude toward Clyff's painting. I had been very intimate with them, but I disagreed with them about that . . . So we kind of formed up into camps. And that was a gap which was never really bridged. Elmer Bischoff and I have become friendly after many years. But there was a fairly profound kind of disagreement which existed in the late 1940s and early 1950s.[113]

To some extent, the antagonism toward Still sprang from professional rivalry. MacAgy recalled that this was particularly the case for Park, who had been the school's star teacher before Still's arrival: "There was jealousy involved—perfectly normal human jealousy. Clyff was getting all the kudos and Dave, who had been there much longer, was not."[114] William Morehouse concurred that Park, Bischoff, and Diebenkorn "felt the sting of Still's influence strongly. Still got the best students, and they resented that, but they also took umbrage at Still's cultish behavior."[115] Diebenkorn, by nature a deeply modest man, was especially offended by Still's shamanistic posturing, which he disparaged as little more than "paranoid pomposity."[116]

But aside from personal animosity and the clash of personalities, there were basic ideological conflicts that fueled the "anti-Still" faction at the California School of Fine Arts. Still's hostility to European modernism was a particular source of dispute. Diebenkorn, Park, and Bischoff were committed to extending the tradition of modernism, not to annihilating it. All three continued to admire Picasso and Miró through the late 1940s, and Diebenkorn was partial to Matisse, whose decorativeness most of the

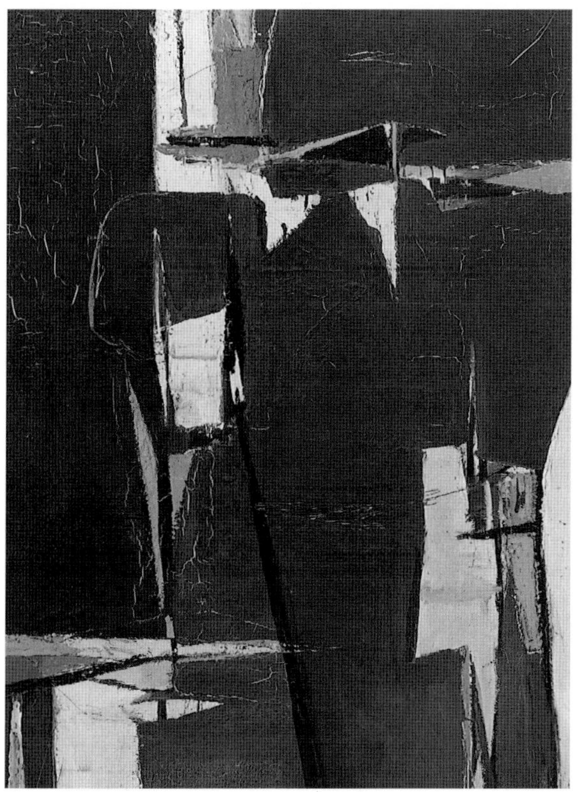

other San Francisco painters disliked. Yet at the height of the Abstract Expressionist movement, they too rejected Parisian polish. In the late 1940s, their paintings had a roughness that few artists of the New York School matched. Nonetheless, a quirky playfulness set them apart from Still and his closest colleagues. Their delight in handling paint found a close parallel in their enthusiasm for Dixieland and Creole jazz.[117] Such a high-spirited, fun-loving, and sensual approach could not have been further removed from the weighty seriousness of Still and many of the artists sympathetic to him.

As the 1940s came to a close, this schism was readily apparent, but in late 1947 and 1948, contrary to Smith's account, the lines of division were not yet clearly drawn. Bischoff and Park may have resisted Still's influence from the start, but Diebenkorn was initially receptive and even a bit awed by the older artist's work. The fourteen canvases in Diebenkorn's one-man exhibition at the California Palace of the Legion of Honor in 1948 revealed that he had studied Still's paintings well. Comparing one of Diebenkorn's paintings from that exhibition to Still's work shows undeniable affinities (fig. 4.36; see fig. 2.24). Although

Diebenkorn's palette lacks Still's ominous tone, both works are composed of sharp, craggy shapes that spread to the outer limits of the canvas. Unlike the paintings Diebenkorn produced during his stay in New York the previous year, his new works have little sense of figure-ground relationship. The shapes are flat compared with those of such earlier Picasso-inspired paintings as *Untitled (Magician's Table)* (1947; see fig. 2.21), which feature relatively conventional abstract motifs, neatly contoured in the center of a shallow, stagelike space.

By late 1948, Still's influence on Diebenkorn had diminished beyond meaningful recognition. The menacing shapes had by then been replaced by freely generated playful forms tending toward the rotund. Diebenkorn described his painting process as "forming with color," and it is clear from these works that he had put aside for a time the loosened Cubist grid that gave structure to the paintings in the Legion of Honor show.[118] Rothko's example may have encouraged Diebenkorn to warm up his palette and concentrate on reds, yellows, and a broad range of oranges. But none of Diebenkorn's paintings from the Sausalito period (1947–49) have the softness of Rothko's

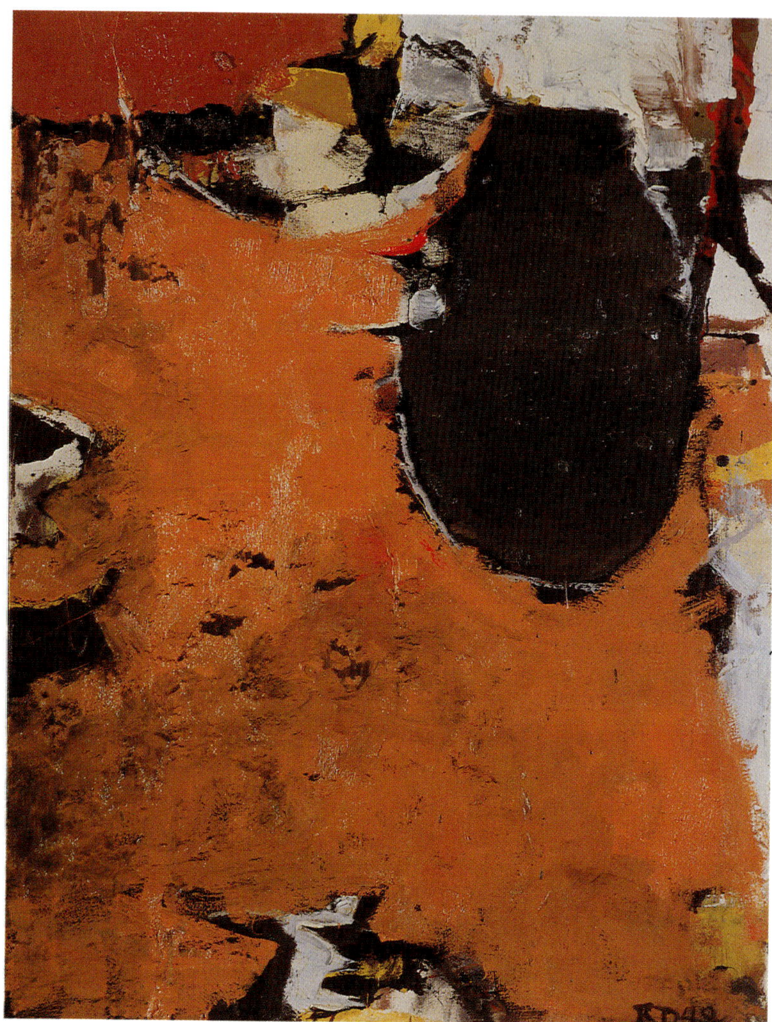

Figure 4.37

Richard Diebenkorn, *Painting II,* 1949. Oil on canvas,
45¾ × 34¾ in. Collection, The Oakland Museum, gift of the
Estate of Howard E. Johnson. Photographer: M. Lee Fatherree.

work. As Diebenkorn told Hultberg at the time, he wanted his paintings to look "ugly up close."[119] Indeed, many of his paintings have the shrapnel-spattered surfaces common to the San Francisco School, with seemingly random clumps and clots of paint. Works such as *Painting II* (1949; fig. 4.37), in the Oakland Museum, also display the scumbled bleed-through effects that can be found in Stillman's paintings and collages of the period. Corbett's work comes to mind as well when looking at this painting. The edges of Diebenkorn's shapes, revealing multiple coats of paint, are comparable to the shredded layerings of Corbett's *Black Paintings.*

Park has often been credited with being Diebenkorn's guiding force in the late 1940s,[120] but the few abstract paintings that survived Park's destruction in 1950 lack the confidence of many works by his contemporaries.[121] Years later, Diebenkorn confessed

that he considered Park's abstract painting "kind of forced."[122] Park's influence on him seems to have been more of a personal nature. Park, besides widening Diebenkorn's artistic horizons, helped him to form his painting conscience. It was Park, with his "overdose of New England morality," as Bischoff put it, who challenged Diebenkorn to push beyond easy formulas.[123] As his teacher, Park saw a danger in Diebenkorn's natural facility with the brush. According to Bischoff, Park used to "chide and ride" Diebenkorn about the ease with which he could resolve a painting, because that ease demeaned the value of the work.[124] Diebenkorn himself seems to have considered his facility something of an obstacle: "A *way* is just what I don't want," he once said. "With each new painting, I find a way all too soon, and that's when the trouble starts."[125]

On a purely aesthetic level, Diebenkorn probably

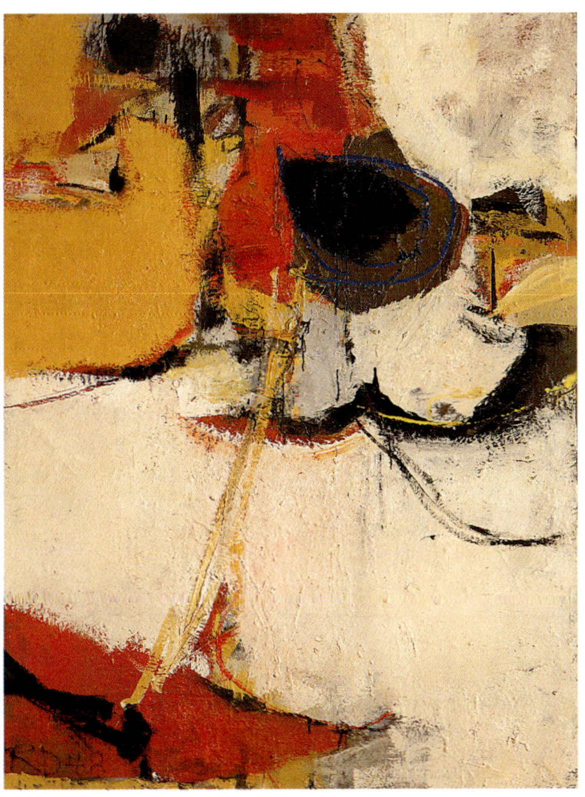

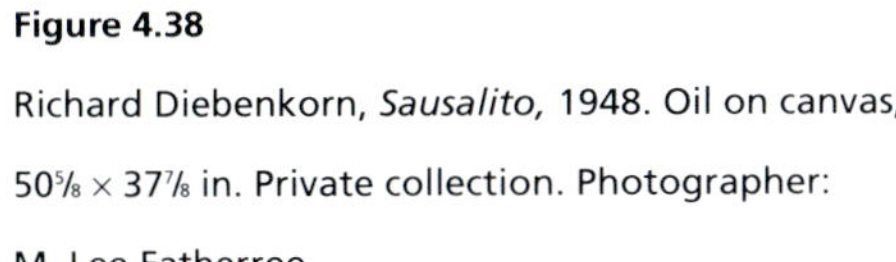

Figure 4.38

Richard Diebenkorn, *Sausalito,* 1948. Oil on canvas,

50⅝ × 37⅞ in. Private collection. Photographer:

M. Lee Fatherree.

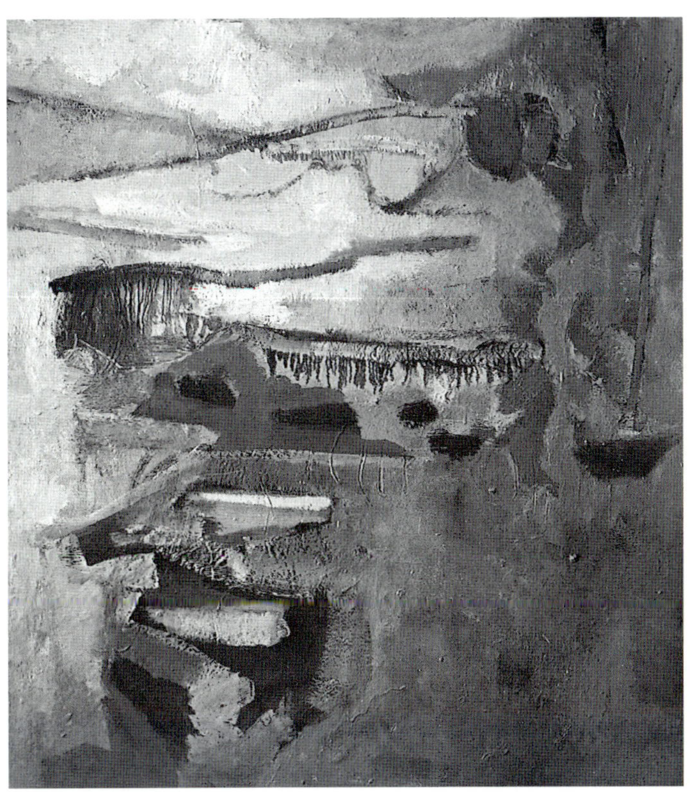

Figure 4.39

Elmer Bischoff, *Untitled* (?), 1948. Oil on canvas, 48 × 40 in.

Whereabouts unknown. Photographer: George Stillman.

learned more from Bischoff than he did from Park. Indeed, for a brief period, Bischoff and Diebenkorn worked together so closely that their paintings were sometimes nearly interchangeable. Paintings such as Diebenkorn's *Sausalito* (1948; fig 4.38) and one of Bischoff's canvases of the same year (fig. 4.39), with their dry, raspy brushwork and "bleeding drip" technique, could almost have come from the same hand. Other paintings feature a similar choppy, angular construction of form. From late 1948 to early 1949, Bischoff and Diebenkorn exchanged numerous motifs, notably the whimsical bulbous shapes and knob-headed tendrils that appear in both Diebenkorn's *Sausalito* (1949; fig. 4.40) and Bischoff's *Object with Black* (1948; fig. 4.41).

Diebenkorn, in one of the more significant developments in his painting at the close of the 1940s, introduced an animated, free-flowing line. De Koon-

ing is generally considered the source for this renewed interest in line, but it seems unlikely that the four small reproductions Diebenkorn might have seen in 1948 could have been a more compelling inspiration than his weekly improvisational drawing sessions in San Francisco and Sausalito.[126] In any case, Diebenkorn's use of line is much closer to the playful naïveté of the San Francisco artists than to the smooth, unerring draftsmanship of de Kooning.[127] Paintings such as his *Sausalito*s of 1948 and 1949 (fig. 4.42; see fig. 4.40) are more profitably compared with Smith's *Alone with the Killer* of 1948 (see fig. 1.7), with its rambunctious line. Despite Smith's self-professed alliance with the "Still camp," he remained close friends with Diebenkorn, Park, and Bischoff in the late 1940s and often participated in their drawing sessions and studio visits. Diebenkorn and Smith shared a fondness for comic strips and liked to swap humor-

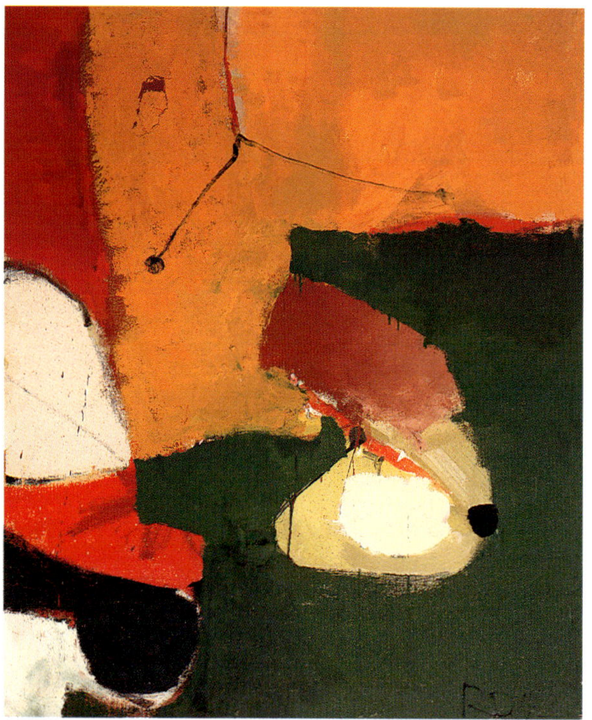 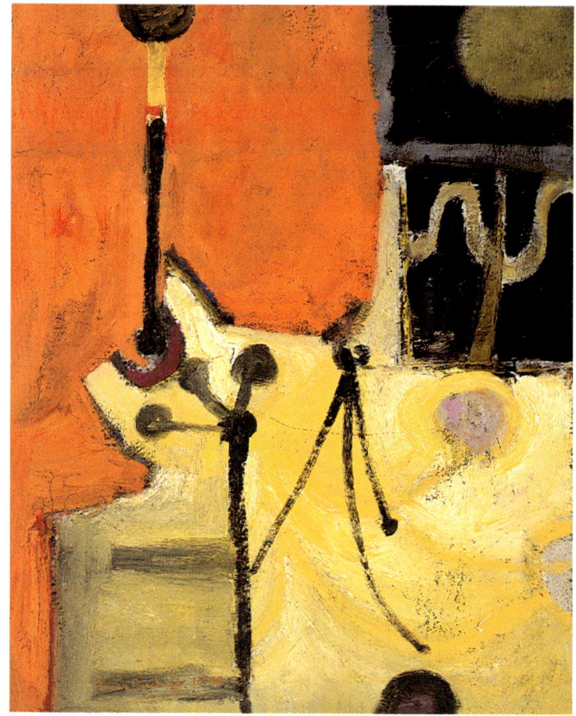

ous doodles. "One can see a kinship in their drawing," Bischoff recalled. "Diebenkorn was keen about Krazy Kat cartoons, cultivating a deliberate awkwardness."[128] Indeed, the kinship between Diebenkorn and Smith was sufficiently close for them to collaborate on a painting circa 1949–50.[129] They also joined in a two-man exhibition at the Lucien Labaudt Gallery in 1950. Frankenstein's review of the show expressed his reluctant but growing appreciation of Abstract Expressionism. He called Smith and Diebenkorn "two of the old masters of the tradition represented at the Metart":

> As is often the case with workers in this style, I found myself repelled at first by their apparently haphazard improvisations, the vast, pretentious size of their canvases, and the reliance upon runs and drippings that remain good in the department of the accidental. After a time, however, it seemed to me that these works communicated a fabulous richness and energy, that they took one into a new domain of visual expression that could be entered by no other road, and that what they had to say was at least important and at best profound.[130]

When Frankenstein's review appeared, Diebenkorn was no longer living in the Bay Area. Taking advantage of free tuition on the GI Bill, he had moved to Albuquerque to enroll in the master's program at the University of New Mexico. By the time he returned in 1953, after briefly teaching at the University of Illinois, he found the artistic landscape of San Francisco considerably changed. MacAgy and Still had moved to New York, Corbett and Spohn to Taos, and Smith, Bischoff, and Park had resigned from their teaching positions at the California School of Fine Arts.[131] The demise of the school is often blamed on MacAgy's successor, Ernest Mundt, whose Bauhaus training and conservative temperament seemed incompatible with the free-spirited nature of Abstract Expressionism. But in truth, Mundt did little to change the administration in ways not mandated by the school's distressed finances.[132] The plummeting enrollment of the former GIs, who constituted the bulk of the student body in the late 1940s, forced severe financial cutbacks. More important, the loss of the veterans changed the tough, no-nonsense atmosphere of the school. MacAgy had apparently seen the handwriting on the wall as early as 1948.[133] "The postwar pool of mature students was dwindling," he recalled later, soon to be replaced by "throngs of girls who can't make college" and students "who would trade being artists for being teachers when the cards

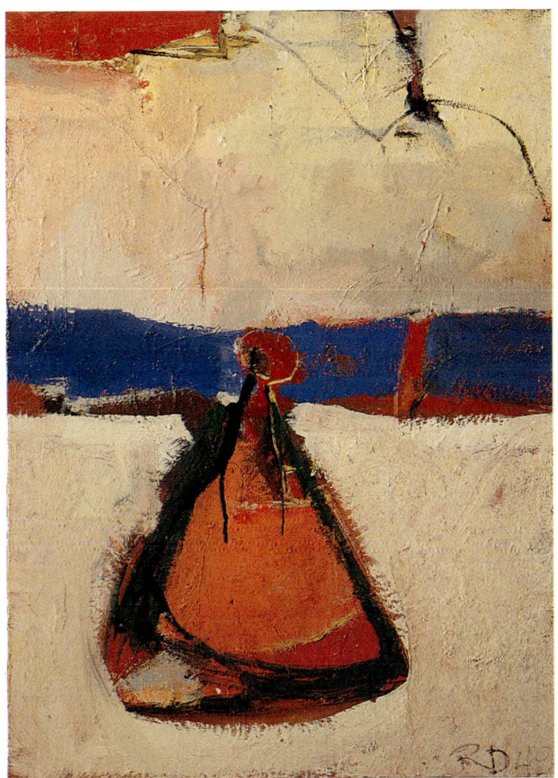

Figure 4.40

Opposite, left: Richard Diebenkorn, *Sausalito,* 1949. Oil on canvas, 44⅞ × 37 in. Private collection. Photographer: M. Lee Fatherree.

Figure 4.41

Opposite, right: Elmer Bischoff, *Object with Black,* 1948. Oil on canvas, 40 × 32⅛ in. Collection, Stephen Bischoff. Photographer: M. Lee Fatherree.

Figure 4.42

Left: Richard Diebenkorn, *Sausalito,* 1949. Oil on canvas, 45⅞ × 33 in. Private collection. Photographer: M. Lee Fatherree.

are down." He concluded: "Socially and economically speaking, what we'd been doing in the school's shelter was shortly to be put out of date by a different school situation."[134] MacAgy was right. Within a few years of his departure, Mundt was recruiting the Junior League in a desperate attempt to fill his classrooms, and the California School of Fine Arts was on the verge of bankruptcy.[135]

5

The End of a Golden Era?

Critics and art historians generally designate 1950 the end of the "golden age" of San Francisco Abstract Expressionism.[1] Certainly, the late 1940s represented the most intense stage of the movement's ferment and group interaction. The period exemplifies what Poggioli called the "activistic" phase of an avant-garde, when "a movement takes shape and agitates for no other end than its own self, out of the sheer joy of dynamism, a taste for action, a sportive enthusiasm, and the emotional fascination of adventure."[2] Much of the excitement in the late 1940s sprang from the newness of the enterprise and the defiance free-form abstraction represented in those years. But after the modernist battle was won, the movement lost much of its fanaticism. By the middle of the decade, the extremist ideology that had prohibited any hint of figuration was losing its grip. Park's defection from abstraction was considered a betrayal in 1950, but Diebenkorn's return to the figure in 1955 barely raised an eyebrow.[3] Even obvious borrowings from the more decorative Parisian artists, such as Bonnard and Matisse, became relatively commonplace. And titles, once frowned upon by nearly everyone at the California School of Fine Arts, became standard. Artists such as Sonia Gechtoff and James Kelly thought nothing of alluding to the poetry of Michael McClure or Dylan Thomas in their work.

In the 1950s, orthodoxy gave way to permissibility, yet ironically, the individualism central to the movement's ideology was never as complete as in the pluralism of this decade. As Walter Kuhlman remarked, "the so-called golden years were the most exciting years, but they were formative, in some respects just the beginning. The real growth occurred after the school broke up."[4] Indeed, even those who place the height of the movement securely in the 1940s agree that the strongest work was produced later. Albright draws the line for the golden years at 1950, yet most of the paintings he discusses in *Art in the San Francisco Bay Area* date from the following decade.[5]

There is an inescapable subjectivity in the gilding of the 1940s in San Francisco. For many artists, the carefree years of the California School of Fine Arts were indeed a thing of the past. It was extremely difficult to make a living as an artist in San Francisco. The city had few reliable collectors of contemporary art, and local galleries began selling appreciable quantities of vanguard painting only in the 1960s. When the GI Bill's support ran out, many artists had to take any job they could find to survive. Frank Lobdell took a full-time position in a printing shop running heavy machinery; Philip Roeber worked as a cook and gardener; and Kuhlman labored as a clay mixer for a ceramics factory. Kuhlman's job was so physically taxing that in a full year, he was able to paint only two canvases.[6]

But the dissolution of the California School of Fine Arts, which had provided a structure for daily exchange, did less to fragment solidarity than might be expected. By the mid-1950s, the center of activity had shifted to North Beach, the original site of San Francisco's bohemia. During the late nineteenth century, the heart of the artists' district had been the antebellum building known as the Montgomery Block (or "Monkey Block"), where Robert Louis Stevenson, Bret Harte, Mark Twain, Jack London, and numerous others held forth in studios and saloons.[7] During the 1940s and 1950s, the block's more than one hundred studios still housed artists—with Edward Dugmore and Elmer Bischoff among them—but it was no longer the fashionable address for the avant-garde.[8] In the early 1950s, poets, painters, filmmakers, and jazz musicians were gathering nearby in such artist-run cafés and bars as Miss Smith's Tea Room, the Cellar, and Vesuvio Café along the upper reaches of Grant and Columbus Avenues. For the poets in particular, "the Grant Avenue places were almost like an office or a classroom. Someone was always around, and the talk—about poetry, painting, music, philosophy, writing—was endless."[9] Within walking distance was the Audiffred Building, a landmark Victorian at the base of Mission Street on the waterfront, where a number of artists rented studios. In the 1950s it housed a concentration of talent, including Hassel Smith, Lobdell, Ernest Briggs, Jack Jefferson, Kelly, Gechtoff, Roeber, Julius Wasserstein, Madeleine Dimond, and Joan Brown.[10]

Toward the mid-1950s a second hub of activity began developing in the Marina District of San Francisco. It started with the opening of several artist-run alternative galleries along Fillmore near Union Street—the King Ubu in late 1952, which became the Six Gallery in 1954; the East and West Gallery in 1955; and Dimitri Grachis's Spatsa Gallery, which opened in 1958.[11] Just up the block from these galleries was the house on Fillmore Street where Brown, Gechtoff, Kelly, Jay DeFeo, Wally Hedrick, and Bruce Conner lived at one time or another during the 1950s.

Although the California School of Fine Arts would never again be the hotbed of activity it had been under MacAgy, the school was not entirely deserted after 1950. The Korean War brought a second wave of veterans in 1953, when the institution was accredited, and in 1956, with the appointment of Gurdon Woods as director, the school experienced something of a renaissance. Shortly after arriving, Woods revamped the faculty to include Bischoff, Diebenkorn, Jefferson, Lobdell, Kuhlman, and Nathan Oliveira. The faculty was fairly evenly split between figurative and abstract painters; as Joan Brown recalled, the school had no "party line."[12] The good-natured rivalry between the groups is reflected in their annual softball games pitting the figurative "Figs" against the nonobjective "Creepy Crawleys."[13]

Arrivals and Departures: Corbett, Dugmore, Briggs, McChesney, Jefferson, and Others

Much has been made of the exodus of San Francisco Abstract Expressionists eastward in search of success. Yet this migration has often been exaggerated.[14] Despite reports to the contrary, the majority of artists who participated in the "golden age" of Abstract Expressionism were not lured east but remained in San Francisco or left for Europe, Mexico, and the Southwest. New Mexico proved one of the more attractive destinations for former CSFA students hoping to extend their GI subsidies. In the early 1950s Taos drew numerous Abstract Expressionists, becoming something of a western counterpart to Provincetown.[15] Although Diebenkorn, Still, and McChesney each made an appearance there, the two artists who stayed long enough to make a lasting impact on the artistic community were Spohn and Corbett (fig. 5.1).

In Taos Spohn produced what critics generally consider his finest work after he moved there in 1951. Some of his most successful paintings express his delight in the cloud formations and dramatic light of the Taos Valley. With their complex orchestration of color and dynamic movement, paintings such as *Ballet of the Elements* strongly suggest music and the dance (1951; fig. 5.2).

Corbett was equally moved to interpret the Taos landscape, but his work has little of Spohn's exuberant physicality. Indeed, many of Corbett's Taos works are masterpieces of understatement. From 1951 to 1954, Corbett concentrated almost exclusively on drawings in charcoal. The Taos drawings make full use of that velvety medium's capacity to register the slightest adjustments of tone. Most are in shades of gray, ranging from light pearl to smoky black. Occasionally Corbett suffused the entire field with plum, amber, or blue pastel, or allowed the colors to flicker and glow from beneath the charcoal like embers in the darkness. Many of Corbett's Taos drawings convey a feel for the horizons and vast distances of the desert landscape. Breadth had been a primary theme in his San Francisco work, but in drawings such as *New Mexico #34* (1954; fig. 5.3) the projection is more emphatically horizontal.

When Corbett's charcoal drawings were included in one of the early group shows of the New York

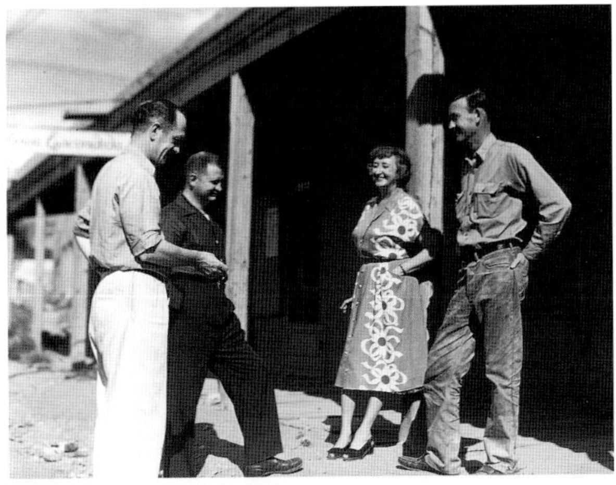
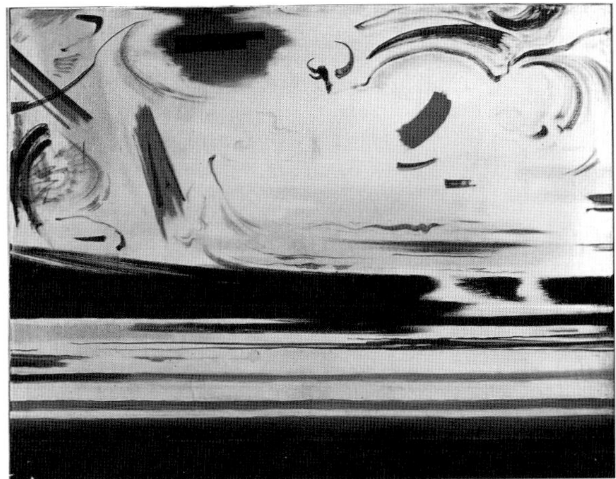
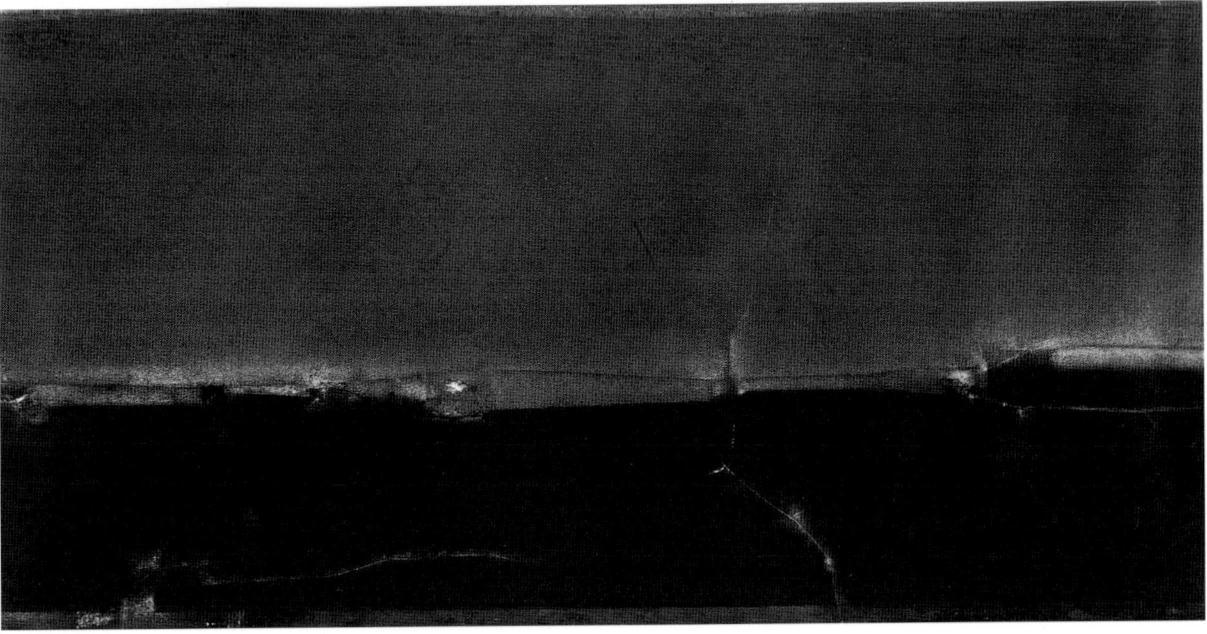

Figure 5.1

Top, left: Clay Spohn, Ad Reinhardt, Eulalia Emetaz, and
Edward Corbett (*left to right*), in front of La Galeria
Escondida, ca. 1952. The Harwood Foundation Museum, Taos,
New Mexico. Mildred Tolbert Collection. Photographer:
Mildred Tolbert.

Figure 5.2

Top, right: Clay Spohn, *Ballet of the Elements,* 1951. Oil on
canvas, 58 × 72½ in. Collection, David Beasley.

Figure 5.3

Above: Edward Corbett, *New Mexico #34,* 1954. Charcoal,
conté crayon, and crayon, 13⅝ × 26¹/₁₆ in. Collection, Hirshhorn
Museum and Sculpture Garden, Smithsonian Institution, gift
of Joseph H. Hirshhorn, 1966.

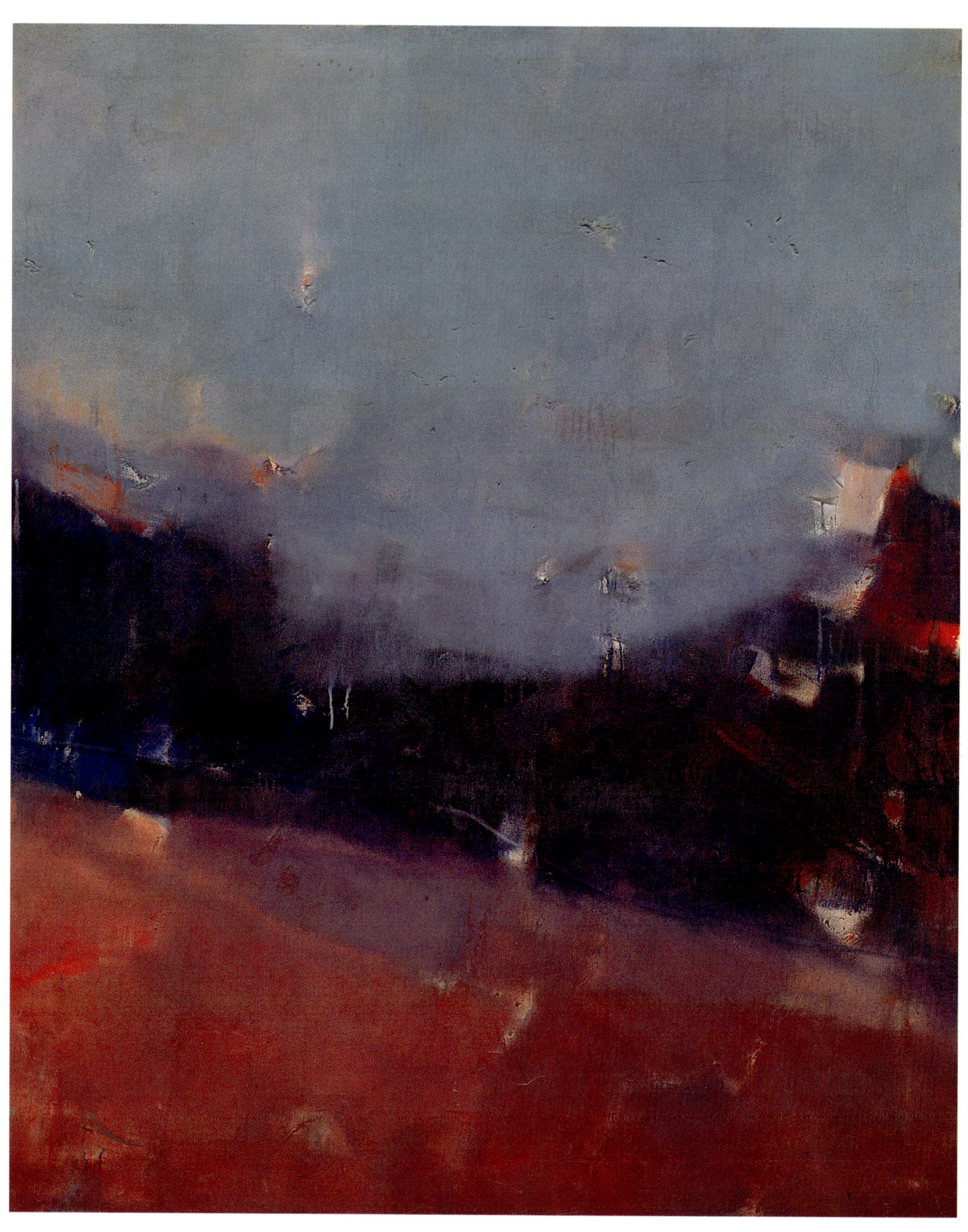

Figure 5.4
Edward Corbett, *Provincetown II,* 1958. Oil on canvas,
56½ × 45 in. Private collection.

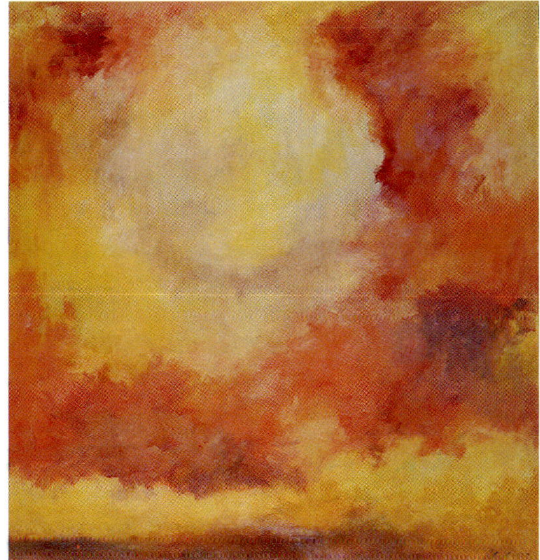

School at the Museum of Modern Art in 1952, they received much critical acclaim. Thomas Hess called Corbett "the most interesting new artist in the show."[16] As a result of the exhibition at MOMA, he was invited to join the artists represented by the Borgenicht Gallery and met Pollock, Kline, and de Kooning. But while he felt a sense of camaraderie with some of these artists, friends recall his resentment of the self-promotional tactics required for survival in New York, resentment he dramatically expressed by refusing to sit for a portrait of the New York School.[17] Instead of staying in New York, Corbett took a position at Mount Holyoke College in Massachusetts in 1953, where he produced a series of white-on-white abstractions appropriately titled *Paintings for Puritans* and, toward the end of the decade, turned to a group of sumptuously radiant abstractions (fig. 5.4).

Three of Still's most devoted students, Briggs, Jon Schueler, and Dugmore, who found New York more sympathetic than Corbett did, were among the few CSFA artists who followed their teacher and developed flourishing careers. All three signed on with the Stable Gallery, an important showcase for new talent in the 1950s. Although Irving Sandler and B. H. Friedman have classified them as members of the second-generation New York School,[18] they never fully shed their identities as San Francisco artists. Indeed, their contemporaries in Manhattan generally viewed them as outsiders.[19] Even Still—who has since become a full-fledged member of the New York School by most accounts—was considered a San Francisco painter in New York art circles. Such branding was

sometimes derogatory, as when Hans Hofmann called Briggs and Dugmore "Stillites," a term that quickly caught on among Tenth Street artists. In part, the segregation persisted because Dugmore, Briggs, Schueler, and Still maintained what amounted to a San Francisco colony in New York. Still was particularly insular; after 1953, he dissociated himself from the New York artists for their overly "practical" concerns and communicated mostly with his colleagues from San Francisco.[20]

This clannishness affected the character of their painting; as a group, Still's circle shared a common ideology and an aesthetic vocabulary distinct from artistic developments in New York. Paradoxically, their painting was less influenced by Tenth Street "action painting" than that of many artists who remained in California, such as Diebenkorn and John Saccaro.

Schueler, the first to follow Still to New York in 1951, was alone in deriving much that was meaningful from New York gesture painting during the 1950s. By his own account, his work in San Francisco amounted to little more than student exercises, but after arriving in New York, he began formulating the *Sky* series that continued to be his consuming subject.[21] The first of these paintings recall his nighttime bombing missions during the war, when he piloted B-17s in the Atlantic theater. Drawing from the San Francisco black painting genre, they are entirely black except for flashes of hot color suggesting bomb trajectories. After the mid-1950s, Schueler lightened his palette to include silvery blues, pinks, and yellows, and softened his brushwork to suggest vapor expanding in all directions (fig. 5.5).

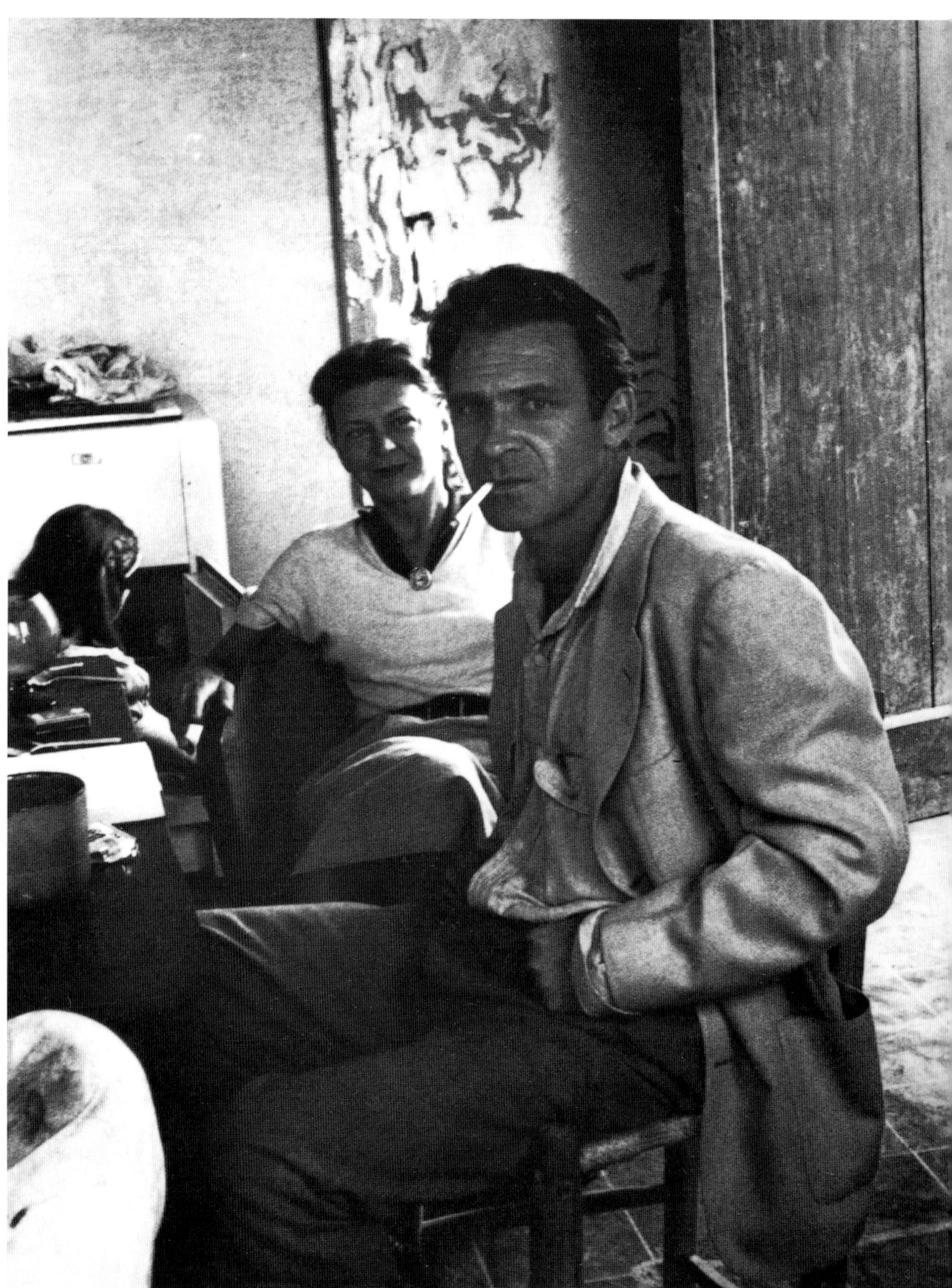

Figure 5.6

Opposite: Edward and Eadie Dugmore, Mexico, ca. 1951–52. Photographer: Naomi Williams.

Figure 5.7

Left: Edward Dugmore, *#30,* 1952. Oil on canvas, 91¼ × 59¾ in. Collection, Linda Dugmore Shannon.

The cloud studies of Turner, which he first saw in a CSFA class with Still, were an important inspiration for these paintings.[22]

Dugmore (fig. 5.6) never made explicit references to nature as Schueler did, although he often evoked an earthy organicism in much the same vein as Still's. Dugmore's work was generally lighter and more linear than that of most other painters at the California School of Fine Arts. His one-man show at the Metart Galleries in 1950 displayed soft washes enlivened with slashing strokes of vibrant color. Echoing the work of Stillman, Dixon, and others, some of these paintings featured the pronounced vertical dimensions of Asian hanging scrolls.[23]

Before leaving San Francisco in 1951 to take up residence in Mexico, Dugmore flattened and simplified his color areas and reduced his dependence upon line. Some of these early paintings, with their liquid planes of shifting color and ambiguous geometry, anticipate Dugmore's later canvases of the 1950s.[24] In Mexico, where Dugmore studied at the University of Guadalajara from 1951 to 1952, he continued along the same lines, often working in shades of brown and black (fig. 5.7). These paintings and his subsequent New York canvases often came closer to the San Francisco parched-earth aesthetic than anything he produced in California. As Dore Ashton observed, Dugmore's paintings consistently drew sustenance from the West Coast tradition of "huge flat forms that seem to spread indefinitely into space."[25]

At Dugmore's urging, Briggs moved to New York in 1953, but not without first making a name for himself in San Francisco. Briggs made his West Coast debut with the opening one-person show of the Metart Galleries in the spring of 1949. The exhibition was eclectic—some paintings consisted of allover compositions of shimmering units in the manner of Tobey, while others showed the influence of Matta, Rothko, and Still. Frankenstein gave the show a favorable review, noting that for Briggs

> painting seems to be a process of thoughtful, ruminative adventure. Unlike many of his colleagues in idiom, he does not repeat himself. Each of his canvases strikes in a different direction, but most of them are admirably consistent and well integrated; if you think this type of painting invariably means an unleashed and unconsidered flinging of brushes and pigment, take a good, long look at Briggs and learn your error.[26]

Frankenstein's use of the term "meditative" was especially appropriate for Briggs, who was a longtime devotee of Asian art and philosophy. He was also disinclined toward the exuberant physicality of "action painting," especially as it was practiced by New York's second generation.[27] Like Still and Dugmore, Briggs preferred a more studied approach. It is significant, too, that all three regarded highly the tradition of craftsmanship in oil painting. None of them used commercial housepaint, and each took satisfaction in grinding and mixing pigments from scratch.[28]

Around 1953, Briggs's work began to take the form that would characterize his painting for the remainder of the decade. That year, in a joint exhibition at the California Palace of the Legion of Honor, Briggs showed several oils worked with a palette knife—some in grisaille with spare touches of jewel-like color, others with strident combinations of red, black, yellow, and sienna. Many of these paintings suggested dynamic natural forces at work, alluding to geological processes through patterns reminiscent of rocky veins and fissures (fig. 5.8). Recognizing this aspect of Briggs's work, Lawrence Ferlinghetti wrote:

> There is a depth and a dynamism in Ernest Briggs' non-objective painting such as is seldom seen in these parts. His work is not of the non-objective kind that seems to be an "explosion" on canvas. His paintings have, rather, a feeling of flood and sway, of a pouring of forces and tensions across the canvas field. It is as if, to use a slightly mixed metaphor, there were a great wind blowing through all his painting. There is a kind of dynamism here which gives the effect of living, abstract gesture.[29]

Although Briggs never returned to California after moving to New York in 1953, he continued to maintain a strong artistic presence in San Francisco, with a solo show at the California School of Fine Arts in 1956.

Robert McChesney, Philip Roeber, Jack Jefferson, and Ronald Bladen were among the San Francisco artists who opted to live and work on the West Coast rather than travel abroad or move to New York in the early 1950s. Jefferson and Roeber both chose to work in virtual isolation, avoiding publicity and declining involvement with profit-making galleries—a stance Roeber continues to maintain in his remote retreat in northern Maine. And Bladen, although he would make a name for himself as a sculptor in New York after moving there in 1956, also kept his distance from the commercial gallery scene. He showed his work on occasion in the alternative artist-run spaces such as King Ubu and the Six, but was more closely associated with the literary underground and with Kenneth Rexroth's anarchist circle than he was with any of the artists' groups in the North Beach and Fillmore districts.

A native of Vancouver, Bladen initially painted abstractions that were quiet and meditative, somewhat akin to the works of Orientalizing mysticism by such painters of the Pacific Northwest as Kenneth Callahan and especially Morris Graves. During the war, while studying at the California School of Fine Arts, Bladen became interested in theosophy and Symbolist poetry. Paintings such as *The Descent* (ca. 1946; fig. 5.9), with its gentle radiance and occult imagery, recall the work of Blake, Redon, and Ryder.

The precise chronology is unclear, but sometime in the mid-1950s, while sharing a house on Scott Street with the poet Michael McClure, Bladen began painting the Abstract Expressionist works for which he is best known: the "mound paintings," as they came to be called. These paintings grew to be as much as four inches thick after Bladen managed to obtain half a dozen or so drums of free paint from the storehouse of the Museum of Modern Art in New York. After that, he approached his work like a mason, using spatulas and sometimes two-by-fours to apply his gritty stucco-like pigment in great slabs.[30] He credited Still as his greatest inspiration,[31] and many paintings exhibit Still's "control of the corners," to borrow Richard Brilliant's phrase.[32] The arrangement of shapes around a central void in works such as *Untitled* (ca. 1958; fig. 5.10) originated with Still and became a hallmark of the San Francisco School. Some of Bladen's paintings also contain hints of California

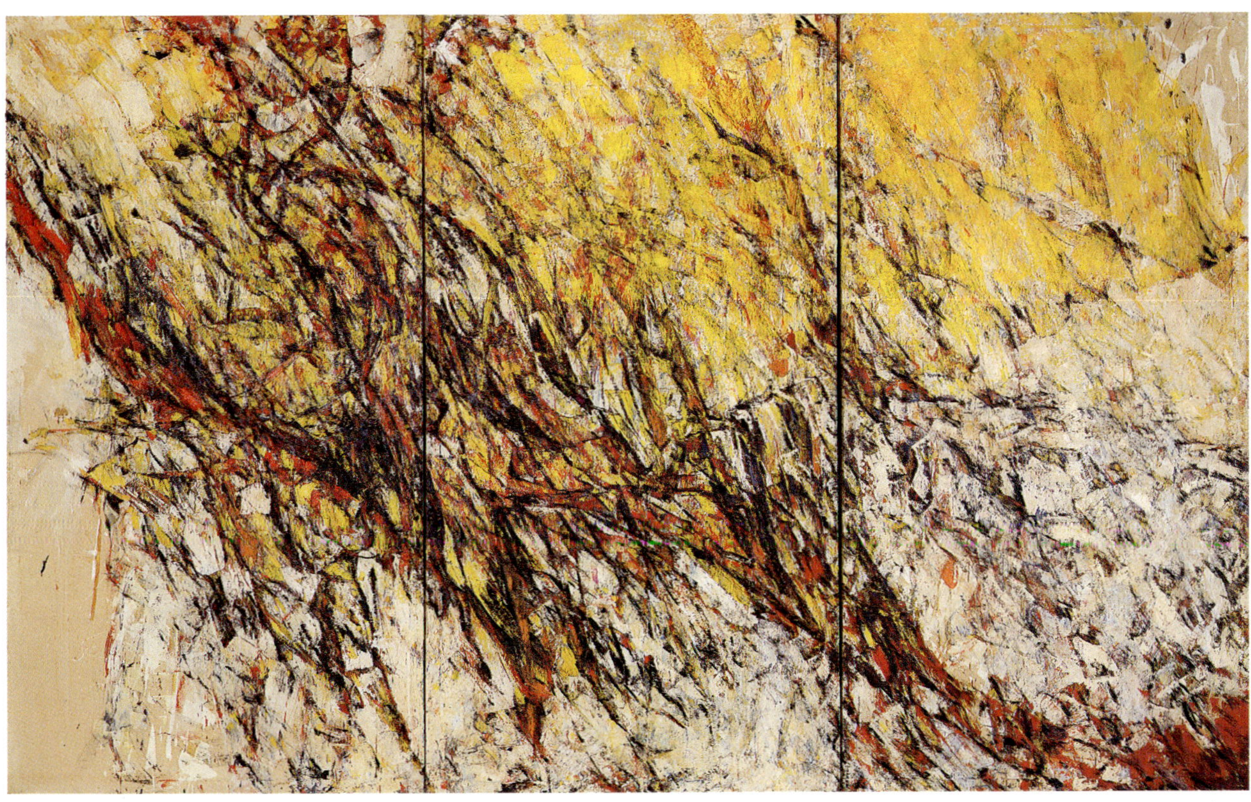

Figure 5.8

Above: Ernest Briggs, *Untitled I, II, III,* 1954. Oil on canvas, 96 × 150 in. Photograph courtesy, Anita Shapolsky Gallery, New York. Photographer: Jos van der Hamsvoord.

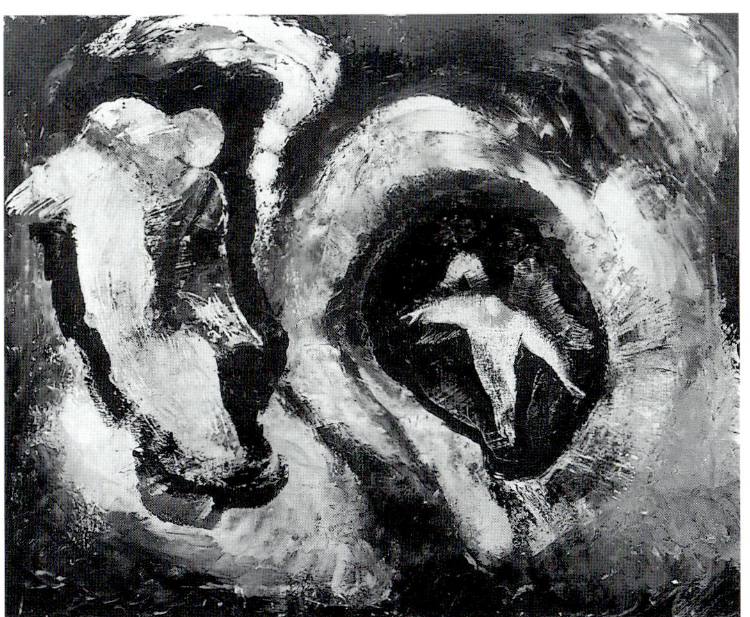

Figure 5.9

Left: Ronald Bladen, *The Descent,* ca. 1946. Oil on canvas, 25¼ × 30¼ in. Collection, Barbara Bladen Porter. Photograph courtesy, San Francisco Museum of Modern Art; photographer: Ben Blackwell.

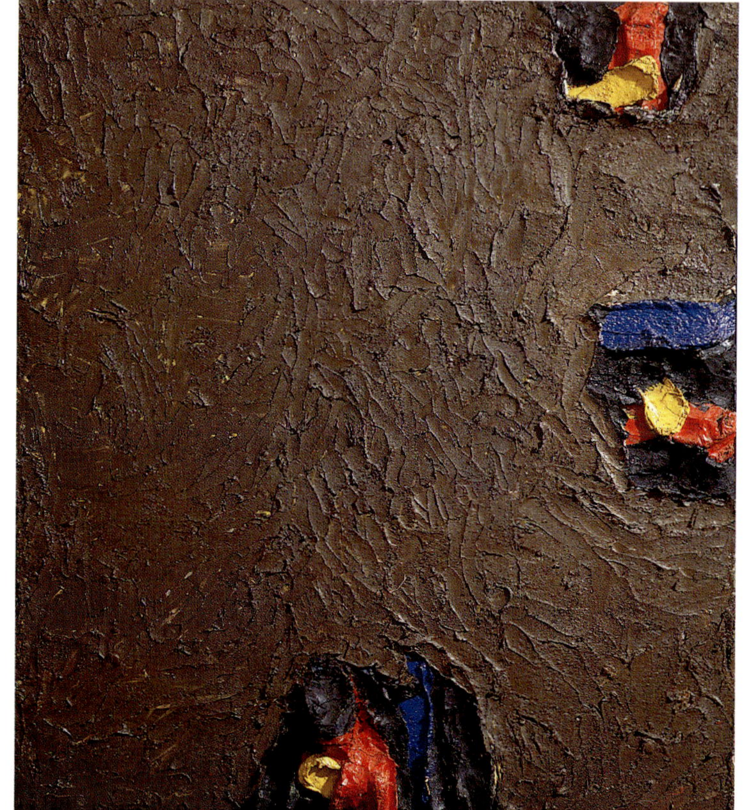

landscape; his *Untitled* (ca. 1956–59; see fig 1.13) for example, calls to mind Diebenkorn's *Berkeley* abstractions (see figs. 1.16, 5.31, 5.32).

Roeber had studied with Still at the California School of Fine Arts, but having been born in 1913, he was older than most of his fellow students and had had a career as an actor and poet. His painting of the late 1940s and early 1950s was often dark and forbidding, inspired by the dream imagery of Blake, Shelley, and other Romantic poets.[33] It ranged from the twisted, ghostly forms of *Abstraction* (ca. 1952) to the smoky evanescence of *Untitled* (1950; see fig. 3.9), which reveals Roeber's debt to his teacher and good friend Corbett. Like Corbett, Roeber was capable of exceeding refinement without becoming precious or decorative. He was best known for his extraordinary handling of collage. Works such as *Untitled* (1958; fig. 5.11), with their finely calibrated balance of ruggedness and subtlety—sooty, pockmarked surfaces combined with soft pinks and delicate patches of sgraffito —led Robert Motherwell to call Roeber "possibly the finest collagist in the country."[34]

Jefferson, like Roeber, initially gravitated toward a rather grim and unforgiving vision. As a CSFA student in the late 1940s, Jefferson had become one of Still's closest friends and confidants. Like Still, he was raised on the Great Plains of the Dakotas, which may have contributed to his strong identification with the harshness of Still's painting, especially the raw, earthen colors of the mid to late 1940s. Jefferson's own palette was similar, with a good deal of brown, ocher, and black—prairie colors, in Jefferson's estimate. But his paint handling was more complex than Still's. Whereas Still tended to work in broad, flat planes, Jefferson liked to create multiple layers of paint, sometimes with threads of color interwoven densely like fabric.

When Jefferson enrolled at the California School of Fine Arts in 1946 after serving in the U.S. Marines, he was working in a semi-Surrealist vein, largely under the influence of De Chirico. His first efforts in nonobjective painting came in 1947, after he had met Lobdell, Anderson, and Briggs, who would remain his closest associates. Jefferson's work

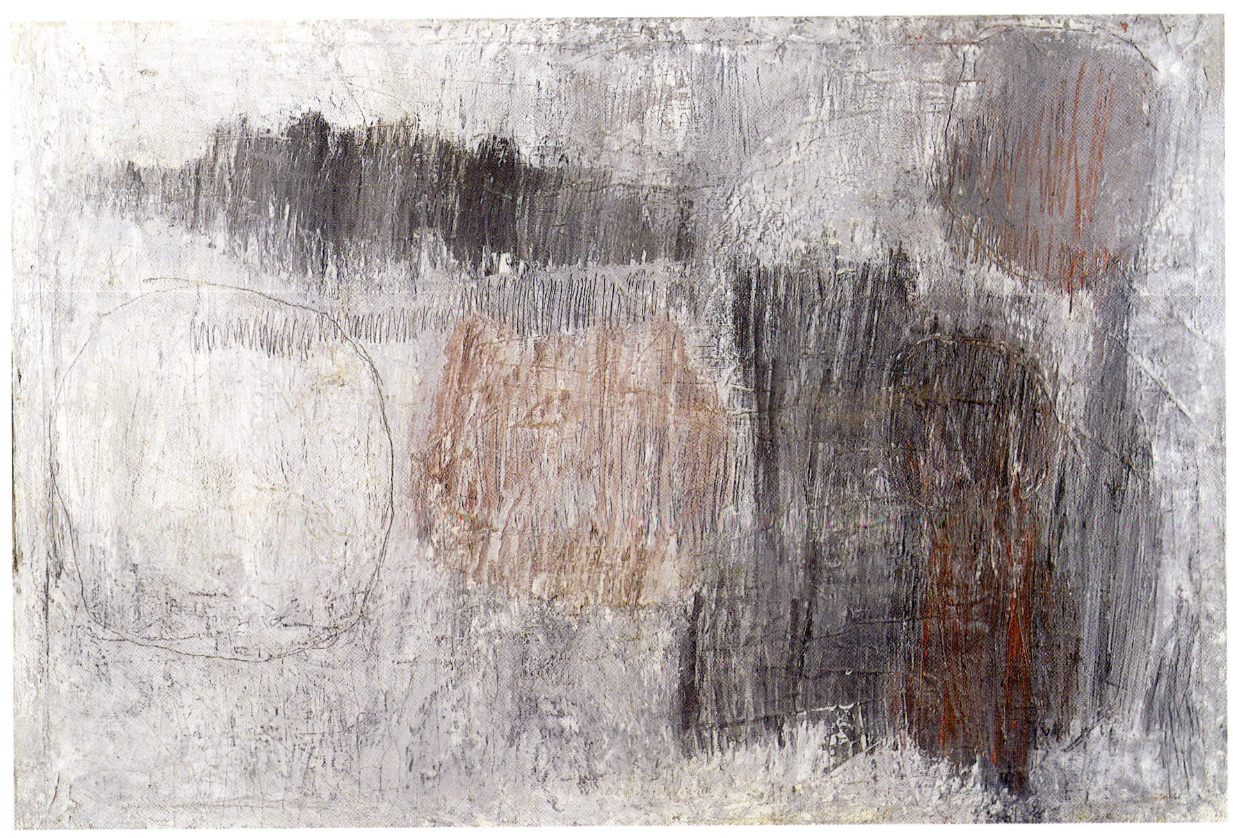

of the late 1940s and early 1950s bears a resemblance to some of Roeber's paintings of the period, with narrow shafts of light emanating from behind a dark screen.

For a brief time in the early 1950s, Jefferson took an interest in the painting of Bradley Walker Tomlin, adopting a rugged version of Tomlin's hooking ribbon motif (see fig. 3.21). By the mid-1950s, however, he had begun to develop the imagery best associated with him: the faint glimmers of form that seem to spread laterally or ascend gradually to the upper reaches of the canvas.[35] Albright vividly describes the enigmatic drama of these works:

> [Jefferson's forms] seem to be locked in an intense struggle to assert themselves as organisms, on the one hand, and, on the other, to resist the appearance of human forms; hence the intense, if understated, tension of these paintings, with their thick-skinned surfaces; evocative shapes that swim in and out of porous, amorphous color areas; and uningratiating, drab or hot and astringent, colors.[36]

Jefferson's *Mission #20* of 1957 (fig. 5.12) exemplifies the work Albright described. A deep blue-black wall of paint is penetrated only by slivered forms that appear to grope their way upward. Although the painting's title, which is repeated in works throughout the late 1950s and early 1960s, refers to Jefferson's studio in the Audiffred Building on Mission Street, one might also surmise that the "mission" of Jefferson's organisms is a metaphor for the artist's own internal quest and, by extension, the spiritual quest of humankind.

Jefferson's inclination toward an essentially romantic vision of painting was shared by his contemporary Robert McChesney, who also explored the expressive possibilities of shadowy, penumbral forms. But McChesney took his cue primarily from nature, from such phenomena as the shimmering heat of the desert or the ripple of moonlight on water. Compared with the epic drama of Jefferson, McChesney's paintings of the 1950s seem poetic and lyrical, with a quiet sense of mystery much like that of Corbett.

Although he had been active in San Francisco's art

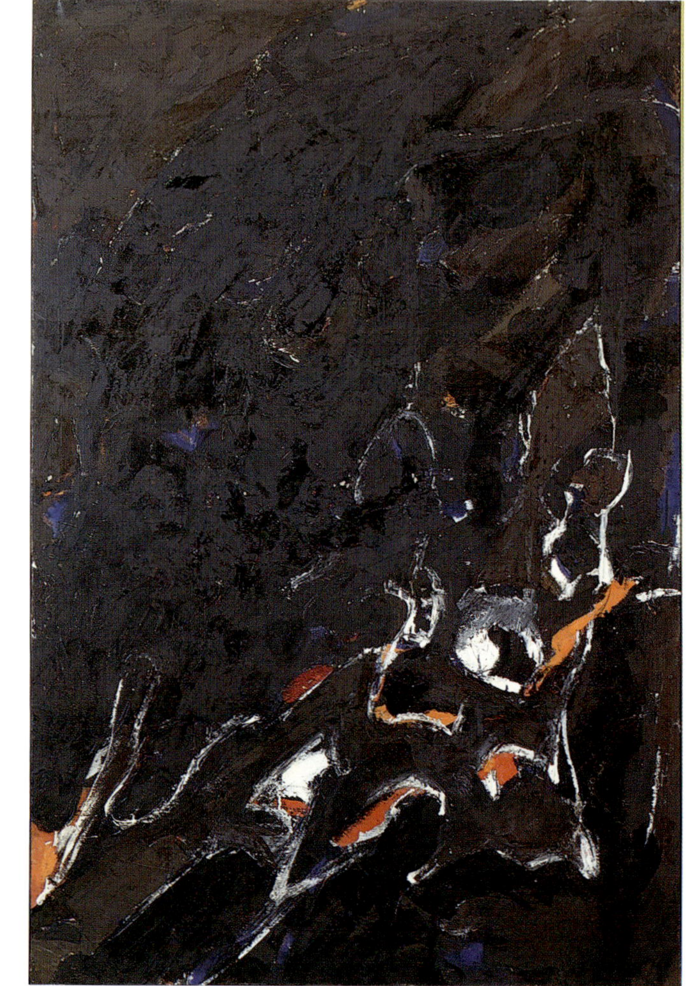

Figure 5.12

Right: Jack Jefferson, *Mission #20,* 1957. Oil on canvas, 77 × 50 in. Collection, David and Bernadette Packard. Photograph courtesy, Gallery Paule Anglim, San Francisco.

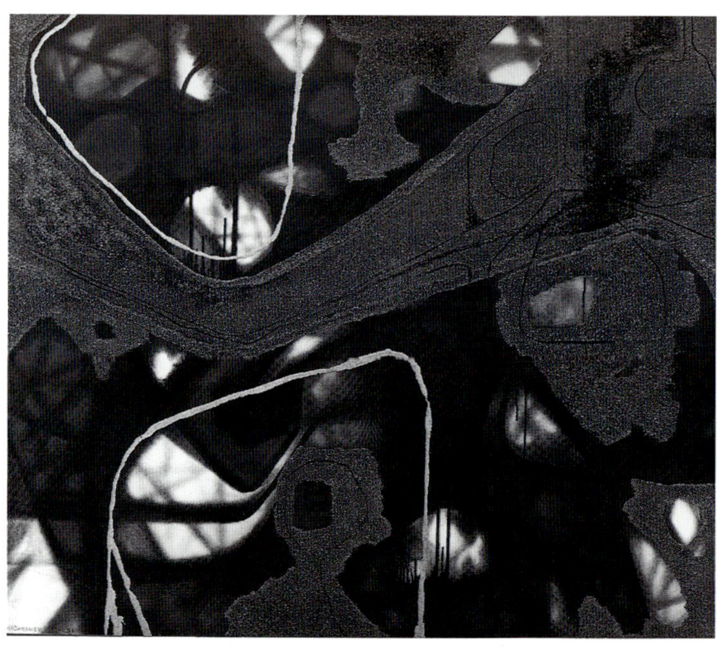

Figure 5.13

Below: Robert McChesney, *A-7,* 1951. Enamel and sand on canvas, 42 × 48 in. Collection of the artist. Photographer: F. W. Quandt.

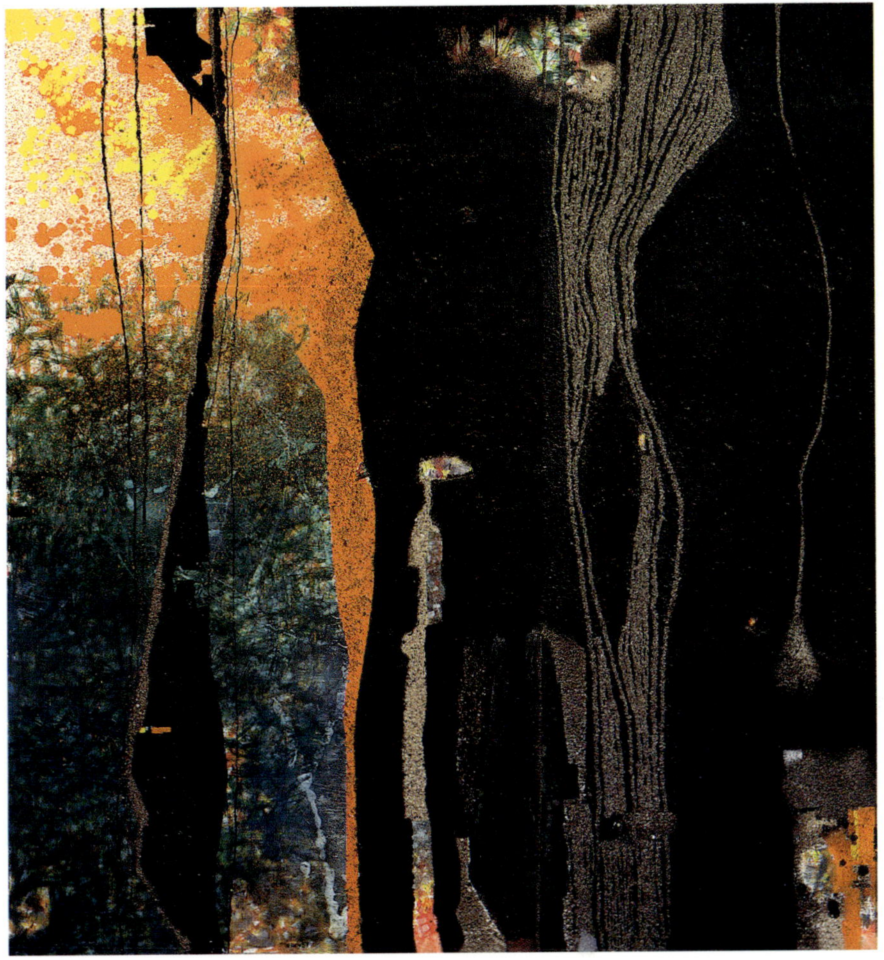

Figure 5.14

Robert McChesney, *Arena #1,* 1958. Enamel and sand on canvas, 60 × 54 in. Collection, Thelma Faltus. Photographer: M. Lee Fatherree.

community since 1938, McChesney was a relative late-comer to Abstract Expressionism. Until 1950, he worked in a stylized form of hard-edge abstraction that owed something to the South Sea Islander art he had seen in the merchant marine, and something to the abstract Surrealism of Charles Howard. While living with Corbett and Smith in Point Richmond from 1950 to 1951, McChesney executed his first expressive nonobjective works, a group of sand and enamel paintings with fluid linear designs emerging from murky depths (fig. 5.13).[37] These were followed in late 1951 and 1952 by a group of paintings he produced in Mexico by soaking paint directly into unsized canvas, a process similar to Helen Frankenthaler's subsequent staining technique (see fig. 1.15).

McChesney's work received a good deal of critical acclaim in San Francisco during the 1950s. Frankenstein emerged as his ardent supporter with a series of reviews in the *San Francisco Chronicle* and *Art in America.*[38] In 1959 Frankenstein pronounced McChesney the undisputed "master" of Bay Area

abstraction, an individualist who nonetheless worked well within San Francisco's tradition of "sublime" abstraction.[39] Reviewing McChesney's *Mountain* series, named after the artist's residence on Sonoma Mountain, Frankenstein wrote of the paintings' "illuminated depths of incalculable distance." Their effect, he wrote, "is one of flux and light, with long black lines moving like rivers through the coloristic cloud pools, lending form to their flow, and carrying it outward far beyond the confines of the frame."[40] Frankenstein's words aptly describe McChesney's work of the late 1950s and 1960s, such as his *Arena* (Spanish for "sand") series, a group of abstractions that exploit the granular texture of sand while evoking the undulating dunes of the desert (fig. 5.14).

Frankenstein may have favored McChesney, but the artists who made the most impact on newcomers to the movement were Smith, Lobdell, and Diebenkorn. Smith and Diebenkorn had the imprimatur of teaching at the California School of Fine Arts in its heyday, and Lobdell was among the school's star students. All three had been central to the Abstract Expressionist movement since the late 1940s, and Smith and Diebenkorn had maintained a strong Bay Area presence through exhibitions of their work.

Hassel Smith, 1948–60

Hassel Smith joined the Abstract Expressionist movement somewhat later than many of his colleagues at the California School of Fine Arts. By Smith's account, his first nonobjective paintings were the result of an overnight conversion after seeing Still's exhibition at the Legion of Honor in 1947: "There's no secret about it," he later explained in an interview. "I just got sick and tired of what I was doing and I liked what these other guys were doing so I decided to see if I could do something like that. Just like that. It was conscious and overnight, based on an overnight decision really. I stopped doing one thing and started doing something else."[41]

But Smith's break with abstraction was not quite as sudden as his account would suggest. Jorge Goya, among others, observed that Smith was initially opposed to Still and his work.[42] Smith's first efforts in abstract painting were not until 1948—a year after Still's exhibition—and throughout the late 1940s and into the 1950s he continued to paint an occasional fig-

urative canvas. Works such as *Untitled (Abstraction)* (1948; fig. 5.15), with its improvised mix of figuration and abstraction, show that Smith went through a transitional phase before making a decisive shift to nonrepresentational painting.

That shift was evident in the paintings Smith showed in a joint exhibition at the San Francisco Museum of Art with Bischoff and Park in the summer of 1948. These canvases, known as the "beast paintings," as much for the ferocity of the brushwork as for their reptilian and insectile imagery, placed Smith in the company of a number of artists in San Francisco, including Diebenkorn, Stillman, and Kuhlman, who also incorporated menacingly spiky forms in their work.

The "beast paintings" constituted a brief episode in Smith's restless career of the late 1940s and early 1950s. From around 1948 to 1953, his work ranged from broad, shaggy color masses to the calligraphic profusion of such paintings as *Little Big Horn* (1953; see fig. 3.17). Many of Smith's canvases from this period feature the dirty, fuscous colors typical of the San Francisco School. For some paintings, Smith applied his paint in lumpy, almost scatological, smears to match a decidedly unappealing mud and vanilla palette. Smith was quite outspoken about his desire to keep his paintings from being appropriated by the art market. As a loyal Marxist, Smith felt that

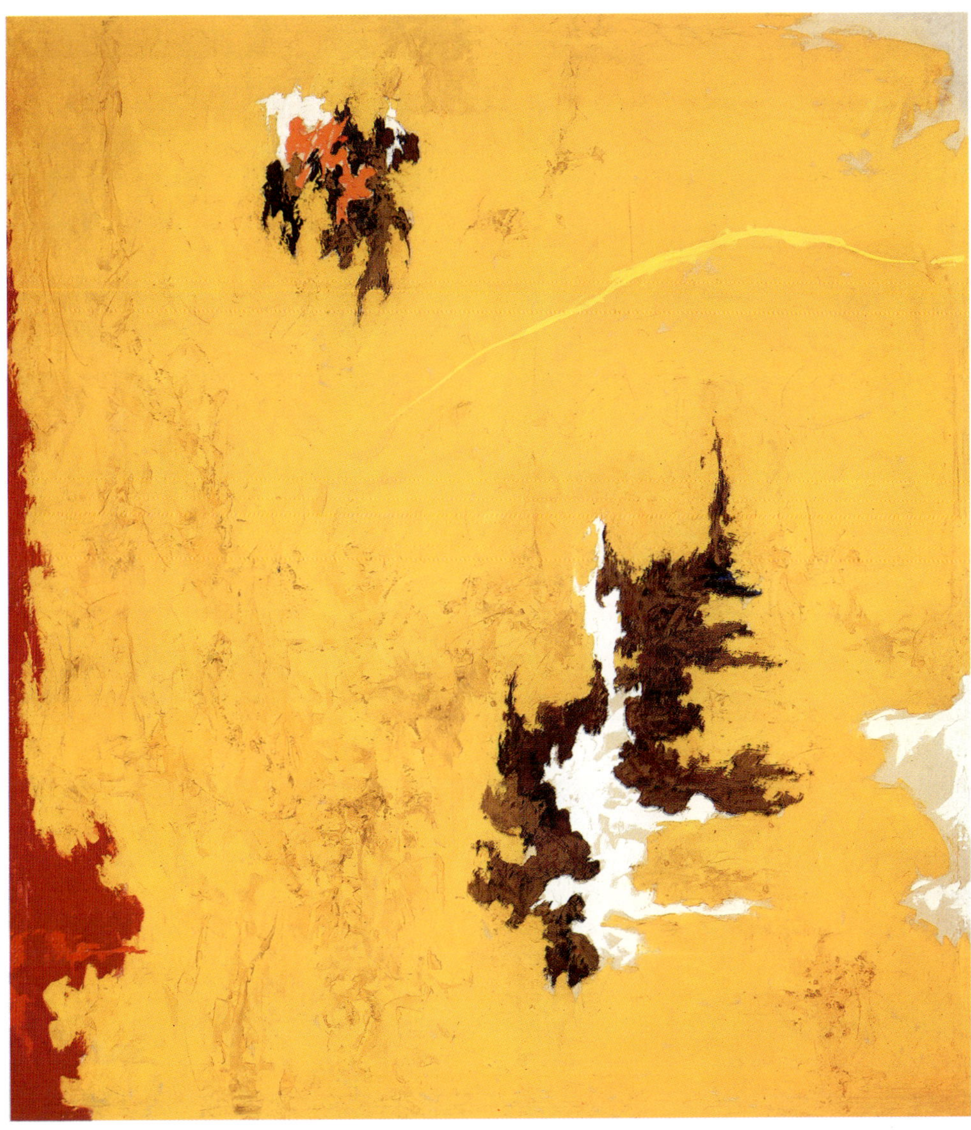

art could never escape its essential social responsibility.[43] "His images were an explosive attack against the materialism of capitalist society," said the collagist Jess, who knew Smith well.[44] In his effort to sabotage materialistic values, Smith intended some paintings to literally self-destruct. At the end of the 1940s, he allegedly painted an entire series of canvases using pigments mixed only with turpentine.[45] These works, like most of his proto-Funk sculptures of 1950 and 1951 made entirely from refuse, have, for obvious reasons, not survived.[46]

A vehement antimaterialism allied Smith closely with Still, the artist Smith credits with having converted him to abstraction. Smith professed an undying allegiance to Still throughout the 1950s and kept one of the older artist's paintings hanging prominently in his house on Potrero Hill. But while he absorbed a good deal from Still's rough-hewn planes and reductive palette, Smith transformed these borrowings into a sensibility very much his own. The transformation is nowhere more evident than in a comparison between the painting by Still that hung in Smith's home (fig. 5.16) and Smith's *Tiptoe Down to Art* (1950; fig. 5.17). Both feature broad expanses of golden yellow, but while Still creates awe-inspiring grandeur, Smith's cartoonish imagery and tongue-in-cheek title irreverently undermine any preconceptions of high art. Still's unrelenting seriousness was often the butt of Smith's jokes. In *Alone with the Killer* of 1948 (see fig. 1.7), for example, Smith paro-

died the fearsome imagery of Still's early crutch and orb paintings.[47]

In 1955 Smith purchased a small apple orchard north of San Francisco, in Sebastopol, where he kept his studio for the next six years. There many of the tendencies evident since the late 1940s began to coalesce into a single recognizable style. The flat masses of shaggy color, still very much in evidence, were now considerably lighter and airier, with less of the intentional coarseness of his earlier *faux-gauche* efforts. Smith's use of line underwent a similar evolution, from the wildly uncontrolled tangles of *Little Big Horn* (1953; see fig. 3.17) to the taut calligraphy of *The Triumph of Gargoylism* (1957; fig. 5.18).

As disciplined as these new works were, they retained much of Smith's former kinesthetic enthusiasm; indeed, because of their lightning-fast draftsmanship the critic Allan Temko called them Smith's "thunderbolt" paintings.[48] Temko noted the propensity of these paintings toward "flying phalli, or something very much like them, spurting ambiguously through wide bursts of color."[49] In works such as *Blue Meets Bloy* (1956–57; fig. 5.19) this allusion is inescapable. Because many of Smith's works of the late 1950s suggest such erotic imagery as buttocks and breasts, critics compared them to the visceral hybrids of Gorky and de Kooning. For his part, Smith has denied any direct influence of these artists.[50] It seems rather, as Diebenkorn has remarked, that Smith's

whiplash line can be traced to his years as a student of Maurice Sterne's.[51] Significantly, both de Kooning and Smith spent many years drawing from the nude, which may well have led to parallel tendencies in their art. But in any case, as Albright observed, if Smith's anatomical notations align him with Gorky and de Kooning, they carry little hint of the New Yorkers' sense of crisis and struggle.[52] "My paintings are intended to be additions to rather than reflections of or upon 'life,'" Smith wrote in 1952.[53] Like Still, Smith wanted his paintings to be affirmative rather than to express the "terrible anxiety" evident in much of the painting of the New York School.[54]

Indeed, as the 1950s advanced, Smith's painting became increasingly exuberant, even joyful. The playfulness that was evident on occasion before 1950 became the overriding characteristic of his work, manifest in titles such as *You, Too, Can Have Lovely Hair* (1953), a reference to the painting's unmanageable linear snarl.[55] Beginning around 1953, Smith began to find absurd titles from such random sources as the daily newspaper, as in *Snubs Money for Love* (1959; fig. 5.20), which came from a tabloid headline.[56] Sometimes his humor was only suggested by graffiti-like scribbles. Like Diebenkorn and Bischoff, Smith was a great admirer of comic strips, and some of his paintings show the whimsical spotting and cross-hatching of cartoon art.

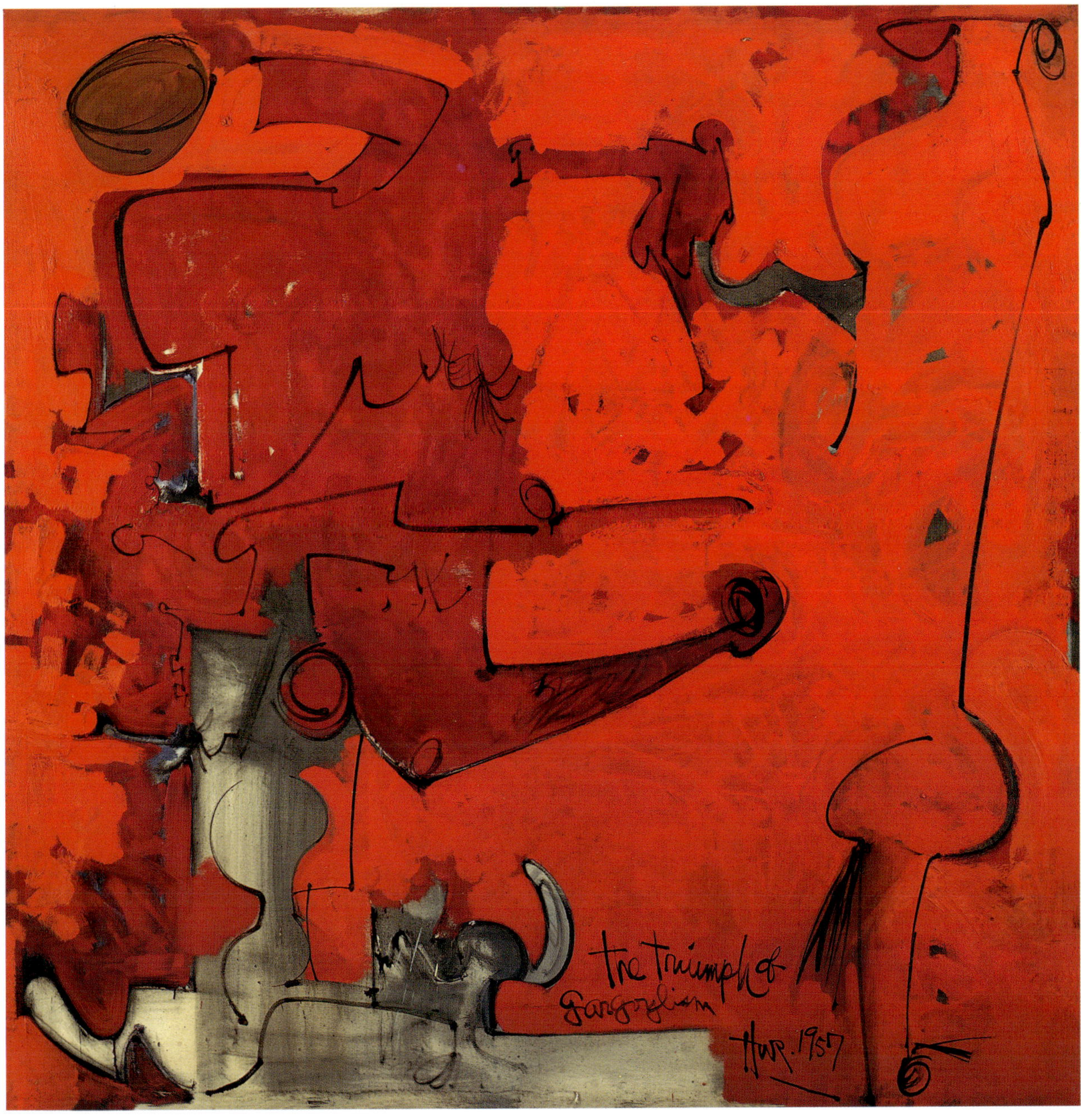

Figure 5.17

Opposite: Hassel Smith, *Tiptoe Down to Art,* 1950. Oil on
canvas, 60 × 96 in. Collection, Norton Simon Museum,
Pasadena, California, gift of Mrs. Sadye J. Moss, 1966.
Photographer: Antoni E. Dolinski.

Figure 5.18

Above: Hassel Smith, *The Triumph of Gargoylism,* 1957. Oil on
canvas, 68 × 68 in. Collection, Gimpel Fils, London.
Photographer: Rodney Todd-White and Son.

Figure 5.19

Right: Hassel Smith, *Blue Meets Bloy,* 1956–57. Oil on canvas, 71¾ × 47¾ in. Private collection. Photograph courtesy, Parkerson Gallery, Houston, Texas; photographer: Rick Gardner.

Figure 5.20

Below: Hassel Smith, *Snubs Money for Love,* 1959. Oil on canvas, 72 × 72 in. Collection, The Museum of Fine Arts, Houston, Texas, gift of Dr. and Mrs. Marc Moldawer.

Figure 5.21

Opposite: Frank Lobdell, Sausalito, ca. 1949. Photographer: George Stillman.

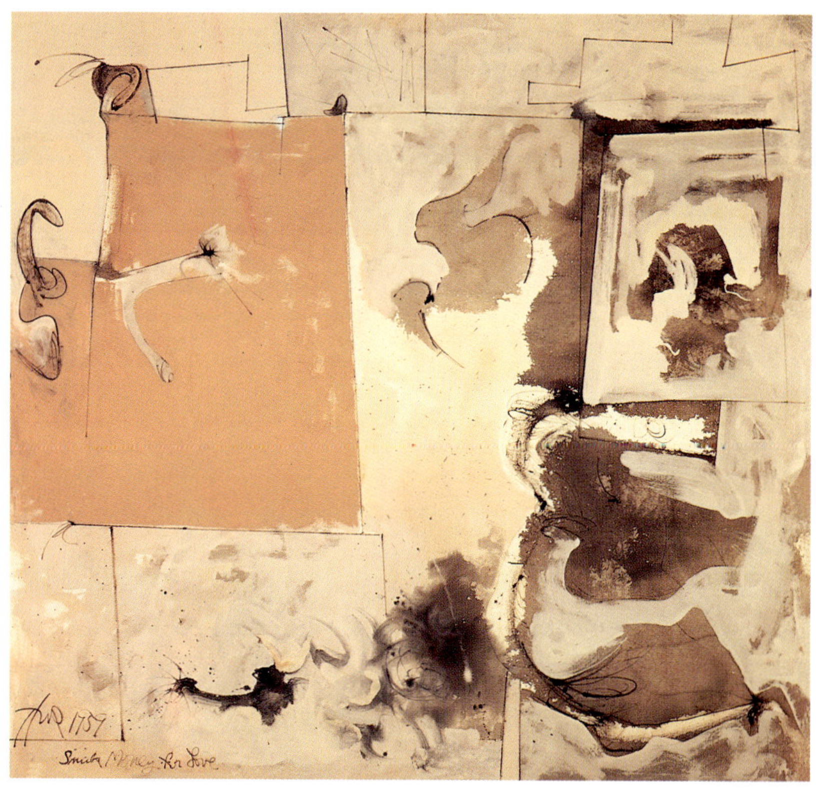

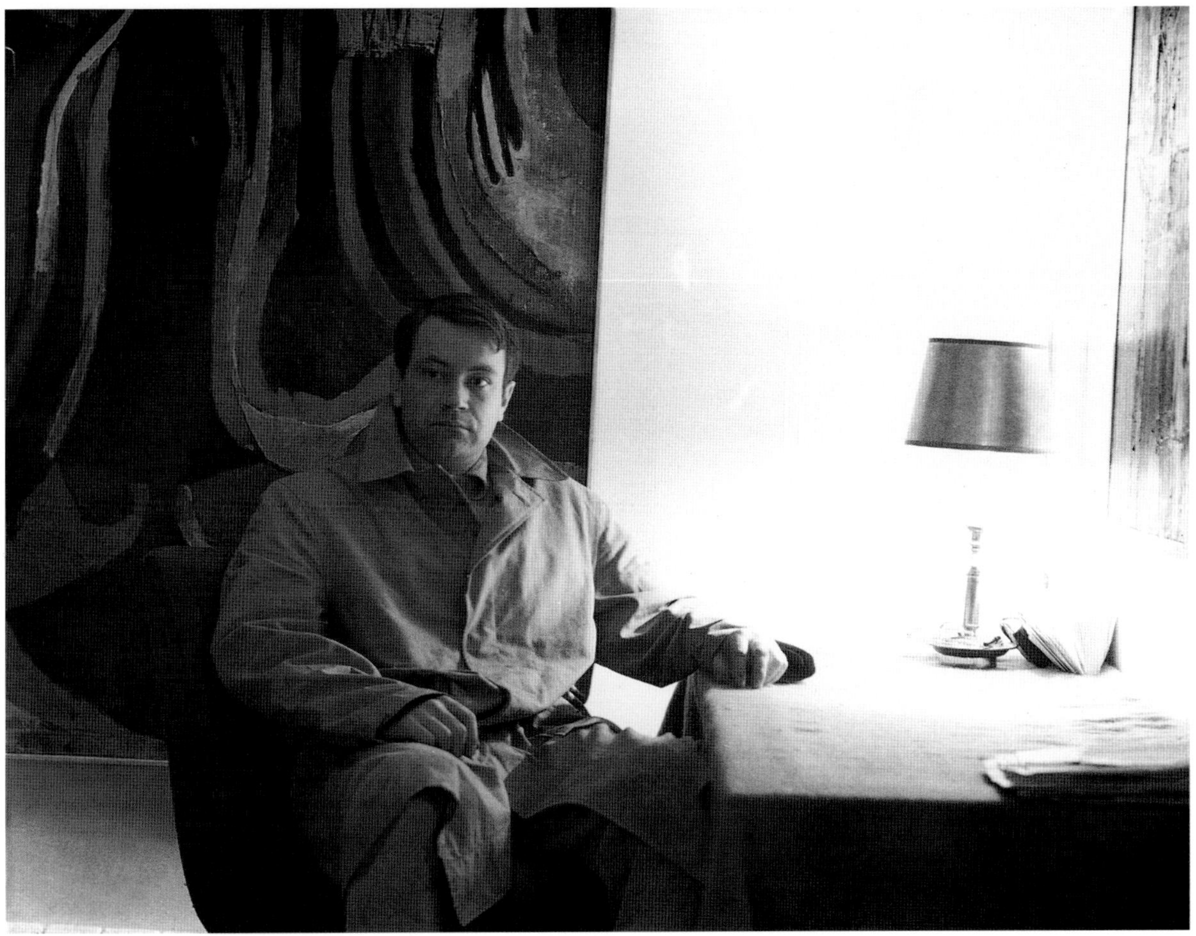

Smith also had a fondness for the silent screen comedians Buster Keaton and Charlie Chaplin, but a more important inspiration came from music, specifically, the energetic Dixieland jazz that became popular in San Francisco during the 1940s. Smith often borrowed his titles from jazz phrases. *Rim Shot* (1959), for example, takes its name from the technique of slamming the metal rim of a snare drum. Borrowing from the cartoonist's vocabulary, Smith's painting makes allusion to the explosion of sound such contact produces, with multiple parallel lines signifying reverberating sound. Smith's work often suggests the boisterous, earthy vitality of jazz artists such as Lu Watters and Bob Scobey, to whom he dedicated several paintings. Smith felt that these musicians, who also included Turk Murphy, Bob Helm, and Wally Rose, were "the real heroes of the 'San Francisco School.'"[57] Certainly, the qualities of their jazz that Smith cited as most significant—virtuoso performance, humor, and cultivated naïveté—are among the salient aspects of his own work.[58]

Frank Lobdell, 1947–62

If Smith's painting epitomizes the witty, energetic, jazz-inspired strain of the San Francisco School, that of Frank Lobdell (fig. 5.21) can be seen as representing an equally compelling inclination toward a dark, introspective, and intensely spiritual art.[59] With their scabrous surfaces and stubborn antagonism to light, Lobdell's paintings could hardly be further removed from the frank sensuality and joie de vivre of Smith's.

Lobdell's fundamentally romantic approach to painting dates back to his years as a student at the St. Paul School of Art in Minnesota, where both he and Kuhlman studied under Cameron Booth. Lobdell remembered Booth, a former student of Hans Hofmann's, as a Regionalist with a rare enthusiasm for

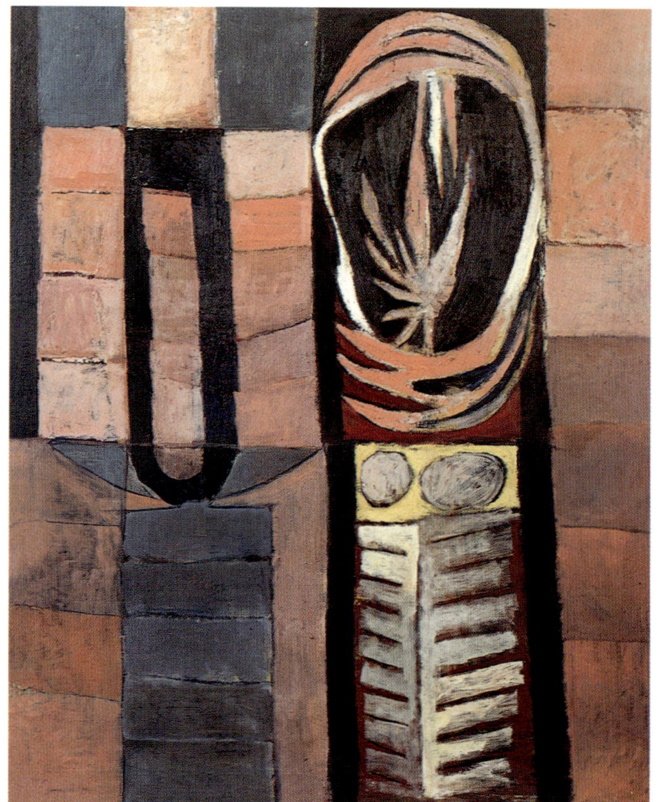

European abstraction. But the Picasso retrospective at the Art Institute of Chicago in 1940 was the pivotal event in Lobdell's early career. After driving through a snowstorm with Kuhlman, Lobdell spent three days absorbing the exhibition, one of them in front of the formidable *Guernica*.[60] "I felt the power of painting to really move," Lobdell recalled of that experience. "I wanted that power, the power to stir emotions as strongly as I was feeling the work I was looking at."[61] While Lobdell was powerfully drawn to Picasso's figurative paintings, the more cerebral Cubist works of the 1910s held little interest for him.

Lobdell's first efforts after the war incorporated motifs drawn from prehistoric cave drawings and early Egyptian sculpture—symbols that would recur in altered form during the 1950s. Some of Lobdell's paintings from this time featured imaginary pictographs in loosened grid compositions somewhat in the manner of contemporary works by Adolph Gottlieb or Joaquín Torres-García, although his acknowledged sources were the later Klee and Miró (fig. 5.22).[62]

Like so many painters attached to the San Francisco movement, Lobdell was deeply impressed by Still's retrospective at the Legion of Honor in 1947. He described the exhibition as a painful revelation. Although he was familiar with the work of Baziotes, Pollock, Rothko, and other future members of the New York School, Still's painting represented the first meaningful challenge to European modernism he had encountered: "I felt my investment was flattened—this raw sensibility was very different from French art . . . I wanted in the worst way to forget it, but I must have seen that show dozens of times."[63] With some reluctance, Lobdell came to feel that the sentimentality of much of the European abstraction he had admired was a cover-up for the harsh reality laid bare by the war. As he later explained, the artist with integrity "can't be content with prettiness when a feeling of turmoil seems most characteristic of our times."[64]

Not long after seeing Still's show, Lobdell dropped his obvious marks of deference to Picasso, Klee, and Miró. Although he credited Still with this newfound independence, it is difficult to trace Still's influence in all but a few examples of Lobdell's work.[65] One notable exception is *November 20, 1948*, in the collection of the Oakland Museum. The painting features the jagged islands of paint typical of Still's work in the late 1940s, and the "dirty color, those Indian reds and siennas, ochers and blacks" that Lobdell singled out as impressing him in Still's show at the Legion of Honor.[66]

More characteristic of this period, however, is Lobdell's *September 3, 1948,* an oil standing more than seven and a half feet tall (fig. 5.23). Composed of twisting lines snaking in and out of a fathomless sea-green expanse, the imagery is disturbing, like that of a good number of Lobdell's paintings. Lobdell seems to have had bones and tendons in mind when he painted the canvas, and the work strongly suggests intestinal coils as well, a connotation that becomes clearer in some of the lithographs Lobdell produced that year.[67]

These images answered Lobdell's call for an art with "substance and guts,"[68] but they also conveyed Lobdell's own nightmarish memories of the war, when as an army lieutenant, he came across scorched and disfigured corpses on the front lines.[69] Caroline Jones, who interviewed Lobdell in 1991–92, related one of his more horrific wartime experiences: "In early April 1944 . . . Lobdell's company entered Gardelegen, a small, prosperous town in eastern Germany. There the Allied troops encountered a stone barn burned by the retreating Nazis, with their prisoners still inside. A corpse's outstretched arm protruded from a chink in the walls, the body within charred beyond recognition."[70]

Although it took Lobdell a number of years to express the horror of that experience, some of it is powerfully communicated in a work of circa 1948 that suggests mangled limbs and an outstretched hand dripping with blood (fig. 5.24). Such imagery characterizes much of Lobdell's output of the late 1940s, although he occasionally digressed into relatively formal exercises in abstraction. Colorful works such as *October 5, 1949* call to mind Rothko's contemporaneous *Multiforms,* which Lobdell admired at the time.[71] But Lobdell's painting has none of the elegance of Rothko's. Instead, he presents us with lopsided squares stacked at a precarious tilt. Never far from suggestive allusion, Lobdell has lined some of their inner contours with small dots, like the steel rivets of military plating. In a related painting from the same year, *September 13, 1949,* these dots metamorphose into gnashing teeth in a headless jaw.

In 1950 Lobdell left the country for Paris, where he enrolled in the Académie de la Grande Chaumière and took a studio in the Académie de la Colarossi. In

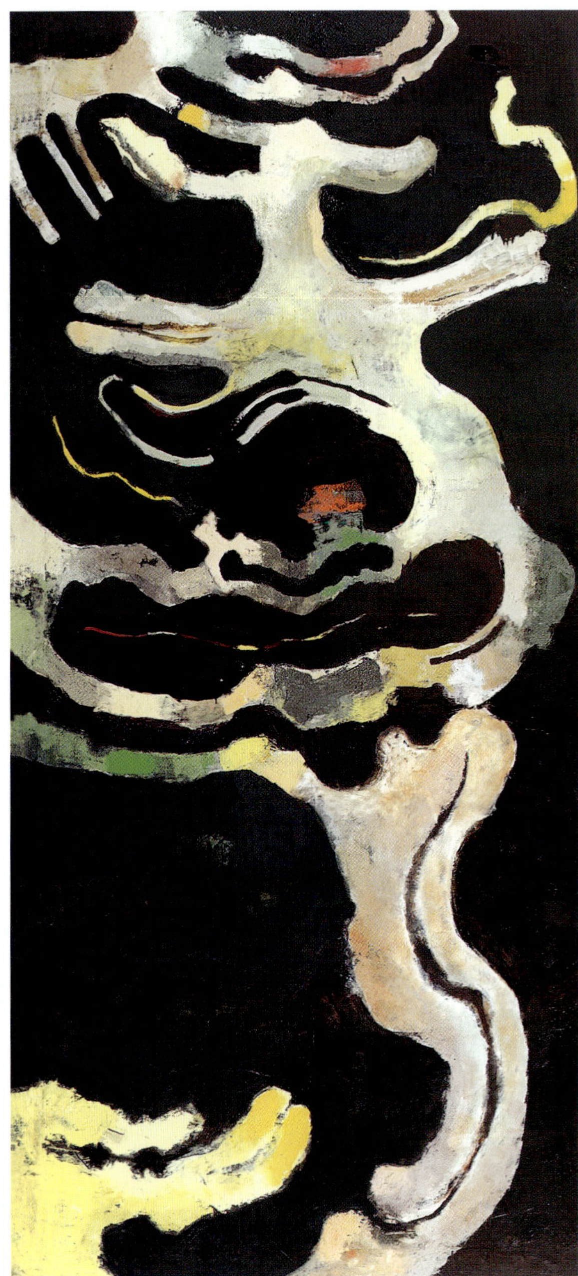

Figure 5.23

Frank Lobdell, *September 3, 1948,* 1948. Oil on canvas, 92½ × 42 in. Photograph courtesy, Campbell-Thiebaud Gallery, San Francisco; photographer: Ira D. Schrank.

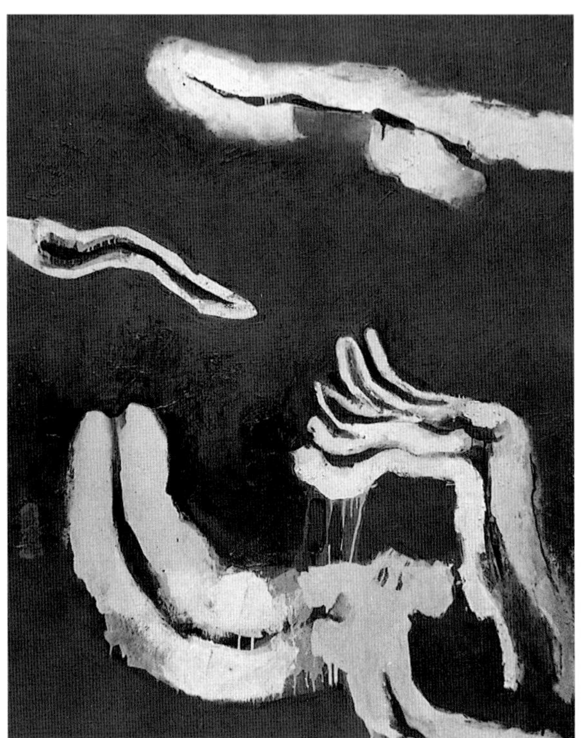

Frank Lobdell, *Untitled* (?), ca. 1948. Oil on canvas, dimensions and whereabouts unknown. Photographer: George Stillman.

Paris, Lobdell exhibited with Kuhlman in one of the earliest displays of American Abstract Expressionism in a French museum, the *6ème Salon des Réalités Nouvelles* at the Petit Palais in 1951. Next to the work of elegant "slide-rule boys" of the School of Paris, that of Lobdell and Kuhlman struck French critics as being in appallingly bad taste.[72] In an epithet that recalls the initial response to the Fauves, French critics dubbed them "wild pigs."[73]

After spending a year in Paris, Lobdell returned to San Francisco and took a studio, first with Briggs and then with Jefferson, in the Audiffred Building at 9 Mission Street. Lobdell's first major effort of the 1950s was a group of paintings done almost entirely in black and white with occasional mixtures of umber, ocher, and burnt sienna, executed during 1953 and 1954. Economics may have been an incentive for the reduced palette—titanium, zinc, and ivory black have long been among the cheapest pigments—but another pressing reason was his need to concentrate on form: "I was fighting for an image and couldn't enjoy the luxury of color," he recalled of the period.[74] *April 1954, Number 1* (fig. 5.25), a painting in this series, contains several motifs that would occupy Lobdell throughout the decade. Heavy, dark lines, which

appear burned into a skin of white paint, look like scratch marks in the lower right-hand corner, but coalesce into a configuration of clutching hands above.[75] A similar motif reappears in the upper center of the painting with the suggestion of a cracked egg, or of interior organs, Lobdell's earlier preoccupation. Much like the early iconography of Still, Lobdell's imagery seems to have evolved gradually out of a searching process in which the artist continually redefined a small vocabulary of emotionally charged, multivalent motifs.

Another painting from the black and white group, *March 1954,* in the collection of the San Francisco Museum of Modern Art, presents a vaguely anthropomorphic shape, suggestive at once of a groping hand and a headless torso rising diagonally across the canvas.[76] The theme of ascension, as we have seen, was explored by a number of artists in San Francisco, notably Jefferson, whose *Mission* series sometimes featured shapes moving in a diagonal trajectory. This was also among Still's most important themes, but in contrast to Still's seemingly confident expansion, Lobdell's forms climb heavily and arduously. As Albright observed, they seem weighted down by a "ponderous existentialist uncertainty."[77]

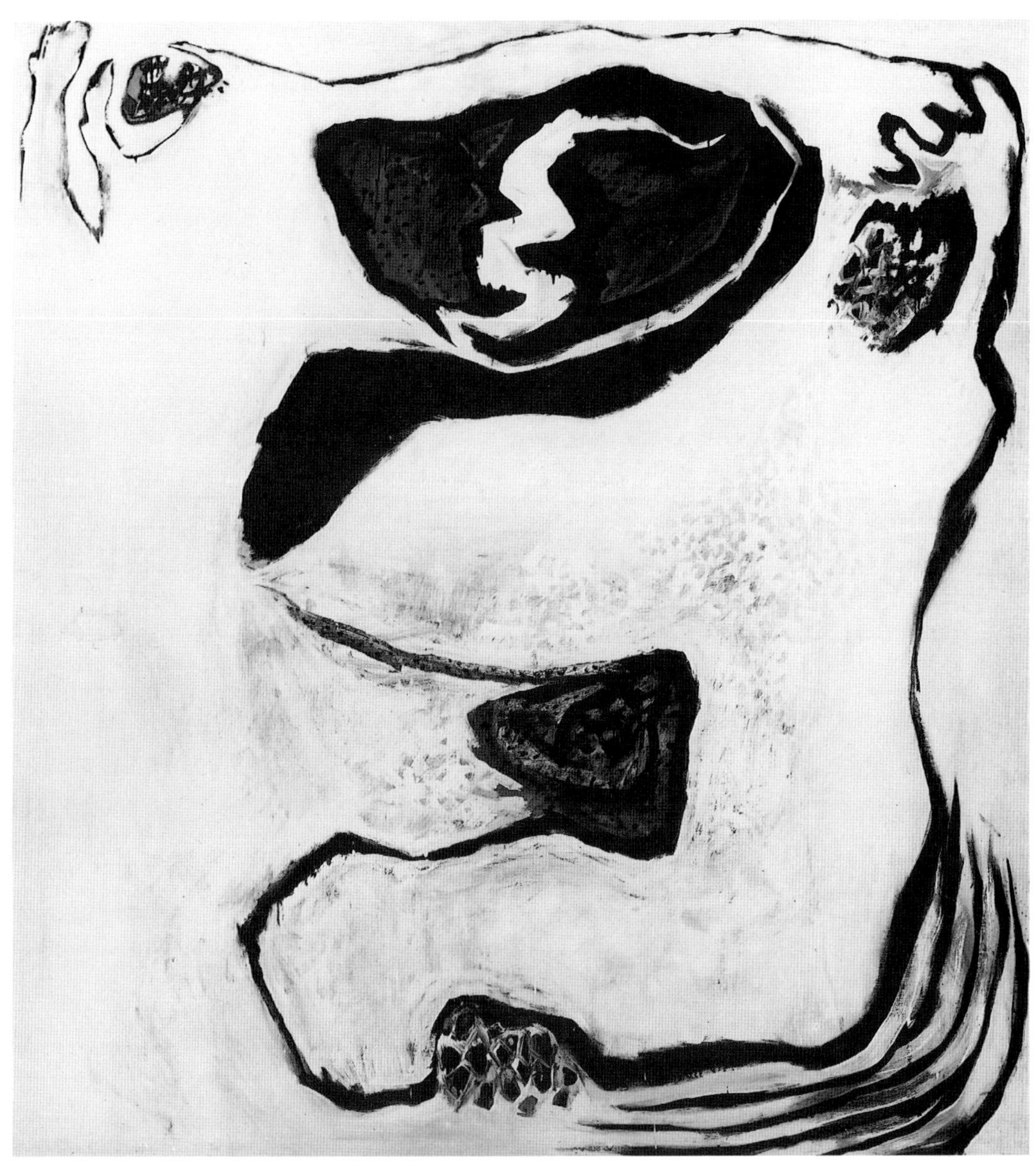

Figure 5.25

Frank Lobdell, *April 1954, Number 1,* 1954. Oil on canvas,
72 × 63½ in. Collection, University Art Museum, University of
California at Berkeley, gift of David K. Anderson, New York, in
memory of Martha Jackson (from the Martha Jackson
Collection). Photographer: Colin McRae.

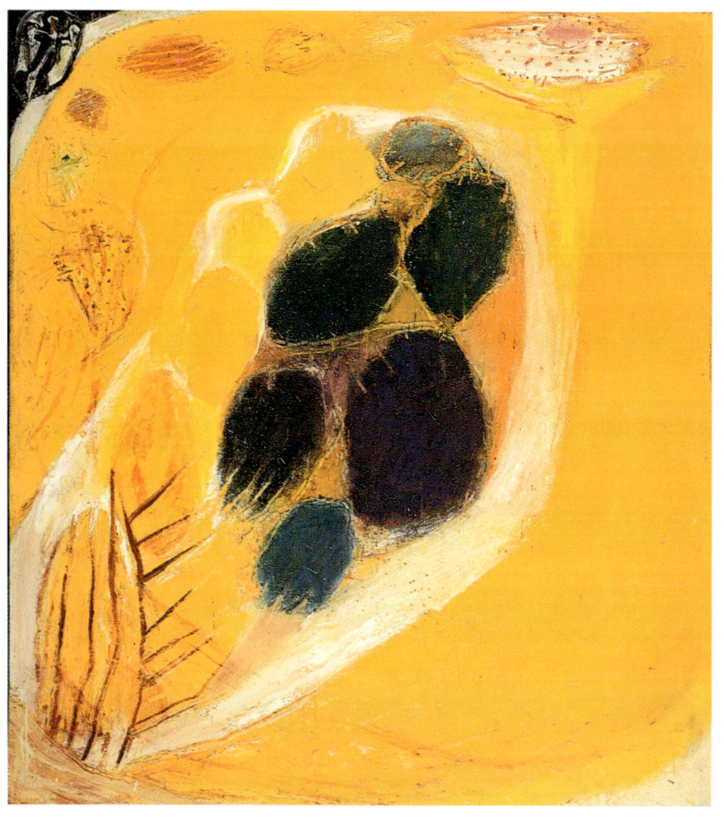

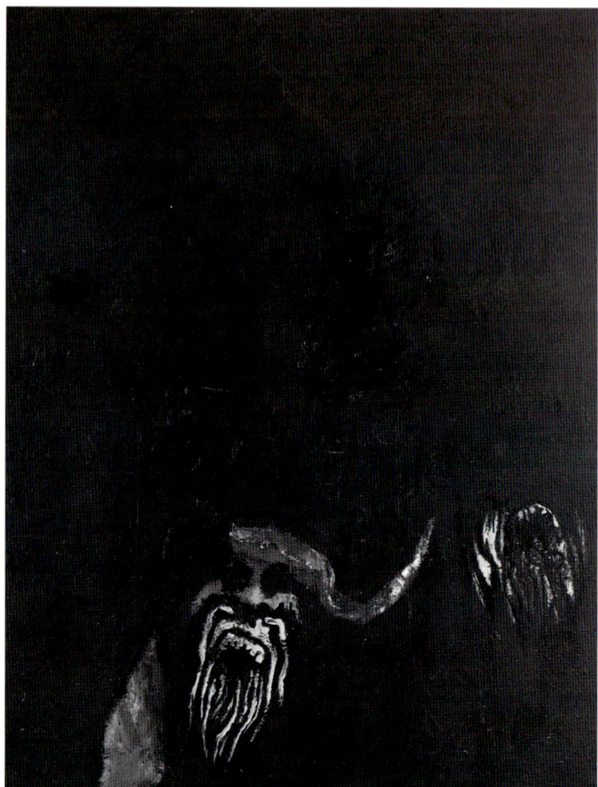

Albright's reference to existentialism is apt, since Lobdell, perhaps more than any of his colleagues except Corbett in San Francisco, was drawn to existentialism.[78] For Lobdell, the senseless brutality of World War II, followed by the Korean War and the McCarthy hearings, was instrumental in shaping his view of the human condition as an endless struggle for meaning, purpose, and dignity.[79] He expressed that struggle, not through de Kooning's turbulent gesture, but through forms, which seem burdened, as Herschel Chipp described them, "with the agony of a human organism confronted with an environment that offers little that is certain—no horizon, no gravity, no substance."[80] Lobdell has acknowledged human vulnerability as one of his chief metaphorical themes, and indeed, his paintings often display forms that are painfully clumsy (fig. 5.26) or wound into a defensive fetal coil.[81]

As the 1950s progressed, Lobdell's paintings became increasingly ominous and brooding. Chalky white grounds gave way to dense and impenetrable grays and blacks in agitated impastos. As in the work of Still, these impastos are divested of all the sensuality usually associated with the technique: they are the product of slow, accretionary buildup rather than of oil-laden brushstrokes. Often, as in *January 1955,* Lobdell's surfaces are as dry and parched as cinder (fig. 5.27). This painting evokes a fire-charred hell—the flickering streaks of red and orange suggesting both flames and mouths open wide in agonizing screams. Lobdell was deeply moved by the Edvard Munch exhibition at the M. H. de Young Memorial Museum in 1951,[82] and the Norwegian artist's embodiment of primal emotion in such paintings as *The Scream* must have charged his imagination.

The religious connotation of much of Lobdell's imagery in the later 1950s has often been noted. Many of his paintings from this period contain figures with arms spread that might be read as crucifixes or as angels. The twisted, spectral forms of *April 1957,* for

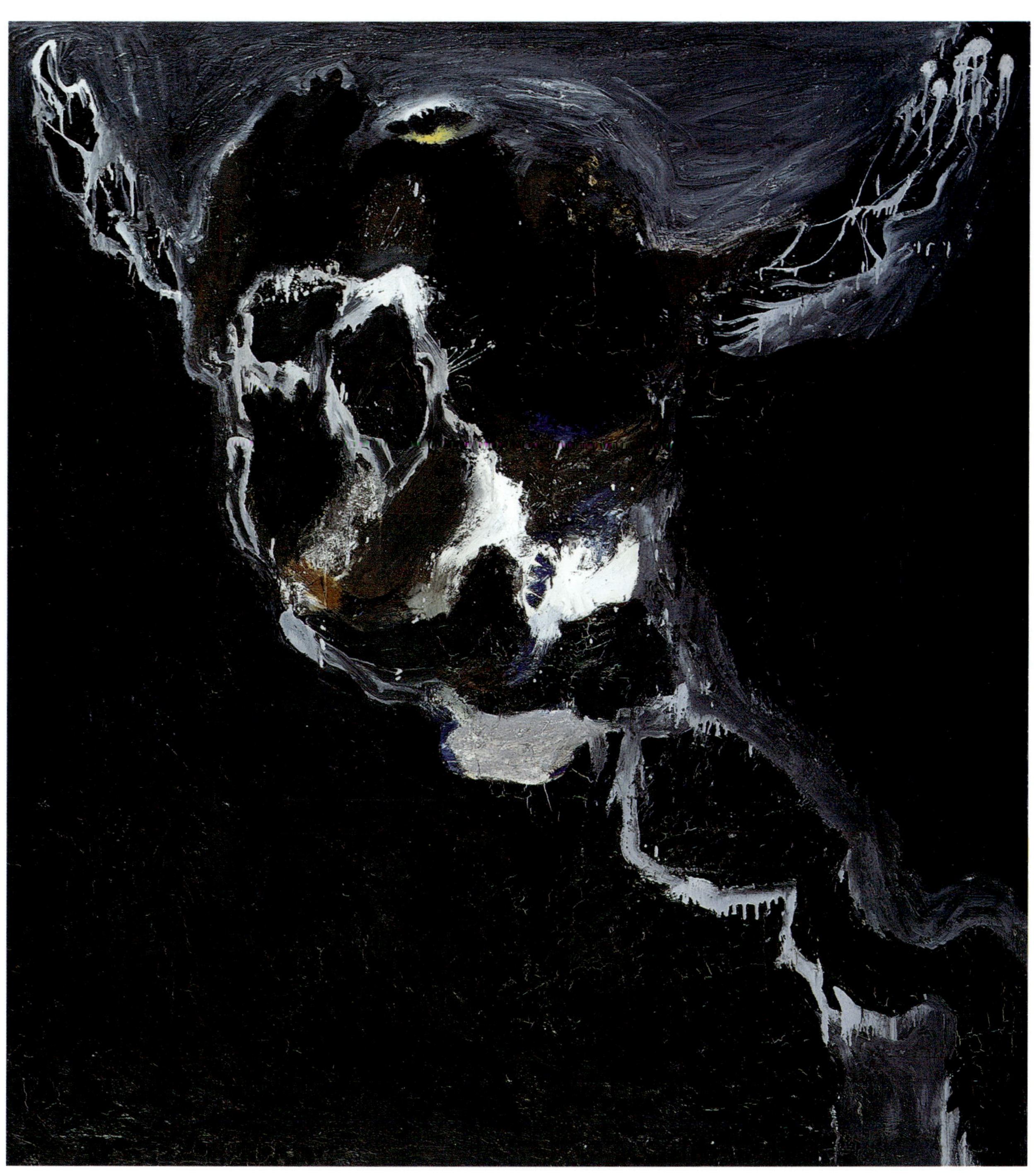

Figure 5.28

Frank Lobdell, *April 1957,* 1957. Oil on canvas, 69½ × 60½ in.

Photograph courtesy of the artist. Photographer:

Ira D. Schrank.

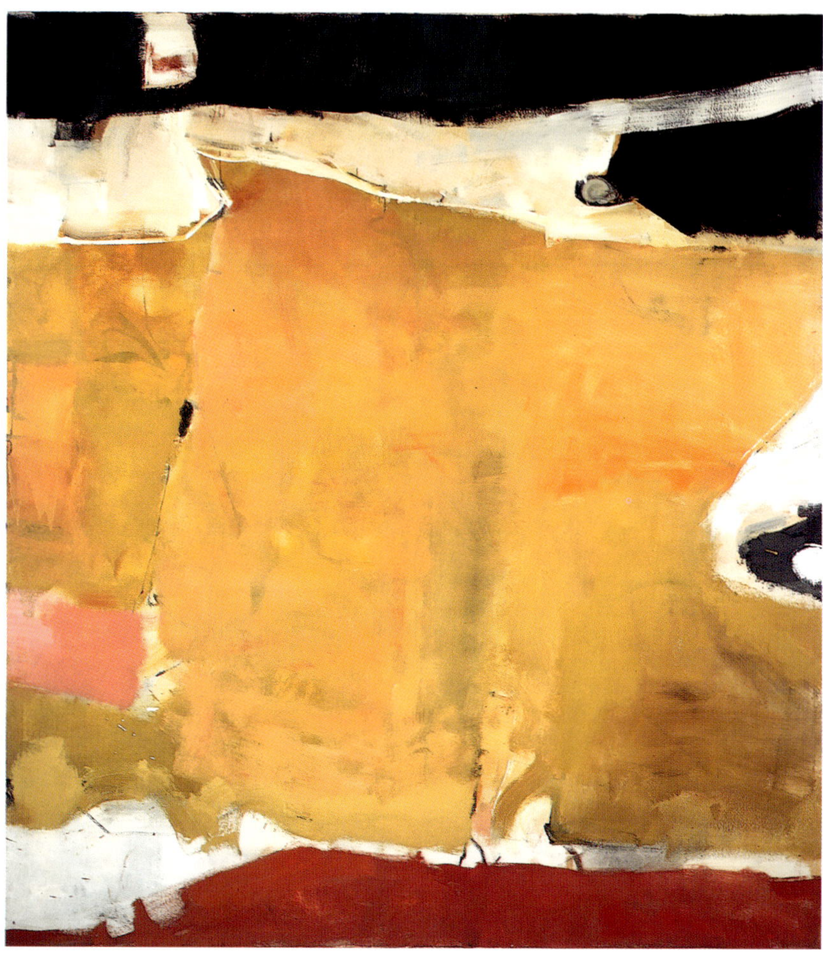

example, prompt both of these interpretations (fig. 5.28). The painting's spiritual implication is reinforced by the suggestion of a halo and the milky white, vaporous rendering of the figure against a black void. Yet Lobdell did not intend these paintings to convey Christianity in any specific sense; they are, rather, universal emblems of spiritual striving. Some scholars have attempted to trace them to the archetypal symbols defined by Jung in his theories of the collective unconscious, but Lobdell has denied ever having had a serious interest in Jung or psychoanalysis.[83] Lobdell's paintings are more profitably compared with Robert Duncan's poems, in which the psyche is fraught with battling divine and demonic powers. Or they might be compared with the epic moral struggles of Milton and Melville, both of whom Lobdell was reading in the 1950s (he was particularly fascinated by *Moby-Dick*).[84] But as the critic Charles Miedzinsky has remarked, Lobdell's personal lexicon does not readily lend itself to literal analysis, since his symbols are "never mere form, but rather

expressions that point beyond themselves to ever-expanding possibilities." Miedzinsky was correct in observing that "Lobdell has retained his awe of the symbolic process, thereby preserving its mystery, integrity, and transformative power."[85]

Richard Diebenkorn, 1950–55

An entirely different variant of San Francisco Abstract Expressionism was forged by Richard Diebenkorn, whose *Berkeley* series of 1953 to 1955 was highly influential in the Bay Area for younger artists such as George Miyasaki and Henry Villierme. Compared with Lobdell, Diebenkorn was little interested in symbolic or thematic content. Although his painting is more a celebration of the optical pleasures of color and light than of unbridled vitality, like Smith, he was basically a sensualist.

When Diebenkorn returned to the Bay Area in 1953 after spending three years in Albuquerque and Urbana, his work had changed significantly. Freed

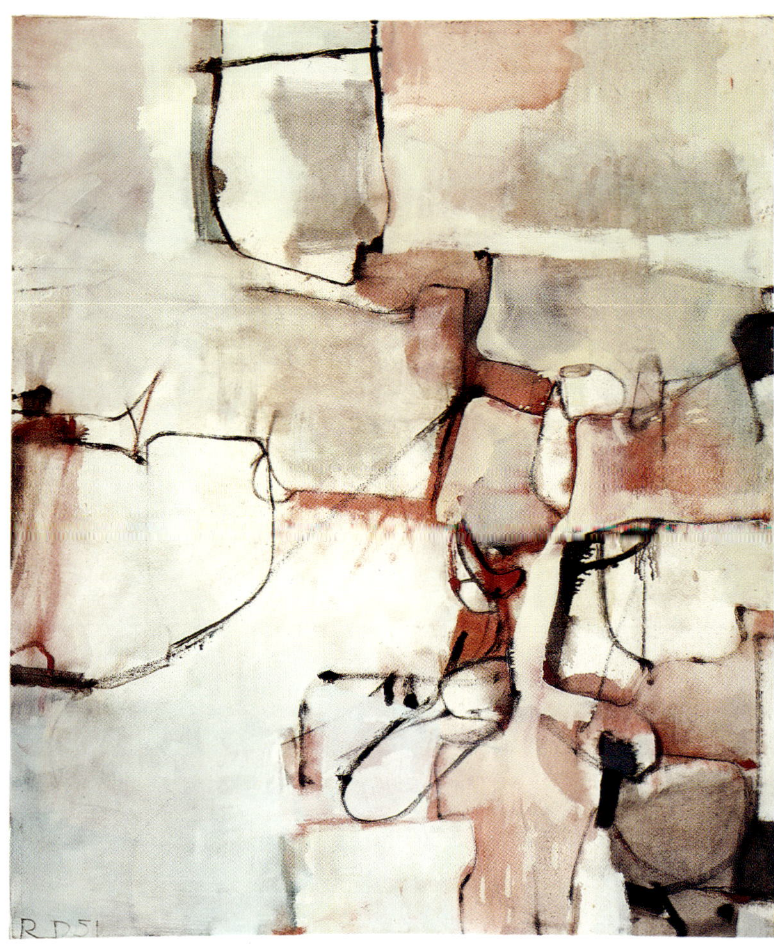

Figure 5.29

Opposite: Richard Diebenkorn, *Albuquerque,* 1952. Oil on canvas, 69 × 60 in. The Buck Collection, Laguna Hills, California. Bliss Photography.

Figure 5.30

Left: Richard Diebenkorn, *Albuquerque #3,* 1951. Oil on canvas, 55¾ × 46 in. Private collection.

from the weight of peer pressure, Diebenkorn had made a decisive move from the rugged aesthetic that dominated the California School of Fine Arts. The shift occurred almost as soon as he settled in New Mexico in 1950. Within a year's time, his lines became more fluid and graceful, and his colors began to soften. He also began to incorporate bits of recognizable imagery into his abstractions, mostly playful animal and sexual motifs. A work such as *Disintegrating Pig* (1950) would have been unthinkable in the late 1940s, when, as Diebenkorn later confessed, a mere hint of a Mickey Mouse fragment discovered in an impromptu scribble could cause him to repaint his entire canvas.[86]

But the most significant development in Diebenkorn's work after he left the California School of Fine Arts in late 1949 was his new willingness to treat landscape themes. Diebenkorn acknowledged that the flat line of the western mesa of Albuquerque strongly influenced his work. "Temperamentally, perhaps, I had always been a landscape painter, but I was fight-ing the landscape feeling," he admitted. "For years I didn't have the color blue on my palette because it reminded me too much of the spatial qualities in conventional landscape. But in Albuquerque I relaxed and began to think of natural forms in relation to my own feelings."[87]

Diebenkorn was not alone in exploring abstractions of the landscape during his stay in New Mexico. In Taos, where he exhibited at Eulalia Emetaz's Galeria Escondida in 1951, Corbett, McChesney, and Spohn were also creating abstractions that drew from the distinctive clear light and vast horizons of the Southwest.[88] Diebenkorn particularly admired Corbett's subtle charcoal drawings of the early 1950s, which show a kindred fondness for the empty spaces and monochromes of the desert. The reference to landscape space is perhaps less obvious in Diebenkorn's paintings than the evocative desert colors, which tended toward sun-bleached tans and tawny golds during his stay in New Mexico from 1950 to 1952 (figs. 5.29, 5.30).

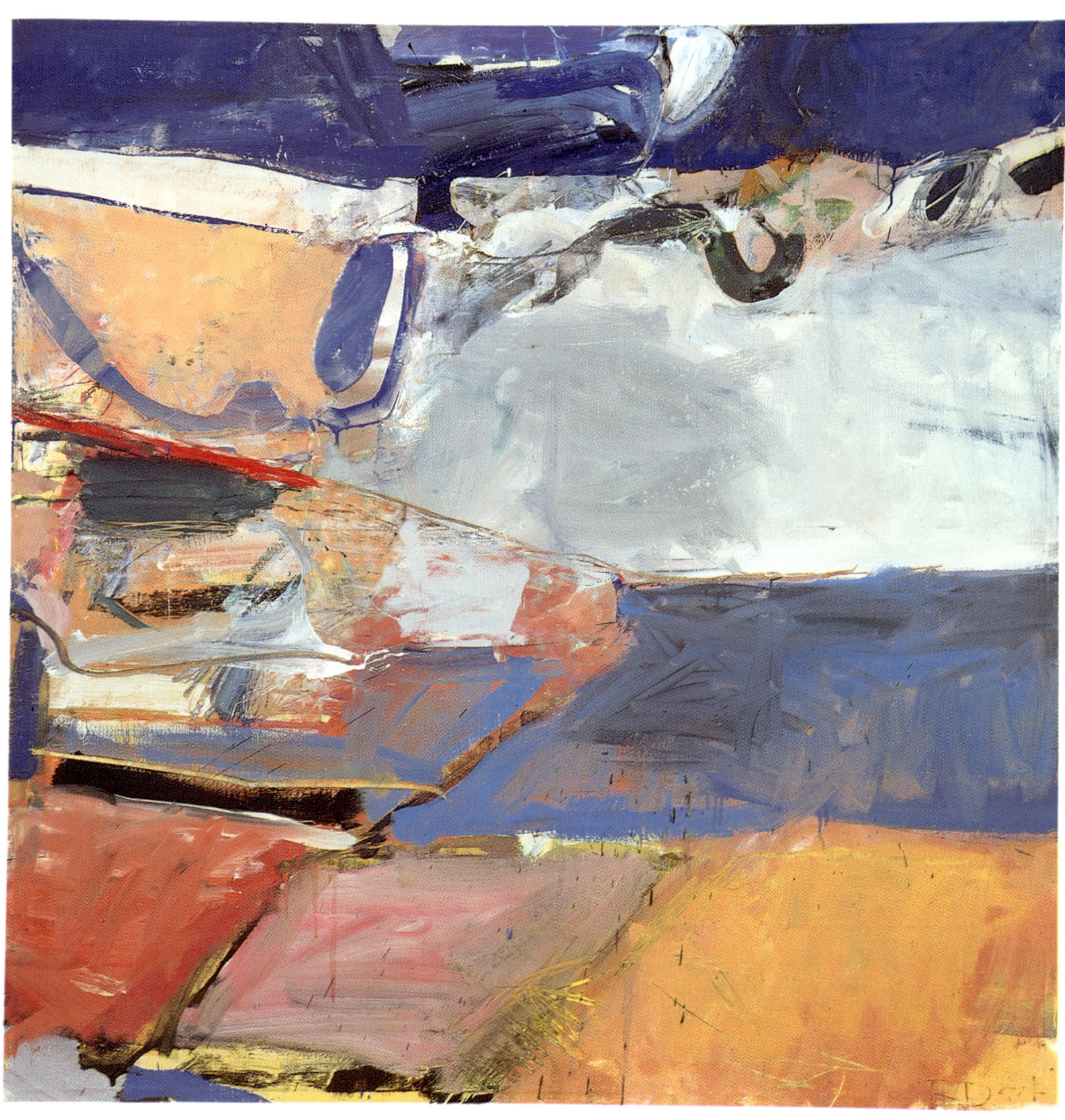

Figure 5.31

Above: Richard Diebenkorn, *Berkeley Number 22,* 1954. Oil on
canvas, 59 × 57 in. Collection, Hirshhorn Museum and
Sculpture Garden, Smithsonian Institution, museum purchase
with funds provided under Regent's Collections Acquisition
Program, 1986.

Figure 5.32

Opposite: Richard Diebenkorn, *Berkeley #57,* 1955. Oil on
canvas, 59½ × 59½ in. Collection, San Francisco Museum of
Modern Art, gift of Joseph M. Bransten in memory of
Ellen Hart Bransten.

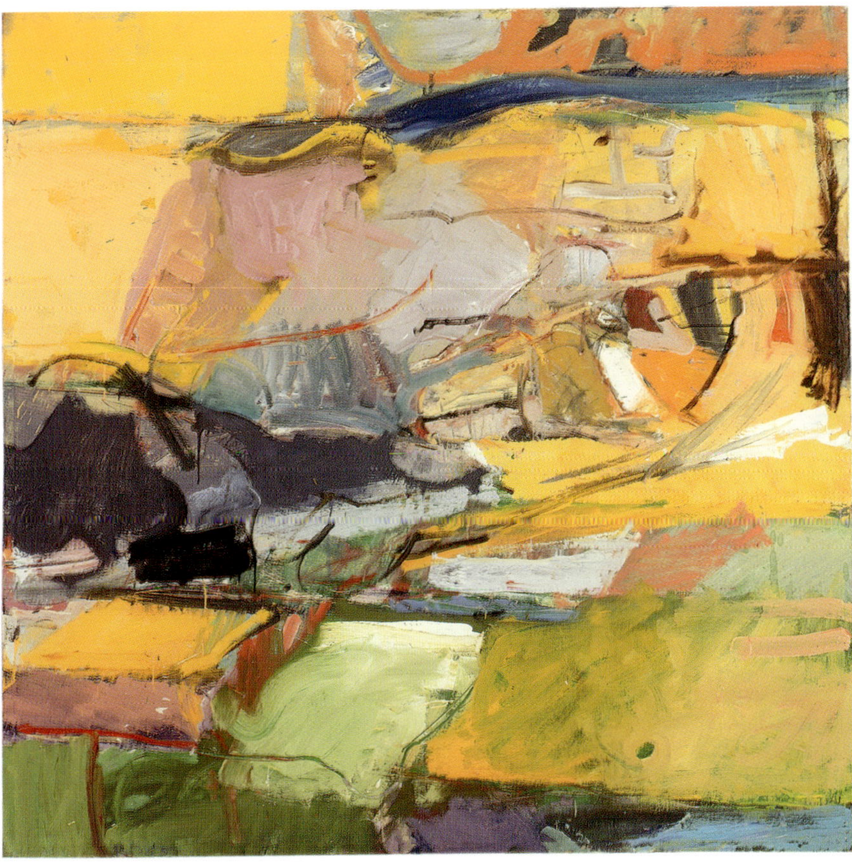

Diebenkorn's landscape allusions became more pronounced after he took up residence in Berkeley in 1953. Anyone who has visited the Berkeley hills and looked westward at the sloping patchwork of city blocks and boulevards leading to San Francisco Bay will recognize their analogue in Diebenkorn's *Berkeley* paintings. But the grid structure evident in these abstractions can also be traced to a revelation Diebenkorn had while flying from Albuquerque to San Francisco in 1951. "The aerial view showed me a rich variety of ways of treating a flat plane," he later recalled.[89] Some of Diebenkorn's paintings from Albuquerque suggest the patterning of land plots that fascinated him, but few conjure the spectacle of water, land, and air found in such paintings as *Berkeley Number 22* (1954; fig. 5.31).

One of the more noticeable elements of the *Berkeley* paintings is their often high-keyed palette (fig. 5.32), a marked departure from the earth tones of Diebenkorn's Albuquerque period. The Matisse retrospective Diebenkorn saw on a visit to Los Angeles in 1952 renewed his long-standing admiration for Fauvist color. Diebenkorn's *Berkeley* abstractions show a close study of Matisse, combining vivid ultramarines and cadmiums with creamy, seductive pastels. In their emphatic use of gesture, they also show the influence of de Kooning and Kline, whose recent work Diebenkorn viewed on a trip to New York in the summer of 1953. Like de Kooning slightly later in his abstract landscapes, Diebenkorn accomplishes a simultaneous flattening and opening up of space through dynamic brushwork and the juxtaposition of complementary colors.

When Diebenkorn participated in the *Younger American Painters* show at the Solomon R. Guggenheim Museum in 1954, his *Berkeley* paintings attracted considerable national attention, the first such recognition bestowed upon an abstract painter working on the West Coast during the 1950s. Diebenkorn's first one-man show in New York, at the Poindexter Gallery, drew enthusiastic responses from collectors; one major critic, Dore Ashton, pronounced him a "born painter."[90] When art dealers in New York, Los Angeles, and Chicago began to launch promotional campaigns, the success of the *Berkeley* abstractions seemed assured. Yet to general dismay, in 1955 Die-

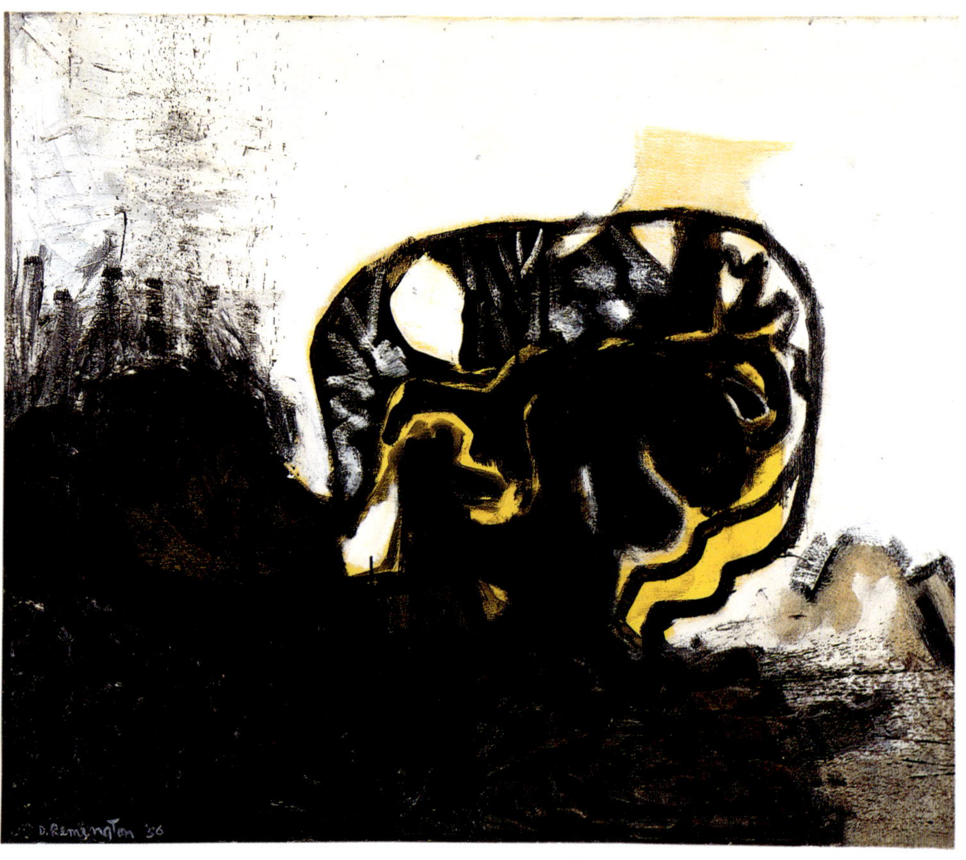

benkorn abruptly began a comparatively traditional group of still lifes, landscapes, and interior scenes. Diebenkorn's shift exemplifies a common tendency among the San Francisco painters: commercial success did not come often to them, but when it did, they were typically uneasy. In Diebenkorn's case, the impetus to deviate from the obvious path of success may have come from his mentor and friend Park, who cautioned him against painting that came effortlessly. "I felt that in the last of the abstract painting around 1955, it was almost as though I could do too much, too easily," he later confessed.[91] With his turn away from abstraction, Diebenkorn took his place alongside Park and Bischoff in the triumvirate of painters who, wittingly or not, launched the Bay Area Figurative movement that would dominate the artistic discourse of the following decade.[92]

Kelly, Gechtoff, Saccaro, DeFeo, and Other Second-Generation Abstract Expressionists

Although his *Berkeley* abstractions were highly influential for the younger generation of Abstract Expres-

sionists in the Bay Area, Diebenkorn's quiet and retiring ways made him less personally accessible than some of his other, more gregarious, colleagues. Lobdell became an inspirational model of artistic commitment and integrity for artists such as Charles Strong, but he too was taciturn and reclusive by nature and did not make many personal contacts outside his small circle of friends from earlier days at the California School of Fine Arts.[93] Smith, on the other hand, emerged as a charismatic leader of a mostly younger group of artists in San Francisco that included Deborah Remington (fig. 5.33), Julius Wasserstein, Madeleine Dimond (fig. 5.34), Lilly Fenichel (fig. 5.35), Adelie Landis, Roy De Forest, and (to a lesser extent) Sonia Gechtoff and James Kelly.[94] After leaving the California School of Fine Arts, Smith operated a kind of atelier at his Mission Street studio and gave an evening lecture series at his home on Potrero Hill entitled "Theories of Nonobjective Painting."[95] Although the discussions often degenerated into raucous drinking parties, there were numerous heated debates about the meaning of contemporary painting, with the garrulous Smith presiding.[96]

It is not surprising that newcomers to the move-

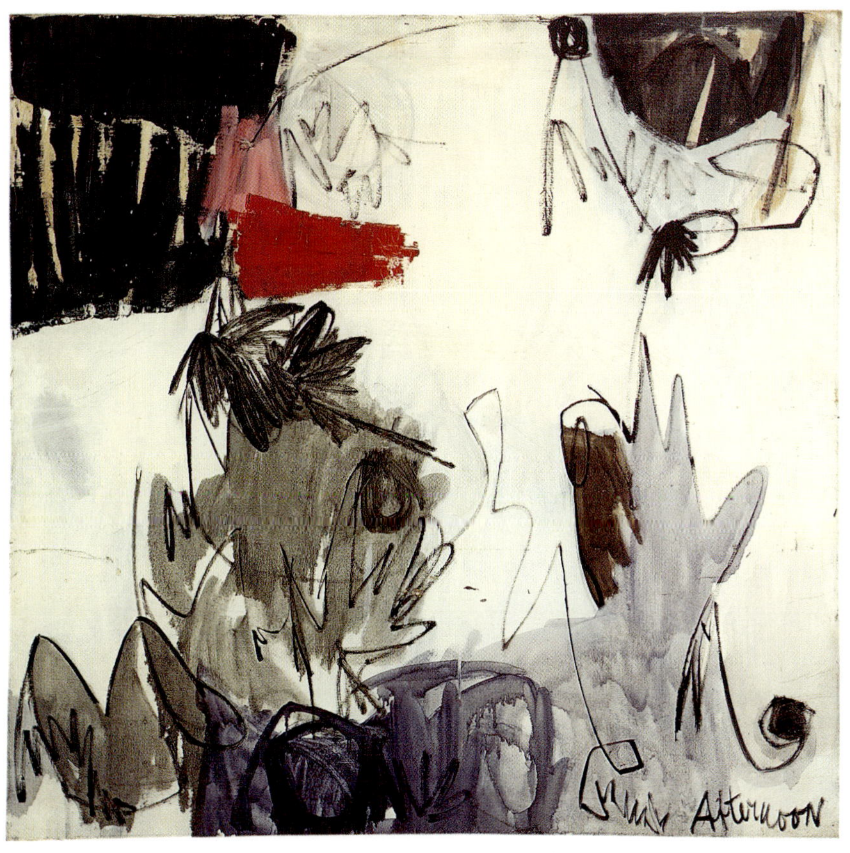

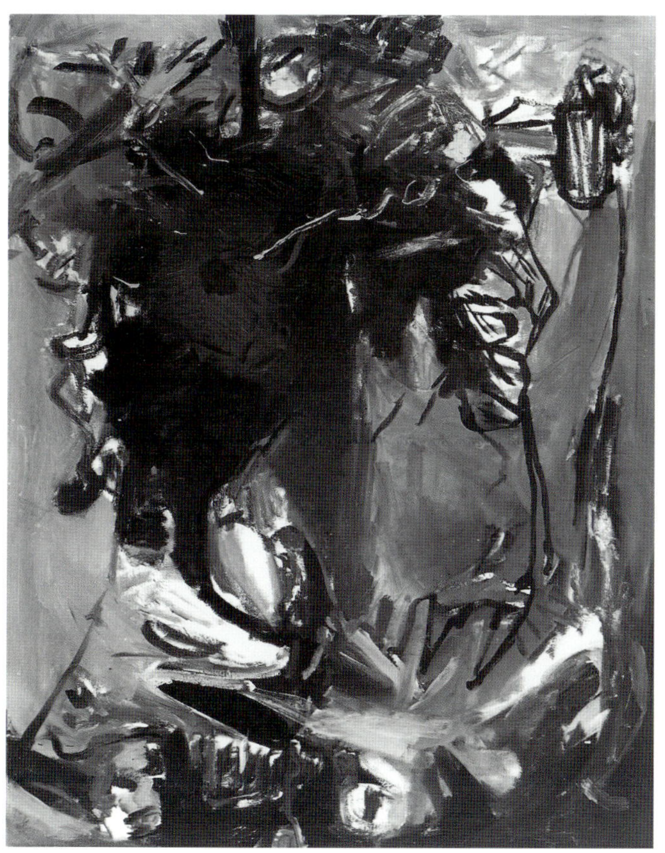

Figure 5.33

Opposite: Deborah Remington, *Dacia,* 1956. Oil on canvas, 40 × 66 in. Collection of the artist. Photographer: D. James Dee. © 1994 Deborah Remington/VAGA, New York.

Figure 5.34

Above: Madeleine Dimond, *Grimy Afternoon,* 1957. Oil on canvas, 49¾ × 49¾ in. Collection, Mag Dimond. Photographer: Ira D. Schrank.

Figure 5.35

Left: Lilly Fenichel, *Untitled,* 1952. Oil on canvas, 48⅞ X 38⅞ in. Photograph courtesy, John Natsoulas Gallery, Davis, California; photographer: Allan Labb, Albuquerque, N.Mex.

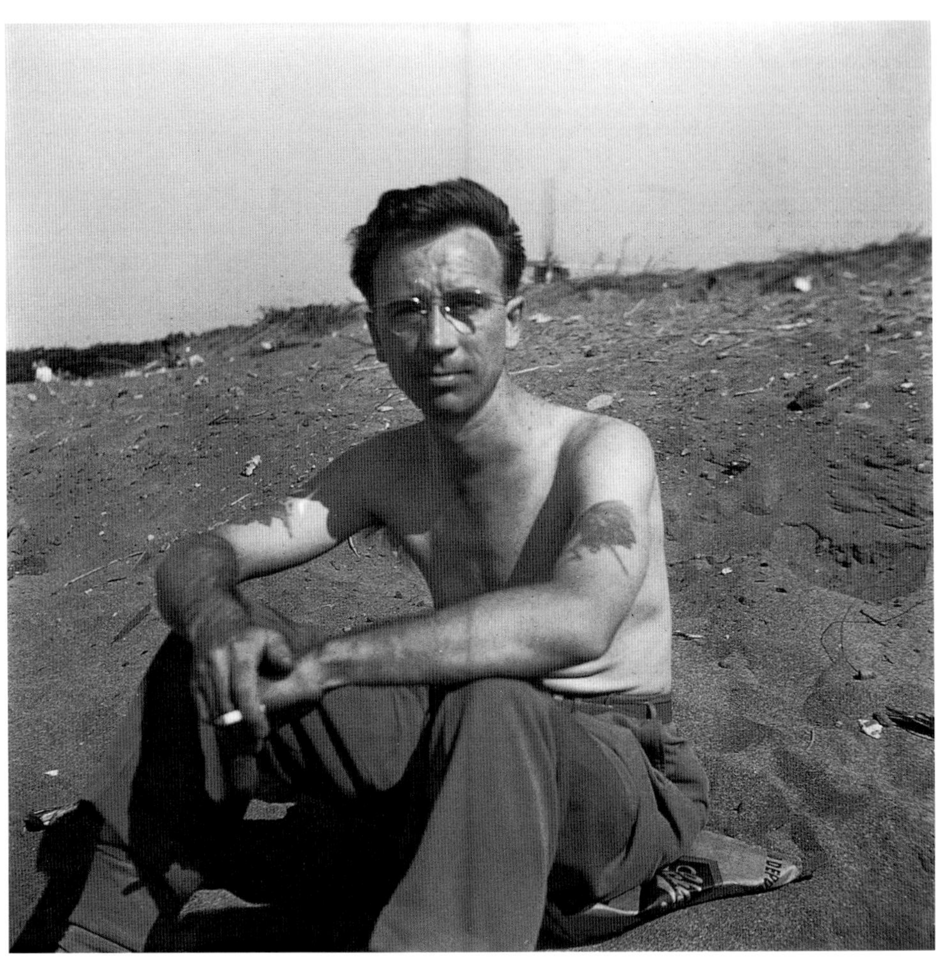

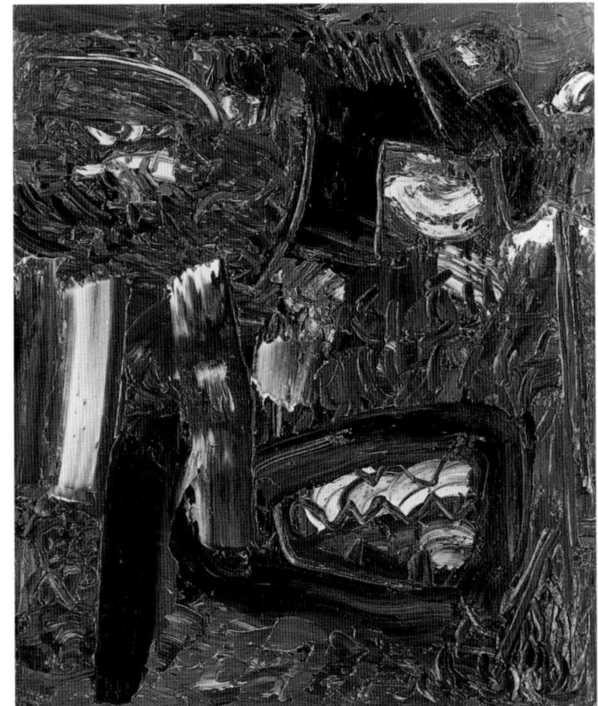

Figure 5.36

Above: James Kelly, San Francisco, 1951.
Photographer: Phyllis Lynch.

Figure 5.37

Right: James Kelly, *Jackknife,* 1956. Oil on canvas, 32 × 26 in.
Collection, Allan Sommer. Photograph courtesy, Wiegand
Gallery, College of Notre Dame, Belmont, Calif.;
photographer: M. Lee Fatherree.

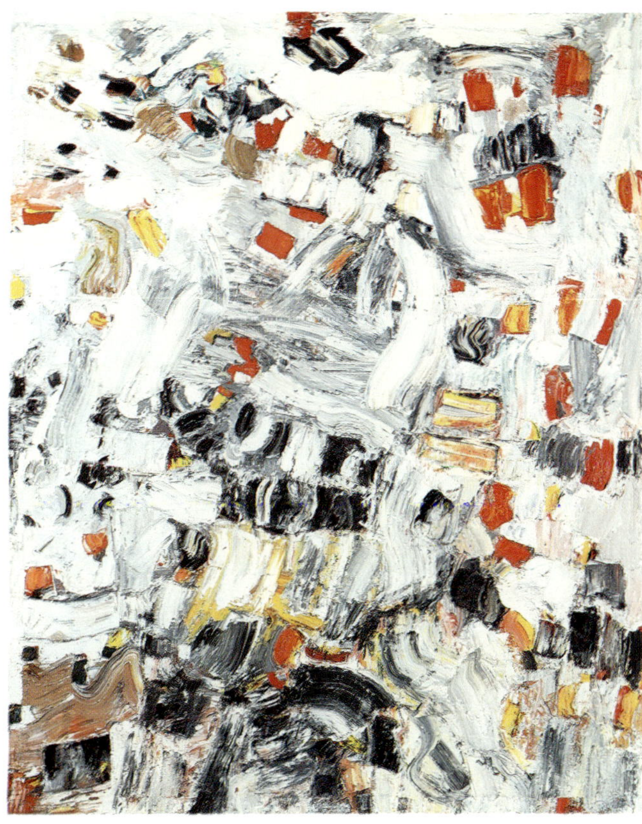

James Kelly, *Assault on K-2,* 1956. Oil on canvas, 84 × 66 in. Collection, San Francisco Museum of Modern Art, gift of Gump's. Photographer: Ben Blackwell.

ment gravitated to Smith rather than to Lobdell or Diebenkorn, for Smith's work was in many respects philosophically and aesthetically more compatible with theirs. Like Smith, many of them were jazz aficionados (although they generally preferred Brubeck to Hines) and tended to be devotees of high-velocity improvisation. The second generation, unlike their predecessors of the late 1940s, had taken in a good dose of New York painting through the pages of *Art News* and trips to the East Coast.[97] The presence of the New York gesture painters Milton Resnick, George McNeil, and Kyle Morris in the art department at the University of California at Berkeley also served to disseminate ideas from the East. By the early 1950s the influence of Manhattan-style "action painting" was readily apparent in the big-brush arm-stretching gestures that began to emerge in the work of Gechtoff, Fenichel, Kelly, Wasserstein, John Saccaro, and others.

Kelly (fig. 5.36) was a good deal older than most of his colleagues in San Francisco, and in strictly chronological terms he belongs to the earlier generation of Abstract Expressionists. Born in 1913, just a year after Pollock, Kelly studied at the Pennsylvania Academy of the Fine Arts in the late 1930s. A fellow-ship at the Barnes Foundation in 1941 brought him in touch with Miró, Picasso, and Matisse, but Kelly recognized van Gogh as the seminal force in his career after seeing the artist's work at the Philadelphia Museum of Art. "Van Gogh's paint was alive [with] tactility," he recalled. "Prior to that, the paintings I saw in museums were well blended, smooth. When I found him it was an explosion."[98]

The paintings Kelly executed after moving to San Francisco in late 1950 paralleled Smith's in their playful spotting and erratic darting lines. In a short time, however, Kelly revealed that he was capable of producing paintings with a dramatic and sometimes epic power all their own. His *Last Days of Dylan Thomas* (1953; see fig. 1.20) is an early example of Kelly's command of abstraction. Composed of a flurry of snowflakelike daubs against a dark abyss, the painting commemorates the recent death of one of Kelly's favorite poets.[99] The snowflake connotation is particularly apt as a reference to Thomas's best-known poem, "A Child's Christmas in Wales."

Kelly's work of the mid to late 1950s became more intensely physical and more involved with the plastic qualities of paint. In canvases such as *Jackknife* (1956; fig. 5.37) and *Assault on K-2* (1956; fig. 5.38), Kelly's

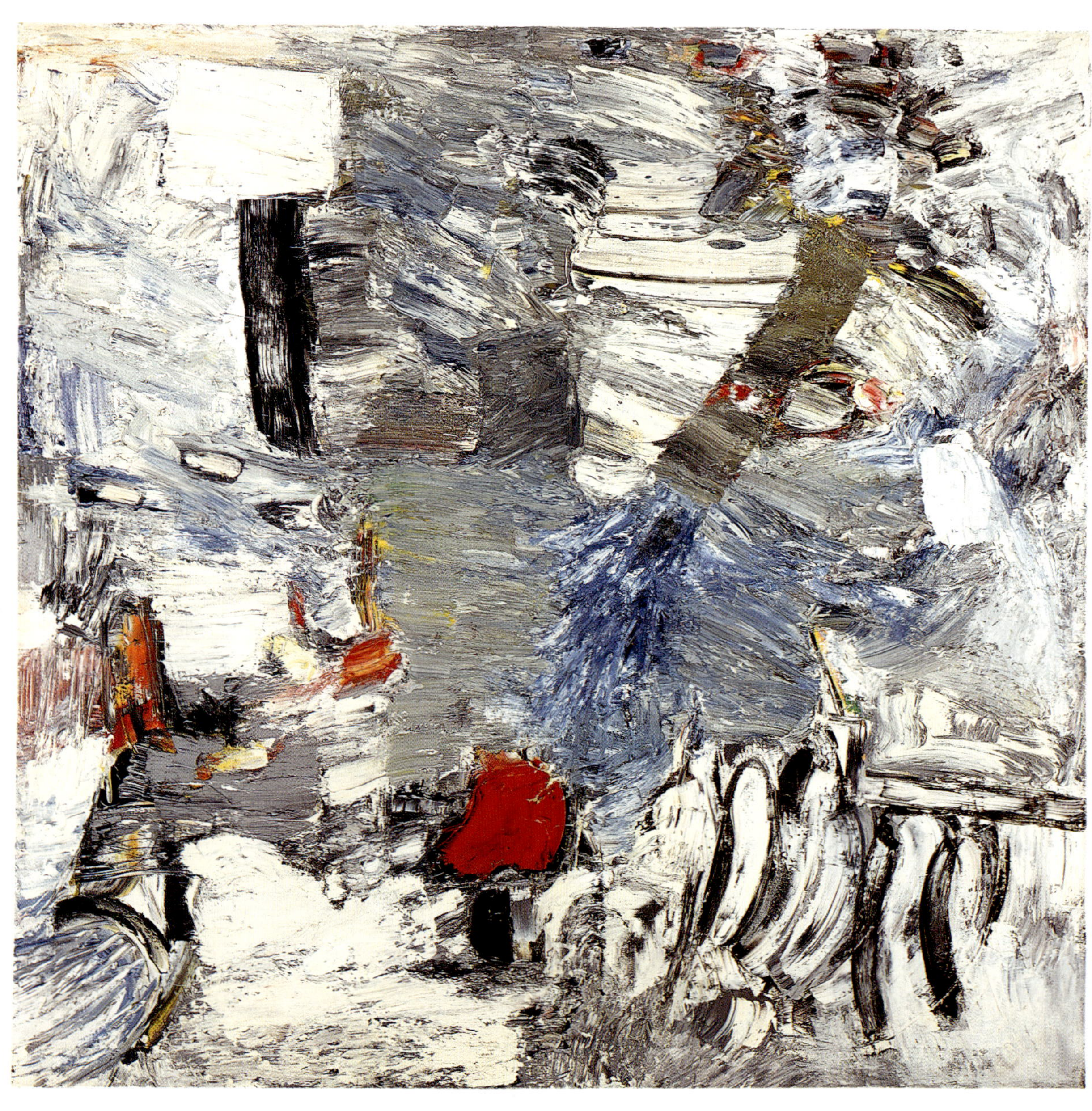

James Kelly, *Mid-Passage*, 1958. Oil on canvas, 60 × 60 in.
Collection, Clinton Reilly. Photograph courtesy, Wiegand
Gallery, College of Notre Dame, Belmont, Calif.

paint is thick, sitting on the surface in high relief. Kelly often used a liberal amount of creamy white, and the smooth ridges formed by his palette knife in paintings such as *Mid-Passage* (1958; fig. 5.39) lend a confectionary character to his surfaces, much like icing on a cake.

Sonia Gechtoff's career as an Abstract Expressionist closely paralleled that of Kelly, whom she married in 1953. Like Kelly, Gechtoff (fig. 5.40) was from Philadelphia, where she received a bachelor's degree from the Philadelphia Museum School of Art in 1950, just before moving to San Francisco. Gechtoff began her career as a Social Realist influenced by Ben Shahn,

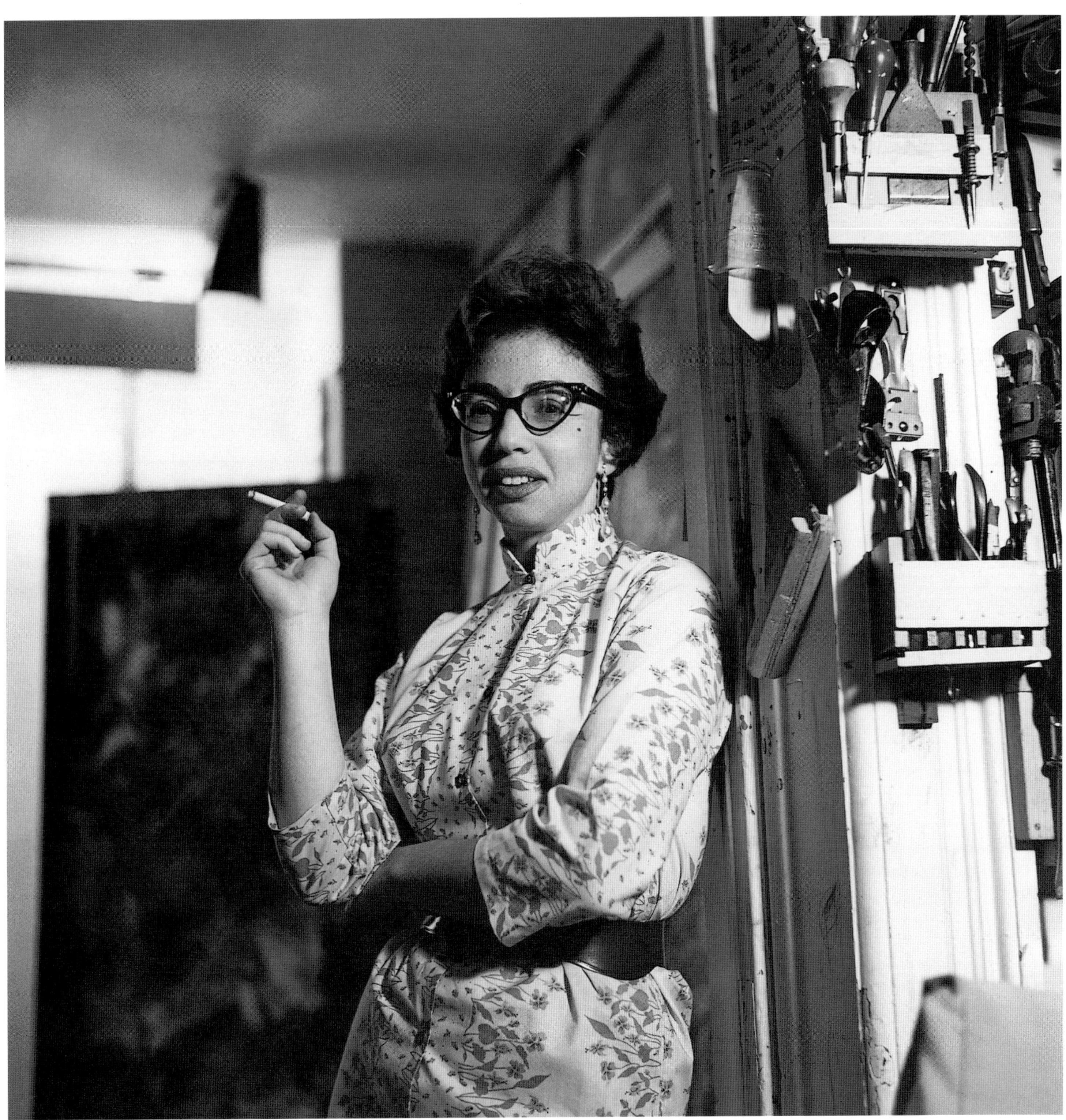

Figure 5.40

Sonia Gechtoff, San Francisco studio, ca. 1957–58.

Photographer: Harry Redl.

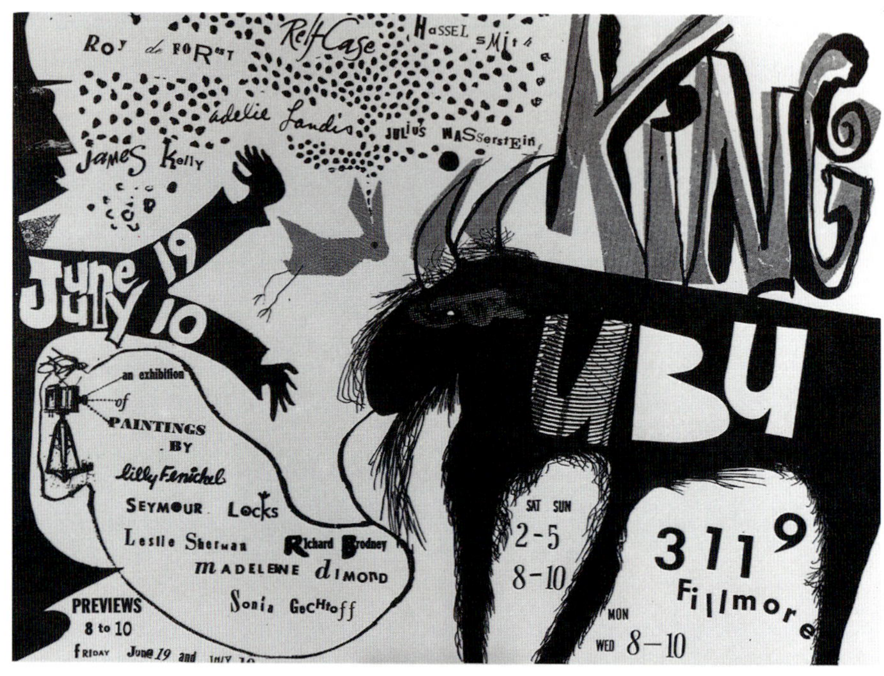

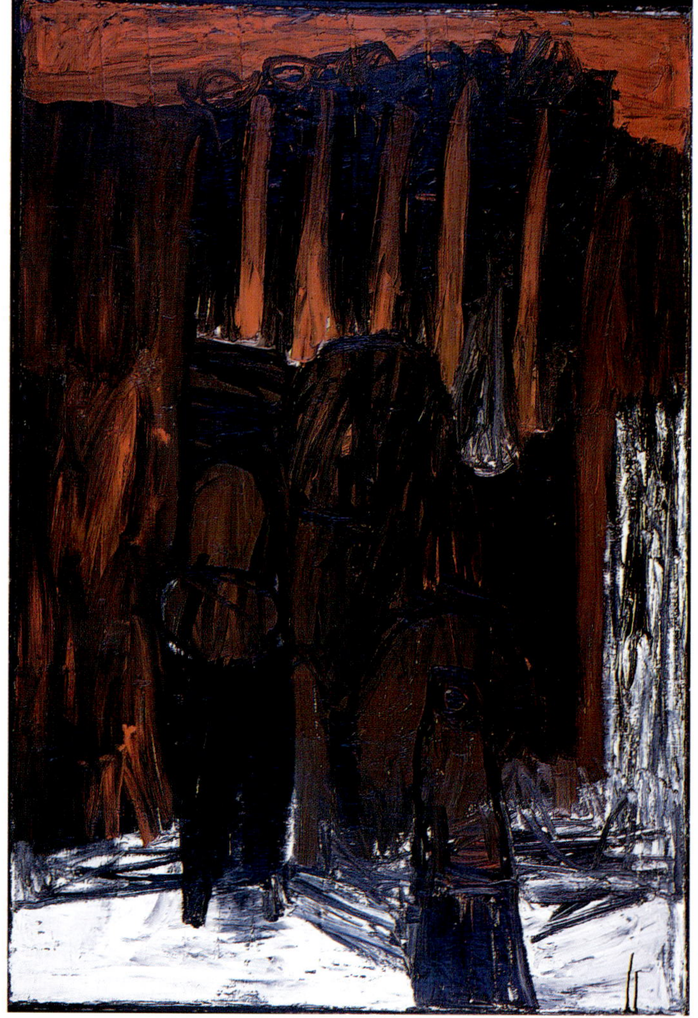

Figure 5.41

Above: Poster for June and July exhibitions, King Ubu Gallery, designed by Roy De Forest, 1953. Collection, Sonia Gechtoff and James Kelly.

Figure 5.42

Right: Sonia Gechtoff, *Anna Karenina,* ca. 1953–55. Oil on canvas, 60 × 48 in. Collection, Herbert Hoover. Photographer: Custom Image.

Figure 5.43

Opposite: Sonia Gechtoff, *Mystery of the Hunt,* 1956. Oil on canvas, 45¼ × 106 in. Collection, San Francisco Museum of Modern Art, gift of Irving Blum.

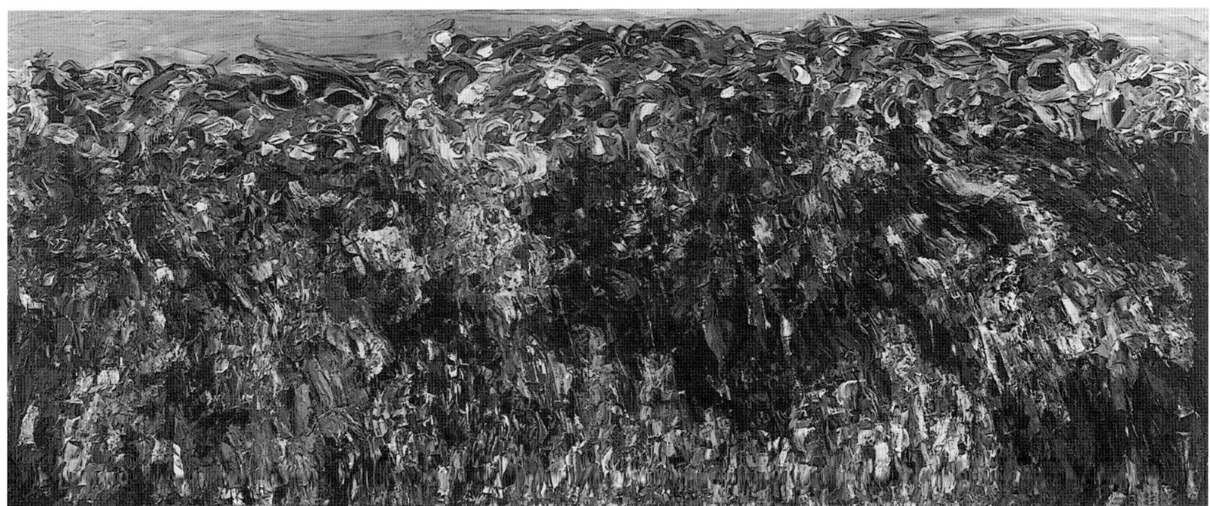

Philip Evergood, and especially Max Beckmann.[100] Her first West Coast paintings were figurative, but in 1952, after meeting Briggs and the Potrero Hill crowd, she launched into vigorous large-scale abstractions. The paintings she showed at King Ubu in a group exhibition of Smith's students during the summer of 1953 (fig. 5.41) featured the exuberant, looping lines common to the group (fig. 5.42).[101]

As the 1950s progressed, Gechtoff came to rely less on drawing and more on relating discrete units of color in her painting. Frankenstein, who reviewed her one-woman show at the M. H. de Young Memorial Museum in 1957, described her work as "a kind of grandly scaled pointillism, with large, thick flecks of paint applied with a palette knife, determining forms, their direction, speed, density, and movement."[102] In many of her canvases, Gechtoff shows a sensuous, hedonistic affection for paint laid on in broad, juicy strokes. Like Kelly, she often wielded her palette knife like a pastry knife, producing lustrous, glossy impastos.

One of the more conspicuous features of Gechtoff's work after the mid-1950s is the suggestion of landscape imagery. Many of her paintings present an identifiable horizon line. Gechtoff readily admits that nature was a primary catalyst of feeling in the later 1950s.[103] Another important inspiration, which she shared with Kelly, was poetry.[104] Gechtoff's exhibition at the de Young in 1957 was accompanied by pages of Michael McClure's poems, which, like her painting, often focused on natural themes. *Mystery of the Hunt* (1956; fig. 5.43)—named after McClure's poem of the same title—features a shimmering field of feathery strokes suggesting a worm's-eye view of a vast undulating grassland.[105]

After 1957 Gechtoff broadened her strokes into flickering, flame-like shapes with a torrential sweep recalling the work of her close friend and mentor Briggs. Many of these paintings are less suggestive of landscape than they are of a human presence. In works such as *The Queen, The Widow,* and *Portrait of Venus*—paintings the artist identified as female portraits—the figure is implied only in the vaguest sense. Gerald Nordland aptly described these canvases as evoking "spectral figures emerging from a fountain of expressionist paint handling."[106] One of Gechtoff's most powerful works in this group is the epic *Children of Frejus* (1959; fig. 5.44), commemorating the tragic mass drowning of children in the French village of Frejus.[107]

While not closely associated with Smith's Potrero Hill group, John Saccaro (fig. 5.45) was among the most innovative and imaginative of the gesture painters in the Bay Area. A native of San Francisco, Saccaro began his career in the late 1930s as a California Regionalist specializing in watercolors. In the years just prior to the war, he worked on the Federal Art Project and painted murals with McChesney for the Golden Gate International Exposition in 1939–40. Although he had explored abstract painting during the 1930s with a group of fluid watercolors much like John Marin's, Saccaro did not take abstraction

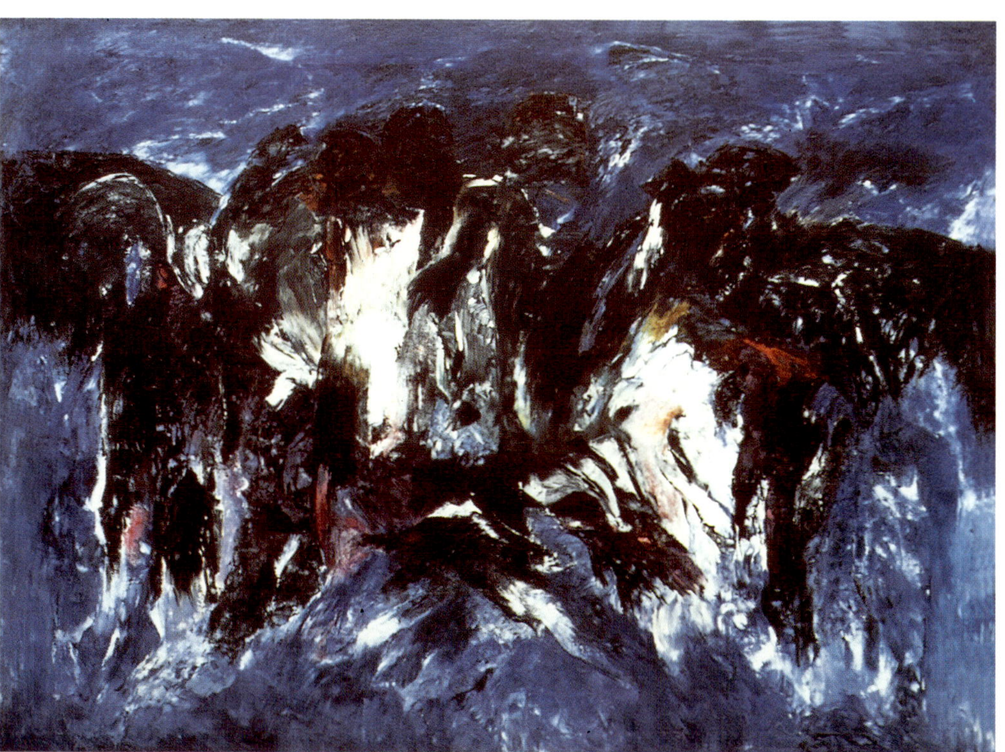

seriously until he enrolled in the California School of Fine Arts in 1951 at the age of thirty-eight, taking classes with Dixon and Bischoff.

Saccaro's initial Abstract Expressionist canvases showed little trace of influence from his teachers. Until about 1954 his work consisted primarily of shaggy, interlocking forms meticulously constructed through multiple layers of delicately scumbled paint (see figs. 1.17 and 5.46). Many paintings from this period show his close study of French Impressionist color, especially that of Bonnard and later Monet, whose soft pinks and frosty blues appear in his work up through the early 1960s.

About 1955 Saccaro began to paint in the manner for which he is best known, using a slashing, angular brushwork that bears some resemblance to the more reductive gestural canvases of Kline but involves a rhythmic play of color closer to the whir and speed of Futurism (fig. 5.47). Saccaro called these paintings "sensory raids," defining sensorism as an approach that favors "the scrape, slash and violence of the sensory."[108] Toward the early 1960s, Saccaro's painting became increasingly high-keyed and multichromatic, with brushstrokes that sometimes proliferated until they animated nearly every inch of the canvas.

Saccaro's bright palette was not typical of the San Francisco painters. Even in the 1950s Abstract Expressionism in the Bay Area was inclined toward earth tones and monochromes, tending to be less colorful than the work being produced in New York.[109] And the Bay Area painters frequently favored the palette knife over the brush, doubtless a legacy of Still's troweled surfaces. Another feature that distinguished San Francisco's second generation was the pronounced bent toward comedy. Parody, camp, and absurdist humor were mainstays of Kelly, Remington, De Forest, and other newcomers to the movement. De Forest, who is best known today for his whimsical paintings of dogs, began his career turning out amusing abstractions with such titles as *The Pattering of Little Feet among the Geraniums* (ca. 1954). Kelly's early work also tended toward antic humor. *Design for an Army Blanket* (1952), with its leopard-spotted frame, is a good example of his prankish wit. The painting, which initially featured a stuffed green rubber glove protruding from its middle, incited something of an uproar when it was displayed in a CSFA group exhibition in 1952. Perceiving, perhaps, a slackening of the Abstract Expressionist ethos, Briggs and Dixon condemned the work as an insult to serious art.[110] Kelly

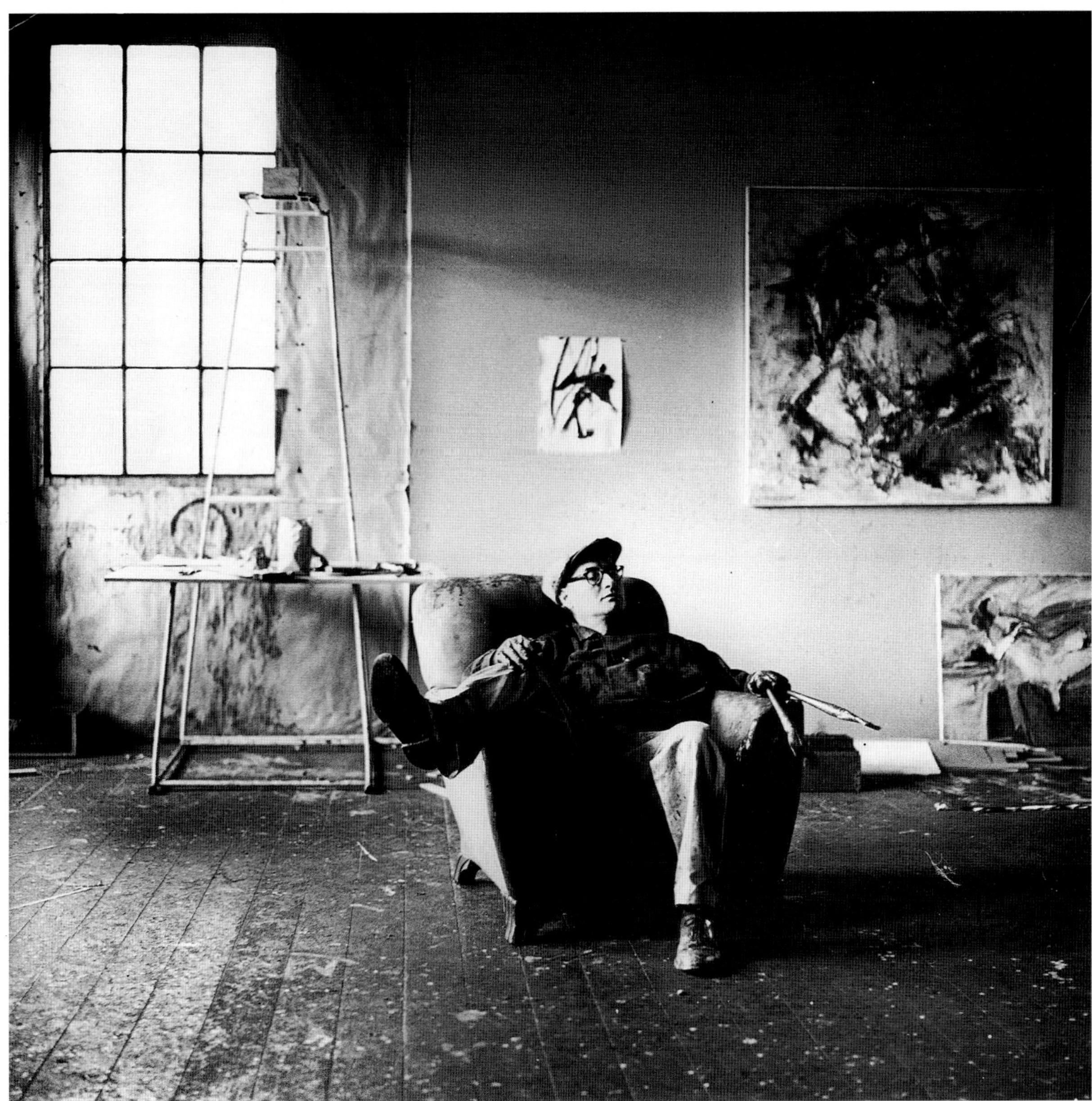

Figure 5.44

Opposite: Sonia Gechtoff, *Children of Frejus,* 1959. Oil on
canvas, 76¾ × 102 in. Collection of the artist. Photograph
courtesy, Kraushaar Galleries, New York; photographer:
Eric Politzer.

Figure 5.45

Above: John Saccaro, San Francisco, 1962. Photographer:
Elaine Mayes.

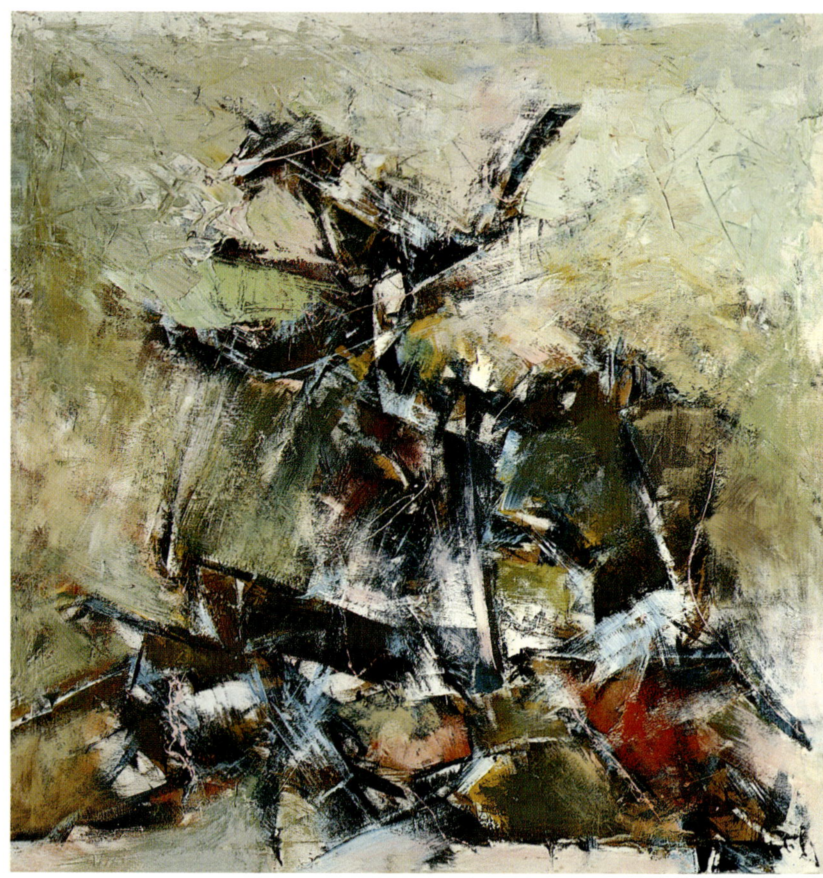

compounded the heresy with another canvas hung in the same show. This painting, reminiscent of Robert Rauschenberg's later challenge to de Kooning's supremacy, impetuously mimicked Clyfford Still.[111]

Such playful irreverence was widespread among the second-generation painters and was an important point of rapprochement with their comrades in letters, the Beat poets. Allen Ginsberg, Michael McClure, Jack Spicer, and numerous others who participated in the San Francisco poetry renaissance of the 1950s, were similarly engaged in supplanting the modernist orthodoxy with an earthy, sometimes raunchy, iconoclasm. In place of the formalist detachment of the New Criticism—the credo of academic poets such as John Crowe Ransom and the laureates of the *Kenyon Review*—the Beats aspired to what D. H. Lawrence called the "direct utterance from the instant whole man," an expression that was emotional, spontaneous, and uninhibited by stylistic considerations.[112] The openly romantic and confessional approach they cultivated, with its emphasis upon organic form and free association, was remarkably similar in conception to Abstract Expressionism. Indeed, the terms "free-form" and "open-form" were used interchangeably to describe this impulse in painting and poetry.

To a large extent, the parallel was spontaneous, the product of shared historical and cultural circumstances.[113] But there were cross-media influences as well. McClure, for example, came to San Francisco to study with Still, only to emulate his painting in poetry. Corbett and Lobdell both made abstract drawings to accompany publications of poetry. An aspiring poet himself, Corbett was particularly close to Robert Duncan, who based a character on him in his first play, *Faust Foutu*.[114] Corbett liked to think of his abstractions as equivalents of poetry, in the Symbolist sense of a non-narrative imagining of experience, evoked through suggestion rather than definition.[115]

But it was the second-generation Abstract Expressionists in San Francisco with whom the Beat poets shared the most and developed the closest dialogue.

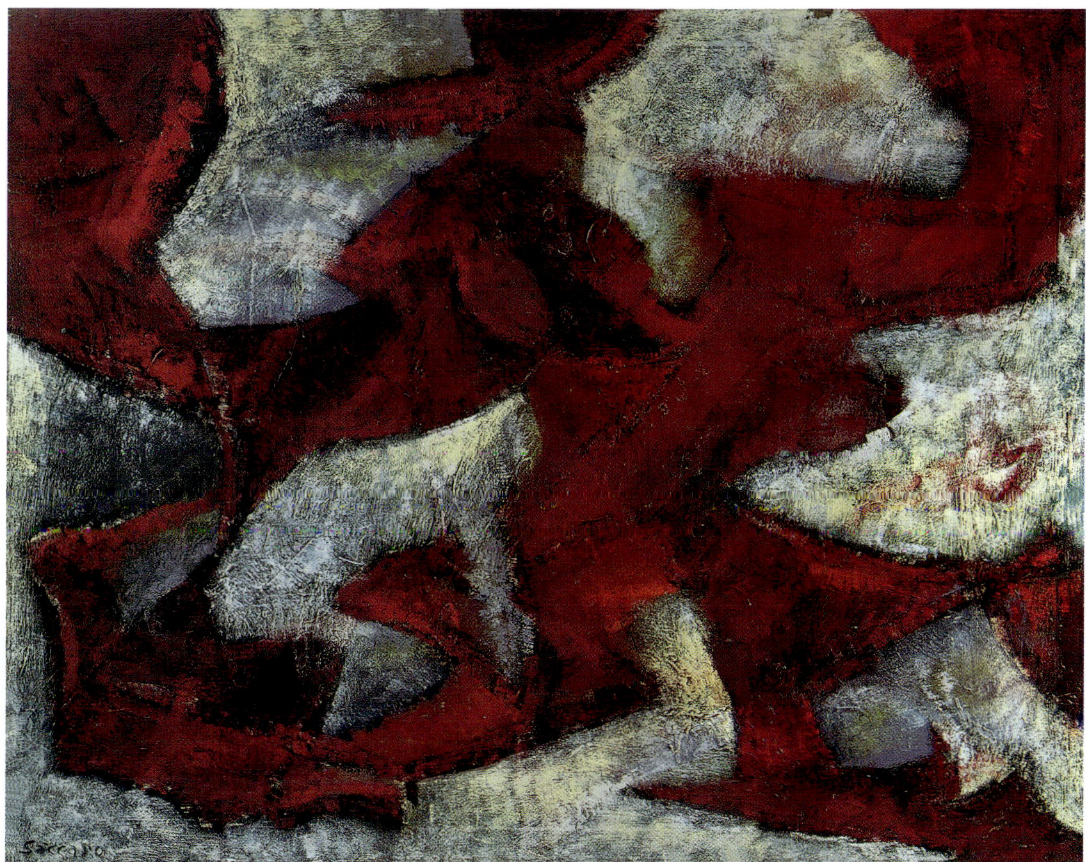

This exchange reached its peak with the artist-and-poet-run cooperative galleries of the 1950s—notably King Ubu and its successor, the Six. Both served as primary venues for second-generation artists such as Gechtoff, Kelly, Remington, and DeFeo while staging poetry readings for a number of important rising poets, notably Duncan, Ginsberg, Spicer, and McClure. King Ubu and the Six were also obligatory ports of call for Jack Kerouac and other writers visiting from the East.

The spirit of Dada, an undercurrent in San Francisco since Spohn's zany assemblages of the early 1940s, was pervasive throughout San Francisco's alternative galleries. King Ubu and the Six styled themselves along the lines of the Cabaret Voltaire, with evenings much like the Dada "manifestation nights," where poets and painters collaborated on spontaneous skits, pranks, and performances. At the Place, a gallery-bar in North Beach where Kelly worked as a bartender, there were open microphone "blabbermouth nights" every week. Wally Hedrick described those sessions as a "re-run of Zurich, 1912–1914, where people could get up and say anything they wanted and then everybody'd pound on the tables and drink their beer, just generally raise hell."[116] The King Ubu gallery, which Duncan, Jess, and the painter Harry Jacobus founded in late 1952, took its name from Alfred Jarry's absurdist play *Ubu Roi*. The graffito Jacobus scrawled on his own drawings in an exhibition at King Ubu—"Eye Don't Giv a Fok Abot Tast"—articulates the rebellious spirit that made Jarry's play a favorite among the Dadaists.[117] Yet the atmosphere at King Ubu was never one of abject nihilism. There were sacred passions shared by poets and painters alike, which included an enthusiasm for Romantic poetry and for the religions of Asia. For all their tongue-in-cheek self-parody, the artists of King Ubu retained their belief in the regenerative capacity of art.

The Six Gallery, which took over King Ubu's space in 1954, derived its name from the number of its founders, Jack Spicer and five of his students from a

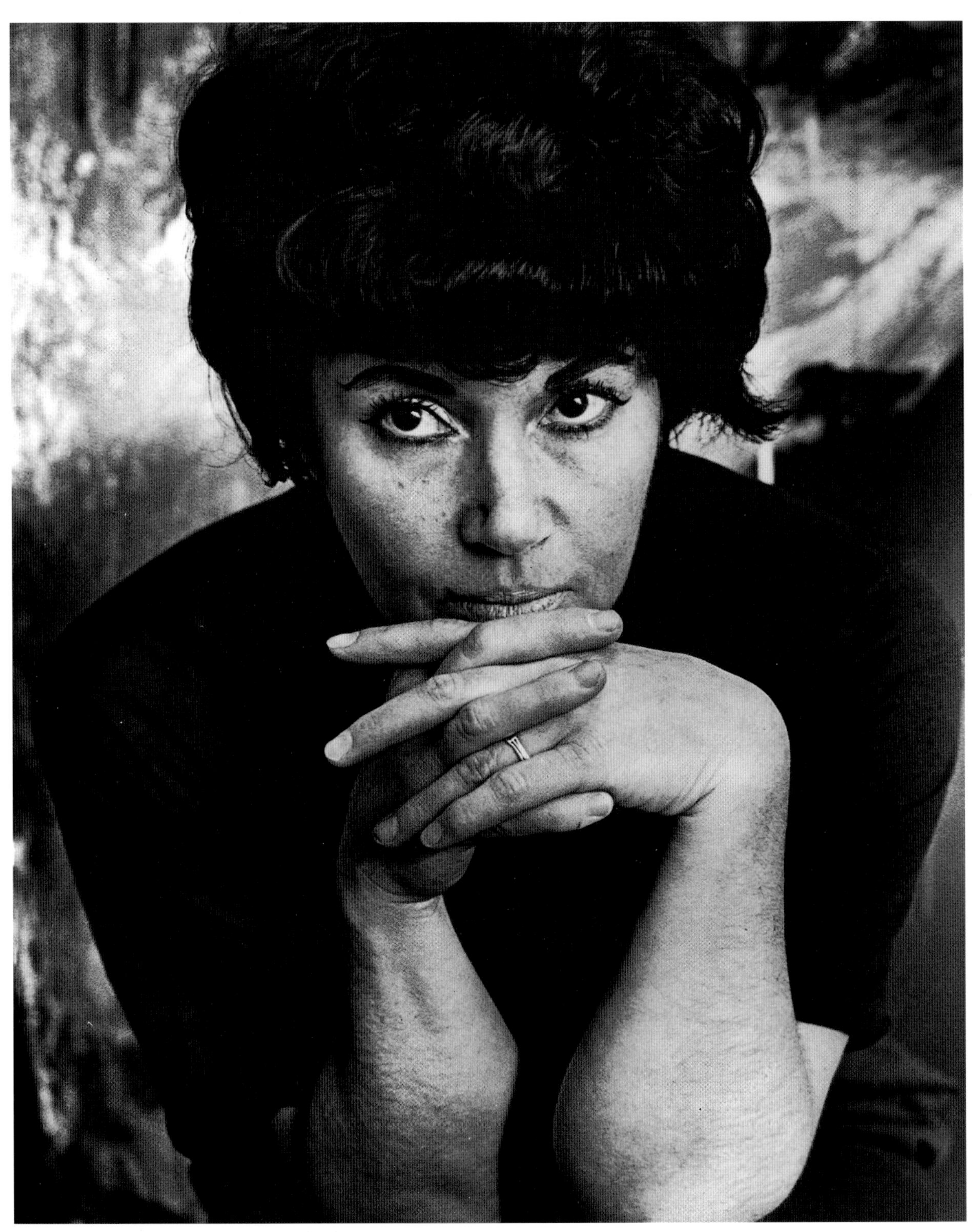

Figure 5.48

Mimi Jacobs, Portrait of Jay DeFeo, 1960. Gelatin silver print,
13½ × 10½ in. Collection, The Oakland Museum, gift of
Mimi Jacobs.

poetry course at the California School of Fine Arts: Remington, Hedrick, John Allen Ryan, Hayward King, and David Simpson. Even more than King Ubu, the Six promoted a cross-pollination of the arts.[118] Its founding charter called for the combination of music, poetry, painting, theater, film, and photography—an ambitious goal that spawned a broad range of experimental art forms such as Hedrick's "color organ," a precursor of rock-and-roll light shows of the 1960s, and the poetry-inspired tragicomic strain of assemblage later known as Funk Art. At the Six, where paintings were often displayed next to pages of poetry, multimedia collaborations became commonplace. One of the first instances of a Happening on the West Coast was the result of such a collaboration between painters and poets at the Six in 1957. Billed as an evening of "collective expressionism," the event consisted of readings by Ginsberg and Kerouac, during which several works of art and a piano were destroyed with an ax.[119]

The Six Gallery figures heavily in the mythic history of the Beats, for it was there, according to Kerouac and other participants, that the movement officially began. On the evening of October 13, 1955, five poets read aloud on the gallery's stage to an audience composed mostly of artists and poets. Each of them —Ginsberg, McClure, Gary Snyder, Philip Whalen, and Philip Lamantia—was introduced, appropriately enough, by San Francisco's senior bard, Kenneth Rexroth. Kerouac's account of the event in *The Dharma Bums* is still the most vivid:

> Anyway I followed the whole gang of howling poets to the reading at the Gallery Six that night, which was, among other important things, the night of the birth of the San Francisco Poetry Renaissance. Everyone was there. It was a mad night. And I was the one who got things jumping by going around collecting dimes and quarters from the rather stiff audience standing around in the gallery and coming back with three huge gallon jugs of California Burgundy and getting them all piffed so that by eleven o'clock when Alvah Goldbook [Ginsberg] was reading his, wailing his poem "Wail" ["Howl"] drunk with arms outspread everybody was yelling "Go! Go! Go!" (like a jam session) and old Rheinhold Cacoethes [Rexroth] the father of the Frisco poetry scene was wiping his tears in gladness.[120]

Among the artists most affected by this manic exchange was Jay DeFeo (fig. 5.48). Although DeFeo's work seldom contains the insurrectionary wit that was typical at the Six, it does embody the attitudes toward art making that set her generation apart from the preceding one and paved the way for the ascendance of Funk Art in the late 1950s. As intensely personal as her painting was, DeFeo refused to become identified with a single style. Like her husband, Hedrick, who was known to destroy repetitive works when he found them, DeFeo employed a variety of idioms and media to challenge aesthetic labels and standards of taste.[121]

DeFeo was one of the few significant Bay Area abstract painters besides Sam Francis to have studied art at the University of California at Berkeley, which promoted American Scene painting and a relatively academic variety of abstraction for most of the 1940s. After receiving a master's degree in 1951, she spent a year and a half traveling through Europe, stopping off in Manhattan on her way back to California to see the work of Philip Guston and other New York Abstract Expressionists. The ink and tempera drawings DeFeo brought back from her trip combined the spontaneity of Abstract Expressionism with the delicacy and finesse of French Tachisme and Asian calligraphy. Many of the motifs would become central to her later work: circles, triangles, and crosses would recur in various media throughout her career.

In 1954 DeFeo quite suddenly burst upon the San Francisco art scene. That year she married Hedrick, moved to San Francisco, and had her first solo show at the Place. The following year she submitted an assemblage work to the annual drawing and print exhibition at the San Francisco Museum of Art that became a succès de scandale in the local art community: a wooden cross approximately twelve feet high, covered with white butcher paper, with a large glass jewel and a splash of tempera at its center. Almost as soon as it was installed, it was defaced with graffiti. One of DeFeo's fellow exhibitors recalled: "The work immediately became a storm center while newspaper critics denounced it and Art Lovers wrote dirty words on it. The Museum finally removed it from the exhibition with the explanation that the burden of inscriptions placed on it had made it an obscene object."[122]

DeFeo's diverse work of the later 1950s ranged from the torrential *Doctor Jazz* (1958; fig. 5.49) to the meticulously rendered and hypnotic painting *The Eyes* (1958), which was inspired by a line of poetry by Philip Lamantia: "Tell him I have eyes only for heaven."[123] After 1956 DeFeo also concentrated on large-scale monochrome abstractions such as *The*

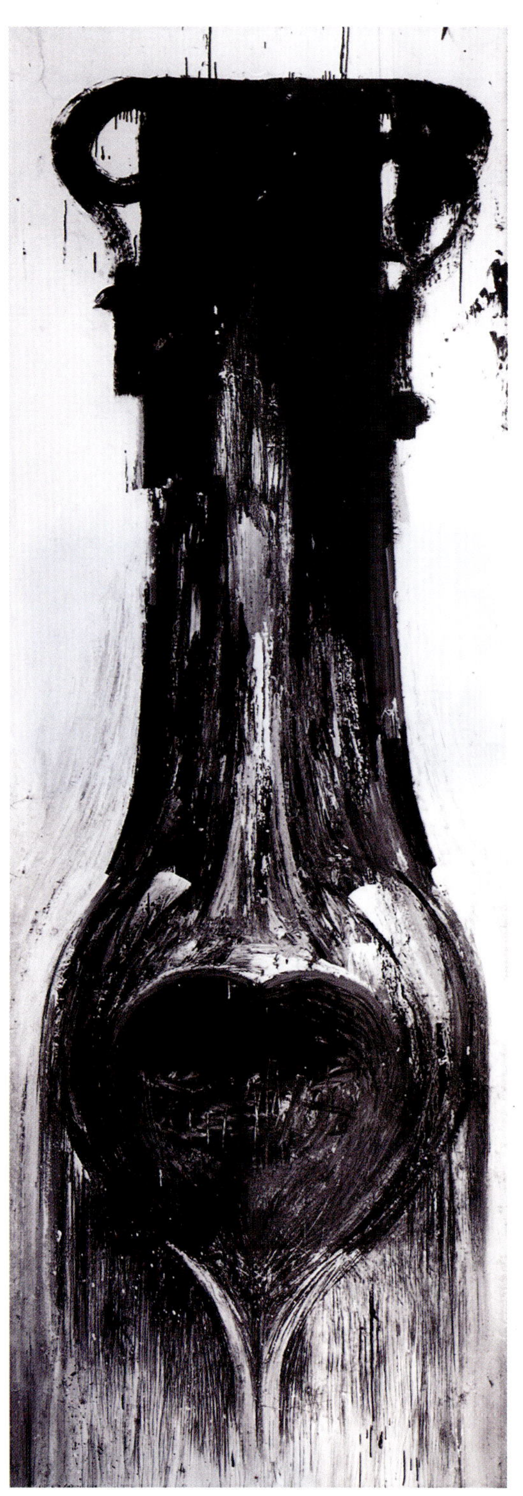

Above: Jay DeFeo, *Doctor Jazz,* 1958. Oil and mixed media on paper, 125½ × 42½ in. Collection, the Estate of Jay DeFeo. Photograph courtesy, Nicole Klagsbrun Gallery, New York; photographer: Ben Blackwell.

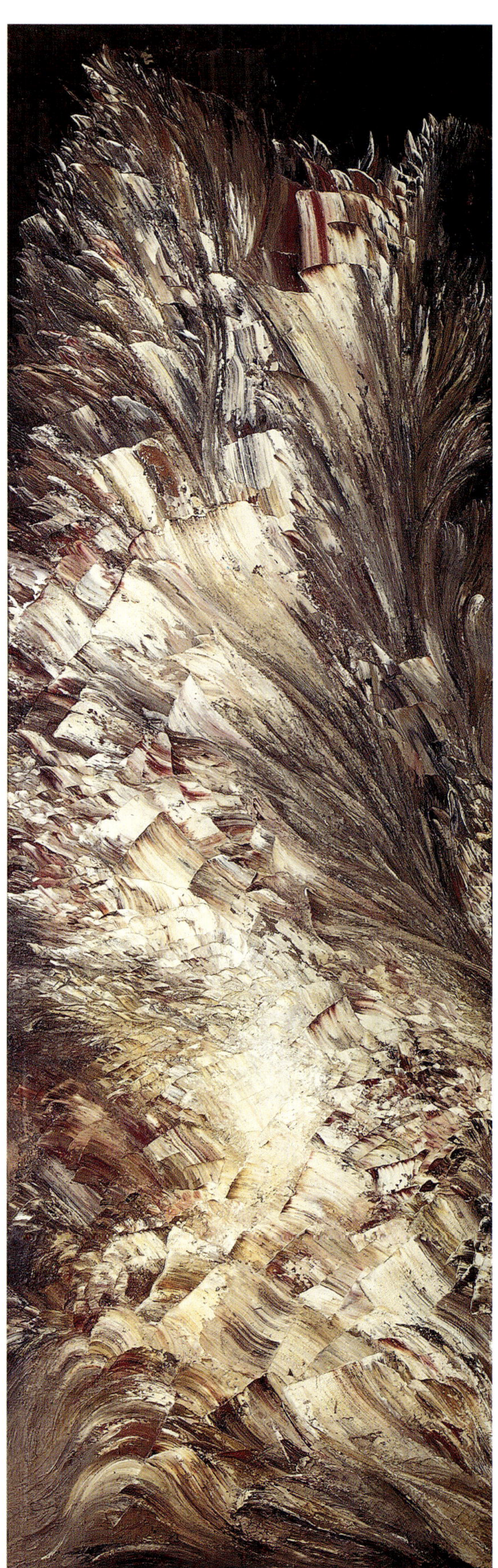

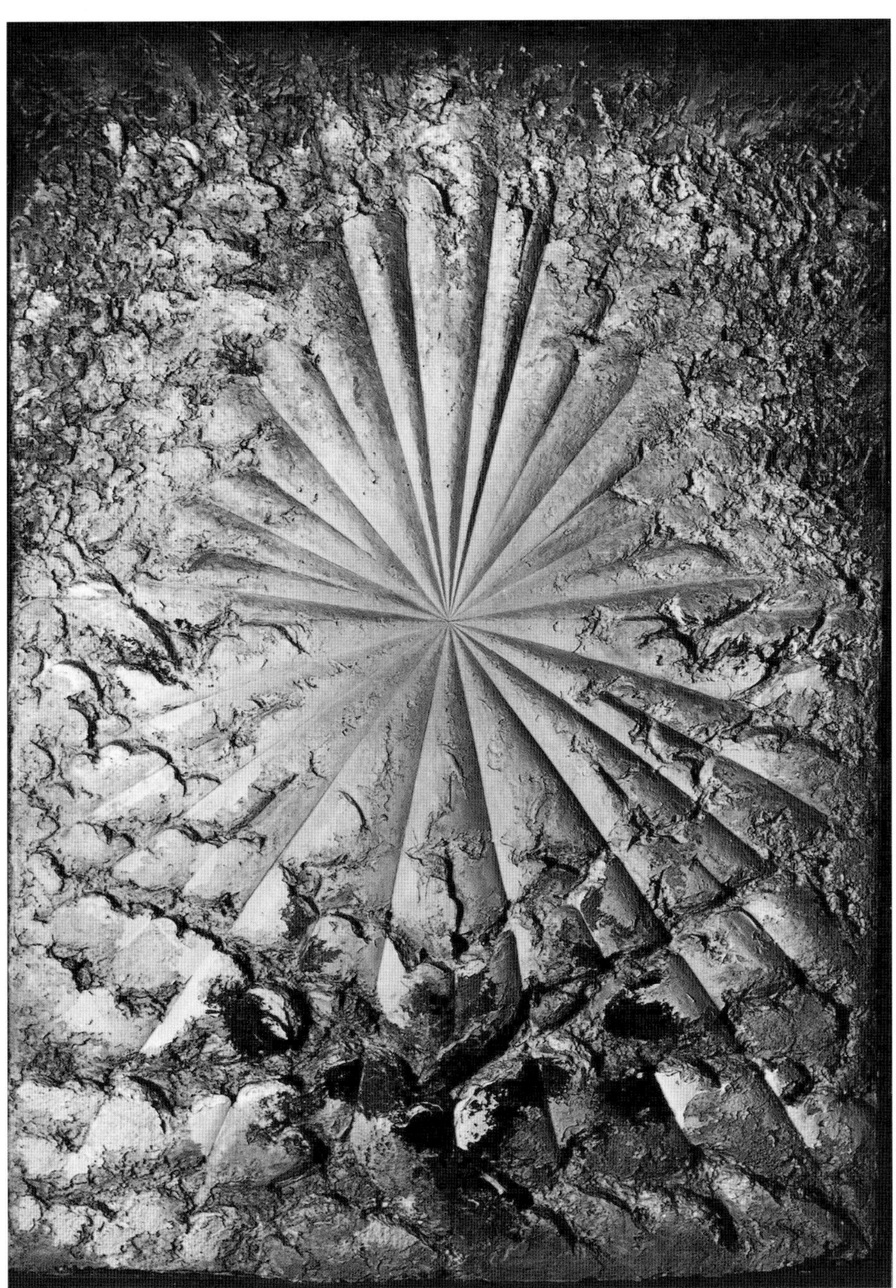

Veronica (1957; fig. 5.50) and *Incision* (1958–61; see fig. 3.7), both of which partake of the organic tonality and ascending sweep of the San Francisco School.[124] While *The Veronica* suggests a tidal wave, *Incision* conveys the impression of a scorched track of lava.

DeFeo took San Francisco's tradition of densely piled surfaces to a greater extreme than any other artist before or since in *The Rose,* her best-known work (fig. 5.51). For more than six years, from 1958 to 1965, DeFeo applied layer upon layer of paint, embedding bits of wire, beads, and other scraps from her

Figure 5.50

Opposite: Jay DeFeo, *The Veronica,* 1957. Oil on canvas, 132 × 42⅜ in. San Francisco Museum of Modern Art, gift of Irving Blum. Photographer: Antoni E. Dolinski.

Figure 5.51

Above: Jay DeFeo, *The Rose,* 1958–65. Oil and mixed media on canvas, 129 × 92 × 8 in. Collection, the Estate of Jay DeFeo. Photographer: Frank Thomas.

jewelry making until she had created a canvas with a surface depth of eight inches. With its radiating image of a mandala, *The Rose* was clearly a product of its time and place, reflecting the San Francisco artists' preoccupation with non-Western religions in the 1950s. But it also addressed issues that were rapidly coming to the fore in New York's art discourse. Like Robert Rauschenberg's contemporaneous "combine" assemblages, DeFeo's piece forced observers to question the aesthetic boundary between painting and sculpture. In a statement written for publication in *Art in America* while *The Rose* was in progress, DeFeo explained:

> Although [I am] a painter by definition, my work as it has emerged in the past two years could more accurately be described as a combination of painting and sculpture. I consider the aspects of each to be inseparable and interdependent . . . It is not my intention to be first a sculptor and subsequently a painter, adorning the three-dimensional form in a painterly manner. To realize satisfaction in this effort I must cope with the problems of both sculpture and painting as we have understood them in the past, and attempt to solve the new problems that emerge out of the dependency of one upon the other in my work.[125]

In 1959 DeFeo took part in the Museum of Modern Art's *Sixteen Americans* exhibition, a roundup of new talent organized by Dorothy Miller, which introduced Rauschenberg, Jasper Johns, Frank Stella, and Ellsworth Kelly. Both DeFeo and Hedrick, who was also in the show, chose not to attend the opening or to follow up on any of the contacts the exposure offered.[126] The Stable Gallery in New York invited DeFeo to join its growing roster of successful artists, but she declined in order to concentrate exclusively on painting *The Rose,* which was itself becoming unmarketably heavy and unwieldy. By 1960, *The Rose* weighed twenty-three hundred pounds and was too large to fit through the studio windows or doors. A friend of DeFeo's later remembered that *The Rose* lent a religious feeling to her high-ceilinged Fillmore Street apartment: "The whole place had it as the fixed focus, which is why it was so dramatic when you went there. It was like a little cathedral."[127] It took an eviction in 1964 to force DeFeo to remove the painting, an event immortalized in Bruce Conner's film *The White Rose.* Appropriately enough, until the mid-1990s the work stood enshrined like an oracle behind a wall, invisible yet potent, in its place of spiritual origin: the California School of Fine Arts.[128]

Epilogue

As with the inception of Abstract Expressionism in San Francisco, no single date can designate the movement's close. Even today, a number of the principal artists—notably Jefferson, Lobdell, and Dugmore—are exploring variations of the themes and objectives they set for themselves in the late 1940s and 1950s. Dixon continued painting his fiery expressionist abstractions until his death in 1967. Other artists shifted their approach in response to the temper of the times. Smith adopted a humorous figuration that made a bow to the Pop culture of the mid-1960s, while Saccaro's reverence for John Cage led to a series of conceptual works based on Cage's musical scores. Bladen was the only San Francisco Abstract Expressionist to become seriously involved with Minimalism, although he did so after moving to the East Coast.[129]

Few artists picked up the Abstract Expressionist torch after the 1950s came to a close. Of those artists, Charles Strong (fig. 5.52) remained perhaps truest to the original ethos of the movement. A former molybdenum miner from the Colorado Rockies, Strong came to San Francisco in late 1959 and studied at the California School of Fine Arts with Jefferson and Lobdell.[130] He seems to have absorbed their stubborn commitment to painterly abstraction in full face of its commercial demise, for the style he developed was nationally unmarketable. Paintings such as *Hemlock* (1962; fig. 5.53), with their roily surfaces and sooty whites, have the epic presence and vertiginous sweep of work by Strong's predecessors. And his "nocturnes" of the early to mid 1960s—so named for their vast expanses of scaly blacks and murky browns—could not have been further removed from the fresh-faced Pop Art that dominated the art magazines (fig. 5.54).

Individual careers aside, it is safe to say that as a group phenomenon, Abstract Expressionism in San Francisco had reached its peak and had begun to wane by 1957. That year, several events signaled the movement's decline. Paul Mills's exhibition at the Oakland Art Museum, *Contemporary Bay Area Figurative Painting,* called attention to the beginning of a new trend. Within a short time, Bischoff, Park, and Diebenkorn were hailed as leaders of a distinctive California movement, which, through a series of articles in *Time* and *Life,* gave Bay Area painting its first national acclaim.[131] The year 1957 also marked the rise of another movement that would soon eclipse Abstract Expressionism in San Francisco. With the

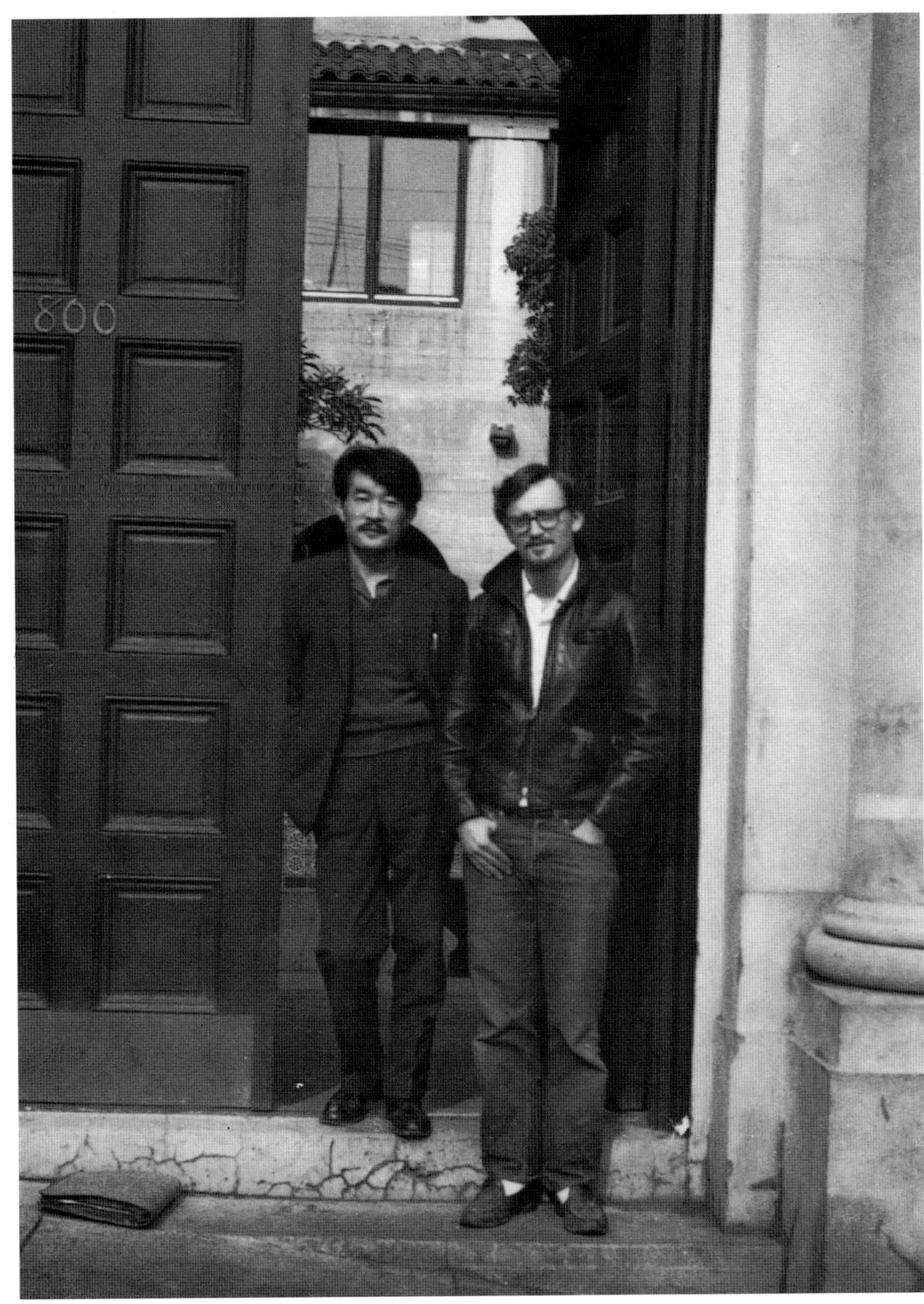

Figure 5.52

Charles Strong (*right*) with Kenji Nanao, at the entrance to

the California School of Fine Arts, September 1960.

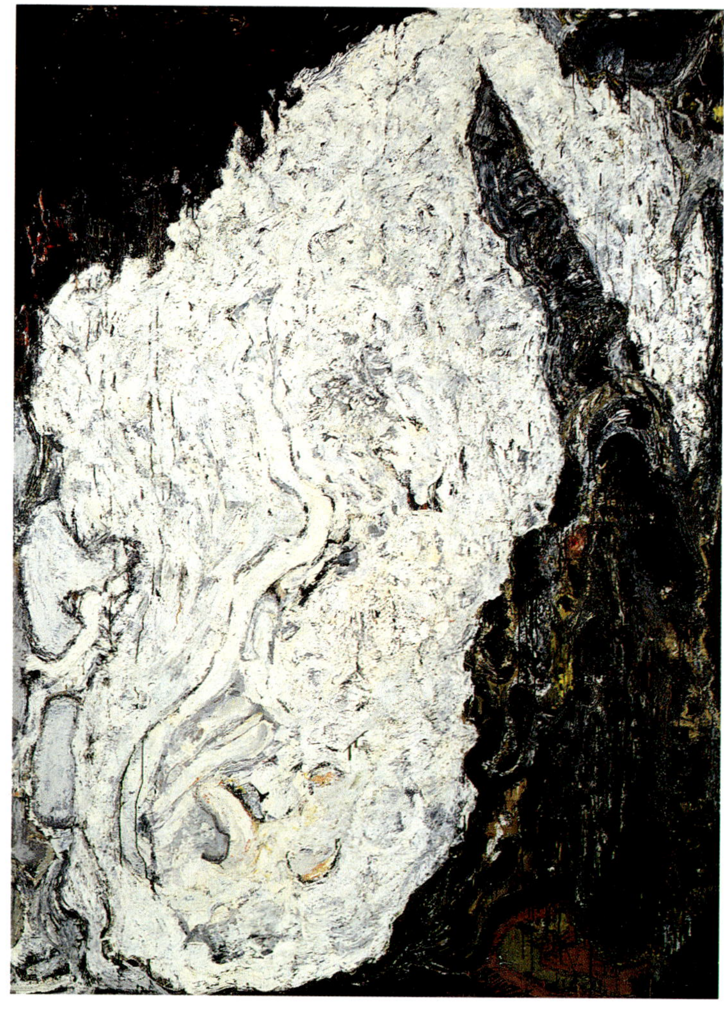

publication of Jack Kerouac's *On the Road* and the start of Allen Ginsberg's obscenity trial for "Howl," the Beat movement was officially under way. On Sunday, May 4, 1958, a three-day exposé in the *San Francisco Examiner* proclaimed San Francisco's North Beach "the headquarters of the Beat Generation."[132] The ensuing droves of Beatniks, columnist Herb Caen's catchy sobriquet for the new breed of bohemian disaffiliates—along with the tourists who gawked at them from crowded Gray Line buses—sent many artists fleeing San Francisco for New York, the Southwest, and Mexico.[133] The publicity also trained critical attention for the first time on the "funky" strain of assemblage art that had largely grown out of the Beat movement in the mid to late 1950s—ultimately known as Funk Art.[134]

The demise of Abstract Expressionism was not debated loudly on a public platform in San Francisco as it was in New York. A few scattered commentators did note a general dilution of quality through popularization. As early as 1954, Frankenstein lamented the movement's spread to the University of California at Berkeley and to the California College of Arts and Crafts, remarking that "the avant-garde has traded its beret and velvet jacket for the cap and gown."[135] Two years later, Herschel Chipp observed somewhat wistfully that with the domination of contemporary abstraction, "there is scarcely even an avant-garde any more."[136]

But unlike New York, San Francisco had neither critics such as John Canaday to attack the movement nor defenders like Thomas Hess to take up its cause.[137] Nor did the artists themselves line up in opposing camps. Although the Bay Area Figurative movement was viewed by a few New York critics as a deliberate challenge to Abstract Expressionism, the

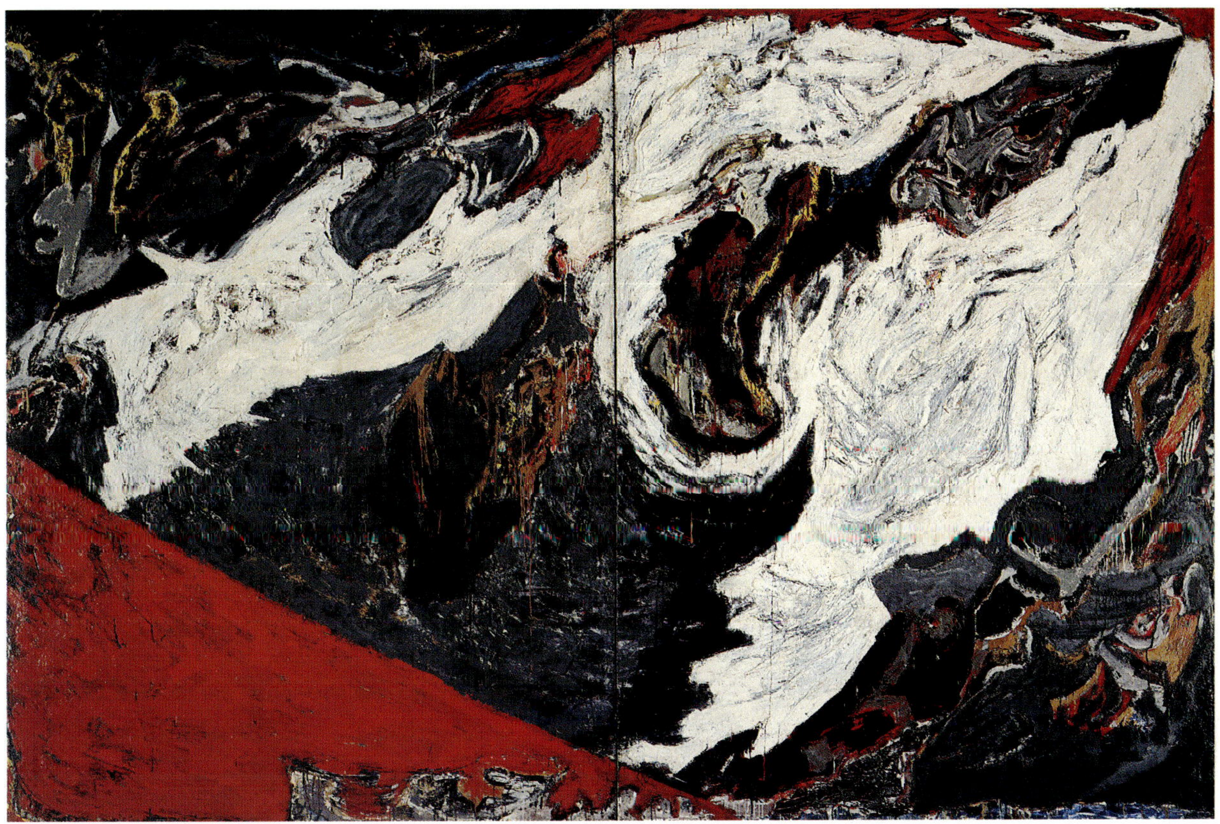

Figure 5.54

Charles Strong, *Untitled (Diptych),* 1962–63. Oil on canvas,
94 × 137¼ in. Collection, Mag Dimond. Photographer:
Ira D. Schrank.

artists tended to agree with the Oakland Art Museum's curator, Paul Mills, that the new figuration was "an abandonment not so much of abstraction in particular as of the whole politics of style."[138]

San Francisco's Funk artists, too, were unconcerned with positing themselves as the new leaders of the avant-garde. Whereas the most vocal antagonists of Abstract Expressionism in New York were the early practitioners of assemblage such as Allan Kaprow, their counterparts in San Francisco tended to admire the older generation.[139] Likewise, while members of the New York School dismissed assemblage as "an anti-art joke at best," many Abstract Expressionists in San Francisco experimented with junk sculpture themselves.[140] Dugmore, Smith, Diebenkorn, and Spohn each had exhibitions of their own assemblage art during the late 1940s and early 1950s.[141]

In fact, what distinguished the Bay Area art community most during the 1950s was its atmosphere of relaxed collegiality. In galleries such as the Six, the Dilexi, and the Spatsa, abstract and figurative paintings hung comfortably side by side, while artists such as Brown (fig. 5.55), Hedrick, and DeFeo moved from one idiom to the next with impunity. The lack of competitive tension among the various forms of art in San Francisco resulted largely from the stakes being lower than in New York. The older generation of artists in San Francisco had not achieved the acclaim that might have motivated the next generation to topple them from their position of privilege. Ultimately, this very absence of rivalry shaped the art that was to follow. Indeed, both the major movements in San Francisco during the 1960s—Figuration and Funk—grew out of, rather than in opposition to, Abstract Expressionism. Meanwhile, Pop, Minimalism, and Hard-Edge abstraction—New York movements that

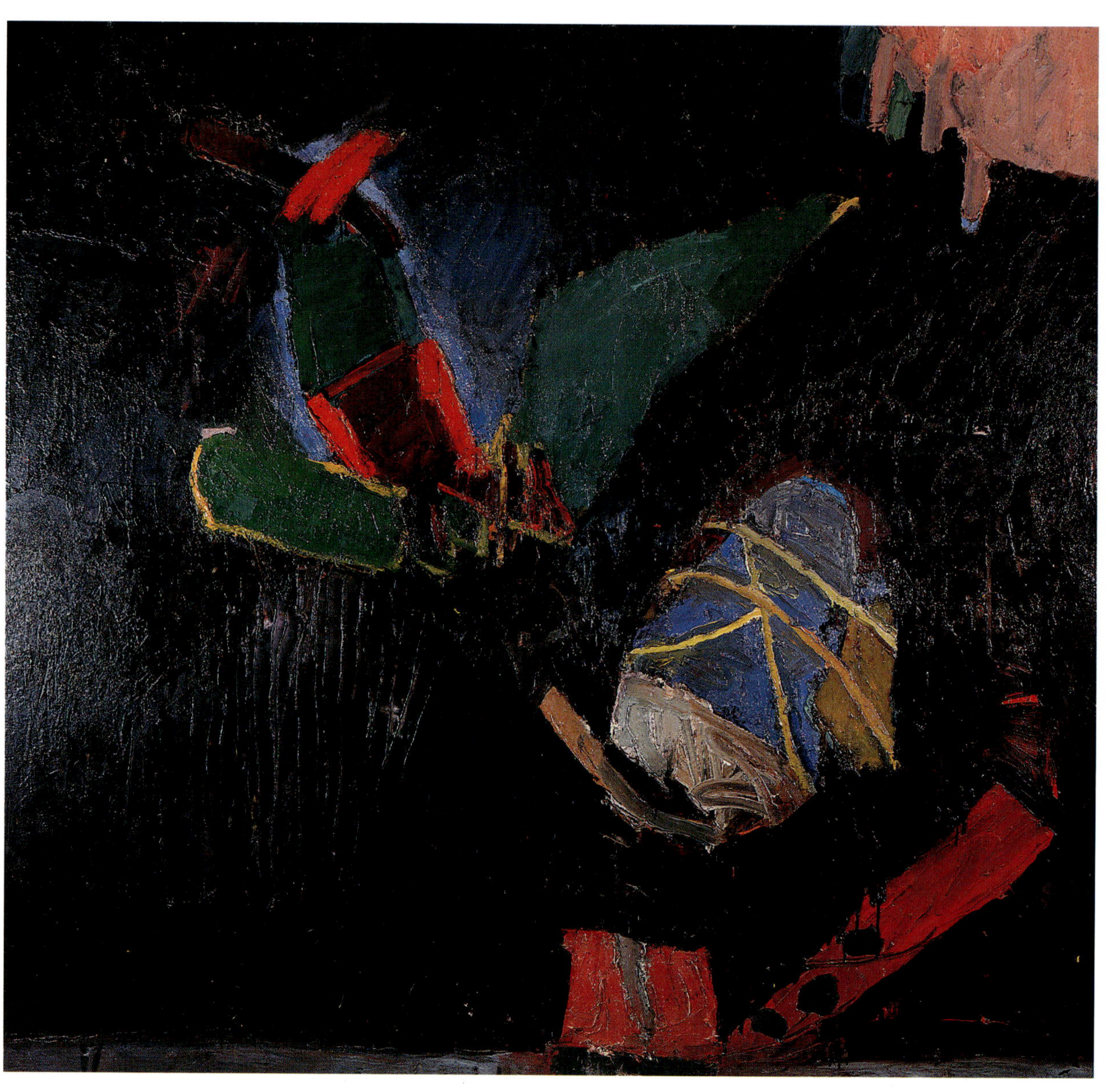

Figure 5.55

Above: Joan Brown, *Fussing Around by the Light of the Moon,* 1959. Oil on canvas, 84 × 88 in. Private collection. Photograph courtesy, Carlson Gallery, Carmel, California.

Figure 5.56

Opposite: Elmer Bischoff, *Figure in Landscape,* ca. 1957. Oil on canvas, 52 × 57½ in. Collection, The Oakland Museum, gift of the Women's Board of The Oakland Museum. Photographer: M. Lee Fatherree.

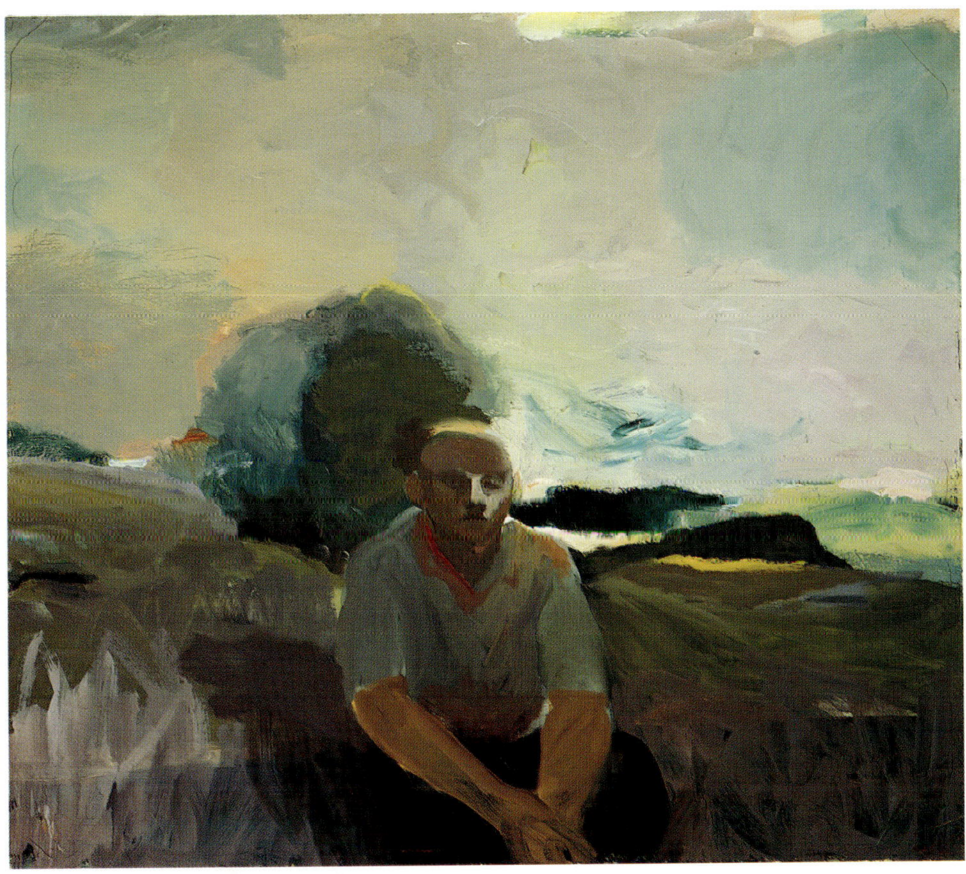

developed in sharp, often bitter, opposition to the tenets of Abstract Expressionism—found few followers in the Bay Area. San Francisco artists may have left Abstract Expressionism behind, but they remained loyal to many of its ideals.

The allegiance of the Bay Area figurative artists to Abstract Expressionism was all too apparent to critics in New York, who generally viewed the tendency as a liability. It is symptomatic of the differing regional expectations that the critic Hilton Kramer, previously supportive of the New York School, could complain in the early 1960s that Diebenkorn's expressive treatment of the figure—as opposed to the comparative realism of an artist like Philip Pearlstein—remained too close to the "taste, physical comportment, and over-all aesthetic loyalty" of gesture painting.[142] Critics in San Francisco, by comparison, mostly considered this family resemblance an asset, as did the artists themselves. Indeed, Park saw virtually no distinction between nonobjective and figurative painting, insisting: "The line between [them] is no different than the line between still life and portrait paintings . . . I think concepts of progress in painting are rather fool-

ish."[143] Well into the 1960s, the Bay Area figurative painters continued to value such Abstract Expressionist ideals as immediacy, spontaneity, and above all, the communication of mood and emotion (fig. 5.56). Even the empathetic premise of Abstract Expressionism—that object and maker were indivisible—persisted in Bay Area Figuration. As Bischoff remarked, speaking for the group, "the complexity of yourself being poured into the painting is the issue."[144]

The legacy of Abstract Expressionism for San Francisco Funk artists is perhaps less apparent on casual glance, but equally significant. Through the 1960s, artists such as Hedrick, Conner, Seymour Locks, and Jess continued to draw from a core of intensely personal experience, ignoring the tendency of assemblage artists in New York to neutralize and dehumanize their subject matter. Like their Abstract Expressionist predecessors, the major practitioners of Funk made fantasy and enigma central to their work. They mined the Victorian ruins of San Francisco's Western Addition for materials, which often gave their assemblages an aura of mystery and nostalgia. This latter characteristic was particularly typical of

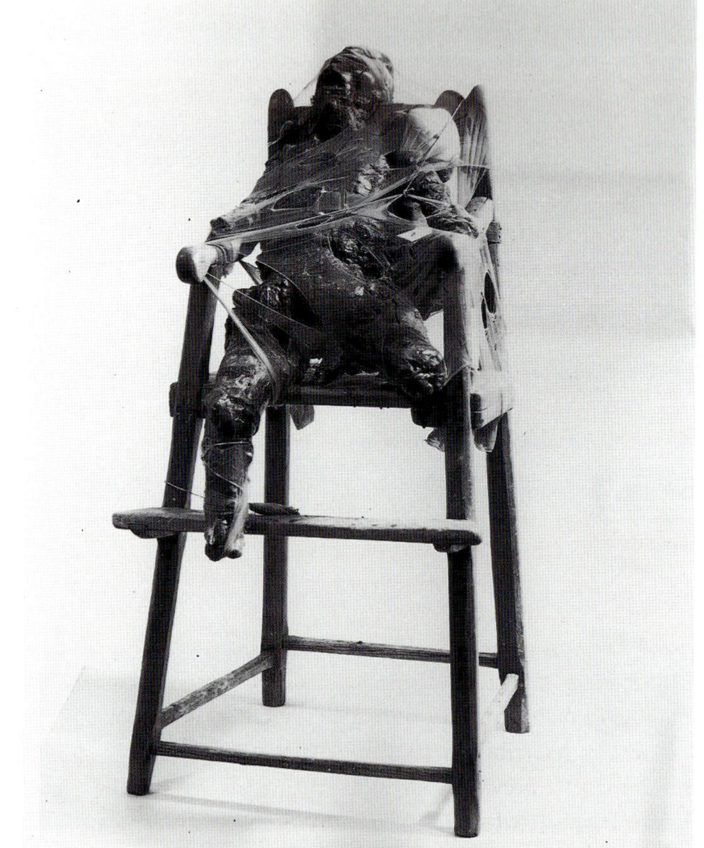

Figure 5.57

Right: Bruce Conner, *Child,* 1959–60. Assemblage: wax figure with nylon, cloth, metal, and twine in a highchair; 34⅝ × 17 × 16½ in. Collection, The Museum of Modern Art, New York, gift of Philip Johnson.

Figure 5.58

Below: Roy De Forest, *Country Dog Gentlemen,* 1972. Polymer on canvas, 66¾ × 97 in. Collection, San Francisco Museum of Modern Art, gift of the Hamilton-Wells Collection. Photographer: Don Myer.

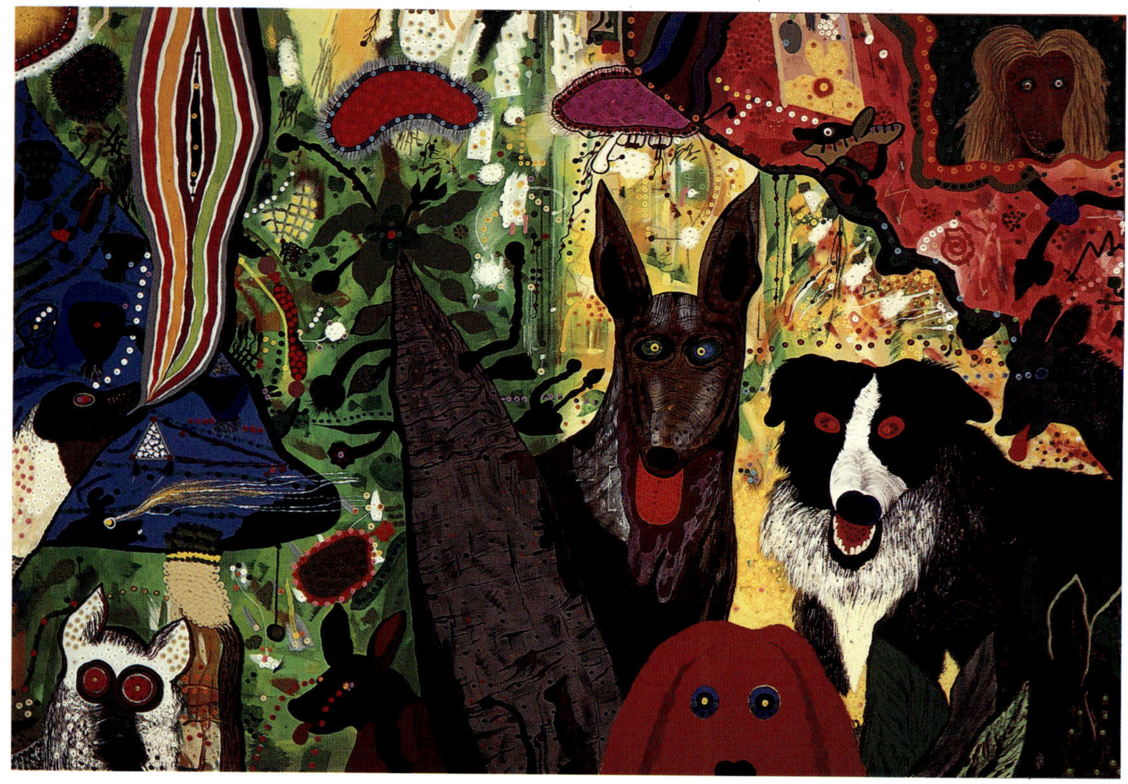

the work of Conner, who found a major source of inspiration in freakish nineteenth-century carnival memorabilia, including such oddities as the midget costumes of Tom Thumb, the mummies, and the mechanical dolls housed in the Sutro Museum.[145] Conner showed a gothic taste for horror in works such as *Child* (1959–60; fig. 5.57), a mutilated doll in a highchair, caught in a web of nylon stockings. Conner aimed, not to exemplify the "aesthetics of boredom" prevalent in New York during much of the 1960s, but to provoke violent emotions.[146]

In addition to their fondness for openly emotional content, Funk artists such as Conner retained the San Francisco School's disregard for technical finesse and durability, taking the dirty, scruffy aesthetic of Abstract Expressionism to new extremes.[147] As Joan Brown remarked, speaking of her peers' predilection for aged, decomposing materials, the general consensus was "the rattier the better."[148] The Funk artists were not alone in appreciating dingy, impermanent objects, but they used them more often than assemblagists in New York or Los Angeles. Lack of audience no doubt contributed to this tendency; as Conner observed, the prevalent attitude at the time was: "No one else cared what we were doing, so why should we?"[149] Wallace Berman's Semina Art Gallery effectively illustrates Conner's comment. Housed in a roofless boathouse that had been abandoned along the Larkspur marshlands, the gallery literally sank into the mud after giving some of Berman's friends exhibitions lasting no more than a few hours each.[150] The spirit of Berman's gallery survived until relatively recently in the Emeryville mudflats, where anonymous assemblages could be seen in various stages of decay along the eastern approach to the Bay Bridge.

The antiformalist ethic expressed in perishable junk sculpture extended well beyond San Francisco's Funk Art circles. Only a minority of artists in Northern California embraced the appealing bright colors and smooth, slick surfaces of Pop, Op, and Formalist Abstraction.[151] The clean, antiseptic L.A. Look, so fashionable in Southern California during the 1960s, never really caught hold in San Francisco. David Simpson and Sam Tchakalian—the Bay Area's best-known formalists of the 1960s—refused to adopt the anonymous painting methods popularized by artists elsewhere. Even Mel Ramos and Wayne Thiebaud,

the artists most closely associated with Pop Art in Northern California, rejected mechanical production techniques that erased the presence of the artist's hand.

Most of San Francisco's artists of the 1960s did not fall into any of the mainstream categories established in New York or Los Angeles. If any single trend can be identified, it is what Hilton Kramer called "Dude Ranch Dada" to describe the eccentric self-styled primitivism of William T. Wiley's work of the 1960s and early 1970s.[152] Wiley's fanciful *Columbus Re-Routed* series and his quirky animal hide constructions, with their tongue-in-cheek references to cowboy and Indian lore, typified the self-conscious regionalism of San Francisco artists who traced their lineage to the faux naïf spoofs of artists such as Spohn, Smith, and Kelly. Among the more excessive examples of this tendency are De Forest's childlike canine fantasies (fig. 5.58) and Brown's Rousseau-inspired animals dressed like people. The imaginary maps of Jeremy Anderson and Fred Martin also epitomize the Bay Area's penchant for intensely subjective and fantastic art—a penchant that would give rise to the drug-induced psychedelic visionary art of the late 1960s and early 1970s.

In sum, many of the most cherished ideals of Abstract Expressionism endured for subsequent generations of artists in San Francisco, whereas in other parts of the country they were repudiated and even ridiculed. Autobiography, fantasy, and subjective feeling continued to be important sources of inspiration, while idiosyncrasy was strongly encouraged. That these ideals were so tenacious may reflect their rootedness in the cultural identity of Northern California rather than the impact of Abstract Expressionism itself. San Francisco's celebration of eccentricity dates back at least as far as 1880, when more than thirty thousand people are said to have attended the funeral of Emperor Norton, a retired banker who believed that he was emperor of North America.[153] Individualism and nonconformity have been central to San Francisco's sense of self since the Gold Rush, and their manifestations are myriad: the anarchist movement of the 1940s, the Beat and Free Speech movements of the 1950s and 1960s, the counterculture of Haight-Ashbury, and the multitude of alternative lifestyles that flourish today.

By Susan Landauer and Andrea Feeser with the assistance of Mara Skov

Specific dates and exhibition venues are provided where possible. Any form of publication with an exhibition is indicated with the reference "cat." In most cases, type of teaching appointment is not specified.

The following Bay Area arts institutions underwent name changes: The California School of Design (founded 1874) became the Mark Hopkins Institute of Art (1893), the San Francisco Institute of Art (1906), the California School of Fine Arts (1916), and the San Francisco Art Institute (from 1961). The Oakland Art Gallery (founded 1916) became the Oakland Art Museum (1953) and the Oakland Museum (from 1969). The San Francisco Museum of Art (founded in 1916) became a private institution devoted to modern art (1935) and the San Francisco Museum of Modern Art (1975). References to these institutions spanning periods of more than one name use the later name.

GEORGE ABEND   Born in New York City (1922). Served in U.S. Army (1942–46). Studied at University of California, Berkeley (1946–47); California School of Fine Arts (1948–50); Académie de la Grande Chaumière, Paris (1951–52); and University of Guadalajara, Mexico (1953–54). Founding member of VORTEX audiovisual happenings group sponsored by California Academy of Sciences, San Francisco (1957–59). Taught at Carnegie Institute of Technology and the Cedar Educational Center in Pittsburgh, Pa. (1962–66). Visiting artist at California State College, Los Angeles, and graphic film consultant at University of Southern California, Los Angeles (1966–69). Worked and exhibited in Big Sur, Calif. (1969–71). Worked in Bonny Doon, near Santa Cruz, Calif. (1971–76). Died in San Francisco (1976).

Selected One-Person Exhibitions   Howard Gallery, San Francisco (1949); Metart Galleries, San Francisco (1950); Lucien Labaudt Gallery, San Francisco (1950, 1952); Galerie de France, Paris (1951); Olivetti Art Gallery, Guadalajara (1954); Batman Gallery, San Francisco (1961); Carnegie Institute of Technology, Pittsburgh, Pa. (1963); Howard Wise Gallery, New York City (1963, 1964, 1965, 1966); New York Six Gallery, New York City (1964); Hewlett Gallery, Pittsburgh, Pa. (1965); Coast Gallery, Big Sur, Calif. (1970); Fulton Gallery, New York City (1973); University of California, Santa Cruz (1976); Hoover Gallery, San Francisco (1983).

RUTH ARMER   Born in San Francisco (1896). Attended California School of Fine Arts (1914–15, 1918–19). Studied with George Bellows, Robert Henri, and John Sloan at Art Students League, New York City; worked as fashion illustrator for *Vogue* magazine (1919–21). Returned to San Francisco; opened portrait studio (1922). Member, Beatrice Judd Ryan's Beaux Arts Club; exhibited in group shows at Galerie Beaux Arts (1924–33). Began first nonobjective paintings, inspired by classical music scores (1930). Established studio school for private instruction (ca. 1931). Faculty member, California School of Fine Arts (1933–40). Showed with Post-Surrealists, San Francisco Museum of Art (1935). Board of Directors, San Francisco Art Institute (1947–52, 1961–68, 1970–77). Died in San Francisco (1977).

Selected One-Person Exhibitions   Vickery, Atkins, & Torrey Gallery, San Francisco (1922, 1931); Gelber-Lilienthal Gallery, San Francisco (1931); Oakland Art Gallery, Oakland, Calif. (1932); Brownell & Lamberton Gallery, New York City (1934); San Francisco Museum of Art (1936, 1939, 1950); Raymond & Raymond Gallery, San Francisco (1952); Eric Locke Gallery, San Francisco (1958); Bolles Gallery,

San Francisco (1963); Gump's Gallery, San Francisco (1967); Quay Gallery, San Francisco (1971, 1972); Braunstein/Quay Gallery, San Francisco (1976, cat.); San Francisco Art Institute (1979).

RICHARD AYER   Born in San Bernardino, Calif. (1909). Spent childhood among Utes in Utah; moved to Fort Bragg, Calif. (1924). Studied at College of Marin, Kentfield, Calif. (1930–31). Studied sculpture at California School of Fine Arts under Ralph Stackpole (1934). Assisted Hilaire Hiler with Aquatic Park murals, San Francisco (decorated second-floor banquet room solo); worked on murals for Hobby and Recreation Pavilion for Golden Gate International Exposition at Treasure Island, San Francisco (1939–40). Served in U.S. Army Air Corps (1942–45). Returned to San Francisco (1945). Studied collage with Jean Varda, sculpture with Zygmund Sazevich, and lithography with Stanley William Hayter at California School of Fine Arts (1946–48). Died in San Francisco (1967).

Selected One-Person Exhibitions   San Francisco Museum of Art (1940); Lucien Labaudt Gallery, San Francisco (ca. 1950); Vesuvio Café, San Francisco (1954); Glad Hand Restaurant, Sausalito, Calif. (1954); I and Thou Coffee House, San Francisco (1967).

MARTIN BAER   Born in Chicago (1894). Attended School of the Art Institute of Chicago (1910–14). Ran commercial design studio in Chicago with brother George (1915–21). Studied art at Munich Staatsakademie with George (1921–24). Spent time in Paris (1924, 1929, 1936, 1937), where he met Chaim Soutine and other painters who had been associated with Amedeo Modigliani (1924). Painted in Algeria and Morocco (1924–28). Exhibited jointly with George in Paris (1926, 1928), Chicago (1926), and New York City, St. Louis, Mo., and Los Angeles (1929). Lived in Ibiza, Spain (1934–36). Lived in St. Tropez, France (1938–40). Lived in Carmel, Calif., and befriended Edward Weston (1941–47). Lived in San Francisco (1947–61). Established studio at 1350 Franklin Street (called "Ghost House") and befriended poets Robert Duncan, Philip Lamantia, Christopher Maclaine, and painters Wally Hedrick, Harry Jacobus, Jess, and Hayward King among others; work evolved toward abstraction (1948–53). Died in San Francisco (1961).

Selected One-Person Exhibitions   Galerie M. Bénézit, Paris (1936); Newhouse Galleries, New York City (1936, cat.; 1941, cat.); The Gordon Beer Art Galleries, Detroit (1937); Dayton Art Institute, Dayton, Ohio (1937); Norfolk Museum of Arts and Sciences, Norfolk, Va. (1937, cat.); Santa Barbara Museum of Art, Santa Barbara, Calif. (1942); Francis Taylor Galleries, Los Angeles (1942); The Fine Arts Gallery of San Diego (1942–43, cat.); California Palace of the Legion of Honor, San Francisco (1943, cat.; 1963, cat.); Carmel Art Association Gallery, Carmel, Calif. (1943); North Point Gallery, Oakland, Calif. (1979); The Oakland Museum, Oakland, Calif. (1979); 871 Fine Arts Gallery, San Francisco (1994, cat. [with Nata Piaskowski photographs in homage to Baer]).

JERROLD BALLAINE   Born in Seattle (1934). Attended San Francisco Art Institute (B.F.A., 1960; M.F.A., 1961), where he befriended Joan Brown and William Morehouse. Taught at Cornish School of Allied Art, Seattle (1963–65). Taught at University of California, Berkeley (1966–94). Board of Trustees, San Francisco Art Institute (1969–73). Lived in Sebastopol, Calif. (1970–75). Creative Arts Institute grant, University of California, Berkeley (1971). Acting director, University Art Museum, University of California, Berkeley (1974–75). Humanities Research Fellowship, University of California, Berkeley (1980). Lives in Sebastopol (since 1986).

Selected One-Person Exhibitions   Zabriskie Gallery, New York City (1960); Gump's Gallery, San Francisco (1961); Robert Schoelkopf Gallery, New York City (1963); Scott Gallery, Seattle (1964; 1965, cat.); Richmond Art Center, Richmond, Calif. (1965, cat.); Mills College Art Gallery, Oakland, Calif. (1967, cat.); Sonoma State College, Rohnert Park, Calif. (1967, cat.; 1975); Galeria Carl van der Voort, San Francisco (1969, cat.); Gallery Reese-Palley, San Francisco (1970, 1971); San Francisco Museum of Art (1970, cat.); Richard White Gallery, Seattle (1970); Bolles Gallery, San Francisco (1974); Stephen Wirtz Gallery, San Francisco (1977); Traver Gallery, Seattle (1978, 1979); San Jose Museum of Art, San Jose, Calif. (1981); Worth Ryder Art Gallery, University of California, Berkeley (1984); Joseph Chowning Gallery, San Francisco (1986); Charles Campbell Gallery, San Francisco (1988); Erickson & Elins Gallery, San Francisco (1988); Stanford University, Stanford, Calif. (1989); Ebert Gallery, San Francisco (1989, 1990, 1991 [two], 1992, 1993 [two]); Collector Gallery, The Oakland Museum, Oakland, Calif. (1992).

ELMER BISCHOFF   Born in Berkeley, Calif. (1916). Studied at University of California, Berkeley (B.A., 1938; M.A., 1939). Served in U.S. Air Force Intelligence Section, England (1942–45). Taught at California School of Fine Arts (1946–52). Resigned from California School of Fine Arts to protest Hassel Smith's dismissal, Douglas MacAgy's departure, and Ernest Mundt's appointment as school director; began painting representationally (1952). Taught at Yuba College, Marysville, Calif. (1953–54). Awarded Abraham Rosenberg Fellowship (1954). Resumed teaching (in 1956) at California School of Fine Arts under administration of Gurdon Woods; appointed chairman of Fine Arts Department (1957–59) and then of Graduate Program (1959–63). Received Ford Foundation grant (1959). Taught at Skowhegan School of Painting and Sculpture, Skowhegan, Maine (summer 1961). Taught at University of California, Berkeley (1963–85). Died in Berkeley, Calif. (1991).

Selected One-Person Exhibitions California Palace of the Legion of Honor, San Francisco (1947); King Ubu Gallery, San Francisco (1953); Paul Kantor Gallery, Los Angeles (1955); San Francisco Art Association Gallery, California School of Fine Arts, San Francisco (1956, cat.); Staempfli Gallery, New York City (1960, 1962, 1964, 1969); M. H. de Young Memorial Museum, San Francisco (1961); E. B. Crocker Art Gallery, Sacramento, Calif. (1964, 1981); Henry Art Gallery, University of Washington, Seattle (1968); Richmond Art Center, Richmond, Calif. (1969); San Francisco Museum of Modern Art (1971, 1986); San Francisco Art Institute (1975); The Oakland Museum, Oakland, Calif. (1975, cat.); Charles Campbell Gallery, San Francisco (1975); University Art Museum, Berkeley (1975, 1982); Art Academy of Cincinnati, Ohio (1975); San Jose Museum of Art, San Jose, Calif. (1979); John Berggruen Gallery, San Francisco (1979, 1980, 1988; 1990, cat.); The Arts Club of Chicago (1980); Contemporary Arts Museum, Houston, Tex. (1980); Grossmont College Art Gallery, El Cajon, Calif. (1981); Hirschl & Adler Modern Inc., New York City (1985, cat.); Laguna Art Museum, Laguna Beach, Calif. (1985, cat.); Wiegand Gallery, College of Notre Dame, Belmont, Calif. (1992, cat.).

RONALD BLADEN Born in Vancouver, British Columbia, Canada (1918). Attended Vancouver School of Art (1937–39). Attended Victoria School of Art and studied privately with Allan Edwards (1938–39). Moved to San Francisco (1939) and attended California School of Fine Arts (until 1945). Received Abraham Rosenberg Fellowship (1946). Co-founded the literary magazine *Ark* (1947), to which he contributed illustrations. Lived in San Carlos, Calif. (1951–55). Moved back to San Francisco (1955) and lived with poet Michael McClure and others in communal house at 707 Scott Street. Illustrated *Ark II,* an anthology of poetry by Michael McClure, Lawrence Ferlinghetti, Kenneth Rexroth, Kenneth Patchen, and other Bay Area poets; met Al Held at 707 Scott Street and at his urging moved to New York, where he co-founded Brata Gallery on Tenth Street (1956). Began freestanding Minimalist sculpture (1963). Received National Endowment for the Arts grants (1964, 1977). Visiting artist, Hunter College, New York City (1967–68). Received John Simon Guggenheim Memorial Foundation fellowship (1968). Visiting artist, Columbia University, New York City (1974). Received Mark Rothko fellowship (1975). Taught at Parsons College, New York City (1976–88). Taught at School of Visual Arts (1978–79).

Artist-in-residence at Skowhegan School of Painting and Sculpture, Skowhegan, Maine (1981). Visiting artist, Yale University, New Haven, Conn. (1983–84). Died in New York City (1988).

Selected One-Person Exhibitions Vancouver Art Gallery, British Columbia, Canada (1946); Raymond & Raymond Gallery, San Francisco (1951); Fine Arts Gallery, University of British Columbia, Vancouver, Canada (1956); Six Gallery, San Francisco (1956); Brata Gallery, New York City (1958, 1960); Green Gallery, New York City (1962); Fischbach Gallery, New York City (1967, 1970, 1971, 1972); Emily Lowe Gallery, Hempstead, N.Y. (1967, cat.); The Hudson River Museum, Yonkers, N.Y. (1977); Hamilton Gallery, New York City (1980); Joan T. Washburn Gallery, New York City (1986, cat.; 1988; 1989, cat.; 1990, cat.; 1992, cat.), CompassRose, Chicago (1987, 1990, cat.); San Francisco Museum of Modern Art (1991, cat.).

RICHARD BOWMAN Born in Rockford, Ill. (1918). Attended School of the Art Institute of Chicago (1938–42). On Edward L. Ryerson Traveling Fellowship, traveled and painted in Mexico, where he met Gordon Onslow-Ford; began *Rock and Sun* series (1943). Traveled to New York; met Max Ernst, Dorothea Tanning, and Fernand Léger (1944). Lived and painted in Chicago (1944–47). Studied at State University of Iowa, Iowa City (M.F.A., 1949). Moved to Sausalito, Calif., and met Clyfford Still and Mark Rothko in San Francisco (1949). Moved to Palo Alto, Calif., and taught at Stanford University; began *Kinetograph* series (1950). Taught at University of Manitoba, Winnipeg, Canada (1950–54). Began *Micromacrocosmos* series (1953). Returned to Palo Alto area (1954). Began *Kinetogenics* series (1956). Began *Environs* series (1960).

Selected One-Person Exhibitions Pinacotheca Gallery, New York City (1945); Milwaukee Art Institute, Wis. (1946); Swetzoff Gallery, Boston (1949); Stanford University Art Gallery, Stanford, Calif. (1950, 1951, 1952, 1953, 1954, 1955; 1956, cat.); Rose Rabow Galleries, San Francisco (every 18 months, 1959–77); San Francisco Museum of Art (1961, cat.; 1970); Roswell Museum and Art Center, Roswell, N.Mex. (1972, cat.); Harcourts Gallery, Inc., San Francisco (1986).

ERNEST BRIGGS Born in San Diego (1923). Served in U.S. Army Air Corps in China, Burma, and India theaters (1943–45). Attended Rudolph Schaeffer School of Design, San Francisco (1946–47). Attended California School of Fine Arts (1947–51). Co-founded Metart Galleries, San Francisco (1949). At Edward Dugmore's urging, moved to New York City (1953). Taught at University of Florida, Gainesville (1958). Taught at Pratt Institute, New York City

(1961–84). Taught at Yale University Graduate School of Art and Architecture (1967–68). Died in New York City (1984).

Selected One-Person Exhibitions   Metart Galleries, San Francisco (1949); Stable Gallery, New York City (1954, 1955); San Francisco Art Association Gallery, California School of Fine Arts, San Francisco (1956, cat.); Howard Wise Gallery, New York City (1960, 1962, 1963); Yale University Art Gallery, New Haven, Conn. (1968); Alonzo Gallery, New York City (1969); Green Mountain Gallery, New York City (1973); Susan Caldwell Gallery, New York City (1975); Aaron Berman Gallery, New York City (1977); Cape Split Place Gallery, Addison, Maine (1979, cat.); Landmark Gallery, New York City (1980); Gruenebaum Gallery, New York City (1980, 1981, 1982; 1984, cat.); Anita Shapolsky Gallery, New York City (1991, 1992, 1994).

JOAN BROWN   Born in San Francisco (1938). Studied at California School of Fine Arts, notably with Elmer Bischoff (B.F.A., 1959; M.F.A., 1960). Took over Sonia Gechtoff and James Kelly's flat at 2330 Fillmore Street studio building, next to 2324 Fillmore, residence of Jay DeFeo, Wally Hedrick, and Michael McClure (1958). Taught at San Francisco Art Institute (1961–68). Named one of "Ten Young Women of the Year" by *Mademoiselle* magazine (1963). Taught at University of Victoria, British Columbia; Sacramento State College, Sacramento, Calif. (1969–70). Faculty member, Academy of Art, San Francisco (1971–74). Taught at University of California, Berkeley (1974–90). Died in Proddatur, India (1990).

Selected One-Person Exhibitions   Six Gallery (1957); The Cellar, San Francisco (1958); Spatsa Gallery, San Francisco (1958); Batman Gallery, San Francisco (1959); Staempfli Gallery, New York City (1960, 1961, 1964); David Stuart Galleries, Los Angeles (1961, 1962, 1964); Hansen Fuller Gallery, San Francisco (1968, 1976, 1978, 1979, 1980); Lawson Gallery, San Francisco (1968, 1970, 1976); San Francisco Museum of Art (1971); San Francisco Art Institute (1973); Charles Campbell Gallery, San Francisco (1974, 1975); University Art Museum, Berkeley (1974, cat.; 1979); Allan Frumkin Gallery, New York City (1974, 1976, 1979, 1981, 1982); Allan Frumkin Gallery, Chicago (1975, 1977); Wadsworth Atheneum, Hartford, Conn. (1977); Newport Harbor Art Museum, Newport Beach, Calif. (1978, cat.); San Jose Museum of Art, San Jose, Calif. (1979); University of Hawaii Art Gallery, Honolulu (1981); Hansen Fuller Goldeen Gallery, San Francisco (1982); Koplin Gallery, Los Angeles (1982, 1983, 1986, 1992); Fuller Goldeen Gallery, San Francisco (1983); Mills College Art Gallery, Oakland, Calif. (1983); Art Museum of Santa Cruz County, Santa Cruz, Calif. (1984); University Art Gallery, San Diego State University, Calif. (1986, cat.); Frumkin/Adams Gallery, New York City (1991, cat.)

LAWRENCE CALCAGNO   Born in San Francisco (1913). After high school, traveled in Asia, working as merchant seaman. Served in U.S. Air Force (1943–46). Attended California School of Fine Arts; studied with Clyfford Still and Mark Rothko (1947–50). Lived and worked in France, Italy, and North Africa (1950–55): studied at Académie de la Grande Chaumière, Paris (1950–51); Istituto d'Arte Statale, Florence (1951–52); worked and studied independently in Paris (1953–55) and helped organize exhibition of American artists in Paris (1953). Visiting artist-in-residence, University of Alabama, Tuscaloosa (1955–56). Artist-in-residence, Albright Art School, Buffalo, N.Y.; traveled in Peru (1956–57). Visiting artist-in-residence, University of Illinois at Urbana-Champaign (1958–59). Taught part-time at New York University, New York City (1960–61). Traveled widely (1961–63). Visiting artist-in-residence, Museum of Fine Arts, Houston, Tex. (1965). Taught at Carnegie Mellon University, Pittsburgh, Pa. (1965–68). Visiting artist-in-residence, Honolulu Academy of Arts, Hawaii (1968). Traveled and lectured in Russia on a U.S. Information Association cultural exchange grant (1988). Received National Endowment for the Arts grant (1989). Died in State College, Pa. (1993).

Selected One-Person Exhibitions   Little Gallery, New Orleans (1945); Lucien Labaudt Gallery, San Francisco (1948, 1954); Studio Paul Facchetti, Paris (1955); Martha Jackson Gallery, New York City (1955, 1958, 1960; 1962, cat.); Albright Art Gallery, Buffalo, N.Y. (1956, cat.); University of Illinois at Urbana-Champaign (1959); Ciudad Universitaria, Mexico City (1961); Carnegie Mellon University, Pittsburgh, Pa. (1965); Houston Museum of Fine Arts, Houston, Tex. (1965); Esther Robles Gallery, Los Angeles (1966); Westmoreland County Museum of Art, Greensburg, Pa. (1967, cat.); Honolulu Academy of Arts, Hawaii (1968, 1969); Ithaca College Museum, Ithaca, N.Y. (1970); Smithsonian Institution, Washington, D.C. (1973–75 [traveling exhibition], cat.); Contemporary Art Center, Honolulu (1976); Mitchell Museum, Mount Vernon, Ill. (1982–83, cat.); Roanoke Museum of Fine Art, Roanoke, Va. (1984); Anita Shapolsky Gallery, New York City (1987, 1992); Anderson Gallery, Buffalo, N.Y. (1992).

EDWARD CORBETT   Born in Chicago, Ill. (1919). Family settled in Bay Area (1934). Attended California School of Fine Arts (1936–41). Served in Merchant Marine running arms; participated in Battle of the Coral Sea (1941–44). Lived and painted in New York City; studied collections at the Museum of Modern Art; joined Communist Party; met

Ad Reinhardt (1944–45). Returned to San Francisco; joined American Abstract Artists (1946). Taught at California School of Fine Arts and University of California, Berkeley (1947–50). Lived with Robert McChesney, Hassel Smith, sculptor Mary Fuller, and poet Weldon Kees in Point Richmond, Calif.; began *Black Paintings* and resigned from California School of Fine Arts (1950). Received Abraham Rosenberg Fellowship and worked in American Southwest (1951). Taught at Mount Holyoke College, South Hadley, Mass. (1953–63). Began *Paintings for Puritans* series (1955). Lived and painted principally in Washington, D.C. (1964–71). Taught at University of California, Santa Barbara (1967–68). Died in Provincetown, Mass. (1971).

Selected One-Person Exhibitions　Pat Wall Gallery, Monterey, Calif. (1946); La Galeria Escondida, Taos, N.Mex. (1951); Borgenicht Gallery, New York City (1954, 1956, 1959, 1961, 1962, 1963, 1964, 1965; 1967, cat.; 1968); Sophie Newcomb College, Tulane University, New Orleans (1957); Massachusetts Institute of Technology, Cambridge (1959); Walker Art Center, Minneapolis (1961, cat.); Quay Gallery, San Francisco (1967); San Francisco Museum of Art (1969, cat.); University of Maryland Art Gallery, College Park (1979, cat.); Richmond Art Center, Richmond, Calif. (1990, cat.).

HAROLD CHRISTOPHER DAVIES　Born in Seattle, Washington (1891). Family moved to Washington, D.C. (1892), and then Cherrydale, Va. (1893). Family lived in Georgetown, Washington, D.C. (1900–09). Attended Corcoran Art Institute, Washington, D.C., where he studied with Edmund C. Messer (1905–09). Moved to Fresno, Calif. (1909). Clerk for San Joaquin Power and Light Company, Calif. (1915). Lieutenant, U.S. Army, Fort Lewis, Wash. (1917–18). Moved to Bay Area and enrolled at Mark Hopkins Institute of Art (1920). Moved to Oakland, Calif.; worked as office manager for Cleveland Metal Products Company and painted at night and on weekends (1921). Traveled to New York City (1923). Comptroller (and later president) of California Spray Chemical Company (1933). Moved to Orinda, Calif. (1938). Moved to Huntsville, Ala., as owner and president of Calabama Chemical Company (1945). Exhibited in Huntsville and started art class (1950). Lectured on Renaissance painting and exhibited at University of the South, Sewanee, Tenn. (1954). Lived and painted in East Hampton, N.Y.; met Adolph Gottlieb, Franz Kline, and Willem de Kooning (1957–69). Moved to Inverness, Calif. (1969). Died in Inverness (1976).

Selected One-Person Exhibitions　Marquoit Gallery, San Francisco (1975); Hoover Gallery, San Francisco (1975, 1979); Fresno Art Museum, Fresno, Calif. (1976); Coe College East Gallery, Cedar Rapids, Iowa (1979); The Haggin

Museum, Stockton, Calif., and Huntsville Museum of Art, Huntsville, Ala. (1981–82, cat.).

JAY DeFEO　Born in Hanover, N.H. (1929). Family moved to Northern California (1932); spent parts of her youth in San Francisco, San Jose, and Oakland. Studied at University of California, Berkeley (B.A., 1950; M.A., 1951). Traveled and painted in Paris and Florence (1951–52). Lived and painted in Berkeley (1952–54). Married Wally Hedrick and moved to San Francisco (1954). Moved into 2324 Fillmore Street studio building, residence of Michael McClure (1956). Began work on *The Rose* (1958). Taught at San Francisco Art Institute (1962–70, 1979). Completed *The Rose* (1965). Lived and painted in Ross and Larkspur, Marin County, Calif.; taught art classes at the San Francisco Museum of Modern Art (1965–80). Taught at Sonoma State University, Rohnert Park, Calif. (1976–80). Taught at California College of Arts and Crafts, Oakland, Calif. (1978–81). Moved to Oakland and began teaching at Mills College, Oakland, Calif. (1980–81). Received Honorary Doctorate from the San Francisco Art Institute (1982). Died in Oakland (1989).

Selected One-Person Exhibitions　The Place, San Francisco (1954); Dilexi Gallery, San Francisco (1959); Ferus Gallery, Los Angeles (1960); Pasadena Art Museum, Calif. (1969, cat.); San Francisco Museum of Art (1969); San Francisco Art Institute (1969, cat.; 1984, cat.); The Oakland Museum, Oakland, Calif. (1970); Wenger Gallery, San Francisco (1974); California College of Arts and Crafts, Oakland, Calif. (1975); University Art Museum, Berkeley (1978, cat.; 1990); The Faith and Charity in Hope Gallery, Hope, Idaho (1979, cat.); Whitman College, Walla Walla, Wash. (1980); Gallery Paule Anglim, San Francisco (1980, 1983); California State University, Chico (1981); Indian Valley College, Novato, Calif. (1981); Nave Museum, Victoria, Tex. (1986, cat.); The Art Museum of Santa Cruz County, Calif. (1990, cat.); The Krannert Art Museum, Champaign, Ill. (1990, cat.); Moore College of Art and Design, Philadelphia (1996, cat.).

RICHARD DIEBENKORN　Born in Portland, Oreg. (1922). Family moved to San Francisco Bay Area (1924). Attended Stanford University, Stanford, Calif. (1940–43). Studied at University of California, Berkeley, under Worth Ryder and Erle Loran (1943). Served in U.S. Marines, Quantico, Va. (1943–45). Attended California School of Fine Arts (1946). Taught at California School of Fine Arts and lived in Sausalito, Calif. (1947–49). Studied at University of New Mexico, Albuquerque (M.F.A., 1951). Taught at University of Illinois at Urbana (1952). Stayed briefly in New York City; moved to Berkeley and began *Berkeley* series (1953).

Began painting representationally (1955). Taught at California College of Arts and Crafts, Oakland, Calif. (1955–59). Taught at San Francisco Art Institute (1959–63). Lived in Santa Monica and taught at University of California, Los Angeles (1966–73). Began *Ocean Park* series (1967). Moved to Healdsburg, Calif. (1988), but spent last years in Berkeley. Died in Berkeley (1993).

Selected One-Person Exhibitions California Palace of the Legion of Honor, San Francisco (1948; 1960, cat.; 1961); Paul Kantor Gallery, Los Angeles (1952, 1954); San Francisco Museum of Art (1954); Poindexter Gallery, New York City (1956, 1958, 1966; 1969, cat.); Pasadena Art Museum, Calif. (1960, cat.); The Phillips Collection, Washington, D.C. (1961, cat.); Washington Gallery of Modern Art, Washington, D.C. (1964, cat.); Stanford University Art Gallery, Stanford, Calif. (1964, cat.); Richmond Art Center, Richmond, Calif. (1968, cat.); Los Angeles County Museum of Art (1969, cat.); Marlborough Gallery, New York City (1971, cat.; 1973, cat.; 1975, cat.); San Francisco Museum of Modern Art (1972–73, cat.; 1983, cat.); John Berggruen Gallery, San Francisco (1975); James Corcoran Gallery, Los Angeles (1975, cat.); Frederick S. Wight Art Gallery, University of California, Los Angeles (1976, cat.); Albright-Knox Art Gallery, Buffalo, N.Y. (1976–77, cat.); M. Knoedler & Co., Inc., New York City (1977, cat.; 1979, cat.; 1980, cat.; 1982, cat.; 1984, cat.; 1985, cat.; 1987, cat.); University of California, Berkeley (1981, cat.); Minneapolis Institute of Art (1981–83 [traveling exhibition], cat.); Crown Point Gallery, Oakland, Calif. (1982, cat.); Sheldon Memorial Art Gallery, University of Nebraska, Lincoln (1983, cat.); Stanford University Museum of Art, Stanford, Calif. (1987, cat.); Museum of Modern Art, New York City (1988–89, cat.); Whitechapel Gallery, London (1991–92, cat.); Whitney Museum of American Art (forthcoming, cat.).

MADELEINE [VIOLETT] DIMOND Born in New York City (1922). Studied with George Grosz at Art Students League (1941–42). Joined U.S. Navy as a Wave. Attended California School of Fine Arts on GI Bill; studied with Edward Corbett and Hassel Smith (1948–51). Joined King Ubu Gallery and Six Gallery co-ops and exhibited with each (1953–55). Lived and painted in Florence and Rome (1956–59). Returned to San Francisco briefly; moved to New York City (1960). Married third husband, Peter Martin (founder of City Lights Bookstore, San Francisco); they founded New Yorker Bookshop, New York City (1965), which they ran until early 1980s. Stopped abstract painting (late 1960s). Moved to San Francisco (1986). Co-founded Peter and Madeleine Martin Foundation for the Creative Arts, San Francisco, with Charles Strong (1990). Died in San Francisco (1991).

One-Person Exhibition Lucien Labaudt Gallery, San Francisco (1954).

JAMES BUDD DIXON Born in San Francisco (1900); family moved to farm estate outside Stockton, Calif. Traveled to Asia (1909 or 1910). Attended San Francisco Polytechnic (1916–20) and University of California, Berkeley (1920–21, 1922–23). Studied at California School of Fine Arts (1923–26, 1929–30; and, on GI Bill, 1946, 1948–49). Worked as art director for Moore Machinery, San Francisco (1935–36). Worked under Beniamino Bufano for Works Progress Administration (mid-1930s). Worked as chief draftsman at Bethlehem Steel, San Francisco (1942–44). Served in U.S. Army, cargo planning, Oakland, Calif. (1944–46). Established storefront studio at 700 Lombard Street, San Francisco, a gathering place for artists (1946). Taught printmaking at California School of Fine Arts (1949–55) and painting at San Francisco Art Institute (1961–65). Died in San Francisco (1967).

Selected One-Person Exhibitions San Francisco Museum of Art (1939); College of Notre Dame Art Gallery, Belmont, Calif. (1977).

EDWARD DUGMORE Born in Hartford, Conn. (1915). Introduced to Surrealism by Wadsworth Atheneum exhibition *Newer Super-Realism* (1931). Attended Hartford Art School, where he met John Grillo (1934–38). With Alexander Calder and Grillo, helped Eugene Berman design sets for *Paper Ball: Le Cirque des Chiffonniers* (costumes by Pavel Tchelitchew and Calder) at Hartford Festival (1936). Spent spring in Kansas City; studied with Thomas Hart Benton at Kansas City Art Institute (1941). Served in U.S. Marine Corps (1943–44). Moved to New York City (1944). Taught at St. Joseph's College, West Hartford, Conn. (1946–47, 1949). At Grillo's urging, moved to San Francisco (1948). Attended California School of Fine Arts on GI Bill (1948–50). Co-founded Metart Galleries, San Francisco (1949). Studied at University of Guadalajara, Mexico, on GI Bill (1951–52). Moved to New York City (1952). Taught part-time at Pratt Institute, Brooklyn (1964–74). Visiting artist, Montana Institute of Arts, Great Falls (1965). Taught summer session at University of Minnesota (1970). Taught summer session at Des Moines Art Center and Drake University (1972). Taught part-time at Maryland Institute, College of Art, Baltimore (1973–82).

Selected One-Person Exhibitions Metart Galleries, San Francisco (1950); Sheldon Street Studio, Hartford, Conn. (1953); Stable Gallery, New York City (1953, 1954, 1956); Holland-Goldowsky Gallery, Chicago (1959); Howard Wise Gallery, New York City (1960, 1961, 1963); M.I.A. Gallery, Great Falls, Mont. (1965); Des Moines Art Center, Des Moines, Iowa (1972, cat.); Green Mountain Gallery, New York City (1973); H. Marc Moyens Gallery, Alexandria, Va. (1975); Carlson Gallery, San Francisco (1990, cat.); Manny Silverman Gallery, Los Angeles (1991, cat.; 1992, cat.; 1993, cat.; 1994, cat.)

LILLY FENICHEL   Born in Vienna, Austria. Family fled Nazis to Great Britain (1939). Moved to Hollywood, Calif. (1940). Attended Chouinard Art Institute, Los Angeles (1946–47). Studied at Los Angeles City College (1947–48). Attended California School of Fine Arts (1950–52). Moved to New York City; shared studio with Harlan Jackson (1952). Painted in Taos, N.Mex.; worked with Clay Spohn (1959). Lived in Hollywood, Calif. (1960–67). Established studio in Taos, N.Mex. (1980–84); began to work three-dimensionally (1983). Moved to Corrales, N.Mex.; established studio in Albuquerque; and studied woodworking and sculpture (1985). Returned to painting (1990).

Selected One-Person Exhibitions   Santa Barbara Museum of Art, Santa Barbara, Calif. (1968); Lutz-Bergerson Gallery, Taos, N.Mex. (1980); Taylor Gallery, Taos, N.Mex. (1981); New Gallery, Taos, N.Mex. (1983); New Gallery, Houston (1987); Carlson Gallery, San Francisco (1990, cat.).

SAM FRANCIS   Born in San Mateo, Calif. (1923). Studied psychology and medicine at the University of California, Berkeley (1941–43). Served in U.S. Army Air Corps; began painting in San Francisco veterans' hospital while recuperating from illness brought on by injury (1943–47). Returned to University of California as an art major; studied with Edward Corbett (B.A., 1949; M.A., 1950). Lived and painted in Paris; became associated with the critic Michel Tapié, Jean-Paul Riopelle, and other abstract painters in Paris (1950–56). Traveled around world, with extended stay in Japan (1957). Traveled back and forth between New York City, Paris, Tokyo, and Bern, Switzerland (1958–61). Lived and worked principally in Santa Monica, Calif. (1962–94). Taught at San Francisco Art Institute (1966). Died in Santa Monica, Calif. (1994).

Selected One-Person Exhibitions   Galerie Rive Droite, Paris (1955, cat.; 1956, cat.); Kornfeld and Klipstein, Bern, Switzerland (1957, cat.; 1959, cat.; 1961, cat.; 1963, cat.); Moderna Museet, Stockholm (1960, cat.); Minami Gallery, Tokyo (1961, cat.); Esther Bear Gallery, Santa Barbara, Calif. (1962, cat.; 1984, cat.); Museum of Fine Arts, Houston, Tex., and University Art Museum, Berkeley, Calif. (1967, cat.; 1994, cat.); San Francisco Museum of Art (1967, cat.); Felix Landau Gallery, Los Angeles (1969–70, cat.); Los Angeles County Museum of Art (1970, cat.; 1980, cat.); Albright-Knox Art Gallery, Buffalo, N.Y. (1972, cat.); Smith Andersen Gallery, Palo Alto, Calif. (1976, cat.); Gemini G.E.L., Los Angeles (1977, cat.); Institute of Contemporary Art, Boston (1979, cat.); The Phillips Collection, Washington, D.C. (1979, cat.); Robert Elkon Gallery, New York City (1979, cat.); André Emmerich Gallery, New York City (1979–80, cat.); Pao Sui Loong Galleries, Hong Kong Arts Center (1981, cat.); Fondation Maeght, Saint-Paul, France (1983, cat.); Gagosian Gallery, New York City (1991, cat.); Kunst- und Ausstellungshalle, Bonn (1993, cat.).

SONIA GECHTOFF   Born in Philadelphia (1926). Studied at Philadelphia Museum School of Art (B.F.A., 1950). Moved to San Francisco (1951). Studied lithography at California School of Fine Arts (1952). Married James Kelly and moved to 2330 Fillmore Street studio building, next to 2324 Fillmore, residence of Jay DeFeo, Wally Hedrick, and Michael McClure (1953). Taught at California School of Fine Arts (1957–58). Moved to New York City (1958). Taught part-time at New York University (1960–70). Received Ford Foundation fellowship to work at Tamarind Lithography Workshop, Los Angeles (1963). Taught at Queens College, N.Y. (1970–74). Taught at University of New Mexico, Albuquerque (1974–75). Took several trips to England and Europe (1968–87). Adolph and Esther Gottlieb Foundation grant (1987). Mid Atlantic Regional National Endowment for the Arts grant for works on paper (1988). Artist-in-residence, Skidmore College, Saratoga Springs, N.Y. (summers 1988–90). Visiting artist, Art Institute of Chicago (1989). Artist-in-residence, Adelphi University, Garden City, N.Y. (1991, 1993). Elected associate, National Academy of Design (1994).

Selected One-Person Exhibitions   Lucien Labaudt Gallery, San Francisco (1952); Six Gallery, San Francisco (1955); M. H. de Young Memorial Museum, San Francisco (1957); Ferus Gallery, Los Angeles (1957, 1959); Poindexter Gallery, New York City (1959, 1960); East Hampton Gallery, New York City (1963, 1966); Albright College, Reading, Pa. (1966); Westbeth Galleries, New York City (1971, 1972); Gallery One, Montclair State College, N.J. (1974, cat.); Gloria Cortella Gallery, New York City (1976, 1978); Gruenebaum Gallery, New York City (1979; 1980, cat.; 1982, cat.; 1983; 1985; 1987, cat.); Witkin Galleries, New York City (1984, 1989); Kraushaar Galleries, New York City (1990; 1992, cat.; 1995, cat.); University Center Gallery, Adelphi University, Garden City, N.Y. (1991); Schick Gallery, Skidmore College, Saratoga Springs, N.Y. (1995, cat.).

JORGE GOYA [-LUKICH]   Born in Cleveland (1924). Studied mathematics and science at Case Western Reserve University, Cleveland (ca. 1941). Served in U.S. Air Force Weather Squadron (ca. 1941–46). Studied painting and printmaking at California School of Fine Arts on GI Bill (1947–50). Obtained teaching credentials from San Francisco State College (ca. 1948). Co-founded Metart Galleries, San Francisco (1949). Taught printmaking at California Labor School, San Francisco (1951). Studied painting at the University of Oregon, Eugene (M.F.A., 1953). Moved to New York City; worked as a technical advisor at Robert Blackburn Graphics Workshop and founded Pennyeach Press (1953). Taught graphics with Abraham Rattner at Rattner's summer school in New York City (1956). Taught mathematics at Fieldston School, New York City (1957–59). Died in San Francisco (1977).

Selected One-Person Exhibitions Lucien Labaudt Gallery, San Francisco (1948); Metart Galleries, San Francisco (1949); Vesuvio Café, San Francisco (1951); Six Gallery, San Francisco (1952); University of Oregon, Eugene (1952); Camillo Gallery, New York City (1956).

JOHN GRILLO Born in Lawrence, Mass. (1917). Attended Hartford Art School, Conn., where he met Edward Dugmore (1935–38). With Alexander Calder and Dugmore, helped Eugene Berman design sets for *Paper Ball: Le Cirque des Chiffonniers* (costumes by Pavel Tchelitchew and Calder) at Hartford Festival (1936). Served in U.S. Navy (1941–46). Discharged from service in San Francisco; attended California School of Fine Arts (1946–47). Studied with Hans Hofmann in New York and at Hans Hofmann School of Fine Arts, Provincetown, Mass. (1948–51). Received Ford Foundation grant to work at Tamarind Lithography Workshop, Los Angeles (1964). Received Ford Foundation artist-in-residence grant, Butler Institute of American Art, Youngstown, Ohio (1964). Taught painting at New School for Social Research, New York City (1964–66). Professor of Fine Arts, University of Massachusetts at Amherst (1967–91). Currently resides in Wellfleet, Mass. (from 1991).

Selected One-Person Exhibitions Daliel's Gallery, Berkeley, Calif. (1947, cat.); Artists' Gallery, New York City (1948); Tanager Gallery, New York City (1952, 1960); Tibor de Nagy Gallery, New York City (1953); Bertha Schaefer Gallery, New York City (1955, 1957, 1959); HCE Gallery, Provincetown, Mass. (1959); Howard Wise Gallery, New York City (1961, 1962, 1963); Ankrum Gallery, Los Angeles (1962–63); Worth Ryder Art Gallery, University of California, Berkeley (1962); Provincetown Art Association and Museum, Mass. (1988, cat.); University of Massachusetts, Amherst (1988, cat.); Carlson Gallery, San Francisco (1990, cat.).

JOHN HULTBERG Born in Berkeley, Calif. (1922). Studied at Fresno State College, Fresno, Calif., as an English major (B.A., 1943). Served in U.S. Navy (1943–46). Attended California School of Fine Arts on GI Bill; lived and painted in Sausalito, Calif. (1947–49). Moved to New York City (1949); attended Art Students League, New York City (until 1951). Moved to Paris and traveled in Europe (1954). Received Guggenheim Fellowship and traveled in Europe (1956). Received Ford Foundation fellowship to work at Tamarind Lithography Workshop, Los Angeles (1963). Taught at San Francisco Art Institute (1963–64). Ford Foundation fellowship (1964). Artist-in-residence at Honolulu Academy of Arts, Hawaii (1966). National Endowment for the Arts grant (1981). Elected member, National Academy of Design (1982). Lived in Portland, Maine

(1986–91), and New York City (since 1991). Has taught at Art Students League, New York City (since 1991). Pollock-Krasner Foundation fellowships (1988, 1992). Adolph and Esther Gottlieb Foundation fellowship (1993). Received Marie Walsh Sharpe residency, New York City (1994).

Selected One-Person Exhibitions Contemporary Gallery, Sausalito, Calif. (1949); Korman Gallery, New York City (1953); Fresno State College, Fresno, Calif. (1954, 1963); Martha Jackson Gallery, New York City (1955, cat.; 1956, cat.; 1958, cat.; 1959, cat.; 1960, cat.; 1961, cat.; 1962; 1963, cat.; 1964, cat.; 1966, cat.; 1967; 1969, cat.; 1972, cat.); Galleria Numero, Florence, Italy (1956, 1958); Institute of Contemporary Arts, London, England (1956); Galerie Rive Droite, Paris (1957); Phoenix Art Museum, Phoenix, Ariz. (1957, cat.); Corcoran Gallery of Art, Washington, D.C. (1958); Rockhill Nelson Gallery and Atkins Museum of Fine Arts, Kansas City, Mo. (1958); Galerie du Dragon, Paris (1959, 1964, 1966; 1970, cat.); Galleria dell'Ariete, Milan, Italy (1959, cat.); Main Street Gallery, Chicago (1959); Fairweather-Hardin Gallery, Chicago (1960); Galleria Galatea, Turin, Italy (1960); Oakland Art Museum, Oakland, Calif. (1960, cat.); Esther Robles Gallery, Los Angeles (1960, 1963, 1964); Piccadilly Gallery, London (1961, 1962; 1965, cat.); Pasadena Art Museum, Calif. (1961, 1962); The Museum of Malmö, Malmö, Sweden (1962); David Andersen Gallery, New York City (1963; 1970, New York and Paris, cat.; 1972, cat.; 1974, cat.; 1976; 1978); Roswell Museum and Art Center, Roswell, N.Mex. (1963); Galerie Anderson-Mayer, Paris (1964, 1966); La Galerie Alice Pauli, Lausanne, Switzerland (1965); Honolulu Academy of Arts, Hawaii (1967); American Cultural Center, Paris (1968); Southampton College, Southampton, N.Y. (1968); Fred L. Emerson Gallery, Hamilton College, Clinton, N.Y. (1985–86, traveling retrospective); Anita Shapolsky Gallery, New York City (1987, 1989); University of Southern Maine, Portland (1989, cat.); The Nicholas Roerich Museum, New York City (1990, cat.); Elaine Wechsler, New York City (1992, 1993); Denise Bibro Gallery, New York City (1994, cat.).

HARLAN JACKSON Born in Cleburne, Tex. (1918). Attended Kansas State Teachers College, Pittsburg (1937–38). Attended California Labor School, San Francisco. Attended California School of Fine Arts (1946–48). Received Abraham Rosenberg Fellowship to study art by American and Caribbean Island (primarily Haitian) artists of African descent (1948). Traveled to Washington, D.C. (stayed with writer and Howard University drama professor Owen Dodson), New York City (visited galleries with John Grillo), New Orleans, Atlanta, and Port-au-Prince, Haiti (1948–49). While in Haiti, worked to represent in abstract form his study of Haitian mysticism and voodooism. Studied with Hans Hofmann (1951) and shared studio with Lilly

Fenichel in New York City (1952). Exhibited in group shows at Howard University Art Gallery, Washington, D.C. (1961, 1970). Died in New York City (1993).

Selected One-Person Exhibitions   Artists' Guild Gallery, San Francisco (1947); Centre d'Art, Port-au-Prince, Haiti (1949, cat.); Barnet Aden Gallery, Washington, D.C. (1950); Palais des Beaux Arts, Port-au-Prince, Haiti (1950); Panoras Gallery, New York City (1955).

JACK JEFFERSON   Born in Lead, S.Dak. (1921). Worked as shoveler in Homestake Mines, Lead, S.Dak. (part of 1939 and 1940). Studied at University of Iowa, Iowa City (1940–42). Served as a sergeant in the U.S. Marine Corps (1942–46); served during height of action at Guadalcanal (mid-September 1942–1 December 1943). Attended California School of Fine Arts on GI Bill (1946–50). Traveled to Pacific Northwest and British Columbia on Abraham Rosenberg Fellowship (1953). Shared Mission Street studio with Frank Lobdell (1954–58). Spent year in Taos, N.Mex., devoted exclusively to drawing (1958). Instructor of painting and drawing, San Francisco Art Institute (1959–78).

Selected One-Person Exhibitions   Metart Galleries, San Francisco (1949); M. H. de Young Memorial Museum, San Francisco (1960; 1962–63, cat.); The Oakland Museum, Oakland, Calif. (1970); College of Notre Dame Art Gallery, Belmont, Calif. (1973); Smith Andersen Gallery, Palo Alto, Calif. (1976); Paule Anglim Gallery, San Francisco (1982, 1984, 1986, 1991).

JAMES KELLY   Born in Philadelphia (1913). Attended Philadelphia Museum School of Art at night and worked in shoe factory during day (1937). Studied at Pennsylvania Academy of the Fine Arts (1938). Studied at the Barnes Foundation, Merion, Pa. (1941). Served in U.S. Air Force (1941–45). Resumed painting in Philadelphia (1946). Moved to San Francisco (late 1950). Attended California School of Fine Arts on GI Bill (1951–54). Married Sonia Gechtoff and moved to 2330 Fillmore Street studio building, next to 2324 Fillmore, residence of Jay DeFeo, Wally Hedrick, and Michael McClure (1953). Taught painting and drawing at University of California, Berkeley (summer 1957). Moved to New York City (1958). Received Ford Foundation grant to work at Tamarind Lithography Workshop, Los Angeles (1963). Received National Endowment for the Arts grant (1977). Received Peter and Madeleine Martin Foundation for the Creative Arts grant (1990).

Selected One-Person Exhibitions   The Place, San Francisco (1954); San Francisco Art Association Gallery, California School of Fine Arts (1956, cat.); Stryke Gallery, New York City (1963); East Hampton Gallery, New York City

(1965, 1969); Albright College, Reading, Pa. (1966); Long Island University, Brooklyn (1968); Westbeth Gallery, New York City (1971, 1972); Wiegand Gallery, College of Notre Dame, Belmont, Ca. (1990, cat.).

MICHAEL KENNEDY   Born in Des Moines, Iowa (1941). Studied at California School of Fine Arts with Elmer Bischoff, Wally Hedrick, Frank Lobdell, and Jack Jefferson (B.F.A., 1963; M.F.A., 1965). Worked at San Francisco Post Office (until 1993). Died in San Francisco (1993).

Selected One-Person Exhibitions   Triangle Gallery, San Francisco (1973, 1974, 1975, 1976, 1978, 1980); Dominican College, San Rafael, Calif. (1974); Wiegand Gallery, College of Notre Dame, Belmont, Calif. (1995, cat.).

HAYWARD KING   Born Little Rock, Ark. (1928). Grew up in Pasadena, Calif. Studied at California School of Fine Arts (1949–50; B.F.A., 1955). Served as a company clerk in Alaska during Korean War (1950–52). Co-founded Six Gallery, San Francisco, with Wally Hedrick, Deborah Remington, David Simpson, poet-painter John Allen Ryan, and poet Jack Spicer (1954). Studied printmaking in Paris on Fulbright scholarship (1955–56). Attended Sorbonne, Paris, on GI Bill (1955–57). Worked as Edward Weston's personal assistant (1957). Registrar for evening/graduate classes, San Francisco Art Institute (1958–62). First African American museum administrator in San Francisco Bay Area (1962–66): Registrar at San Francisco Museum of Art; Director, Richmond Art Center, Richmond, Calif. (1966–70). Second vice president, Western Association of Art Museums (1968–70). Curator, Bolles Gallery, San Francisco (1970–74). Taught at San Francisco State University (1971–78). Curatorial consultant, Palo Alto Cultural Center, Calif. (1972–76). Director, Stuart Gallery, Berkeley, Calif. (1978–79). Died in San Francisco (1990).

Selected One-Person Exhibitions   Six Gallery, San Francisco (1955); Public Library, Sierra Madre, Calif. (1957); Spatsa Gallery, San Francisco (1959); Edward Dean Gallery, San Francisco (1960); University of California, Davis (1963).

WALTER KUHLMAN   Born in St. Paul, Minn. (1918). Studied with Cameron Booth at St. Paul School of Art, where he met Frank Lobdell (1936–39). Went to Chicago with Lobdell to see Picasso show (1940). Studied at University of Minnesota (from 1937; B.A., 1941). Instructor, St. Paul School of Art (1940–41). Served in U.S. Navy as medical illustrator in the Hospital Corps (1943–45). Attended Tulane University, New Orleans (1945–46). Lived and painted in Virgin Islands (1946–47). Studied at California

School of Fine Arts on GI Bill; lived and painted in Sausalito (1947–50). Taught at University of Michigan, Ann Arbor (summer 1948). Built current house in Sausalito, Calif. (1949). Traveled to Paris; took studio at Académie de la Grande Chaumière (1950–51). Returned to Sausalito (1951). Awarded Graham Fellowship; traveled to Chicago and met Buckminster Fuller, Mies van der Rohe (1957). Taught at California School of Fine Arts (1957–60). Taught at University of California, Berkeley (summer 1959). Taught at University of New Mexico, Albuquerque (1960–65). Taught at San Francisco Art Institute (summers 1964 and 1965). Taught at Stanford University, Stanford, Calif. (1966–67). Taught at University of Santa Clara, Santa Clara, Calif. (1967–69). Taught at Sonoma State University, Rohnert Park, Calif. (1969–88). Awarded Maestro Grant as outstanding California working artist and teacher (1982).

Selected One-Person Exhibitions Walker Art Center, Minneapolis (1940); Berkshire Museum, Pittsfield, Mass. (1942); La Jolla Museum of Art, La Jolla, Calif. (1943); Santa Barbara Museum of Art, Santa Barbara, Calif. (1943); California Palace of the Legion of Honor, San Francisco (1956, 1964); New Arts Gallery, Houston (1959, 1960, 1961); Raymond Jonson Gallery, University of New Mexico, Albuquerque (1963, 1964, 1965); De Saisset Museum, Santa Clara, Calif. (1969, cat.); University Art Gallery, Sonoma State University, Rohnert Park, Calif. (1969; 1988, cat.); Gump's Gallery, San Francisco (1976, 1992); Charles Campbell Gallery, San Francisco (1981, 1983, 1985); Djurovich Gallery, Sacramento, Calif. (1986); Carlson Gallery, San Francisco (1989, cat.); John Natsoulas Gallery, Davis, Calif. (1992); Albuquerque Museum of Art, Albuquerque, N.Mex. (1994); Robert Green Fine Arts Gallery, Ross, Calif. (1994).

ADELIE LANDIS Born (1926) and raised in Brooklyn. Studied with Elmer Bischoff, David Park, and Hassel Smith at California School of Fine Arts (1951–52). Studied with Smith at his Potrero Hill/Mission Street school (1952–53). Studied at University of California, Berkeley (B.A., 1958; M.F.A., 1959). Married Elmer Bischoff (1962). Has continued to paint and exhibit in Bay Area; resides in Berkeley.

Selected One-Person Exhibition Kennedy Art Center, Holy Names College, Oakland, Calif. (1993).

FRANK LOBDELL Born in Kansas City, Mo. (1921). Studied with Cameron Booth one semester at the St. Paul School of Art, St. Paul, Minn., where he met Walter Kuhlman (1939). Painted independently in Minneapolis (1940–42). Served in U.S. Army (1942–46). Lived and painted in Sausalito, Calif. (1946–49). Attended California School of Fine Arts on GI Bill (1947–50). Traveled to France; attended Académie de la Grande Chaumière, Paris (1950–51). Returned to San Francisco; shared studio with Ernest Briggs, 645 Chestnut Street (1951). Established studio at 9 Mission Street (1953), where Jack Jefferson joined him the following year. Taught at San Francisco Art Institute (1957–64). Awarded first Nealie Sullivan Award by San Francisco Art Association (1960). Appointed chair of Graduate Program Committee, San Francisco Art Institute (1963). Artist-in-residence at Stanford University, Stanford, Calif. (1965). Received fellowship at Tamarind Lithography Workshop, Los Angeles (1966). Taught at Stanford University, Stanford, Calif. (1966–91). Medal for Distinguished Achievement in Painting from the American Academy and Institute of Arts and Letters (1988).

Selected One-Person Exhibitions Martha Jackson Gallery, New York City (1960, cat.; 1963; 1964; 1972, cat.; 1974, cat.); M. H. de Young Memorial Museum, San Francisco (1960); Ferus Gallery, Los Angeles (1962); Galerie D. Benador, Geneva, Switzerland (1964, cat.); Galerie Anderson-Mayer, Paris (1965, cat.); Pasadena Art Museum, Calif. (1966, cat.); Marylhurst College, Portland, Oreg. (1967); San Francisco Museum of Modern Art (1969, cat.; 1983, cat.); Hearst Art Gallery, St. Mary's College of California, Moraga, Calif. (1971); Smith Andersen Gallery, Palo Alto, Calif. (1977, 1981, 1988); College of Notre Dame Art Gallery, Belmont, Calif. (1981, cat.); Oscarsson-Hood Gallery, New York City (1983; 1985, cat.); John Berggruen Gallery, San Francisco (1987); Charles Campbell Gallery, San Francisco (1988, cat.); Stanford University Museum of Art, Stanford, Calif. (1988); Campbell-Thiebaud Gallery, San Francisco (1990; 1992, cat.; 1995); Printworks, Chicago (1991); Stanford University Museum of Art, Stanford, Calif. (1993, cat.).

PETER LOWE Born in Los Angeles (1913). Went to southern China, where he studied Chinese Buddhist sculpture (1916–22). Studied at California School of Fine Arts. Studied painting with fellow Chinese Americans at Carpenters' Hall, Montgomery Street, San Francisco; group hired Otis Oldfield as instructor. Owned garment factory in Chinatown. Worked as welder in Vallejo shipyards. Worked as a gardener under federal relief, and subsequently on Works Progress Administration mural project: worked under Herman Volz with Robert McChesney and John Saccaro on design and painting of Federal Building murals and on mosaic at Fine Arts Building (mosaic later moved to San Francisco City College), Treasure Island, for the Golden Gate International Exposition (1939–40). Worked as chicken farmer near Auburn, Calif. (1943). Traveled between China and United States (1945–47). Elected member of San Francisco Art Association (1946). Helped with ideograms for carved animals in Portsmouth Square, Chinatown, San Francisco.

ROBERT McCHESNEY Born in Marshall, Mo. (1913). Attended Washington University School of Fine Arts, St. Louis, Mo. (1933–34). Attended Otis Art Institute, Los Angeles (1936). Worked as a bus driver in Glacier Park, Mont., and for the Army Corps of Engineers during the building of Fort Peck Dam, Fort Peck, Mont. (1935–36). Worked in mural division of Works Progress Administration (1938–40): under Herman Volz, with Peter Lowe and John Saccaro, on design and painting of Federal Building murals and on mosaic at Fine Arts Building (mosaic later moved to San Francisco City College), Treasure Island, for the Golden Gate International Exposition (1939–40). Worked with Clay Spohn on his Los Gatos Union High School mural, Los Gatos, Calif. (1939). Served in the merchant marine transporting military personnel and arms to Pacific theater (1942–46). Assisted Anton Refregier on Rincon Annex Post Office mural, San Francisco (1946). Taught at California Labor School, Art Department (1948–49). Lived with Edward Corbett; Hassel Smith; sculptor and wife, Mary Fuller; and poet Weldon Kees in Point Richmond, Calif. (1948–51). Taught at California School of Fine Arts (1949–51). Began enamel and sand canvases (late 1950–early 1951). Traveled to Guadalajara, Ajijic, and San Miguel de Allende, Mexico, and Taos, N.Mex.; began *Mexico* series of large stained canvases (1951–52). Built current house and studios on Sonoma Mountain, Petaluma, Calif. (1952). Began *Mountain* series (1953). Operated Sonoma Open-Air Art School in rural Sonoma County with Hassel Smith (1957). Began *Arena* series (1958). San Francisco Art Institute Board of Directors (1965–66).

Selected One-Person Exhibitions Raymond & Raymond Gallery, San Francisco (1944); Pat Wall Gallery, Monterey, Calif. (1946); Lucien Labaudt Gallery, San Francisco (1947, 1951); Marquis Gallery, Los Angeles (1949); San Francisco Museum of Art (1949, 1953); Daliel's Gallery, Berkeley, Calif. (1950); Gump's Gallery, San Francisco (1952, 1953, 1955); San Francisco Art Association Gallery, California School of Fine Arts (1957, cat.); Todes Art Gallery, Chicago (1958); Reed College, Portland, Oreg. (1959); Bolles Gallery, San Francisco (1959, 1961, 1962 [New York City], 1970, 1971); Parsons Gallery, Los Angeles (1960, 1961); Hobb's Gallery, San Francisco (1961); Bon Marché Gallery, Seattle, Wash. (1963); Marshall Art Gallery, Marshall, Calif. (1964); San Francisco Art Center (1964); Studio C Gallery, Berkeley, Calif. (1965); Twentieth Century West, New York City (1965); Triangle Gallery, San Francisco (1966); San Francisco Theological Seminary, San Anselmo, Calif. (1966, 1969); Sonoma State College Art Gallery, Cotati, Calif. (1970, cat.); Both Up Gallery, Berkeley, Calif. (1973, 1974); San Francisco Art Commission Gallery (1974, cat.); University Gallery, California State University, Hayward, Calif. (1977, cat.); Lincoln Arts Center, Santa Rosa, Calif. (1978); San Francisco Cultural Center (1984); F. J. Michael's Gallery, San Francisco (1985); California Museum of Art, Santa Rosa, Calif. (1988); Edward S. Curtis Gallery, San Anselmo, Calif. (1989); Carlson Gallery, San Francisco (1990, cat.); E. L. Wiegand Gallery, Nevada Museum of Art, Reno (1994, cat.).

GEORGE MIYASAKI Born in Kalopa, Hawaii (1935). Studied painting and printmaking with Richard Diebenkorn and Nathan Oliveira at California College of Arts and Crafts, Oakland, Calif. (B.F.A. and B.A.Ed., 1957; M.F.A., 1958). Executed first Abstract Expressionist color lithographs using asphaltum (1956). John Hay Whitney Opportunity Fellowship (1957–58). Showed color lithographs in thirteen juried exhibitions across the country (1958). Taught at California College of Arts and Crafts, Oakland, Calif. (1958–64). Helped Willem de Kooning pull his first lithographs (1960). Worked at Tamarind Lithography Workshop, Los Angeles (summer 1961). Taught at Stanford University, Stanford, Calif. (winter 1963). Received John Simon Guggenheim fellowship (1963–64). Taught at University of California, Berkeley (1963–94). Guest artist, State University of Oregon, Corvallis (1967). National Endowment for the Arts artist's fellowship (1980–81, 1985–86). Associate member, National Academy of Design (1993).

Selected One-Person Exhibitions Gump's Gallery, San Francisco (1957); Paul Kantor Gallery, Los Angeles (1961, cat.); Richmond Art Center, Richmond, Calif. (1961); Achenbach Foundation for Graphic Arts, California Palace of the Legion of Honor, San Francisco (1963, cat.); Worth Ryder Gallery, University of California, Berkeley (1963); Lanyon Gallery, Palo Alto, Calif. (1963, 1964); The Original Prints Gallery, San Francisco (1964, 1965, 1966, 1967); Gallery of Modern Art, Washington, D.C. (1966); La Jolla Museum of Art, La Jolla, Calif. (1967); San Francisco Museum of Art (1967); Carnegie Hall, University of Maine at Orono (1968); Berkeley Gallery, San Francisco (1969, 1970); San Marco Gallery, Dominican College, San Rafael, Calif. (1971); Stephen Wirtz Gallery, San Francisco (1979, cat.; 1981, cat.; 1982; 1984; 1988; 1992, cat.); Honolulu Academy of Fine Arts, Hawaii (1980); Matthews Center, Arizona State University, Tempe (1980); The Dillon Gallery, Seattle, Wash. (1981); Portland Art Museum, Oreg. (1983); Rubiner Gallery, Bloomfield Hills, Mich. (1984); 311 Site Gallery, Pacific Grove, Calif. (1987); Gallery of the American Cultural Center, Belgrade, Yugoslavia (1987); Paul Klein Gallery, Chicago (1989); Mary Ryan Gallery, New York City (1993).

WILLIAM MOREHOUSE Born in San Francisco (1929). Studied at California School of Fine Arts (1947–50; B.F.A., 1954). Worked as a bartender at the Vesuvio Café, San Francisco (1950–51). Combat tour in Korea and military service in Hokkaido, Japan (1951–52). Attended California College of Arts and Crafts, Oakland, Calif. (1953). Lived in Oaxaca, Mexico (summer–fall 1955). Studied at San Francisco State College (M.A., 1956). California School of Fine Arts Board of Directors (1956–59). Taught at San Francisco Art Institute (1958–67). Destroyed fourteen years of abstract work; began working figuratively (1961). Traveled in Europe, North Africa, and Great Britain; spent winter through spring in Balearic Islands, Spain (1961–62). Traveled in South Pacific, New Zealand, and Australia (fall 1966). Moved to Sonoma County, Calif. (1967). Taught at Sonoma State University, Rohnert Park, Calif. (1967–93). Moved to Bodega, Sonoma County, Calif. (1970). Died in Bodega (1993).

Selected One-Person Exhibitions   Telegraph Hill Gallery, San Francisco (1954); Six Gallery, San Francisco (1956); Bolles Gallery, San Francisco (1958, 1961 [and New York City], 1963, 1981); Atherton Gallery, Menlo Park, Calif. (1960); California Palace of the Legion of Honor, San Francisco (1960, cat.); Discovery Gallery, Monterey, Calif. (1960); Spatsa Gallery, San Francisco (1960); Realities Gallery, Taos, N.Mex. (1961); Millberry Union, University of California Medical Center, San Francisco (1964); Harbor Gallery, Oakland, Calif. (1965); Richmond Art Center, Richmond, Calif. (1967); Lester Gallery, Inverness, Calif. (1976); San Jose Museum of Art, San Jose, Calif. (1977); Dana Reich Gallery, San Francisco (1982).

ANN MORENCY   Born in New York City. Attended Academy of Advertising Art, San Francisco (1948). Worked as freelance fashion artist in Oakland and San Francisco (1950–56). Worked as designer and fashion artist at Joseph Magnin's, San Francisco (1956–58). Founded and co-owned Fairfield Advertising Agency, San Francisco (1958). Received Reginald A. Fessenden Educational Fund grant to study in Japan (1984). Traveled to Hong Kong (1984, 1985, 1986), China (1984, 1986), Japan (1985, 1986), and Taiwan and Korea (1985) to study and practice traditional and contemporary Asian art-making techniques. Recognition for Achievement in Art award, National League of American Pen Women (1989). Awarded first rank, Sho-Dan degree in calligraphy and calligraphy instructor license, Kampo Cultural Center, Tokyo (1994).

Selected One-Person Exhibitions   College of Notre Dame Art Gallery, Belmont, Calif. (1979, 1984); Smith-Andersen Gallery, Palo Alto, Calif. (1981, 1991); Charles Campbell Gallery, San Francisco (1982, 1984); San Jose City College Art Gallery, San Jose, Calif. (1983).

EMIKO NAKANO   Born in Sacramento, Calif. (1925). Studied at California School of Fine Arts and Mills College, Oakland, Calif. Won second prize, Modern Oils Division, State Fair Art Exhibition, Sacramento, Calif. Assistant teacher in children's art program, Mills College, Oakland, Calif. (summer 1952). Exhibited in numerous group shows in the 1950s.

DAVID PARK   Born in Boston, Mass. (1911). Studied at Otis Art Institute, Los Angeles (1928–29). Moved to Berkeley, Calif. (1929). Worked on murals and designed tapestries for Works Progress Administration Federal Arts Project (1930). Taught at California School of Fine Arts (1945–52). Discarded recent abstract work and began painting figuratively (1949–50). Resigned from teaching position at California School of Fine Arts to protest Hassel Smith's dismissal (1952). California School of Fine Arts Board of Directors (1953–60). Taught at University of California, Berkeley (1955–60). Died in Berkeley, Calif. (1960).

Selected One-Person Exhibitions   East West Gallery of Fine Arts, San Francisco (1934); Oakland Art Gallery, Oakland, Calif. (1934, 1957, 1960); San Francisco Museum of Art (1939, 1940); California Palace of the Legion of Honor, San Francisco (1946); King Ubu Gallery, San Francisco (1953); Paul Kantor Gallery, Los Angeles (1954); Richmond Art Center, Richmond, Calif. (1955); College of Architecture, University of California, Berkeley (1956); M. H. de Young Memorial Museum, San Francisco (1959, cat.); Staempfli Gallery, New York City (1959, cat.; 1961, cat.; 1962, cat.); Artists Cooperative Gallery, Sacramento, Calif. (1961); La Jolla Art Center, La Jolla, Calif. (1961); Obelisk Gallery, Washington, D.C. (1962); University Art Gallery, Berkeley, Calif. (1964, cat.); E. B. Crocker Art Gallery, Sacramento, Calif. (1966); San Jose State College, San Jose, Calif. (1968); Santa Barbara Museum of Art, Santa Barbara, Calif. (1968); Maxwell Galleries, San Francisco (1970, cat.; 1973, cat.; 1976, cat.); Newport Harbor Art Museum, Newport Beach, Calif. (1977, cat.); Salander-O'Reilly Gallery, New York City (1983, 1985, 1987, 1990); Stanford Art Gallery, Stanford, Calif. (1988, cat.); Whitney Museum of American Art, New York City (1989, cat.); John Berggruen Gallery, San Francisco (1992); Palo Alto Cultural Center, Palo Alto, Calif. (1994, cat.).

DEBORAH REMINGTON   Born in Haddonfield, N.J. (1935). Studied at California School of Fine Arts (B.F.A., 1955). Co-founded Six Gallery, San Francisco, with Wally Hedrick, Hayward King, David Simpson, poet-painter John Allen Ryan, and poet Jack Spicer (1954). Traveled and studied Chinese and Japanese calligraphy in Japan and India (1955–58). Taught at Waseda University, Tokyo (1956). Lived and worked in San Francisco (1958–65). Taught at San Francisco Art Institute (1960–65). Taught at University of California, Davis (1962). Taught at San Francisco State College (1965). Moved to New York City (1965). Awarded fellowship to work at Tamarind Lithography Workshop, Los Angeles (1973). Teaches at Cooper Union Art School, New York City (since 1973).

Selected One-Person Exhibitions   King Ubu Gallery, San Francisco (1953); Six Gallery, San Francisco (1955); San Francisco State College (1961); Dilexi Gallery, San Francisco (1962, 1963 [Los Angeles], 1965); San Francisco Museum of Art (1964); Bykert Gallery, New York City (1967, 1969, 1972, 1974); Galerie Darthea Speyer, Paris (1968, cat.; 1971; 1973; 1992, cat.); Obelisk Gallery, Boston (1971); Pyramid Galleries, Washington, D.C. (1973, 1976); Brooke Alexander Inc., New York City (1974); Michael Berger Gallery, Pittsburgh, Pa. (1974, 1979); Zolla-Lieberman Gallery, Chicago (1976); Hamilton Gallery, New York City (1977); Portland Center for the Visual Arts, Oreg. (1977); University of Missouri Museum, Kansas City (1977); Art Gallery, Miami-Dade Community College, South Campus, Miami (1978, cat.); Bonfoey Gallery, Cleveland (1980); Mary Ryan Gallery, New York City (1982); Newport Harbor Art Museum, Newport Beach, Calif. (1983, cat.); Raymon Osuna Gallery, Washington, D.C. (1983); Gallery Paule Anglim, San Francisco (1984); The Oakland Museum, Oakland, Calif. (1984); Gallery at Greenville, Greenville, Del. (1985, cat.); Jack Shainman Gallery, New York City (1987); Shoshana Wayne Gallery, Los Angeles (1988).

PHILIP ROEBER   Born in Lamborn Mesa, Colo. (1913). Attended Cornish School of the Theatre, Seattle, Wash. (1936–37). Met Morris Graves and published poetry in little magazines *Furioso, Kaleidoscope, Poetry: A Magazine of Verse,* and *Prairie Schooner* (1937–40). Served in U.S. Navy (1941–46). Moved to San Francisco; worked as commercial display designer (1946–48). Studied at California School of Fine Arts on GI Bill (1948–52). Spent year in Provincetown, Mass., on Lannan Foundation grant (1960). Lived and painted winters in New York City, summers in Provincetown (1962–68). Lived in Provincetown (1968–83). Moved to Jonesport, Maine (1983).

Selected One-Person Exhibitions   East and West Gallery, San Francisco (1955, 1956, 1957); Dilexi Gallery, San Francisco (1959); HCE Gallery, Provincetown, Mass. (1962, mid-1960s); Westerly Gallery, New York City (1965, ca. 1967); Jules Brenner Gallery, Provincetown, Mass. (1970); Depot Gallery, Wellfleet, Mass. (1971); Krannert Drawing Room, Purdue University, West Lafayette, Ind. (1971); Provincetown Art Association and Museum, Mass. (1981, cat.); Napi's Restaurant, Provincetown, Mass. (1983).

JOHN SACCARO   Born in San Francisco (1913). Wrote plays and short stories (1932–53). Worked on Easel Painters

and Mural Sections of the Federal Art Project (1939–41): worked under Herman Volz with Peter Lowe and Robert McChesney on design and painting of Federal Building murals and on mosaic at Fine Arts Building (mosaic later moved to San Francisco City College), at Treasure Island, for the Golden Gate International Exposition (1939–40); supervisor of murals and facade of Aquatic Park Building (1940–42). Served in U.S. Army as camoufleur in France, Germany, and Belgium (1942–46). Studied at California School of Fine Arts with Elmer Bischoff, David Park, and James Budd Dixon (1951–54). Taught at University of California, Los Angeles (1963–64). Died in San Francisco (1981).

Selected One-Person Exhibitions   San Francisco Museum of Art (1939; 1959–60, cat.); M. H. de Young Memorial Museum, San Francisco (1946, 1956, 1960); Oakland Art Museum, Oakland, Calif. (1958, cat.); Bolles Gallery, New York City (1962); Museo Italo Americano, San Francisco (1981, cat.); Carlson Gallery, San Francisco (1990, cat.).

JON SCHUELER   Born in Milwaukee, Wis. (1916). Studied at University of Wisconsin, Madison (B.A. in economics, 1938; M.A. in English literature, 1940). Served as B-17 navigator in U.S. Air Force, stationed in England (1941–44). Started painting in Los Angeles (1945). Attended California School of Fine Arts (1948–51); studied with Clyfford Still. Moved to New York City (1951). Traveled and painted in Mallaig, Scotland (1957–58), and Paris (1958–59). Returned to New York City (1959). Taught at Yale University, New Haven, Conn. (1960–62); Maryland Institute, College of Art, Baltimore (1963–67); University of Pennsylvania, Philadelphia (1965); and University of Illinois at Urbana (1968–69). Lived in Mallaig, Scotland (1970–75). Lived in New York City, with periods of work in Mallaig (1975–92). Died in New York City (1992).

Selected One-Person Exhibitions   Metart Galleries, San Francisco (1950); Contemporary Gallery, Sausalito, Calif. (1950); Stable Gallery, New York City (1954, cat.; 1961; 1963); Leo Castelli Gallery, New York City (1957, 1959); Hirschl & Adler Modern, Inc., New York City (1960, cat.); Maryland Institute, College of Art, Baltimore (1967); Richard Demarco Gallery, Edinburgh (1971, cat.); The Edinburgh College of Art (1973, cat.); Dayton's Gallery 12, Minneapolis (1974); Whitney Museum of American Art, New York City (1975, cat.); John Stoller Gallery, Minneapolis (1980); The Talbot Rice Art Center, University of Edinburgh (1981); Dorothy Rosenthal Gallery, Chicago (1981, cat.; 1984); Dorry Gates Gallery, Kansas City, Mo. (1982, 1986, 1991); A. M. Sachs Gallery, New York City (1983, 1984); William Sawyer Gallery, San Francisco (1984); Katharina Rich Perlow Gallery, New York City (1986, 1987, 1989, 1991); The Scottish Gallery, Edinburgh (1991, cat.;

1994); The Highland Regional Council, Scotland (1991, cat.).

PETER SHOEMAKER   Born in Newport, R.I. (1920). Spent youth in Paris, France (1923–33). Served in U.S. Army (1941–46). Studied at University of California, Berkeley (1938–41; B.A. in art, 1951). Studied at California School of Fine Arts on GI Bill (1947–50). Taught at California College of Arts and Crafts (1960–85), Oakland, Calif.

Selected One-Person Exhibitions   Gump's Gallery, San Francisco (1953); California Palace of the Legion of Honor, San Francisco (1955, 1961); Oakland Art Museum, Oakland, Calif. (1957); Hollis Gallery, San Francisco (1962, 1963, 1964, 1965); Adele Bednarz Galleries, Los Angeles (1966); Trutton Gallery, San Francisco (1968); Bolles Gallery, San Francisco (1971, 1972, 1974); Marquoit Galleries, San Francisco (1975); Holy Names College, Oakland, Calif. (1988); Carlson Gallery, San Francisco (1990, cat.).

NELL SINTON   Born in San Francisco (1910). Studied at California School of Fine Arts (1920–25, 1926–28, 1937–38) with Lucien Labaudt and Maurice Sterne (1937–38). Apprentice to Sterne on Federal Art Project murals done in San Francisco for U.S. Department of Justice (1938–40). Named one of the Ten Most Distinguished Bay Area Women of the Year (1959). Served on San Francisco City and County Art Commission (1959–63). Member, Board of Trustees, San Francisco Art Institute (1966–72). Studied at Institute for Creative and Artistic Development, Oakland, Calif. (1968). Taught at San Francisco Art Institute (1970–71). Taught at Institute for Creative and Artistic Development, Oakland, Calif. (1974–85). Visiting artist, Louisiana State University, Baton Rouge (1976). Artist-in-residence and participant in National Organization of Women Conference, University of Illinois at Urbana-Champaign (1978; guest artist, 1984). Taught for emeritus program, College of Marin, Kentfield, Calif. (1981–87).

Selected One-Person Exhibitions   Raymond & Raymond, San Francisco (1947); California Palace of the Legion of Honor, San Francisco (1949); Santa Barbara Museum of Art, Santa Barbara, Calif. (1950); Bolles Gallery, New York and San Francisco (1962); Quay Gallery, San Francisco (1966, 1969, 1971, 1974); San Francisco Museum of Art (1970, cat.); Jacqueline Anhalt Gallery, Los Angeles (1972, cat.); University of California Extension, Berkeley (1975); Louisiana State University, Baton Rouge (1976); Temple Emanu-El, San Francisco (1977); Braunstein/Quay Gallery, San Francisco (1977, 1978, 1989); Braunstein Gallery, San Francisco (1980, 1983, 1986, 1987); Mills College Art Gallery, Oakland, Calif. (1981, cat.); The Oakland Museum, Oakland, Calif. (1990).

HASSEL SMITH   Born in Sturgis, Mich. (1915). Studied at Northwestern University, Evanston, Ill. (B.S. in art history and practice, 1936). Studied with Maurice Sterne at California School of Fine Arts (1936–40). Worked for the California State Relief Administration, San Francisco (1939). Received Abraham Rosenberg Fellowship and moved to Angels Camp in the Sierra foothills, Calif. (1940). Worked for the Farm Security Administration, Arvin, Calif. (1942). Worked for the U.S. Forest Service as a timber scaler on McKenzie River in Oregon (1943). Taught at San Francisco State College (1945–46). Taught at California School of Fine Arts (1945–47, 1948–52). Taught at University of Oregon, Eugene (1947–48). Lived with Edward Corbett, Robert McChesney, sculptor Mary Fuller, and poet Weldon Kees in Point Richmond, Calif. (1948–50). Resigned from California School of Fine Arts after clash with Ernest Mundt and Board of Directors; established Potrero Hill/Mission Street school (1952). Taught at Presidio Hill School, San Francisco (1952–53). Purchased apple orchard and built studio in Sebastopol, Calif. (1955). Operated Sonoma Open-Air Art School in rural Sonoma County with Robert McChesney (1957). Moved to Mousehole, Cornwall, England (1961–62). Returned to Sebastopol (1962). Taught at University of California, Berkeley (1963–65, 1977–78, 1979–80). Moved to Los Angeles and taught at University of California, Los Angeles (1965–66). Moved to Bristol, England, where he currently resides (1966). Taught at Bristol Polytechnic, Bristol, England (1966–81). National Endowment for the Arts Award for Distinguished Service to American Art (1967). Taught at University of California, Davis (1973, 1976). Taught at San Francisco Art Institute (summers 1978–80, 1981 as guest artist). Taught at Cardiff College of Art, Cardiff, Wales (1978–81). Artist-in-residence, College of Notre Dame, Belmont, Calif. (1988).

Selected One-Person Exhibitions   Iron Pot Restaurant, San Francisco (1946); University of Oregon Gallery, Eugene (1947); California Palace of the Legion of Honor, San Francisco (1947, 1953); Lucien Labaudt Gallery, San Francisco (1949, 1950); East and West Gallery, San Francisco (1955, 1956); King Ubu Gallery, San Francisco (1955); New Arts, Houston, Tex. (1956, 1958, 1959, 1961); Dilexi Gallery, San Francisco (1956, 1957, 1958, 1959, 1960, 1961; 1962, cat.; 1964, cat.; 1965); California School of Fine Arts (1957, cat.; 1958; 1959); Ferus Gallery, Los Angeles (1958, 1959, 1961, 1962); Reed College, Portland, Oreg. (1959); Gimpel Fils, London (1960; 1963, cat.); Pasadena Art Museum, Calif. (1961, cat.); André Emmerich Gallery, New York City (1961, cat.; 1962; 1963); Galleria dell'Ariete, Milan (1962, cat.); Gallery Lounge, San Francisco State College (1964); University of Minnesota Art Gallery, Minneapolis (1964); Worth Ryder Gallery, University of California, Berkeley (1964); David Stuart Galleries, Los Angeles (1964, 1965, 1966, 1968, 1969, 1973); Suzanne Saxe Gallery, San Francisco (1970, 1973); Bristol Art Gallery, Bristol, England (1972); Sarah Campbell Blaffer Gallery, University of Houston, Tex. (1974); San Francisco Museum of Modern Art (1975); Gallery Paule Anglim, San Francisco (1977, 1978, 1979, 1980, 1982, 1984, 1987); Atlantic-Richfield Center for Visual Arts, Los Angeles (1978); The Oakland Museum, Oakland, Calif. (1981, cat.); San Jose Museum of Art, San Jose, Calif. (1983); John Berggruen Gallery, San Francisco (1985); Blum Helman Gallery, Santa Monica, Calif. (1987); Wiegand Gallery, College of Notre Dame, Belmont, Calif. (1988, cat.); Cleveland Bridge Gallery, Bath, England (1988); Gallery 44, Oakland, Calif. (1988); Monterey Peninsula Museum of Art, Monterey, Calif. (1988); Iannctti-Lanzoni Gallery, San Francisco (1988, 1989); Natsoulas/Novelozo Gallery, Davis, Calif. (1989, cat.); Harcourts Gallery, San Francisco (1995).

FRANN SPENCER [REYNOLDS]   Born in Oakland, Calif. Studied art under Erle Loran, Worth Ryder, and Margaret Peterson at University of California, Berkeley (A.A., 1945; B.A., 1947; M.A. 1950). Commissioned to paint screens and murals (no longer extant) for main lounge and Indian Room of Ahwahnee Hotel, Yosemite National Park, Calif. (1946). Attended California School of Fine Arts (1946–47) and studied with Ruth Armer and Stanley William Hayter. Attended Rhode Island School of Design, Providence (spring 1948).

Selected One-Person Exhibitions   Metart Galleries, San Francisco (1950); Ansel Adams's studio, San Francisco (1953); Area Arts Gallery, San Francisco (1955).

CLAY SPOHN   Born in San Francisco (1898); raised in Piedmont, Calif. Attended California College of Arts and Crafts, Oakland, Calif. (1910–16). Studied at the California School of Fine Arts (1914, 1920–21). Majored in economics and studied art with Perham Nahl and Eugen Neuhaus at University of California, Berkeley (1919–22). Studied landscape painting with Armin Hansen, Monterey, Calif. (summer 1921). Studied with Guy Pène du Bois, George Luks, Kenneth Hayes Miller, and Boardman Robinson at Art Students League, New York City, where he befriended Alexander Calder (1922–24). Traveled in Italy and France; attended the Académie Moderne, Paris, run by Fernand Léger and Othon Friesz (studied with latter); met Surrealists; worked with Calder on kinetic sculpture, precursor of the mobile (1926–27). Returned to San Francisco (1927). Worked for Works Progress Administration Federal Arts Project on murals: painted Montebello, Calif., Post Office murals (1938) and Los Gatos Union High School mural (1939). Worked on decorations for first San Francisco Open Air Show (1941). Executed *Fantastic War Machines and Guerragraphs* (1941–42). Served as technical illustrator for

the U.S. Navy (1942–44). Taught at California School of Fine Arts (1945–50). Created *Museum of Unknown and Little-Known Objects* (1949). Lived in New York City (1950–51). Lived in Taos, N.Mex. (1951–57). Taught at Mount Holyoke College, South Hadley, Mass. (1958). Moved to New York City (fall 1958). Taught at School of Visual Arts, New York City (1964–69). Lived in Taos (1969–71). Moved to New York City (1971). Died in New York City (1977).

Selected One-Person Exhibitions   San Francisco Art League and Art Center Gallery (1931); San Francisco Museum of Art (1942); Rotunda Gallery, City of Paris department store, San Francisco (1946); Stables Gallery, Taos, N.Mex. (1947); Artium Orbis Corp., Santa Fe, N.Mex. (1971, cat.); The Oakland Museum, Oakland, Calif. (1974, cat.)

CLYFFORD STILL   Born in Grandin, N.Dak. (1904); raised in Spokane, Wash., and southern Alberta, Canada. Visited New York City (1925). Graduated from Spokane University, Wash. (1933). Taught at Washington State College, Pullman (1933–41). Lived in San Francisco Bay Area; worked in Oakland shipyards and for Hammond Aircraft in San Francisco (1941–43). Met Mark Rothko in Berkeley, Calif. (1943). Taught at Richmond Professional Institute, College of William and Mary, Richmond, Va. (1943–45). Lived and painted in New York City (1945). Taught at California School of Fine Arts (1946–50). Visited New York City; cofounded Subjects of the Artist, a short-lived school (1948). Lived in New York City; maintained contact with Bay Area artists through correspondence and occasional trips to San Francisco (1950–61). Moved to Maryland, near Westminster (1961). Died in Baltimore (1980).

Selected One-Person Exhibitions   San Francisco Museum of Art (1943); Art of This Century, New York City (1946); California Palace of the Legion of Honor, San Francisco (1947); Betty Parsons Gallery, New York City (1947, 1950, 1951); Metart Galleries, San Francisco (1950); Albright Art Gallery, Buffalo, N.Y. (1959, cat.); Institute of Contemporary Art, University of Pennsylvania, Philadelphia (1963, cat.); Albright-Knox Art Gallery, Buffalo, N.Y. (1966, cat.; 1978; 1980); Marlborough-Gerson Gallery, New York City (1969, cat.); San Francisco Museum of Modern Art (1976, cat.); The Metropolitan Museum of Art, New York City (1979, cat.); Los Angeles County Museum of Art (1980); Mary Boone Gallery, New York City (1990, cat.); San Francisco Museum of Modern Art, Albright-Knox Art Gallery, Buffalo, N.Y., and Kunsthalle, Basel (1992, cat.).

GEORGE STILLMAN   Born in Laramie, Wyo. (1921); spent most of his childhood in Ontario, Calif. Studied at Chaffey

College, Alta Loma, Calif. (A.A., 1941). Attended University of California, Berkeley (1941–42). Drafted into U.S. Army (1942). Served as chief of U.S. Signal Corps Photographic Laboratory (until 1946). Studied collections at Museum of Modern Art, New York (1942–46). Studied at New York University (1943). Operated Stillman Studios (photography) in Oakland (1946–49). Studied at California School of Fine Arts on GI Bill (1946–49). Taught photography and lithography at University of Guadalajara, Mexico (1950–51). Lived in New York City; declined offer to show work at Museum of Modern Art (1951). Chief, Reproduction Branch and head instructor for photolithography in Latin America, Civilian U.S. Army (1953–60). Received Civilian Army Award for development of color proofing reproduction system (1954). Communications Media Officer, U.S. State Department, Brazil and Bolivia (1960–66). Publisher of national audiovisual magazine, Brazil (1960–66). Publisher of technical publications, northeast Brazil, and training films and publications in Bolivia (1960–66). Producer-director for Arizona State University television station, Tempe (1966–70). Attended Arizona State University, Tempe (from 1967; B.F.A., 1968; M.F.A., 1970). Taught at Columbus College, Columbus, Ga. (1970–72). Taught at Central Washington University, Ellensburg (1972–88). Awarded National Endowment for the Arts fellowship (1990).

Selected One-Person Exhibitions   Artists' Guild Gallery, San Francisco (1948); Galería Arte Moderna, Mexico City (1951); Galería Camarauz, Guadalajara, Mexico (1951); Arizona State University, Tempe (1970, cat.); LaGrange College Gallery, LaGrange, Ga. (1970); Columbus Museum of Art, Columbus, Ga. (1972); Gallery of Art, Phoenix, Ariz. (1974); Yakima Public Library, Yakima, Wash. (1974); Community Art Gallery, Ellensburg, Wash. (1979); Foster/White Gallery, Seattle (1986); Gallery Imago, San Francisco (1986); Heller Gallery, University of California, Berkeley (1989); Allied Arts Association, Richland, Wash. (1991); Sarah Spurgeon Gallery, Central Washington University, Ellensburg (1991, cat.); Gallery One, Ellensburg, Wash. (1993); North Light Gallery, Everett, Wash. (1993).

CHARLES STRONG   Born in Greeley, Colo. (1938). Attended Coronado School of Art, San Diego (1957–58). Studied at San Francisco Art Institute with Elmer Bischoff, Richard Diebenkorn, Jack Jefferson, and Frank Lobdell (from 1959; M.F.A., 1963). Met Clyfford Still (1960). Studied at Skowhegan School of Art, Skowhegan, Maine, where he befriended Bischoff. Awarded Fulbright scholarship to England; met Hassel Smith (1963). Traveled through Europe: examined works by Blake, Goya, and Fra Angelico (1963–64). Taught at San Francisco State College (1965–68). Began teaching at College of Notre Dame, Belmont, Calif.

(1970); founded, and curated exhibitions for, College of Notre Dame Art Gallery, Belmont, Calif. (1970–79). Taught at University of California, Berkeley (1979–80). National Endowment for the Arts fellowship (1982). Founded Wiegand Gallery, College of Notre Dame, Belmont, Calif. (1987). Co-founded Peter and Madeleine Martin Foundation for the Creative Arts, San Francisco, with Madeleine Martin (1990).

Selected One-Person Exhibitions   Richmond Art Center, Richmond, Calif. (1969); University of California, Santa Cruz (1972); Smith Andersen Gallery, Palo Alto, Calif. (1972, 1975); Sonoma State University, Rohnert Park, Calif. (1973); James Willis Gallery, San Francisco (1973, 1976); College of Notre Dame Art Gallery, Belmont, Calif. (1980, cat.; 1985); De Saisset Museum, Santa Clara, Calif. (1985); San Jose Art Museum, San Jose, Calif. (1985); Gregory Ghent Gallery, San Francisco (1987); Iannetti-Lanzone Gallery, San Francisco (1988, cat.); Bolinas Museum, Bolinas, Calif. (1991, cat.); Natsoulas/Novelozo Gallery, Davis, Calif. (1991, cat.); Hearst Art Gallery, St. Mary's College of California, Moraga, Calif. (1991, cat.); Rancho de Talpa Gallery, Talpa, N.Mex. (1992); Triton Museum of Art, Santa Clara, Calif. (forthcoming).

SAM TCHAKALIAN   Born in Shanghai, China (1929). Moved to San Francisco (1947). Received A.A. from San Francisco City College (1950). Studied at San Francisco State College (B.A. in psychology, 1952; M.A. in art, 1958). Served in U.S. Army, Military Intelligence battalion, Washington, D.C. (1952–54). Taught at California College of Arts and Crafts, Oakland, Calif. (1962–63). Taught at College of San Mateo, San Mateo, Calif. (1964–65). Taught at California State College, Los Angeles (summer 1965). Began teaching at San Francisco Art Institute (1966–present). Taught at University of California, Davis (1970). Guest lecturer, Cooper Union Art School, New York City (1973); Hampshire College, Amherst, Mass., and Pratt Institute, Brooklyn, N.Y. (1974); and College of Creative Studies, University of California, Santa Barbara (1979). National Endowment for the Arts fellowships (1975, 1981, 1989). Taught at University of California, Berkeley (1979–80). Adaline Kent Award, San Francisco Art Institute (1981).

Selected One-Person Exhibitions   Dilexi Gallery, San Francisco (1960, 1963); M. H. de Young Memorial Museum, San Francisco (1962, cat.); Art Unlimited Gallery, San Francisco (1963); Bolles Gallery, San Francisco (1966); Balboa Pavilion Gallery, Balboa, Calif. (1967, cat.); San Francisco Museum of Art (1967); Molly Barnes Gallery, Los Angeles (1968–69); Emanuel Walter Art Gallery, San Francisco Art Institute (1970, 1982); Quay Gallery, San Francisco (1972, 1973); Ruth Braunstein/Quay Gallery, New York City (1975); Susan Caldwell Gallery, New York City (1977); The Oakland Museum, Oakland, Calif. (1978, cat.); Portland Center for the Visual Arts, Portland, Oreg. (1979); Stephen Wirtz Gallery, San Francisco (1981); Modernism Gallery, San Francisco (1986; 1987, cat.; 1991, cat.); The National Museum of Contemporary Art, Seoul, Korea (1989, cat.)

HORST TRAVE   Born in Reinfeld, Germany (1918). Attended Meisterschule für Grafik und Buchkunst, Berlin (1937–39); saw 1937 *Entartete Kunst* (Degenerate Art) exhibition in Munich organized by the Nazis. When called to report for military induction, left Germany for Sweden, where he studied at Royal Academy, Stockholm, and participated in antifascist artists' forum Realisten (1940). Emigrated to United States (1941). Served in U.S. Army overseas (1943–46). Intelligence Service, U.S. War Department, European theater (1946–47). Attended California School of Fine Arts (1947–49); studied at California College of Arts and Crafts, Oakland, Calif. (B.A.Ed., 1950; M.F.A., 1951). Served in U.S. Army (1952). Worked as an art instructor in San Francisco (1954–78). Has painted independently since 1978. Traveled to Germany (1987). Taught at Santa Rosa Junior College, Santa Rosa, Calif. (1988–90).

Selected One-Person Exhibitions   Raymond & Raymond Gallery, San Francisco (1948); Metart Galleries, San Francisco (1950); San Francisco State College Gallery (1958); Dilexi Gallery, San Francisco (1961); Green Gallery, San Francisco (1968); College of Notre Dame Art Gallery, Belmont, Calif. (1976); Triangle Gallery, San Francisco (1979); Santa Rosa Junior College Gallery, Santa Rosa, Calif. (1980); California Museum of Art, Santa Rosa, Calif. (1987); Ebert Gallery, San Francisco (1991); Ironwood Ridge Gallery, Healdsburg, Calif. (1991); Soundscape Gallery, Healdsburg, Calif. (1991).

JULIUS WASSERSTEIN   Born in Providence, R.I. (1924); moved to San Francisco (1925). Attended California School of Fine Arts (1950–53). Gallery superintendent, San Francisco Museum of Modern Art (1952–85). Studied at San Francisco State College (1955–58). Taught at San Francisco Art Institute (1960–63). Received San Francisco Art Association Nealie Sullivan Award (1961). Died in San Francisco (1985).

Selected One-Person Exhibitions   King Ubu Gallery, San Francisco (1953); Lucien Labaudt Gallery, San Francisco (1954); Six Gallery, San Francisco (1956); Syndell Studio, Los Angeles (1956); East and West Gallery, San Francisco (1957); Ferus Gallery, Los Angeles (1957); Spatsa Gallery, San Francisco (1959); Rose Rabow Galleries, San Francisco (1959, 1961, 1968, 1973, 1975); Staempfli Gallery, New York City (1961); San Francisco Art Institute (1961); California Palace of the Legion of Honor, San Francisco (1962); Dilexi Gallery, San Francisco (1962); San Francisco Museum of Modern Art (1953, 1962, 1964, 1985); Gallery Paule Anglim, San Francisco (1979, 1981, 1984).

By Susan Landauer and Andrea Feeser, with the assistance of Mara Skov

Exact exhibition titles, dates, and catalogue references are provided where possible. For traveling exhibitions, venues listed are those of organizing institutions.

1940   Golden Gate International Exposition, Palace of Fine Arts, San Francisco. Included James Budd Dixon, Nell Sinton, Hassel Smith, and Clay Spohn. Cat.

Sixtieth Annual Exhibition: Oil, Tempera, and Sculpture, San Francisco Art Association, San Francisco Museum of Art. Included Ruth Armer, Peter Lowe, Robert McChesney, and John Saccaro. Cat.

1941   [Fifth] *Annual Exhibition of Drawings and Prints, San Francisco Art Association,* San Francisco Museum of Art. Included Ruth Armer, James Budd Dixon, Peter Lowe, and Clay Spohn. Cat.

Sixty-first Annual Exhibition: Oil, Tempera on Panel, and Sculpture, San Francisco Art Association, San Francisco Museum of Art. Included Ruth Armer, Richard Ayer, Elmer Bischoff, Richard Bowman, David Park, and Hassel Smith. Cat.

1942   [Sixth] *Annual Exhibition of Drawings and Prints, San Francisco Art Association,* San Francisco Museum of Art. Included Ruth Armer and Hassel Smith. Cat.

Sixty-second Annual Exhibition: Oil, Tempera on Panel, and Sculpture, San Francisco Art Association, San Francisco Museum of Art. Included Richard Ayer, Elmer Bischoff, and Peter Lowe. Cat.

1944   [Eighth] *Annual Exhibition of Drawings and Prints, San Francisco Art Association,* San Francisco Museum of Art. Included Ronald Bladen and Hassel Smith. Cat.

Sixty-fourth Annual Exhibition: Oil, Tempera on Panel, and Sculpture, San Francisco Art Association, San Francisco Museum of Art. Included Ruth Armer, Ronald Bladen, Hassel Smith, and Clay Spohn. Cat.

1945   *Art of Our Time,* San Francisco Museum of Art. Included David Park and Clay Spohn. Cat.

Contemporary American Painting, California Palace of the Legion of Honor, San Francisco. Included Hassel Smith and Clay Spohn. Cat.

Ninth Annual Drawing and Print Exhibition of the San Francisco Art Association, San Francisco Museum of Art. Included James Budd Dixon and Clay Spohn. Cat.

Sixty-fifth Annual Exhibition: Oil, Tempera, and Sculpture, San Francisco Art Association, San Francisco Museum of Art. Included Peter Lowe, David Park, Hassel Smith, and Clay Spohn. Cat.

Twentieth Annual Exhibition, San Francisco Society of Women Artists, San Francisco Museum of Art [?]. Included Ruth Armer and Nell Sinton. Cat.

1946   *Faculty Exhibition,* California Palace of the Legion of Honor, San Francisco. Included Elmer Bischoff, David Park, Hassel Smith, Clay Spohn, and Clyfford Still. Cat.

First Spring Annual Exhibition, California Palace of the Legion of Honor, San Francisco. Included Martin Baer, Robert McChesney, David Park, and Clay Spohn. Cat.

Group exhibition, Pat Wall Gallery, Monterey, Calif. Included Edward Corbett, Robert McChesney, and Richard Diebenkorn.

Sixty-sixth Annual Exhibition: Oil, Tempera, and Sculpture, San Francisco Art Association, San Francisco Museum of Art. Included Ruth Armer, Elmer Bischoff, Ronald Bladen, Edward Corbett, Richard Diebenkorn, James Budd Dixon, Sam Francis, John Grillo, Harlan Jackson, Robert McChesney, David Park, Hassel Smith, and Frann Spencer. Cat.

Tenth Annual Drawing and Print Exhibition, San Francisco Art Association, San Francisco Museum of Art. Included Ruth Armer, Peter Lowe, Robert McChesney, Hassel Smith, and Clay Spohn. Cat.

1947   *Eleventh Annual Drawing and Print Exhibition, San Francisco Art Association,* San Francisco Museum of Art. Included Robert McChesney and Hassel Smith. Cat.

Group exhibition, Artists' Guild Gallery, San Francisco. Included Edward Corbett, Robert McChesney, and Hassel Smith.

New Bay Region Artists, San Francisco Museum of Art. Included Ruth Armer, Elmer Bischoff, Peter Lowe, Robert McChesney, David Park, and Clay Spohn.

Twenty-second Annual Exhibition, San Francisco Women Artists, San Francisco Museum of Art. Included Ruth Armer, Nell Sinton, and Frann Spencer. Cat.

1947–48   *Daliel's Opening: Group Show,* Daliel's, Berkeley, Calif. Included Elmer Bischoff, David Park, and Clay Spohn.

Second Annual Exhibition of Painting, California Palace of the Legion of Honor, San Francisco. Included Richard Ayer, Elmer Bischoff, John Grillo, Harlan Jackson, Walter Kuhlman, Frank Lobdell, Clay Spohn, Clyfford Still, and George Stillman. Cat.

1948   *Abstract and Surrealist American Art,* The Art Institute of Chicago. Included Elmer Bischoff, Edward Corbett, and Robert McChesney. Cat.

Current Trends in Bay Region Art, California College of Arts and Crafts, Oakland, Calif. Included John Hultberg, Walter Kuhlman, Frank Lobdell, and George Stillman.

Five Young Moderns, Seashore Gallery of Modern Art, Sausalito, Calif. Included John Hultberg, Walter Kuhlman, Frank Lobdell, and George Stillman.

Group exhibition, Contemporary Gallery, Sausalito, Calif. Included Richard Diebenkorn, James Budd Dixon, John Hultberg, Walter Kuhlman, and Frank Lobdell.

Group exhibition, Letterman Hospital, San Francisco. Included Robert McChesney and Hassel Smith.

Group exhibition, North Beach Studio Gallery, San Francisco. Included Richard Diebenkorn, John Hultberg, Frank Lobdell, and George Stillman.

Group exhibition [five-man show], Reed College, Portland, Oreg. Included Frank Lobdell, John Hultberg, Walter Kuhlman, George Stillman, and James Budd Dixon.

Group exhibition, Schillerhaus, Sausalito, Calif. Included Lawrence Calcagno, Richard Diebenkorn, John Hultberg, Walter Kuhlman, and Frank Lobdell.

Group Show—Bischoff, Park, and Smith, San Francisco Museum of Art.

Group Show, Sixteen Lithographs, Lawson Galleries, San Francisco. Included Richard Diebenkorn, James Budd Dixon, John Hultberg, Walter Kuhlman, Frank Lobdell, and George Stillman.

Oakland Art Gallery's Annual Exhibition of Oil Paintings and Sculpture, Oakland Art Gallery, Oakland, Calif. Included Frank Lobdell and George Stillman. Cat.

Sixty-seventh Annual Exhibition: Oil, Tempera, and Sculpture of the San Francisco Art Association, San Francisco Museum of Art. Included Elmer Bischoff, Richard Diebenkorn, James Budd Dixon, Sam Francis, Jorge Goya, John Hultberg, Harlan Jackson, Walter Kuhlman, Frank Lobdell, Robert McChesney, David Park, Hassel Smith, Clay Spohn, and George Stillman. Cat.

Twelfth Annual Drawing and Print Exhibition, San Francisco Art Association, San Francisco Museum of Art. Included Richard Ayer, Edward Corbett, Richard Diebenkorn, James Budd Dixon, Jorge Goya, John Hultberg, Frank Lobdell, Peter Lowe, Robert McChesney, David Park, Hassel Smith, and George Stillman. Cat.

Young Artists of the Bay Area, California Palace of the Legion of Honor, San Francisco. Included John Hultberg, Frank Lobdell, and George Stillman.

1948–49   *Third Annual Exhibition of Painting,* California Palace of the Legion of Honor, San Francisco. Included Ruth Armer, James Budd Dixon, Frank Lobdell, and Clyfford Still. Cat.

1949   *First Annual Selections Show,* Metart Galleries, San Francisco. Included Ernest Briggs, Edward Dugmore, Jack Jefferson, Jorge Goya, Horst Trave, Frann Spencer [and Clyfford Still?].

Frank Lobdell/George Stillman, Lucien Labaudt Gallery, San Francisco.

Group exhibition, Alta Mira Hotel, Sausalito, Calif. Included James Budd Dixon, John Hultberg, Walter Kuhlman, Frank Lobdell, and George Stillman.

Hassel Smith/Richard Diebenkorn, Lucien Labaudt Gallery, San Francisco.

New Bay Region Artists, San Francisco Museum of Art. Included Ruth Armer, Elmer Bischoff, Richard Diebenkorn, Sam Francis, Robert McChesney, David Park, Frann Spencer, and Clay Spohn.

Paintings by Philip Roeber, Robert McChesney, Byron Randall, Emmy Lou Packard, and Edward Corbett, San Francisco Museum of Art.

Sixty-eighth Annual Exhibition, San Francisco Art Association, San Francisco Museum of Art. Included George Abend, Ruth Armer, Ernest Briggs, Lawrence Calcagno, Edward Corbett, Richard Diebenkorn, John Hultberg, Walter Kuhlman, Robert McChesney, Nell Sinton, Hassel Smith, Frann Spencer, and George Stillman. Cat.

Thirteenth Annual American Abstract Artists Exhibition, Riverside Museum, New York City. Included John Grillo and Clay Spohn. Cat.

Thirteenth Annual Drawing and Print Exhibition, San Francisco Art Association, San Francisco Museum of Art. Included Ruth Armer, Elmer Bischoff, and George Stillman. Cat.

Twenty-fourth Annual Exhibition, San Francisco Women Artists, San Francisco Museum of Art. Included Ruth Armer and Nell Sinton. Cat.

1950 *Bay Area Painters,* Studio C Gallery, Berkeley, Calif. Included Edward Corbett and Robert McChesney.

Fifteen Paintings by Nine Artists in San Francisco, Henry Art Gallery, University of Washington, Seattle. Included Elmer Bischoff, Edward Corbett, Richard Diebenkorn, Jack Jefferson, Hassel Smith, David Park, George Stillman, and Clyfford Still. Cat.

Fourteenth Annual Drawing and Print Exhibition, San Francisco Art Association, San Francisco Museum of Art. Included Richard Bowman, Jay DeFeo, James Budd Dixon, Sam Francis, Jorge Goya, Frank Lobdell, Peter Shoemaker, George Stillman, and Horst Trave. Cat.

Joint exhibition, Lucien Labaudt Gallery, San Francisco. Included Richard Diebenkorn and Hassel Smith.

Large Scale Drawings by Modern Artists, California Palace of the Legion of Honor, San Francisco. Included Elmer Bischoff, Edward Corbett, Richard Diebenkorn, Jack Jefferson, David Park, Hassel Smith, and Clay Spohn. Cat.

New Bay Region Artists (Fifteenth Anniversary), San Francisco Museum of Art. Included Ruth Armer, Elmer Bischoff, Ernest Briggs, Lawrence Calcagno, Richard Diebenkorn, James Budd Dixon, John Hultberg, Walter Kuhlman, Frank Lobdell, David Park, Hassel Smith, Frann Spencer, and George Stillman.

Sixty-ninth Annual Oil, Tempera, and Sculpture Exhibition of the San Francisco Art Association, San Francisco Museum of Art. Included George Abend, Ruth Armer, Richard Ayer, Elmer Bischoff, Richard Bowman, Lawrence Calcagno, James Budd Dixon, Sam Francis, John Hultberg, Walter Kuhlman, Frank Lobdell, Robert McChesney, David Park, Peter Shoemaker, Hassel Smith, Frann Spencer, George Stillman, and Horst Trave. Cat.

Twenty-fifth Annual Exhibition, San Francisco Women Artists, San Francisco Museum of Art. Included Ruth Armer, Nell Sinton, and Frann Spencer. Cat.

1950–51   *Fourth Annual Exhibition of Contemporary American Painting,* California Palace of the Legion of Honor, San Francisco. Included Ruth Armer, Jorge Goya, Peter Shoemaker, and Clyfford Srill. Cat.

1951   *Bay Region Painting and Sculpture,* San Francisco Museum of Art. Included Ruth Armer, Richard Ayer, Elmer Bischoff, Ernest Briggs, James Budd Dixon, Jorge Goya, Frann Spencer [Reynolds], Peter Shoemaker, Nell Sinton, Hassel Smith, and Horst Trave.

California School of Fine Arts fourth faculty exhibition, M. H. de Young Memorial Museum, San Francisco. Included Elmer Bischoff, James Budd Dixon, Robert McChesney, David Park, and Hassel Smith.

Fifteenth Annual Drawing and Print Exhibition, San Francisco Art Association, San Francisco Museum of Art. Included Ruth Armer, Jay DeFeo, Jorge Goya, Emiko Nakano, Deborah Remington, and Nell Sinton. Cat.

Group exhibition, La Galeria Escondida, Taos, N.Mex. Included Edward Corbett, Richard Diebenkorn, Robert McChesney, and Clay Spohn.

Group exhibition, Lucien Labaudt Gallery, San Francisco. Included Lilly Fenichel and Philip Roeber.

Hassel Smith/Edward Corbett, San Francisco Art Association Gallery, California School of Fine Arts.

1951 Annual Exhibition, Oakland Art Gallery, Oakland, Calif. Included Lawrence Calcagno, Jorge Goya, and George Kuhlman. Cat.

6ème Salon des Réalités Nouvelles, Petit Palais, Paris. Included Walter Kuhlman and Frank Lobdell.

Seventieth Annual Oil and Sculpture Exhibition of the San Francisco Art Association, San Francisco Museum of Art. Included Ruth Armer, Elmer Bischoff, Sam Francis, Walter Kuhlman, David Park, Philip Roeber, Nell Sinton, George Stillman, and Horst Trave. Cat.

Twenty-sixth Annual Exhibition, San Francisco Women Artists, San Francisco Museum of Art. Included Ruth Armer and Nell Sinton. Cat.

1951–52   Contemporary American painting annual, Whitney Museum of American Art, New York City. Included Ruth Armer and Frann Spencer.

1952   *Bay Region Painting and Sculpture,* San Francisco Museum of Art. Included Ruth Armer, Richard Ayer, Elmer Bischoff, James Budd Dixon, Walter Kuhlman, Frank Lobdell, David Park, Frann Spencer [Reynolds], Nell Sinton, and Hassel Smith.

Fifteen Americans, Museum of Modern Art, New York City. Included Edward Corbett and Clyfford Still. Cat.

Fifth Annual Exhibition of Contemporary American Painting, California Palace of the Legion of Honor, San Francisco. Included Ruth Armer and Nell Sinton. Cat.

First Annual Pacific Art Festival, Exposition Building, Oakland, Calif. Included Walter Kuhlman, David Park, and Nell Sinton. Cat.

Large Scale Drawings, King Ubu Gallery, San Francisco (inaugural exhibition). Included Elmer Bischoff, David Park, Philip Roeber, and Hassel Smith.

Metropolitan Museum of Art annual exhibition of watercolors, drawings, and prints, New York City. Included Ruth Armer, Emiko Nakano, and Nell Sinton.

The Mirror Five, San Francisco Art Association Gallery, California School of Fine Arts. Included James Kelly and John Saccaro.

Seventy-first Annual Painting and Sculpture Exhibition of the San Francisco Art Association, San Francisco Museum of Art. Included Richard Diebenkorn, Nell Sinton, and Horst Trave. Cat.

Sixteenth Annual Drawing and Print Exhibition, San Francisco Art Association, San Francisco Museum of Art. Included Ruth Armer, Sam Francis, Jorge Goya, Emiko Nakano, Deborah Remington, Peter Shoemaker, Nell Sinton, and Horst Trave. Cat.

Sixteenth Annual Watercolor Exhibition, San Francisco Art Association, San Francisco Museum of Art. Included James Budd Dixon and Sonia Gechtoff. Cat.

State Fair art exhibition, modern oils division, Sacramento, Calif. Included Emiko Nakano, David Park, Frann Spencer, and Horst Trave.

Twenty-seventh Annual Exhibition, San Francisco Women Artists, San Francisco Museum of Art. Included Ruth Armer and Nell Sinton. Cat.

1953   *Deborah Remington/Jorge Goya,* King Ubu Gallery, San Francisco.

Four Contemporary Artists, California Palace of the Legion of Honor, San Francisco. Included Ernest Briggs and Hassel Smith.

Group exhibition, King Ubu Gallery, San Francisco. Included James Kelly, Adelie Landis, Hassel Smith, and Julius Wasserstein.

Group exhibition, King Ubu Gallery, San Francisco. Included Madeleine Dimond, Lilly Fenichel, and Sonia Gechtoff.

Seventeenth Annual Drawing and Print Exhibition, San Francisco Art Association, San Francisco Museum of Art. Included George Abend, Ruth Armer, Jay DeFeo, Sonia Gechtoff, Emiko Nakano, Deborah Remington, Nell Sinton, Horst Trave, and Julius Wasserstein. Cat.

Seventeenth Annual Watercolor Exhibition of the San Francisco Art Association, San Francisco Museum of Art. Included Jay DeFeo, Sonia Gechtoff, and Nell Sinton. Cat.

Seventy-second Annual Painting and Sculpture Exhibition of the San Francisco Art Association, San Francisco Museum of Art. Included Ruth Armer, Elmer Bischoff, Ernest Briggs, Madeleine Dimond, Walter Kuhlman, Robert McChesney, David Park, Philip Roeber, John Saccaro, Peter Shoemaker, Nell Sinton, and Horst Trave. Cat.

Six San Francisco Painters, Felix Landau Gallery, Los Angeles. Included James Budd Dixon and Frank Lobdell.

State Fair art exhibition, Sacramento, Calif. Included Ruth Armer, Emiko Nakano, and Nell Sinton.

1954   *Eighteenth Annual Drawing and Print Exhibition, San Francisco Art Association,* San Francisco Museum of Art. Included Jay DeFeo, Emiko Nakano, Nell Sinton, and Julius Wasserstein. Cat.

Fourth Annual Exhibition: Oil and Sculpture, Richmond Art Center, Richmond, Calif. Included Jay DeFeo, Richard Diebenkorn, Sonia Gechtoff, David Park, and Hassel Smith. Cat.

From San Francisco: A New Language in Painting, Kaufmann Art Gallery, YM-YWHA, New York City. Included Madeleine Dimond, Sonia Gechtoff, James Kelly, Hassel Smith, and Julius Wasserstein.

Group exhibition, Six Gallery, San Francisco (inaugural exhibition). Included Madeleine Dimond, Hayward King, Deborah Remington, and Peter Shoemaker.

Individualités d'aujourd'hui, Galerie Rive Droite, Paris. Included Sam Francis and John Hultberg.

Seventy-third Annual Painting and Sculpture Exhibition of the San Francisco Art Association, San Francisco Museum of Art. Included Ruth Armer, Richard Ayer, Richard Diebenkorn, James Budd Dixon, Sonia Gechtoff, Walter Kuhlman, William Morehouse, David Park, John Saccaro, Peter Shoemaker, Clay Spohn, and Julius Wasserstein. Cat.

Spring Annual Exhibition of Oil Painting and Related Media, Oakland Art Museum, Oakland, Calif. Included Ruth Armer, John Saccaro, and Nell Sinton. Cat.

Third Annual Exhibition: Watercolor, Print, Decorative Arts, Richmond Art Center, Richmond, Calif. Included Ruth Armer, Jay DeFeo, and James Budd Dixon. Cat.

Three Bay Region Artists: Ruth Armer, Richard Diebenkorn, Ralph Du Casse, San Francisco Museum of Art.

Twenty-ninth Annual Exhibition, San Francisco Women Artists, San Francisco Museum of Art. Included Ruth Armer and Nell Sinton. Cat.

Younger American Painters, Solomon R. Guggenheim Museum, New York City. Included Richard Diebenkorn, Sonia Gechtoff, and William Morehouse. Cat.

1955   *Action 1,* Merry-Go-Round Building, Santa Monica, Calif. Included Jay DeFeo, Roy De
        Forest, Madeleine Dimond, James Budd Dixon, Sonia Gechtoff, James Kelly, Philip Roeber,
        Hassel Smith, and Julius Wasserstein.

        Art in the Twentieth Century, San Francisco Museum of Art. Included Ruth Armer, Lawrence
        Calcagno, Sam Francis, John Hultberg, Walter Kuhlman, and John Saccaro. Cat.

        Bay Region Painting and Sculpture, San Francisco Museum of Art. Included Ruth Armer,
        Richard Diebenkorn, Walter Kuhlman, Robert McChesney, Emiko Nakano, David Park, and
        Nell Sinton.

        Fifth Annual Oil and Sculpture Exhibition, Richmond Art Center, Richmond, Calif. Included
        Elmer Bischoff, Jay DeFeo, Richard Diebenkorn, Emiko Nakano, David Park, and Deborah
        Remington. Cat.

        Group exhibition, East and West Gallery and Six Gallery, San Francisco, and Syndell Studio
        and Now Gallery, Los Angeles. Included Jay DeFeo, Sonia Gechtoff, James Kelly, and Julius
        Wasserstein.

        Invitational Group Show, Six Gallery, San Francisco. Included Ronald Bladen, Richard
        Diebenkorn, James Budd Dixon, David Park, and Julius Wasserstein.

        Nine Painters, East and West Gallery, San Francisco (inaugural exhibition). Included
        Madeleine Dimond, Sonia Gechtoff, James Kelly, Hassel Smith, and Julius Wasserstein.

        Nineteenth Annual Drawing and Print Exhibition, San Francisco Art Association, San Francisco
        Museum of Art. Included Ruth Armer, Jay DeFeo, Sonia Gechtoff, James Kelly, George
        Miyasaki, Emiko Nakano, Deborah Remington, Nell Sinton, and Julius Wasserstein. Cat.

        Second Annual Group Show, Six Gallery, San Francisco. Included Jay DeFeo, Madeleine
        Dimond, Sonia Gechtoff, James Kelly, William Morehouse, and Julius Wasserstein.

        Seventy-fourth Annual Painting and Sculpture Exhibition of the San Francisco Art Association,
        San Francisco Museum of Art. Included Richard Bowman, Hayward King, Walter Kuhlman,
        Ann Morency, David Park, and Peter Shoemaker. Cat.

        Third Biennial, Museu de Arte Moderna, São Paulo, Brazil. Included Ruth Armer, Frank
        Lobdell, Richard Diebenkorn, Walter Kuhlman, Robert McChesney, Emiko Nakano, David
        Park, John Saccaro, and Peter Shoemaker. Cat.

        Thirtieth Annual Exhibition of Art, San Francisco Women Artists, San Francisco Museum of
        Art. Included Ruth Armer and Nell Sinton. Cat.

        Vanguard 1955, Walker Art Center, Minneapolis, Minn. Included Ernest Briggs, Richard
        Diebenkorn, Edward Dugmore, John Grillo, and Jon Schueler. Cat.

1955–56 *1955 Western Painters' Annual Exhibition,* Oakland Art Museum, Oakland, Calif. Included
        Richard Diebenkorn, George Miyasaki, David Park, Nell Sinton, and Julius Wasserstein. Cat.

1956   *California Painters Exhibit,* University of Minnesota, Minneapolis. Included Jay DeFeo,
        Sonia Gechtoff, James Kelly, and Julius Wasserstein.

California Painting: Forty Painters, The Municipal Art Center, Long Beach, in collaboration with the San Francisco Museum of Art. Included Ruth Armer, Richard Diebenkorn, Walter Kuhlman, Frank Lobdell, David Park, John Saccaro, and Peter Shoemaker. Cat.

California School, Yes or No? Oakland Art Museum, Oakland, Calif. Included Elmer Bischoff, Jay DeFeo, Richard Diebenkorn, Sam Francis, Sonia Gechtoff, James Kelly, Walter Kuhlman, Frank Lobdell, David Park, Hassel Smith, and Clyfford Still.

East Bay Artists Association Inaugural Exhibition, Oakland Art Museum, Oakland, Calif. Included Ruth Armer and Peter Shoemaker. Cat.

Pacific Coast Art: United States' Representation at the Third Biennial of São Paulo, San Francisco Museum of Art. Included Ruth Armer, Richard Diebenkorn, Walter Kuhlman, Frank Lobdell, Robert McChesney, David Park, John Saccaro, and Peter Shoemaker. Cat.

41 Aquarellistes américains d'aujourd'hui, Musée A. Lecuyer, Saint-Quentin, France. Included Lawrence Calcagno, Edward Corbett, Richard Diebenkorn, Edward Dugmore, and John Hultberg. Cat.

Seventy-fifth Annual Painting and Sculpture Exhibition of the San Francisco Art Association, San Francisco Museum of Art. Included Ruth Armer, Elmer Bischoff, Richard Diebenkorn, Sonia Gechtoff, James Kelly, Walter Kuhlman, Robert McChesney, William Morehouse, David Park, Deborah Remington, John Saccaro, Peter Shoemaker, Horst Trave, and Julius Wasserstein. Cat.

Sixth Annual Oil and Sculpture Exhibition, Richmond Art Center, Richmond, Calif. Included Elmer Bischoff, Richard Diebenkorn, and John Saccaro. Cat.

The Third Annual Group Show, Six Gallery, San Francisco. Included Jay DeFeo, Sonia Gechtoff, James Kelly, and Julius Wasserstein.

Thirty-first Annual Exhibition, San Francisco Women Artists, San Francisco Museum of Art. Included Emiko Nakano and Nell Sinton. Cat.

Twentieth Annual Drawing and Print Exhibition, San Francisco Art Association, San Francisco Museum of Art. Included Ruth Armer, Sonia Gechtoff, George Miyasaki, William Morehouse, Emiko Nakano, and Julius Wasserstein. Cat.

1957   *American Paintings, 1954–1957,* Minneapolis Institute of Arts, Minn. Included Richard Diebenkorn, James Kelly, and David Park. Cat.

Directions: Bay Area Painting, 1957, Richmond Art Center, Richmond, Calif. Included Elmer Bischoff, Richard Diebenkorn, Sonia Gechtoff, James Kelly, and David Park. Cat.

Drawings by Local Artists, Six Gallery, San Francisco. Included Joan Brown and Julius Wasserstein.

1957 California Painters' Exhibition, Oakland Art Museum, Oakland, Calif. Included Elmer Bischoff, Richard Diebenkorn, James Kelly, and David Park. Cat.

Objects on the New Landscape Demanding of the Eye, Ferus Gallery, Los Angeles (inaugural exhibition). Included Jay DeFeo, Richard Diebenkorn, James Budd Dixon, Sonia Gechtoff,

Jack Jefferson, James Kelly, Frank Lobdell, Hassel Smith, Clyfford Still, and Julius Wasserstein.

Pacemakers, Contemporary Arts Museum, Houston, Tex. Included Walter Kuhlman, Peter Shoemaker, and Hassel Smith. Cat.

Painting and Sculpture Now, San Francisco Museum of Art. Included Ruth Armer, Elmer Bischoff, Richard Diebenkorn, Sonia Gechtoff, James Kelly, Walter Kuhlman, Frank Lobdell, Robert McChesney, Emiko Nakano, David Park, and Julius Wasserstein. Cat.

Paintings by Richard Diebenkorn and David Park from the Collection of Walter P. Chrysler, Jr., Oakland Art Museum, Oakland, Calif. Cat.

Second Pacific Coast Biennial Exhibition of Paintings and Watercolors, Santa Barbara Museum of Art, Santa Barbara, Calif. Included Richard Diebenkorn, Sonia Gechtoff, James Kelly, and Walter Kuhlman. Cat.

Seventh Annual Exhibition: Oil and Sculpture, Richmond Art Center, Richmond, Calif. Included Elmer Bischoff, Joan Brown, Jay DeFeo, and George Miyasaki. Cat.

Seventy-sixth Annual Painting and Sculpture Exhibition of the San Francisco Art Association, San Francisco Museum of Art. Included Ruth Armer, Elmer Bischoff, Richard Diebenkorn, James Budd Dixon, Sonia Gechtoff, James Kelly, Walter Kuhlman, Frank Lobdell, George Miyasaki, Philip Roeber, Nell Sinton, and Julius Wasserstein. Cat.

Six West Coast Painters, Brata Gallery, New York City. Included James Budd Dixon and Philip Roeber.

[Twenty-first] *Annual Watercolor, Drawing, and Print Exhibition of the San Francisco Art Association,* San Francisco Museum of Art. Included Sonia Gechtoff, George Miyasaki, Emiko Nakano, Nell Sinton, and Julius Wasserstein. Cat.

1958   *American Painting, 1958,* Virginia Museum of Fine Arts, Richmond. Included Lawrence Calcagno, Edward Corbett, Richard Diebenkorn, Sam Francis, Sonia Gechtoff, John Hultberg, Walter Kuhlman, David Park, and John Saccaro. Cat.

Bay Area Invitational Exhibition, Gump's Gallery, San Francisco. Included Elmer Bischoff, Richard Diebenkorn, Sonia Gechtoff, James Kelly, and David Park.

Contemporary Images, San Francisco Museum of Art. Included Richard Diebenkorn, Sonia Gechtoff, James Kelly, Walter Kuhlman, John Saccaro, and Nell Sinton.

Eighth Annual Exhibition: Oil and Sculpture, Richmond Art Center, Richmond, Calif. Included Elmer Bischoff, Richard Diebenkorn, George Miyasaki, Emiko Nakano, David Park, Nell Sinton, and Sam Tchakalian. Cat.

Fresh Paint—1958: A Selective Survey of Recent Western Painting, Stanford Art Gallery, Stanford, Calif. Included Richard Bowman, Richard Diebenkorn, Sonia Gechtoff, and Walter Kuhlman. Cat.

Group exhibition, Dilexi Gallery, San Francisco. Included Sonia Gechtoff and James Kelly.

Group exhibition, Ferus Gallery, Los Angeles. Included Jay DeFeo, Frank Lobdell, Hassel Smith, and Julius Wasserstein.

Group exhibition, Ferus Gallery, Los Angeles. Included Richard Diebenkorn, Sonia Gechtoff, Frank Lobdell, David Park, Hassel Smith, and Julius Wasserstein.

1958 California Painters' Exhibition, Oakland Art Museum, Oakland, Calif. Included Ruth Armer, Elmer Bischoff, Joan Brown, Richard Diebenkorn, David Park, and George Miyasaki. Cat.

The 1958 Pittsburgh Bicentennial International Exhibition of Contemporary Painting and Sculpture, Carnegie Institute, Pittsburgh, Pa. Included Lawrence Calcagno, Richard Diebenkorn, Sam Francis, Sonia Gechtoff, John Hultberg, and Peter Shoemaker. Cat.

Paintings by Six Artists, Stanford Research Institute, Stanford, Calif. Included Richard Diebenkorn, Sonia Gechtoff, and Walter Kuhlman.

Seventeen American Painters, Brussels World's Fair, Brussels, Belgium. Included Lawrence Calcagno, Richard Diebenkorn, and Sonia Gechtoff. Cat.

The Seventeen Brussels Fair Painters, Bolles Gallery, San Francisco. Included Lawrence Calcagno, Richard Diebenkorn, and Sonia Gechtoff.

Seventh Annual Exhibition: Watercolor, Graphic, Ceramic Sculpture, Richmond Art Center, Richmond, Calif. Included Ruth Armer, Jay DeFeo, and Sam Tchakalian. Cat.

Seventy-seventh Annual Painting and Sculpture Exhibition of the San Francisco Art Association, San Francisco Museum of Art. Included Elmer Bischoff, Joan Brown, Richard Diebenkorn, Sonia Gechtoff, James Kelly, Walter Kuhlman, George Miyasaki, David Park, Philip Roeber, Nell Sinton, Sam Tchakalian, and Horst Trave. Cat.

Three Bay Area Artists: Claire Falkenstein, James Budd Dixon, Walter Kuhlman, San Francisco Museum of Art. Cat.

Tribute to Mrs. Leonid Gechtoff, Ferus Gallery, Los Angeles. Included Jay DeFeo, Sonia Gechtoff, James Kelly, Philip Roeber, Hassel Smith, and Julius Wasserstein.

Twenty-second Annual Drawing and Print Exhibition of the San Francisco Art Association, San Francisco Museum of Art. Included Ruth Armer, James Kelly, George Miyasaki, Emiko Nakano, Deborah Remington, Nell Sinton, Sam Tchakalian, and Julius Wasserstein. Cat.

West Coast Artists, The American Federation of Arts, New York City [traveled through United States and Canada]. Included Sonia Gechtoff, James Kelly, and Nell Sinton.

1959   *California Painters Exhibition,* Oakland Art Museum, Oakland, Calif. Included Elmer Bischoff, David Park, Peter Shoemaker, and Nell Sinton. Cat.

Eighth Annual Exhibition: Watercolor—Graphic—Ceramic Sculpture, Richmond Art Center, Richmond, Calif. Included Emiko Nakano, Deborah Remington, and Sam Tchakalian. Cat.

First Anniversary Group Show, Dilexi Gallery, San Francisco. Included Jay DeFeo, Richard Diebenkorn, Frank Lobdell, Philip Roeber, and Hassel Smith.

Group exhibition, Bolles Gallery, San Francisco. Included Walter Kuhlman and Sam Tchakalian.

Group exhibition, Everett Ellin Gallery, Los Angeles. Included Walter Kuhlman and Peter Shoemaker.

Group exhibition, Ferus Gallery, Los Angeles. Included Jay DeFeo, Sonia Gechtoff, Frank Lobdell, and Hassel Smith.

Group exhibition, Ferus Gallery, Los Angeles. Included Joan Brown, James Kelly, and Julius Wasserstein. Cat.

Group Show: Small Works in Varied Media, Dilexi Gallery, San Francisco. Included Joan Brown, Jay DeFeo, Sam Francis, Deborah Remington, Sam Tchakalian, and Julius Wasserstein.

Ninth Annual Exhibition: Oil and Sculpture, Richmond Art Center, Richmond, Calif. Included Joan Brown, Emiko Nakano, Nell Sinton, and Sam Tchakalian. Cat.

San Francisco Women Artists Thirty-fourth Annual Exhibition, San Francisco Museum of Art. Included Ruth Armer and Nell Sinton. Cat.

Seventy-eighth Annual Painting and Sculpture Exhibition of the San Francisco Art Association, San Francisco Museum of Art. Included Elmer Bischoff, Lawrence Calcagno, Richard Diebenkorn, Hayward King, Robert McChesney, George Miyasaki, William Morehouse, Emiko Nakano, John Saccaro, Peter Shoemaker, Nell Sinton, and Sam Tchakalian. Cat.

1960   [First] *Winter Invitational Exhibition.* California Palace of the Legion of Honor, San Francisco. Included George Abend, Ruth Armer, Martin Baer, Elmer Bischoff, Richard Diebenkorn, James Budd Dixon, Hayward King, Walter Kuhlman, William Morehouse, David Park, Peter Shoemaker, Nell Sinton, Hassel Smith, Sam Tchakalian, and Julius Wasserstein. Cat.

Group exhibition, Dilexi Gallery, San Francisco. Included Jay DeFeo, Deborah Remington, Philip Roeber, Hassel Smith, and Sam Tchakalian.

Group exhibition, Ferus Gallery, Los Angeles. Included Jay DeFeo, Sonia Gechtoff, Frank Lobdell, and Hassel Smith.

A Look at Recent Bay Area Art, San Francisco Museum of Art. Included Richard Bowman, Frank Lobdell, William Morehouse, Hassel Smith, Sam Tchakalian, and Julius Wasserstein.

1960 California Painters' Exhibition, Oakland Art Museum, Oakland, Calif. Included George Miyasaki, Philip Roeber, and Sam Tchakalian. Cat.

Seventy-ninth Annual Paining and Sculpture Exhibition of the San Francisco Art Association, San Francisco Museum of Art. Included George Abend, Ruth Armer, Richard Diebenkorn, James Kelly, Robert McChesney, William Morehouse, Deborah Remington, John Saccaro, Peter Shoemaker, Nell Sinton, Sam Tchakalian, Horst Trave, and Julius Wasserstein. Cat.

Sixty American Painters, Walker Art Center, Minneapolis, Minn. Included Lawrence Calcagno, Edward Corbett, Sam Francis, and Sonia Gechtoff. Cat.

Tenth Annual Oil and Sculpture Exhibition, Richmond Art Center, Richmond, Calif. Included Joan Brown, Deborah Remington, Nell Sinton, and Sam Tchakalian. Cat.

The Twenty-third Annual Drawing, Print, and Watercolor Exhibition of the San Francisco Art Association, San Francisco Museum of Art. Included Ruth Armer, Jerrold Ballaine, George Miyasaki, Deborah Remington, Nell Sinton, and Julius Wasserstein. Cat.

Young America, Whitney Museum of American Art, New York City. Included Joan Brown and Sonia Gechtoff. Cat.

1960–61   *Gangbang,* Batman Gallery, San Francisco. Included Joan Brown and Jay DeFeo.

1961   *Drawings by Richard Diebenkorn and Frank Lobdell,* Pasadena Art Museum, Pasadena, Calif.

Eightieth Annual Painting Exhibition of the San Francisco Art Institute, formerly the San Francisco Art Association, San Francisco Museum of Art. Included George Abend, Deborah Remington, Peter Shoemaker, Sam Tchakalian, Horst Trave, and Julius Wasserstein. Cat.

Faculty Exhibition, San Francisco Art Institute. Included Elmer Bischoff, Richard Diebenkorn, Jack Jefferson, and Frank Lobdell.

Group exhibition, Dilexi Gallery, San Francisco. Included Jay DeFeo, Philip Roeber, Hassel Smith, Sam Tchakalian, and Horst Trave.

Group exhibition, Ferus Gallery, Los Angeles. Included Jay DeFeo, Sonia Gechtoff, Frank Lobdell, and Hassel Smith.

Second Winter Invitational, California Palace of the Legion of Honor, San Francisco. Included Elmer Bischoff, Richard Bowman, Richard Diebenkorn, Hayward King, William Morehouse, Peter Shoemaker, Nell Sinton, Hassel Smith, Sam Tchakalian, and Julius Wasserstein. Cat.

Sixth Biennial São Paulo, 1961, Museu de Arte Moderna, São Paulo, Brazil. Included Richard Diebenkorn and Sonia Gechtoff.

Twenty-fifth Annual Drawing, Print, and Sculpture Exhibition of the San Francisco Art Association, San Francisco Museum of Art. Included George Miyasaki and Sam Tchakalian. Cat.

1961?   Group exhibition, Dilexi Gallery, San Francisco. Included Jay DeFeo, Deborah Remington, Philip Roeber, Hassel Smith, and Sam Tchakalian.

A Selection of Drawings, Dilexi Gallery, San Francisco. Included Jay DeFeo, Frank Lobdell, Deborah Remington, and Sam Tchakalian.

1961–62   *The 1961 Pittsburgh International Exhibition of Painting and Sculpture,* Carnegie Institute, Pittsburgh, Pa. Included Richard Bowman, Ernest Briggs, Lawrence Calcagno, Richard Diebenkorn, Sam Francis, and Hassel Smith. Cat.

Third Winter Invitational, California Palace of the Legion of Honor, San Francisco. Included Ruth Armer, Richard Bowman, Richard Diebenkorn, Jack Jefferson, William Morehouse,

Robert McChesney, John Saccaro, Peter Shoemaker, Nell Sinton, Hassel Smith, Sam Tchakalian, and Julius Wasserstein. Cat.

1962   *The Artist Looks at Peace,* Kaiser Center, Oakland, Calif. Included Elmer Bischoff, Richard Diebenkorn, and Hassel Smith. Cat.

The Artist's Environment: West Coast, The Amon Carter Museum of Western Art, Fort Worth, Tex. Included Elmer Bischoff, Richard Diebenkorn, Sam Francis, Frank Lobdell, David Park, John Saccaro, Hassel Smith, Clyfford Still, and Sam Tchakalian. Cat.

Eighty-first Annual Painting Exhibition of the San Francisco Art Institute, San Francisco Museum of Art. Included Ruth Armer and George Miyasaki. Cat.

Faculty Annual, California College of Arts and Crafts, Oakland, Calif. Included George Miyasaki and Peter Shoemaker. Cat.

Fifteen San Francisco Bay Area Painters, Poindexter Gallery, New York City. Included Jack Jefferson, Peter Shoemaker, Sam Tchakalian, and Julius Wasserstein.

Fifty California Artists, San Francisco Museum of Art and Los Angeles County Museum of Art. Included Elmer Bischoff, Richard Bowman, Richard Diebenkorn, Frank Lobdell, Hassel Smith, and Julius Wasserstein. Cat.

San Francisco Nine, Contemporary Arts Museum, Houston, Tex. Included James Budd Dixon and Frank Lobdell. Cat.

Some Points of View—Sixty-two: San Francisco Bay Area Painting and Sculpture, Stanford University Art Gallery, Stanford, Calif. Included Elmer Bischoff, Richard Bowman, Richard Diebenkorn, Jack Jefferson, Frank Lobdell, John Saccaro, Hassel Smith, Sam Tchakalian, and Julius Wasserstein. Cat.

Treasures from East Bay Collections, Oakland Art Museum, Oakland, Calif. Included Richard Diebenkorn, Sonia Gechtoff, and David Park. Cat.

Vanguard American Painting, American Embassy, United States Information Service Gallery, London. Included Richard Diebenkorn, Sam Francis, David Park, and Clyfford Still. Cat.

1962?   *Large Works,* Dilexi Gallery, San Francisco. Included Deborah Remington, Hassel Smith, and Sam Tchakalian.

1962–63   *Fourth Winter Invitational,* California Palace of the Legion of Honor, San Francisco. Included Ruth Armer, Elmer Bischoff, Richard Bowman, Richard Diebenkorn, Deborah Remington, John Saccaro, Peter Shoemaker, Nell Sinton, Hassel Smith, Sam Tchakalian, and Julius Wasserstein. Cat.

1963   *Drawings by Bischoff, Diebenkorn, Lobdell,* Achenbach Foundation for Graphic Arts, California Palace of the Legion of Honor, San Francisco.

Eighty-second Annual Exhibition of the San Francisco Art Institute, San Francisco Museum of Art. Included Jerrold Ballaine, Elmer Bischoff, Joan Brown, Jay DeFeo, Richard Diebenkorn,

James Budd Dixon, Jack Jefferson, Frank Lobdell, George Miyasaki, Deborah Remington, Nell Sinton, Hassel Smith, Sam Tchakalian, and Julius Wasserstein. Cat.

Group exhibition, Ferus Gallery, Los Angeles. Included Jay DeFeo and Frank Lobdell. Cat.

Recent American Paintings, University Art Museum, University of Texas, Austin. Included Edward Dugmore, Sam Francis, and Walter Kuhlman. Cat.

Some New Art in the Bay Area, San Francisco Art Institute. Included Joan Brown and Jay DeFeo. Cat.

1964   *Current Painting and Sculpture in the Bay Area,* Stanford Museum, Stanford University, Stanford, Calif. Included Elmer Bischoff and Joan Brown. Cat.

Eighty-third Annual Exhibition of the San Francisco Art Institute, San Francisco Museum of Art. Included Richard Diebenkorn, James Budd Dixon, and Deborah Remington. Cat.

Exhibition of drawing, Solomon R. Guggenheim Museum, New York City. Included Richard Diebenkorn and Frank Lobdell.

Fifth Winter Invitational, California Palace of the Legion of Honor, San Francisco. Included Richard Bowman, George Miyasaki, William Morehouse, Robert McChesney, Peter Shoemaker, and Sam Tchakalian. Cat.

New Dimensions in Lithography, University of California, Los Angeles. Included Richard Diebenkorn, Sam Francis, Sonia Gechtoff, John Hultberg, and James Kelly.

The 1964 Pittsburgh International Exhibition of Contemporary Painting and Sculpture, Museum of Art, Carnegie Institute, Pittsburgh, Pa. Included Elmer Bischoff, Richard Bowman, Richard Diebenkorn, and John Hultberg. Cat.

Seven California Painters, Staempfli Gallery, New York City. Included Elmer Bischoff, Joan Brown, Richard Diebenkorn, and David Park.

1965   *Eighty-fourth Annual Exhibition of the San Francisco Art Institute,* San Francisco Museum of Art. Included Deborah Remington and Sam Tchakalian. Cat.

The San Francisco Collector, M. H. de Young Memorial Museum, San Francisco. Included Richard Diebenkorn, Frank Lobdell, Hassel Smith, and Clyfford Still.

Some Aspects of California Painting and Sculpture, La Jolla Museum of Art, La Jolla, Calif. Included George Miyasaki and Deborah Remington. Cat.

The interviews and conversations, from 1988 to 1994, cited in the notes are my own unless otherwise stated. The following abbreviations are used throughout the notes: AAA (Archives of American Art, Smithsonian Institution), ACA (Archives of California Art, The Oakland Museum), CSFA (California School of Fine Arts, San Francisco), and SFAI (Archives of the Anne Bremer Memorial Library, San Francisco Art Institute).

Chapter 1

1. Michael Auping et al., *Abstract Expressionism: The Critical Developments* (New York: Harry N. Abrams, 1987), 10.

2. The text of this banner reads: "Gleetings, Happy New Lear, Flome San Francisco Grup to New York Annex. Goot Yontiff. Flom the . . . Zen flicks." While obviously intended as good-humored parody of the ethnic images of the two cities, the sign reflects the racial stereotyping of Asian Americans then prevalent in the American media. Although it would be unfair to read the banner as prejudice rather than insensitivity, it is significant that however interested the San Francisco painters were in Asian culture, few Asians participated in the movement, and even such artists as Peter Lowe and Emiko Nakano remained only marginally a part.

3. Auping et al., *Abstract Expressionism,* 12.

4. These surveys include William Seitz, *Abstract Expressionist Painting in America* (Cambridge: Harvard University Press, 1983); Maurice Tuchman, *New York School: The First Generation,* 2d ed. (Greenwich, Conn.: New York Graphic Society, 1970); Irving Sandler, *The Triumph of American Painting: A History of Abstract Expressionism* (New York: Harper and Row, 1970); David Anfam,

Abstract Expressionism (London: Thames and Hudson, 1990); and Stephen Polcari, *Abstract Expressionism and the Modern Experience* (Cambridge: Cambridge University Press, 1991). Only Dore Ashton, *The New York School: A Cultural Reckoning* (New York: Penguin Books, 1972), makes passing reference to the San Francisco Abstract Expressionists (202).

5. Irving Sandler, *The New York School: The Painters and Sculptors of the Fifties* (New York: Harper and Row, 1978), 322–23.

6. Michael Kimmelman, "Links amid Diversity in Two Retrospectives," *New York Times,* 19 November 1991; William Rubin, "Arshile Gorky, Surrealism, and the New American Painting," *Art International* 7 (February 1963): 38.

7. For example, Peter Plagens asserted that San Francisco Abstract Expressionism was "plotted by curators, writers, and scholastics eminently familiar with [New York's] mainstream model" in *Sunshine Muse: Contemporary Art on the West Coast* (New York: Praeger, 1974), 20. Similarly, the *Los Angeles Times* critic Christopher Knight wrote that Abstract Expressionism was "largely a received style in the small province of San Francisco [having been] transplanted from the intensely urban milieu in which it had originated by way of imported teachers, reproductions, journals and popular magazines" (*The Figurative Mode: Bay Area Figurative Painting, 1956–1966* [New York: Grey Art Gallery and Study Center, New York University, 1984], 6).

8. Eugene Victor Thaw, "The Abstract Expressionists," *The Metropolitan Museum of Art Bulletin* 44 (Winter 1986–87): 3.

9. Auping et al., *Abstract Expressionism,* book jacket.

10. Serge Guilbaut, *How New York Stole the Idea of*

Modern Art: Abstract Expressionism, Freedom, and the Cold War (Chicago: University of Chicago Press, 1983), 10.

11. Ann Gibson, "Recasting the Canon: Norman Lewis and Jackson Pollock," *Artforum* 30 (March 1992): 66. Gibson has pointed out that only since the early 1980s have museums paid attention to first-generation women Abstract Expressionists such as Lee Krasner and Hedda Sterne, and African Americans like Norman Lewis have fared worse.

12. Michael Leja, "The Formation of an Avant-Garde in New York," in Auping et al., *Abstract Expressionism* (as in note 1), 24.

13. Ibid.

14. Guilbaut has suggested that Abstract Expressionism may have appeared in Paris and Montreal at the same time as in New York under the name "Abstraction Chaude." But he concentrates almost exclusively on the comparative politics of propaganda and market forces in France, Canada, and New York and spends little time examining the art. See Serge Guilbaut et al., *Reconstructing Modernism: Art in New York, Paris, and Montreal, 1945–1964* (Cambridge: MIT Press, 1990).

15. Leja, "The Formation of an Avant-Garde," 14.

16. As late as 1945, the savvy art dealer Samuel Kootz was still pessimistic about the prospects for modern art in the United States: "Under the present circumstances the probability is that the future of painting lies in America. The pitiful fact is, however, that we offer little better than a geographical title to the position of the world's headquarters for art . . . I probably have haunted the galleries during the past decade as much as have the critics, because of my anxiety to see new talent, intelligent invention. My report is sad. I have not discovered *one* bright white hope. I have not seen one painter veer from his established course. I have not seen one attempt to experiment, to realize a new method of painting" (quoted in Hilaire Hiler, Henry Miller, and William Saroyan, *Why Abstract?* [New York: New Directions, 1945], 55–56).

17. The exhibition opened at the Cincinnati Art Museum and traveled to the Denver Art Museum, the Seattle Art Museum, and the Santa Barbara Museum of Art before ending its tour at the San Francisco Museum of Art in July 1944.

18. Robert Coates, *New Yorker* 20 (23 December 1944): 45. For more on the synthetic nature of Abstract Expressionism during and immediately after the war, see Leja, "The Formation of an Avant-Garde," 13–33; and Charles Harrison, "Abstract Expressionism," in *Concepts of Modern Art*, ed. Nikos Stangos (New York: Harper and Row, 1974), 171.

19. Robert Coates, "The Art Galleries," *New Yorker* 22 (30 March 1946): 75. Guilbaut states in *How New York Stole the Idea of Modern Art*, 230, that Hilda Loveman used the term earlier than Coates in a review of the Whitney annual exhibition of 1945, but Loveman was describing a broader category of painting that included such figurative expressionists as Abraham Rattner and John Marin.

20. Daniel Catton Rich, "Freedom of the Brush," *Atlantic Monthly* 181 (February 1948): 47.

21. See especially the national surveys of Allen S. Weller and C. V. Donovan at the College of Fine and Applied Arts of the University of Illinois, Urbana. Although this chapter does not survey the full scope of these pan-national tendencies, a partial list of experimental abstract artists working outside New York and San Francisco in the 1940s might include (from the Midwest) Leonard Beck, Claude Bentley, Richard Bowman, Eleanor Harris, Medard Klein, Felix Ruvolo, William Saltzman, and Emerson Woelffer; (from the South) Worden Day and William Fett; (from New England) Calvert Coggeshall and Karl Knaths; (from the Southwest) Ward Lockwood, Beatrice Mandelman, Louis Ribak, Agnes Sims, and Cady Wells; (from the Pacific Northwest) Guy Anderson, Kenneth Callahan, William Cummings, Mark Tobey, and Margaret Tomkins; (from Los Angeles and other parts of California outside the San Francisco Bay Area) Hans Burkhardt, Dan Harris, Frederick Heidel, Fred Kahn, John McNee, Knud Merrild, and Florence Saltzman.

22. Quoted in Guilbaut, *How New York Stole the Idea of Modern Art*, 116–17.

23. Alfred Barr, *Painting and Sculpture in the Museum of Modern Art* (New York: Museum of Modern Art, 1948), 203–4.

24. Alfred Barr, "Seven Americans Open in Venice: Gorky, De Kooning, Pollock," *Art News* 49 (Summer 1950): 22.

25. See also Manny Farber's reviews in the *Nation;* Coates's coverage for the *New Yorker;* and the columns by Howard Devree and Edward Alden Jewell in the *New York Times* during the late 1940s.

26. Harold Rosenberg, "Introduction to Six American Artists," *Possibilities* 1 (Winter 1947–48): 75.

27. Clement Greenberg, statement in "The State of American Art: A Symposium," *Magazine of Art* 42 (March 1949): 92. During the late 1940s, Greenberg viewed Adolph Gottlieb, Barnett Newman, Rothko, and Still as a distinct group, however. In late 1947 he described them as members of "a new indigenous school of symbolism," which he deemed "half-baked and revivalist, in a familiar American way" (quoted in Sandler, *The Triumph of American Painting,* 88).

28. Clement Greenberg, "The Present Prospects of American Painting and Sculpture," *Horizon* 93–94 (October 1947): 29. Greenberg's tally approximates the number of artists admitted to the Club in 1950, but even that number falls short of gauging the true size of the movement in New

York. Some of the experimental modernists whose names are less familiar today include (in addition to those mentioned elsewhere in this chapter): Gertrude Barrer, Forrest Bess, Fritz Bultman, Rollin Crampton, Robert DeNero, Seymore Franks, Lee Hersch, Hisako Hibi, Fannie Hillsmith, Martha Hoskins, Harry Jackson, Gerome Kamrowski, Weldon Kees, Norman Lewis, John Little, Boris Margo, George McNeil, Raymond Parker, Reginald Pollack, Jeanne Reynal, Ralph Rosenborg, Alfred Russel, Anne Ryan, Ethel Schwabacher, Sonia Sekula, Harold Shapinsky, Sal Sirugo, Janet Sobel, Max Spivak, Hedda Sterne, Reuben Tam, and Steve Wheeler.

29.   These early group shows were as follows: David Porter Gallery, Washington, D.C., *Painting Prophecy—1950,* February 1945; 67 Gallery, *A Problem for Critics,* May–July 1945 (organized by Howard Putzel); Kootz Gallery, *The Intrasubjectives,* September–October 1949; and Kootz Gallery, *Talent 1950,* April–May 1950.

30.   The protest led to Nina Leen's famous group portrait published in *Life* magazine in 1951 that has been enormously influential in shaping the pantheon of the New York School. According to Ad Reinhardt, however, the portrait represented little more than the bringing together of two rival factions from the Kootz and Parsons galleries. Reinhardt explained: "Neither Still nor Rothko were around. Rothko was in Europe and Still was on the West Coast and it was due to Newman and myself that we got those two guys in, so when they had this big picture in *Life* magazine, it looks like a document . . . I mean that's the way these things are created and then, you know, you see the picture now where these eighteen people got together, they started the New York School or a revolution of the avant-garde. Gee, it was funny. All it was [was] a sort of rivalry between the Betty Parsons and the Kootz galleries at the time" (Ad Reinhardt, interview with Mary Fuller McChesney, 27 April and 15 June 1966, transcript in private collection).

31.   Paul Bird, "Big Met Show Finds Americans Now Speak Universal Language," *Art Digest* 25 (1 December 1950): 7.

32.   Robert Motherwell, *Seventeen Americans: The School of New York* (Los Angeles: Frank Perls Gallery, 1951), n.p. William Seitz echoed Motherwell's caveat in his dissertation of 1955, the first major study of Abstract Expressionism. While Seitz used the term "School of New York," he was careful to point out that the "region designated by that label is more ideological than geographical" (see Seitz, *Abstract Expressionist Painting in America,* 4). Ten years later, however, in the first museum retrospective of the movement, this detail was forgotten or ignored by Maurice Tuchman, who neatly reversed Seitz's observation: "The term 'New York School,' as a geographical indicator," Tuchman wrote, "is more valid in application to the first generation than in relation to its followers, for the proliferation and dispersal of the achievements and ideas of the earlier group of artists make it impossible to impose such localized restraints on the younger generation" (Tuchman, *New York School,* 7).

33.   Barnett Newman, "The New York School Question," *Art News* 64 (September 1965): 39.

34.   *Modern Artists in America,* ed. Robert Motherwell and Ad Reinhardt (New York: Wittenborn, Schultz, 1951). Motherwell's ambition to place modern American art on an equal footing with modern European art can be seen in his reprinting of an article entitled "Paris New York, 1951" by the French critic Michel Seuphor. Seuphor's article praised recent developments in American art and proclaimed New York and Paris the two artistic capitals of the Western world. But Seuphor also observed that while American art matched the quality of French art, it was not superior (122). This seems to have been the view of Motherwell and Reinhardt as well. They took special pains to include reproductions of paintings by a number of contemporary French artists, including Jean Bazaine, Nicholas De Staël, Jean Dubuffet, Hans Hartung, and André Lanskoy. One could argue that the editors of *Modern Artists in America* viewed Abstract Expressionism as both a national and an international phenomenon.

35.   Ibid., 6.

36.   Daniel Catton Rich, quoted in ibid., 147.

37.   Michel Seuphor, quoted in ibid., 120. Significantly, the exhibition that impressed Seuphor most was the Metropolitan Museum of Art's annual of 1950, which the "Irascibles" protested.

38.   For more on the Western Round Table on Modern Art, which was held at the San Francisco Museum of Art in 1949 and included Marcel Duchamp, Douglas MacAgy, Mark Tobey, and Frank Lloyd Wright, see Bonnie Clearwater, "Trying Very Hard to Think: Duchamp and the Western Round Table on Modern Art, 1949," in *West Coast Duchamp,* ed. Clearwater (Miami Beach: Grassfield Press, 1991), 46–59.

39.   Barr and the curators who succeeded him during the war, James Thrall Soby and James Johnson Sweeney, demonstrated a pronounced European bias in their curatorial programs. Morley was a good deal more adventurous in her exhibitions of contemporary American artists. Under her aegis, the San Francisco Museum of Art gave many of the earliest shows by New York Abstract Expressionists: *Paintings by Arshile Gorky,* 9–24 August 1941; *Paintings by Clyfford Still,* 2–21 March 1943; *Jackson Pollock,* 7–26 August 1945; *Mark Tobey: Ten Years of His Painting,* 8–30 September 1945; *Oils and Watercolors by Mark Rothko,* 13 August–8 September 1946; *Paintings by Hans Hofmann,* 17 September–6 October 1946; and *Robert Motherwell,* 26 March–14 April 1946. By contrast, the first museum solos in New York were not mounted until the 1950s. Both were memorial shows,

the first for Gorky at the Whitney Museum of American Art, in 1951, and the second for Pollock at the Museum of Modern Art, in 1956.

40.   A partial report of the survey conducted by the Addison Gallery in Andover, Massachusetts, can be found in Bartlett H. Hayes, Jr., "Art Schools U.S.A.," *Art News* 47 (September 1948): 46–47, 60. See also William Hall, "School of Fine Arts Acquires World Fame," *San Francisco Examiner*, 11 July 1948.

41.   Weldon Kees, "San Francisco Artists Set a Pace," *New York Times*, 31 December 1950.

42.   The phrase is Barnett Newman's in "The New York School Question," 39, but the notion has frequently been summoned as an apology for the marked differences between the artists, first by Thomas Hess in his criticism in *Art News* and his book *Abstract Painting: Background and American Phase* (New York: Viking, 1951), and then by Irving Sandler.

43.   That the Abstract Expressionists were bound together by their centrist politics is a fundamental premise of Guilbaut's *How New York Stole the Idea of Modern Art*. See also Max Kozloff, "American Painting during the Cold War," *Artforum* 11 (May 1973): 43–54; David and Cecile Shapiro, "Abstract Expressionism: The Politics of Apolitical Painting," *Prospects* 3 (1977): 175–214; and Fred Orton and Griselda Pollock, "*Avant-Gardes* and Partisans Reviewed," *Art History* 4 (September 1981): 305–27. More recently, David Craven has argued that the Abstract Expressionists harbored anarchist sympathies; see Craven, "Abstract Expressionism, Automatism, and the Age of Automation," *Art History* 13 (March 1990): 72–103. Yet none of the San Francisco painters besides Ronald Bladen evidenced any significant loyalty toward anarchism or its libertarian off-shoots, which flourished among San Francisco's literary avant-garde during the 1940s and 1950s.

44.   Since the late 1970s, art historians have treated Abstract Expressionism iconographically, emphasizing the New York School's abstract Surrealism of the war years. These studies are too numerous to list here, but a good place to start would be the endnotes in Stephen Polcari's excellent book *Abstract Expressionism and the Modern Experience* (1991). See also note 6 of Polcari's article "Abstract Expressionism: 'New and Improved,'" *Art Journal* 47 (Fall 1988): 179.

45.   Many Abstract Expressionists in San Francisco, especially Still, regarded William Baziotes, Arshile Gorky, and Ad Reinhardt as too close to European modernism to be major figures in the movement.

46.   William Seitz, "Spirit, Time, and Abstract Expressionism," quoted in Mary Fuller McChesney, *A Period of Exploration: San Francisco, 1945–1950* (Oakland, Calif.: The Oakland Museum, 1973), introduction.

47.   Evidence for the importance of this controversy for the Abstract Expressionists can be found in the painstaking chronicle in *Modern Artists in America*, ed. Motherwell and Reinhardt, 143–56.

48.   Other artists in Northern California who worked in hybrids of Surrealism and Cubism in the mid-1940s included Ronald Bladen, Richard Diebenkorn, James Budd Dixon, Claire Falkenstein, Dan Harris, Charles Howard, Harlan Jackson, Adaline Kent, Robert McChesney, André Moreau, Alexander Nepote, David Park, Bern Porter, Bezalel and Zahara Schatz, Clay Spohn, Jean Varda, and W. Edwin Ver Becke.

49.   *The Montgomery Street Skylight*, an artist-run weekly newspaper billed as the "Bulletin of San Francisco's Bohemia," reported that "a mass conversion" to abstraction had occurred in the painting and sculpture annual of 1945 at the San Francisco Museum of Art, and that even "veterans of the picturesque flower pot" had "stepped onto the bandwagon." See G. P. Hitchcock, "Annual Drunkenly Abstract," *Montgomery Street Skylight*, 9 November 1945.

50.   Alexander Fried, "San Francisco Region, 1947," *Art News* 46 (June 1947): 27.

51.   The San Francisco Art Association's twelfth annual exhibition in October 1948 was the first in the country to be dominated by abstract painting. See Alfred Frankenstein, "Local Art Galleries in Review," *San Francisco Chronicle*, 31 October 1948.

52.   Peter Selz, "Between Friends: Still and the Bay Area," *Art in America* 63 (November–December 1975): 72. Although there is little evidence that many critics outside San Francisco were aware of the city's progressive tendency at this early date, the art critic for the *Los Angeles Times* was well apprised of it. In a review of the second annual at the California Palace of the Legion of Honor in 1947, Arthur Millier wrote that the West Coast paintings were "far more 'advanced' than most of the Eastern ones" and that "San Francisco's moderns luxuriate in the abstract and non-objective" ("San Francisco Opens Second National Annual," *Art Digest* 22 [15 November 1947]: 12).

53.   The show Erle Loran described consisted of recent works by Elmer Bischoff, David Park, and Hassel Smith. See his "San Francisco," *Art News* 48 (September 1949): 44. A number of critics were also outraged by the new nonobjective expressionism, especially Alexander Fried of the conservative Hearst-run *San Francisco Examiner*, but also Jehanne Bietry-Salinger, a former champion of modernism for the *Argus*. Bietry-Salinger condemned the preponderance of experimental abstract painting at the San Francisco Museum of Art's annual of 1948 as a "complete breakdown of esthetic standards." It was her impression that the "nonrepresentational schools" had "sprung from nowhere over night" and had "taken over everywhere in the country" ("Painting for Whom, If You Please?" *Opera and Concert* 13 [March 1948]: 25).

54.   Aline Louchheim, "San Francisco: Division and Vitality," *New York Times,* 24 October 1948.

55.   There were also vanguard reviews in the Bay Area that CSFA artists read widely during the late 1940s, notably the East Bay magazines *Circle* (1944–48) and *Berkeley: A Journal of Modern Culture* (1947–50). *Circle* was published in Berkeley by George Leite, who also operated Daliel's, a short-lived gallery on Telegraph Avenue that showed the work of Bischoff, John Grillo, Park, Bezalel Schatz, and Spohn in 1947. *Circle's* editorial program was vaguely Surrealist, although Leite was careful to avoid categorization. In the fourth issue, *Circle* defined its credo: "When a technique becomes a school, death of creation is the result. Eclecticism is the only approach to Art in which there is no death. CIRCLE is completely eclectic." Contributors to *Circle* included Philip Lamantia, MacAgy, Henry Miller, Anaïs Nin, Bern Porter, Kenneth Rexroth, Spohn, W. Edwin Ver Becke, and William Carlos Williams. The slightly later journal *Berkeley,* published by one of *Circle's* editors, followed this editorial policy of eclecticism but widened its cultural range considerably. *Berkeley* drew contributions from Sibyl Moholy-Nagy, Wolfgang Paalen, Man Ray, Jean Paul Sartre, and Frank Lloyd Wright.

56.   See Karen Tsujimoto, *Mark Rothko 1949: A Year in Transition: Selections from the Mark Rothko Foundation* (San Francisco: San Francisco Museum of Modern Art, 1983).

57.   See Susan Landauer, *Edward Corbett: A Retrospective* (Richmond, Calif.: Richmond Art Center, 1990), 24–25.

58.   Cf. Sandler, *The Triumph of American Painting,* 1.

59.   This important phase of American painting has been eclipsed by Abstract Expressionism in the present-day art-historical literature. For more on neo-romantic painting of the 1940s, see James Thrall Soby and Dorothy Miller, *Romantic Painting in America* (New York: Museum of Modern Art, 1943); Frederick Sweet, *Fifty-sixth Annual of American Paintings* (Chicago: Art Institute of Chicago, 1945–46); Alfred Frankenstein, "A Summary of Art in Our Time," *San Francisco Chronicle,* 12 December 1948; Frederick Wight, *Milestones of American Painting in Our Century* (New York: Chanticleer Press, 1949); and Alfred Barr et al., "State of American Painting: A Symposium," *Magazine of Art* 42 (March 1949): 83–104.

60.   See Piri Halasz, "Figuration in the Forties: The Other Expressionism," *Art in America* 70 (December 1982): 110–19, 145–47.

61.   Guilbaut has described this equation of modernism and democracy in *How New York Stole the Idea of Modern Art* as "an excellent weapon [for liberals] with which to combat Soviet authoritarianism" (143). It was not necessary, however, to join the "vital center" to oppose totalitarianism. In San Francisco, a number of artists, including Ronald Bladen, Corbett, McChesney, and Smith, remained faithful to left-wing politics after the war, while Still was politically conservative. All these artists were just as much against totalitarian censorship as their more centrist colleagues.

62.   See, for example, Edward Alden Jewell, "'Globalism' Pops into View," *New York Times,* 13 June 1943; or Wendell Willkie's best-seller, *One World* (New York: Simon and Schuster, 1943).

63.   Elmer Bischoff, quoted in Susan Klein [Landauer], "Elmer Bischoff," *Issue* 4 (Fall 1985): 11.

64.   See Taylor D. Littleton and Maltby Sykes, *Advancing American Art: Painting, Politics, and Cultural Confrontation at Mid-Century* (Tuscaloosa: University of Alabama Press, 1989); Margaret Lynne Ausfeld and Virginia M. Mecklenburg, *Advancing American Art* (Montgomery, Ala.: Montgomery Museum of Fine Arts, 1984); and Serge Guilbaut, "The Frightening Freedom of the Brush," in *Dissent: The Issue of Modern Art in Boston* (Boston: Institute of Contemporary Art, 1985).

65.   Renato Poggioli, *The Theory of the Avant-Garde,* trans. Gerald Fitzgerald (Cambridge: Harvard University Press, 1968), 26. Although Poggioli's model of avant-garde dynamics has come under criticism in the context of postmodernist discourse, I find it still an accurate depiction of modernist ideology.

66.   Considering the sudden and pervasive appearance of this phenomenon, I would argue that what Stephen Polcari, Robert Rosenblum, and others have disparaged as the "big bang" theory of Abstract Expressionism misses the mark in its failure to provide a convincing explanation.

67.   In a letter to me, dated 1 June 1989, George Stillman remembered the controversy as a major topic at the California School of Fine Arts at that time. A number of faculty members sent letters to the State Department concerning its recall of the State Department's traveling exhibition of 1947 (SFAI). See also Grace McCann Morley, "Tour of Some Paintings Is Stopped and a Controversy Seems to Be On," *San Francisco Chronicle,* 25 May 1947.

68.   See, for example, the art criticism of John Garth for the *Argonaut.* The modern art controversy boiled over in San Francisco once again in 1951, when the Society for Sanity in Art, spearheaded by Garth, attacked Anton Refregier's murals in the Rincon Hill Post Office for being "subversive." Morley, who defended the murals, was labeled a Communist by Congressman George Dondero. For a summary of the controversy, see Alfred Frankenstein, "A Discussion of the Charges That Communists Influence Modern Art," *San Francisco Chronicle,* 23 March 1952.

69.   Wallace Stevens, quoted in *Modern Artists in America,* ed. Motherwell and Reinhardt, 40.

70.   Caroline A. Jones, *Bay Area Figurative Art, 1950–1965* (San Francisco: San Francisco Museum of Mod-

ern Art; and Berkeley and Los Angeles: University of California Press, 1990), 11. Jones's assessment echoes Peter Selz's view; see Selz, "Between Friends" (as in note 52), 72.

71.   Thomas Albright, *Art in the San Francisco Bay Area, 1945–1980: An Illustrated History* (Berkeley and Los Angeles: University of California Press, 1985), 39, xvi. Albright's two chapters on Abstract Expressionism in this book provide the most detailed historical discussion to date. Another important source of information is Mary Fuller McChesney's publication, *A Period of Exploration* (as in note 46), which draws from extensive interviews McChesney conducted with the artists in 1965–66.

72.   Patrick Frank also expressed this opinion in his dissertation on San Francisco Abstract Expressionism: "If 'school' is defined as a style adopted by a group of artists which has a distinctly recognizable look (such as Venetian or Flemish), then there probably is not a San Francisco School" (Patrick L. Frank, "Abstract Expressionism in San Francisco, 1945–1950," Ph.D. diss., George Washington University, 1992, 6).

73.   Rosenberg, "Introduction to Six American Artists" (as in note 26), 75.

74.   Mark Tobey, statement in Dorothy Miller, *Fourteen Americans* (New York: Museum of Modern Art, 1946), 24.

75.   Robert Motherwell, quoted in ibid., 36.

76.   Elmer Bischoff, lecture presented at the Oakland Museum, 27 October 1973, transcript in SFAI. The search for a regional identity is doubly problematic considering that the group at the California School of Fine Arts was composed of so many recent immigrants to California. Indeed, they formed a demographic cross section of America: Edward Dugmore and John Grillo were from Connecticut; Jack Jefferson was from South Dakota; Walter Kuhlman came from Minnesota; McChesney was from Missouri; Park was from Massachusetts; and Still was from North Dakota and went to school in Washington state.

77.   Tapié's conception of an *école du Pacifique* was debated in a round table discussion in 1954, which included Julien Alvard, Claire Falkenstein, Sam Francis, and Fitz Simmons. Although Francis argued that to define a Pacific Coast school was to "make an abstraction out of particulars," most participants agreed that the artists at the California School of Fine Arts were more influenced by the Asian, and less dependent upon the European, tradition. For a partial transcript of the discussion, see Tapié, "L'école du Pacifique," *Cimaise* 1 (June 1954): 6–9.

78.   The idea of a "San Francisco School" may predate Tapié's efforts in the early 1950s. Dorr Bothwell remembered hearing talk of a "School of San Francisco" in Paris as early as 1951. See Mary Fuller [McChesney], "Was There a San Francisco School?" *Artforum* 9 (January 1971): 47. That

year, Lobdell and Kuhlman sparked a controversy over their paintings in the *6ème Salon des Réalités Nouvelles* at the Petit Palais (Kuhlman, interview with author, 5 July 1988). George Abend, Lawrence Calcagno, and Sam Francis also showed in various group exhibitions in Paris between 1950 and 1953. According to Calcagno, in an interview, 21 October 1992, talk began circulating of a "San Francisco School" in 1953, when a scandal erupted over the American Students Club's refusal to hang the work of Francis, Calcagno, and other West Coast artists. The group formed a committee and showed the rejected work at the Galerie Craven.

79.   Brazilian critics viewing the Pacific Coast section of the São Paulo Third Biennial in 1955—which included work by Ruth Armer, Diebenkorn, Kuhlman, Lobdell, McChesney, and Peter Shoemaker—also distinguished an alternative to Abstract Expressionism in New York. According to Morley: "They appeared to feel that the artists included reflect contemporary currents in Europe far less directly than do artists from the Eastern seaboard whose works they know. They believed that they could recognize in the Pacific Coast artists' works the effects of a different light and climate; a sensibility stirred by the Orient; a youthfulness, freshness and optimism, and a scale inspired by the distances of the West about which they had heard" (Grace McCann Morley, "The Pacific Coast Artists Brought Their Climate to São Paulo," *San Francisco Chronicle,* 2 October 1955).

80.   Kenneth Sawyer, "L'expressionnisme abstrait: La phase du Pacifique," *Cimaise* 1 (June 1954): 3 (my translation).

81.   See James Johnson Sweeney, *Younger American Painters* (New York: Solomon R. Guggenheim Museum, 1954). Sweeney's exhibition did not posit a "California School," but the exhibition was commented upon by the art press as representative of the "California School" (Hubert Crehan, "Is There a California School?" *Art News* 54 [January 1956]: 33). Sweeney's show included nine artists active in California: Diebenkorn, Ralph Du Casse, Sonia Gechtoff, Karim Khosrovi, William Morehouse, Kyle Morris, Kenneth Nack, Richard White, and Paul Wonner.

82.   Crehan, "Is There a California School?" 33.

83.   Ibid., 34.

84.   Dore Ashton, "An Eastern View of the San Francisco School," *Evergreen Review* 1 (1957): 148–59. This issue, entitled the "San Francisco Scene," also contained essays by Kenneth Rexroth and Henry Miller on the cultural milieu and by Ralph J. Gleason on West Coast jazz, as well as a short story by Jack Kerouac and poems by Robert Duncan, Brother Antoninus (William Everson), Lawrence Ferlinghetti, Michael McClure, Gary Snyder, Jack Spicer, and Philip Whalen.

85.   See Joshua C. Taylor, "Introduction," *Art of the*

Pacific Northwest: From the 1930s to the Present (Washington, D.C.: National Collection of Fine Arts, 1974), n.p.

86.   No transcript or tape recording of the discussion, which took place on 22 February 1956, appears to have survived. The Oakland Art Museum's exhibition included work by Bischoff, Jay DeFeo, Diebenkorn, Francis, Sonia Gechtoff, Walter Kuhlman, Lobdell, Park, Rothko, Smith, and Still.

87.   According to the panel's moderator, Fred Martin, who took notes on the discussion, it was generally agreed there had been a "San Francisco Style" in the late 1940s. See Martin, "The Birth of the Thing, or Some Recent Developments in the Art of the San Francisco Bay Area," ca. 1956, in the Martin papers, roll 1129, frames 450–63, AAA.

88.   Clyfford Still, letter to Paul Mills, 6 May 1956, ACA.

89.   Hassel Smith, with the assistance of Mary McChesney, "Sulla scuola di San Francisco," *Evento delle arti 2* (1958): 24–27. The article was based on Smith's presentation for the Oakland Art Museum panel discussion "California School—Yes or No?" in 1956. A humorous version of the article as a mystery story by Smith and Joe Rayter (pseud. of Mary Fuller McChesney) about the search for the San Francisco School can be found in the Smith papers, roll 2009, frames 283–300, AAA.

90.   Smith felt that the work of Still, Corbett, Briggs, and McChesney was aesthetically distinct from the San Francisco School (Hassel Smith papers, roll 2009, AAA). Fred Martin also specifically excluded Still from the San Francisco School. He considered Bischoff, Diebenkorn, and Park the true exemplars of San Francisco Abstract Expressionism, arguing that by comparison with Still they developed a style more "rooted in the sights of the Bay Area" ("The Birth of the Thing," ca. 1956, Martin papers, roll 1129, frame 454, AAA).

91.   A survey Mary Fuller McChesney conducted in 1965–66 found that of thirty-three artists, nineteen said there had been a school in San Francisco, six said there had not, and eight expressed no opinion. See McChesney, *A Period of Exploration* (as in note 46), 73–74.

92.   Elmer Bischoff, lecture presented at the Oakland Museum, 27 October 1973, transcript in SFAI.

93.   This is Barbara Rose's phrase for the Ash Can School in *American Art since 1900: A Critical History* (New York: Praeger, 1967), 11.

94.   Alfred Frankenstein, review in *San Francisco Chronicle*, 24 July 1949; Clement Greenberg, "'American-Type' Painting," (1955); reprinted in *Art and Culture: Critical Essays* (Boston: Beacon Press, 1961), 224; Thomas B. Hess, "The Outsider," *Art News* 68 (December 1969): 37.

95.   As distinct as their aesthetics were, Still and Spohn became very close in later years, signing their letters to each other "Your brother." Some of these letters can be found in the unfilmed Spohn papers, AAA.

96.   See Sandra Leonard Starr, *Lost and Found in California: Four Decades of Assemblage Art* (Santa Monica, Calif.: James Corcoran Gallery, Shoshana Wayne Gallery, and Pence Gallery, 1988).

97.   By contrast, the only major New York Abstract Expressionist who served in uniform was Reinhardt. Although most of the New Yorkers were of draft age (between twenty and forty-five when the United States entered the war), they were exempted for having dependents or for various disabilities.

98.   William Ivey, interview with Barbara Johns, 24 May 1983, Northwest Oral History Project, roll 3593, frames 758–59, AAA.

99.   Elmer Bischoff, lecture presented at the Oakland Museum, 27 October 1973, transcript in SFAI.

100.   As the historian Paul Fussell observed, during World War II expletives were indispensable to military life: "Indeed, without *ass,* military discourse would be virtually dumb" ("Chickenshit: An Anatomy," in Fussell, *Wartime: Understanding and Behavior in the Second World War* [Oxford: Oxford University Press, 1989], 91). For more on the impact of World War II on the San Francisco Abstract Expressionists, see Susan Landauer, "Painting under the Shadow: California Modernism and the Second World War," in *On the Edge of America: California Modernist Art, 1900–1950* ed. Paul J. Karlstrom (Washington, D.C., and San Francisco: Archives of American Art of the Smithsonian Institution in Association with Fine Arts Museums of San Francisco; and Berkeley and Los Angeles: University of California Press, 1996).

101.   In an interview, 1 April 1989, William Morehouse said these artists were viewed as Surrealists in San Francisco during the 1940s. Ernest Briggs, interviewed by Mary Fuller McChesney, 20 April 1966, recalled that San Franciscans were particularly disdainful of Gorky: "We put Gorky down because there was too much French painting in it, you know. Too much Surrealism, too much Joan Miró and so on" (transcript in private collection).

102.   Still told Betty Freeman in an interview, 24 May 1961, that he could not paint in a horizontal work even if he were forced to work with a horizontal canvas (Freeman papers, roll 4060, frame 288, AAA).

103.   Dorr Bothwell, interviewed by Mary Fuller McChesney, 30 August 1965, transcript in private collection.

104.   Lilly Fenichel, quoted in Susan Landauer, *Lilly Fenichel: The Early Paintings,* Abstract Expressionists, An Exhibition and Historical Survey of Northern California

Abstract Expressionists Active 1945–1960 (San Francisco: The Carlson Gallery, 1990), 11.

105. Grillo, interview, 10 March 1993. MacAgy's praise was a variation on Renoir's famous declaration "I paint with my prick."

106. Robert T. Buck, Jr., et al., *Richard Diebenkorn: Paintings and Drawings, 1943–1976* (Buffalo, N.Y.: Albright-Knox Art Gallery, 1976), 12.

107. See Irving Sandler, *The Triumph of American Painting* (as in note 4), 3. Of course, the same argument could be (and has been) made for the New York School; see Anfam, *Abstract Expressionism* (as in note 4), 135.

108. Harry Jacobus, quoted in Christopher Wagstaff, "An Interview with Harry Jacobus," *Northern Lights: Studies in Creativity* 2 (1985–86): 88.

109. Cf. Bill Berkson, *Ronald Bladen: Early and Late* (San Francisco: San Francisco Museum of Modern Art, 1991), 8. Berkson credits Al Held with introducing Bladen to thickly painted canvases, but there were many sources in San Francisco for this approach. Held himself spent time in San Francisco during the mid-1950s, where he could have seen numerous examples of the heavy use of pigment.

110. Lawrence Alloway, "The Biomorphic Forties," *Artforum* 4 (September 1965): 18–22. Even industrial design reflected this pervasive organicism in the 1940s. See, for example, the pages of *Arts and Architecture* during the war.

111. The layering of meanings art historians attach to the nature imagery of the New York School has grown increasingly complex; see, for example, Jeffrey Weiss, "Science and Primitivism: A Fearful Symmetry in the Early New York School," *Arts* 57 (March 1983): 81–87; and Stephen Polcari's interpretations of Abstract Expressionist nature themes in his *Abstract Expressionism and the Modern Experience* (as in note 4).

112. *Painting and Sculpture in California: The Modern Era* (San Francisco: San Francisco Museum of Modern Art, 1976), 27.

113. Beginning with the Sierra Club's rechartering as a conservation organization in the 1940s, the Bay Area was the seat of a national environmental movement that reached its peak in the 1960s. KPFA, a radio station in Berkeley owned and run by local writers and artists, broadcast numerous programs on environmental themes in the late 1940s. Alan Watts and Kenneth Rexroth were among the key speakers in these broadcasts.

114. According to Fred Martin, Still played a recording of Robinson Jeffers's adaptation of *Medea* (1948) for his students at the California School of Fine Arts; see "Remembering 'the School,' Part 2," *Artweek* 6 (8 November 1975): 7. Others who particularly admired Jeffers in the late 1940s were Bladen, Hultberg, Jefferson, and Kuhlman.

115. Edward Dugmore, interview, 1 March 1988.

116. In an interview, 1 April 1989, William Morehouse noted that he, Briggs, and Jefferson were particularly interested in the philosophical connections between their painting and Zen, especially its emphasis on intuition and spontaneity. The writings of Daisetz Suzuki and Ananda Coomaraswamy were well known in San Francisco during the late 1940s. Alan Watts, who shared a ferryboat in Sausalito with the CSFA instructor Jean Varda, also helped to popularize Zen in the Bay Area through broadcasts on KPFA beginning in the late 1940s and through writings such as *Spirit of Zen* (1936; rpt. 1948).

117. This was the Six Gallery, co-founded in 1954 by the poets John Allen Ryan and Jack Spicer and the artists Wally Hedrick, Hayward King, Deborah Remington, and David Simpson. This reading of "Howl" is often designated the first, but Ginsberg had recited the poem earlier in the year at the Nourse Auditorium in San Francisco (Flyer, San Francisco Art Festival, Nourse Auditorium, 16 September 1955, John Allen Ryan papers, private collection).

118. Albright, *Art in the San Francisco Bay Area* (as in note 71), 53.

Chapter 2

1. Jermayne MacAgy, *Contemporary American Painting* (San Francisco: California Palace of the Legion of Honor, 1945), n.p.

2. Nancy Boas has astutely noted that the exhibition was considerably tamer than generally acknowledged, and certainly more conservative than New York's Armory Show of 1913; see *The Society of Six: California Colorists* (San Francisco: Bedford Arts, 1988), 59. The Armory Show's most controversial painting, Marcel Duchamp's *Nude Descending a Staircase,* was not included, although a San Francisco print dealer, who had purchased the work in 1913, displayed it in his Sutter Street gallery in 1914 to the general incomprehension of San Francisco viewers. See Francis M. Naumann, "Frederic C. Torrey and Duchamp's *Nude Descending a Staircase,*" in *West Coast Duchamp,* ed. Bonnie Clearwater (Miami Beach: Grassfield Press, 1991), 17–18.

3. Beatrice Judd Ryan, "The Bridge between Then and Now," unpublished manuscript, before 1966, Bancroft Library, University of California, Berkeley, 3.

4. Erle Loran, who began his career as an instructor at Berkeley in the 1930s, stated categorically that "modernism came to Northern California when Worth Ryder was appointed to the U.C. Art Department in 1927" (symposium "Earthquake to Albright: Modernism in Northern California, 1906 to 1945," California Palace of the Legion of Honor, 6 May 1988). Ryder had painted with Hans Hofmann and Vaclav Vytlacil in the mid-1920s in Germany and had seen Picasso's Synthetic Cubism in Paris. But German Expressionism was introduced to the East Bay slightly ear-

lier. The collector Galka Scheyer had promoted the "Blue Four," consisting of Feininger, Jawlensky, Kandinsky, and Klee, whose works were shown at the Oakland Art Gallery (now the Oakland Museum) in 1926. During the 1930s, this group also exhibited at the Mills College Art Gallery. It appears that these exhibitions helped to spawn a tradition of German Expressionist–style painting in Oakland (for example, in the work of certain members of the Society of Six) that eventuated in the appointments of Max Beckmann and Lyonel Feininger to the summer faculty of Mills College.

5. "Glenn A. Wessels: Education of an Artist," interview by Suzanne Bassett Riess, Regional Oral History Office, Bancroft Library, University of California, Berkeley, 1960, 164.

6. The Oakland Art Gallery regularly featured the Society of Six and organized a few exhibitions of German Expressionists and Constructivists in the late 1920s and 1930s.

7. In the latter part of the 1920s and 1930s the East West Gallery of Fine Arts and the Courvoisier Gallery mounted a few shows that included contemporary works by New Yorkers. The columns of Jehanne Bietry-Salinger, the art critic for the *Argus*, are an excellent source of information on the activities of modernists in the Bay Area during these decades.

8. The 1935 incarnation of the San Francisco Museum of Art was its second; the museum had been founded in 1916, a year after the Panama-Pacific International Exposition, by the San Francisco Art Association, and its original location was the Palace of Fine Arts, with J. Nilsen Laurvik as director.

9. "Grace L. McCann Morley: Art, Artists, Museums, and the San Francisco Museum of Art," interview by Suzanne Bassett Riess, Regional Cultural History Project, General Library, University of California, Berkeley, 1960, 146. Morley's international concerns eventuated in her appointment (1946–49) as director of UNESCO's museum division, where she worked to promote international exchange and, as she put it, to prevent political and economic developments from "dividing the world into little paddocks" ("A Talk with Dr. Morley of UNESCO," *San Francisco Chronicle*, 11 September 1949).

10. See San Francisco Museum of Art, *1934–35 Carnegie International, European Section, Including a Representative Showing of Contemporary American Painting* (San Francisco: San Francisco Museum of Art, 1935).

11. Grace McCann Morley, *Art of Our Time* (San Francisco: San Francisco Museum of Art, 1945), 11.

12. Frederick S. Wight, *The Artist's Environment: West Coast* (Fort Worth, Tex.: The Amon Carter Museum of Western Art, 1962–63), 20. See also "Ten Year Tenure of the Moderns in San Francisco," *Art News* 43 (February 1945):

22. From 1935 to 1945, Morley mounted an average of 110 to 120 exhibitions annually.

13. Picasso's *Guernica* made its debut at the San Francisco Museum of Art in the summer of 1939 before traveling to New York for display at the Museum of Modern Art the following November; for a detailed itinerary of the painting's tour of the country in 1939, see William Rubin, ed., *Pablo Picasso: A Retrospective* (New York: Museum of Modern Art, 1980), 349.

14. Morley recalled that "people came and gasped" when she first installed the exhibition of works by Miró in 1935, but "when they saw them a second time it wasn't quite as bad, you see, and they began to decide they liked this one better than that. It was an educational method—exposure, familiarity, and eventually discrimination" (quoted in "Grace L. McCann Morley," interview by Riess [as in note 9], 124).

15. The museum's bulletin asserted that more than fifty newspapers reported the incident. See *Quarterly Bulletin of the San Francisco Museum of Art* 1 (Summer 1940): 20.

16. Morley recalled that there was no real abstraction in the *Bay Region Styles* exhibition at the San Francisco Museum of Art in 1935: "there was some stylization, some decorative use of color, some simplification of form and design allied to expressionism; but the majority of entries were solid, technically able, representational in subject" ("The Museum's Fifteenth Birthday," *San Francisco Chronicle*, 22 January 1950).

17. In the view of at least one anonymous editor of *Art Digest*, San Francisco in 1941 was more inclined toward modernism than New York: "While the art trend in the East continues toward an assimilated union of modernism and conservatism, with middle-of-the-road works taking the bulk of exhibition honors, across the continent in San Francisco the more radical phases of aesthetic experience maintain their hold. Until stronger competition comes, San Francisco may well be called the capital of ultra-modern art in America." The remark was prompted by Charles Howard's receiving first prize from the San Francisco Museum of Art for his Surrealist abstraction, *First War Winter* (1939–40). While perhaps a bit overblown, the comment reflects the unusually high level of support the museum extended to local avant-garde artists. See "Abstraction Wins San Francisco Honor," *Art Digest* 15 (1 January 1941): 21.

18. Martin Leuer, "Recipe Art Moderne," *Montgomery Street Skylight* (6 December 1940).

19. This group, the first Surrealist movement in America with its own name and program, premiered in Hollywood at the Centaur Gallery in 1934, three years after the introduction of Surrealism to the United States at the Wadsworth Atheneum in Connecticut. It should be noted, however, that some of the principles espoused by these

artists were at odds with Surrealist ideology, particularly their emphasis on "ordered" introspection. See Henry T. Hopkins and Diane Degasis Moran, *Lorser Feitelson and Helen Lundeberg: A Retrospective Exhibition* (San Francisco: San Francisco Museum of Modern Art, 1980), 13.

20.   Merrild's "flux" paintings feature a pouring technique that predates Pollock's. See Henry Miller, "Knud Merrild: A Holiday in Paint," *Circle* 1 (1944): 41–47; and Victoria Dailey, "Knud Merrild," *Art of California* 4 (November 1991): 52–56. Other artists who anticipated drip painting were Harold Christopher Davis and Fred Kahn, who operated the Circle Gallery in Los Angeles.

21.   This show, which traveled to the Brooklyn Museum in 1936, was apparently the inspiration for Alfred Barr's *Fantastic Art, Dada, Surrealism* show in the winter of 1936–37; see Robert R. Petta, "Surrealism in Northern California," in Joseph Armstrong Baird, Jr., ed., *From Exposition to Exposition: Progressive and Conservative Northern California Painting, 1915–1939* (Sacramento, Calif.: Crocker Art Museum, 1981), 46.

22.   Howard Putzel served as advisor to the Paul Elder Gallery and Julien Levy, to the Courvoisier, helping to organize shows of paintings by Dalí, De Chirico, Ernst, Miró, and Picasso during the 1930s. Both were early promoters of Surrealism in New York as well; Putzel went on to become Peggy Guggenheim's advisor at Art of This Century gallery and an important early supporter of many New York Abstract Expressionists. See Melvin P. Lader, "Howard Putzel: Proponent of Surrealism and Early Abstract Expressionism in America," *Arts* 56 (March 1982): 85–96.

23.   Catherine Church Holland, *From the Collection: The Gifts of Jermayne MacAgy* (San Francisco: San Francisco Museum of Modern Art, 1983), 3. Morley's emphasis on Surrealism in the 1940s came from a conviction that, as she stated in 1945, it offered the contemporary artist "almost the only valid and living manner of expressing non-visual, abstract and symbolic statements in painting, and there was never a time that felt more keenly the need of doing so" (quoted in *Art of Our Time* [as in note 11], 24).

24.   The most significant of these group shows was *European Artists in America* in 1946, which included Eugene Berman, Marc Chagall, Max Ernst, Stanley William Hayter, Jean Hélion, Fernand Léger, Jacques Lipchitz, André Masson, Amédée Ozenfant, Kurt Seligmann, Yves Tanguy, and Pavel Tchelitchew. The critic Alfred Frankenstein remarked that "all of them are well known, and none of them needs any introduction or apology at this late date" (*San Francisco Chronicle,* 19 May 1946).

25.   Jeffrey Wechsler has argued that small size alone should not exclude a work from the precinct of Abstract Expressionism; see *Abstract Expressionism: Other Dimensions. An Introduction to Small Scale Painterly Abstraction in America, 1940–1965* (New Brunswick, N.J.: The Jane Voorhees Zimmerli Art Museum, 1989). Although most of the artists Wechsler discusses generally painted on a large scale, he introduces several artists who received comparatively little critical attention in the 1950s, presumably because of the small scale of their work, including Edward Corbett, Rollin Crampton, Ralph Rosenborg, Ethel Schwabacher, Sonia Sekula, and Janet Sobel.

26.   Schatz was a Jewish refugee who left Palestine in the late 1930s and came to California, where he befriended Henry Miller. In 1947, Miller and Schatz collaborated on a book, *Into the Night Life,* which was exhibited that year at the San Francisco Museum of Art. Schatz's slashing abstractions paralleled Miller's equally vehement and torrential prose. Although Schatz won a good deal of praise from local critics, he remains a virtually unknown artist.

27.   Bischoff, Dixon, Grillo, Park, and, to a lesser extent, Diebenkorn belonged to the small contingent of CSFA Abstract Expressionists who were seriously involved with Surrealism and mythic symbolism after the war. Other artists who were perhaps too much in the Surrealist camp to be classified as Abstract Expressionists in the 1940s include Peter Shoemaker and Lawrence Calcagno.

28.   See Peter Selz, "Between Friends: Still and the Bay Area," *Art in America* 63 (November–December 1975): 72; and Joan Roebuck, "Northern California and New York, 1940s–1960s," in Joseph Armstrong Baird, Jr., ed., *Directions in Bay Area Painting: A Survey of Three Decades, 1940s–1960s* (Davis, Calif.: Richard L. Nelson Gallery and The Fine Arts Collection, Department of Art, University of California, Davis, 1983), 6.

29.   For more on Hayter's and Onslow-Ford's influence on Bay Area art, see Susan M. Anderson, *Pursuit of the Marvelous: Stanley William Hayter, Charles Howard, Gordon Onslow Ford* (Laguna Beach, Calif.: Laguna Art Museum, 1990), 6–9, 14–25.

30.   Although critics were quick to link the mysterious and fantastic imagery of Still's paintings of the early 1940s with Surrealism, Still himself denied ever having gone through a Surrealist phase. His published diary notes, written in the fall of 1945, explicitly disavowed any connection with "Surrealist theology." See San Francisco Museum of Modern Art, *Clyfford Still* (San Francisco: San Francisco Museum of Modern Art, 1976), 111. Still also denied having any affiliation with Newman and Rothko's "band of Mythmakers" in an open letter to the Art of This Century gallery in 1946 (quoted in Buffalo Fine Arts Academy, *Paintings by Clyfford Still* [Buffalo, N.Y.: Buffalo Fine Arts Academy, 1959], n.p.). In the late 1940s, Still's distaste for Surrealism was well known by his colleagues and students at the California School of Fine Arts. Jefferson recalled, when he was interviewed by Mary Fuller McChesney, 21 December 1965: "I got a strong impression from him that anything that was out of the unconscious, he wasn't going for" (transcript in private collection).

31.   I owe this insight to Frank Lobdell (interview, 20

June 1988). Free associative techniques were widespread among the literary avant-garde in the Bay Area, with Henry Miller the most prominent and influential practitioner. The concept of "stream of consciousness" had, of course, been used by critics to describe the linguistic experiments of Gertrude Stein and James Joyce. Joyce was widely admired in Bay Area avant-garde circles in the 1940s.

32. Diebenkorn, Dugmore, Walter Kuhlman, and Still were among the artists who admired the dripped and kneaded expressionist paintings of the Oregon painter C. S. Price in the late 1940s (interviews with Dugmore and Kuhlman, 21 November 1988 and 5 July 1988, respectively; and letter to me from Diebenkorn, 23 September 1991).

33. The anti-Surrealist ethic at the California School of Fine Arts was so strong in the late 1940s that even those who wanted to experiment with automatism were discouraged from doing so by their peers. George Stillman, in an interview, 12 July 1988, remembered that "people played with it, but were ashamed of it."

34. Frank Lobdell, interview, 20 June 1988. John Hultberg, interviewed by Mary Fuller McChesney, 6 May 1966, remembered that Lobdell liked to draw spontaneously in the manner of automatism but preferred to think of such an approach as analogous to jazz improvisation (transcript in private collection).

35. George Stillman, interview, 12 July 1988. Peter Shoemaker appears to be among the few artists from the California School of Fine Arts who were significantly influenced by Hayter's taut, linear style.

36. In San Francisco these characteristics often carried associations with Pacific Northwest artists, such as Kenneth Callahan, Ambrose Patterson, Mark Tobey, and others whose work was well known through several exhibitions at the City of Paris Rotunda Gallery and the San Francisco Museum of Art beginning in the mid-1940s. Of the CSFA artists, only Ernest Briggs, Lawrence Calcagno, and James Budd Dixon seem to have been significantly interested in the work of Tobey.

37. Jeffrey Wechsler, *Surrealism and American Art, 1931–1947* (New Brunswick, N.J.: Rutgers University Art Gallery, 1977), 50. See, for example, Lawrence Alloway et al., *The Interpretive Link: Abstract Surrealism into Abstract Expressionism: Works on Paper, 1938–1948* (Newport Beach, Calif.: Newport Harbor Art Museum, 1986).

38. Ernest Briggs, quoted in Mary Fuller McChesney, *A Period of Exploration: San Francisco, 1945–1950* (Oakland: The Oakland Museum, 1973), 77.

39. See Thomas Albright, *Art in the San Francisco Bay Area, 1945–1980: An Illustrated History* (Berkeley and Los Angeles: University of California Press, 1985), 16.

40. Douglas MacAgy, quoted in ibid., 17.

41. Douglas MacAgy, quoted in Dore Ashton, *The New York School: A Cultural Reckoning* (New York: Penguin Books, 1980), 200.

42. Douglas MacAgy, interviewed by Mary Fuller McChesney, 6 June 1966 (transcript in private collection).

43. Jermayne MacAgy, *Large Scale Drawings by Modern Artists* (San Francisco: California Palace of the Legion of Honor, 1950). The exhibition included Jeremy Anderson, Bischoff, Corbett, Diebenkorn, Claire Falkenstein, George Harris, Jefferson, Adaline Kent, James McCray, Park, Sidney Peterson, Smith, and Spohn. To my knowledge, only Falkenstein's twenty-three-foot drawing has survived. For more information on San Francisco Abstract Expressionist works on paper, see Susan Landauer, *Paper Trails: San Francisco Abstract Expressionist Prints, Drawings, and Watercolors* (Santa Cruz, Calif.: The Art Museum of Santa Cruz County, 1993).

44. Walter Kuhlman, in a telephone conversation, July 1991, insisted that it was a well-known but little-publicized fact that Jermayne was "the real mover and shaker of the pair."

45. Smith was probably the first to tell the story; see McChesney, *A Period of Exploration,* 8. Since then, the curtain incident has been mentioned in nearly every account of the period, including Albright, *Art in the San Francisco Bay Area,* 17; Michael Leonard, "The Golden Age of Bay Area Painting," *Art of California* 2 (August–September 1989): 13; Richard Armstrong, *David Park* (Berkeley and Los Angeles: University of California Press; and New York: Whitney Museum of American Art, 1989), 24; and Patrick L. Frank, "Abstract Expressionism in San Francisco, 1945–1950" (Ph.D. diss., George Washington University, 1992), 128–29. Frank adds an interesting variation to the story with the suggestion that the mural was covered to deflect anti-Communist attention. It is possible that the incident occurred during Ernest Mundt's reign in the early 1950s, at the peak of the McCarthy era.

46. Most of the artists interviewed for this study—including William Morehouse, whose custodial duties in the late 1940s involved sweeping the Rivera room—remembered that the mural was left uncovered except during special exhibitions. Moreover, photographs of the school's commencement ceremony of 1948 in the archives of the SFAI show the Rivera mural in full glory. Finally, the course catalogue for the 1945–46 school year, a publication MacAgy personally supervised, boasted that the mural was one of the special attractions of the California School of Fine Arts.

47. William Morehouse, quoted in McChesney, *A Period of Exploration,* 12.

48. Clyfford Still, quoted in Albright, *Art in the San Francisco Bay Area,* 17.

49. Douglas MacAgy, quoted in William Hall, "School of Fine Arts Acquires World Fame," *San Francisco*

Examiner, 11 July 1948. When interviewed by Mary Fuller McChesney, 30 May 1966, MacAgy complained that "cheesy Bohemianism was very strong in San Francisco" in the late 1940s (transcript in private collection).

50.   Grades and attendance were not a factor for "advanced" students like the artists in the present study. MacAgy recognized these students as another breed altogether and exempted them from formal requirements. Many of them painted in makeshift studios in the school (such as stairwells and other nooks), and some of them worked at home. For most of these artists, attendance required no more than showing up and working in the physical space of the school. However, MacAgy's requirements for less experienced artists were much more strict. Faculty memoranda and transcripts of meetings (which were held on campus, not at MacAgy's apartment, and were serious, no-nonsense affairs) show that MacAgy asked monitors to call roll fifteen minutes after the start and fifteen minutes before the close of each period and that students with more than three absences were dropped.

51.   William M. Ivins, Jr., quoted in Douglas MacAgy, "The Contemporary Art School," *Arts and Architecture* 65 (November 1948): 25. In this article (24) MacAgy cited Lewis Mumford's *Culture of Cities* to support his view that an artistic avant-garde was crucial to the health of society.

52.   MacAgy, "The Contemporary Art School," 24. This view of the school concurs with that of the *Montgomery Street Skylight.* In 1946, the *Skylight* called the CSFA program markedly "progressive" and quoted an instructor as saying: "It is the school's desire to place more emphasis on association of line and color, on imagination and individuality, than on the more formal concepts of artistic representation" ("Embryo Potsters Take Show," *Montgomery Street Skylight* [4 June 1946]).

53.   MacAgy, "The Contemporary Art School," 24. This view is also discussed in MacAgy's lecture "Contemporary Painting," presented at Dominican College, San Rafael, Calif., 17 February 1947, transcript in SFAI.

54.   Hassel Smith added to the swell of MacAgy mythology by reporting that "Douglas MacAgy came in and he threw all those old cats out and hired a lot of new people. That was sort of a palace revolution. Doug turned out the rascals, the dead wood" (quoted in McChesney, *A Period of Exploration,* 8). But MacAgy said he took the position as director for the very reason that "there weren't any teachers left from the preceding faculty, so there wasn't the embarrassment of having to fire people" (MacAgy, interviewed by Mary Fuller McChesney, 30 May 1966, transcript in private collection).

55.   See Minor White, "Photography Is an Art," *Design* 49 (December 1947): 6–8, and "Photography in an Art School," *U.S. Camera* 12 (July 1949): 49–51.

56.   Peterson's Workshop 20 was highly influential in fostering experimental filmmaking in the Bay Area; the group that gathered around Peterson included Jordan Belson, James Broughton, and Frank Stauffacher. At the same time, the San Francisco Museum of Art's Art in Cinema Society (1946–49), a forerunner of the Museum of Modern Art's Cinema 16, screened vanguard films by Dalí, Maya Deren, Duchamp, Oskar Fischinger, Léger, Francis Picabia, and Man Ray. See San Francisco Museum of Art, *Art in Cinema—San Francisco Museum of Art* (San Francisco, 1947). For more on the history of avant-garde film in San Francisco, see James Broughton, "Experimental Film in San Francisco: How It All Began," in Thomas Albright et al., *Rolling Renaissance: San Francisco Underground Art in Celebration, 1945–1968,* 2d ed. (San Francisco: Intersection, Center for Religion and the Arts, 1975), 25–26.

57.   Elmer Bischoff, lecture presented at the Oakland Museum, 27 October 1973, transcript in SFAI.

58.   Ibid.

59.   Alfred Frankenstein, review of a faculty exhibition at the California School of Fine Arts, *San Francisco Chronicle,* undated clipping in the collection of Bischoff's former wife, Jean Tickle, Walnut Creek, Calif.

60.   Hassel Smith, interviewed by Mary Fuller McChesney, 20 July 1965, recalled that Bischoff was "rather keen about" Rothko's biomorphic Surrealism of the mid-1940s, as well as the work of Baziotes, David Hare, and Matta (transcript in private collection).

61.   In a review of Bischoff's show at the California Palace of the Legion of Honor in 1947, Alfred Frankenstein described Bischoff's new works as "large, totally abstract, full of whirling movement and tension, large and strong for all their rhapsodic heat and speed" (*San Francisco Chronicle,* 8 June 1947).

62.   Hassel Smith, interviewed by Paul Karlstrom, 5 September 1978, roll 3199, frames 586–87, AAA.

63.   Alfred Frankenstein, review of Smith's one-man show at the California Palace of the Legion of Honor, *San Francisco Chronicle,* 18 May 1947.

64.   Richard Armstrong, *David Park* (as in note 45), 19–20.

65.   For an example of these paintings, see Park's *Divining* (ca. 1946), reproduced in "Exhibition: Faculty of the California School of Fine Arts," *Bulletin of the California Palace of the Legion of Honor* 4 (October 1946).

66.   Alexander Calder, quoted in Mary Fuller [McChesney], "Portrait: Clay Spohn," *Art in America* 51 (December 1963): 80.

67.   Ibid., 80.

68.   "Fly Swatter Painting: Entry Mystifies Art Judges," *San Francisco Examiner,* 30 September 1941.

69.   Hassel Smith stated unequivocally that "Clay Spohn brought Surrealism and Dada to San Francisco"

("Sulla scuola di San Francisco," *Evento delle arti* 2 [1958]: 26). See also Albright, *Art in the San Francisco Bay Area,* 42; and Peter Plagens, *Sunshine Muse: Contemporary Art on the West Coast* (New York: Praeger, 1974), 78–79.

70. Although there are certainly affinities between Spohn's assemblages and Dada and it is hard to imagine Spohn's work without the European precedent, Spohn asserted in a letter to Mary Fuller McChesney, dated 25 April 1963, that he had never been interested in Dada, explaining that in contrast with the anti-art ideology of Duchamp, his own assemblages were created purely in a spirit of fun (roll D169, frames 1239, 1246, 1297, 1330, AAA).

71. Douglas MacAgy organized Spohn's first one-man museum exhibition, *Fantastic War Machines and Guerragraphs,* at the San Francisco Museum of Art in 1942. MacAgy coined the term "guerragraph" after the Spanish word for war. See Douglas MacAgy, "Clay Spohn's War Machines," *Circle* 5 (1945): 38–43. For more on Spohn's *War Machines,* see Susan Landauer, "Painting under the Shadow: California Modernism and the Second World War," in *On The Edge of America: California Modernist Art, 1900–1950* ed. Paul J. Karlstrom (Washington, D.C., and San Francisco: Archives of American Art of the Smithsonian Institution in Association with Fine Arts Museums of San Francisco; and Berkeley and Los Angeles: University of California Press, 1996).

72. Clay Spohn, draft of a letter to Alfred Frankenstein, 1974, quoted in David Beasley, "The Boundless Spirit of Clay Edgar Spohn," unpublished manuscript, 1991, 65.

73. William Ivey, interviewed by Barbara Johns, 24 May 1983, Northwest Oral History Project, roll 3593, frame 755, AAA.

74. Clay Spohn, undated notes, unfilmed Spohn papers, AAA.

75. Clay Spohn, "To the Student," teaching notes, 31 August 1949, unfilmed Spohn papers, AAA.

76. Clay Spohn, teaching notes for watercolor painting, California School of Fine Arts, summer session, 22 June 1948, unfilmed Spohn papers, AAA.

77. George Stillman, interview, 12 July 1988.

78. Edward Corbett, interviewed by Mary Fuller McChesney, 16 May 1966, transcript in private collection.

79. Dorr Bothwell, quoted in McChesney, *A Period of Exploration* (as in note 38), 75.

80. Hassel Smith, quoted in McChesney, *A Period of Exploration,* 9.

81. By the fall of 1946 the enrollment of veterans accounted for nearly three-quarters of the entire student body. Curriculum papers, SFAI.

82. In 1948 the average age for students at the California School of Fine Arts was reportedly twenty-seven; see Hall, "School of Fine Arts Acquires World Fame" (as in note 49). Most of the students who participated in the movement, including Briggs, Dixon, Dugmore, Sonia Gechtoff, Grillo, Kelly, Kuhlman, Lobdell, and John Saccaro, had previous art training.

83. Mark Rothko, letter to Barnett Newman, 24 June 1947, Barnett Newman papers, roll 3481, frame 329, AAA.

84. William Ivey, interviewed by Barbara Johns, 24 May 1983, Northwest Oral History Project, roll 3593, frame 759, AAA.

85. Elmer Bischoff, interviewed by Paul Karlstrom, 10 August 1977, transcript in AAA.

86. Most of the biographical information here is based on a series of interviews with Grillo I conducted in 1990. For more on Grillo, see Susan Landauer, "John Grillo: The San Francisco Years," *Art of California* 3 (May 1990): 56–61.

87. Douglas MacAgy, *John Grillo: Oils and Watercolors* (Berkeley, Calif.: Daliel's Gallery, 1947), n.p.

88. John Hultberg, quoted in Mary Fuller [McChesney], "Was There a San Francisco School?" *Artforum* 9 (January 1971): 51.

89. Gerald Nordland, *Richard Diebenkorn* (New York: Rizzoli International Publications, 1987), 23.

90. "Triple Enrollment," *Art Digest* 20 (February 1946): 31, curriculum papers, SFAI.

91. Henry Miller, "Varda: The Master Builder," *Circle* 1 (1944): 26–38; see also Grace Clements, "Varda," *Arts and Architecture* 62 (November 1945): 28–30.

92. Jean Varda, statement in "Teaching Art—by Instructors of the California School of Fine Arts," wall text for faculty show, 1952, SFAI.

93. Ibid., 14–15.

94. For more on Corbett's early work, see Susan Landauer, *Edward Corbett: A Retrospective* (Richmond, Calif.: Richmond Art Center, 1990), 14–18.

95. Edward Corbett, draft of a Guggenheim Fellowship application, 1951, Corbett papers, roll 4381, frame 962, AAA. Although Corbett quickly became dissatisfied with Surrealism, he did continue to admire Alberto Giacometti and Paul Delvaux, according to Mary and Norman Jackman, interview, 13 July 1989.

96. Unidentified clipping, unfilmed Edward Corbett papers, AAA.

97. Edward Corbett, application for Abraham Rosenberg Fellowship, 28 March 1947, SFAI.

98. Ibid. Corbett wrote in his Rosenberg Fellowship application: "The nature of the change which must occur in my work is suggested by the divided sum of modern painting. I recognize two contrasting and energetic traditions—the Formalist and the Expressionist. There is, I believe, a determinable orthodoxy in both traditions. In

Formalism the orthodoxy is intellective, in Expressionism the orthodoxy is affective. Both traditions are probably mature, and their apparent maturity as well as the incipient standardization in the works of their exemplars, indicates, to me, the need and possibility of synthesis . . . The aesthetic nature of this synthesis is certainly unknown to me. To pretend an exact knowledge of it would be preposterous—painting alone can give the answer."

99.   Corbett, draft of Guggenheim Fellowship application, 1951, Corbett papers, roll 4381, frame 964, AAA.

100.   Nordland, *Richard Diebenkorn,* 16.

101.   Ibid.

102.   Intimations of Surrealist influence appeared in Diebenkorn's painting while he was a student at the California School of Fine Arts, probably with the encouragement of Spohn and especially Park, whose painting drew heavily from Picasso and Miró.

103.   Frank Lobdell, in an interview, 20 July 1988, remembered that Diebenkorn returned to San Francisco from Woodstock speaking enthusiastically of Rothko's "Surrealist work."

104.   Nordland, *Richard Diebenkorn,* 23–24.

105.   Ibid., 24.

106.   See McChesney, *A Period of Exploration* (as in note 38), 5; Albright, *Art in the San Francisco Bay Area* (as in note 39), 20; Armstrong, *David Park* (as in note 45), 24–25.

107.   Clay Spohn, letter to Thomas Albright, 2 April 1976, quoted in Albright, *Art in the San Francisco Bay Area,* 20.

108.   Still never forgave Alfred Frankenstein for his unflattering review of this exhibition: "Mr. Still, to be frank about it, I did not like at all. I found his portraits on the commonplace side, and his large abstractions, some of them vaguely like Picasso's macabre 'bone' pictures, seem to me perfect examples of modern experiment misunderstood and misapplied. Sorry" (*San Francisco Chronicle,* 14 March 1943).

109.   San Francisco Museum of Modern Art, *Clyfford Still* (as in note 30), 107. I have found conflicting information regarding Still's art training in the exhibition catalogue *Contemporary Art in the United States* (New York: International Business Machines, Inc., 1940), n.p., which states that Still studied with Worth D. Griffin and Vaclav Vytlacil at the Art Students League.

110.   Still, quoted in David Anfam, "'Of the Earth, the Damned, and of the Recreated': Aspects of Clyfford Still's Earlier Work," *Burlington Magazine* 135 (April 1993): 262.

111.   When I interviewed Edward Dugmore, 1 March 1988, and Jon Schueler, 29 February 1988, former CSFA students, both recalled Still's telling them that his father was a cruel man who frequently beat him, until finally one day, in his late teens, his father came after him with a whip. After

112.   These last two subjects are depicted in paintings from the period, photographs of which are in the ACA.

113.   Martha Kingsbury, "Seattle and the Puget Sound," in *Art of the Pacific Northwest: From the 1930s to the Present* (Washington, D.C.: National Collection of Fine Arts, 1974), 48–49.

114.   Clyfford Still, quoted in Albright, *Art in the San Francisco Bay Area,* 22.

115.   See Stephen Polcari, *Abstract Expressionism and the Modern Experience* (Cambridge: Cambridge University Press, 1991), 91–116. David Anfam has done some impressive detective work, pulling together clues from diverse sources to pin Still's work to Harrison's *Themis* and other texts. See Anfam, "'Of the Earth, the Damned, and of the Recreated': Aspects of Clyfford Still's Earlier Work," 260–69.

116.   Clay Spohn remembered Still frequently recited "The Tyger" in the late 1940s. See David Beasley, "The Boundless Spirit of Clay Edgar Spohn," unpublished manuscript, 1991, 33.

117.   Susan Landauer, "Clyfford Still and Abstract Expressionism in San Francisco," in *Clyfford Still, 1904–1980: The Buffalo and San Francisco Collections,* ed. Thomas Kellein (Munich: Prestel, 1992), 93.

118.   Jim Eakle, one of Still's students in 1946, in a telephone interview, 17 February 1991, remembered that Still pointed to a recent painting leaning against a wall in his studio that had a circular form suggesting a halo and referred to it as "one of his saints."

119.   Review of Still's one-man show at Art of This Century gallery, *Art News* 44 (February 1946): 92.

120.   Glenn Wessels, who took Still's place on the faculty at Washington State, remembered that Northwest Indian art was "the big thing at Pullman" while Still was there; see Riess, "Glenn A. Wessels: Education of an Artist" (as in note 5), 282.

121.   I believe this painting is in the estate of Clyfford Still in New Windsor, Maryland. It is reproduced in John P. O'Neill, ed., *Clyfford Still* (New York: Metropolitan Museum of Art, 1979), 180.

122.   Paraphrase of Betty Freeman's interview notes, 2 April 1963, Freeman papers, roll 4060, frame 321, AAA.

123.   In 1947 vestigial figurative references, such as hands, eyes, and halos, were still appearing on occasion in Still's work. At least one, untitled, work from that year shows a vaguely canine figure, with gaping jaws thrust skyward. See the reproduction in *Art International* 17 (January 1973): 58.

124.   Later in the 1940s, Still would expand his chromatic range to include oranges, purples, and beautiful lapis and navy blues, but the paintings he displayed at the Legion

of Honor in 1947 featured the brutal palette that made the defining impression in San Francisco.

125.   Kenneth Sawyer, "U.S. Painters Today, No. 1: Clyfford Still," *Portfolio and Art News Annual* 2 (1960): 80.

126.   Still, quoted in O'Neill, ed., *Clyfford Still,* 180.

Chapter 3

1.   Frank Lobdell, interview, 20 June 1988. The epigraph to this chapter is from "Americani a Parigi," *Numero: Arte e letteratura* 1 (31 January 1951): 4.

2.   Edward Corbett, quoted in Mary Fuller McChesney, *A Period of Exploration: San Francisco, 1945–1950* (Oakland: The Oakland Museum, 1973), 16.

3.   James Budd Dixon, quoted in McChesney, *A Period of Exploration,* 54.

4.   Elmer Bischoff, lecture presented at the Oakland Museum, 27 October 1973, transcript in SFAI.

5.   Stewart Buettner quotes both Pollock and Gottlieb as saying that "painting is self-discovery" (*American Art Theory, 1945–1970* [Ann Arbor: UMI Research Press, 1981], 168).

6.   See Malcolm Bradbury and James McFarlane, "The Name and Nature of Modernism," in *Modernism, 1890–1930,* ed. Bradbury and McFarlane (New York: Penguin Books, 1976), 29.

7.   John Ferren, "Epitaph for an Avant-Garde," *Arts* 33 (November 1958): 25; reprinted in Herschel Chipp, *Theories of Modern Art: A Source Book by Artists and Critics* (Berkeley and Los Angeles: University of California Press, 1968), 573.

8.   Stewart Buettner, *American Art Theory,* 64.

9.   Renato Poggioli defined "agonism" as the "concept of the artist as victim-hero" running through modernism; see *The Theory of the Avant-Garde,* trans. Gerald Fitzgerald (Cambridge: Harvard University Press, 1968), 65–68.

10.   Clyfford Still, for example, described his experience of the late 1940s as "free, lively, [and] without fear . . . I didn't paint to eat; but ate to live. In those days I felt an exultation in the freedom of life" (quoted in Gerald Nordland, *Edward Corbett* [San Francisco: San Francisco Museum of Art, 1969], n.p).

11.   This sense of collectivity is indicated by John Hultberg's remark "We were all painting pretty much alike. We didn't *want* identities" (quoted in Shirley Jacks, *John Hultberg: Painter of the In-Between: Selected Paintings, 1953–1984* [Clinton, N.Y.: Fred L. Emerson Gallery, 1985], 35). Cf. Michael Leja, "The Formation of an Avant-Garde in New York," in Michael Auping et al., *Abstract Expressionism: The Critical Developments* (New York: Harry N. Abrams, 1987), 13–33.

12.   John Hultberg, interviewed by Mary Fuller McChesney, 6 May 1966, transcript in private collection.

13.   Edward Corbett, letter to Mary Fuller [McChesney], ca. early 1950s, Corbett papers, roll 4382, frame 19, AAA.

14.   Joseph Warren Beach, *The Twentieth-Century Novel: Studies in Technique* (New York: Appleton-Century, 1932), 530. Although Beach used this term to describe a post–World War I phenomenon, it is equally applicable to the anti-intellectualism accompanying World War II.

15.   William Morehouse, interview, 1 April 1989.

16.   Walter Kuhlman, interview, 5 July 1988.

17.   "Disdain for the thesis" is André Breton's phrase, quoted in Herbert Read, *A Concise History of Modern Painting,* 3d ed. (New York: Praeger, 1964), 137. That Breton was referring to Marcel Duchamp does not make the phrase any less pertinent to the San Francisco painters. Duchamp, who was among the speakers Douglas MacAgy invited to participate in his Western Round Table on Modern Art in 1949, was one of the few European émigrés who was widely admired by the San Franciscans. The sympathetic relationship between Duchamp and the CSFA artists regarding matters of exposition is marvelously encapsulated by an anecdote told by William Morehouse: "Of the luminaries who came and went at that time, the sharpest . . . recollection that I have is of a visit by Marcel Duchamp . . . I was in an advanced painting group so there were five or six of us that squatted in this one studio working and MacAgy and Still came in with Duchamp in tow . . . I was working on a great big . . . nonobjective thing and Duchamp said, 'What are you doing there, young man?' and I said, 'Frankly, I don't know,' and he said, 'Fine, Fine. Keep up the good work'" (quoted in Bonnie Clearwater, "Trying Very Hard to Think: Duchamp and the Western Round Table on Modern Art, 1949," in *West Coast Duchamp,* ed. Clearwater [Miami Beach: Grassfield Press, 1991], 50–51).

18.   Clyfford Still, diary notes, 1945, quoted in San Francisco Museum of Modern Art, *Clyfford Still* (San Francisco: San Francisco Museum of Modern Art, 1976), 110–11.

19.   While not a primary interest among modern painters, the notion that conventional usage had "de-potentiated" language, to use Roland Barthes's phrase, was a major concern for modern poets, from Yeats to Breton. See Richard Sheppard, "The Crisis of Language," in *Modernism, 1890–1930* (as in note 6), 323–36.

20.   As a group phenomenon, this disinclination to title works was more common in San Francisco than in New York during the late 1940s. Although Rothko stopped giving his paintings titles in 1947 (probably with Still's encouragement) and Pollock assigned numbers after 1949, most of the New York artists—including Baziotes, de Kooning, Gottlieb, Kline, Motherwell, and Newman—preferred to title their works. In 1950, during the 22 April artists' session at Studio 35, no one raised a hand when Alfred Barr asked who preferred to leave their paintings untitled (*Modern Artists in America,* ed. Robert Motherwell

and Ad Reinhardt [New York: Wittenborn, Schultz, 1951], 14).

21. See, for example, *The Renaissance Philosophy of Man,* ed. Ernst Cassirer, Paul Oskar Kristeller, and John Herman Randall, Jr. (Chicago: University of Chicago Press, 1948).

22. This belief that mass culture was a threat was particularly strong for those associated with, or influenced by, the Frankfurt School; see, for example, Paul Lazarsfeld and Robert Merton, "Mass Communication, Popular Taste, and Organized Social Action," in *The Communication of Ideas,* ed. Lyman Bryson (New York: Harper and Brothers, 1948), 95–118.

23. Douglas MacAgy, "Contemporary Painting," lecture presented at Dominican College, San Rafael, Calif., 17 February 1947, transcript in SFAI.

24. Many of the New York Abstract Expressionists were similarly reluctant to discuss their work, no doubt for some of the same reasons. But the explanations generally offered by art historians are inapplicable to the San Francisco painters. Their reticence cannot be explained as a reaction to the invasive effects of art criticism, since there was no appreciable critical discourse in San Francisco beyond Alfred Frankenstein's generally timid reviews. And Michael Auping's argument that it was a matter of "a cautious awareness of their positions in history and the advantage of signaling a content that was anything but static" suggests a cynical success motive not applicable to the San Francisco artists. See Michael Auping, introduction to Auping et al., *Abstract Expressionism* (as in note 11), 11. Of course, as Ann Gibson has pointed out, the attitudes that might lead to a mistrust of verbalizing about art were widespread. She has located such ideas in a variety of intellectual sources in Jungian psychology, New Criticism, Russian Formalism, and existentialism (see Gibson, "Abstract Expressionism's Evasion of Language," *Art Journal* 47 [Fall 1988]: 208–14).

25. Edward Corbett, undated notes, unfilmed portion of the Corbett papers, AAA.

26. Walter Kuhlman, quoted in [Judy Stone], "New Art Explained by Sausalitans," *San Rafael Daily Independent and Marin Journal,* 22 January 1949.

27. Spohn, personal notes, ca. 1947–48, unfilmed Spohn papers, AAA.

28. See, for example, Alfred Frankenstein, "A Summary of Art in Our Time," *San Francisco Chronicle,* 12 December 1948. Frankenstein noted in this review that this romantic tendency was characteristic of figurative painters as well.

29. Robert McChesney went so far as to call himself an "abstract-Romanticist" (quoted in McChesney, *A Period of Exploration,* 64).

30. Jermayne MacAgy, brochure for *Fifteen Paintings by Nine Artists in San Francisco,* Henry Art Gallery, University of Washington, Seattle, 1950. The show consisted of untitled paintings by Bischoff, Calcagno, Corbett, Diebenkorn, Jefferson, Park, Smith, Still, and Stillman. That MacAgy's statement has the abrasive, heavy-handed tone characteristic of Still suggests that Still had a part in writing it. This exhibition deeply shocked Seattle viewers. One reviewer noted that "our own Mark Tobey shapes up like an old European master" compared to the nine San Francisco artists in the show. The critic was especially perplexed by the work of Corbett, who showed two canvases "that appear to be utterly bare, being just expanses of mottled gray with faint soot-like discolorations in the upper corners" (Douglass Welch, "Art from S.F.—Just Out of Our World!" *Seattle Post-Intelligencer,* February 1950, clipping in Corbett papers, roll 4376, frame 174, AAA).

31. Clay Spohn, "To the Student," 31 August 1949, unfilmed Spohn papers, AAA.

32. André Breton, quoted in Read, *A Concise History of Modern Painting* (as in note 17), 133.

33. Irving Sandler, *The Triumph of American Painting: A History of Abstract Expressionism* (New York: Harper and Row, 1970), 31.

34. Frank Lobdell confirmed in an interview, 20 June 1988, that the CSFA artists "didn't make value judgements; the question was rather does something really strike a nerve—does something really reach you?" See also Hubert Crehan, "Art Schools Smell Alike," *San Francisco Sunday Examiner and Chronicle,* 4 October 1970.

35. Thomas Albright stated that Spohn put together the "Abstract Expressionist Kit" in 1950 (Albright, *Art in the San Francisco Bay Area, 1945–1980: An Illustrated History* [Berkeley and Los Angeles: University of California Press, 1985], 42). But according to Spohn, Douglas MacAgy tried unsuccessfully to get a contract for him with Simon and Schuster as early as 1948. Originally entitled "Foundations of Understanding in the Contemporary Approach to Painting: A Manual of Understanding," the project was never completed, according to Spohn, interviewed by Paul Cummings, 9 January 1976, transcript in AAA. Notes for the text can be found in the unfilmed Spohn papers, AAA, and a set of playful diagrams from the manuscript is on file in the ACA.

36. Diebenkorn, quoted in Dan Hofstadter, "Profiles: Almost Free of the Mirror," *New Yorker* 63 (7 September 1987): 63. George Stillman recalled in an interview, 12 July 1988, that Still could not even bear praise of his own work if he felt it suggested an aesthetic judgment: "I remember being at an opening one time," Stillman said, "and Still, myself, and some other people were standing around one of his paintings, when someone said to Still, 'God, that's a beautiful painting,' and Still was silent for a moment and then said: 'It's just another rag I wiped my ass on.' Still never accepted a compliment."

37.   Douglas MacAgy observed this consensus by negation when he described the ideological exchange at the California School of Fine Arts in the late 1940s to Frederick Wight: "In a ferment that was far from being only local (we all recognized its symptoms elsewhere as well), individual vision was our objective. At that point procedures and their outcome had not been tabbed—catch-all terms such as 'action painting' and 'abstract-expressionism' were yet to be coined—and for a while it seemed in speech that these people were drawn together by what they negated. Irrelevant concepts and styles had already been named and could be talked about. There was no verbal settlement on matters that seemed relevant. They were approached in conversation by indirection, by analogy—most often by metaphor" (quoted in Frederick S. Wight, *The Artist's Environment: West Coast* [Fort Worth, Tex.: The Amon Carter Museum of Western Art, 1962–63], 22). Sandler noted a similar tendency among the New Yorkers in his book *The Triumph of American Painting*, 3.

38.   Renato Poggioli similarly noted that it is common for avant-garde aesthetics to be "directly and rigidly determined by an inverse relation to traditional conventions." See *The Theory of the Avant-Garde* (as in note 9), 56.

39.   Interview with George Stillman, 12 July 1988, and with Jon Schueler, 13 November 1988. The New York artists were less rigorously programmatic about nonobjectivity. Quite a few had some degree of figuration in their work in 1948, including Baziotes, Gottlieb, Guston, Kline, Motherwell, Pousette-Dart, and sometimes de Kooning. In the 1950s, however, San Francisco artists became at least as lax about the issue of representation as the New Yorkers.

40.   On the strictness of this standard, Hubert Crehan observed that "should one detect among the collision of shapes and colors the vestige of a dog's head, or the enigmatic smile on the face of a Buddha, or a movement across the picture plane suggesting a horizon line, or the color of blue at the top of the canvas evoking a patch of sky—such banalities were to be obliterated" (Crehan, "Art Schools Smell Alike," *San Francisco Sunday Examiner and Chronicle*, 4 October 1970).

41.   Spohn recalled, when interviewed by Paul Cummings, 9 January 1976, that Still "didn't want the word 'abstract' because it came from France" (transcript in AAA).

42.   Clay Spohn, letter to Judson Crews, 6 August 1952, unfilmed Spohn papers, AAA.

43.   John Hultberg, quoted in Robert T. Buck, Jr., et al., *Richard Diebenkorn: Paintings and Drawings, 1943–1976* (Buffalo, N.Y.: Albright-Knox Art Gallery, 1976), 8.

44.   Weldon Kees, "Robert Motherwell," *Magazine of Art* 41 (March 1948): 87.

45.   Clyfford Still, quoted in J. Benjamin Townsend, "An Interview with Clyfford Still," *Gallery Notes,* Albright-Knox Art Gallery (Summer 1961): 11. Few of Still's CSFA

colleagues found Still's disavowal of natural imagery convincing. When Mary Fuller McChesney interviewed them for *A Period of Exploration,* many echoed John Baur's remark that the influence of nature on artists is virtually inescapable since it is "obviously the ultimate source of visual experience" (Baur, *Nature in Abstraction* [New York: Macmillan, 1958], 6). Spohn, who was Still's closest friend in San Francisco, indicated that Still considered nature more important to his work than he was willing to admit publicly. According to Spohn, interviewed by Mary Fuller McChesney, 23 April 1966, Still told him sometime around 1947 that he, Spohn, was the only person who understood his painting when he described it as "the sort of thing you experience if you were out on the plains someplace and you were sitting there on the grass—the earth and all these relationships, the nature forces" (transcript in private collection).

46.   Clay Spohn, notes, ca. late 1940s, unfilmed Spohn papers, AAA.

47.   This was Walter Kuhlman's own interpretation of the painting, although he maintained that he was not conscious of the subject until after it was finished (telephone interview, July 1990).

48.   See, for example, José Ortega y Gasset, "The Dehumanization of Art," in *The Dehumanization of Art and Notes on the Novel,* trans. Helene Weyl (Princeton, N.J.: Princeton University Press, 1948).

49.   Meyer Schapiro discussed this antipathy as a general tendency among both figurative and abstract artists after the Second World War in "The Liberating Quality of Avant-Garde Art," *Art News* 56 (Summer 1957): 38–39.

50.   Herbert Read, "Surrealism and the Romantic Principle" (1936); reprinted in *The Philosophy of Modern Art: Collected Essays by Herbert Read,* 2d ed. (London: Faber and Faber, 1969), 107.

51.   This was Douglas MacAgy's central argument in "Contemporary Painting," lecture presented at Dominican College, San Rafael, Calif., 17 February 1947, transcript in SFAI.

52.   Richard Diebenkorn, quoted in Buck et al., *Richard Diebenkorn,* 12; interview with Edward Corbett by Mary Fuller McChesney, 16 May 1966, transcript in private collection; Clyfford Still, quoted in Dorothy Miller, *Fifteen Americans* (New York: Museum of Modern Art), 21.

53.   MacAgy, "Contemporary Painting," SFAI.

54.   The threads of paint that Grillo allowed to cross the lower margins of his works function in much the same way as the "spirit lines" that the Navajo Indians wove across the borders of their textiles to free the spirit of the maker.

55.   In an interview, 12 July 1988, George Stillman pointed out that studio space was a primary determinant in the size of an artist's work in San Francisco during the late 1940s. He noted that the artists who routinely painted on a

large scale, such as Bischoff, Lobdell, Smith, and Still, had relatively large studios. Stillman's own work more than doubled in size in 1950, when he found a large studio in Berkeley.

56.   Pollock was actually paraphrasing a critic's remark about his work when he used this oft-quoted phrase, but he said he considered it "a fine compliment" (see "Unframed Space," *New Yorker* 26 [5 August 1950]: 16).

57.   See, for example, Michael Auping, "Beyond the Sublime," in Auping et al., *Abstract Expressionism,* 146. It should be noted that on the matter of scale, the Abstract Expressionists had an immediate precedent in the work of Matta and Picasso. Besides *Guernica* (138 × 308 in.), Picasso had painted several mural-sized canvases during the war. After 1946, Matta also routinely painted canvases as large as fifteen feet wide. The Museum of Modern Art's *Large-Scale Painting* exhibition of 1947, which included Wilfredo Lam, Matta, Picasso, Siqueiros, and Ben Shahn, showed that painting on a large scale was both a European and an American phenomenon in the 1940s.

58.   For more on Kiesler's design, see *VVV* 1 (1943): 76–83.

59.   See Bern Porter, "New Projection," *College Art Journal* 3 (November 1943): 26–28. Although it is not clear how influential Porter's theories were in the Bay Area, Porter himself had a high profile among local literary and artistic circles throughout the 1940s. A poet, photographer, and former physicist on the Manhattan Project, he taught at the University of California at Berkeley during the war and edited the little magazines *Circle* and *Berkeley.* He also published books and folios by Robert Duncan, Philip Lamantia, Henry Miller, and Kenneth Patchen. In the late 1940s Porter operated two galleries in Sausalito that catered to CSFA artists: the Contemporary Gallery and Schillerhaus. His exhibitions in 1948 were among the first group shows of Bay Area Abstract Expressionism. Some of the artists who showed in Porter's galleries were Jeremy Anderson, Calcagno, Diebenkorn, Dixon, Francis, Hultberg, Kuhlman, Lobdell, and Stillman.

60.   Bern Porter, "All Over the Place," *Circle* 1 (1944): 50.

61.   Irving Sandler seems to have extrapolated from statements by Newman and Rothko that Still was concerned with increasing viewers' intimacy with his work; see *The Triumph of American Painting* (as in note 33), 154. Yet there is little evidence that this was Still's primary intention; in fact, he claimed that communication with the public was "both presumptuous and irrelevant" (statement in Dorothy Miller, *Fifteen Americans,* 22).

62.   The theme of upward expansion seems to have been peculiar to San Francisco; among the artists of the New York School, only Newman (who himself was probably influenced by Still) developed the idea in his "zip"

paintings. Both Rothko and Pollock often circumscribed their paintings with margins, producing what David Anfam has called an "inner equilibrium" that for Pollock tended to loop toward itself and for Rothko often created a pictorial space that projected forward rather than upward (Anfam, *Abstract Expressionism* [London: Thames and Hudson, 1990], 130). Kenneth Sawyer suggested that the theme of expansion was especially common in San Francisco when he wrote in 1952: "Members of the so-called 'San Francisco School,' a few New York artists, [and] a scattering of frontiersmen elsewhere have discovered that a painting not only may function within its frame, but evoke the illusion of motion and space beyond it" (Sawyer, "Lawrence Calcagno," *Numero: Arte e letteratura* 4 [December 1952]: 11).

63.   Still, quoted in San Francisco Museum of Modern Art, *Clyfford Still* (San Francisco: San Francisco Museum of Modern Art, 1976), 123–24.

64.   That Still drew from the Romantic aesthetic of the sublime for some of his ideas about pictorial space has been well documented; see, for example, Michael Auping, "Beyond the Sublime," in Auping et al., *Abstract Expressionism,* 146; Robert Rosenblum, "The Abstract Sublime," *Art News* 59 (February 1961): 38–41, 56–58; and Lawrence Alloway, "The American Sublime" (1963), reprinted in *Topics of Modern Art since 1945,* ed. Alloway (New York: W. W. Norton, 1975), 31.

65.   See Henry Nash Smith, *Virgin Land: The American West as Symbol and Myth* (Cambridge: Harvard University Press, 1978).

66.   See David Perkins, *A History of Modern Poetry: Modernism and After* (Cambridge: Harvard University Press, 1987), 541.

67.   See Gerald Nash, *The American West Transformed* (Bloomington: University of Indiana Press, 1985). Nash's research shows that the war transformed California from a "colony" dependent upon the East to "a path-breaking self-sufficient region with unbounded optimism for its future" (216).

68.   Earl Warren, quoted in Nash, *The American West Transformed,* 204.

69.   Gifford Phillips, "Today's Frontier," *Frontier: The Voice of the New West* 1 (15 November 1949): 2. Phillips's optimistic rhetoric was echoed by numerous politicians and journalists in the late 1940s, especially during the centennial of the Treaty of Guadalupe Hidalgo of 1848, which gave California to the United States.

70.   William Morehouse, interview, 1 April 1989. Of course, living in the West was not a prerequisite for conceiving of the American artist as a pioneer conquering aesthetic frontiers. Harold Rosenberg invoked the mythology of the West to give a distinctly American cast to avant-garde activities of the New York School in his essay "The Ameri-

can Action Painters," *Art News* 51 (December 1952): 22–23, 48–50, and in a later article in which he compared Pollock, who had been raised in the West, with Daniel Boone, claiming that Pollock's tough, taciturn deportment was a frontiersman's means of defying "European esthetic superiority and snobbishness" ("The Search for Jackson Pollock," *Art News* 59 [February 1961]: 35).

71.   Elmer Bischoff, lecture presented at the Oakland Museum, 27 October 1973, transcript in SFAI.

72.   Peter Selz has observed that while the concept of empathy has its roots in Romantic aesthetics and found its apogee in German Expressionism, the theory appears in many aesthetic doctrines of the twentieth century, including Neo-Impressionism, Cubism, and the Bauhaus writings of Kandinsky and Klee (Selz, *German Expressionist Painting* [Berkeley and Los Angeles: University of California Press, 1957], 7).

73.   Still, letter to Alfonso Ossorio 25 June 1952, Ossorio papers, roll 3888, frame 681, AAA; notes from interview with Still by Betty Freeman, 4 October 1960, Freeman papers, roll 4060, frame 269, AAA.

74.   James Budd Dixon, quoted in McChesney, *A Period of Exploration* (as in note 2), 54. Even John Saccaro, who is often classified as an "action painter," stressed the importance of discipline: "I used to knock myself out with these paintings," he said. "Sometimes I'd wait forty minutes to an hour before I'd make a stroke on the damn thing" (quoted in McChesney, *A Period of Exploration,* 63).

75.   Elmer Bischoff, lecture presented at the Oakland Museum, 27 October 1973, transcript in SFAI.

76.   William Morehouse, interview, 1 April 1989. Diebenkorn was also chastised by his older colleagues for being facile with the brush. See Buck et al., *Richard Diebenkorn* (as in note 43), 10.

77.   Clyfford Still, quoted in Ti-Grace Sharpless, *Clyfford Still* (Philadelphia: Institute of Contemporary Art, University of Pennsylvania, 1963), n.p.

78.   Rosenberg stated that according to the American vanguard, "Form, color, composition, drawing, are auxiliaries" that "can be dispensed with," and "the gesture on the canvas was a gesture of liberation, from Value—political, aesthetic, moral" ("The American Action Painters," *Art News* 51 [December 1952]: 23).

79.   When Rosenberg's article "The American Action Painters" first appeared, in 1952, Still sent Rosenberg a furious letter of protest, calling the effort "a hatchet job" (Still, letter, 14 December 1952, unfilmed Jon Schueler papers, AAA).

80.   Corbett elaborated: "I think random marking by anyone or random actions are the opposite of what leads to art. Art is design. It is intentions, careful concentrations, acute awareness. It's the employment of all of your faculties and these paint pushers and paint splatterers and so on who were moved or encouraged by the notion of Action Painting were simply misled . . . Art is purposeful. It is not accident" (quoted in McChesney, *A Period of Exploration,* 73).

81.   Lawrence Hatterer, quoted by Edward Corbett, who was interviewed by Gerald Nordland, February 1966, transcript in private collection.

82.   John Saccaro, interviewed by Mary Fuller McChesney, 1 September 1965, transcript in private collection.

83.   Richard Shiff has argued that Rosenberg's ideal of unpremeditated action did not match the actual practice of the New York School. He noted that Pollock contradicted himself when he said, "When I'm in the painting, I don't know what I'm about" and then insisted that he controlled his spilling and dripping. Shiff concluded that "Pollock organized compositions just as Manet invented and arranged subjects" (see Shiff, "Performing an Appearance: On the Surface of Abstract Expressionism," in Auping et al., *Abstract Expressionism* [as in note 11], 96). It is worth noting, in this regard, that Still seems to have been the only Abstract Expressionist to make copies of his own paintings down to the last stroke. Still's gestural *1947-H,* for example, survives in three versions: the first was purchased from the artist by Phillippe Dotremont, the second was a gift from the artist to Douglas and Jermayne MacAgy (it is now in the Menil Collection in Houston, Tex.), and the third was given by the artist to the San Francisco Museum of Modern Art.

84.   Pollock's drip paintings, begun in the winter of 1946–47, may have been a partial catalyst, but it is important to remember that they did not achieve notoriety until after *Life* magazine reproduced them in 1949. Pollock's dripping and pouring of paint, however, would not have been entirely new to San Franciscans, as similar methods were used by the California artists Harold Christopher Davies, Grillo, Fred Kahn, Knud Merrild, and Bezalel Schatz. In addition, the drip technique the San Francisco artists tended to use, as Stillman pointed out in an interview, 12 July 1988, was very different from Pollock's. Rather than place the canvas on the floor and drip from above, they propped the canvas upright so that the drips bled and streaked. This method was closer to that of John Little, whose *Personage and Serpent* of 1947 was something of a succès de scandale at the San Francisco Museum of Art's spring annual of 1948. See Jehanne Bietry-Salinger, "Notes on Art: Painting for Whom, If You Please?" *Opera and Concert* 13 (March 1948): 24–25.

85.   When he was interviewed by Jan Butterfield, ca. 1975, Hassel Smith said: "I think we all had a go at throwing paint around all over the place and I think we all discovered rather quickly that it produced within us certain kinds of responses in relation to the material and so on, that we became pretty quickly disillusioned about" (Smith papers, roll 2008, AAA). Stillman also remembered a brief

"drip explosion" that occurred around 1948. In his case, however, he had already been applying drip motifs in his figurative works. He explained in an interview, 1 June 1989: "I had been doing female figures in some cases with one eye, and one time a drip occurred at the eye and progressed down the face and onto the figure. Normally we were taught to hold the rag in one hand and paint with the other so that any drips could be stopped using the rag. But since the drip looked like a tear, I left it. This element so fascinated me as an element of our postwar trauma and a reminder of the recent past that I began to use it throughout my paintings."

86. Spencer Macky, who was president of the California College of Arts and Crafts in the late 1940s, used the phrase "drip and drool school"; it is conceivable that it was coined as a result of an exhibition there in 1948 that consisted of works by Hultberg, Kuhlman, Lobdell, and Stillman. The exhibition raised such a storm of protest that several students felt compelled to slash some of the paintings with razors. One student was so distraught that he threw a chair through a canvas of Kuhlman's (interview with Kuhlman, 5 July 1988, and with Stillman, 5 October 1990). According to Smith, Still took to using the phrase; see Caroline A. Jones, *Bay Area Figurative Art, 1950–1965* (San Francisco: San Francisco Museum of Modern Art; and Berkeley and Los Angeles: University of California Press, 1990), 8.

87. George Stillman, "Self-Interview," 1966, transcript in ACA.

88. Ernest Briggs, quoting Still in an interview with Mary Fuller McChesney, 20 April 1966, transcript in private collection.

89. Still, letter to Smith, 20 March 1977, Smith papers, roll 2008, AAA, and letter to Alfonso Ossorio, 30 January 1955, Alfonso Ossorio papers, roll 3888, frame 710, AAA; interview with Dugmore, 1 March 1988, and with Schueler, 13 November 1988.

90. Jack Jefferson, quoted in McChesney, *A Period of Exploration* (as in note 3), 43–44.

91. When interviewed by Mary Fuller McChesney, 2 May 1966, Jorge Goya remembered Still telling his class that pink and baby blue "could never be used in painting again because they had been so corrupted by their usage in American advertising" (transcript in private collection). One of the San Francisco Museum of Art's few Picasso paintings, *Jug of Flowers* (1937), was a still life in soft pastel blues and pinks. Still detested Picasso for pandering to popular taste. He told Peter Shoemaker, one of his CSFA students, that he considered Picasso a "commercial painter" (Shoemaker, interview, 10 April 1989).

92. Ernest Briggs, quoted in McChesney, *A Period of Exploration,* 64.

93. In 1958 Hassel Smith considered the absence of buyers "the number one influence on the San Francisco School," pointing out that in the Bay Area, "there is

absolutely no market for avantgarde or 'modern' painting . . . Painters occasionally sell paintings (for prices under five hundred dollars), but the possibility of sale is so remote that it might just as well not exist at all" (see Smith, "Sulla scuola di San Francisco," *Evento delle arti* 2 [1958]: 26).

94. Smith, "Sulla scuola di San Francisco," 26.

95. Stillman, interview, 9 February 1994.

96. Still, quoted in Albright, *Art in the San Francisco Bay Area* (as in note 35), 31.

97. San Francisco Museum of Modern Art, *Clyfford Still* (as in note 18), 113.

98. Dugmore, interview, 1 March 1988.

99. The list of members in San Francisco Museum of Modern Art, *Clyfford Still,* 135, is incorrect. The initial roster consisted of Jeremy Anderson, Ernest Briggs, W. Cohantz, Hubert Crehan, Edward Dugmore, Jorge Goya, William Huberich, Jack Jefferson, Kio Kiozumi, Zoe Longfield, Frann Spencer, and Horst Trave. Each member paid ten dollars per month to cover the rent of one hundred and twenty. The order of exhibitions was determined in the most democratic manner possible, by pulling straws. In 1950, the membership more than doubled to include nonartist members (interview with Zoe Longfield Etigson, April 1989, and with Dugmore, 21 November 1988).

100. Press release, probably written by Hubert Crehan, ca. April 1949, private collection.

101. Letter to prospective patron members from "participating artists of Metart Galleries," ca. 1950, private collection.

102. In 1949, two stores—Gump's and the City of Paris—also sometimes showed experimental abstraction, and there were a few receptive galleries, in Berkeley (Daliel's) and Sausalito (the Seashore Gallery and Bern Porter's Contemporary Gallery). But in San Francisco, the Lucien Labaudt Gallery was the only reliable venue for contemporary abstraction. Operated by the widow of the local artist Lucien Labaudt, the nonprofit Lucien Labaudt Gallery gave a number of San Francisco Abstract Expressionists, including Diebenkorn, Lobdell, McChesney, Smith, and Stillman, shows between 1946 and 1958. For more on the gallery, see Lawrence Ferling [Ferlinghetti], "The Labaudt Gallery," *Counterpoint: Magazine of Music and Applied Arts* (May 1952): 22–23; and Mary Fuller [McChesney], "Lucien Labaudt: In Memoriam," *Artforum* 1 (August 1962): 24–25.

103. Dugmore, interviewed by Mary Fuller McChesney, 4 May 1966, transcript in private collection. When I interviewed Dugmore, 21 November 1988, he said that members were "screened by honesty," not style, but nonetheless admitted that most of them ended up painting in a nonobjective expressionist manner.

104. Alfred Frankenstein, "The Art Galleries," *San Francisco Chronicle,* 12 March 1950. In 1950 Erle Loran

noted that the Metart represented "the ultra-advance-garde in painting," the sort that "is by no means unfamiliar to readers of *Art News* since the official annuals at the San Francisco Museum have been dominated by this type of painting for over two years" (see Loran, "Scheduled for San Francisco," *Art News* 49 [Summer 1950]: 54).

Chapter 4

1. In an interview, 5 July 1988, Walter Kuhlman remembered that Still was notorious in San Francisco for painting over his canvases and leaving the old dates on the back.

2. Still's annotation of the manuscript by Betty Freeman, "Clyfford Still: A Critical Study," ca. 1963, Freeman papers, roll 4060, frame 925, AAA.

3. Clement Greenberg, "'American-Type' Painting" (1955); reprinted in Greenberg, *Art and Culture* (Boston: Beacon Press, 1961), 225.

4. Still, quoted in Freeman "Clyfford Still: A Critical Study," ca. 1963, Freeman papers, roll 4060, frames 930–31, AAA.

5. Susan Landauer, "Clyfford Still and Abstract Expressionism in San Francisco," in *Clyfford Still, 1904–1980: The Buffalo and San Francisco Collections,* ed. Thomas Kellein (Munich: Prestel, 1992), 91.

6. Still, interviewed by Betty Freeman, undated, Freeman papers, roll 4060, frame 322, AAA. Under Morley, the San Francisco Museum of Art amassed an impressive collection of Latin American art. Orozco was a local favorite, and his painting *Sleeping* (1930) in the museum's collection is especially evocative of Still's work. For a history of the museum's policy of collecting Mexican art, see Sarah Newmeyer, "Mexican Art and the Museum," *San Francisco Museum of Art Quarterly Bulletin,* supplement, ser. 2, 3 (1954): 1–12.

7. Still, quoted in Katherine Kuh, "Clyfford Still, the Enigma," *Vogue* 155 (1 February 1970): 219.

8. Still confided to Betty Freeman that he used his first name because it expressed his individuality better than his surname, which he shared with his family. He told her that he believed Rembrandt did it for the same reason (notes from an interview with Still by Betty Freeman, ca. early 1960s, Freeman papers, roll 4060, frame 322, AAA).

9. Jon Schueler, interview, 13 November 1988.

10. Notes from interviews with Still by Betty Freeman, 6 and 21 April 1961, Freeman papers, roll 4060, frame 281, AAA.

11. Ironically, Spanish *duende* has been cited as the chief characteristic of Still's nemesis, Picasso; see John Richardson, *A Life of Picasso* (New York: Random House, 1991), 1, 4.

12. Landauer, "Clyfford Still," 93.

13. Interview with William Morehouse, 1 April 1989, and with Edward Dugmore, 1 March 1988.

14. Edward Dugmore, interview, 21 November 1988.

15. Betty Freeman reported that Still made "neither studies nor sketches for the large works, and he has the total concept of the painting fully laid out in his mind before he begins to paint, much as Mozart had his music complete before he wrote it down" (Freeman, "Clyfford Still: A Critical Study," third draft, 1968, Freeman papers, roll 4060, frame 588, AAA). Elmer Bischoff, in an interview, 7 July 1985, confirmed Freeman's observation. In the late 1940s at the California School of Fine Arts, he had occasion to watch Still complete an entire painting in one session without hesitating.

16. "Aristocratic radicalism" is Georg Brandes's term for Nietzsche, quoted in *Modernism, 1890– 1930,* ed. James MacFarlane and Malcolm Bradbury (New York: Penguin Books, 1976), 79.

17. Bischoff, transcript of lecture presented at the Oakland Museum, 27 October 1973, SFAI.

18. Lobdell, quoted in [Judy Stone], "New Art Explained by Sausalitans," *San Rafael Daily Independent and Marin Journal,* 22 January 1949.

19. Hubert Crehan, "Art Schools Smell Alike," *San Francisco Sunday Examiner and Chronicle,* 4 October 1970.

20. Schueler, quoted in Mary Fuller McChesney, *A Period of Exploration: San Francisco, 1945–1950* (Oakland: The Oakland Museum, 1973), 46.

21. See the San Francisco Art Association annual exhibitions at the San Francisco Museum of Art after 1950.

22. Fenichel, telephone conversation, January 1990.

23. Frankenstein, review, *San Francisco Chronicle,* 24 July 1949.

24. These comments are reproduced in Alfred Frankenstein, "Backtalk to a Critic and a Critic's Comments," *San Francisco Chronicle,* 7 August 1949.

25. For more on Still's teaching methods, see McChesney, *A Period of Exploration,* 34–51.

26. The course has been referred to as the "graduate painting class at the California School of Fine Arts by which the school became especially known throughout the world" (San Francisco Museum of Modern Art, *Clyfford Still* [San Francisco: San Francisco Museum of Modern Art, 1976], 113).

27. The class became official only in the fall of 1949, when it appeared in the course catalogue.

28. Notes from an interview with Clyfford Still by Betty Freeman, 2 April 1963, Freeman papers, roll 4060, frames 325–26, AAA.

29. According to Still, it was he who initially conceived of the school (San Francisco Museum of Modern Art, *Clyfford Still,* 113).

30.   Ibid.

31.   Still, letter to Spohn, 25 June 1948, unfilmed Spohn papers, AAA.

32.   See Michael Leja, "The Formation of an Avant-Garde in New York," in Michael Auping et al., *Abstract Expressionism: The Critical Developments* (Buffalo, N.Y.: Albright-Knox Art Gallery, 1987), 17.

33.   Barnett Newman, "The Sublime Is Now" (1948); reprinted in *Theories of Modern Art: A Source Book by Artists and Critics,* ed. Herschel B. Chipp (Berkeley and Los Angeles: University of California Press, 1968), 553.

34.   Most of the San Francisco artists remember that Rothko was generally amiable, but Hassel Smith contends that "there were quite a lot of complaints about his approach in the classroom. People would ask him things and his response was 'Why should I tell you? You're going to become a competitor. So why should I let you in on my secrets?'" (Smith, quoted in McChesney, *A Period of Exploration,* 33).

35.   Dore Ashton, *The New York School: A Cultural Reckoning* (New York: Penguin Books, 1972), 202.

36.   Although Rothko billed these sessions as a lecture course, he never lectured, according to William Morehouse, in an interview, 1 April 1989. The format was one of informal exchange; Rothko would introduce some ideas and the other artists would "hash them out with him."

37.   Hultberg, quoted in Shirley Jacks, *John Hultberg, Painter of the In-Between: Selected Paintings, 1953–1984* (Clinton, N.Y.: Fred L. Emerson Gallery, 1985), 36.

38.   See Douglas MacAgy, "Mark Rothko," *Magazine of Art* 42 (January 1949): 20–21. As Bonnie Clearwater has noted, this article, which MacAgy drafted in 1947, was among the first to address Rothko's breakthrough abstractions. See "Trying Very Hard to Think: Duchamp and the Western Round Table on Modern Art, 1949," in *West Coast Duchamp,* ed. Clearwater (Miami Beach: Grassfield Press, 1991), 48.

39.   In a letter to me, dated 1 June 1989, George Stillman recalled Rothko's speaking of "a universal language and a belief in the commonality of the origins of man. He made references to the cultural background of the race that made him feel that what he put down in paint could be understood as a universal symbol or language . . . there was a good deal of talk, perhaps even conflict, between Rothko, Still, Park and Smith with regard to the motivation of painters, be it Jungian, Freudian, or Gestalt theories . . . However, there was some care taken not to admit to having too much interest in psychology."

40.   Many of the San Francisco artists were still finishing up their military duties in the summer of 1946, but for those who were in San Francisco, Rothko's exhibition at the San Francisco Museum of Art was an important event. The show, *Oils and Watercolors by Mark Rothko* (13 August–8 September 1946), included twenty-nine paintings and was partially circulated to the Santa Barbara Museum of Art.

41.   Briggs, quoted in McChesney, *A Period of Exploration* (as in note 20), 33.

42.   Rothko, letter to Spohn, May 1948, unfilmed Spohn papers, AAA. In an earlier letter, Rothko spoke of his recurrent "nostalgia" about that summer "which pops up over and over again at any provocation." In wistful tones, he asked Spohn, "What was there about last summer that seems now to have been so magical? As I remember, there were a lot of pulls and twists which made me at that time wish it were over. Yet you, Clyff, Doug [MacAgy], etc. set up tensions which made us exist, I believe, on a very desirable plane, and I miss it." Uncannily suggesting his suicide more than twenty years later, Rothko continued: "The best that can be said about living here [in New York] is that one lives nowhere at all, which, too, I wish were over" (letter to Spohn, February 1948, unfilmed Spohn papers, AAA).

43.   Although Rothko had painted a few fully nonobjective works in 1946, he did not make his decisive move toward abstraction until after the summer of 1947; see Diane Waldman, *Mark Rothko, 1903–1970: A Retrospective* (New York: The Solomon R. Guggenheim Museum, 1978), 272. In an interview, 1 April 1989, William Morehouse remembered that the question whether or not to paint nonobjectively was one Rothko "hashed out" in his Friday afternoon discussion sessions at the California School of Fine Arts in 1947. The sculptor Claire Falkenstein confirmed this recollection when she stated unequivocally in a telephone interview, 2 November 1993: "Rothko came to San Francisco a Surrealist and left an abstractionist. I remember that quite clearly."

44.   Rothko, "The Romantics Were Prompted," *Possibilities* 1 (Winter 1947–48): 84, quoted in Irving Sandler, *The Triumph of American Painting: A History of Abstract Expressionism* (New York: Harper and Row, 1970), 149.

45.   Spohn, interviewed by Mary Fuller McChesney, 23 April 1966, transcript in private collection.

46.   For a discussion of Rothko's work of 1949, see Karen Tsujimoto, *Mark Rothko 1949: A Year in Transition, Selections from the Mark Rothko Foundation* (San Francisco: San Francisco Museum of Modern Art, 1984).

47.   Briggs, interviewed by Barbara Shikler, 12 July 1982, "Mark Rothko and His Times," transcript in AAA. The incident must have taken place in the summer of 1949, when Briggs met Rothko for the first time.

48.   Briggs, paraphrasing Rothko, ibid. When interviewed by McChesney, 23 April 1966, Spohn also recalled Rothko's telling him that Still had been a major impetus for him (transcript in private collection).

49.   Susan Landauer, *Edward Corbett: A Retrospective* (Richmond, Calif.: Richmond Art Center, 1990), 19.

50.   Draft of Guggenheim Fellowship application 1951, Corbett papers, roll 4381, frame 965, AAA.

51.   In an earlier publication, I incorrectly dated this drawing 1947; see Landauer, *Edward Corbett,* 19.

52.   Two good examples are the drawing in the collection of Lilly Fenichel in Corrales, New Mexico, and the one in the collection of the San Francisco Museum of Modern Art. The latter work was owned by Diebenkorn until the 1980s. Both drawings are untitled and dated 1948.

53.   Rothko, quoted in Seldon Rodman, *Conversations with Artists* (New York: Capricorn Books, 1961), 93–94.

54.   Still, quoted in Thomas Albright, *Art in the San Francisco Bay Area, 1945–1980: An Illustrated History* (Berkeley and Los Angeles: University of California Press, 1985), 38.

55.   See Irving Sandler, *The New York School: The Painters and Sculptors of the Fifties* (New York: Harper and Row, 1978), 82. Francis never met Rothko, although he was surely aware of his work in the late 1940s.

56.   A color reproduction of this painting can be found in Peter Selz, *Sam Francis,* rev. ed. (New York: Harry N. Abrams, 1982), 145.

57.   Francis told Peter Selz that his acquaintance with Corbett had been of considerable value in the late 1940s; see Selz, *Sam Francis,* 27. Francis and Corbett remained in contact through the early 1950s. Their correspondence can be found in the unfilmed portion of the Corbett papers, AAA. Corbett's *Black Paintings* and his white-on-white paintings, which Francis probably saw at Corbett's exhibition in Berkeley at the Studio C Gallery in 1950, may well have been a stimulus for Francis's own black monochromes and white paintings of the early 1950s.

58.   Priscilla Colt, "The Painting of Sam Francis," *Art Journal* 22 (Fall 1962): 2.

59.   Alfred Frankenstein, "Works by Corbett, Smith Hung at Fine Arts School," *San Francisco Chronicle,* 14 January 1951.

60.   This drawing is reproduced in Landauer, *Edward Corbett,* 28. Another charcoal of the same vintage in Jess's collection is so pale that it cannot be reproduced.

61.   "Redon: Drawings and Lithographs," *The Museum of Modern Art Bulletin* 19 (Winter 1952): 5; Corbett's copy is in Corbett papers, roll 4381, AAA.

62.   Copies of these poems can be found in the filmed and unfilmed Corbett papers, AAA.

63.   Draft of Guggenheim Fellowship application, 1951, Corbett papers, roll 4381, frame 967, AAA.

64.   Corbett, statement in "New Works by Two Painters," *San Francisco Art Association Bulletin* 17 (January 1951): n.p.

65.   Reinhardt's letter is reproduced in Henry Niese and Gerald Nordland, *Edward Corbett* (College Park: University of Maryland Art Gallery, 1979), 18; the original letter appears to have been lost. The catalogue Reinhardt refers to in the letter probably accompanied his exhibition at the Jewish Museum in New York in 1967. Reinhardt implies that Corbett had earlier asked him to "mention" him in this catalogue. However, Corbett is not mentioned in this publicaton or any other on Reinhardt except the essay by Lucy Lippard, in which she remarks that Corbett "dealt with near-monochrome" around the same time that Reinhardt began his black paintings in the early to mid 1950s; see Lippard, *Ad Reinhardt* (New York: Harry N. Abrams, 1981), 35, note 103.

66.   In an interview, 13 July 1989, Mary Fuller and Robert McChesney remembered that Reinhardt was a frequent visitor to the house they shared with Corbett in Point Richmond. In addition, Reinhardt took a number of photographs of Corbett's Point Richmond *Black Paintings* and included one in *Modern Artists in America,* ed. Robert Motherwell and Ad Reinhardt (New York: Wittenborn, Schultz, 1951), 79.

67.   In an interview, 1 March 1988, Edward and Eadie Dugmore described Corbett's white-on-white paintings of 1950 as having faint, almost transparent, rectangular and "sail-like" forms. The architectural critic Allan Temko recalled in a conversation, August 1989, that Corbett at that time was much enamored of Malevich's white-on-white square paintings.

68.   Still was strongly opposed to Reinhardt's aestheticism and allegiance to Neoplastic and Bauhaus traditions. In a letter to Sidney Janis, 4 April 1955, he wrote: "Openly and for many years I have rejected the sadistic Bauhaus devices and sterile color parodies of Adolph Reinhardt" (Ossorio papers, roll 3888, frames 726–27, AAA).

69.   Reinhardt shared these views in his six-week lecture course, "The Artist Today," at the California School of Fine Arts in July and August 1950. According to a letter Reinhardt sent an administrator at the school, he planned to give a lecture he had delivered at the Subjects of the Artist, entitled "Purity and Decency." He explained that "purity" referred to "a kind of 'artistic integrity' problem" and "decency" to "artists' responsibilities" (letter to Dorothy Colodny, 15 April 1950, SFAI).

70.   Mary Fuller McChesney and Robert McChesney, interview, 13 July 1989.

71.   Briggs, quoted in McChesney, *A Period of Exploration* (as in note 20), 26.

72.   Robert McChesney, quoted in McChesney, *A Period of Exploration,* 23.

73.   See Ad Reinhardt, "An Artist Asks . . . ," *San Francisco Art Association Bulletin* 16 (August–September 1950): n.p.

74.   Reinhardt, quoted in McChesney, *A Period of Exploration,* 23.

75.   Lobdell, interviewed by Terry St. John, 9 April 1980, The Oral History Collections of the AAA, roll 3198, frame 373, AAA; John Hultberg, interviewed by Mary Fuller McChesney, 6 May 1966, transcript in private collection.

76.   The portfolio, entitled *Drawings* and dated 1948, appears to have been the first group portfolio of American Abstract Expressionist prints; see Susan Landauer, *Paper Trails: San Francisco Abstract Expressionist Prints, Drawings, and Watercolors* (Santa Cruz, Calif.: The Art Museum of Santa Cruz County, 1993), 24–25. According to Lobdell, Stillman, and Kuhlman, in conversations in the fall of 1992, approximately seventy-five portfolios were ultimately printed out of a projected edition of two hundred, each containing sixteen or seventeen lithographs. The artists used a then-experimental process to make original drawings with litho and wax crayons on direct image sheets of paper and aluminum, which were run on the offset press of Eric Liden in Mill Valley. According to MacAgy, the group's intention was to bring "a visual testament of their beliefs" to "a wider public" by making their work inexpensive to acquire. Each portfolio sold for a single dollar. Copies of these portfolios can be found in the Metropolitan Museum of Art and the British Museum. See [Judy Stone], "New Art Explained by Sausalitans" (as in note 18).

77.   Stillman never shared a studio with Lobdell, as Albright asserted in *Art of the San Francisco Bay Area* (as in note 54), 316.

78.   Peter Plagens incorrectly described the Sausalito group as consisting only of Diebenkorn, Hultberg, and Lobdell in *Sunshine Muse: Contemporary Art on the West Coast* (New York: Praeger, 1974), 36–37, an error repeated in Gerald Nordland, *Richard Diebenkorn* (New York: Rizzoli International Publications, 1987), 25; and Caroline A. Jones, *Bay Area Figurative Art, 1950–1965* (San Francisco: San Francisco Museum of Modern Art; and Berkeley and Los Angeles: University of California Press, 1990), 27.

79.   Hultberg, interviewed by Mary Fuller McChesney, 6 May 1966, transcript in private collection.

80.   Although Hultberg did produce some impressive abstract work in San Francisco (notably the Oakland Museum's *Untitled,* 1948), he said, when interviewed by Mary Fuller McChesney, 6 May 1966, that he was never fully comfortable with nonobjective painting but that peer pressure compelled him to abandon figuration until after he moved to New York in 1950, when he resumed representational work (transcript in private collection).

81.   Observing that the Metart artists organized discussions and lectures on metaphysical topics, Hultberg, interviewed by Mary Fuller McChesney, 6 May 1966, noted that the Sausalito artists were more pragmatic about their art. "We thought they were too mystical, too spiritualistic" (transcript in private collection).

82.   Dugmore, interviewed by Mary Fuller McChesney, 4 May 1966, transcript in private collection.

83.   Unless otherwise noted, information pertaining to Stillman's life and work is based on interviews, 12 July 1988 and 26 March 1989.

84.   In *Art in the San Francisco Bay Area* (316), Thomas Albright described Stillman's early work as taking its inspiration from Gottlieb's painting, but in an interview, 12 July 1988, Stillman insisted there was no connection. A look at the work yields little correlation. Albright probably based his statement on a review Alfred Frankenstein wrote in 1947, in which he compared Stillman's tendency to compartmentalize his compositions to Gottlieb's pictographs (see Frankenstein, "Around the Local Galleries," *San Francisco Chronicle,* 4 April 1948).

85.   See Landauer, *Paper Trails* (as in note 76), 19–25.

86.   Stillman explained in an interview, 26 March 1989, that he destroyed his works, not because he no longer cared for them, but for a purely practical reason: they were cluttering his studio.

87.   Kuhlman disapproved of his peers' use of Bay City house paint. He attributed their carelessness about the permanence of their work to nihilism bred by the war (interview with Kuhlman by Mary Fuller McChesney, 28 November 1965, transcript in private collection).

88.   One of Kuhlman's patrons in this period was Duncan Phillips, who purchased an early landscape for the Phillips Collection.

89.   Kuhlman, letter to me, 1 October 1993.

90.   Ibid. Caroline A. Jones has described a similar delay in Lobdell's artistic response to the war. See Jones, *Frank Lobdell: Works, 1947–1992* (Stanford, Calif.: Stanford University Museum of Art, 1993), 6–7.

91.   Kuhlman wrote me, in a letter dated 1 October 1993: "Much of my time as a medical illustrator was spent in the operating room, sketch book in hand. Nights I went to the wards and made portrait drawings of the wounded. I saw the horrible effects of war. The spikes in some of my paintings are not only frightening sea forms, but surgical knives. Consequently, the darkness in my work stems not only from my Nordic heritage but from my war experiences."

92.   Such images characterize Kuhlman's *Untitled* (1948), in my own collection. I owe this insight to Mara Skov (in conversation, May 1994).

93.   Picasso's influence seems to have lain dormant for several years; in 1940, Kuhlman had driven through a blizzard with his classmate Lobdell to spend three days absorbing the Picasso retrospective at the Art Institute of Chicago.

94.   Walter Kuhlman, application for the Abraham Rosenberg Fellowship, 20 January 1950, SFAI; The Carlson Gallery, *Walter Kuhlman* (San Francisco: The Carlson Gallery, 1989), 11.

95.   See, for example, Albright, *Art in the San Francisco Bay Area* (as in note 54), 292. Kuhlman was probably

indebted to Rothko's *Multiforms,* which he first saw at the California Palace of the Legion of Honor in the winter of 1948–49. In an interview, 5 July 1988, he said he considers Rothko to have been at best "a minor influence" compared with Still.

96.   Byron McClintock, interview, 20 March 1989, and miscellaneous documents in McClintock's personal collection (McClintock was a friend of Dixon's).

97.   "State Supreme Court Awards $ to 13 Year Old," *San Francisco Examiner,* 8 November 1913, cited in Patrick L. Frank, "Abstract Expressionism in San Francisco, 1945–1950" (Ph.D. diss., George Washington University, 1992), 258.

98.   Interview with Byron McClintock, 20 March 1989.

99.   There is considerable discrepancy in the Dixon literature as to dates of his attendance, but the San Francisco Art Institute's records show that Dixon initially studied at the California School of Fine Arts from 1923 to 1926 and from 1929 to 1930.

100.   Spearheaded by Millard Sheets in Southern California, the California Watercolor School stretched from Los Angeles to Sacramento in the 1930s and 1940s. See Susan M. Anderson, *Regionalism: The California View* (Santa Barbara, Calif.: Santa Barbara Museum of Art, 1988). Anderson (48) reproduces Dixon's undated *Untitled (Furniture Store),* in the collection of the Oakland Museum.

101.   See Alfred Frankenstein's review of this show, "Around the Art Galleries," *San Francisco Chronicle,* 1 October 1939.

102.   One of these was reproduced on the cover of the *San Francisco Art Association Bulletin* (March 1945).

103.   Some of Dixon's prints of the late 1940s, however, do make recognizable figurative references.

104.   Byron McClintock, interview, 20 March 1989.

105.   Thomas Albright, "'Period of Exploration'—at Oakland Museum," *San Francisco Sunday Examiner and Chronicle,* 9 September 1973.

106.   Albright, *Art in the San Francisco Bay Area* (as in note 54), 53.

107.   Thomas Albright stated, ibid., that Dixon began teaching at the California School of Fine Arts in 1950, but the school's records show that he joined the faculty in the fall of 1949, during the last year of the MacAgy administration. For more on Dixon's printmaking, see Landauer, *Paper Trails* (as in note 76), 20–21.

108.   According to Susan M. Anderson, Dixon was Hayter's class monitor; see Anderson, *Pursuit of the Marvelous: Stanley William Hayter, Charles Howard, Gordon Onslow Ford* (Laguna Beach, Calif.: Laguna Art Museum, 1990–91), 9.

109.   For more on this exhibition, which introduced San Francisco Abstract Expressionism to many artists in Los Angeles, see Betty Turnbull, *The Last Time I Saw Ferus, 1957–1966* (Newport Beach, Calif.: Newport Harbor Art Museum, 1976), n.p.

110.   See Michel Tapié, *Morphologie autre* (Turin: Edizioni d'Arte Fratelli Pozzo, 1960). Tapié helped place Dixon's paintings in collections in Bern, Switzerland; Turin, Italy; Osaka, Japan; and Paris.

111.   Interview, 14 March 1989, with Elmer Bischoff's former wife, Jean Tickle.

112.   Interview with Hassel Smith by Paul Karlstrom, 5 September 1978, roll 3199, frame 599, AAA.

113.   Interview with Smith by Jan Butterfield, ca. 1975, Smith papers, roll 2008, frame 331, AAA.

114.   Interview with Douglas MacAgy by Mary Fuller McChesney, 30 May 1966, transcript in private collection.

115.   Morehouse, interview, 1 April 1989. For a fuller discussion of the schism between Still and his competitors, see Jones, *Bay Area Figurative Art, 1950–1965* (as in note 78), 16–18.

116.   Diebenkorn, quoted in Dan Hofstadter, "Profiles: Almost Free of the Mirror," *New Yorker* 63 (7 September 1987): 63.

117.   Elmer Bischoff felt that jazz was of paramount importance in the late 1940s. When Lu Watters, Earl Hines, Mugsey Spanier, and Kid Ory played at local clubs like the Hangover Club on Bush Street, he remembered, "we would all pile in and eat it up. We loved it! Of course we had all their recordings . . . [jazz] was very much a part of the spirit . . . the very physical and keyed-up spirit of the time. It fit very well with the paintings Park, Diebenkorn, Smith and I were doing. It had least kinship with Clyfford Still's work" (Susan Klein [Landauer], "Elmer Bischoff," *Issue: A Journal for Artists* 4 [Fall 1985]: 11).

118.   Diebenkorn, quoted in Gerald Nordland, *Richard Diebenkorn* (Washington, D.C.: Washington Gallery of Modern Art, 1964), 11.

119.   Hultberg, quoted in ibid.

120.   See, for example, Nordland, *Richard Diebenkorn* (New York: Rizzoli International Publications, 1987), 19; see also Herschel B. Chipp, "Diebenkorn Paints a Picture," *Art News* 56 (May 1957): 44.

121.   In an interview, 12 July 1991, Stillman, who commuted daily with Park to Berkeley in the late 1940s, suggested that Park destroyed most of his abstract paintings from the late 1940s because of his discomfort with abstraction and his insecurity about the reception of his work (he had great difficulty getting his paintings accepted by museum juries while students such as Stillman had little trouble). For more on Park's Abstract Expressionist period, see Richard Armstrong, *David Park* (New York: Whitney Museum of American Art; Berkeley and Los Angeles: University of California Press, 1989), 26–30; and Jones, *Bay Area Figurative Art,* 9.

122.   Diebenkorn, quoted in Armstrong, *David Park*, 28–29.

123.   Bischoff, quoted in Nordland, *Richard Diebenkorn,* (as in note 120), 20.

124.   Bischoff, quoted in Robert T. Buck, Jr., et al., *Richard Diebenkorn: Paintings and Drawings, 1943–1976* (Buffalo, N.Y.: Albright-Knox Art Gallery, 1976), 10.

125.   Diebenkorn, quoted in Hofstadter, "Profiles," 59.

126.   Gerald Nordland and Dan Hofstadter both contend that Diebenkorn first saw de Kooning's work reproduced in the *Partisan Review* in 1948 (see Hofstadter, "Profiles" [as in note 116], 63; and Nordland, *Richard Diebenkorn* [as in note 120], 35); Maurice Tuchman argues that Diebenkorn did not see the 1948 issue featuring de Kooning's work until 1950; see Buck et al., *Richard Diebenkorn,* 15.

127.   It is also worth noting that the subject Diebenkorn taught at the California School of Fine Arts from 1947 to 1949 was drawing, and his use of line seems a natural outcome of this concentration.

128.   Bischoff, quoted in Nordland, *Richard Diebenkorn* (as in note 120), 34.

129.   This painting is often dated 1950, but Diebenkorn could not have worked on it that year, as he was in Albuquerque. Smith may have finished the painting in 1950 after Diebenkorn was gone (Phyllis Diebenkorn, in conversation, June 1994).

130.   Alfred Frankenstein, "The Art Galleries," *San Francisco Chronicle,* 12 March 1950.

131.   According to Jess, they resigned because of a dispute between Mundt and Smith over a constitution that Smith and some other instructors had drawn up giving the faculty more power in administrative decision making (letter to Edward Corbett, 24 February [ca. 1952], Corbett papers, roll 4377, frames 198–201, AAA). After learning of Smith's impending termination, Park and Bischoff tendered their resignations in January 1952. Copies of these letters can be found in the SFAI.

132.   In an interview, 6 January 1989, Mundt himself attributed the faculty cutbacks to financial hardship, not personal animosity. His contention is supported by the minutes of the San Francisco Art Association Board, which show that Mundt employed delaying tactics to avoid reducing the faculty of the painting department in the early 1950s. Records of these meetings can be found in the SFAI.

133.   In a memorandum dated 6 October 1948, MacAgy informed the president of the San Francisco Art Association that the school was likely to suffer a significant decline beginning in the summer of 1949 because of a sharply reduced enrollment of veterans (administrative papers, SFAI).

134.   MacAgy, quoted in McChesney, *A Period of Exploration* (as in note 20), 84.

135.   File marked "Junior League," 1951–52, SFAI. In 1954, the San Francisco Art Association announced that the California School of Fine Arts would not reopen in the fall, but a fund-raising campaign and auction helped the school out of bankruptcy (see Lawrence Ferlinghetti, "San Francisco: Bay Area Roundup," *Art Digest* 28 [1 August 1954]: 16–17).

Chapter 5

1.   See Mary Fuller McChesney, *A Period of Exploration: San Francisco, 1945–1950* (Oakland: The Oakland Museum, 1973); Thomas Albright, "The Golden Years of Abstract Expressionism," in *Art in the San Francisco Bay Area, 1945–1980: An Illustrated History* (Berkeley and Los Angeles: University of California Press, 1985), 37–55; Michael Leonard, "The Golden Age of Bay Area Painting," *Art of California* 2 (August–September 1989): 12–19; and Rebecca Solnit, *Secret Exhibition: Six California Artists of the Cold War Era* (San Francisco: City Lights Books, 1990), 29.

2.   Renato Poggioli, *The Theory of the Avant-Garde,* trans. Gerald Fitzgerald (Cambridge: Harvard University Press, 1968), 25.

3.   For reactions of the abstract painters to Park's defection, see Caroline A. Jones, *Bay Area Figurative Art, 1950–1965* (San Francisco: San Francisco Museum of Modern Art; and Berkeley and Los Angeles: University of California Press, 1990), 16–17.

4.   Kuhlman, interview, 5 July 1988.

5.   See Albright's chapter "The Golden Years of Abstract Expressionism," in *Art in the San Francisco Bay Area,* 37–55.

6.   Kuhlman, in an interview, 5 July 1988, said things improved when he and Lobdell took jobs as chefs for the Glad Hand, the restaurant that preceded Scoma's on the Sausalito wharf. Although they put in long hours in the kitchen at night, the job gave them time to paint during the day.

7.   Built in 1853 by Henry Wagner Halleck, Abraham Lincoln's future chief of staff, the Montgomery Block was torn down in the 1970s to make room for the Transamerica Building. For a fascinating history, see Idwal Jones, *Ark of Empire: San Francisco's Montgomery Block* (New York: Doubleday Books, 1951).

8.   The *Montgomery Street Skylight,* the weekly paper that was the building's semi-official organ, shows that by the end of World War II the Montgomery Block was occupied mostly by an older generation of modernists including Matthew Barnes, Beniamino Bufano, Luke Gibney, Dong

Kingman, Dorr Bothwell, Sargent Johnson, and Justin Murray.

9.   Bruce Nixon, paraphrasing Deborah Remington, in John Natsoulas et al., *Lyrical Vision: The Six Gallery, 1954–1957* (Davis, Calif.: Natsoulas/Novelozo Gallery, 1990), 36.

10.   For a history of the building, see Stephen Hall, "Historic Building Gutted," *San Francisco Chronicle,* 24 July 1978.

11.   Ethel Gechtoff's East and West Gallery on Fillmore Street should not be confused with the East West Gallery of Fine Arts, which was operated by the San Francisco Western Women's Club during the 1920s and 1930s in the San Francisco Women's Building on Sutter Street. Another gallery with a similar name was Rudolph Schaeffer's East-West Arts Gallery, which opened in 1950 in Chinatown. Like the earlier East West Gallery of Fine Arts, Schaeffer's gallery was "devoted to the showing of the ancient Oriental arts alternating with Western contemporary arts," according to the gallery's initial press release (quoted in Alfred Frankenstein, "The Local Galleries in Brief Review," *San Francisco Chronicle,* 5 March 1950). Gechtoff's East and West Gallery, by contrast, endeavored to bring together the art of the East and West Coasts—she had earlier operated a gallery in Philadelphia (interview with Gechtoff's daughter, Sonia Gechtoff, 3 March 1988).

12.   Interview with Brown by Paul Karlstrom, 1 July 1975, roll 3196, frame 1028, AAA.

13.   Sandra Leonard Starr, *Lost and Found in California: Four Decades of Assemblage Art* (Santa Monica, Calif.: James Corcoran Gallery, Shoshana Wayne Gallery, and Pence Gallery, 1988), 75.

14.   See Leonard, "The Golden Age of Bay Area Painting" (as in note 1), 19; Peter Plagens, *Sunshine Muse: Contemporary Art on the West Coast* (New York: Praeger, 1974), 56. Calcagno and Grillo are often described as being part of this exodus in 1950, but Grillo moved to New York much earlier, in 1947, and Calcagno did not settle there until 1955.

15.   See David L. Witt, *Taos Moderns: Art of the New* (Santa Fe, N.Mex: Red Crane Books, 1992).

16.   Thomas B. Hess, "The Modern Museum's Fifteen: Where U.S. Extremes Meet," *Art News* 51 (April 1952), quoted in Susan Landauer, *Edward Corbett: A Retrospective* (Richmond, Calif.: Richmond Art Center, 1990), 11.

17.   Landauer, *Edward Corbett,* 27. There is some evidence that this exclusion was mutually determined. Irving Sandler is quoted as having said that Newman "and the group" intentionally excluded Corbett from a show in New York. See Jeffrey Wechsler, *Abstract Expressionism: Other Dimensions. An Introduction to Small Scale Painterly Abstraction in America, 1940–1965* (New Brunswick, N.J.: The Jane Voorhees Zimmerli Art Museum, 1989), 77.

18.   Irving Sandler, *The New York School: The Painters and Sculptors of the Fifties* (New York: Harper and Row, 1978), 75–78; *School of New York: Some Younger Artists,* ed. B. H. Friedman (New York: Grove Press, 1959).

19.   Mary Fuller [McChesney], "Was There a San Francisco School?" *Artforum* 9 (January 1971): 47–48.

20.   Still, letter to Spohn, 22 November 1957, Spohn papers, AAA.

21.   Jon Schueler, interview, 3 March 1988.

22.   Ibid.

23.   In an interview, 4 September 1989, Dugmore said he had been interested in Asian calligraphy since the 1930s.

24.   See, for example, his *Untitled SF B-3* (1950), reproduced in Susan Landauer, *Paper Trails: San Francisco Abstract Expressionist Prints, Drawings, and Watercolors* (Santa Cruz, Calif.: The Art Museum of Santa Cruz County, 1993), plate 9.

25.   Dore Ashton, "Art: A Dugmore Show," *New York Times,* 29 April 1960. See also, Dore Ashton, *Edward Dugmore, Burning Bright: Paintings, 1950–1959* (Los Angeles: Manny Silverman Gallery, 1991).

26.   Alfred Frankenstein, "Around the Local Art Galleries," *San Francisco Chronicle,* 10 April 1949.

27.   Edward Dugmore, interview, 4 September 1989.

28.   Still was probably the least knowledgeable of the three about the physical properties of oil paint, and indeed, many of his paintings have not survived well. Still's comparative lack of formal instruction may have hurt him in this regard. By contrast, Dugmore had a thorough classical training in the tradition of oil painting at the Hartford School of Art, and Briggs learned how to grind and mix pigments from Dugmore (Edward Dugmore, interview, 4 September 1989).

29.   Lawrence Ferling [Ferlinghetti], "Coast-to-Coast: San Francisco," *Art Digest* 28 (15 October 1953): 12.

30.   Connie Reyes, interview, 17 February 1994.

31.   Ibid.

32.   Richard Brilliant, in conversation, 18 February 1994.

33.   See the issue of the *Artist's View* by and about Philip Roeber (March 1954). This short-lived little magazine was edited and published by the San Francisco figurative painter Claire Mahl. The journal, reportedly the brainchild of Robert Duncan, ran for eight numbers, each authored by a single San Francisco artist.

34.   Motherwell, quoted by Ciro Cozzi, in conversation, 27 November 1993.

35.   In a letter to me, dated 3 January 1989, Jefferson stated that Tomlin was only of superficial interest to him in the early 1950s: "For a short time I was interested in the all

over aspect," he wrote, "but turned off by the decorative aspect of Tomlin's work."

36. Thomas Albright, "A Rare Look at a Pair of Local Artists," *San Francisco Chronicle,* 23 February 1984.

37. McChesney seems never to have been interested in the work of Stanley William Hayter, as Thomas Albright has written. Although McChesney's fluid line bears some resemblance to that of Hayter, a look at McChesney's watercolors of the early 1940s shows that he was working in this mode long before seeing Hayter's work. McChesney himself, in an interview, 14 July 1988, denied that Hayter was ever an influence. Cf. Albright, *Art in the San Francisco Bay Area* (as in note 1), 297.

38. Alfred Frankenstein, review, *San Francisco Chronicle,* 29 November 1953; "McChesney's Paintings Reflect a Full Life," *San Francisco Chronicle,* 19 April 1957; and "Northern California: David Park, Fenton Kastner, Robert McChesney," *Art in America* 42 (Winter 1954): 48–53.

39. Alfred Frankenstein, *San Francisco Chronicle,* 8 November 1959.

40. Alfred Frankenstein, "McChesney's Paintings Reflect a Full Life," *San Francisco Chronicle,* 19 April 1957.

41. Smith, quoted in McChesney, *A Period of Exploration* (as in note 1), 21.

42. Interview with Jorge Goya by Mary Fuller McChesney, 2 May 1966, transcript in private collection.

43. That Smith remained a Marxist after the war is indicated by his contribution of a linocut to *The Communist Manifesto in Pictures* (San Francisco: International Book Store, 1948), a publication to which McChesney and Corbett also submitted illustrations. Stillman, in conversation, 9 February 1994, remembered discovering that Smith was a member of the Communist Party by accident. Sometime between 1948 and 1949 Smith was giving Stillman a ride in his Packard, when they were pulled over by the police for speeding. When the officer asked for indentification, Smith mistakenly handed over his Communist Party card.

44. Jess, interview, 28 April 1989.

45. James Keeney, telephone interview, 15 June 1990.

46. Smith's interest in assemblage art began with his contribution to Clay Spohn's *Museum of Unknown and Little-Known Objects* (1949), which consisted of what Smith described as a "wildly reorganized bent-wood chair" (Smith, handwritten answers to questions posed by Kevin Power for an interview published under the title "A Conversation with Hassel Smith," ca. 1975, Smith papers, roll 2008, frame 358, AAA). In 1950 Smith and Diebenkorn showed assemblage works in a joint exhibition at the Lucien Labaudt Gallery. Some of the works in the show included, according to Frankenstein, "sculpture made of old weathered boards and a miscellany of other objects,

including deceased electric bulbs, and in one case, a piece of radiator hose from an automobile" (Alfred Frankenstein, *San Francisco Chronicle,* 12 May 1950).

47. See Susan Landauer, "Clyfford Still and Abstract Expressionism in San Francisco," in *Clyfford Still, 1904–1980: The Buffalo and San Francisco Collections,* ed. Thomas Kellein (Munich: Prestel, 1992), 99–100.

48. Allan Temko, *Hassel Smith: Paintings, 1954–1975* (San Francisco: San Francisco Museum of Modern Art: 1975), n.p.

49. Ibid.

50. According to Lilly Fenichel, in a telephone interview, 16 April 1990, Smith "detested de Kooning's work" in the 1950s.

51. Diebenkorn told Gerald Nordland that "Hassel's drawing had grown out of Maurice Sterne's teaching at the CSFA, an exuberant system of lines in opposition" (Gerald Nordland, *Richard Diebenkorn* [New York: Rizzoli International Publications, 1987], 35). This exuberant application of line can be seen in a drawing by Smith entitled *Street Scene, Columbia Number 2,* which was reproduced in the catalogue for the San Francisco Art Association's *Annual Exhibition of Drawings and Prints* at the San Francisco Museum of Art in 1942.

52. Thomas Albright, "Outspoken Man with a Brush, "*San Francisco Chronicle,* 18 May 1978.

53. Hassel Smith, *The Artist's View,* no. 1 (July 1952), n.p. (see note 33).

54. Interview with Still by Betty Freeman, 6 and 21 April 1961, Freeman papers, roll 4060, frame 283, AAA.

55. This painting is reproduced upside down and without its proper title in Peter Plagens, *Sunshine Muse* (as in note 14), 39. It is currently in the collection of Mag Dimond.

56. Smith, interview, 25 March 1988.

57. Hassel Smith, "Sulla scuola di San Francisco," *Evento delle arti* 2 (1958): 27.

58. Ibid.

59. Thomas Albright made a similar observation: "In general, Bay Area Abstract Expressionism in the 1950s separated into two district branches, the extremes of which were defined by the painting of Frank Lobdell and Hassel Smith" (see Albright, *Art in the San Francisco Bay Area* [as in note 1], 46–47).

60. Caroline A. Jones, *Frank Lobdell: Works, 1947–1992* (Stanford, Calif.: Stanford University Museum of Art, 1993), 6.

61. Interview with Lobdell by Terry St. John, 9 April 1980, roll 3198, frame 315, AAA.

62. Lobdell, interview, 20 June 1988.

63. Ibid.

64.   Lobdell, quoted in [Judy Stone], "New Art Explained by Sausalitans, "*San Rafael Daily Independent and Marin Journal,* 22 January 1949.

65.   Interview with Lobdell by Terry St. John, 9 April 1980, roll 3198, frame 327, AAA.

66.   Ibid.

67.   Lobdell, interview, 20 June 1988.

68.   Lobdell, quoted in [Stone], "New Art Explained by Sausalitans."

69.   Walter Kuhlman, in a telephone conversation, 15 February 1991, remembered that in the late 1940s Lobdell had recurring nightmares about the "blood and guts spilling out of men" he had seen overseas during the war.

70.   Jones, *Frank Lobdell,* 7.

71.   Lobdell, interview, 20 June 1988. *October 5, 1949* is reproduced in Walter Hopps, *Frank Lobdell: Paintings and Graphics from 1948 to 1965* (Pasadena, Calif: Pasadena Art Museum, 1966), n.p.

72.   Kuhlman, in an interview, 5 July 1988, related that this was what he and Lobdell called Auguste Herbin, Victor Vasarely, and other Parisian hard-edge abstractionists.

73.   Ibid.

74.   Interview with Lobdell by Terry St. John, 9 April 1980, roll 3198, frame 341, AAA.

75.   Lobdell's use of heavy dark lines that appear burned may stem from his study of the newly discovered caves of Lascaux (interview, 4 October 1993).

76.   This painting is reproduced in Diana C. duPont et al., *San Francisco Museum of Modern Art: The Painting and Sculpture Collection* (New York: Hudson Hills Press, 1985), 191.

77.   Thomas Albright, "Lobdell's Monastic Commitment," *San Francisco Chronicle,* 30 January 1983.

78.   In an interview, 20 June 1988, Lobdell acknowledged the importance of existentialism in his thinking during the late 1940s and 1950s.

79.   Lobdell, interview, 20 June 1988.

80.   Herschel B. Chipp, "This Summer in San Francisco," *Art News* 57 (Summer 1958): 48.

81.   Lobdell, interview, 20 June 1988.

82.   Ibid.

83.   Ibid. Peter Boswell has traced some of Lobdell's symbols to Jung; see Thomas Albright and Peter Boswell, *Frank Lobdell: Paintings and Monotypes* (San Francisco: San Francisco Museum of Modern Art, 1983), 16.

84.   Lobdell also took some of his imagery from Goya's *Caprichos* (interview, 11 December 1991).

85.   Charles Miedzinsky, "Frank Lobdell: Painting the Spiritual Quest," *Artweek* 14 (12 February 1983): 1.

86.   Robert T. Buck, Jr., et al., *Richard Diebenkorn: Paintings and Drawings, 1943–1976* (Buffalo, N.Y.: Albright-Knox Art Gallery, 1976), 12.

87.   Diebenkorn, quoted in Joseph Pulitzer, Jr., *Modern Painting, Drawing, and Sculpture Collected by Louise and Joseph Pulitzer, Jr.* (Cambridge: Fogg Art Museum, Harvard University, 1957), 31.

88.   See Phyllis Dorset, "La Galeria Escondida: A Taos Retrospective," *Artspace* 11 (Fall 1987): 43–49.

89.   Diebenkorn, quoted in Nordland, *Richard Diebenkorn* (as in note 51), 43.

90.   Dore Ashton, "Art," *Arts and Architecture* 73 (April 1956): 11.

91.   Richard Diebenkorn, quoted in Phillip Brookman and Walker Melion, *Richard Diebenkorn, Drawings, 1944–1973* (Santa Cruz, Calif.: Mary Porter Sesnon Gallery, University of California at Santa Cruz, 1974), 8.

92.   Caroline A. Jones has appropriately called it "the reluctant movement" (*Bay Area Figurative Art, 1950–1965* [San Francisco: San Francisco Museum of Modern Art; Berkeley and Los Angeles: University of California Press, 1990], 37).

93.   I use the term "second-generation" here to denote the artists who entered the San Francisco School's milieu in the 1950s and were not part of the germinal period of Abstract Expressionism, from about 1947 to 1950.

94.   Gechtoff and Kelly were part of this group as well, but they should not be viewed as followers of Smith. Although his imprint is apparent in their early San Francisco work, Gechtoff was influenced as much by Still and Briggs, and Kelly, by Post-Impressionism.

95.   A bulletin dated 25 August 1952, advertising his course for a fee of thirty dollars, describes the "informal lecture and discussion meetings" as focusing on "the idea of painting as metaphor [and] painting as the transmutation of experience into a form of itself." Smith's suspicion of such critical rhetoric as Harold Rosenberg's freshly minted term "action painting" is implied by his promise that "every effort will be made to avoid those clichés of criticism which, appearing constantly in newspapers, magazines, books and talk, have made it necessarily difficult for the person in search of it to discover a significant attachment for painting, even in its presence" (SFAI).

96.   Smith initially planned a full-fledged school rather than an informal lecture series. He tried to recruit Edward Corbett's help with a program that would have included three afternoon painting classes and one evening seminar per week. It was Smith's hope that if the school could get GI accreditation, it might "clean CSFA out" (letter to Corbett, ca. 1952, Corbett papers, roll 4377, frame 223, AAA).

97.   Sonia Gechtoff, in an interview, 3 March 1988, remembered that she and her peers used to "pore over *Art News* to see what was happening in the East" in the 1950s.

"De Kooning was the artist most admired in San Francisco then," she recalled.

98. Kelly, quoted in Stacey Moss, *Mediating Abstraction and Figuration: The Paintings of James Kelly, 1952–1990* (Belmont, Calif.: Wiegand Gallery, College of Notre Dame, 1990), n.p.

99. Kelly, interview, 3 March 1988.

100. Whitney Museum of American Art, *Young America 1960* (New York: Whitney Museum of American Art, 1960), 21.

101. King Ubu hosted two group exhibitions of the artists associated with Smith's Potrero Hill/Mission Street atelier, both in the summer of 1953: the first featured Relf Case, Roy De Forest, James Kelly, Adelie Landis, Hassel Smith, and Julius Wasserstein; the second included Richard Brodney, Madeleine Dimond, Lilly Fenichel, Sonia Gechtoff, Seymour Locks, and Leslie Sherman. Smith, Kelly, Gechtoff, Wasserstein, De Forest, and Dimond also showed at the Kaufmann Art Gallery in New York in an exhibition in 1954 entitled *From San Francisco: A New Language in Painting.* See the review "San Francisco Group," signed A. N., *Art Digest* 29 (1 March 1954): 18.

102. Alfred Frankenstein, "Sonia Gechtoff Exhibit Blazes with Vision," *San Francisco Chronicle,* 23 January 1957.

103. Gechtoff, interview, 3 March 1988.

104. Ibid.

105. Ibid.

106. Gerald Nordland, "Art," *Frontier* 10 (January 1959): 21.

107. Gechtoff, in conversation, 4 December 1993.

108. John Saccaro, quoted in George P. Tomlin, *Saccaro: Sensorist Paintings* (Oakland: Oakland Art Museum, 1958), n.p.

109. In an interview, 3 March 1988, Gechtoff recalled her surprise when she visited New York galleries in 1956 after a five-year absence from the East. "The colors were so brilliant," she said, "compared with San Francisco's earth tones—browns, whites, grays, and ochers."

110. In an interview, 3 March 1988, Kelly recalled that Briggs in particular "had apoplexy over that work."

111. Kelly, ibid., explained that he was simply curious to know whether he could "paint a Still."

112. D. H. Lawrence, quoted in David Perkins, *A History of Modern Poetry: Modernism and After* (Cambridge: Harvard University Press, 1987), 494.

113. For an excellent discussion of the development of open-form poetry in San Francisco and New York during the 1940s and 1950s, see Perkins, *A History of Modern Poetry,* 486–552. See also Michael Davidson, *The San Francisco Renaissance: Poetics and Community at Mid-Century* (Cambridge: Cambridge University Press, 1989).

114. Jess, interview, 14 August 1989.

115. Susan Landauer, *Edward Corbett* (as in note 16), 27.

116. Hedrick, interview with Paul Karlstrom, 10 June 1974, transcript in AAA.

117. For more on the King Ubu, see Christopher Wagstaff, *An Art of Wondering: The King Ubu Gallery, 1952–1953* (Davis, Calif.: Natsoulas/Novelozo Gallery, 1989).

118. For more on the Six, see John Natsoulas et al., *Lyrical Vision: The Six Gallery, 1954–1957* (Davis, Calif.: Natsoulas/Novelozo Gallery, 1990).

119. Albright, *Art in the San Francisco Bay Area* (as in note 1), 83. Several versions of the event are recounted in Natsoulas et al., *Lyrical Vision,* 41. According to Rebecca Solnit, Spicer staged Happenings as early as 1954 under the pretext of teaching a poetry course at the California School of Fine Arts; see her *Secret Exhibition* (as in note 1), 47.

120. Jack Kerouac, *The Dharma Bums* (New York: New American Library, 1958), 13; quoted in Davidson, *The San Francisco Renaissance,* 3.

121. Solnit, *Secret Exhibition,* 53.

122. Fred Martin, "The Birth of the Thing, or Some Recent Developments in the Art of the San Francisco Bay Area," ca. 1956, in the Martin papers, roll 1129, frames 458–59, AAA.

123. Albright, *Art in the San Francisco Bay Area,* 93.

124. DeFeo often spoke of the "polychromatic" qualities she hoped to achieve in her grisaille abstractions, much as the *sumi-e* artists of Asia spoke of the infinite "colors" of black. She may well have come under the influence of the renown *sumi-e* artist Chiura Obata, who taught at the University of California at Berkeley for many years.

125. DeFeo, statement in "New Talent, U.S.A.: Painting," *Art in America* 49 (Spring 1961): 30; quoted in Sidra Stich, with essays by Michael McClure and Brigid Doherty, *Jay DeFeo: Works on Paper* (Berkeley: University Art Museum, University of California, 1989), 19.

126. DeFeo later remembered: "Wally and I didn't realize the prestige of being included in such a show. It really surprises people that we were the only people included in that show who didn't make an effort to go to the opening. The whole show was a kind of coming out party, I discovered later" (quoted in Solnit, *Secret Exhibition,* 77).

127. Fred Martin, quoted in Solnit, *Secret Exhibition,* 78.

128. *The Rose* was removed to the California School of Fine Arts (now the San Francisco Art Institute), ostensibly for a short time while awaiting funds for conservation. After a number of years, when the money could not be raised, it was decided that the work should be covered, and a wall was built in front of it, closing it off from viewers. It is now in the collection of the Whitney Museum of American Art.

129.   Corbett's *Paintings for Puritans* (1955–57), for all their reductive starkness, constituted a short-lived Minimalist phase well *avant la lettre*.

130.   For more on Charles Strong, see Bruce Nixon, *Charles Strong* (Davis, Calif.: Natsoulas/ Novelozo Gallery, 1991).

131.   See "The Human Figure Returns in Separate Ways and Places," *Life* 52 (8 June 1962): 54–61; and "Up from Goopiness," *Time* 69 (27 April 1962): 48–49.

132.   Cited in Thomas Albright et al., *Rolling Renaissance: San Francisco Underground Art in Celebration, 1945–1968,* 2d ed. (San Francisco: Intersection, Center for Religion and the Arts, 1976), 13.

133.   The artists' response to this deluge of popular attention is typified by the following passage from a letter to Edward Dugmore from a friend in 1958: "Have been bartending at Vesuvio's three nights a week, but the place is starting to bug me. North Beach, especially Grant Ave., has had so much publicity with all this crap about Beatniks [who] knock themselves out more than ever to live up to the myths created by the newspapers. Not a day goes by without picking up a paper and finding some article on the Beat set . . . the phonies have moved in, in full force . . . If you found it hard before, you would puke now . . . I want to get the hell out of there" (letter from unknown correspondent to Dugmore, 5 August 1958, unfilmed Dugmore papers, AAA).

134.   The term Funk Art came into general usage after Peter Selz's exhibition at the University Art Museum in Berkeley in 1967. See Selz, *Funk* (Berkeley: University Art Museum, University of California, 1967). The etymology of "funky" is less clear, but probably the word was initially used by jazz musicians. By the early 1950s, according to Manuel Neri, "artists were using the term to describe, not content, but a certain look, a disregard for finish" (quoted in Sandra Leonard Starr, *Lost and Found in California* (as in note 13), 94.

135.   Alfred Frankenstein, "Northern California: David Park, Fenton Kastner, Robert McChesney," *Art in America* 42 (Winter 1954): 48.

136.   Herschel B. Chipp, "Summer Events: San Francisco," *Art News* 55 (Summer 1956): 22.

137.   For a detailed chronicle of the critical debate on the decline of the New York School, see Irving Sandler, *The New York School* (as in note 18), 278–87.

138.   Paul Mills, "Bay Area Figurative," *Art in America* 52 (June 1964): 43.

139.   See Sandler, *The New York School,* 283.

140.   Ibid., 146.

141.   Dugmore exhibited assemblage works in his one-man show at Metart Galleries in 1949. For reproductions of Smith's and Diebenkorn's assemblage art of the early 1950s,

see Starr, *Lost and Found in California,* 24–25. Other San Francisco artists who considered themselves principally painters explored assemblage art during the 1950s, notably Joan Brown and Jay DeFeo.

142.   Hilton Kramer, "Pure and Impure Diebenkorn," *Arts Magazine* 38 (December 1963): 46. Writing about Park, Bischoff, and Diebenkorn as a group in 1960, Kramer protested: "These painters leave painting in exactly the same state of exhaustion in which they found it. They refuse to bring any ideas to their work which might violate the painting method they favor, a method they have inherited but not enlarged" (quoted in Sandler, *The New York School*, 284).

143.   Park, quoted in Paul Mills, *Contemporary Bay Area Figurative Painting* (Oakland: Oakland Art Museum, 1957), 7.

144.   Bischoff, quoted in Buck et al., *Richard Diebenkorn* (as in note 86), 9.

145.   Thomas Albright, *Art in the San Francisco Bay Area* (as in note 1), 98.

146.   Sam Hunter used "aesthetics of boredom" as a play on Susan Sontag's "aesthetics of silence" to characterize the general artistic sensibility in New York during the 1960s (Sam Hunter and John Jacobus, *American Art of the Twentieth Century: Painting, Sculpture, Architecture* [New York: Harry N. Abrams, 1973], 372).

147.   As Sandra Starr has noted, the first-generation assemblage artists cultivated "a muted, almost monochromatic palette of burnt sepias, beige, umber, black, brown and gray"—in other words, a palette very much like that of the San Francisco School (Starr, *Lost and Found in California,* 16).

148.   Brown, quoted in Solnit, *Secret Exhibition* (as in note 1), 68.

149.   Bruce Conner, quoted in Albright, *Art in the San Francisco Bay Area,* 98.

150.   Among the artists who exhibited at Berman's Semina Art Gallery in 1960 were Paul Beattie, Charles Brittin, George Herms, John Reed, Arthur Richer, and Edmund Teskin.

151.   See Thomas Albright, "Mythmakers," *The Art Gallery* 18 (February 1975): 12–17, 44–45.

152.   Hilton Kramer, "Wiley of the West: Dude Ranch Dada," *New York Times,* 16 May 1971. See also Albright, "Mythmakers," 12–17, 44–45.

153.   Even in the 1940s San Franciscans regarded Emperor Norton fondly; when his remains were moved to a cemetery south of San Francisco, an infantry detachment fired a military salute and taps were played over his grave. See Workers of the Writer's Program of the Work Projects Administration in Northern California, *San Francisco: The Bay and Its Cities* (New York: Hastings House, 1947), 132.

Books and Exhibition Catalogues

Albright, Thomas. *Art in the San Francisco Bay Area, 1945–1980: An Illustrated History.* Berkeley and Los Angeles: University of California Press, 1985.

———. *On Art and Artists: Essays by Thomas Albright.* Edited by Beverly Hennessey. San Francisco: Chronicle Books, 1989.

Albright, Thomas, et al. *Rolling Renaissance: San Francisco Underground Art in Celebration, 1945–1968,* 2d ed. San Francisco: Intersection, Center for Religion and the Arts, 1975.

Baird, Joseph Armstrong, Jr., ed. *Directions in Bay Area Painting: A Survey of Three Decades, 1940s–1960s.* Cat. Davis, Calif.: Richard L. Nelson Gallery and The Fine Arts Collection, Department of Art, University of California, Davis, 1983.

California Palace of the Legion of Honor. *First Spring Annual Exhibition.* Foreword by Jermayne MacAgy, introduction by Alfred Frankenstein. Cat. San Francisco: California Palace of the Legion of Honor, 1946.

———. *Second Annual Exhibition of Painting.* Foreword by Thomas Carr Howe, Jr., introduction by Jermayne MacAgy. Cat. San Francisco: California Palace of the Legion of Honor, 1947–48.

———. *The Third Annual Exhibition of Painting.* Foreword by Thomas Carr Howe, Jr., essay by Jermayne MacAgy. Cat. San Francisco: California Palace of the Legion of Honor, 1948–49.

———. *The Fourth Annual Exhibition of Contemporary American Painting.* Essays by Thomas Carr Howe, Jr., Jermayne MacAgy, and Frederick S. Bartlett. Cat. San Francisco: California Palace of the Legion of Honor, 1950–51.

Coplans, John. *West Coast, 1945–1969.* Exh. cat. Pasadena, Calif.: Pasadena Art Museum, 1969.

Crocker-Citizens National Bank. *A Century of California Painting, 1870–1970.* Exh. cat. Los Angeles: Crocker-Citizens National Bank, 1970.

Dallas Museum of Fine Arts. *Poets of the Cities: New York and San Francisco, 1950–1965.* Exh. cat. Dallas: Dallas Museum of Fine Arts, 1974.

Di Suvero, Victor. *A Survey of Bay Area Art.* San Francisco: Broadcast Productions, 1953.

duPont, Diana C., Katherine Church Holland, Garna Garren Muller, and Laura L. Sueoka. *San Francisco Museum of Modern Art: The Painting and Sculpture Collection.* Foreword by Henry T. Hopkins. New York: Hudson Hills Press, 1985.

Frankenstein, Alfred, et al. *Art and Artist.* Berkeley and Los Angeles: University of California Press, 1956.

Goodrich, Lloyd. *Fifty California Artists.* Exh. cat. New York: Whitney Museum of American Art, 1962.

Holland, Katherine Church. *From the Collection: The Gifts of Jermayne MacAgy.* Exh. cat. San Francisco: San Francisco Museum of Modern Art, 1983.

Jones, Caroline A. *Bay Area Figurative Art, 1950–1965.* Exh. cat. San Francisco: San Francisco Museum of Modern Art; and Berkeley and Los Angeles: University of California Press, 1990.

Karlstrom, Paul J., ed. *On the Edge of America: California Modernist Art, 1900–1950.* Washington, D.C., and San Francisco: Archives of American Art of the Smithsonian Institution in Association with Fine Arts Museums of San Francisco; and Berkeley and Los Angeles: University of California Press, 1996.

Landauer, Susan. *Paper Trails: San Francisco Abstract Expressionist Prints, Drawings, and Watercolors.* Exh. cat. Santa Cruz, Calif.: The Art Museum of Santa Cruz County, 1993.

Leering, Jan. *Kompas 4: West Coast U.S.A.* Exh. cat. Eindhoven, The Netherlands: Stedelijk van Abbemuseum, 1969.

Long Beach Municipal Art Center. *California Painting: Forty Painters.* Exh. cat. Long Beach, Calif.: Municipal Art Center, 1956.

Loran, Erle, Weldon Kees, and Ernest Mundt. *Painting and Sculpture: The San Francisco Art Association.* Berkeley and Los Angeles: University of California Press, 1952.

MacAgy, Douglas. *Faculty Exhibition.* Cat. San Francisco: California Palace of the Legion of Honor, 1946.

————, ed. "The Western Round Table on Modern Art." In *Modern Artists in America,* ed. Robert Motherwell and Ad Reinhardt. New York: Wittenborn, Schultz, 1951.

MacAgy, Jermayne. *Contemporary American Painting.* Exh. cat. San Francisco: California Palace of the Legion of Honor, 1945.

————. *Fifteen Paintings by Nine Artists in San Francisco.* Exh. brochure. Seattle: Henry Art Gallery, University of Washington, Seattle, 1950.

————. *Large Scale Drawings by Modern Artists.* Exh. cat. San Francisco: California Palace of the Legion of Honor, 1950.

McChesney, Mary Fuller. *A Period of Exploration: San Francisco, 1945–1950.* Exh. cat. Oakland: The Oakland Museum, 1973.

Monte, J. *Late Fifties at the Ferus.* Exh. cat. Los Angeles: Los Angeles County Museum of Art, 1968.

Morley, Grace McCann. *Art of Our Time.* Exh. cat. San Francisco: San Francisco Museum of Art, 1945.

————. *Art in the Twentieth Century.* Exh. cat. San Francisco: San Francisco Museum of Art, 1955.

————. *Pacific Coast Art: United States' Representation at the Third Biennial of São Paulo.* Exh. cat. San Francisco: San Francisco Museum of Art, 1956.

Moss, Stacey. *The Abstract Expressionist Years and After: Jack Jefferson, Frank Lobdell, Alvin Light.* Exh. cat. Belmont, Calif.: Wiegand Gallery, College of Notre Dame, 1989.

Natsoulas, John, Rebecca Solnit, Michael McClure, and Bruce Nixon. *Lyrical Vision: The Six Gallery, 1954–1957.* Exh. cat. Davis, Calif.: Natsoulas/Novelozo Gallery, 1990.

Newman, Jim, and Terry St. John. *The Dilexi Years, 1958–1970.* Exh. cat. Oakland: The Oakland Museum, 1984.

Orr-Cahall, Christina, ed. *The Art of California: Selected Works from the Collection of The Oakland Museum.* Oakland: The Oakland Museum, 1984.

Painting and Sculpture in California: The Modern Era. Preface by Henry T. Hopkins. Exh. cat. San Francisco: San Francisco Museum of Modern Art, 1976.

Plagens, Peter. *Sunshine Muse: Contemporary Art on the West Coast.* New York: Praeger Publishers, 1974.

Richmond Art Center. *Fourth Annual Exhibition: Oil and Sculpture.* Cat. Richmond, Calif.: Richmond Art Center, 1954.

————. *Directions: Bay Area Painting, 1957.* Exh. cat. Richmond, Calif.: Richmond Art Center, 1957.

Sandler, Irving. *The Triumph of American Painting: A History of Abstract Expressionism.* New York: Harper and Row, 1970.

————. *The New York School: The Painters and Sculptors of the Fifties.* New York: Harper and Row, 1978.

San Francisco Art Association. *Sixtieth Annual Exhibition: Oil, Tempera, and Sculpture.* Cat. San Francisco Museum of Art, 1940.

————. *[Fifth] Annual Exhibition of Drawings and Prints, San Francisco Art Association.* Cat. San Francisco Museum of Art, 1941.

————. *Sixty-first Annual Exhibition: Oil, Tempera on Panel, and Sculpture.* Cat. San Francisco Museum of Art, 1941.

————. *[Sixth] Annual Exhibition of Drawings and Prints, San Francisco Art Association.* Cat. San Francisco Museum of Art, 1942.

————. *Sixty-second Annual Exhibition: Oil, Tempera on Panel, and Sculpture.* Cat. San Francisco Museum of Art, 1942.

————. *[Eighth] Annual Exhibition of Drawings and Prints, San Francisco Art Association.* Cat. San Francisco Museum of Art, 1944.

————. *Sixty-fourth Annual Exhibition: Oil, Tempera on Panel, and Sculpture.* Cat. San Francisco Museum of Art, 1944.

————. *Ninth Annual Drawing and Print Exhibition of the San Francisco Art Association.* Cat. San Francisco Museum of Art, 1945.

————. *Sixty-fifth Annual Exhibition: Oil, Tempera, and Sculpture.* Cat. San Francisco Museum of Art, 1945.

————. *Sixty-sixth Annual Exhibition: Oil, Tempera, and Sculpture.* Cat. San Francisco Museum of Art, 1946.

————. *Tenth Annual Drawing and Print Exhibition, San Francisco Art Association.* Cat. San Francisco Museum of Art, 1946.

————. *Eleventh Annual Drawing and Print Exhibition, San Francisco Art Association.* Cat. San Francisco Museum of Art, 1947.

————. *Sixty-seventh Annual Exhibition: Oil, Tempera, and Sculpture of the San Francisco Art Association.* Cat. San Francisco Museum of Art, 1948.

————. *Twelfth Annual Drawing and Print Exhibition, San Francisco Art Association.* Cat. San Francisco Museum of Art, 1948.

————. *Sixty-eighth Annual Exhibition.* Cat. San Francisco Museum of Art, 1949.

————. *Thirteenth Annual Drawing and Print Exhibition.* Cat. San Francisco Museum of Art, 1949.

————. *Fourteenth Annual Drawing and Print Exhibition,*

San Francisco Art Association. Cat. San Francisco Museum of Art, 1950.

———. *Sixty-ninth Annual Oil, Tempera, and Sculpture Exhibition of the San Francisco Art Association*. Cat. San Francisco Museum of Art, 1950.

———. *Fifteenth Annual Drawing and Print Exhibition, San Francisco Art Association*. Cat. San Francisco Museum of Art, 1951.

———. *Seventieth Annual Oil and Sculpture Exhibition of the San Francisco Art Association*. Cat. San Francisco Museum of Art, 1951.

———. *Seventy-first Annual Painting and Sculpture Exhibition of the San Francisco Art Association*. Cat. San Francisco Museum of Art, 1952.

———. *Sixteenth Annual Drawing and Print Exhibition, San Francisco Art Association*. Cat. San Francisco Museum of Art, 1952.

———. *Sixteenth Annual Watercolor Exhibition*. Cat. San Francisco Museum of Art, 1952.

———. *Seventeenth Annual Drawing and Print Exhibition, San Francisco Art Association*. Cat. San Francisco Museum of Art, 1953.

———. *Seventeenth Annual Watercolor Exhibition of the San Francisco Art Association*. Cat. San Francisco Museum of Art, 1953.

———. *Seventy-second Annual Painting and Sculpture Exhibition of the San Francisco Art Association*. Cat. San Francisco Museum of Art, 1953.

———. *Eighteenth Annual Drawing and Print Exhibition, San Francisco Art Association*. Cat. San Francisco Museum of Art, 1954.

———. *Seventy-third Annual Painting and Sculpture Exhibition of the San Francisco Art Association*. Cat. San Francisco Museum of Art, 1954.

———. *Nineteenth Annual Drawing and Print Exhibition, San Francisco Art Association*. Cat. San Francisco Museum of Art, 1955.

———. *Seventy-fourth Annual Painting and Sculpture Exhibition of the San Francisco Art Association*. Cat. San Francisco Museum of Art, 1955.

———. *Seventy-fifth Annual Painting and Sculpture Exhibition of the San Francisco Art Association*. Cat. San Francisco Museum of Art, 1956.

———. *Twentieth Annual Drawing and Print Exhibition, San Francisco Art Association*. Cat. San Francisco Museum of Art, 1956.

———. *Seventy-sixth Annual Painting and Sculpture Exhibition of the San Francisco Art Association*. Cat. San Francisco Museum of Art, 1957.

———. *[Twenty-first] Annual Watercolor, Drawing, and Print Exhibition of the San Francisco Art Association*. Cat. San Francisco Museum of Art, 1957.

———. *Painting and Sculpture in the Art Bank of the San Francisco Art Association*. San Francisco Art Association, 1958.

———. *Seventy-seventh Annual Painting and Sculpture Exhibition of the San Francisco Art Association*. Cat. San Francisco Museum of Art, 1958.

———. *Twenty-second Annual Drawing and Print Exhibition of the San Francisco Art Association*. Cat. San Francisco Museum of Art, 1958.

———. *Seventy-eighth Annual Painting and Sculpture Exhibition of the San Francisco Art Association*. Cat. San Francisco Museum of Art, 1959.

———. *Painting and Sculpture in the Art Bank of the San Francisco Art Association*. San Francisco Art Association, 1960.

———. *Seventy ninth Annual Painting and Sculpture Exhibition of the San Francisco Art Association*. Cat. San Francisco Museum of Art, 1960.

———. *The Twenty-third Drawing, Print and Watercolor Exhibition of the San Francisco Art Association*. Cat. San Francisco Museum of Art, 1960.

Santa Barbara Museum of Art. *Second Pacific Coast Biennial Exhibition of Paintings and Watercolors*. Exh. cat. Santa Barbara, Calif.: Santa Barbara Museum of Art, 1957.

Smith, Richard Cándida. *Utopia and Dissent: Art, Poetry, and Politics in California*. Berkeley and Los Angeles: University of California Press, 1995.

Solnit, Rebecca. *Secret Exhibition: Six California Artists of the Cold War Era*. San Francisco: City Lights Books, 1990.

Stanford Art Gallery. *Fresh Paint—1958: A Selective Survey of Recent Western Painting*. Exh. cat. Stanford, Calif.: Stanford Art Gallery, Stanford University, 1958.

Starr, Sandra Leonard. *Lost and Found in California: Four Decades of Assemblage Art*. Exh. cat. Santa Monica, Calif.: James Corcoran Gallery, Shoshana Wayne Gallery, and Pence Gallery, 1988.

Sweeney, James Johnson. *Younger American Painters*. Exh. cat. New York: Solomon R. Guggenheim Museum, 1954.

Tapié, Michel. *Morphologie autre*. Turin, Italy: Edizioni d'Arte Fratelli Pozzo, 1960.

Turnbull, Betty. *The Last Time I Saw Ferus, 1957–1966*. Exh. cat. Newport Beach, Calif.: Newport Harbor Art Museum, 1976.

University of St. Thomas. *Jermayne MacAgy: A Life Illustrated by an Exhibition*. Cat. Houston, Tex.: University of St. Thomas, 1969.

Wagstaff, Christopher. *An Art of Wondering: The King Ubu Gallery, 1952–1953*. Exh. cat. Davis, Calif.: Natsoulas/ Novelozo Gallery, 1989.

Walker Art Center. *Vanguard 1955*. Exh. cat. Minneapolis: Walker Art Center, 1955.

———. *Sixty American Painters*. Exh. cat. Minneapolis: Walker Art Center, 1960.

Wight, Frederick S. *The Artist's Environment: West Coast*. Exh. cat. Fort Worth, Tex.: The Amon Carter Museum of Western Art in collaboration with the

UCLA art galleries and the Oakland Art Museum, 1962–63.

Articles and Reviews

Albright, Thomas. "Looking Back on Bay Area Art." Review. *San Francisco Sunday Examiner and Chronicle,* 18 August 1968.

———. "'Period of Exploration'—at Oakland Museum." Review. *San Francisco Sunday Examiner and Chronicle,* 9 September 1973.

———. "Mythmakers." *Art Gallery* 18 (February 1975): 12–17, 44–45.

———. "The California School of Fine Arts, c. 1945–1960." In *Reflections: Alumni Exhibitions.* San Francisco: San Francisco Art Institute, 1981.

———. "The Beat Artists Revisited." Review. *San Francisco Chronicle,* 23 October 1983.

Ashton, Dore. "An Eastern View of the San Francisco School." *Evergreen Review* 1 (1957): 148–59.

Bengston, Billy Al. "Late Fifties at the Ferus." *Artforum* 7 (January 1969): 33–35.

Bietry-Salinger, Jehanne. "A Critical Study of San Francisco Museums." *Opera and Concert* 12 (October 1947): 20–21, 31.

———. "Notes on Art: Painting for Whom, If You Please?" Review. *Opera and Concert* 13 (March 1948): 24–25.

Bogat, Regina. "Fifty California Artists." Review. *Artforum* 1 (December 1962): 23–26.

"California School of Fine Arts." *Fortnight* 15 (20 July 1953): 22.

Chipp, Herschel B. "Art News from San Francisco." Review. *Art News* 55 (March 1956): 12, 72–73.

———. "Art News from San Francisco." Review. *Art News* 55 (April 1956): 20.

———. "Summer Events: San Francisco." Review. *Art News* 55 (Summer 1956): 22, 61–62.

———. "Art News from San Francisco." Review. *Art News* 55 (September 1956): 18, 57–58.

———. "Art News from San Francisco." Review. *Art News* 55 (February 1957): 20, 60–61.

———. "Art News from San Francisco." Review. *Art News* 56 (December 1957): 50.

———. "Art News from San Francisco." Review. *Art News* 57 (April 1958): 48.

———. "This Summer in San Francisco." Review. *Art News* 57 (Summer 1958): 48.

———. "Art News from San Francisco." Review. *Art News* 57 (December 1958): 50.

———. "San Francisco." Review. *Art News* 58 (Summer 1959): 24.

———. "Art News from San Francisco." Review. *Art News* 59 (Summer 1960): 58, 62.

Coffelt, Beth. "The Big Wave Was Rising." *San Francisco Sunday Examiner and Chronicle,* 9 November 1975.

Coplans, John. "Circle of Styles on the West Coast." *Art in America* 52 (June 1964): 24–41.

Crehan, Hubert. "Is There a California School?" *Art News* 54 (January 1956): 32–35, 64–65.

———. "Art Schools Smell Alike." *San Francisco Sunday Examiner and Chronicle,* 4 October 1970.

Dorset, Phyllis. "La Galeria Escondida: A Taos Retrospective." *Artspace* 11 (Fall 1987): 43–49.

Falkenstein, Claire. "Exhibition of Students' Work." Review. *Arts and Architecture* 65 (June 1948): 14–16.

———. "Painting Today: A Round Table Discussion." *Arts and Architecture* 66 (April 1949): 16–21.

Farber, Manny. "Art." *Nation* 172 (6 January 1951): 19.

Ferling [Ferlinghetti], Lawrence. "Expressionism in San Francisco Painting Today." *Counterpoint: Magazine of Music and Applied Arts* 17 (January 1952): 16–19.

———. "The Labaudt Gallery." *Counterpoint: Magazine of Music and Applied Arts* 17 (May 1952): 22–23.

———. "Coast-to-Coast: San Francisco." Review. *Art Digest* 28 (15 October 1953): 12–13.

———. "San Francisco: 'Hour of Absinthe.'" Review. *Art Digest* 28 (15 March 1954): 15.

———. "San Francisco: Bay Area Roundup." Review. *Art Digest* 28 (1 August 1954): 16–17.

———. "San Francisco." Review. *Art Digest* 29 (15 January 1955): 13.

———. "Bay Area Painting and Sculpture." Review. *Art Digest* 29 (1 May 1955): 16.

———. "San Francisco." Review. *Art Digest* 29 (1 August 1955): 26–27, 30.

Frankenstein, Alfred. "The Legion of Honor Separates the Sheep from the Goats." Review. *San Francisco Chronicle,* 10 June 1945.

———. "Quality in Art Is Quite Independent of Idiom." Review. *San Francisco Chronicle,* 17 March 1946.

———. "An Answer to an Article on Modern Art by George Biddle." *San Francisco Chronicle,* 4 January 1948.

———. "A Look at the Local Galleries." Review. *San Francisco Chronicle,* 15 August 1948.

———. "Local Galleries in Review." *San Francisco Chronicle,* 31 October 1948.

———. "A Summary of Art in Our Time." *San Francisco Chronicle,* 12 December 1948.

———. "The Past Year in the Field of Art and Music." *San Francisco Chronicle,* 2 January 1949.

———. "Around the Local Art Galleries." Review. *San Francisco Chronicle,* 3 July 1949.

———. "The Local Galleries." Review. *San Francisco Chronicle,* 24 July 1949.

———. "Backtalk to a Critic and a Critic's Comments." *San Francisco Chronicle,* 7 August 1949.

———. "Around the Local Galleries." Review *San Francisco Chronicle,* 28 August 1949.

———. "The Art Association Annual and Other Shows." Review. *San Francisco Chronicle,* 19 February 1950.

———. "A Review of the Local Art Galleries." *San Francisco Chronicle,* 26 February 1950.

———. "The Art Galleries." Review. *San Francisco Chronicle,* 12 March 1950.

———. "Graphic Arts Come to the Fore in the Local Galleries." Review. *San Francisco Chronicle,* 28 June 1953.

———. "A New Exhibition of the Works of Recent Prize-Winning Artists." Review. *San Francisco Chronicle,* 11 October 1953.

———. "A New Abstraction Is Evident at the Art Association Annual." Review. *San Francisco Chronicle,* 28 February 1954.

———. "'Six'—Informal Gallery with More Than Visual Arts." Review. *San Francisco Chronicle,* 17 November 1954.

———. "The Avant-Garde Is Busy at the Fillmore-Union Galleries." Review. *San Francisco Chronicle,* 15 May 1955.

———. "Oakland Shows There Was No 'California School.'" Review. *San Francisco Chronicle,* 26 February 1956.

———. "San Francisco's Trail Blazer in Modern Art." *San Francisco Chronicle,* 10 August 1958.

———. "The Role of Nature in Abstract Art . . ." Review. *San Francisco Chronicle,* 28 September 1958.

———. "What Ever Happened To . . . ?" *San Francisco Chronicle,* 26 October 1969.

———. "The Birth of Avant-Garde Art in the Bay Area." *San Francisco Chronicle,* 30 October 1975.

Fried, Alexander. "San Francisco Region, 1947." *Art News* 46 (June 1947): 24–28, 38–39.

———. "One Juror's Views of the Legion's Third Annual." Review. *San Francisco Examiner,* 12 December 1948.

———. "Abstracts with New Objects? An Exhibit Which May Mean an Epoch's End." Review. *San Francisco Sunday Examiner and Chronicle,* 22 January 1956.

Garth, John. "California School of Fine Arts." *Argonaut* 136 (1 November 1957): 15.

Grissom, Sarah. "San Francisco." Review. *Arts* 32 (February 1958): 22–23.

———. "San Francisco." Review. *Arts* 32 (May 1958): 20.

Hagan, R. H. "San Francisco Museum Showing Variety of Works by Local Artists." Review. *San Francisco Chronicle,* 9 July 1950.

———. "Union-Fillmore Galleries Challenge Sutter Street." Review. *San Francisco Chronicle,* 11 February 1955.

Hall, William. "School of Fine Arts Acquires World Fame." *San Francisco Examiner,* 11 July 1948.

Hunter, Sam. "Guggenheim Sampler." Review. *Art Digest* 28 (15 May 1954): 8–9, 31.

Kees, Weldon. "San Francisco Artists Set a Pace." *New York Times,* 31 December 1950.

———. "San Francisco." *Art News* 54 (June 1955): 58.

Kramer, Hilton. "Wiley of the West: Dude Ranch Dada." *New York Times,* 16 May 1971.

———. "A Survey of California Art." Review. *New York Times,* 19 June 1977.

Lamantia, Philip. "Letter from San Francisco." *Horizon* 93–94 (October 1947): 118–23.

Lee, Anthony W. "The Gang of Six." Review. *Artweek* 21 (25 January 1990): 1, 20.

Leider, Philip, and John Coplans. "West Coast Art: Three Images." *Artforum* 1 (June 1963): 21–25.

Leonard, Michael. "The Golden Age of Bay Area Painting." *Art of California* 2 (August– September 1989): 12–19.

Loran, Erle. "San Francisco." Review. *Art News* 48 (September 1949): 44–45, 52–53.

———. "Art News from San Francisco." Review. *Art News* 49 (April 1950): 50, 61–62.

———. "Scheduled for San Francisco." Review. *Art News* 49 (Summer 1950): 34, 54.

———. "San Francisco." Review. *Art News* 50 (March 1951): 53.

———. "Art News from San Francisco." Review. *Art News* 51 (March 1952): 50–51.

———. "Art News from San Francisco." Review. *Art News* 52 (March 1953): 41, 50.

———. "San Francisco." Review. *Art News* 53 (January 1954): 22–23.

Louchheim, Aline. "San Francisco: Division and Vitality." *New York Times,* 24 October 1948.

MacAgy, Douglas. "The School's New Program." *San Francisco Art Association Bulletin* (July– August 1945), n.p.

———. "But—Can They Draw?" *San Francisco Art Association Bulletin* (September 1946), n.p.

———. "Exhibition of Work of the Faculty." *California Palace of the Legion of Honor Bulletin* (October 1946), 51–55.

———. "From Student to Artist." *Design* 48 (January 1947): 18–19.

———. "The Art School Problem." *College Art Journal* 7 (Summer 1948): 297–301.

———. "A Margin of Chaos." *Circle* 10 (Summer 1948): 39–42.

———. "The Contemporary Art School." *Arts and Architecture* 65 (November 1948): 24–25.

———. "Mark Rothko." *Magazine of Art* 42 (January 1949): 20–21.

———. "The State of American Art: A Symposium." *Magazine of Art,* 42 (March 1949): 94–95.

———. "A Note on the Western Round Table on Modern Art." *San Francisco Art Association Bulletin* 15 (April–May 1949), n.p.

———. "Fine and Commercial Arts Re-defined." *College Art Journal* 9 (Summer 1950): 406–11.

———. "Accounting Poet Kings." *Arts and Architecture* 69 (February 1952): 16, 32–33.

MacCawley, Nancy. "Art News from San Francisco." Review. *Art News* 56 (May 1957): 50, 59–60.

[McChesney], Mary Fuller. "Was There a San Francisco School?" *Artforum* 9 (January 1971): 46–53.

Martin, Fred. "Remembering 'the School,'" part 1. *Artweek* 6 (1 November 1975): 1, 16–18; part 2: 6 (8 November 1975), 6–7; part 3: 6 (15 November 1975): 3–4.

———. "San Francisco Letter." *Art International* 19 (20 November 1975): 52–55.

Millier, Arthur. "San Francisco Opens Second National Annual." Review. *Art Digest* 22 (15 November 1947): 12.

———. "San Francisco Visit." *Art Digest* 23 (15 November 1948): 8.

———. "The Pacific Coast: Artists Are Stimulated by Its Diverse Climates." *Art Digest* 26 (1 November 1951): 30–31.

Morley, Grace McCann. "Tour of Some Paintings Is Stopped and a Controversy Seems to Be On." *San Francisco Chronicle,* 25 May 1947.

———. "A Modern Art Museum." *Opera and Concert* 15 (August 1950): 38–40.

———. "The Pacific Coast Artists Brought Their Climate to São Paulo." *San Francisco Chronicle,* 2 October 1955.

———. "Growth of Museum Collections." *San Francisco Museum of Art Quarterly Bulletin* 5 (1956): 11–22.

Nordland, Gerald. "Art." Review. *Frontier* 8 (May 1957): 25–26.

———. "Art." Review. *Frontier* 9 (January 1958): 20–21.

Plagens, Peter. "A Period of Exploration, San Francisco, 1945–1950." Review. *Artforum* 12 (December 1973): 91–92.

———. "Seventy Years of California Modernism in 340 Works by 200 Artists." Review. *Art in America* 65 (May–June 1977): 63–69.

[Porter, Bern(?)]. "The New School of Painting." *Berkeley: A Journal of Modern Culture* 7 (1949): 7.

Rexroth, Kenneth. "San Francisco." Review. *Art News* 54 (October 1955): 10–15.

———. "San Francisco Letter." *Evergreen Review* 1 (1957): 5–14.

Rohr, Nora Lee. "Faculty Exhibition Reviewed." *San Francisco Art Association Bulletin* (November 1945), n.p.

Ryan, Beatrice Judd. "The Rise of Modern Art in the Bay Area." *California Historical Society Quarterly* 38 (March 1959): 1–5.

"San Francisco Group." Review, signed N.A. *Art Digest* 29 (1 March 1954): 18.

Sawyer, Kenneth. "L'expressionisme abstrait: La phase du Pacifique." *Cimaise: Revue de l'Art Actuel* 1 (June 1954): 3–5.

Selz, Peter. "Between Friends: Still and the Bay Area." *Art in America* 63 (November–December 1975): 70–73.

Shere, Charles. "Exhibit Requires Two Visits." Review. *Oakland Tribune,* 23 September 1973.

Smith, Hassel, with the assistance of Mary McChesney. "Sulla scuola di San Francisco." *Evento delle arti* 2 (1958): 24–27. English translation by Ann Lee, in Archives of California Art, The Oakland Museum.

[Stone, Judy]. "New Art Explained by Sausalitans." *San Rafael Daily Independent and Marin Journal,* 22 January 1949.

Stone, Judy. "Former Atom Scientist Now Promotes Experimental Art." *Daily Independent Journal* (San Rafael, Calif.), 8 April 1950.

Tapié, Michel. "L'école du Pacifique." Roundtable, with Julien Alvard, Claire Falkenstein, Sam Francis, and Fitz Simmons. *Cimaise: Revue de l'Art Actuel* 1 (June 1954): 6–9.

Temko, Allan. "The Flowering of San Francisco." *Horizon: A Magazine of the Arts* 1 (January 1959): 4–23.

Timberman, Marcy. "Crossing into the Other Camp: Abstract Expressionists in Northern California, 1945–1960." Review. *Artweek* 21 (30 August 1990): 1, 20.

Tory, Alan. "Six Young Hopefuls." Review. *Fortnight Magazine* 17 (15 December 1954): 31.

Ventura, Anita. "The Prospect over the Bay." Review. *Arts* 37 (May 1963): 19–21.

———. "The Bay Climate." Review. *Arts* 37 (December 1963): 29–33.

Waddington, Peter. "Buy a Painting with Your Dinner: The Story of the Bay Area Artists Group." *Opera, Concert, and Symphony* 12 (July 1947): 14–15.

Wagstaff, Christopher. "An Interview with Harry Jacobus." *Northern Lights: Studies in Creativity* 2 (1985–86): 81–118.

Welch, Douglass. "Fifteen Paintings by Nine San Francisco Painters." Review. *Seattle Post-Intelligencer,* 1 February 1950.

———. "Art from S.F.—Just Out of Our World!" Review. *Seattle Post-Intelligencer,* February 1950.

White, Nan. "Free Form Abstractions Stir Up Controversy in This Area: Leaders of New School, Variously Known as 'Spiritist' and 'Blob,' Tell Theories." *San Francisco News,* 18 March 1950.

Unpublished Manuscripts

Frank, Patrick L. "Abstract Expressionism in San Francisco, 1945–1950." Ph.D. diss., George Washington University, Washington, D.C., 1992.

"Grace L. McCann Morley: Art, Artists, Museums, and the San Francisco Museum of Art." Interview by Suzanne Bassett Riess, 1960. Regional Cultural History Project, General Library (manuscript in Bancroft Library), University of California, Berkeley.

Leonard, Michael. "A History of Painting at the California School of Fine Arts, 1940–1960." Master's thesis, San Francisco State University, 1985.

Elmer Bischoff

Frankenstein, Alfred. Review. *San Francisco Chronicle,* 8 June 1947.

Frash, Robert M. *Elmer Bischoff, 1947–1985.* Exh. cat. Laguna Beach, Calif.: Laguna Art Museum, 1985.

Hirschl and Adler Modern. *Elmer Bischoff.* Exh. cat. New York: Hirschl and Adler Modern, 1985.

Jones, Caroline A. *Bay Area Figurative Art, 1950–1965.* Exh. cat. San Francisco: San Francisco Museum of Modern Art; and Berkeley and Los Angeles: University of California Press, 1990.

[Landauer], Susan Klein. "Elmer Bischoff." *Issue: A Journal for Artists* 4 (Fall 1985): 8–11.

San Francisco Art Association. *Elmer Bischoff.* Exh. cat. San Francisco Art Association Gallery, California School of Fine Arts, 1956.

Strong, Charles. *The Drawings of Elmer Bischoff: From the Collections of Family and Friends.* Exh. cat. Belmont, Calif.: Wiegand Gallery, College of Notre Dame, 1993.

University Art Museum and Pacific Film Archive. *On Painting: The Work of Elmer Bischoff and Joan Brown.* Exh. cat. Berkeley: University Art Museum and Pacific Film Archive, University of California, Berkeley, 1992.

Ronald Bladen

Ark I. San Francisco, 1947.

Ark II. San Francisco, 1956.

Berkson, Bill. *Ronald Bladen: Early and Late.* Exh. cat. San Francisco: San Francisco Museum of Modern Art, 1991.

Bladen [Porter], Barbara. "Sculptor's Death Stirs Glowing Memories." *San Mateo Times,* 8 February 1988.

Ferling [Ferlinghetti], Lawrence. "Expressionism in San Francisco Painting Today." *Counterpoint: Magazine of Music and Allied Arts* 17 (January 1952): 16–19.

Sandler, Irving. *Ronald Bladen: The 1950s.* Exh. cat. New York: Washburn Gallery, 1989.

Washburn Gallery. *Ronald Bladen.* Exh. cat. New York: Washburn Gallery, 1990.

Ernest Briggs

Ashton, Dore. "Art." Review. *Arts and Architecture* 7 (December 1955): 10, 33–34.

Campbell, Lawrence. *Ernest Briggs, 1922–1984: Memorial Exhibition.* Cat. New York: Gruenebaum Gallery, 1984.

"Ernest Briggs." Review, signed N.A. *Art Digest* 28 (1 May 1954): 18.

Ferlinghetti, Lawrence. "Coast to Coast: San Francisco." Review. *Art Digest* 28 (15 October 1953): 12–13.

Frankenstein, Alfred. "Around the Local Art Galleries." Review. *San Francisco Chronicle,* 10 April 1949.

Kingsley, April. *Ernest Briggs: New Paintings.* Exh. cat. New York: Gruenebaum Gallery, 1982.

Miller, Dorothy. *Twelve Americans.* Exh. cat., with statement by Briggs. New York: Museum of Modern Art, 1956.

Sandler, Irving. *The Triumph of American Painting: A History of Abstract Expressionism.* New York: Harper and Row, 1970.

San Francisco Art Association. *Ernest Briggs.* Exh. cat. San Francisco: San Francisco Art Association Gallery, California School of Fine Arts, 1956.

Edward Corbett

Curl, Huldah. *Paintings and Drawings by Edward Corbett.* Exh. cat. Minneapolis, Minn.: Walker Art Center, 1961.

Frankenstein, Alfred. "Works by Corbett, Smith Hung at Fine Arts School." Review. *San Francisco Chronicle,* 14 January 1951.

Fuller [McChesney], Mary. "Edward Corbett: A Profile." *Art Digest* 28 (1 January 1954): 21–23.

Hess, Thomas B. "The Modern Museum's Fifteen: Where U.S. Extremes Meet." Review. *Art News* 51 (April 1952): 16–19.

Landauer, Susan. *Edward Corbett: A Retrospective.* Exh. cat. Richmond, Calif.: Richmond Art Center, 1990.

———. "The Quiet Mystery of Edward Corbett." *Art of California* 4 (January 1991): 18–22.

Lenoir, Henri Villon. "Skylight Sketch." *Montgomery Street Skylight,* 22 July 1946.

McCann, Cecile N. "Fifty Paintings by Corbett." Review. *Westart* 7 (21 April 1969): 7.

Miller, Dorothy. *Fifteen Americans.* Exh. cat., with statement by Corbett. New York: Museum of Modern Art, 1952.

"New Works by Two Painters." *San Francisco Art Association Bulletin* 17 (January 1951), n.p.

Niese, Henry, and Gerald Nordland. *Edward Corbett.* Exh. cat. College Park: University of Maryland Art Gallery, 1979.

Nordland, Gerald. *Edward Corbett.* Exh. cat. San Francisco: San Francisco Museum of Art, 1969.

Jay DeFeo

Albright, Thomas. "Just One Single Rose—a Glorious Anachronism." *San Francisco Chronicle,* 11 April 1968.

———. "Their Own Artistic Paths." *San Francisco Chronicle,* 15 July 1971.

———. "Massive Restoration on 'White Rose.'" *San Francisco Chronicle,* 7 July 1973.

———. "The Re-emergence of a Forceful Artist." *San Francisco Chronicle,* 8 July 1978.

———. "Strong Works by Powerful Artist." *San Francisco Chronicle,* 7 February 1980.

———. "Twenty-three-hundred-pound Rose." *Art News* 79 (May 1980): 141–43.

Davis, D. M. "Miss DeFeo's Awesome Painting Is Like Living Thing Under Decay." *National Observer,* 14 July 1969.

Dunham, Judith L. "Cabbage Rose." *Artweek* 6 (27 September 1975): 16.

———. "Jay DeFeo." *Arts and Architecture* 1 (Fall 1981): 16–17.

Fried, Alexander. "After Six Years and Twenty-three-hundred Pounds of Paint." *San Francisco Chronicle,* 11 April 1969.

Frizzelle, N. "The Sad Story of the 'Rose.'" *San Francisco Examiner,* 10 July 1973.

Kienholz, Edward. *J. DeFeo.* Exh. cat. Hope, Idaho: The Faith and Charity in Hope Gallery, 1979.

Miller, Dorothy. *Sixteen Americans.* Exh. cat. New York: Museum of Modern Art, 1959.

San Francisco Art Institute. *Jay DeFeo: Selected Works, Past and Present.* Exh. cat. San Francisco: San Francisco Art Institute, 1984.

Shere, Charles. "DeFeo's Paintings Show Commitment." *Oakland Tribune,* 19 September 1974.

———. "DeFeo's Paintings Achieve a New Level." *Oakland Tribune,* 1 March 1983.

Stich, Sidra, with essays by Michael McClure and Brigid Doherty. *Jay DeFeo: Works on Paper.* Exh. cat. Berkeley: University Art Museum, University of California, Berkeley, 1989.

Stiles, Knute. "Jay DeFeo at the University Art Museum." *Art in America* 67 (March–April 1979): 157.

Wallace, Dean. "Review: Dilexi Gallery." *San Francisco Chronicle,* 27 July 1959.

Winter, David. "Jay DeFeo." *Art News* 85 (December 1986): 28.

Richard Diebenkorn

Buck, Robert T., Jr., Linda L. Cathcart, Gerald Nordland, and Maurice Tuchman. *Richard Diebenkorn: Paintings and Drawings, 1943–1976.* Exh. cat. Buffalo, N.Y.: Albright-Knox Art Gallery, 1976.

Butterfield, Jan. *Resource/Response/Reservoir, Pentimenti: Seeing and Then Seeing Again.* Exh. cat. San Francisco: San Francisco Museum of Modern Art, 1983.

Chipp, Herschel B. "Diebenkorn Paints a Picture." *Art News* 56 (May 1957): 44–47, 54–55.

Elderfield, John. *The Drawings of Richard Diebenkorn.* Exh. cat. New York: Museum of Modern Art, 1988.

———. *Richard Diebenkorn.* Exh. cat. London: Whitechapel Art Gallery, 1991.

Frankenstein, Alfred. "The Art Galleries." Review. *San Francisco Chronicle,* 12 March 1950.

Hofstadter, Dan. "Profiles: Almost Free of the Mirror." *New Yorker* 63 (7 September 1987): 54–55, 58–70, 72–73.

Jones, Caroline A. *Bay Area Figurative Art, 1950–1965.* Exh. cat. San Francisco: San Francisco Museum of Modern Art; and Berkeley and Los Angeles: University of California Press, 1990.

Lavatelli, Mark. "Richard Diebenkorn: The Albuquerque Years." *Artspace* 4 (June 1980): 20–25.

Nordland, Gerald. *Richard Diebenkorn*. New York: Rizzoli International Publications, 1987.

James Budd Dixon

Albright, Thomas. "A Vital Look at a Neglected Painter." Review. *San Francisco Chronicle*, 7 March 1977.

Chipp, Herschel B. Review. *Art News* 57 (December 1958). 50.

Hodel, Emilia. Review. *San Francisco News*, 7 October 1939.

Moss, Stacey. "James Budd Dixon and the Painting Process." Review. *Artweek* 8 (2 April 1977): 6.

Strong, Charles. "James Budd Dixon, Non-Objective Paintings, 1948–1960." Unpublished manuscript, 1977. Archives of California Art, The Oakland Museum.

Tapié, Michel. *Morphologie autre*. Turin, Italy: Edizioni d'Arte Fratelli Pozzo, 1960.

Edward Dugmore

Ashton, Dore. "Art." Review. *Arts and Architecture* 73 (February 1956): 10–11.

———. "About Art and Artists: Recent Paintings by Dugmore." Review. *New York Times*, 20 October 1956.

———. "Art: A Dugmore Show." Review. *New York Times*, 29 April 1960.

———. *Edward Dugmore, Burning Bright: Paintings, 1950–1959*. Exh. cat. Los Angeles: Manny Silverman Gallery, 1991.

Crehan, Hubert. "Edward Dugmore: A Second One-Man Show by One of the Younger Romantic Painters." Review. *Art Digest* 29 (15 October 1954): 9.

Frankenstein, Alfred. "A Look at the Shows in the Local Galleries." Review. *San Francisco Chronicle*, 12 February 1950.

Gross, Stephen. "A 'Philosopher with a Brush.'" Review. *Des Moines Tribune*, 10 June 1972.

Ruhe, Barnaby. *Edward Dugmore: Paintings, 1948–1953*. Abstract Expressionists: An Exhibition and Historical Survey of Northern California Abstract Expressionists Active 1945–1960, no. 8. Exh. cat. San Francisco: The Carlson Gallery, 1990.

Sandler, Irving. *The Triumph of American Painting: A History of Abstract Expressionism*. New York: Harper and Row, 1970.

Sam Francis

Albright, Thomas. "A Huge Sam Francis Show." Review. *San Francisco Chronicle*, 14 June 1973.

Alloway, Lawrence. "Sam Francis: From Field to Arabesque." *Artforum* 11 (February 1973): 37–41.

Belz, Carl. "Fitting Sam Francis into History." *Art in America* 61 (January–February 1973): 40–45.

Buck, Robert T., Jr., Franz Meyer, and Wieland Schmied. *Sam Francis: Paintings, 1947–1972*. Exh. cat. Buffalo, N.Y.: Albright-Knox Art Gallery, 1972.

Butterfield, Jan. "Sam Francis." *Arts* 55 (November 1980): 19.

Chipp, Herschel B. "Art News from San Francisco." Review. *Art News* 58 (Summer 1959): 24.

Colt, Priscilla. "The Painting of Sam Francis." *Art Journal* 22 (Fall 1962): 2–7.

Hulten, Pontus. *Sam Francis*. Exh. cat. Stuttgart, Germany: Edition Cantz, 1993.

Miller, Dorothy. *Twelve Americans*. Exh. cat. New York: Museum of Modern Art, 1956.

The Museum of Fine Arts. *Sam Francis*. Exh. cat. Houston, Tex.: The Museum of Fine Arts, 1967.

Selz, Peter. *Sam Francis*. Rev. ed. New York: Harry N. Abrams, 1982.

Sonia Gechtoff

"Americans at Brussels: Soft Sell, Range, and Controversy." Review. *Time* 71 (16 June 1958): 70–75.

Frankenstein, Alfred. Review. *San Francisco Chronicle*, 13 January 1952.

———. Review. *San Francisco Chronicle*, 30 October 1955.

———. "Sonia Gechtoff Exhibit Blazes with Vision." Review. *San Francisco Chronicle*, 23 January 1957.

Fried, Alexander. "Smell the Paint: Sonia Gechtoff Puts Furious Energy into Her Oils." Review. *San Francisco Examiner*, 3 February 1957.

Langsner, Jules. "Art News from Los Angeles." Review. *Art News* 56 (Summer 1957): 64, 81.

Lipman, Jean, and Cleve Gray. "The Amazing Inventiveness of Women Painters." *Cosmopolitan* 151 (October 1961): 62–69.

Nordland, Gerald. "Art." Review. *Frontier* 10 (January 1959): 20–22.

Schick Art Gallery. *Out of Abstract Expressionism: Roy De Forest, Sonia Gechtoff, Philip Wofford*. Exh. cat. Saratoga Springs, N.Y.: Schick Art Gallery, Skidmore College, 1991.

Sweeney, James Johnson. *Younger American Painters*. Exh. cat. New York: Solomon R. Guggenheim Museum, 1954.

Whitney Museum of American Art. *Young America, 1960*. Exh. cat. New York: Whitney Museum of American Art, 1960.

John Grillo

Fuller [McChesney], Mary. "Was There a San Francisco School?" *Artforum* 9 (January 1971): 46–53.

Landauer, Susan. *John Grillo: Works on Paper, 1946–1948.* Exh. cat. Abstract Expressionists: An Exhibition and Historical Survey of Northern California Abstract Expressionists Active 1945–1960, no. 2. San Francisco: The Carlson Gallery, 1990.

———. "John Grillo: The San Francisco Years." *Art of California* 3 (May 1990): 56–61.

MacAgy, Douglas. *John Grillo: Oils and Watercolors.* Exh. brochure. Berkeley, Calif.: Daliel's Gallery, 1947.

———. "John Grillo." *Art International* 6 (April 1962): 38–40.

Provincetown Art Association and Museum. *John Grillo: A Selection of Works from Nineteen Fifties through Nineteen Eighties.* Exh. cat. Provincetown, Mass.: Provincetown Art Association and Museum, 1988.

John Hultberg

Alloway, Lawrence. "Art News from London." Review. *Art News* 55 (November 1956): 46.

Beem, Edgar Allen. "John Hultberg: Apocalypse Now and Again." Review. *Maine Times,* 14 June 1985.

Jacks, Shirley. *John Hultberg, Painter of the In-Between: Selected Paintings, 1953–1984.* Exh. cat. Clinton, N.Y.: Fred L. Emerson Gallery, 1985.

Kuh, Katherine. "Foreword . . . New Talent in the U.S.A." *Art in America* 44 (February 1956): 10–11.

Miller, Sherry. "Hultberg: The Man Who Would Be Painting's Wagner." Review. *Maine Sunday Telegram,* 30 March 1986.

Tapié, Michel. *Morphologie autre.* Turin, Italy: Edizioni d'Arte Fratelli Pozzo, 1960.

Jack Jefferson

Albright, Thomas. "The Realm of Jack Jefferson." Review. *San Francisco Chronicle,* 16 February 1982.

———. "Jack Jefferson." Review. *Art News* 81 (May 1982): 136.

———. "A Rare Look at a Pair of Local Artists." Review. *San Francisco Chronicle,* 23 February 1984.

Frankenstein, Alfred. "Around the Local Galleries." Review. *San Francisco Chronicle,* 16 October 1949.

French, Christopher. "More Than History." Review. *Artweek* 15 (18 February 1984): 5.

"Jack Jefferson, Rosenberg Fellowship Winner." *San Francisco Art Association Bulletin* 19 (February–May 1953): n.p.

M. H. de Young Memorial Museum. *Jack Jefferson.* Exh. cat. San Francisco: M. H. de Young Memorial Museum, 1963. Statement by Jefferson.

Moss, Stacey. *The Abstract Expressionist Years and After: Jack Jefferson, Frank Lobdell, Alvin Light.* Exh. cat. Belmont, Calif.: Wiegand Gallery, College of Notre Dame, 1989.

Ventura, Anita. "The Prospect over the Bay." Review. *Arts* (May 1963): 19–21.

James Kelly

Chipp, Herschel B. "San Francisco." Review. *Art News* 55 (Summer 1956): 22, 61.

Escher, Earl, and F[red] M[artin]. *James Kelly.* Exh. cat. San Francisco: San Francisco Art Association Gallery, California School of Fine Arts, 1956.

Frankenstein, Alfred. "Touring the Local Galleries." Review. *San Francisco Chronicle,* 25 May 1952.

———. "Graphic Arts Come to the Fore in the Local Galleries." Review. *San Francisco Chronicle,* 28 June 1953.

———. "James Kelly's Art Expresses Serenity." Review. *San Francisco Chronicle,* 2 May 1956.

Moss, Stacey. *Mediating Abstraction and Figuration: The Paintings of James Kelly, 1952–1990.* Exh. cat. Belmont, Calif.: Wiegand Gallery, College of Notre Dame, 1990.

Walter Kuhlman

The Carlson Gallery. *Walter Kuhlman.* Abstract Expressionists: An Exhibition and Historical Survey of Northern California Abstract Expressionists Active 1945–1960, no. 1. Exh. cat. San Francisco: The Carlson Gallery, 1989.

Chipp, Herschel B. "Art News from San Francisco." Review. *Art News* 57 (December 1958): 50.

Frankenstein, Alfred. "A Look at the Current Exhibitions." Review. *San Francisco Chronicle,* 22 January 1956.

———. "The Role of Nature in Abstract Art . . ." Review. *San Francisco Chronicle,* 28 September 1958.

Fried, Alexander. Review. *San Francisco Examiner,* 2 August 1964.

Goldberg, Beth. *Walter Kuhlman: A Forty-Year Retrospective.* Exh. cat. Rohnert Park, Calif.: Sonoma State Art Gallery, Sonoma State University, 1988.

Taylor, Dan. "Painting in the Moment." *Press Democrat* (Santa Rosa, Calif.), 9 September 1988.

Van der Meulen, Jack. "Arts." Review. *Pacific Sun* (Santa Rosa, Calif.), 3 June 1983.

Walker, Dorothy. "The Art World: Praise for Local Artists." Review. *San Francisco News,* 13 September 1958.

Frank Lobdell

Albright, Thomas. "Frank Lobdell Painting—Memorial and Milestone." Review. *San Francisco Chronicle,* 24 January 1969.

———. "On the Lighter Side of Frank Lobdell." Review. *San Francisco Chronicle,* 15 March 1982.

———. "Lobdell's Monastic Commitment." Review. *San Francisco Chronicle,* 30 January 1983.

———. "The Value of a 'Bad' Painting to an Artist." Review. *San Francisco Chronicle*, 3 March 1983.

Albright, Thomas, and Peter Boswell. *Frank Lobdell: Paintings and Monotypes.* Exh. cat. San Francisco: San Francisco Museum of Modern Art, 1983.

Ashton, Dore. "Frank Lobdell's Work on View." Review. *New York Times,* 19 April 1960.

F[actor], D[on]. "Frank Lobdell: Pasadena Art Museum." Review. *Artforum* (May 1966): 13–14.

Frankenstein, Alfred. "The Depth and Radiance of Lobdell." Review. *San Francisco Sunday Examiner and Chronicle,* 8 May 1966.

———. "Two Bay Area Masters." Review. *San Francisco Chronicle,* 20 May 1971.

Galerie Anderson-Mayer. *Frank Lobdell.* Exh. cat. Paris: Galerie Anderson-Mayer, 1965.

Gibson, Ann, ed. "Frank Lobdell." *Issue* 4 (Fall 1985): 30–32. Statement by Lobdell.

Hopps, Walter. *Frank Lobdell: Paintings and Graphics from 1948 to 1965.* Exh. cat. Pasadena, Calif.: Pasadena Art Museum, 1966.

Jones, Caroline A. *Frank Lobdell: Works, 1947–1992.* Exh. cat. Stanford, Calif.: Stanford University Museum of Art, 1993.

Lobdell, Frank, and Kenneth Sawyer. *Poems and Drawings.* Sausalito, Calif.: Bern Porter, 1949.

Martha Jackson Gallery. *Frank Lobdell.* Exh. cat. New York: Martha Jackson Gallery, 1960.

———. *Frank Lobdell: Paintings and Drawings, 1955–1973.* Exh. cat. New York: Martha Jackson Gallery, 1974.

Miedzinsky, Charles. "Frank Lobdell: Painting the Spiritual Quest." Review. *Artweek* 14 (12 February 1983): 1.

Moss, Stacey. *The Abstract Expressionist Years and After: Jack Jefferson, Frank Lobdell, Alvin Light.* Exh. cat. Belmont, Calif.: Wiegand Gallery, College of Notre Dame, 1989.

Shere, Charles. "Exhibit Requires Two Visits." Review. *Oakland Tribune,* 23 September 1973.

Tapié, Michel. *Morphologie autre.* Turin, Italy: Edizioni d'Arte Fratelli Pozzo, 1960.

Wallace, Dean. "Director's Choice—San Francisco: Frank Lobdell." Review. *Art in America* 50 (Winter 1962): 127.

Robert McChesney

Bloomfield, Arthur. Review. *San Francisco News Call-Bulletin,* 17 May 1961.

Frankenstein, Alfred. "Northern California: David Park, Fenton Kastner, Robert McChesney." *Art in America* 42 (Winter 1954): 48–53.

———. "McChesney's Paintings Reflect a Full Life." Review. *San Francisco Chronicle,* 19 April 1957.

———. Review. *San Francisco Chronicle,* 8 November 1959.

Lenoir, Henri. "Skylight Sketch: Robert McChesney." *Montgomery Street Skylight,* 24 December 1945.

[McChesney], Mary Fuller. *Robert McChesney: From Arena to Barranca, Nineteen Years.* Exh. cat. Hayward, Calif.: University Gallery, California State University, Hayward, 1977.

McChesney, Mary Fuller. *Robert McChesney: The Arena Series Paintings, 1958–1962.* Exh. cat. Abstract Expressionists: An Exhibition and Historical Survey of Northern California Abstract Expressionists Active 1945–1960, no. 4. San Francisco: The Carlson Gallery, 1990.

Sonoma State College Art Gallery. *Robert McChesney: A Decade of Painting, 1960–1970.* Exh. cat. Cotati, Calif.: Sonoma State College Art Gallery, 1970.

Spencer, Howard DaLee. *Robert McChesney: A Retrospective.* Exh. cat. Reno: Nevada Museum of Art, 1994.

Temko, Allan. "Robert McChesney." *Artforum* 2 (November 1963): 39.

Temko, Allan, Robert McChesney, and Mary Fuller [McChesney]. *Robert McChesney.* Exh. cat. San Francisco: San Francisco Art Association Gallery, California School of Fine Arts, 1957.

Wallace, Dean. Review. *San Francisco Chronicle,* 29 May 1961.

Philip Roeber

Hagan, R. H. "Philip Roeber, an Artist with Subtle Colors, Form." Review. *San Francisco Chronicle,* 22 July 1955.

Roeber, Philip. *The Artist's View,* no. 7 (March 1954). Issue devoted to Roeber.

Vevers, Tony. *Phil Roeber, A Retrospective Exhibition.* Cat. Provincetown, Mass.: Provincetown Art Association and Museum, 1981.

John Saccaro

Cooney, Gibbons J. *John Saccaro: Paintings, 1952–1962.* Exh. cat. Abstract Expressionists: An Exhibition and Historical Survey of Northern California Abstract Expressionists Active 1945–1960, no. 5. San Francisco: The Carlson Gallery, 1990.

Frankenstein, Alfred. Review. *San Francisco Chronicle,* 26 May 1946.

———. "Europe vs. the U.S. in Two Brilliant Exhibitions." Review. *San Francisco Chronicle,* 12 February 1956.

———. "John Saccaro's 'Sensory Raids.'" Review. *San Francisco Chronicle,* 18 May 1958.

———. "The Torch Passes to a Berkeley Loft." Review. *San Francisco Chronicle,* 18 May 1958.

Fried, Alexander. "Today's Artist Talks Too Much." Review. *San Francisco Examiner,* 26 December 1959.

Museo Italo Americano. *New Paintings by John Saccaro.* Exh. cat. San Francisco: Museo Italo Americano, 1981.

"Saccaro." *Westart* 4 (15 January 1966): 6.

S[andler], I[rving] H. "John Saccaro." Review. *Art News* 61 (May 1962): 18.

"Sketch." *Argonaut* 135 (2 March 1956): 17.

Stanford Art Gallery. *Contemporary American Painters, 1950–1955.* Exh. cat. Stanford, Calif.: Stanford University, 1956.

Tomlin, George P. *Saccaro: Sensorist Paintings.* Exh. cat. Oakland: Oakland Art Museum, 1958.

Jon Schueler

Balliett, Whitney. "Profiles: City Voices: Jon Schueler and Magda Salvesen." *New Yorker* 61 (25 February 1985): 35–40, 43–44, 48–49, 51.

Crehan, Hubert. "Exhibition at Castelli." Review. *Art News* 58 (April 1959): 56.

Feinstein, Sam. "Jon Schueler: A Vision of Nature." Review. *Art Digest* 29 (1 March 1954): 14, 25.

Friedman, B. H., ed. *School of New York: Some Younger Artists.* New York: Grove Press, 1959.

Munsterberg, Hugo. "Exhibition at Castelli." Review. *Arts* 33 (May 1959): 65.

Porter, Fairfield. "Jon Schueler." Review. *Art News* 52 (February 1954): 61–62.

———. "Exhibition at Castelli Gallery." Review, signed F. P. *Art News* 56 (March 1957): 12.

Sandler, Irving. *The New York School: The Painters and Sculptors of the Fifties.* New York: Harper and Row, 1978.

Stable Gallery. *Jon Schueler: A Statement by the Artist.* New York: Stable Gallery, 1954.

Hassel Smith

Albright, Thomas. "Outspoken Man with a Brush." Review. *San Francisco Chronicle,* 18 May 1978.

Beauchamp, Toni. *Hassel Smith in Houston.* Exh. cat. Houston, Tex.: Sarah Campbell Blaffer Gallery, University of Houston, 1974.

Coplans, John. "Re-discovering Hassel Smith." *Artforum* 2 (May 1964): 28–31.

Frankenstein, Alfred. Review. *San Francisco Chronicle,* 18 May 1947.

———. "Works by Corbett, Smith Hung at Fine Arts School." Review. *San Francisco Chronicle,* 14 January 1950.

———. "The Art Galleries." Review. *San Francisco Chronicle,* 12 March 1950.

———. Review. *San Francisco Chronicle,* 22 November 1953.

Hopps, Walter. *Hassel Smith: A Selection of Paintings, 1948–1961.* Exh. cat. Pasadena, Calif.: Pasadena Art Museum, 1961.

Lenoir, Henri Zola. "Skylight Sketch." *Montgomery Street Skylight* (1 July 1946).

MacAgy, Douglas. *First New York Exhibition: Hassel Smith.* Exh. cat. New York: André Emmerich Gallery, 1961.

"New Works by Two Painters." *San Francisco Art Association Bulletin* 17 (January 1951), n.p.

Nixon, Bruce. *Hassel Smith.* Exh. cat. Davis, Calif.: Natsoulas/Novelozo Gallery, 1989.

Nordland, Gerald. "Art." Review. *Frontier* 9 (February 1958): 25.

St. John, Terry. *Hassel Smith: Selected Works, 1945–1981.* Exh. cat. Oakland, Calif.: The Oakland Museum, 1981.

San Francisco Art Association. *Hassel Smith.* Exh. cat. San Francisco: San Francisco Art Association Gallery, California School of Fine Arts, 1957.

Shere, Charles. "Hassel Smith Show Recalls Golden Age." Review. *Oakland Tribune,* 9 November 1975.

———. *Hassel Smith: Recent Paintings, 1986–1987; Selected Works, 1948–1963.* Exh. cat. Belmont, Calif.: Wiegand Gallery, College of Notre Dame, 1988.

Smith, Hassel. *The Artist's View,* no. 1 (July 1952). Issue devoted to Smith.

Smith, Hassel, and Bern Porter. *Constructions.* San Francisco: Bern Porter, 1955.

Smith, Hassel, with the assistance of Mary Fuller McChesney. "Sulla scuola di San Francisco." *Evento delle arti* 2 (1958): 24–27. English translation by Ann Lee, in Archives of California Art, The Oakland Museum.

Temko, Allan. *Hassel Smith: Paintings, 1954–1975.* Exh. cat. San Francisco: San Francisco Museum of Modern Art, 1975.

Tromble, Meredith. "'. . . We Were Making It Up from Day to Day . . .': A Conversation with Hassel Smith." *Artweek* 23 (17 December 1992): 13–14.

Clay Spohn

Beasley, David. "Life of a Painter: Clay Spohn Remembered." Lives of the Obscure, no. 7. *Bulletin of Research in the Humanities* 86 (Summer 1983): 162–215.

———. "The Boundless Spirit of Clay Edgar Spohn." Unpublished manuscript, 1991, private collection.

Fuller, [McChesney], Mary. "Portrait: Clay Spohn." *Art in America* 51 (December 1963): 78–85.

MacAgy, Douglas. "Clay Spohn's War Machines." *Circle* 5 (1945): 38–43.

St. John, Terry. *Clay Spohn.* Exh. cat. Oakland, Calif.: The Oakland Museum, 1974.

Clyfford Still

Albright, Thomas. "Acquisitions from an American Abstract Giant." *San Francisco Chronicle,* 18 May 1975.

————. "Having Lunch with a Legend." *San Francisco Chronicle,* 8 January 1976.

————. "A Conversation with Clyfford Still." *Art News* 75 (March 1976): 30–35.

————. "The Painted Flame." *Horizon: A Magazine of the Arts* 22 (November 1979): 24–33.

————. "The Giant Dimensions of Still's World." *San Francisco Sunday Examiner and Chronicle,* 6 July 1980.

————. "Clyfford Still: 'Seeking the Vastness and Depth of a Beethoven Sonata or a Sophocles Drama.'" *Art News* 79 (September 1980): 159–60.

Anfam, David. "Clyfford Still." Ph.D. diss., Courtauld Institute of Art, University of London, 1984.

————. "'Of the Earth, the Damned, and of the Recreated': Aspects of Clyfford Still's Earlier Work." *Burlington Magazine* 135 (April 1993): 260–69.

Barefoot, Spencer. Review. *San Francisco Chronicle,* 13 July 1947.

"Clyfford Still." *Magazine of Art* 41 (March 1948): 96.

Coffelt, Beth. "The Big Wave Was Rising." *San Francisco Sunday Examiner and Chronicle,* 9 November 1975.

Crehan, Hubert. "Clyfford Still's Exhibition." Review. *San Francisco Chronicle,* 9 July 1950.

————. "Clyfford Still: Black Angel in Buffalo." *Art News* (December 1959): 32, 58–60.

"Exhibition Notes." *San Francisco Art Association Bulletin* 13 (April 1947), n.p.

Hess, Thomas B. "The Outsider." *Art News* 68 (December 1969): 34–37, 67–69.

Hopkins, Henry T. "Clyfford Still." *Currant* 1 (December 1975–January 1976): 18–25.

————. "Clyfford Still's Gift to the San Francisco Museum of Modern Art." *American Art Review* 3 (January–February 1976): 85–99.

————. "Clyfford Still, 1904–1980." *Art in America* 68 (October 1980): 11.

Kuh, Katherine, and Ethel Moore. *Clyfford Still: Thirty-three Paintings in the Albright-Knox Art Gallery.* Exh. cat. Buffalo, N.Y.: Albright-Knox Art Gallery, 1966.

Landauer, Susan. "Clyfford Still and Abstract Expressionism in San Francisco." In *Clyfford Still, 1904–1980: The Buffalo and San Francisco Collections,* Exh. cat., ed. Thomas Kellein, 91–102. Munich: Prestel, 1992.

Loran, Erle. "Art News from San Francisco." Review. *Art News* 49 (October 1950): 52, 58–59.

"New Faculty Members: Clyfford Still." *San Francisco Art Association Bulletin* 13 (January 1947): n.p.

O'Neill, John P., ed. *Clyfford Still.* Exh. cat. New York: Metropolitan Museum of Art, 1979.

Polcari, Stephen. "The Intellectual Roots of Abstract Expressionism: Clyfford Still." *Art International* 25 (May–June 1982): 18–35.

San Francisco Museum of Modern Art. *Clyfford Still.* Exh. cat. San Francisco: San Francisco Museum of Modern Art, 1976.

Sawyer, Kenneth. "U.S. Painters Today, No. 1: Clyfford Still." *Portfolio and Art News Annual* 2 (1960): 76–86.

Selz, Peter. "Between Friends: Still and the Bay Area." *Art in America* 63 (November–December 1975): 70–73.

Sharpless, Ti-Grace. *Clyfford Still.* Exh. cat. Philadelphia: Institute of Contemporary Art, University of Pennsylvania, 1963.

Temko, Allan. "Clyfford Still's Cosmic Supermanland." *San Francisco Chronicle,* 10 February 1980.

Townsend, Benjamin J. "An Interview with Clyfford Still." *Gallery Notes* (Albright-Knox Art Gallery, Buffalo Fine Arts Academy) 24 (Summer 1961): 8–16.

George Stillman

[Frankenstein, Alfred]. "Around the Local Galleries." Review. *San Francisco Chronicle,* 4 April 1948.

Loran, Erle. "Art News from San Francisco." Review. *Art News* 49 (February 1950): 52.

Ludtka, Karol. "Painting: From Past to Present." Review. *The Daily Record* (Ellensburg, Wash.), 5 October 1991.

Sarah Spurgeon Gallery. *George Stillman Up 'Til Now: A Selection of Work since 1947. Paintings, Drawings, Prints.* Exh. cat. Ellensburg, Wash.: Sarah Spurgeon Gallery, Central Washington University, 1991.

Stillman, Lillian. "Exhibit Paints Picture of Artist's Work." Review. *The Daily Record* (Ellensburg, Wash.), 21 October 1991.

Charles Strong

Albright, Thomas. "Three at Oakland Museum: Gut-Level Painters Present Top-Notch Show." Review. *San Francisco Chronicle,* 11 September 1971.

————. "Strong Paints Up a Storm." Review. *San Francisco Chronicle,* 26 May 1973.

————. Review. *Art News* 75 (November 1976): 102.

————. "Reflections on a Subcurrent of Abstract Expressionism." Review. *San Francisco Chronicle,* 18 March 1980.

Bell, Michael S. "Savants in Color." Review. *Artweek* 15 (6 October 1984): 3.

Conal, Robbie. *Charles Strong: A Survey of Works on Paper, 1961–1979.* Exh. cat. Belmont, Calif.: College of Notre Dame Art Gallery, 1980.

Gibbon, John Fitz. *Charles Strong: The Bolinas Years, 1965–1966.* Exh. cat. Bolinas, Calif.: Bolinas Museum, 1991.

Heller, Jules. *Paper-Making.* New York: Watson-Guptill, 1978.

McCombie, Mel. "Strength in Simplicity." Review. *Artweek* 11 (22 March 1980): 1, 16.

Moss, Stacey. "One-Artist Shows: A Satisfying One and One with Bravado Minus Impact." Review. *Peninsula Times Tribune* (Palo Alto, Calif.), 17 March 1980.

Nixon, Bruce. *Charles Strong.* Exh. cat. Davis, Calif.: Nat-
soulas/Novelozo Gallery, 1991.
Shere, Charles. *Charles Strong: New Paintings: China, Ezra,
Joan.* Exh. cat. Moraga, Calif.: Hearst Art Gallery,
Saint Mary's College of California, 1991.
"The Three Painters." Review. *Artweek* 2 (9 October 1971):
2.

Sam Tchakalian

Albright, Thomas. "Tchakalian Art Eloquent, Sensual."
Review. *San Francisco Chronicle,* 29 May 1970.
———. "Two Decades of Tchakalian." Review. *San Fran-
cisco Chronicle,* 1 October 1978.
Dunham, Judith. "Sam Tchakalian's History in Painting."
Review. *Artweek* 9 (28 October 1978): 1, 16.
The National Museum of Contemporary Art. *Sam
Tchakalian—Paintings.* Exh. cat. Foreword by Kyung-
Sung Lee, essay by Kenneth Baker. Seoul, Korea: The
National Museum of Contemporary Art, 1989.

Designer: Steve Renick
Compositor: TBH Typecast, Inc.
Text: Adobe Garamond
Display: Frutiger & Bodoni
Printer & Binder: Dai Nippon